John —

I love the windows in your home. We have been looking at Anderson Tilt & Wash replacement windows. These windows seem comparable. Do you have information on your windows I could look at?

Prices — styles — sizes
snap-ins — etc.

Carol T.

11/2
1:45/pm — (Ray Paccini ?) called — will call you tomorrow.

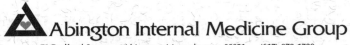

Abington Internal Medicine Group

79 Bedford Street - Abington, Massachusetts 02351 - (617) 878-1700

Timothy R. Lynch, M.D.
Diplomate, American Board of Internal Medicine

Joseph L. Raduazzo, M.D.
Diplomate, American Board of Internal Medicine

905-279-0321

Bobby Fischer

Complete Games of the American World Chess Champion

Compiled and edited by Lou Hays

Condensed annotations by Senior Master John Hall

Hays Publishing
Dallas

Editor: Lou Hays
Condensed annotations: Senior Master John Hall
Computer typeset: Lou Hays
Cover design and Fischer illustration: Carolyn Hoefelmeyer
Cover illustration produced from photo courtesy of British Chess Magazine (Bobby Fischer at the 1966 Havana Olympiad)
File Creation: David Sewell, Sid Pickard, Ken Artz, Will Brugge, Joe Drake, Lou Hays
Proofreaders: David Sewell, John Hall, Sid Pickard, David King

Hays, Lou, 1947–
    Bobby Fischer – Complete games of the American World Chess Champion

Includes indices.
1. Fischer, Bobby, 1943–   2. Chess–Collections of games.   I. Title.
ISBN 1-880673-99-1

Printed in the United States of America   *July, 1995*

Hays Publishing
P.O. Box 797623
Dallas, Texas 75379

CONTENTS

BOBBY FISCHER'S TOURNAMENT
AND MATCH GAMES

BOBBY FISCHER
1943-

Born: March 9, 1943 Chicago, Illinois
Learned the rules of chess: 1949
First recorded tournament game: 1954
International Grandmaster title: 1958
U.S. Champion eight times (in eight attempts): 1957, 1958, 1959, 1960, 1962, 1963, 1965, 1966
Winner of every tournament and match in which he participated from December, 1962 through World Championship rematch 1992 with the exceptions of Capablanca Memorial, 1965, (2nd place - 1/2 point behind Smyslov), and Piatigorsky Cup, 1966, (2nd place - 1/2 point behind Spassky).
World Champion: 1972

Bobby Fischer is generally recognized as the strongest player in the history of chess.

HINTS FOR ENJOYING YOUR BOBBY FISCHER BOOK

Bobby Fischer–Complete Games of the American World Chess Champion was created with the serious student of chess in mind. These games, like the work of any truly great artist are more profound than they might at first appear. Fischer's uncompromising style represents everything known about the game of chess through the middle of the twentieth century, blended with his desire to win *every* game, whether playing the White or the Black pieces.

The 1995 edition contains 1043 listings and 972 actual game scores. Except for the new listings at the end of the book, games are presented in chronological order. Some might be surprised to find the high number of annotations throughout which suggest improved play in the openings. This does not mean that the players were committing known opening errors; rather it reflects the numerous changes in opening theory over the past twenty years. In some of the tournaments it appears that Fischer missed playing in one or more rounds. In nearly every case this simply means that he had the bye. In the Olympiads players do not necessarily play in every round so many round numbers may be missing in these events.

The industrious player will want to take full advantage of the multiple indexing. The book is indexed by opponent, opening, ECO code, and ending. An in depth study of Fischer's games is possible from many angles through these indexes (Opening, ECO, and Ending indexes do not include the blitz, exhibition, or simultaneous games).

Players of every level are advised to begin by turning to "100 notable games in Bobby Fischer's career" (page 15) and play through these games. You will start with Fischer's first Najdorf Sicilian defense, pass soon to the "Game of the Century" vs. Donald Byrne and then to the draw with Gligoric which gave Bobby the Grandmaster title at age fifteen. The section continues with an overview of the most important, best played and most exciting games of Bobby Fischer's career, right through his winning of the World Championship. After going through these hundred games, go back and slowly digest and enjoy the rest of the book. A thorough study of Bobby Fischer's chess games amounts to the equivalent of a college degree in chess.

ACKNOWLEDGEMENTS

I am grateful to the many chessplayers who took part in the creation of this book. I wish in particular to acknowledge the efforts of David Sewell, John Hall, and Mike Richards, all of whom were active on the project from the beginning. I am indebted to International Master John Donaldson, a virtual "walking encyclopedia of chess" for his assistance in tracking down new games, and to Kenneth R. Smith for encouraging me to make the start.

David Sewell—*Game input, diagrams, proofreading;* John Hall—*Condensed annotations, ECO codes, proofreading;* Mike Richards—*Condensed annotations for games from the 1955 US Junior tournament, "100 notable games in Bobby Fischer's chess career", assistance on "The evolution of Bobby Fischer's opening Repertoire";* Billy Patteson—*Games from the Houston, Texas simultaneous exhibition;* Jim Warren —*Games from the Chicago and Cicero, Illinois simultaneous exhibitions;* Jude Acers and Frank Chavez—*Information and games from Fischer's visit to Louisiana, 1964;* Carolyn Hoefelmeyer—*Cover Illustration of Bobby Fischer;* Chess Informant— Opening codes; British Chess Magazine–use of photo (Fischer at the 1966 Havana Olympiad) to produce cover illustration; John G. White Collection of the Cleveland, Ohio Public Library.

Bibliography: *Die gesammelten Partien von Robert J. Fischer* by Christiaan M. Bijl (Vermande Zonen); *The games of Robert J. Fischer* R. G. Wade and Kevin J. O'Connell (Batsford); *A Legend on the Road* by IM John Donaldson (ICE, Seattle); *Chess Life and Review magazine; Inside Chess* Magazine, Seattle; *Encyclopedia of Chess Openings* (Chess Informant); Numerous state chess publications and newspaper articles were used as game sources.

Lou Hays
Dallas, Texas
May, 1995

Bobby Fischer's Tournament and Match Record (1955-1992)

Tournaments	+	=	-	Place
1955				
US Junior Championship Lincoln	2	6	2	10-20
1956				
US Amateur Championship, New Jersey	3	2	1	21
US Junior Championship, Philadelphia	8	1	1	1
US Open, Oklahoma City	5	7	0	4-8
Canadian Open, Montreal	6	2	2	8-12
Rosenwald Memorial, New York	2	5	4	8
Eastern States Open, Washington, D.C.	4	3	0	2-4
Manhattan Chess Club Championship, New York (1/2 final)	2	1	2	4
1957				
Log Cabin Open, West Orange	4	0	2	6
Log Cabin 50-50, West Orange	3	2	0	?
New Western Open, Milwaukee	5	2	1	7
US Junior, San Francisco	8	1	0	1
US Open, Cleveland	8	4	0	1
New Jersey Open, East Orange	6	1	0	1
North Central Open, Milwaukee	4	2	1	5-11
US Championship, New York	8	5	0	1
1958				
Interzonal, Portoroz	6	12	2	5-6
US Championship, New York	6	5	0	1
1959				
Mar del Plata	8	4	2	3-4
Santiago, Chile	7	1	4	4-7
Zurich	8	5	2	3-4
Candidate's Tournament, Belgrade/Bled/Zagreb	8	9	11	5-6
US Championship, New York	7	4	0	1
1960				
Mar del Plata	13	1	1	1-2
Buenos Aires	3	11	5	13
Reykjavik	3	1	0	1
Leipzig Olympiad (First board)	10	6	2	-
US Championship, New York	7	4	0	1
1961				
Bled	8	11	0	2
1962				
Interzonal, Stockholm	13	9	0	1
Candidate's Tournament, Curacao	8	12	7	4
Varna Olympiad (First board)	8	6	3	-
US Championship, New York	6	4	1	1

1963	+	=	-	Place
Western Open, Bay City	7	1	0	1
New York State Open, Poughkeepsie	7	0	0	1
US Championship, New York	11	0	0	1
1965				
Capablanca Memorial, Havana	12	6	3	2-4
US Championship, New York	8	1	2	1
1966				
Piatigorsky Cup, Santa Monica	7	8	3	2
Havana Olympiad (First board)	14	2	1	-
US Championship, New York	8	3	0	1
1967				
Monaco	6	2	1	1
Skopje	12	3	2	1
Interzonal, Sousse	7	3	0	Withdrew
1968				
Netanya	10	3	0	1
Vinkovci	9	4	0	1
1970				
USSR vs. the Rest of the World, Belgrade (Second Board)	2	2	0	-
Rovinj/Zagreb	10	6	1	1
Buenos Aires	13	4	0	1
Siegen Olympiad (First board)	8	4	1	
Interzonal, Palma de Mallorca	15	7	1	1

Matches

1957				
vs. Cardoso, New York	5	2	1	won
vs. Euwe, New York	0	1	1	lost
1958				
vs. Janosevic, Belgrade	0	2	0	drew
vs. Matulovic, Belgrade	2	1	1	won
1961				
vs. Reshevsky, New York/Los Angeles	2	7	2	drew
1971				
vs. Taimanov, Vancouver (Candidates quarterfinal)	6	0	0	won
vs. Larsen, Denver (Candidates semifinal)	6	0	0	won
vs. Petrosian, Buenos Aires (Candidates final)	5	3	1	won
1972				
vs. Spassky, Reykjavik (World Championship)	7	11	3	won
1992				
vs. Spassky, Sveti Stefan-Belgrade (World Championship Rematch)	10	15	5	won

THE EVOLUTION OF BOBBY FISCHER'S OPENING REPERTOIRE

Bobby Fischer's opening repertoire can be divided into three general periods. **Early years:** 1955 through 1962 (Games 1 through 409). **Middle years:** 1964 through 1969 (Games 410 through 574). **The Road to the World Championship years:** 1970 through 1972 (Games 575 through 690). After each of the first two periods, Bobby took time off, only to return to competition a much stronger player as was evidenced by the modifications to his opening repertoire. A sampling of games is given at the end of most listings. For a complete look, however, be sure to use the main index. [**Game numbers are bolded and given in brackets**]

Early years: 1955-1962 (Games 1-409)

Fischer as White

From the beginning of his career, Fischer has been a devotee of 1.e4.

vs. Alekhine's Defense

The only examples of this defense in this period show Bobby playing the solid 5.ed6 variation, avoiding possible surprises against the Four pawn's attack. [**295, 401**]

vs. the Caro Kann Defense

During this period Fischer played the Two Knights variation almost exclusively. (1.e4 c6 2.Nc3 d5 3.Nf3) He doggedly used this setup, which generally results in a closed center and long maneuvering games. It can be viewed as a young player's method of having <u>one</u> system to always be played against a particular defense. Bobby can be seen playing this variation most effectively against Addison (U.S. Open Cleveland, 1957). In 1960, Bobby switched to the sharper Panov attack (1.e4 c6 2.d4 d5 3.ed5 cd5 4.c4). Few players challenged Fischer in this line due to his decisive victory over Euwe at the Leipzig Olympiad, 1960. In 1961 he tried out the Classical 3.Nc3 against Petrosian at Bled, winning the game without a clear edge in the opening. [**65, 85, 142, 186, 197, 202, 203, 211, 217, 219, 221, 226, 250, 253, 286**]

vs. the French Defense

When faced with the French Defense, Fischer almost invariably invited the Winawer with 1.e4 e6 2.d4 d5 3.Nc3. After the further moves 3...Bb4 4.e5 c5 5.a3 Bc3 6.bc3, we arrive at the theoretically crucial position. [**112, 171, 257, 284, 291, 298, 353, 383, 399**]

vs. Petroff's Defense

There were but two encounters against the Petroff Defense during this period: vs. Bisguier (U.S. Championship, 1959), and German (Stockholm Interzonal). Bobby played 3.Ne5 vs. Bisguier and 3.d4 vs. German, winning both games. **[224, 343]**

vs. the Pirc Defense

Fischer nearly always used the direct Austrian Attack (characterized by 4.f4) or the Byrne system(4.Bg5). **[72, 116, 228, 326, 358]**

Four Knights Game

This opening (1.e4 e5 2.Nf3 Nc6 3.Nc3 Nf6) occurred only one time during this period. Bobby scraped a draw with this early experiment in the U.S. Junior Championship, 1955, vs. Ames. **[4]**

King's Indian Attack

Bobby once said of the King's Indian Attack, *"This used to be my favorite."* Indeed, there are numerous examples throughout his career of his using this opening. The opening is characterized by the White setup 1.Nf3 2.g3 3.Bg2 4.d3 5.0-0 and 6.e4. Bobby often played this formation against the Caro Kann, French defense and occasionally even the Sicilian (see main index for game numbers).

Ruy Lopez

The Ruy Lopez has been a potent weapon for Bobby throughout his entire career. Strategic play across the board suited Bobby's talents from the start. During this early period, Fischer was so proficient in the main lines that many of his opponents chose irregular setups when defending the Ruy (see main index for game numbers).

vs. the Sicilian

This early period is marked by a search for attacking formations against all of the main lines of the Sicilian. It was during this period that Bobby finally settled on the 6.Bc4 Sozin-like attacking system for White. Once this system jelled, Bobby was prepared for virtually all Black Open Sicilian variations, and began to introduce theoretical novelties which popularized the system (see main index for game numbers).

Fischer as Black

vs. Queenside openings (1.d4, 1.c4, etc.)

King's Indian Defense

This modern, active defense found a place in Fischer's repertoire when he was but twelve years old at the 1955 U.S. Junior Championship. During this period Bobby played the King's Indian almost exclusively against non-1.e4 openings. The King's Indian is characterized by flexible piece play and pawn formations which allowed Bobby to play for a win and create dynamically unbalanced positions straight from the opening (see main index for game numbers).

Grunfeld Defense

Fischer's Grunfeld defenses from this period are among his most famous games, including the "Game of the Century" vs. D. Byrne, and Botvinnik at the Varna Olympiad. [**35, 270, 390, 397, 402, 406**]

Queen's Gambit

Fischer occasionally adopted this solid, but basically passive line in order to avoid prepared variations against his usual hypermodern defenses. In these games he demonstrated that he was very capable of playing a solid, classical type of game. [**133, 218, 242, 254, 306, 308, 321, 327, 331, 346, 352, 373, 377, 380, 381**]

vs. 1.e4

The story of Fischer's adoption of the Sicilian Defense is essentially a study in the Najdorf variation, for this has been virtually the only variation of the Sicilian he has ever played. Against 6.f4 (after 1.e4 c5 2.Nf3 d6 3.d4 cd4 4.Nd4 Nf6 5.Nc3 a6), he usually played 6...e5 followed by an early ...b5. Against 6.Be2 he played 6...e5 again with the idea of early Queenside play which is so thematic in the Sicilian. Against 6.g3, 6...e5 was still the prescription. Finally, against the currently popular 6.Bg5 he played an early ...h6 followed by ...g5 (the Goteberg variation), which leads to extremely complicated tactical play (see main index for game numbers).

Middle years: 1963-1969 (Games 410-574)

Fischer as White

vs. Alekhine's Defense

Bobby encountered Alekhine's Defense only once in this period, drawing with Ciocaltea at the Capablanca Memorial, 1965. [**437**]

vs. the Caro Kann Defense

Fischer continued with the Two Knights variation, but also tried the Panov attack and the Exchange variation. **[526, 550, 552, 559, 564]**

vs. the French Defense

During this period, Fischer had uneven results against the French defense. He maintained his allegiance to 3.Nc3 inviting the Winawer variation, but many of his opponents chose less critical variations like the MacCutcheon and Burn variations. **[414, 445, 464, 497, 504, 542]**

vs. the Pirc Defense

During this period Fischer played only the Austrian attack, winning all six games. **[420, 433, 453, 456, 556, 562]**

Ruy Lopez

Fischer began to face the world's strongest players with the Ruy Lopez, scoring well against all defenses. His opponents continued to avoid the long, closed variations by trying new move orders and the Marshall Attack (See main index for game numbers).

vs. the Two Knights Defense

The only examples of the Two Knights in this period of Fischer's career are his games against Bisguier and Radoicic, both from the 1963 New York State Open. Fischer won both games while reviving an old Steinitz line characterized by 9.Nh3. **[422, 423]**

vs. the Sicilian Defense

Against the ever popular Sicilian, Fischer has been challenged by a variety of Black systems. Against the Schevenigen and Najdorf lines he often used his pet 6.Bc4, scoring many brilliant victories. Against the Dragon he invariably played the sharp Yugoslav Attack, which is without doubt the most serious attempt to maintain the initiative (see main index for game numbers).

Fischer as Black

vs. Queenside openings

vs. the English

Against the English Bobby mixed his reliable King's Indian formation with systems employing an early ...c5. **[428, 434, 452, 465, 498, 505, 507, 528, 545, 565, 569, 574]**

King's Indian Defense

The King's Indian remained Fischer's main weapon against all non 1.e4 openings, and he demonstrates greater knowledge of move orders and often takes over the initiative early in the game (see main index for game numbers).

Grunfeld Defense

Fischer increased the number of Grunfelds he played, adopting this alternative to his normal King's Indian. Bobby maintains that Black obtains excellent play against White's center in the Exchange variation, while other, less sharp lines give Black no problems. **[418, 419, 426, 442, 473, 521]**

Nimzo-Indian Defense

Fischer occasionally played the Nimzo-Indian, especially when facing a King's Indian specialist. One of his favorite setups involved the "extended" fianchetto of the Queen Bishop to a6. **[455, 457, 461, 463, 476]**

Queen's Gambit

Although Fischer was famous now for his play of the hypermodern defenses, he also played two Queen's gambits as Black, winning both games. **[417, 573]**

vs. 1.e4

During this period Fischer continued to play the Najdorf variation of the Sicilian Defense almost exclusively. Against the most popular 6.Bg5 variation he played both the solid ...Be7 and the ultra-sharp ...Qb6 poisoned pawn variation. **[439, 514, 520, 543, 551, 557, 567]**

On the Road to the World Championship: 1970-1972
(Games 575 - 690)

Fischer as White

vs. the Caro Kann Defense

During this period Bobby all but abandoned the Two Knights variation and went back to his early favorite, the King's Indian Attack with 2.d3. Also of interest is his adoption of the ancient line 1.e4 c6 2.d4 d5 3.ed5 cd5 4.Bd3 vs. Petrosian **[575]** in the USSR vs. the rest of World match. Fischer's 11.a4! was an important improvement in this opening. **[575, 577, 582, 617, 624, 626]**

vs. the French Defense

Bobby stayed with 3.Nc3, still inviting the Winawer. He successfully experimented with 4.a3 vs. Uhlmann at Zagreb, 1970, but lost against Kovacevic with this move later in the same tournament. [**584, 586, 599, 616, 655, 663, 669**]

vs. Petroff's Defense

Fischer essayed the classical 3.Ne5 twice in this period, beating Gheorghiu and drawing with Petrosian. [**598, 665**]

vs. the Pirc Defense

Bobby continued with the Austrian Attack, but adds a new twist with an early h3, g4 Kingside expansion, defeating Udovic with this plan. [**590, 686**]

vs. the Sicilian Defense

Fischer stayed with the Yugoslav Attack vs. the Dragon and the Sozin against other main systems, but several times against the popular Taimanov move order (1.e4 c5 2.Nf3 Nc6 3.d4 cd4 4.Nd4 e6) he chose the solid 5.Nb5. [**592, 650, 654, 661**]

Ruy Lopez

Bobby continued to score well against all defenses to the Ruy Lopez, and broadened his arsenal with the Exchange variation, 4.Bc6 (see main index for game numbers).

Fischer as White not playing 1.e4

Fischer broadened his repertoire during this period, playing an occasional English, (1.c4), Nimzowitsch/Larsen Attack (1.b3), and Queen's Gambit, usually by transposition from the English. [**596, 629, 636, 646, 648, 675, 677, 681, 683**]

Fischer as Black

vs. 1.e4

Alekhine's Defense

Fischer adopted Alekhine's Defense six times during this period (3 wins, 3 draws) usually fianchettoing his King Bishop in order to strike at White's center. [**593, 639, 641, 645, 682, 688**]

Sicilian Defense

Throughout Fischer's mature period he remained faithful to his beloved Najdorf variation, expanding on known theory with regularity. Against the closed Sicilian he introduced the theoretical idea ...Bg4 followed by the capture of White's Nf3, thus eliminating one of White's strongest attacking pieces (see main index for game numbers).

vs. the Queen pawn openings

vs. the English

Bobby continued with the flexible King's Indian Defense and occasionally tried the symmetrical variation (...c5) while still fianchettoing the King Bishop. [**576, 600, 606, 611, 627, 631, 633**]

Benoni

Fischer added to his King's Indian repertoire the Modern Benoni (2...c5), playing very aggressively and scoring well against his unsuspecting opponents. [**635, 643, 647, 672**]

Grunfeld Defense

Fischer saved this defense for top level encounters. The Grunfeld's tendency to lead to a build up of increasingly greater tension, with Black firing a direct volley at White's center, creates the preconditions for decisive chess which so admirably suits Fischer's uncompromising style. [**578, 608, 621, 637, 653, 662**]

King's Indian Defense

Always Fischer's first string against the 1.d4 systems, he innovated in this period with the double fianchetto, as well as 5...c5 against the Samisch attack (See main index for game numbers).

Nimzo-Indian Defense

Bobby played this opening successfully on the road to the World Championship as well as in his match with Spassky. [**610, 625, 670**]

vs. the Queen's Gambit

Fischer showed flexibility when playing against King's Indian specialists and adds the Semi-Tarrasch to his ever-widening repertoire. [**602, 678**]

100 NOTABLE GAMES IN BOBBY FISCHER'S CHESS CAREER

07) Grossguth-Fischer [7/2/56] Bobby's first tournament Najdorf Defense, a real squeeze.

20) Donovan-Fischer [7/28/56] Black cooks up a Kingside attack to force a superior ending in an early King's Indian.

35) Byrne,D-Fischer [10/17/56] Thirteen year old Fischer stuns the chess world with a fascinating Queen sacrifice and celebrated victory over Donald Byrne. The game was subsequently dubbed "Game of the Century" by Hans Kmoch.

39) Fischer-di Camillo [11/56] A tactical bolt clears up an unclear endgame.

78) Fischer-Rinaldo [8/8/57] A theoretical error is efficiently converted to a winning endgame.

82) Fischer-Mednis [8/12/57] A slight advantage is used to bring about a nice *zugzwang* finish.

88) Fischer-Green [8/31/57] White shows maturity in converting a superior minor piece ending.

93) Fischer-Sherwin [9/2/57] White launches a Kingside breakthrough resulting in a King hunt.

101) Fischer-Cardoso [9/57] A positional rout caps a match victory.

103) Fischer-Sandrin [11/30/57] Another successful opposite-colored Bishop *zugzwang*.

108) Fischer-Feuerstein [12/17/57] Dark-square weaknesses around Black's King are exploited to win the exchange.

110) Fischer-Reshevsky [12/21/57] Bobby's first draw with U.S. giant Reshevsky.

114) Fischer-Sherwin [12/27/57] Execution of a familiar attacking theme.

128) Fischer-Bronstein [8/13/58] The young American champion holds on against a Soviet giant.

130) Fischer-Larsen [8/16/58] Fischer stakes out his reputation as a "Dragonslayer".

135) Petrosian-Fischer [8/27/58] Black survives the first of many "bear hugs" with his powerful opponent.

143) Gligoric-Fischer [9/10/58] A theoretical novelty secures the draw, Bobby's Grandmaster title, and a berth in the World Championship Tournament.

149) Fischer-Reshevsky [12/58] White uncorks a published refutation and blows Reshevsky out.

161) Fischer-Shocron [3/30/59] Technical problems are solved by tactical means in this sharp Ruy Lopez.

165) Fischer-Rossetto [4/5/59] Black gets rattled and is reduced to another execution of *zugzwang*.

169) Fischer-Sanchez [4/59] Black is pushed to the ropes and caught in a mating net.

180) **Ader-Fischer** [5/6/59] Black uses a stock sacrifice to generate a King hunt.

181) **Walther-Fischer** [5/19/59] Bobby hangs on in a dead lost position to earn a miracle draw.

184) **Fischer-Kupper** [5/59] Bobby's pet Sozin attack. The Sicilian and a small tactical error add up to a quick crush.

188) **Fischer-Unzicker** [5/59] An enterprising pawn sacrifice in the Ruy Lopez leads to a textbook Bishop vs. Knight endgame.

192) **Fischer-Keres** [6/59] A landmark game. Fischer shows brilliance and staying power in grinding this one out.

195) **Tal-Fischer** [6/59] A courageous last round game proving that Bobby isn't to be intimidated.

196) **Keres-Fischer** [9/7/59] Bobby coolly refutes an enterprising Queen sacrifice.

205) **Fischer-Benko** [9/22/59] A move order error is met with a blistering Kingside attack.

210) **Keres-Fischer** [10/3/59] A rare blunder notches another win against this World Championship candidate.

211) **Fischer-Petrosian** [10/4/59] This incredible four Queens game swings to a draw.

220) **Gligoric-Fischer** [10/22/59] Bobby expands existing theory and holds his own.

223) **Smyslov-Fischer** 10/29/59] Ruthless technique punishes an opening inaccuracy.

235) **Wexler-Fischer** [3/29/60] Fischer piles up on the f-pawn and wins material. An excellent example of gradually building initiative before the final breakthrough.

236) **Spassky-Fischer** [3/30/60] This well-known King's gambit shows that Fischer is not afraid of Spassky but at this time, he is not quite up to Spassky's resourcefulness. Both players employ their typical style, although Fischer spoils a winning position and loses a critical game.

252) **Fischer-Rossetto** [6/25/60] Bobby rolls the dice, aiming to complicate and squeeze.

263) **Fischer-Korchnoi** [7/11/60] An important theoretical game for the Smith-Morra gambit.

267) **Fischer-Wade** [7/19/60] Black commits a slight error in the Ruy Lopez and White converts it with a clean technical victory.

278) **Letelier-Fischer** [10/24/60] An inexact opening forces White to regroup his pieces to defend material and Fischer crashes through, first sacrificing the exchange, then delivering a surprising Queen sacrifice. A nice miniature.

279) **Fischer-Unzicker** [10/26/60] Fischer solves technical problems with a combinative solution, seizing the initiative on the Kingside with a piece sacrifice, forcing a won ending.

284) **Fischer-Tal** [11/1/60] Slight inaccuracies by both sides in a French defense result in fireworks and a slugfest ending in a quick draw. A classic game of titans.

286) Fischer-Euwe [11/3/60] Fischer uncorks a theoretical novelty and wins the ending in a topical line.

290) Uhlmann-Fischer [11/8/60] Fischer gains equality then a slight edge with a Bishop vs. Knight ending, grinding out a technical win.

303) Fischer-Reshevsky [7/61] Bobby sacks a pawn and although Reshevsky is resourceful, he makes the last mistake as Fischer evens the match.

306) Reshevsky-Fischer [7/27/61] Bobby is out-calculated in the middlegame but has some compensation for the material deficit, then plays consistent chess to bring home the victory in Reshevsky's time pressure.

314) Fischer-Tal [9/4/61] Fischer's first victory against Tal. Fischer takes advantage of an early opening mistake and wins with accurate play. An important psychological victory for Bobby.

318) Fischer-Geller [9/10/61] Geller adopts a theoretically dubious line and is hit with a thunderbolt (19.Qb3!) for one of the quickest losses on Grandmaster Geller's record.

324) Fischer-Trifunovic [9/20/61] This game shows Bobby at his technical best by turning a pawn weakness into an advantage and continuing the pressure to win a long ending.

327) Portisch-Fischer [9/25/61] Fischer once again wins the opening duel and has the better minor piece. Bobby squeezes out a win against a famous opponent.

330) Fischer-Petrosian [9/30/61] Fischer keeps a slight edge against the man known as "The hardest man in the world to beat." Black cracks against the young Grandmaster and Bobby notches his first victory against Petrosian.

335) Fischer-Portisch [1/31/62] A very instructive Rook and pawn ending where Fischer takes small advantages and nurses them into a win against one of the world's top players.

336) Bilek-Fischer [2/3/62] Fischer unleashes a novelty in the highly theoretical Poisoned Pawn variation of the Sicilian and earns a nice win against the Grandmaster.

342) Yanofsky-Fischer [2/14/62] A little-studied game because of its length, but this game reveals a glimpse of Fischer the World Champion. Bobby takes Knight versus Bishop and keeps the proper number of pieces on the board with a pawn up and grinds out a nice 112-move victory.

349) Fischer-Korchnoi [2/27/62] Another cut-and-thrust struggle with "Victor the Terrible." Both players make inexact moves in the opening and early middlegame, but once again the clock is Fischer's friend as he wins another game in time pressure.

352) Bertok-Fischer [3/4/62] Fischer caps a brilliant Stockholm win with a positional squeeze on the Black side of a Tartakower. This game shows Fischer's classical style and continuing will to win even though he leads the field in the event.

364) Fischer-Tal [5/19/62] Rarely is the Latvian tactical genius put so much on the defensive, but Fischer combines superior King position and a better minor piece to grind out a win against the Soviet titan.

389) Fischer-Najdorf [9/28/62] A unique exchange sacrifice which has a blend of positional and tactical qualities. Najdorf is taken down in 24 moves. This one is a true classic.

391) Fischer-Robatsch [9/30/62] A quick crunch of the Center Counter with Bobby demonstrating his Dragon-slaying tactics to pry open Black's Kingside and go home early.

394) Unzicker-Fischer [10/4/62] Bobby plays his pet Najdorf Sicilian with great accuracy and finishes Unzicker off with a tactical shot.

397) Botvinnik-Fischer [10/7/62] An instructive Rook and pawn ending in which Botvinnik luckily draws an inferior ending thanks to the Soviet team approach of adjourned analysis. This game suggests careful study and shows Bobby's outstanding theoretical preparation. Botvinnik had completely overlooked 17...Qf4! when analyzing this position in preparation for a match with Smyslov some years earlier.

417) Berliner-Fischer [7/7/63] Fischer throws in a tactical shot (20...g5!!) to seal the victory. An example of International Master vs. Super Grandmaster.

426) Byrne,R.-Fischer [12/18/63] Fischer spurns the exchange for a Kingside attack and wins a miniature. Many of the players in the press room thought that Byrne stood better at the moment he resigned. This game is one of Bobby's greatest efforts and demonstrates his delicate handling of the initiative.

429) Fischer-Steinmeyer [12/22/63] A humorous 17-move miniature in which Fischer engineers a Queen trap.

433) Fischer-Benko [12/30/63] Fischer's 19.Rf6!! puts the lid on the game after a few minor inaccuracies by Black. This game typifies Fischer's dominance over Benko throughout his career.

436) Smyslov-Fischer [8/26/65] A game from the Havana Telex Olympiad. Fischer nurses a slight material advantage against his opponent and wins a classic game.

439) Tringov-Fischer [8/31/65] Fischer brings out a theoretical novelty with 15...fxe6! and wins quickly with natural moves against another Grandmaster.

443) Robatsch-Fischer [9/9/65] Bobby takes advantage of an innocuous opening novelty by White and dominates first the dark squares and soon the whole board.

458) Fischer-Benko [12/65] Bobby wins a long Ruy Lopez with a cute tactical finish.

473) Spassky-Fischer [7/28/66] Fischer's second loss to Spassky from a better position. This game showed that at this point in time Bobby's style did not yet match up well against Spassky.

480) Larsen-Fischer [8/10/66] A Benoni position where Larsen is beaten by exact moves at every turn.

485) Fischer-Durao [10/28/66] Fischer plays his favorite King's Indian Attack and pushes on both sides of the board, finally breaking through with a brilliant Knight sacrifice.

492) Fischer-Portisch [11/10/66] Bobby dusts off the Ruy Lopez Exchange variation and takes down Portisch in a very instructive ending. This game characterizes Fischer's classical style and ability to play unexpected, but sound moves.

495) Najdorf-Fischer [11/13/66] Fischer plays the Modern Benoni with Black, taking enormous chances to win a pawn, voluntarily walking into a pin, realizing that White's attack will soon run out of steam.

496) Fischer-Spassky [11/14/66] Fischer's first real chance to win against Boris. In time pressure, Fischer takes a pawn allowing Spassky counterplay. While Fischer didn't win this game, he proved that he could compete with World Champion caliber players.

505) Byrne,D.-Fischer [12/66] Fischer is Black in a Dutch-like English where he shows accurate play to take out International Master Byrne.

516) Larsen-Fischer [3/28/67] A classical King's Indian where Fischer plays a drawish variation, engineers a slightly better ending and outplays Larsen. This game can be seen as a blueprint for Bobby's overwhelming victory in their Candidates match of 1970.

537) Fischer-Sofrevski [8/67] Fischer shows that when given the opportunity, he can attack with the best of them. 15.Nd5 is a bolt that ends in a quick smash.

540) Fischer-Miagmasuren [10/18/67] A King's Indian Attack showing Fischer's gradual build up, resulting in a decisive Queen sacrifice. A game well worth replaying.

544) Fischer-Stein [10/24/67] A battle of titans. Fischer wins the slugout in a Ruy Lopez. No doubt one of the finest games of 1967.

547) Byrne,R.-Fischer [10/31/67] Fischer shows a theoretical novelty on move 13, literally pushing Byrne off the board.

555) Bernstein-Fischer [6/25/68] Bobby castles Queenside against the Closed Sicilian and takes advantage of the tactical mistakes made by his confused opponent.

557) Ciocaltea-Fischer [6/27/68] This game shows Fischer's ability to defend over a long period of time. White puts a Knight on d5, but Bobby forces him to play the best move for many, many turns, and Black finally emerges victorious.

563) Matulovic-Fischer [9/9/68] This game demonstrates Bobby's originality with 13 ...Kxe7!, gaining time for a Queenside initiative. Fischer once again grinds down a Grandmaster from the Black side of a Sicilian.

566) Fischer-Minic [9/14/68] Fischer essays the King's Gambit, in which he demonstrates the potency of his Kingside attack with a profound exchange sacrifice.

574) Saidy-Fischer [1969] Bobby's only serious game of 1969. It was awarded the "second best game of the first half of the year" by the *Chess informator* judges. Bobby uses boa-constrictor tactics on both sides of the board.

575) Fischer-Petrosian [3/29/70] Bobby plays the previously considered innocuous exchange variation of the Caro-Kann and blows Petrosian off the board.

598) Fischer-Gheorghiu [7/21/70] An excellent example of a blend of space, time, and mobility as Bobby puts on the clamp. Each one of White's pieces is slightly better placed, and he squeezes out a victory in under 40 moves.

599) Fischer-Schweber [7/23/70] One of Fischer's longest combinations, he executes a Queen sacrifice resulting in a brilliant ending. This game deserves multiple replays.

606) Szabo-Fischer [8/4/70] A little-known game which shows Bobby's excellent feel for which pieces should remain on the board as he wins an instructive ending.

637) Geller-Fischer [11/24/70] A landmark game. As Geller was Fischer's nemesis, Bobby refused an early draw offer with the Black pieces and continued to play. Geller finally cracked with an optical illusion in the ending.

646) Fischer-Mecking [12/8/70] Fischer switches openings with 1.b3 and positionally and tactically outstrips his young Grandmaster opponent.

649) Taimanov-Fischer [5/16/71] Bobby wins a topsy-turvy King's Indian and sets the tone for the match.

652) Fischer-Taimanov [5/25/71] Fischer puts together another Bishop vs. Knight ending with Rooks on the board. Bobby wins with another positional squeeze. To play Black against Fischer at this stage in his career is torture. Bobby wins the match 6-0.

655) Fischer-Larsen [7/6/71] Candidates Semifinal match in Denver. Game one stands out as Fischer finally gets a grip on the Winawer French, winning a cut and thrust struggle against Grandmaster Larsen. Bobby goes on to win this match by a 6-0 score.

661) Fischer-Petrosian [9/30/71] Candidates Match game one. Bobby wins after being surprised by an opening novelty. This is a sloppy game, but a good way to start a match against Petrosian.

667) Petrosian-Fischer [10/17/71] Candidates Match game six. The match score was tied, and this game breaks Petrosian. Bobby has a space advantage and converts the extra pawn in a long ending. Fischer shows superior analysis and great technical virtuosity after the adjournment. Bobby wins the last four games of the match to qualify for the World Championship match with Spassky.

672) Spassky-Fischer [7/16/72] Fischer wins with the Benoni against a nervous Spassky. This game was Bobby's first victory over Boris Spassky.

674) Spassky-Fischer [7/20/72] Fischer wins again with Black in a Nimzo-Indian. This could have been the psychological turning point of the match, as Boris was showing extreme problems with his nerves. Fischer wins in 27 moves.

679) Fischer-Spassky [8/3/72] A favorite game of many Grandmasters, Bobby sacrifices material for the initiative with 26.Bb3! winning a classic game.

690) Spassky-Fischer [8/31/72] Fischer essays an old variation of the Sicilian defense. Boris plays accurately, but falters late in the middlegame. The game is adjourned, but Spassky resigns without further play on September 1, 1972 and Bobby becomes the first official American World Chess Champion in history.

Twenty years later (1992) Bobby and Boris Spassky played a World Championship rematch for a $5 million purse. The match ended with Bobby winning by a score of 10-5 with 15 draws (see page 239).

EXPLANATION OF SYMBOLS

∞	Unclear position
Δ	With the idea of
1-0	White won
0-1	Black won
1/2-1/2	Drawn game
!	Strong move
!!	Brilliant move
?	Weak move
??	Blunder
!?	Interesting move
?!	Dubious move
#	Checkmate
0-0	Castles Kingside
0-0-0	Castles Queenside
+=	White has a slightly better position
=+	Black has a slightly better position
+ -	White has the better position
- +	Black has the better position
++-	White has a winning advantage
-++	Black has a winning advantage
+=/+-	White is slightly to clearly better
[D]	Diagrammed position
[E:	Ending contained in this game (followed by type of ending)

1955

1) Fischer,R-Warner,K [7/15/55] US Junior Championship [1] B72/06 Sicilian **1.e4 c5 2.Nf3 Nc6 3.d4 cd4 4.Nd4 Nf6 5.Nc3 d6 6.Be2 g6 7.Be3 Bg7 8.f3** [8.0-0] **0-0 9.Qd2 a6 10.0-0-0 Qa5 11.Kb1 Rd8 12.g4** [12.Nb3!] **Nd4 13.Bd4 Be6 14.Qe3** [14.Bf6 Bf6 15.Nd5 Qd2 16.Nf6 =] **Nd7 15.f4 Bd4 16.Qd4 Nf6 17.f5 Bd7 18.h4 Bb5! 19.Bf3 Rac8 20.Nb5** [20.Nd5!] **ab5 21.h5 Rc4 22.Qe3? Ra8 23.a3 Qa4 24.c3 Ne4 25.Be4 Re4 26.Qh6** [D] **Re2 27.Rd2?** [27.Qc1] **Rd2 28.Qd2 Qe4 0-1**

After 26.Qh6

2) Whisler,W-Fischer,R [7/16/55] US Junior Championship [2] E81/01 King's Indian **1.d4 Nf6 2.c4 g6 3.Nc3 Bg7 4.e4 d6 5.f3 0-0 6.Bg5 Nbd7** [6...c5!?] **7.Qd2 e5 8.d5** [8.Nge2] **a5 9.h4 Nc5 10.Nge2 Bd7 11.Ng3** [11.g4 △ 12.Ng3] **h5 12.Be2 Qc8 13.Bh6 Kh7 14.Bg7 Kg7 15.Rf1?!** Qd8 16.0-0-0 Ne8 17.Rh1 f5 18.ef5 Bf5 19.Nf5 Rf5 20.g4 Rf4 21.gh5 gh5 22.Rdg1 Kh8 23.Qc2 Ng7 24.Qg6 Qf6 25.Qf6 Rf6 [D] 1/2-1/2

Final position

3) Thomason, J-Fischer,R [7/16/55] US Junior Championship [3] E90/04 King's Indian **1.d4 Nf6 2.c4 g6 3.Nc3 Bg7 4.e4 d6 5.Nf3 0-0 6.Bd3?!** Bg4 **7.0-0** [7.d5] **Nc6 8.Be3 Nd7 9.Be2 Bf3 10.Bf3 e5 11.d5 Ne7** [11...Nd4!] **12.Be2 f5 13.f4?** [13.f3] **h6 14.Bd3 Kh7** [14...ef4! 15.Bf4 g5 16.Bd2 Ne5 =+] **15.Qe2 fe4! 16.Ne4 Nf5 17.Bd2 ef4 18.Bf4 Ne5 19.Bc2?** [19.Rad1] **Nd4 20.Qd2 Nc4 21.Qf2** [D] **Rf4 22.Qf4 Ne2 23.Kh1 Nf4 0-1**

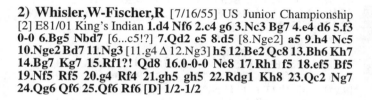

After 21.Qf2

4) Fischer,R-Ames,D [7/18/55] US Junior Championship [4] C55/05 Four Knights **1.e4 e5 2.Nf3 Nc6 3.Nc3 Nf6 4.Bc4! Ne4!** **5.Bf7 Kf7 6.Ne4 d5 7.Neg5 Kg8 8.d4 h6 9.Nh3 Bg4 10.de5 Ne5 11.Nf4 c6 12.h3 Nf3 13.gf3 Bf5 14.Be3 Bb4 15.c3 Ba5 16.Rg1 Qe8?** [16...Kh7] [D] **17.Nd5! Qf7 18.Nf4 Re8 19.Qb3 Bc7 20.Qf7 Kf7 21.Nh5 g6 22.Ng3 Bh3 23.0-0-0 Rd8 24.Rd8 Bd8 25.Rh1 Bg2 26.Rh6 Rh6 27.Bh6 Bf3 28.Be3 1/2-1/2**

After 16...Qe8?

5) Fischer,R-Pupols,V [7/21/55] US Junior Championship [7] C40/08 Latvian Gambit **1.e4 e5 2.Nf3 f5 3.Ne5 Qf6 4.d4 d6 5.Nc4 fe4 6.Nc3 Qg6 7.Ne3** [7.Bf4] **Nf6 8.Bc4 c6 9.d5 Be7 10.a4 Nbd7 11.a5? Ne5 12.Be2 0-0 13.0-0 Bd7 14.Kh1 Kh8 15.Nc4 Nfg4 16.Qe1 Rf7 17.h3 Nf6 18.Ne5 de5 19.Bc4 Rff8 20.Be3 Nh5 21.Kh2** [21.Rd1] **Bd6 22.Bb3 Nf4 23.Bf4 ef4 24.Qe4 f3 25.g3 Bf5 26.Qh4 Rae8 27.Rae1 Be5 28.Qb4 Qh6 29.h4** [D] **g5 30.Rh1 gh4 31.Kg1 h3 32.dc6 bc6 33.Qc5 Qg7 34.Kh2 Qf6 35.Qa7** [35.Rhf1] **Bd4 36.Qc7 Bf2 37.Re8 Re8 38.Rf1 Bd4 39.Rf3 Bc3 40.bc3 Re2 41.Kh1 Be4 42.Qc8 Kg7 43.Qg4 Qg6 44.Qd7 Kh6 0-1** [Time]

After 29.h4

1956

After 29...f5

6) Fischer,R-Nash,E [5/27/56] US Amateur Championship [5] Ashbury Park, New Jersey, A07/07 King's Indian Attack **1.Nf3 Nf6 2.g3 g6 3.Bg2 Bg7 4.0-0 0-0 5.d3 d5 6.Nbd2 Bg4 7.h3 Bd7?!** [7...Bf3] **8.e4 Qc8 9.Kh2 de4 10.de4 Rd8 11.Qe2 Na6 12.Re1** [12.Nb3] **Nb4 13.Nb3 a5 14.c3?!** [14.Ne5 +=] **Nc6 15.Nc5 Be8 16.e5 Nd7 17.Nd3 Nf8 18.h4 Bd7 19.h5 Bg4 20.h6 Bh8 21.Bf4 Qf5 22.Nc5** [22.Rad1] **g5! 23.Bg5 Bf3 24.Bf3 Qg5 25.e6 Qh6 26.Kg2 Ne6 27.Rh1 Qg6 28.Rh4 Ne5 29.Be4 f5** [D] **30.Rah1 Nc5 31.Rh6 Qg4 32.f3 Ne4! 33.fg4 Rd2 34.Qd2 Nd2 35.Rh7 Bg7 36.gf5 Rf8 37.R7h5 Ndc4 38.b3 Ne3 39.Kf2 Nf5 40.g4 Ng4 41.Kf3 Nfe3 42.Ke2 Bc3 43.Rc5 Bb4 44.Rc7 Rf2 45.Kd3 Ra2 46.Rg1 b6 47.Ke4 Rg2 48.Rg2 Ng2 49.Kf5 N4e3 50.Kg6 Nf4 51.Kh6 Nf5 0-1** [52.Kg5 Ne6]

After 19.Na4

7) Grossguth,C-Fischer,R [7/2/56] US Junior Championship [2] Philadelphia B92/07 Sicilian,Najdorf **1.e4 c5 2.Nf3 d6 3.d4 cd4 4.Nd4 Nf6 5.Nc3 a6 6.Be2 e5 7.Nb3 Be7 8.Be3 0-0** [8...Be6!?] **9.Qd2** [9.g4!?] **b5 10.f3 Be6 11.g4?** [11.0-0-0] **d5 12.g5 d4 13.gf6 Bf6 14.0-0-0 de3 15.Qd8 Rd8 16.Nc5 Nc6 17.Ne6 fe6 18.Rhf1 b4 19.Na4** [D] **Nd4 20.Rd4 Rd4 21.Bd3 Rad8 22.Kd1 Bg5 23.Ke2 Bf4 24.h3 Rc8 25.Rd1 Rc6 26.b3 Kf7 27.h4 Kf6 28.h5 a5 29.Nb2 Rd3 0-1** [30.Nd3 Rc2 31.Ke1 Bg3 32.Kf1 e2]

After 20.Bc4

8) Blake,K-Fischer,R [7/6/56] US Junior Championship [9] B72/00 Sicilian **1.e4 c5 2.Nf3 Nc6 3.d4 cd4 4.Nd4 Nf6 5.Nc3 d6 6.Be2 e5 7.Nb3 Be7 8.O-O O-O 9.f4 a5 10.a4 Be6 11.f5 Bb3 12.cb3 Nb4 13.Bg5 Re8 14.Bf3 Qb6 15.Kh1 Rac8 16.Rg1 Qf2 17.Qe2 Qe2 18.Be2 Nc2 19.Rac1 Nd4 20.Bc4** [D] **Ng4 0-1!** [Blake said he did not at the time see how to stop both 21...Nf2# and 21...Bg5. He resigned at this point, but later realized that after 21.h4! he could have continued playing!]

After 41...a5

9) Swank,A-Fischer,R [7/16/56] US Open, Oklahoma City [1] B20/00 Sicilian [E:King + pawn] **1.e4 c5 2.Ne2 Nc6 3.b3 Nf6 4.Nbc3 e6 5.Bb2 d5 6.Ng3 Bd6 7.Bb5 0-0 8.Bd3?** [8.Bc6] **Ne5 9.Be2 Ng6 10.Nb5?** **Ne4 11.Ne4 de4 12.Nd6 Qd6 13.g3 e5 14.c4 Bh3 15.Bf1 Bf1 16.Rf1 f5 17.Qc2 Ne7 18.0-0-0 Nc6 19.Bc3 Nd4 20.Bd4 ed4 21.Kb1 Rae8 22.Rfe1 Re5 23.d3 Rfe8 24.Qd2 ed3 25.Re5 Qe5 26.Qd3 Qe2 27.Rd2 Qd3 28.Rd3 Re1 29.Kc2 Re2 30.Rd2 Rd2 31.Kd2 f4! 32.Kd3 Kf7 33.a3 Kf6 34.b4 b6 35.Ke4 Kg5 36.gf4 Kg4 37.f3 Kh3 38.f5 Kh2 39.f4 Kg3 40.bc5 bc5 41.a4 a5** [D] **42.Kd5 d3 43.Kc5 d2 0-1**

Final position

10) Fischer,R-Gross,H [7/17/56] US Open [2] A07/05 King's Indian Attack **1.Nf3 Nf6 2.g3 d5 3.Bg2 Bf5 4.0-0** [4.c4!?] **e6 5.d3 Bc5 6.Nbd2 Nc6 7.a3** [7.c3! a5 8.b3 0-0 9.a3! Δ 10.Bb2, 11.Qc2 12.b4 +=] **a5 8.Qe1 Bg6 9.e4 de4 10.Ne4 Ne4 11.de4 0-0 12.Be3 Qe7 13.Qc3 Be3 14.Qe3 Rad8 15.Rad1 Rd1 16.Rd1 Rd8 17.Rd8** [D] **1/2-1/2**

11) Tears,C-Fischer,R [7/18/56] US Open [3] B25/00 Sicilian [E:Bishop + pawn] **1.e4 c5 2.Nc3 Nc6 3.d3 g6 4.g3 Bg7 5.Bg2 d6 6.f4 e6 7.Nf3 Nge7 8.0-0 0-0 9.Rb1 Rb8** [9...Bd7 10.Be3 Nd4 11.Ne2 Nf3 12.Bf3 Bc6 =] **10.Ne2 f5 11.Be3 b5 12.e5 Nd5 13.Bf2 de5 14.Bc5 Re8 15.fe5 Ne5 16.Ne5 Be5 17.c4** [17.Ba7 Ra8 Δ 18...Ra2] **Qc7 18.cd5 Qc5 19.Kh1** [19.d4 Qb6] **Qd6 20.d4 Bg7 21.de6 Be6 22.d5 Bf7 23.b3 Rbd8 24.Nf4 Be5 [D] 25.Ne6 Be6 26.de6 Qe6 27.Qe2 a6 28.Rfe1 Qf7 29.Rbd1 Bc3 30.Rd8 Rd8 31.Rd1 Rd1 32.Qd1 Kg7 33.Qf3 Qf6 34.Qb7 Kh6 35.Qb8 Qd4 36.Qf8 Qg7 37.Qg7 Kg7 38.a4 Kf6 39.Bb7 ba4 40.ba4 a5 41.Kg2 Ke5 42.h4 f4 43.Bc6 Be1 44.gf4 Kf4 45.Kh3 1/2-1/2**

After 24...Be5

12) Fischer,R-Lapiken,P [7/19/56] US Open [4] A07/10 King's Indian Attack **1.Nf3 Nf6 2.g3 d5 3.Bg2 Bf5 4.0-0 e6 5.d3 c6 6.Nbd2 Na6 7.a3! Nc5 8.c4** [8.b4! Na4 9.c4 Nc3 10.Qe1 Δ Bb2 +=] **b5 9.Nd4! Qd7 10.Nf5 ef5 11.Nb3 h6 12.Be3 Ne6 13.Nd4 g6 14.Qb3 Rb8 [D] 15.Nc6 Qc6 16.cd5 Nc5 17.Qc3 Qd6** [17...Qb6 18.b4] **18.Bc5 Qc5 19.Qf6 1-0**

After 14...Rb8

13) Owens,B-Fischer,R [7/20/56] US Open [5] E68/07 King's Indian Defence **1.d4 Nf6 2.c4 g6 3.Nc3 Bg7 4.g3 0-0 5.Bg2 d6 6.Nf3 Nbd7 7.0-0 e5 8.e4 ed4 9.Nd4 Nc5 10.Re1 a5** [10...Re8] **11.h3 Re8 12.Bg5!? h6 13.Bf4 Nfd7 14.Be3 c6 15.Qd2 Ne5 16.Qe2** [16.b3 a4] **a4 17.Rad1 Qa5 18.f4 Ned7 19.Kh2 a3 20.Qc2 ab2 21.Qb2 Nb6 22.Bf1 Nba4 23.Na4 Qa4 24.Qg2 [D] Re4** [24...Ne4] **25.Nb3 Re8 26.Nc5 dc5 27.Bc5 Be6 28.Rb1 Bc4 29.Re8 Re8 30.Rb4 Bf1 31.Ra4 Bg2 32.Kg2 Re2 33.Kf3 Rc2 34.Ra8 Kh7 35.Be3 b5 36.Ra7 Kg8 37.Ra8 Bf8 38.f5 g5 39.f6 Rc3 40.Ke4 Rc4 41.Kf5 Rc3 42.Ke4 Rc4 43.Kd3 1/2-1/2**

After 24.Qg2

14) Fischer,R-Santasiere,A [7/22/56] US Open [6] D02/06 King's Indian Attack **1.Nf3 d5 2.g3 Nc6 3.d4 Bg4 4.Bg2 Qd7 5.0-0 g6 6.c4 Bg7 7.cd5 [D] Bf3 8.Bf3 Nd4 9.Bg2 e5 10.de6** [10.Nc3] **Ne6 11.Bb7 Rb8 12.Bg2 Qd1 13.Rd1 Bb2 14.Bb2 Rb2 15.Nc3 Ne7 16.Rab1 Rb6 17.Nb5 0-0 18.Na7 Rfb8 19.Rb6 1/2-1/2**

After 7.cd5

15) Smith,K-Fischer,R [7/23/56] US Open [7] B95/01 Sicilian,Najdorf [E:Bishop + pawn] **1.e4 c5 2.Nf3 d6 3.d4 cd4 4.Nd4 Nf6 5.Nc3 a6 6.Bg5 e6 7.Qd2?!** [7.f4] **h6! 8.Be3** [8.Bh4 Ne4!] **Ng4 9.Be2 Ne3 10.Qe3 Be7 11.f4 Qc7 12.f5 0-0 13.Bg4 Nc6 14.Nc6 bc6 15.0-0 Bg5 16.Qf2 Rb8 17.Rab1 d5 =+ 18.fe6 Be6 19.Bf3 Qe5 20.Qc5 Bf4 21.g3 d4 22.Qe5 Be5 23.Na4 Ba2 24.Rbe1 Rb4 25.Nc5 Rb2 26.Nd3 Rb5 27.Ra1 Be6 28.Ra6 Rc8 29.Be2 g6 30.Re1 Bh3 31.Rd1 Be6 32.Nf4 Rc5 33.Ne6 fe6 34.Bd3 Kf7 35.Ra7 Rc7 36.Rc7 Bc7 37.Ra1 Ke7 38.Ra4 e5 39.Kg2 Kd6 40.Kf3 Ra5 41.Ra5 Ba5 42.Ke2 Kc5 43.Ba6 Kb4 44.Kd3 [D] Ka3 45.g4 g5 46.Bb7 c5 47.Bc6 Kb2 48.Ba4 Kc1 49.Kc4 Kd2 50.Kc5 Ke3 51.Kd5 Bc7 1/2-1/2**

After 44.Kd3

After 11.Bc2

16) Fischer,R-Stevens,W [7/24/56] US Open [8] C82/14 Ruy Lopez **1.e4 e5 2.Nf3 Nc6 3.Bb5 a6 4.Ba4 Nf6 5.0-0 Ne4 6.d4 b5 7.Bb3 d5 8.de5 Be6 9.c3 Bc5 10.Nbd2 0-0 11.Bc2 [D] Nf2 12.Rf2 Bf2 13.Kf2 f6 14.ef6 Qf6 15.Kg1 Rae8 16.Nf1 Ne5 17.Ne3** [17.Be3! Nf3 18.Qf3 Qf3 19.gf3 +=] **Nf3 18.Qf3 Qf3 19.gf3 Rf3 20.Bd1 Rf7 1/2-1/2**

After 16.ed5

17) Ruth,D-Fischer,R [7/25/56] US Open [9] B92/03 Sicilian **1.e4 c5 2.Nf3 d6 3.d4 cd4 4.Nd4 Nf6 5.Nc3 a6 6.Be2 e5 7.Nf3 Be7 8.0-0 0-0 9.h3 Nbd7 10.Re1 b5 11.a4 b4 12.Nd5 Nd5 13.Qd5 Qc7 14.Qb3** [14.Qa8? Nb6] **Nc5 15.Qb4 d5 16.ed5 [D] e4 17.Nd2 Nd3 18.Qe4 Ne1 19.d6 Bd6 20.Qa8 Bb7 21.Qf8 Kf8 22.Kf1 Nc2 23.Rb1 Nd4 24.Bd3 Bb4 0-1**

18) Fischer,R-Popovych,O [7/26/56] US Open [10] A05/08 King's Indian Attack [E:Rook vs. Bishop] **1.Nf3 Nf6 2.g3 g6 3.Bg2 Bg7 4.0-0 0-0 5.d3 d6 6.Nbd2 e5 7.e4 Ne8** [7...c5] **8.c3 f5** [8...c5] **9.d4 f4** [9...ed 10.Nd4]**10.de5 de5 11.Nc4 Qd1 12.Rd1 Nc6 13.gf4 ef4 14.Nd4 Nd4 15.cd4 f3 16.Bf1 Nf6 [D] 17.Ne5!** Be6 [17...Ne4 18.Bc4 Kh8 19.Nf7 Kg8 20.Nd6 Δ 21.Ne4]**18.d5 Ng4 19.Nd3 Bc8 20.Bf4 Rf4 21.Nf4 Be5 22.Nd3 Bh2 23.Kh1 Bd6 24.Bh3 Ne5 25.Ne5 Be5 26.Be6 Kg7 27.Rd3 Be6 28.de6 Kf6 29.Rad1 Re8 30.Rf3 Ke6 31.Kg2 a5 32.a4 b6 33.Rd2 h5 34.Rfd3 Rf8 35.Rf3 Bf4 36.Rc2 c5 37.Rb3 Bc7 38.Rd2 Rf4 39.Rg3 Rf6 40.Rf3 Bf4 41.Rd8 g5 42.Rfd3 Rf7 43.Rh8 Ke5 44.f3 h4 45.Rh6 Rf6 46.Rf6 Kf6 47.Rd7 Ke5 48.Rb7 Kd4 49.Rb6 c4 50.Rb5 Bc7 51.Rd5 Ke3 52.Rg5 1-0**

After 16...Nf6

19) Fischer,R-Popel,S [7/27/56] US Open [11] A04/16 King's Indian Attack [E:Rook + pawn] **1.Nf3 Nf6 2.g3 g6 3.Bg2 Bg7 4.0-0 0-0 5.d3 d6 6.e4 c5 7.Nbd2 Nc6 8.a4 a6 9.Nc4 Rb8 10.a5 Be6 11.Nfd2 d5 12.ed5 Bd5 13.Nb3** [13.Bh3!?] **[D] Bg2 14.Kg2 Nd4 15.Nd4** [15.Nc5? Qd5] **cd4 16.Bf4 Rc8 17.Be5 Qd5 18.Qf3 Qf3 19.Kf3 Nd5 20.Bg7 Kg7 21.Rfe1 e6 22.Ra3 Rfd8 23.Rb3 Rc7 24.Ke2 Ne7 25.Kd2 Nc6 26.Rb6 Rd5 27.Ra1 Kf8 28.Ra3 Ke7 29.Rab3 Nd8 30.f4 g5 31.fg5 Rg5 32.Nd6 Rgc5 33.c4 dc3 34.bc3 Ra5 35.Nb7 Ra2 36.Ke3 Rh2 37.Nd8 Kd8 38.Ra6 Ke7 1/2-1/2**

After 13.Nb3

20) Donovan,J-Fischer,R [7/28/56] US Open [12] E94/10 King's Indian [E:Rook vs. minor piece] **1.d4 Nf6 2.c4 g6 3.Nc3 Bg7 4.e4 d6 5.Nf3 0-0 6.Be2 Nbd7 7.0-0 e5 8.h3** [8.Re1 Δ 9.Bf1 +=] **c6** [8...ed4! 9.Nd4 Re8] **9.Be3 Qe7 10.Qc2 a6 11.a4** [11.d5] **Re8** [11...a5!] **12.de5 de5 13.a5 Nh5 14.Rfd1 Nf4 15.Bf1 Nf8 16.c5 N8e6 17.Na4 Ng5 18.Ng5 Qg5 19.Kh2 Be6! 20.g3 Bh6 [D] 21.gf4 ef4 22.Bc1 Qh4 23.Ra3 Rad8 24.Rad3 Rd3 25.Rd3 Bg7! 26.b3 f5 27.Rf3 fe4 28.Qe4 Bf7 29.Qc2 Re1! 30.Bc4 Qg5 31.Bf7 Kf8!** [31...Kf7 32.Rf4] **32.Rg3 fg3 33.fg3 Qc1 34.Qc1 Rc1 35.Be6 Re1 36.Bc8 Re2 37.Kh1 Re7 38.Kg2 Ke8 39.h4 Kd8 40.Bg4 Re3 0-1**

After 20...Bh6

21) Sobel,R-Fischer,R [8/26/56] Canadian Open, Montreal [2]
B70/04 King's Indian **1.d4 Nf6 2.Nf3 g6 3.g3 Bg7 4.Bg2 0-0
5.0-0 d6 6.Nc3 c5 7.e4** [7.d5] **cd4 8.Nd4 Nc6 9.Nde2 Bd7
10.b3** [10.Nf4] **Qc8 11.Bb2 Bh3 12.f3 Bg2 13.Kg2 d5! 14.ed5
Rd8 15.Qc1 Nb4 16.a3 Nbd5 17.Nd5 Nd5 18.Bg7 Kg7 19.c4
Qe6?** [19...Nf6] **20.Qb2 Nf6 21.Nf4 Qf5 22.Nd5 e6 23.g4 Qg5
24.h4 Qh4 25.Rh1 Qg5** [D] **26.Rh7! Kf8 27.Qf6 1-0**

After 25...Qg5

22) Fischer,R-Fox,M [8/27/56] Canadian Open, Montreal [4]
A05/08 King's Indian Attack [E:Rook + pawn] **1.Nf3 Nf6 2.g3 d6
3.Bg2 g6 4.0-0 Bg7 5.d3 0-0 6.e4 e5 7.Nbd2 c6 8.c3** [8.a4] **Qc7 9.Nh4
a5 10.f4 Nbd7 11.f5 Nc5 12.Nb3 Nb3 13.ab3 Nd7 14.g4 Re8 15.Qf3
Nc5 16.f6** [16.Ra3!] **Bf8 17.Nf5 d5 18.Qg3 de4 19.de4 Kh8 20.Qh4
Qd8 21.Ng7 Bg7 22.fg7 Kg8** [22...Kg7 23.Bg5 ++-] **23.Qf2 Qe7
24.Bg5 Nd3 25.Qe3 Qd7 26.Rab1** [26.Rad1] **Qg4 27.Bh6 Nf4 28.Bf4
ef4 29.Rf4 Qh5 30.Rbf1 Be6 31.Qf2 Re7 32.c4 Qe5 33.Rf6 Kg7 34.h4
Bf5 35.Rf5 gf5 36.ef5 f6 37.Kh1 Qe3 38.Qc2 Rd8 39.Rf3 Qe1 40.Kh2
Rd2 41.Qc3 Qh4 42.Rh3 Rg2 43.Kg2 Re2 44.Kg1 Qe1 45.Qe1 Re1
46.Kf2 Rb1 47.Ke3 Rb2 48.Kd4 b6 49.Kc3 Rf2 50.Rh5 Rf3 51.Kb2
Rg3 52.Rh2 Rg5 53.Rf2 Kf7 54.Kc3 Ke7 55.Re2 Kd7 56.Rd2 Kc7
57.Rf2 Kd6 58.Kd4 Rg4 59.Kd3 Ke5 60.Rh2** [D] **Rg3 61.Kc2 Rg7
62.Rh6 Kf5 0-1**

After 60.Rh2

23) Walz,W-Fischer,R [8/29/56] Canadian Open, Montreal [6]
B25/14 Sicilian **1.e4 c5 2.Nc3 Nc6 3.g3 g6 4.Bg2 Bg7 5.d3 d6 6.f4
e6 7.Nf3 Nge7 8.Be3 0-0 9.0-0 Rb8 10.e5 Nf5 11.Bf2 b6 12.ed6
Qd6 13.Ne4 Qc7 14.c3?** [14.Rab1] **Ba6 15.Qc2 Rfd8 16.Rad1 Rd7
17.Rfe1 Rbd8 18.g4 Nfe7 19.Bg3 Bd3 20.Rd3 Rd3 21.f5 Ne5 22.f6
Nf3 23.Bf3 Qd7 24.fe7 Qe7 25.Bg2 Qd7 26.g5 Rd1 27.Kf1 Kf8
28.Ke2 Re1 29.Ke1 Qd5 30.b3 Be5 31.Be5 Qe5 32.Bf3 h6 33.h4
Qf4 34.Qf2 Qc1 35.Ke2 Rd1 36.gh6 f5 37.h5 e5 38.Bg2** [D] **Qc2
39.Kf3 Rd3 40.Qe3 fe4 0-1**

After 38.Bg2

24) Fischer,R-Matthai,H [8/30/56] Canadian Open, Montreal
[7] B77/14 Sicilian [E:Queen vs. 2 Rooks + pawn] **1.e4 c5 2.Nf3 d6
3.d4 cd4 4.Nd4 g6 5.Nc3 Bg7 6.Be3 Nf6 7.f3 Nc6 8.Qd2 0-0 9.Bc4
Bd7 10.h4 Rc8 11.Bb3 Qa5 12.0-0-0 Nh5 13.g4 Nd4 14.Bd4 Bd4
15.Qd4 Nf4 16.Kb1 Ne6 17.Qd2 Rfe8 18.f4 Nc5 19.h5** [19.f5!]
Nb3 20.ab3 Bg4 21.Rdg1 f5 [21...Bh5 22.Rg5 ++-] **22.hg6 hg6** [D]
**23.b4 Qb4 24.Rg4 fg4 25.f5 Rc3 26.fg6 Rh3 27.Qb4 Rh1 28.Ka2
Kg7 29.e5 de5 30.Qb7 Rhh8 31.Qe4 Kf6 32.Qg4 Reg8 33.b4 Rg6
34.Qf3 Kg7 35.Qe3 Re6 36.Qa7 Rd8 37.Qg1 Kf7 38.b5 Rdd6
39.c4 e4 40.c5 Rd2 41.Kb3 e3 42.Kc3 Rf2 43.c6 Rf5 44.Qh1 Kf6
45.Kd3 e2** [D] **46.c7 Rc5 47.b6 e1=Q 48.Qe1 Re1 49.b7 Rc7
50.b8=Q Rd7 51.Kc2 Re2 52.Kc3 Re3 53.Kc2 Rd6 54.Qh8 Kg5
55.Qg8 Kf4 56.Qg2 Re5 57.Qh2 Kf5 58.Qh5 Ke6 59.Qg4 Rf5
60.Qe4 Re5 61.Qg4 Kd5 62.Qf3 Re4 63.Kd3 Ke5 64.Kc3 Rdd4
65.Qh5 Kd6 66.Qg6 Kc7 67.Qg7 Rd6 68.Qh7 Re5 69.Qg7 Re3
70.Kc4 Re4 71.Kc3 Kd7 72.Qf7 Re5 73.Kc4 Ra5 74.Kb4 Rdd5
75.Kc4 Rac5 76.Kb3 Re5 77.Qg6 Rf5 78.Qg7 Rce5 79.Kc4 Rg5
80.Qh7 Ref5 81.Kd4 Ra5 82.Ke3 Ra3 83.Kf4 Rga5 84.Qf7 Rc5
85.Ke4 Rg5 86.Kf4 Rga5 87.Ke4 R5a4 88.Kd5 Ra5 89.Ke4 Rh3
90.Kf4 Kd6 91.Qg6 e6 92.Qe8 Ra4 93.Kg5 Rg3 94.Kh5 Ra5
95.Kh4 Rga3 96.Qd8 Ke5 97.Qc7 Ke4 98.Qc4 Ke5 99.Qc7 Kf6
100.Qf4 Rf5 101.Qd4 Kg6 102.Qe4 Ra6 103.Qc4 Rd6 104.Qc8
e5 105.Qg8 Kf6 106.Qf8 Ke6 107.Qe8 Kd5 108.Qb5 1/2-1/2**

After 22...hg6

After 45...e2

After 30...Rc2

25) Fischer,R-Sharp,C [8/31/56] Canadian Open, Montreal [8] C84/10 Ruy Lopez **1.e4 e5 2.Nf3 Nc6 3.Bb5 a6 4.Ba4 Nf6 5.0-0 b5 6.Bb3 Be7 7.d4 d6 8.c3 0-0 9.h3 Rb8?! 10.Nbd2 Bd7 11.Re1 Qe8 12.Nf1 Bd8 13.Ng3 Na5 14.Bc2 c5 15.de5 de5 16.Qd6! Nc6 17.Qc5 Bb6 18.Qa3 Qc8 19.Be3 Re8 20.Bb6 Rb6 21.Qc5 Rb7 22.Rad1 Rc7 23.Qd6 Rd8 24.Qa3 a5 25.Rd2 b4 26.cb4 Nb4 27.Bb3 Rc5 28.Red1 Qc7 29.Ng5 Nc2 30.Rc2 Rc2** [D] **31.Qe7 Be8 32.Bf7 Bf7 33.Rd8 1-0**

After 14...Nc6!

26) Bernstein,S-Fischer,R [9/1/56] Canadian Open, Montreal [9] A48/04 Queen's pawn **1.d4 Nf6 2.Nf3 g6 3.Nc3 d5 4.Bf4 Bg7 5.e3 0-0 6.Be2 Nh5 7.Bg5** [7.Be5] **h6 8.Bh4 g5 9.Bg3 Ng3 10.hg3 c5 11.Qd3 e6 12.Ne5 f5 13.g4 f4 14.0-0-0 Nc6!** [D] **15.Rh6 Bh6 16.Qg6 Bg7 17.Bd3 Ne5 18.de5 Rf7 19.Nb5 Kf8! 20.Nd6 Rd7 21.Bb5 Rd6 22.ed6 Bd7 23.Bd7 Qd7 24.Qg5 fe3 25.Qf4 Kg8 26.fe3 Rf8 27.Qg5 Qd6 28.Rh1 Qe5 29.Qh4 Qb2 30.Kd1 Qb1 31.Kd2 Qb4 32.Kd1 Qe4 33.Qh5 Rf2 0-1**

Final Position

27) Anderson,F-Fischer,R [9/2/56] Canadian Open, Montreal [10] B93/12 Sicilian **1.e4 c5 2.Nf3 d6 3.d4 cd4 4.Nd4 Nf6 5.Nc3 a6 6.f4 e5** [6...Qc7] **7.Nf3 Qc7 8.Bd3** [8.a4] **b5 9.a3 Nbd7 10.0-0 Bb7 11.Kh1 g6 12.Qe1 Bg7 13.Qh4 0-0 14.fe5 de5 15.Bh6 Nh5 16.Bg7 Kg7 17.Ng5 Ndf6** [17...h6? 18.Rf7! Rf7 19.Ne6] **18.Nh3 Rae8 19.Rae1 Qe7** [D] **1/2-1/2**

After 32...Rf6

28) Bisguier,A-Fischer,R [10/7/56] Rosenwald Memorial, New York City [1] E78/02 King's Indian **1.d4 Nf6 2.c4 g6 3.Nc3 Bg7 4.e4 d6 5.f4 0-0 6.Nf3 c5 7.Be2** [7.d5] **cd4 8.Nd4 Nc6 9.Nc2 Bd7 10.0-0 Rc8 11.Be3 Na5** [11...a6 12.Qe1 Na5 13.b3 b5∞] **12.b3 a6** [12...b6] **13.e5! de5 14.fe5 Ne8 15.Nd5 Rc6 16.Nd4 Rc8 17.Nc2 Rc6 18.Ncb4! Re6 19.Bg4 Re5 20.Bb6 Qc8 21.Bd7 Qd7 22.Ba5 e6 23.Nd3 Rh5 24.N3f4 Rf5** [24...Ba1 25.Qa1 ed5 26.Nh5 gh5 27.Bb4 Nd6 28.Qe5 Rd8 29.Rd1 ++-] **25.Bb4 ed5 26.Bf8 Ba1 27.Qa1 Kf8 28.Qh8 Ke7 29.Re1 Kd8 30.Nd5 Qc6 31.Qf8 Qd7 32.Rd1 Rf6** [D] **33.Qe8 1-0**

Final position

29) Turner,A-Fischer,R [10/8/56] Rosenwald Memorial [2] E63/00 King's Indian [E:Rook + minor pieces] **1.d4 Nf6 2.c4 g6 3.g3 Bg7 4.Bg2 0-0 5.Nc3 d6 6.Nf3 Nc6 7.0-0 a6 8.e3** [8.h3; 8.d5] **Rb8 9.Nd2 e5** [9...Bd7] **10.Nb3 Bg4?!** [10...ed4!?] **11.f3 Bd7 12.d5 Ne7 13.c5! Ne8 14.e4 f5 15.Be3 f4** [15...Nf6] **16.Bf2 fg3 17.hg3 g5 18.Nd2 Ng6 19.Nc4 h5 20.Qb3 h4 21.g4 h3 22.Bh1 Nh4 23.Bg3 b5 24.cb6 cb6 25.Ne3! b5 26.Nf5 b4 27.Nd1 Nf5 28.gf5 Nf6 29.Ne3! Nh5 30.Kh2 Rc8** [30...a5] **31.Qb4 Ng3 32.Kg3 g4 33.fg4 Bh6 34.Rf3 Bb5 35.Qd2 Bf4 36.Rf4! ef4 37.Kf4 Qf6 38.g5 Qe5 39.Kg4 Rf7 40.g6 Rfc7 41.Bf3 Kg7 42.Rh1 Rh8 43.Rh3 Rcc8 44.Rh8 Rh8 45.Qc3 Qc3 46.bc3 Kf6 47.Kf4 Rh3 48.Bg2 Rh4? 49.Ng4 Kg7 50.Kg5** [D] **1-0**

30) Fischer,R-Bernstein,S [10/9/56] Rosenwald Memorial [3] C70/00 Ruy Lopez [E:Rook vs. minor pieces] **1.e4 e5 2.Nf3 Nc6 3.Bb5 a6 4.Ba4 b5 5.Bb3 d6 6.0-0 Bg4?! 7.c3** [7.h3 +-] **Qf6 8.a4 b4 9.a5 Nge7 10.Ba4! Kd8 11.d3 Bf3 12.gf3 g5 13.Be3 Rg8 14.Nd2 Rg6 15.Nc4 Qe6 16.Kh1 Bg7 17.Rg1 Bf6 18.Rc1 Rb8 19.cb4 Nd4 20.Bd4 ed4 21.Qc2 Rb4 22.e5?!** [22.Ne5!] **[D] Rc4 23.dc4 Qe5 24.Rge1 Qf4 25.Qe4 Be5 26.Qf4 Bf4 27.Rcd1 c5 28.b4! cb4 29.Rd4 Re6 30.Rb1 Nf5 31.Rd3 Re2 32.Kg1 Rd2 33.Rd2 Bd2 34.Rd1 Nd4 35.c5! b3 36.Rb1 Ne2 37.Kf1 Nc3 38.Rb3 Na4 39.cd6 Kd7 40.Rb7 Kd6 41.Rf7 Nc5 42.Rh7 Ba5 43.f4 gf4 44.h4 Bc3 45.h5 Ne6 46.h6 Nf8 47.Ra7 Ke6 48.Ra6 Kf5 49.Ke2 Ng6 50.h7 Bh8 51.Ra8 Bf6 52.Kf3 Ne5 53.Ke2 Nf7 54.Rf8 Kg6 55.Rf7 Kf7 56.Kf3 1/2-1/2**

After 22.e5?!

31) Feuerstein,A-Fischer,R [10/10/56] Rosenwald Memorial [4] E63/04 King's Indian **1.c4 Nf6 2.Nc3 g6 3.g3 Bg7 4.Bg2 0-0 5.d4 d6 6.Nf3 Nc6 7.0-0 a6 8.b3** [8.h3 △ 9.Be3] **Rb8 9.Bb2 b5 10.cb5 ab5 11.d5 Na5 12.Rc1 b4** [12...e6] **13.Na4 e6 14.de6 fe6 15.Qc2 c5 16.Rfd1 Nb7 17.Ne5 Na5 18.Qd3 Ne8 [D] 19.Rc5 Bb7 20.Rc2 Bg2 21.Kg2 Qe7 22.Qa6 de5 23.Qa5 Qb7 24.f3 e4 25.Rf1 Bb2 26.Nb2 Rf5 27.Qa4 Ra8 28.Qc6 Qc6 29.Rc6 Ra2 30.Rb1 ef3 31.ef3 1/2-1/2**

After 18...Ne8

32) Fischer,R-Seidman,H [10/14/56] Rosenwald Memorial [5] A08/03 King's Indian Attack **1.Nf3 Nf6 2.g3 c5 3.Bg2 Nc6 4.0-0 e5 5.d3 d5 6.e4 Be7 7.Nbd2 0-0 8.Re1 de4** [8...d4 9.Nc4 Nd7 10.a4 Qc7 11.Bh3!] **9.de4 Qc7 10.c3 b6 11.Qe2 a5?!** [11...Bb7] **12.a4! [b5 and c4 are weak] Ba6 13.Nc4 b5? 14.ab5 Bb5 15.Bf1 Rad8 16.Qc2 Ng4 17.h3 Nf6 18.Nfd2 Rfe8 19.Nb3 Qc8 20.Kh2 Qe6 21.Nba5 Na5 22.Na5 Bf1 23.Rf1 c4? 24.Qe2 Rd3 25.Ra4 Red8 26.Nc4 h6 27.Re1 Bc5 28.Kg2 g5 29.Nd2 Qd7 30.Ra5 Bb6 31.Ra6 Qb7 32.Ra1 Qd7 33.Nc4 [D] Bf2? 34.Qf2 Nh5 35.Ne5 Qe6 36.Nd3 Rd3 37.Re3 Rd8 38.Qf3 Qb3 39.Qh5 1-0**

After 33.Nc4

33) Reshevsky,S-Fischer,R [10/15/56] Rosenwald Memorial [6] E63/04 King's Indian **1.c4 Nf6 2.d4 g6 3.g3 Bg7 4.Bg2 0-0 5.Nc3 d6 6.Nf3 Nc6 7.0-0 a6 8.b3 Rb8 9.Bb2 b5 10.cb5 ab5 11.Rc1 Na5 12.e4 b4** [12...Nd7] **[D] 13.e5 bc3 14.Bc3 Nb7 15.ef6 Bf6 16.b4 Bf5 17.d5! Bc3 18.Rc3 Qd7 19.Qc1 Rfc8 20.Qh6 f6 21.Nd4 Nd8 22.a3 Nf7 23.Qe3 Ne5 24.f4 Ng4 25.Qd2 h5 26.Re1 Ra8 27.h3 Nh6 28.Kh2 Kf7 29.Qe2 Ng8 30.Rec1 Ra7 31.Qe3 1-0** [Time]

After 12...b4

34) Fischer,R-Mednis,E [10/16/56] Rosenwald Memorial [7] B76/02 Sicilian [E:Rook + pawn; King + pawn] **1.e4 c5 2.Nf3 d6 3.d4 cd4 4.Nd4 Nf6 5.Nc3 g6 6.Be3 Bg7 7.f3 0-0 8.Qd2 Be6 9.Ne6 fe6 10.Bc4** [10.e5! Ne8 11.ed ed 12.0-0-0 +-] **Qc8 11.Bb3 Nc6 12.Ne2 Kh8 13.Nf4 d5! [D] 14.Ne6! Qe6 15.ed5 Nd5 16.Bd5 Qe5 17.Bc6** [17.c3 Rad8 △ 18...e6] **Qb2 18.Rd1 bc6 19.Bd4 Bd4 20.Qd4 Qd4 21.Rd4 Rad8 22.Rd1 Rd1 23.Kd1 Rf5 24.Re1 Rd5 25.Kc1 e5 26.Re4 Kg7 27.Ra4 Rd7 28.Ra6 Rc7 29.Kd2 Kf6 30.Ke3 Ke6 31.Ke4 Kd6 32.Ra3 Rb7 33.Rb3 Rb3 34.ab3 c5 35.c4 Ke6 36.h4 h6 37.f4 ef4 38.Kf4 Kf6 39.Ke4 Ke6 40.Kf4 Kf6 1/2-1/2**

After 13...d5!

After 17.Kf1

35) Byrne,D-Fischer,R [10/17/56] Rosenwald Memorial [8] D97/03 Grunfeld *Fischer's famous "Game of the Century"* **1.Nf3 Nf6 2.c4 g6 3.Nc3 Bg7 4.d4 0-0 5.Bf4 d5 6.Qb3 dc4 7.Qc4 c6 8.e4 Nbd7 9.Rd1 Nb6 10.Qc5 Bg4 11.Bg5?** [11.Be2] **Na4!! 12.Qa3 Nc3 13.bc3 Ne4! 14.Be7 Qb6 15.Bc4 Nc3! 16.Bc5 Rfe8 17.Kf1 [D] Be6!! 18.Bb6** [18.Qc3 Qc5!; 18.Be6 Qb5 19.Kg1 Ne2 20.Kf1 Ng3 21.Kg1 Qf1! 22.Rf1 Ne2#] **Bc4 19.Kg1 Ne2 20.Kf1 Nd4 21.Kg1 Ne2 22.Kf1 Nc3 23.Kg1 ab6 24.Qb4 Ra4! 25.Qb6 Nd1 26.h3 Ra2 27.Kh2 Nf2 28.Re1 Re1 29.Qd8 Bf8 30.Ne1 Bd5 31.Nf3 Ne4 32.Qb8 b5 33.h4 h5 34.Ne5 Kg7 35.Kg1 Bc5 36.Kf1 Ng3 37.Ke1 Bb4 38.Kd1 Bb3 39.Kc1 Ne2 40.Kb1 Nc3 41.Kc1 Rc2# 0-1**

Final position

36) Fischer,R-Pavey,M [10/21/56] Rosenwald Memorial [9] B45/08 Sicilian [E:Bishop + pawn] **1.e4 c5 2.Nf3 Nc6 3.d4 cd4 4.Nd4 Nf6 5.Nc3 e6 6.Ndb5 Bb4 7.Nd6** [7.a3!] **Ke7! 8.Nc8 Rc8 9.Bd3 d5 10.ed5 Qd5 11.0-0 Qh5 12.Qh5 Nh5 13.Ne4 Ne5 14.Be2 Nf6 15.Nf6 gf6 16.c3 Bc5 17.Bf4 Rhd8 18.Rfd1 Bb6 19.Be5 Rd1 20.Rd1 fe5 21.Bf3 Rc7 22.Re1 Rd7 23.Rd1 Rd1 24.Bd1 e4 25.Kf1 Bc7 26.g3 Kd6 27.Ke2 Ke5 28.Ba4 f5 29.Bd7 Bd8 30.Bc8 b6 31.Bd7 Bg5 32.b3 Bf6 33.Bc8 Kd5 34.Kd2 Bg5 35.Ke2 [D] ½-½**

After 22.Bc6

37) Shainswit,G-Fischer,R [10/22/56] Rosenwald Memorial [10] E68/07 King's Indian **1.Nf3 Nf6 2.c4 g6 3.g3 Bg7 4.Bg2 0-0 5.0-0 d6 6.Nc3 e5 7.d4 Nbd7 8.e4 ed4** [8...c6; 8...Re8] **9.Nd4 Nc5 10.Nb3 Be6 11.Nc5 dc5 12.Qe2 c6 13.Rd1 Qa5!** [13...Qe7 14.Bf4 Rad8 15.Na4 Rd4 16.Rd4 cd4 17.c5 b5! -+] **14.Bd2 Rad8 15.e5 Ng4 16.Ne4 Qa6 17.Nc5 Qc4 18.Qc4 Bc4 19.Bc3! Rd1 20.Rd1 b6 21.Nd7 Rd8 22.Bc6 [D] Ba2 23.Ra1 Be6 24.Ra7 Bd7 25.Rd7 Rd7 26.Bd7 Ne5 27.Be5 ½-½**

After 28.Bf7

38) Fischer,R-Hearst,E [10/24/56] Rosenwald Memorial [11] C64/05 Ruy Lopez **1.e4 e5 2.Nf3 Nc6 3.Bb5 Bc5 4.0-0 Nd4 5.Nd4 Bd4 6.c3 Bb6 7.d4 c6 8.Ba4 d6 9.Na3 Nf6** [9...Qe7 10.d5!; 9...Bc7 10.Bc2 +=] **10.Re1** [10.Bc2 Be6 11.Bg5 h6 12.Bf6 Qf6 +=] **Qe7 11.Bg5 h6 12.Bh4** [12.Bf6] **g5 13.Bg3 h5 14.f3 h4 15.Bf2 g4 16.Nc4 g3 17.hg3 hg3 18.Bg3 Nh5 19.Bh2 Bc7 20.Ne3 Qh4 21.Qd2 Bd7 22.Bb3 Rh7 23.Qf2 Qg5 24.Rad1 Nf4 25.Bf4 ef4 26.Nf5 0-0-0 27.Kf1 Rh2 28.Bf7 [D] d5 29.Rd2 Rf8 30.Qg1 Rh7 31.ed5 Rhf7 32.dc6 Bc6 33.d5 Bb5 34.Ree2 Rf5 35.Qa7 Rd5 36.c4 Bc4 37.Qa8 Bb8 38.Rc2 Rc5 39.Ke1 Be2 40.Qa5 Qg3 0-1**

After 39...Rb7

39) Fischer,R-di Camillo,A [11/56] Washington D.C. C78/09 Ruy Lopez **1.e4 e5 2.Nf3 Nc6 3.Bb5 a6 4.Ba4 Nf6 5.0-0 b5 6.Bb3 d6 7.c3 Bg4 8.h3?! Bh5 9.d3 Be7 10.Nbd2 0-0 11.Re1 Qd7 12.Nf1 Na5 13.Bc2 h6 14.g4! Bg6 15.Ng3 Nh7 16.Nf5 Nb7 17.d4 ed4 18.cd4 Nd8 19.Ne7 Qe7 20.d5! c5 21.Bf4 Nb7 22.Bg3 Rfe8 23.a4! Qf6 24.ab5 ab5 25.Kg2 Ng5 26.Ng5 hg5 27.Ra8 Ra8 28.e5! Bc2 29.Qc2 de5 30.Be5 Qd8 31.d6 c4 32.Qe4 Nc5 33.Qc6 Nd3 34.Re3 Rc8 35.Qb7 Rb8 36.Qd5 Nb4 37.Qc5 Nd3 38.Qd4 Rb6 39.d7 Rb7 [D] 40.Bc7! Nf4 41.Kf1 1-0**

40) Nash,E-Fischer,R [11/56] Washington D.C. B95/01
Sicilian, Najdorf [E:Rook vs. Bishops] **1.e4 c5 2.Nf3 d6 3.d4 cd4
4.Nd4 Nf6 5.Nc3 a6 6.Bg5 e6 7.Qd2 h6! 8.Be3 Ng4 =+** [Bishop
pair] **9.Nb3 Ne3 10.Qe3 Nc6 11.Be2 Be7 12.0-0 0-0 13.Rad1 b5
14.f4 Bd7 15.Bf3 Na5 16.Be2 Nc4 17.Bc4 bc4 18.Nd2 Qc7 19.Kh1
Rfc8 20.Nf3 Rab8 21.Rb1 a5 22.f5 a4 23.fe6 fe6 24.a3 Qc5 25.Qc5
Rc5 26.Na2 Rcb5 27.Nb4 c3! 28.Nd4 Rc5 29.Na6 Rb2 30.Nc5
dc5 31.Nf3 c4 32.Ne5 Bb5 33.Rb2 cb2 34.c3 Bf6 [D] 35.Rb1 Be5
36.Rb2 Be8 37.Rb4 Bc3 38.Rc4 Bb2 39.Rb4 Ba3 40.Rb6 Kf7
41.Rb7 Be7 42.e5 a3 43.Kg1 Bc6 44.Ra7 Bd5 45.Kf1 a2 46.Ke2
Kg6 47.g4 Bc5 48.Ra5 Bd4 0-1**

After 34...Bf6

41) Marchand,E-Fischer,R [11/56] Washington D.C. A15/13
English **1.c4 Nf6 2.Nf3 g6 3.b3 Bg7 4.Bb2 0-0 5.g3 d6 6.Bg2 e5 7.d3
Nbd7 8.0-0 Ne8 9.Qc2 f5 10.d4 e4 11.Ne1 c6 12.e3 Qe7 13.Nc3 h5
14.Rd1 h4 15.Qe2 hg3 16.fg3 Ndf6 17.Nc2 Bd7 18.Rb1 Kh7 19.Nd1
Rh8 20.Nf2 Kg8 21.Rfe1 Nh7 22.Nh3 Nef6 23.Nf4 Qf7 24.Rf1 g5
25.Nh3 g4 26.Nf4 Ng5 27.Kf2 Rh2 28.Nh1 Rh1 29.Rh1 Ne6 30.Ne6
Be6 31.Ba3 d5 32.c5 Qc7 33.Qd2 Bf7 34.Bf1 Nh5 35.Rg1 Bf6 36.Qe1
Kg7 37.Ke2 Rh8 38.Qf2 Kg6 39.Bb4 Ng7 40.Kd1 Ne6 41.Ne1 b6
42.Be2 Bg5 43.Rf1 Ng7 44.Ng2 Be6 45.cb6 ab6 46.Nf4 Bf4 47.gf4
c5 48.dc5 bc5 49.Bc3 d4! 50.Bb2** [50.ed cd 51.Bd4 Rd8 -++] **d3
51.Bg4 fg4 52.f5 Bf5 53.Bg7 Rh5 54.Ba1 Qh2 55.Bc3 g3 [D] 0-1**

Final Position

42) Goldhamer-Fischer,R [11/56] Washington D.C. B92/07
Sicilian,Najdorf **1.e4 c5 2.Nf3 d6 3.d4 cd4 4.Nd4 Nf6 5.Nc3 a6
6.Be2 e5 7.Nb3 Be7 8.Be3 0-0 9.f3?!** [9.g4!?; 9.f4] **Be6 10.Qd2 b5
11.Rd1** [11.g4 d5!; 11.0-0-0] **Nbd7 12.g4 Rc8 13.h4 Nb6 14.g5
Nh5! 15.Kf2 f5! 16.Kg2 fe4 17.Bb6 Qb6 18.Nd5** [18.fe Qf2#;
18.Ne4 d5 -++] **ef3 19.Bf3 Bd5 20.Bd5 Kh8 21.Be4 [D] d5 22.Bf3
Nf4 23.Kg3 Bd6 24.Rhf1 e4 25.Bg4 e3 0-1**

After 21.Be4

43) Fischer,R-Hurttlen,N [11/56] Washington D.C. C85/07
Ruy Lopez **1.Nf3 Nc6 2.e4 e5 3.Bb5 a6 4.Ba4 Nf6 5.0-0 Be7
6.Re1 0-0?** [6...b5] **7.Bc6 dc 8.Ne5 Bc5 9.c3?!** [9.Nf3 ++-] **Re8
10.d4 Bd6 11.Bg5??** [11.f4++-] **Be5 12.de5 Qd1 13.Rd1 Ne4
14.Be3 Bf5 [D] 1/2-1/2**

Final position

44) Feuerstein,A-Fischer,R [11/56] Washington D.C. King's
Indian **1.Nf3 Nf6 2.c4 g6 3.g3 Bg7 4.Bg2 0-0 5.0-0 d6 6.d4 Nbd7
7.Nc3 e5 8.e4 ed4 9.Nd4 Nc5 10.f3 Nfd7 11.Be3 a5 12.Qc2 a4
13.Rf2 c6 14.Bf1 Qe7 15.Qd2 Re8 16.Nc2 Ne5 [D] 17.Rd1 Bf8
18.Bh6 Bh6 19.Qh6 f5 20.ef5 Bf5 21.Nd4 Bd3 22.Bd3 Ned3
1/2-1/2**

After 16...Ne5

After 7...a6

45) Fischer,R-Vine,K [1956/7] Manhattan Club Ch. B32/02 Sicilian [E:Rook + minor piece] **1.e4 c5 2.Nf3 Nc6 3.d4 cd4 4.Nd4 d5 5.Bb5** [5.Nc3 de4 6.Nc6 Qd1 7.Kd1 bc6 8.Ne4 Bf5 9.Bd3 0-0-0 10.Ke2 e6 11.Bf4 +-] **de4 6.Nc6 Qd1 7.Kd1 a6 [D] 8.Ba4 Bd7 9.Nc3 Bc6 10.Bc6 bc6 11.Ne4 e6 12.Ke2 Rd8 13.Be3 Nf6 14.Nf6 gf6 15.Rhd1 Be7 16.c4 e5 17.g4 h5 18.h3 hg4 19.hg4 Rh4 20.Kf3 Bd6 21.b3 Ke7 22.Rd2 Bc7 23.Rd8 Bd8 24.b4 Ke6 25.a4 f5 26.gf5 Kf5 27.b5 ab5 28.cb5 cb5 29.a5 Bg5 30.Bb6 Bf4 31.a6 e4 32.Ke2 Rh8 33.a7 Ra8 34.Ra5 Ke6 35.Rb5 Bd6 36.Ke3 Be5 1/2-1/2**

After 12...Qc7

46) Tamargo,J-Fischer,R [1956/7] Manhattan Club Ch. B22/00 Smith Morra Gambit Declined [E:Rook + pawn] **1.e4 c5 2.d4 cd4 3.c3 Nf6 4.e5 Nd5 5.cd4 Nc6 6.Nc3** [6.Nf3] **Nc3 7.bc3 d5** [7...d6] **8.Bd3 e6 9.Ne2 Be7 10.0-0 Bd7 11.f4 g6 12.g4 Qc7 [D] 13.f5 gf5 14.gf5 ef5 15.Ng3 0-0-0 16.Nf5 Be6 17.Kh1 h5 18.Qf3 Rdg8 19.Nh6 Rf8 20.Bf5 Qd7 21.Bd2 f6 22.Be6 Qe6 23.Qf5 Qf5 24.Nf5 fe5 25.Ne7 Ne7 26.de5 Kd7 27.Bg5 Ke6 28.Bf6 Rhg8 29.Rab1 b6 30.Rfd1 Rc8 31.Be7 Ke7 32.Rd5 Rc3 33.a4 Ke6 34.Rdb5 Ra3 35.a5 ba5 36.R1b3 Rb3 37.Rb3 Rg5 38.Rb7 Ke5 39.Ra7 Kd4 40.h4 Rg4 0-1**

After 29...Re5

47) Fischer,R-Pavey,M [1956/7] Manhattan Club Ch. A05/08 King's Indian Attack [E:Bishop + pawn] **1.Nf3 Nf6 2.g3 g6 3.Bg2 Bg7 4.0-0 0-0 5.d3 d6 6.e4 Nbd7 7.Nbd2 e5 8.Ne1** [8.a4 a5 9.Nc4 Nc5 10.Bd2 Bd7 11.b3 b6 12.Qc1 +=] **Nc5 9.f4 ef4 10.gf4 Ng4! 11.Ndf3 f5 12.h3 fe4 13.de4 Nf6 14.e5 de5 15.Qd8 Rd8 16.fe5 Nh5 17.Be3 Ne6 18.Nd3 Ng3 19.Rfd1 Nf5 20.Bf2 Bd7 21.Nh4 Nh4 22.Bh4 g5 23.Bf2 c6 24.Rd2 Be8 25.Be3 Bg6 26.Rad1 Re8 27.Bf1 Re7 28.Nc5 Nc5 29.Bc5 Re5 [D] 30.Bc4 Kh8 31.Rd8 Rd8 32.Rd8 Re8 33.Re8 Be8 34.c3 b6 35.Be3 Bf6 36.a4 Kg7 37.a5 Bd8 38.Kg2 h6 39.Bd4 Bf6 40.Bf2 c5 41.Bd5 Be5 42.Be3 Bf7 43.Bc6 Be6 44.b4 Bd6 45.ab6 ab6 46.bc5 bc5 47.Bf3 Kf6 48.Bg4 Bg4 49.hg4 Ke5 50.Kf3 Kd5 51.Ke2 Kc4 52.Kd2 Bf4 0-1**

After 19...Rae8

48) Turner,A-Fischer,R [1956/7] Manhattan Club Ch. E69/25 King's Indian [E:Rook + minor pieces] **1.Nf3 Nf6 2.g3 g6 3.Bg2 Bg7 4.0-0 0-0 5.d4 d6 6.c4 Nbd7 7.Nc3 e5 8.e4 ed4** [8...c6] **9.Nd4 Nc5 10.h3 Re8 11.Re1 a5 12.Qc2 c6** [12...Nfe4? 13.Ne4 Bd4 14.Bg5! ++-] **13.Be3 Nfd7 14.Rad1 a4 15.f4 Qa5 16.Bf2 Nb6 17.Bf1 Bd7 18.Kh2 Re7 19.g4! Rae8 [D] 20.Bh4 f6 21.f5 Rf8 22.Bg3 Nc8 23.Qd2 Qc7 24.Kh1 Be8 25.b4 ab3 26.ab3 Bf7 27.b4 Nd7 28.Nf3 Ne5 29.Ne5 de5 30.Bf2 Ree8 31.Qd7 Re7 32.Qd2 Ree8 33.Qd7 Re7 34.Qc7 Rc7 35.Na4 Re8 36.Nc5 Bf8 37.Nd7 Be7 38.Bc5 gf5 39.ef5 Bd5 40.cd5 Rd7 41.dc6 Rd1 42.Rd1 bc6 43.Bc4 Kg7 44.Rd7 Kh6 45.Rc7 Kg5 46.Rc8 Rc8 47.Be7 e4 48.Kg2 h5 49.Kg3 hg4 50.Be6 Rb8 51.Bd6 Rg8 52.Bf4 Kh5 53.Bf7 1-0**

49) Fischer,R-Baron,S [1956/7] Manhattan Club Ch. C98/09 Ruy
Lopez **1.e4 e5 2.Nf3 Nc6 3.Bb5 a6 4.Ba4 Nf6 5.0-0 Be7 6.Re1 b5
7.Bb3 d6 8.c3 0-0 9.h3 Na5 10.Bc2 c5 11.d4 Qc7 12.Nbd2 Nc6
13.dc5 dc5 14.Nf1 Be6 15.Ne3 Rad8 16.Qe2 Rd7?!** [Better would
have been 16...Rfe8] **17.Ng5 Rfd8 18.Ne6 fe6 19.a4 c4 20.ab5 ab5
21.b3! [D] Nd4 22.cd4 ed4 23.bc4 de3 24.Be3 bc4 25.Ra6! e5
26.Bb6 Qc8 27.Ra4 Rd2 28.Qc4 Qc4 29.Rc4 Rb8 30.Be3 Rd7
31.Ra1 Rbb7 32.Ra5 Bd6 33.Rc6 Bb8 34.Rb6 h6 35.g3 Kf7
36.Rb7 Rb7 37.Kg2 Rb2 38.Bd3 Rb4 39.Kf3 Rb2 40.Bc4 Kg6
41.Ra6 Rb4 42.Rc6 Ra4 43.Be6 Re4 44.Bc4 Re3 45.Ke3 Ba7
46.Kf3 e4 47.Ke2 Bd4 48.Rc7 h5 49.Bb3 Bb6 50.Rb7 Bc5 51.Bc2
Kh6 52.Rc7 Bf8 53.Rc4 1-0**

After 21.b3!

1957

After 21...Rg5

50) Avram,H-Fischer,R [2/22/57] Log Cabin Open [1] E87/05 King's Indian,Samisch **1.d4 Nf6 2.c4 g6 3.Nc3 Bg7 4.e4 d6 5.f3 e5 6.d5 Nh5 7.Be3 0-0 8.Qd2 f5 9.0-0-0 f4 10.Bf2 Bf6** [Trying to exchange his bad Bishop for White's good Bishop with ...Bh4] **11.Nge2 Bh4 12.Bg1!** [Avoiding the trade] **Be7 13.Kb1 Nd7 14.Nc1 Kh8 15.Nd3 a6 16.Qc2 Rf7 17.Ne2 Qf8 18.Qc3 g5 19.c5!** dc5 **20.h4 Rg7 21.hg5 Rg5 [D] 22.Rh5! Rh5 23.Nef4 Rh1 24.Ne6 Qf6 25.Be3 Bd6 26.Nf2 Rh5 27.Be2 Nf8 28.Nf8 Bf8 29.f4 Rh2 30.fe5 Qg6 31.Bf3 b6 32.Bf4 Rh4 33.g3 Rh2 34.Qe1 Bh6 35.e6 Bf4 36.gf4 h5 37.Nd3 h4 38.Qc3 Qg7 39.Ne5 Bb7 40.Bh5 Rg8 41.e7 Qe7 42.Ng6 Kh7 43.Ne7 1-0**

Final position

51) Santasiere,A-Fischer,R [2/24/57] Log Cabin Open [5] E67/03 King's Indian **1.Nf3 Nf6 2.c4 g6 3.Nc3 Bg7 4.g3 0-0 5.Bg2 d6 6.d4 Nbd7 7.0-0 e5 8.de5** [Playable, but insipid] **de5 9.Bg5?! h6!** ["Putting the question to the Bishop" - Nimzowitsch] **10.Bf6 Qf6 11.Nd2 Nc5 12.Rc1** [12.b4 Ne6] **a5 13.Nb3 Rd8 14.Nd5 Qd6 15.Nc5 Qc5 16.Qb3 Bf8 17.Rfd1 Kg7 18.Qf3 Ra6! 19.e4 Rad6 20.a3 a4 21.Bf1 h5 22.h3 c6 23.Nc3 Rf6 24.Qf6 Kf6 25.Rd8 Bh6 26.Rcd1 Be6 27.Na4 Qa5 28.Nc3 h4 29.Kg2 hg3 30.fg3 Be3 31.R8d3 Bd4 32.b4 Qa7 33.Ne2 c5 34.Nd4 cd4 35.Rf3 Kg7 36.c5 f5 37.Bd3 Qa3 38.Kg1 Qb4 39.Rb1 Qc5 40.Rb7 Kf6 41.ef5 Qd5?** [41...gf5] **42.fe6 [D] 1-0**

After 11...0-0

52) Fischer,R-Goldsmith,J [2/24/57] Log Cabin Open [6] C41/06 Philidor [E:Rook + minor pieces] **1.e4 c6 2.Nc3 d6** [Unusual but playable] **3.d4 Nd7 4.Nf3 e5 5.Bc4 Be7** [Now it's a Philidor's Defence] **6.de5 Ne5?** [6...de5 7.Ng5! Bg5 8.Qh5 g6 9.Qg5 +=] **7.Ne5 de5 8.Qh5 g6 9.Qe5 ++- Nf6 10.Bg5 Bd7 11.0-0-0 0-0 [D] 12.Rd7 Qd7 13.Bf6 Bf6 14.Qf6 Rae8 15.f3 Qc7 16.h4 Qe5 17.Qe5 Re5 18.Rd1 Re7 19.Rd6 Kg7 20.a3 f5 21.Kd2 fe4 22.Ne4 Rf4 23.h5 gh5 24.Rd8 h4 25.Rg8 Kh6 26.Ke3 Rf5 27.Rg4 Rh5 28.Kf2 Rg7 29.Rg7 Kg7 30.Bf1 Rd5 31.Bd3 h6 32.Ke3 Rh5 33.Nd6 h3 34.gh3 Rh3 35.Nb7 Rh5 36.b4 Re5 37.Kf4 Re7 38.Nd8 c5 39.bc5 Kf6 40.c6 Rc7 41.Be4 Ke7 42.Nb7 Kf6 43.Nd6 Re7 44.c7 1-0**

After 17...Kf8

53) Euwe,M-Fischer,R [3/57] Match, New York [1] D50/01 Nimzo-Indian **1.d4 Nf6 2.c4 e6** [Varying from his usual King's Indian] **3.Nc3 d5 4.cd5 ed5 5.Bg5 Bb4** [Ragozin's system, employed several times by Fischer with mixed results] **6.e3 h6 7.Bh4 c5 8.Bd3 Nc6 9.Ne2 cd4 10.ed4 0-0 11.0-0 Be6?** [11...Be7 +=] **12.Bc2! Be7 13.Nf4! Qb6 14.Bf6 Bf6 15.Qd3 Rfd8 16.Rae1! Nb4 17.Qh7 Kf8 [D] 18.a3! Nc2 19.Ncd5 Rd5 20.Nd5** [20...Bd5 21.Qh8#] **1-0**

54) Fischer,R-Euwe,M [3/57] Match, New York [2] C83/19
Ruy Lopez **1.e4 e5 2.Nf3 Nc6 3.Bb5 a6 4.Ba4 Nf6 5.0-0 Ne4** [Euwe
often preferred the Open Defence to the Ruy Lopez] **6.d4 b5 7.Bb3
d5 8.de5 Be6 9.c3 Be7 10.Nbd2 0-0 11.Qe2 Nc5 12.Nd4** [12.Bc2
d4!] **Nb3 13.N2b3 Qd7 14.Nc6 Qc6 15.Be3 Qc4** [D] **16.Qc2**
1/2-1/2

After 15...Qc4

55) Feuerstein,A-Fischer,R [3/31/57] Log Cabin 50-50 [2]
E87/08 King's Indian [E:Rook + minor piece] **1.Nf3 Nf6 2.g3 g6
3.Bg2 Bg7 4.0-0 0-0 5.c4 d6 6.d4 c5** [6...Nc6; 6...Nbd7] **7.h3** [7.d5;
7.dc5] **cd4 8.Nd4 Nc6! 9.e3** [9.Nc6 bc6 10.Bc6 Bh3 =+] **d5**
[9...Bd7] **10.cd5 Nd5 11.Nc6 bc6 12.e4 Nb4 13.Qb3 Rb8 14.a3
Be6 15.Qa4 Nd3 16.Nc3 Nb2 17.Bb2 Rb2 18.Rac1 Qb6 -++**
**19.Nd1 Rb5 20.Qc2 Rb3 21.Qc6 Qc6 22.Rc6 Ra3 23.Rc7 Rd8
24.Ne3 Bd4 25.Nd5 Bd5 26.ed5 Kf8 27.Re1 Bf6 28.Re2 a5
29.Kh2 Ra1 30.Ra7 a4 31.Bf3 Rd6 32.Re4 Rd5** [D] **33.Ree7 Be7
34.Bd5 a3 35.Ra8 Kg7 36.Ra7 Rd1 37.Bf3 Re1 38.Kg2 Bc5
39.Ra4 Rc1 40.Be4 Kf6 41.f4 Ke6 42.Ra6 Ke7 43.g4 Rc4 44.Kf3
Rc3 45.Kg2 Rb3 46.Bd5 Rb2 47.Kf3 Rh2 48.Kg3 Rd2 49.Bc4
Rc2 50.Bd5 Bd6 1/2-1/2**

After 32...Rd5

56) Hurttlen,N-Fischer,R [3/31/57] Log Cabin 50-50 [3]
A02/04 Bird's **1.f4 Nf6 2.Nf3 g6 3.b3** [3.e3] **Bg7 4.Bb2 0-0 5.d3?**
[Weakens e3; correct was 5.e3] **d5 6.Nbd2? Ng4! 7.Bg7 Ne3! 8.Qc1
Kg7 9.Qb2 f6 10.d4 Bf5 11.Rc1 Nc6 12.Qc3 Nf1 13.Nf1 Qd6!
14.e3 Nb4 15.Qb2** [D] **Bc2! 16.Kd2** [16.Rc2 Nd3] **Be4 17.Ne1
Rae8 18.Ng3 e5 19.Rf1 ed4 20.Qd4 b6 21.a3 c5 22.Qb2 Nc6
23.Ne4 Re4 24.Nf3 d4 25.Qc2 Re3 0-1**

After 15.Qb2

57) Fischer,R-Saidy,A [3/31/57] Log Cabin 50-50 [4] B57/00
Sicilian **1.e4 c5 2.Nf3 Nc6 3.d4 cd4 4.Nd4 Nf6 5.Nc3 d6 6.Bc4 e5?**
[A positional mistake, weakening d5 and f5. Better was 6...e6] **7.Nf5
Be6 8.Bb3 Bf5 9.ef5 Be7 10.Bg5 0-0 11.0-0 Nd4 12.Bf6 Bf6
13.Qd3 Qd7 14.f4 Nb3** [14...Nf5 15.fe ++-] **15.ab3 ef4 16.Rf4 Be5
17.Rf3 Qd8 18.Nd5! Qh4** [18...Bb2 19.f6! Ba1 20.Ne7 Kh8 21.Qh7
Kh7 22.Rh3#] **19.Ra4! Qh2 20.Kf2 Qh5 21.Ne7 Kh8 22.Rh3 Qg5**
[D] **23.Rh7! Kh7 24.f6 g6 25.Qh3 Qh5 26.Rh4 Bf6 27.Rh5 gh5
28.Qh5 Kg7 29.Nf5 Kg8 30.c3??** [30.Qh6! wins] **Rae8 31.Nd6
Re5 32.Qg4 Rg5 33.Qf4 Rg6 34.Ne4 Bg7 35.g3 Re8 36.Kg2 Be5
37.Qf5 b6 38.b4 Bg7 39.Qf3 Rge6 40.Ng5 Rf6 41.Qh5 Re5
42.Qh7 Kf8 43.Ne4? Rg6?** [43...Rh6] **44.Qh4 Re8 45.Qf4 Be5
46.Qf5 1/2-1/2**

After 22...Qg5

58) Sherwin,J-Fischer,R [3-31-57] Log Cabin 50-50 [?]
E87/08 King's Indian **1.c4 Nf6 2.d4 g6 3.Nc3 Bg7 4.e4 0-0 5.f3 d6
6.Be3 e5 7.d5 Nh5 8.Qd2 f5 9.ef5 gf5 10.0-0-0 a6 11.Bd3 Nd7
12.Nge2 Nc5 13.Bc2 b5 14.Ng3 Nf4 15.Nge2 b4 16.Na4 Ne2
17.Qe2 Na4 18.Ba4 Bd7 19.Bc2 a5 20.c5 a4 21.c6 b3 22.ab3 ab3
23.Bb3 Qb8 24.Qc4 Be8 25.h4 f4 26.Bf2 Bg6 27.h5 Bf5 28.h6 Bf6
29.Kd2 Ra5 30.Ra1 Rb5 31.Ba7** [D] **Rb3 32.Bb8 Rb2 33.Kc1 Rfb8
34.Rd1 Bh4 35.Ra2 R2b4 36.Qa6 R8b5 37.Kd2 Rd5 38.Ke2 Rd1
39.Kd1 Rd4 40.Ke2 Bd3 41.Qd3 1-0**

After 31.Ba7

After 29.Nc5

59) Hearst,E-Fischer,R [5/25/57] New York Metropolitan League [5] B93/00 Sicilian [E:Rook + pawn] **1.e4 c5 2.Nf3 d6 3.d4 cd4 4.Nd4 Nf6 5.Nc3 a6 6.f4 e5 7.Nf3 Qc7 8.Bd3 Nbd7 9.0-0 b5 10.a3 Bb7 11.Kh1 g6 12.Be3 Ng4 13.Bd2 Bg7 14.f5 Ngf6 15.Ng5 h6 16.Nh3 g5 17.Nf2 Nc5 18.b4 Nd3 19.cd3 Qd7 20.Qe2 Rc8 21.a4 0-0 22.ab5 ab5 23.Ra5 d5! 24.ed5 Nd5 25.Nd5 Qd5 26.Ne4 Rfd8 27.Be1 Qd3 28.Qd3 Rd3 29.Nc5 [D] Rd1! 30.Nb7 Rcc1 31.Kg1 Re1 32.Re1 Re1 33.Kf2 Re4 34.Rb5 Bf8 35.Nc5 Rb4! 36.Ra5** [36.Rb4 Bc5] **Bc5 37.Rc5 Rf4 38.Ke3 Rf5 39.g4 Rf4 40.h3 e4 41.Rc4 Rf3 42.Ke4 Rh3 43.Ke5 Re3 44.Kf6 Rf3 45.Ke5 Kg7 46.Kd5 Kg6 47.Rc1 Rf4 48.Rg1 f5 49.gf5 Kf5 50.Rh1 Kg6 51.Ke5 h5 52.Rd1 h4 53.Rg1 Kh5 54.Rh1 Rf8 55.Rd1 h3 56.Ke4 Kh4 57.Rd7 Rf1 58.Rd2 g4 59.Rd8 h2 0-1**

Final position

60) Fischer,R-Fauber,R [7/4/57] Milwaukee New Western Open [1] A05/08 King's Indian Attack **1.Nf3 Nf6 2.g3 g6 3.Bg2 Bg7 4.0-0 0-0 5.d3 d6 6.e4 e5 7.Nbd2 Nbd7 8.a4 Re8** [8...a5] **9.Nc4 h6?! 10.Ne1!** [preparing f4] **Nf8 11.f4 d5 12.fe5 dc4 13.ef6 Bf6 14.Bh6 Bb7 15.Rb1 Bg7 16.Bg7 Kg7 17.Qf3** +- [Central pawns + f-file] **Qe7 18.d4 Ne6 19.Qc3! Ng5 20.Qc4 Bh3 21.Rb7 Bg2 22.Ng2 Qe4 23.Rc7 Qe2 24.Qe2 Re2 25.h4 Nh3 26.Kh2 Nf2 27.Nf4 Rd2 28.Kg1 Ng4 29.Ne6 Kh8 30.Rff7 [D] 1-0**

After 19.Bd6

61) Elo,A-Fischer,R [7/4/57] Milwaukee New Western Open [2] B93/00 Sicilian,Najdorf [E:Bishop + pawn] **1.e4 c5 2.Nf3 d6 3.d4 cd4 4.Nd4 Nf6 5.Nc3 a6 6.f4 e5 7.Nf3 Qc7 8.Bd3 Nbd7 9.0-0 b5 10.Qe1 Bb7 11.a3 g6 12.Qh4 Bg7 13.g4 ef4 14.Bf4 0-0 15.Qg3 Ne5 16.Ne5 de5 17.Be5 Qc5 18.Rf2 Nh5 19.Bd6 [D] Qc3 20.bc3 Ng3 21.Bf8 Rf8 22.hg3 Bc3 23.Rb1 Bd4 24.a4 Bc8 25.ab5 ab5 26.Rb5 Bg4 27.Kg2 Bf2 28.Kf2 Be6 29.Rc5 Kg7 30.Kf3 Kf6 31.Kf4 Ra8 32.g4 h6 33.g5 hg5 34.Rg5 Rh8 35.Rg2 g5 36.Kf3 Rh3 37.Rg3 Rg3 38.Kg3 Ke5 39.c3 Bd7 40.Bc4 f6 41.Bd5 Be8 42.c4 Kd4 43.Kg4 Bg6 44.Kf3 Bh5 45.Kf2 Bd1 46.Kg3 Be2 47.c5 Kc5 48.Be6 Kd4 49.Bf5 Ke3 0-1**

After 30...Qc6

62) Otteson,M-Fischer,R [7/5/57] Milwaukee New Western Open [3] A05/11 Reti/Sokolsky **1.Nf3 Nf6 2.g3 g6 3.b4** [Sokolsky's Opening] **Bg7 4.Bb2 0-0 5.Bg2 d6 6.d4 e5 7.de5 Ng4 8.Nbd2 Nc6 9.b5 Nce5 10.Ne5 Ne5 11.0-0!?!** [11.Rb1] **Nf3** [Going for the Bishop pair] **12.Bf3 Bb2 13.Rb1 Bg7 14.Nc4 Bh3 15.Re1 Bc3 16.Bb7 Be1 17.Qe1** [17.Ba8 Qa8 threatens mate] **Rb8 18.Bf3 Qg5 19.a4 Qc5 20.Ne3 Be6 21.c4** [White has good compensation for the exchange since his minor pieces are active and Black's Rooks are passive] **a6 22.Rd1 ab5 23.cb5 Bb3 24.Rc1 Qd4 25.Rc7 Qa4 26.Qc3 Be6 27.Bc6 Rfc8 28.Re7** [28.b6? Qa6] **d5 29.Qf6 Rc6 30.bc6 Qc6 [D] 31.Ng4! Qc1 32.Kg2 Rf8 33.Re6** [33.Rc7! Qd2 (33...Qc7 34.Na6#) 34.Rc2!! ++-] **fe6 34.Qe6 Kg7 35.Qe5 Kf7 36.f4 Rc8 37.Nh6 Kf8 38.Qh8 Ke7 39.Qh7 Kd6 40.Qg6 Kc5 41.Qd3 Qc4 42.Ng4 Rg8 43.Ne5 Qf4? 44.Qc3 Kb5 45.Qc6 Ka5 46.Qd5 Ka4 47.Qg8 Qe5 48.Qc4 Ka3 49.h4 1-0** (Based on notes by the winner)

63) Fischer,R-Donnelly,W [7/5/57] Milwaukee New Western Open [4] C90/03 Ruy Lopez [E:Rook + minor pieces] **1.e4 e5 2.Nf3 Nc6 3.Bb5 a6 4.Ba4 Nf6 5.0-0 Be7 6.Re1 d6 7.c3 b5 8.Bb3 Na5 9.Bc2 c5 10.d4 Qc7 11.Nbd2** [11.a4! b4 12.cb4 cb4 13.Nbd2 0-0 14.h3 Be6 15.Nf1+=] **0-0 12.Nf1 Nc6** [Better was 12...cd4 13.cd4 Bg4 14.Ne3 Bf3 15.Qf3 Nc6=] **13.Ne3 Re8 14.Nd5 Nd5? 15.ed5 Na5 16.de5 de5 17.Ne5 Bd6 18.Bf4 Bb7 19.Qd3 g6 20.Qg3 Rad8** [20...Bd5 21.Ng6] **21.Nd3 Nc4 22.b3 Bf4 23.Qf4 Qf4 24.Re8 Re8 25.Nf4 Na3 26.Bd3 c4 27.bc4 bc4 28.Bf1 g5 29.Nh5 Re5 30.d6 Kf8** [D] **31.Nf6 Re6 32.Rd1 1-0**

After 30...Kf8

64) Surgies,M-Fischer,R [7/6/57] Milwaukee New Western Open [5] E72/09 King's Indian **1.d4 Nf6 2.c4 g6 3.g3 Bg7 4.Bg2 0-0 5.e4 d6 6.Ne2** [6.Nc3] **e5** [6...c5] **7.0-0** [7.d5 a5 8.0-0 Na6 9.h3 Nc5=+] **Nbd7 8.Nbc3 c6 9.Qc2** [9.h3 and 10.Be3] **Re8 10.Re1 a6 11.a4?! a5! 12.f3 ed4 13.Nd4 Ne2** [14.Be3 Ng4!] [D] **Ne4 15.fe4 Bd4 16.Nd4 Qd4 17.Be3 Qf6 18.Rad1 Ne5 19.Rf1 Qe7 20.b3 Bg4 21.Rd2 Qe6 22.Bg5 Bh3 23.Rf6 Qg4 24.Bf4 Nf3 25.Bf3 Qf3 26.Qd1 Qe4 27.Rfd6 Qe1 28.Qe1 Re1 29.Kf2 Rae8 30.Bh6 Rf1# 0-1**

After 14.Ne2

65) Fischer,R-Kampars,N [7/6/57] Milwaukee New Western Open [6] B11/00 Caro-Kann,Two Knights [E:Bishop vs. Knight] **1.e4 c6 2.Nc3 d5 3.Nf3 Bg4 4.h3 Bf3 5.Qf3 e6 6.d4 Nd7** [6...de4] **7.Bd3 de4 8.Ne4 Ngf6 9.0-0 Ne4 10.Qe4 Nf6 11.Qe3 Nd5 12.Qf3 Qf6 13.Qf6 Nf6 14.Rd1+=** [Bishop pair] **0-0-0 15.Be3 Nd5 16.Bg5 Be7 17.Be7 Ne7 18.Be4 Nd5 19.g3 Nf6 20.Bf3 Kc7 21.Kf1 Rhe8 22.Be2 e5 23.de5 Re5 24.Bc4 Rd1 25.Rd1 Re7 26.Bb3 Ne4 27.Rd4 Nd6 28.c3 f6 29.Bc2 h6 30.Bd3 Nf7 31.f4 Rd7 32.Rd7 Kd7 33.Kf2 Nd6 34.Kf3 f5 35.Ke3 c5 36.Be2 Ke6 37.Bd3** [D] **1/2-1/2**

Final position

66) Marchand,E-Fischer,R [7/7/57] Milwaukee New Western Open [7] A15/13 King's Indian **1.c4 Nf6 2.Nf3 g6 3.b3 Bg7 4.Bb2 0-0 5.g3 d6 6.Bg2** [6.d4] **e5 7.d4** [7.d3] **e4 8.Nfd2 Re8** [8...e3!?] **9.e3 c6 10.Nc3 Bf5 11.h3 h5 12.Qc2 d5 13.c5** [13.cd5 cd5 14.Nb5 Nc6 =+] **Na6! 14.a3 Nc7 15.Ne2 Ne6 16.Qd1 b6 17.b4 a5 18.Bc3 bc5 19.bc5 Nc7 20.Rb1 Nb5 21.Qc1 Qd7 22.Nb3 Qc7 23.Bd2 a4 24.Na1 h4 25.g4 Bd7 26.Bb4 Nh7 27.Nc2 Ng5 28.Qd1 Bc8 29.Kd2 Ba6 30.Kc1 Ne6 31.Bf1 Rf8 32.Qe1 f5 -++ 33.gf5 Rf5 34.Nc3 Nc3 35.Bc3 Bf1 36.Rf1 Raf8 37.Rb6 Ng5 38.Qe2 Nh3 39.Be1** [D] **Qh2 40.Rc6 Nf2 41.Kb1 Qg2 42.Nb4 h3 43.Nd5 Rd5 44.Qc4 Kh7 45.Bf2 Rf2 46.Rc1 h2 47.Rg6 Kg6 48.c6 h1=Q 49.c7 Rb2 0-1**

After 39.Be1

67) Fischer,R-Bennett,J [7/8/57] US Junior Championship [1] B60/01 Sicilian **1.e4 c5 2.Nf3 Nc6 3.d4 cd4 4.Nd4 Nf6 5.Nc3 d6 6.Bg5 g6?!** [Too weakening] [D] **7.Bf6 ef6 8.Bc4 Bg7 9.0-0** [9.Ndb5+-] **0-0 10.Ndb5 f5 11.ef5 Bf5 12.Nd6 Ne5 13.Bb3 Qd7 14.Nf5 Qf5 ++- [A sound extra pawn] 15.Nd5 Nc6 16.Ne3 Qc5 17.c3 Rad8 18.Qf3 Rd7 19.Rad1 Rd6 20.Rd6 Qd6 21.Rd1 Qc5 22.h3 b5 23.Rd5 Qb6 24.Rd6 Ne5 25.Qd5 Qc7 26.f4 Nc4 27.Nc4 bc4 28.Bc4 Kh8 29.Bb3 f5 30.g3 Re8 31.Qc6 Qb8 32.Rd7 Re1 33.Kf2 Qe8 34.Qf3 Rb1 35.Rd1 Rb2 36.Kg1 Qc8 37.h4 Bc3 38.Rd8! Qd8 39.Qc3 Qf6 40.Qf6# 1-0**

After 6...g6?!

Final position

68) Schoene,A-Fischer,R [7/57] US Junior Championship [2] E70/01 King's Indian [E:Rook + minor piece] **1.d4 Nf6 2.c4 g6 3.Nc3 Bg7 4.e4 0-0!?** [4...d6] **5.e5 Ne8 6.f4** [6.Bf4 d6 7.h3 c5 8.dc5 Qa5 =] **d6 7.Nf3** [7.Be3] **de5 8.fe5?** [8.de5 =] **Bg4 9.Be2** [9.c5!?] **c5! 10.Bf4 cd4 11.Qd4 Nc6 12.Qd8 Rd8 13.Rd1 Rd1 14.Nd1 Bf3 15.Bf3 Ne5 16.Be5 Be5 17.Bb7 Nd6 18.Ba6 Rb8 19.c5 Ne4 20.c6 Rb6 21.Bb7 Nd6 22.b3 Nb7 23.cb7 Rb7 24.g3 Bd4 25.Ke2 Rc7 26.Kd3 e5 27.Re1 Rc1! 28.a4 f5 29.Kd2 Rb1 30.Kc2 Ra1 31.Re2 Ra2 32.Kd3 e4 [D] 0-1**

After 18.Kh1

69) Thacker,R-Fischer,R [7/57] US Junior Championship [3] B50/05 Sicilian **1.e4 c5 2.Nf3 d6 3.c3 Nf6 4.Bd3 g6** [4...Nc6 5.Bc2 Bg4 =] **5.Bc2 Bg7 6.d4 0-0 7.h3 cd4 8.cd4 Nc6 9.Nc3 e5 10.d5 Nd4! 11.Nd4 ed4 12.Ne2** [12.Qd4 Ne4! 13.Qe4 Re8 -++] **Re8 13.f3 Qb6 14.Bd3 Nd7 15.Qa4 Rf8 16.0-0 Nc5 17.Qd1 Bd7 18.Kh1 [D] f5 19.Ng3** [19.ef Nd3 20.Qd3 Bb5 21.Qd1 d2 22.Nf4 d2 -++] **Nd3 20.Qd3 Bb5 21.Qd1 Bf1 22.Qf1 f4 23.Ne2 g5 24.Qd1 Rac8 25.Rb1 Qa6 26.Qb3? Qe2 27.Bf4 gf4 28.Qb7 d3 29.Qa7 d2 30.Qg7 Kg7 31.Re1 de1=Q 32.Kh2 0-1**

After 19.Qd2

70) Fischer,R-Hains,W [7/57] US Junior Championship [4] C97/13 Ruy Lopez **1.e4 e5 2.Nf3 Nc6 3.Bb5 a6 4.Ba4 Nf6 5.0-0 Be7 6.Re1 b5 7.Bb3 d6 8.c3 0-0 9.h3 Na5 10.Bc2 c5 11.d4 Qc7 12.Nbd2 Bd7 13.Nf1 Rfe8 14.Ne3 cd4 15.cd4 Nc4** [15...Rac8 16.b3 +=] **16.Nc4 bc4** [16...Qc4? 17.de ++-] **17.Bd2 Rad8 18.Bc3 Bf8 19.Qd2 [D] g6? 20.Ba5 Qb8 21.Bd8 Qd8 22.b3 cb3 23.Bb3 Qb6 24.Rab1 Qd8 25.Bc4 Ne4 26.Re4 Bf5 27.Ree1 Bb1 28.Rb1 e4 29.Nh2 Qh4 30.Rb7 Bh6 31.Qe2 Rf8 32.Ng4 Qg5 33.Qe3 Qg4 34.hg4 Be3 35.fe3 h6 36.Rd7 Kg7 37.Rd6 Rc8 38.Bb3 1-0**

After 15.g4

71) Ramirez,G-Fischer,R [7/57] US Junior Championship [5] E67/04 King's Indian [E:Rook + minor pieces] **1.Nf3 Nf6 2.g3 g6 3.Bg2 Bg7 4.0-0 0-0 5.c4 d6 6.Nc3 e5 7.d4 Nbd7 8.h3 Re8** [8...c6] **9.Qc2 ed4 10.Nd4 Nb6 11.b3** [11.Nc4 12.Ncb5!] **c5! 12.Ndb5 a6 13.Na3 Bf5! 14.Qd2 d5 -+ 15.g4 [D] Bg4? 16.hg4 Ng4 17.Bh3 Qh4 18.Kg2 d4 19.Qg5 Qg5 20.Bg5 f5 21.Bg4 fg4 22.Nd5 Nd5 23.cd5 d3 24.ed3 Ba1 25.Ra1 Re5 1/2-1/2**

After 8...Nd5

72) Fischer,R-Sholomson,S [7/57] US Junior Championship [6] B08/07 Pirc **1.Nf3 g6 2.e4 Bg7 3.d4 d6 4.Nc3** [4.c4; 4.c3] **Nf6 5.Bc4 0-0** [5...Ne4! 6.Ne4 d5 =; 5...Ne4! 6.Bf7 Kf7 7.Ne4 h6=] **6.0-0 c6 7.Qe2 Nbd7?** [7...b5] **8.e5 Nd5 [D] 9.Bd5 cd5 10.ed6 ed6 11.Nd5 Qa5 12.c4 Nf6 13.Bd2 Qd8 14.Ne7 Kh8 15.Nc8 Rc8 16.b3 Qd7 17.Qd3 h6 18.Rfe1 g5 19.d5 Nh5 20.Rad1 Rg8 21.Nd4 Qg4 22.Nf5 Nf4 23.Bf4 gf4 24.Nd6 Bf6 25.Nf7 Kg7 26.Ne5 Be5 27.Re5 Kh8 28.g3 fg3 29.hg3 Rcf8 30.Re7 1-0**

73) Bredoff,M-Fischer,R [7/57] US Junior Championship [7]
B92/03 Sicilian **1.e4 c5 2.Nf3 d6 3.d4 cd4 4.Nd4 Nf6 5.Nc3 a6
6.Be2 e5 7.Nf3** [7.Nb3] **Be7** [7...h6! stops Bg5] **8.Bg5 Nbd7 9.Nh4?**
[Useless decentralization] **h6 10.Be3** [10.Bf6 Nf6 11.Nf5 Ne4!
12.Ng7 Kf8 13.Ne4 Kg7 =+ center pawns + Bishop pair] **Nb6
11.Nf3 Be6 12.0-0 Nc4 13.Bc4 Bc4 14.Re1 0-0 15.Nd2 Be6 16.f4?**
**ef4 17.Bf4 Qb6 18.Kh1 Qb2 19.Nd5 Bd5 20.ed5 Nd5 21.Nc4 Qb5
22.Nd6 Qc6 23.Nf5 Bf6 24.Be5 Rad8 25.Qg4 Be5 26.Re5 Qf6
27.Rae1 Nc7 28.Qe4 Ne6 29.Qb7 [D] Qe5 0-1** [30.Re5 Rd1#]

After 29.Qb7

74) Fischer,R-Walker,R [7/57] US Junior Championship [8]
C70/00 Ruy Lopez **1.e4 e5 2.Nf3 Nc6 3.Bb5 a6 4.Ba4 b5 5.Bb3
Na5** [Taimanov's Variation] **6.0-0** [6.Ne5 Nb3 7.ab3 Qe7 8.d4 d6
9.Nf3 Qe4 -+] **Nb3 7.ab3 d6 8.d4 f6 9.Nh4** [9.c4! +=] **Ne7 10.Nc3
Be6 11.Be3 g5 12.Qf3!** [12...gh4 13.Qf6 +-] **Bg7** [12...gh4 13.Qf6 +-] **11.Qf3!
14.Nf5 Bf5 15.ef5 0-0 16.Rfd1 Qc8 17.Bc5 Nf5** [17...Rf7 18.Be7
Re7 19.Nb5 ++-] **18.Bf8 Bf8 19.Nd5 Kg7 [D] 20.g4 1-0**

After 19...Kg7

75) Hill,L-Fischer,R [7/14/57] US Junior Championship [9]
B92/00 Sicilian **1.e4 c5 2.Nf3 d6 3.d4 cd4 4.Nd4 Nf6 5.Nc3 a6
6.Be2 e5 7.Nb3 Be7 8.0-0 0-0 9.Be3 Be6 10.f3!?** [10.f4; 10.a4]
Nbd7! [10...d5 11.ed5 Nd5 12.Nd5 Bd5 13.c4 +=] **11.Qd2** [11.Nd5]
**Nb6 12.Rfd1 Qc7 13.Qe1 d5! 14.ed5 Nfd5 15.Nd5 Nd5 16.Bf2
Qc2 17.Qd2 Rac8 18.Rac1 Qd2 19.Rd2 Bg5 20.Rc8 Rc8 21.Rd1
Rc2 [D] 0-1**

Final position

76) Fischer,R-Stephans,E [8/6/57] US Open Cleveland [2]
B77/02 Sicilian,Dragon **1.e4 c5 2.Nf3 d6 3.d4 cd4 4.Nd4 Nf6 5.Nc3
g6 6.Be3 Nc6 7.f3** [The famous Yugoslav Attack - just coming into
fashion at that time] **Bg7 8.Qd2 0-0 9.Bc4 a6** [9...Bd7] **10.0-0-0 Qc7?!**
11.Bb3 b5? 12.Nc6 Qc6 13.Nd5 [D] Kh8 [13...Re8 14.Nf6 Bf6 15.Bd5]
14.Nf6 e6 [14...Bf6 15.Bd5] **15.Bh6 Bb7 16.Bg7 Kg7 17.Ng4 f5
18.ef5 Rf5 19.Qd6 h5 20.Qe7 Rf7 21.Qf7 Kf7 22.Ne5 Ke7 23.Nc6
Bc6 24.Rhe1 Bd7 25.Rd7 1-0**

After 13.Nd5

77) Pitschak,R-Fischer,R [8/7/57] US Open [3] A36/16
English [E:Rook vs. minor piece + pawn] **1.c4 Nf6 2.Nc3 g6 3.g3
Bg7 4.Bg2 0-0 5.e4 d6 6.Nge2 c5 7.0-0 Nc6 8.h3** [8.a3 and 9.Rb1
aiming for b4] **Rb8 9.d3 a6 10.f4 Bd7** [10...b5? 11.e5] **11.a4 Ne8
12.Kh2 Nc7 13.Be3 b5?!** [13...Ne6 14.f5 Nd4 followed by ...b5]
**14.ab5 ab5 15.Qd2 bc4 16.dc4 Rb4 17.e5 de5 18.Bc5 Rc4 19.Bb6
Qb8 20.b3 Qb6 21.bc4 Nd4 22.Nd4 Qd4 23.Qd4 ed4 24.Ne4 +-
Bc6 25.Ra7 Rc8 26.Rd1 Kf8 [D] 27.Nd6 ed6 28.Bc6 Ne6 29.Ra8
Ra8 30.Ba8 Nc5 31.Kg2 d3 32.Kf3 Bc3 33.Rb1 Na4 34.Ke3 Nb2
35.Bf3 d2 36.Be2 f5 37.g4 Ke7 38.g5 Kd7 39.h4 Kc6 40.h5 gh5
41.Bh5 ½-½**

Aftet 26...Kf8

Final position

78) Fischer,R-Rinaldo,,J [8/8/57] US Open [4] C97/15 Ruy Lopez **1.e4 e5 2.Nf3 Nc6 3.Bb5 a6 4.Ba4 Nf6 5.0-0 Be7 6.Re1 b5 7.Bb3 d6 8.c3 0-0 9.h3 Na5 10.Bc2 c5 11.d4 Qc7 12.Nbd2 Bd7 13.Nf1 Rfe8 14.Ne3 g6 15.Bd2** [15.b4; 15.de de 16.Nh2 Rad8 17.Qf3 Be6 18.Nhg4] **Bf8 16.Rc1 Bg7** [16...ed 17.cd Ne4 18.Nd5 Qb7 19.Be4 Re4 20.Nf6 ++-] **17.b4! Nc6 18.Nd5! Nd5 19.ed5 Ne7 20.dc5 Nd5** [20...dc5 21.Be3++-] **21.Bb3 Nf6 22.cd6 Qd6 23.Ng5 Rf8 24.Be3! Qd1 25.Red1 h6 26.Ne4 Ne4 27.Rd7 Rac8 28.c4 Ng5 29.Bg5 hg5 30.c5 [D] 1-0**

Final position

79) Bisguier,A-Fischer,R [8/9/57] US Open [5] B92/09 Sicilian,Najdorf **1.e4 c5 2.Nf3 d6 3.d4 cd4 4.Nd4 Nf6 5.Nc3 a6 6.Be2 e5 7.Nb3 Be7 8.0-0 0-0 9.Bg5 Nbd7** [9...Be6 10.Bf6 Bf6 11.Qd3 Nc6 12.Nd5 Bg5 =] **10.a4 h6 11.Bh4 e6 12.Bc4!** [Pressing on d5] **Bb7 13.Qe2 Qc7 14.Rfd1 Rfe8** [14...Rfc8 ∞] **15.Nd2** [15.Bf6! +-] **g5! 16.Bg3 Nf8 17.h4 Ng6 18.hg5 hg5 19.Bb3 Kg7 20.Nc4 Nf4 21.Bf4 gf4 22.a5 ba5 23.Na5 Rh8 24.Nb7 Qb7 25.Nd5 Rh6 26.Rd3 Rah8 27.Rh3 Rh3 28.gh3 Qd7** [28...Rh3 29.Nf6 Kf6 30.Qg4 Rh7 31.Qf5 ++-] **29.Nf6 Kf6 30.Qg4 Qg4 31.hg4 f3 32.Ba4 Ke6 33.Bb3 Kf6 [D] 1/2-1/2**

After 15...Bc6

80) Fischer,R-Witte,V [8/10/57] US Open [6] B86/04 Sicilian,Najdorf [E:Rook + minor piece] **1.e4 c5 2.Nf3 d6 3.d4 cd4 4.Nd4 Nf6 5.Nc3 a6 6.Bc4 e6 7.0-0 Bd7** [7...b5!] **8.Bb3 Be7 9.Be3 0-0 10.f4 Qc7?!** [10...Nc6] **11.g4! Kh8 12.g5 Ng8 13.f5 e5 14.Nd5 +- Qd8 15.Nf3 Bc6 [D] 16.Bb6 Qc8 17.Ne7 Ne7 18.Qd6 Qe8** [18...Re8 19.Bf7] **19.Bc5 b6 20.f6 Ng6** [20...bc5 21.fe7 Rg8 22.Ne5] **21.fg7 Kg7 22.Qf6 Kg8 23.Bf8 Qf8 24.Rad1 Be8 25.Qd6 Nd7 26.Qf8 Kf8 27.h4 Rc8 28.Rd2 Ke7 29.h5 Nf4 30.Ne5 Nh3 31.Kh2 Ng5 32.Nd7 Bd7 33.Rdf2 Bc6 34.Bf7 Ne4 35.Rf5 Bb5 36.Re5 Kd6 37.Re6 Kc5 38.Rf4 Nd6 39.Re5 Kc6 40.c4 Nf7 41.cb5 Kd6 42.Re2 Ne5 43.Rf6 Kd5 44.Rf5 1-0**

Final position

81) Garais,I-Fischer,R [8/11/57] US Open [7] B91/07 Sicilian,Najdorf **1.e4 c5 2.Nf3 d6 3.d4 cd4 4.Nd4 Nf6 5.Nc3 a6 6.g3 e5** [The sharpest; also playable is 6...e6] **7.Nde2 Be7 8.Bg2 0-0 9.0-0 Nbd7 10.h3 b5 11.Be3 Bb7 12.f4 Qc7 13.g4 b4 14.Nd5 Nd5 15.ed5 ef4 16.Rf4 Bg5 17.Re4 Be3 18.Re3 Rae8 19.Re8 Re8 20.Qd2 Qc5 21.Kh1 Qf2 [D] 0-1**

After 44...Ke6

82) Fischer,R-Mednis,E [8/12/57] US Open [8] A08/05 King's Indian Attack [E:Minor piece] **1.e4 c5 2.Nf3 Nc6 3.d3 e6 4.g3 g6 5.Bg2 Bg7 6.0-0 Nge7 7.Nbd2 0-0** [7...d5 8.Re1 b6 9.c3 a5 10.Nf1 +=] **8.Re1 b6 9.e5 d5 10.Nf1 Qc7?!** [10...a5 and ...Ba6, ...Ra7] **11.Bf4 d4 12.Qd2 Re8 13.Bh6 Bh8 14.h4** [White attacks vulnerable dark squares on Black's Kingside] **Bb7 15.N1h2 Ne5?! 16.Ne5 Bg2 17.Nf7 Qc6 18.Nh8 Bh3 19.f3 Kh8 20.g4 Nd5 21.Qg5 e5** [21...Qd6 22.Re5 ++-] **22.Re5 Ne3 23.Re1 Qd6 24.Re8 Re8 25.Qf4 Qf4 26.Bf4 h5 27.Be3 de3 28.g5 Bd7 29.Nf1 Bc6 30.Re3 Re3 31.Ne3 Bf3 32.Kf2 Bb7 33.Kg3 Kg7 34.Kf4 Kf7 35.Ke5 Ke7 36.Nd5 Kf7 37.Kd6 Bc8 38.Nf4 Bg4 39.Kc7 Bf3 40.c3 b5 41.d4 cd4 42.cd4 b4 43.d5 Bd5 44.Nd5 Ke6 [D] 45.Nf4 Kf5 46.Ng6 Kg6 47.b3 Kf5 48.Kb7 Kg4 49.g6 Kh4 50.g7 1-0**

83) Byrne,D-Fischer,R [8/13/57] US Open [9] A15/12 Reti
**1.Nf3 Nf6 2.c4 g6 3.b3 Bg7 4.Bb2 0-0 5.e3 d6 6.Be2 e5 7.0-0 Nbd7
8.Nc3 Re8 9.Rc1** [9.d3] **e4 10.Ne1 Ne5 11.d3 Bf5 12.de4 Ne4** =+
[More active, centralized pieces] **13.Ne4 Be4 14.Bc3** [14.f3 Bc6
15.e4? Nf3 16.any Bb2 -++] **f5** [To control e4] **15.b4 b6 16.Qb3
Qe7 17.c5 Kh8 18.c6!** Qe6 [18...Nc6 19.f3; 18...Bc6 19.Be5 ++-]
**19.Qb2 Qf7 20.b5 g5 21.a4 f4 22.f3 Bf5 23.e4 Be6 24.Nc2 Qg6
25.Nd4 Rf8 26.a5 Rae8 27.ab6 ab6 28.Ra1 g4 29.fg4 Qe4?!**
[Better was 29...Bg4] **30.Rae1 Qd5 31.h3 Ra8 32.Ne6 Qe6
33.Qb4! Qd5 34.Kh1?** [34.Rf4] **f3! 35.gf3 Nf3 36.Rd1??** [36.Bg7]
Nd4 37.Rf3 [D] Rf3 38.Rd4 Rh3 [38...Rf1!] **39.Kg1 Qh1 40.Kf2
Rf8 41.Rf4 Qh2 0-1**

After 37.Rf3

84) Byrne,R-Fischer,R [8/14/57] US Open [10] E62/19 King's
Indian [E:Bishop vs. Knight] **1.d4 Nf6 2.c4 g6 3.g3 Bg7 4.Bg2 0-0
5.Nc3 d6 6.Nf3 Nc6 7.0-0 e5 8.e3** [Passive. Better is 8.d5 Ne7 9.c5!
+=] **Bg4** [8...Bf5 9.Re1 a5 10.d5 Nb4! =+] **9.h3 Bf3 10.Bf3 Nd7
11.de5 Nce5 12.Be2 Nb6 13.Qb3 Qd7 14.Kh2 Qc6 15.Nd5 Rfe8
16.Nb6 ab6 17.f3 Nd7 18.a3 Nc5 19.Qc2 Qa4** =+ [Better
development] **20.Bd1 Qc2 21.Bc2 Rad8 22.Ra2** [22.e4 f5! since
23.ef Re2] **c6 23.b4 Ne6 24.Rd1 d5 25.cd5 Rd5 26.Rd5 cd5
27.Kg2 Rc8 28.Bd2 Bc3 29.Bb3 d4 30.ed4 Nd4 31.Bd5 Bd2
32.Rd2 Rc2 33.Rc2 Nc2 34.Bb7 Na3 35.Be4 Nb5 36.Kf2 Kf8
37.Ke3 Ke7 38.Bd3 Nc7 39.Kd4 Kd6 40.Bc4 Ke7 41.f4 f6 42.Bg8
Kf8 43.Bc4 Ke7 44.h4 Kd6 45.Bg8 h6 46.Bf7 g5 47.fg5 fg5 48.hg5
hg5 49.Bc4 [D] b5 50.Bd3 Na6 ½-½**

After 49.Bc4

85) Fischer,R-Addison,W [8/15/57] US Open [11] B10/18
Caro-Kann [E:Bishop vs. Knight] **1.e4 c6 2.Nc3 d5 3.Nf3 de4**
[Better would be 3...Bg4 4.h3 Bf3 5.Qf3=] **4.Ne4 Nf6 5.Nf6 ef6
6.Bc4** += [Queenside pawn majority + lead in development] **Bd6
7.Qe2 Qe7 8.Qe7 Ke7 9.d4 Bf5 10.Bb3 Re8 11.Be3 Kf8 12.0-0-0
Nd7 13.c4 Rad8 14.Bc2 Bc2 15.Kc2 f5 16.Rhe1 f4 17.Bd2 Nf6
18.Ne5 g5 19.f3 Nh5 20.Ng4 Kg7 21.Bc3 Kg6 22.Re8 Re8 23.c5!
Bb8 24.d5 cd5 25.Rd5 f5 26.Ne5 Be5 27.Re5 Nf6 28.Re8 Ne8
29.Be5!** [Hemming in the Knight] **Kh5 30.Kd3 g4 31.b4 a6 32.a4
gf3 33.gf3 Kh4 34.b5 ab5 [D] 35.a5! Kh3 36.c6 1-0**

After 34...ab5

86) Fischer,R-Shipman,W [8/16/57] US Open [12] C92/02
Ruy Lopez **1.e4 e5 2.Nf3 Nc6 3.Bb5 a6 4.Ba4 Nf6 5.0-0 Be7 6.Re1
b5 7.Bb3 0-0 8.c3 d6 9.h3 a5 10.d4 ed4 11.Nd4** [11.cd4 a4 12.Bc2
Nb4 13.d5! +-] **Nd4 12.cd4 Bb7** [12...d5 =] **13.Nc3 b4 14.Nd5 Nd5
15.Bd5 Bd5 16.ed5 Bg5 17.Qg4! Bf6!** [17...Bc1? 18.Rac1 with
pressure] **18.Be3 [D] ½-½**

Final position

87) Saltzberg,M-Fischer,R [8/30/57] New Jersey Open [1]
E67/05 King's Indian **1.d4 Nf6 2.c4 g6 3.Nc3 Bg7 4.g3 0-0 5.Bg2
d6 6.Nf3 Nbd7 7.0-0 e5 8.h3** [8.e4 +=] **Re8** [8...c6 9.de de 10.Be3
Qe7 =] **9.Be3 c6 10.Qb3 Qa5 11.Rad1 a6 12.Rfe1 Rb8 13.a3 h6
14.Nd2 ed4 15.Bd4 Nc5 16.Qc2 Qc7 17.e4 Ne6 18.Be3 Nd7 19.f4
Nd4 20.Qb1 b5 21.Nf1 c5 22.cb5 ab5 23.Nd5 Qa7 24.Qc1 Bb7
[D] 25.e5** [Loses, but Black is =+ in any case] **de5 26.f5 Nf5 27.Nc7
Red8 28.Nb5 Qb6 29.a4 Bg2 30.Kg2 Nd4 31.Bd4 cd4 32.Nd2 Nc5**

After 24...Bb7

33.Nc4 Qc6 34.Kg1 Na4 35.Nba3 Qf3 36.Rd2 Qg3 37.Rg2 Qh3 38.Ne5 Be5 39.Re5 Re8 40.Qc6 Re5 41.Rg6 Kh7! [Not 41...fg6? 42.Qg6 Kf8 43.Qf6] **0-1**

88) **Fischer,R-Green,M** [8/31/57] New Jersey Open [2] A04/16
King's Indian Attack [E:Bishop + pawn] **1.Nf3 Nf6 2.g3 g6 3.Bg2 Bg7 4.0-0 0-0 5.d3 c5 6.Nbd2 Nc6 7.e4 d6 8.a4 Rb8 9.Nc4 b6** [9...Bd7] **10.e5! += de5 11.Nfe5 Ne5 12.Ne5 Bb7 13.Nc6 +=** [Bishop pair] **Bc6 14.Bc6 Nd5 15.Re1 e6 16.c3 Qd6 17.Bb5 Rbd8 18.Qf3 h6 19.Bd2 Kh7 20.Bc4 a5?!** [Stopping a5, but also weakening] **21.Qe4 e5 22.Re2 f5?!** [Too aggressive in an inferior position] **23.Qh4 f4 24.Qh3 Rf5 25.g4 Rf7 26.Qf3 Rfd7 27.Kh1 Qf6 28.Rg1 Qg5 29.Bc1 Rd6 30.h3 R6d7 31.Kg2 Qh4 32.Rge1 Qg5 33.Qe4 h5 34.Qf3 Bf6 35.Kh2 hg4 36.Qg4 Qg4 37.hg4 Kh6 38.Kg2 g5 39.Kf3 Kg6 40.Rh1 Bg7 41.Ree1 Rh8 42.Rh8 Bh8 43.Rh1 Bg7 44.Ke2 Rd6 45.Bd2 Nf6 46.f3 Rd8 47.b4** [D] **Rh8 48.Rh8 Bh8 49.ba5 ba5 50.Be6 Ne8 51.c4 Kf6 52.Bd7 Ke7 53.Be8 Ke8 54.Ba5 Kd7 55.Bb6 Kc6 56.Bd8 Bg7 57.Bg5 Kb6 58.Bd8 1-0**

After 47.b4

89) **Mengarini,A-Fischer,R** [8/31/57] New Jersey Open [3]
E60/00 King's Indian, Yugoslav [E:Rook + minor piece] **1.d4 Nf6 2.c4 g6 3.Qc2!?** [Mengarini's pet move and quite playable] **Bg7** [3...c5 4.dc5 Qa5] **4.Nc3 0-0 5.Bg5 c5 6.d5 d6 7.e4 Na6 8.Qd2 Qa5 9.Bd3** [9.Bh6? Bh6 10.Qh6 Ne4] **Nc7 10.Nge2 a6 11.0-0** [11.a4 b5!] **b5 12.Bh6 bc4 13.Bc4 Bh6 14.Qh6 Nb5 15.Qd2 Nd7 16.f4 Nb6 17.Bb3 Qb4 18.f5 Nd7 19.Rf4 Nd4 20.Nd4 cd4 21.Nb1 a5 22.fg6 hg6 23.Qb4 ab4 24.Nd2 Nc5 25.Bc4 Ba6 26.a3 Bc4 27.Nc4 ba3 28.ba3 Rfb8 29.e5 Ra4 30.Rd4 de5 31.Rg4 e4 32.Ne5** [D] **1/2-1/2**

Final position

90) **Fischer,R-di Camillo,A** [9/1/57] New Jersey Open [4]
A08/06 King's Indian Attack **1.e4 e6 2.d3 d5 3.Nd2 Bd6** [Irregular, but not bad] **4.Ngf3 c5 5.g3 Nc6 6.Bg2 Nge7 7.0-0 0-0 8.Re1 Qc7 9.c3 Bd7 10.Qe2 f6 11.a3 Rae8** [11...a5!?] **12.b4 b6 13.d4! cd4 14.cd4 de4 15.Ne4** [The isolated pawn is compensated by easier development and the exposed Queen on the c-file] **Nd5 16.Bb2 Qb8 17.Nfd2 Nd8 18.Nd6 Qd6 19.b5 Bc8 20.a4 Qd7 21.Ba3 +-;** [Bishop pair] **Rf7 22.Nc4 Nb7 23.Qd3 Rd8 24.Be4 g5 25.Rac1 Ne7 26.Bb7 Bb7 27.Nd6** [D] **Nf5** [27...Rg7 28.Nb7 Qb7 29.Re6++-] **28.Nf7 Qd5 29.Qe4! Qd7 30.Qe6 Qe6 31.Re6 Kf7 32.Ree1 Kg6 33.Rc7 Bf3 34.Bb2 h5 35.Ra7 Rc8 36.Rc1 Re8 37.Ra6 h4 38.g4 Bg4 39.Rb6 Re2 40.Bc3 h3 41.d5 Nh4 42.Rf6 Kh5 43.b6 Nf3 44.Rf3 Bf3 45.b7 Re8 46.Be5! Re5 47.b8=Q Re4 48.Qg3 Rg4 49.d6 1-0**

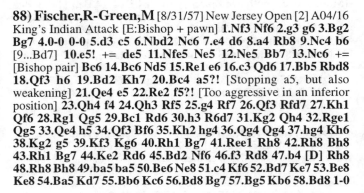

After 27.Nd6

91) **Sobel,R-Fischer,R** [9/1/57] New Jersey Open [5] A49/02
Flank [E:Rook + minor piece] **1.Nf3 Nf6 2.b3 g6 3.Bb2 Bg7 4.g3 0-0 5.Bg2 d6 6.d4 e5 7.de5 Ng4?** [7...Nfd7!] **8.Qc1?!** [8.h3 +-] **Ne5 9.0-0 Nbc6 10.Ne5 Ne5 11.f4 Nc6 12.Bg7 Kg7 13.Qb2 Qf6 14.Qf6 Kf6 15.Nc3 Be6 16.e4 Kg7 17.Rad1 a6 18.Rfe1 Rfe8 19.Rd2 Rad8 20.h3 f6 21.Kf2 Bf7 22.Red1 Re7 23.Re1 Rde8 24.Red1 Nb8** [D] **25.e5 fe5 26.fe5 de5 27.Bb7 c6 28.Ne4 Rb7 29.Nd6 Rd7 30.Ne8 Be8 31.Ke3 Kf6 32.Ke4 Ke6 33.c4 g5 34.Ke3 Bg6 35.b4 e4 36.Rd7 Nd7 37.c5 Nf6 38.Rd6 Ke5 39.Rc6 Nd5 40.Ke2 Nb4 41.Rd6 Bh5 42.g4 Be8 43.Rh6 Bg6 44.a3 Nd3 45.c6 Kd6 46.Ke3 Kc6 47.Kd4 Ne1 48.Rg6 hg6 49.Ke4 Kd6 0-1**

After 24...Nb8

92) Fischer,R-Saidy,A [9/2/57] New Jersey Open [6] B88/06
Sicilian,Sozin **1.e4 c5 2.Nf3 Nc6 3.d4 cd4 4.Nd4 Nf6 5.Nc3 d6 6.Bc4 Bd7** [6...e6] **7.Bb3 e6 8.0-0 Be7 9.Be3 0-0 10.f4 Nd4 11.Bd4 Bc6 12.Qe2 b5 [D] 13.Nb5 Be4?**[13...Ne4] **14.Na7 e5 15.fe5 de5 16.Be3 ++- Qb8 17.Nb5 Bc6 18.Nc3 Qb4 19.Rad1 Ra5 20.Rd2 Qh4 21.Bb6 Rc5 22.Rd3 Rb8 23.Bc5 Bc5 24.Kh1 h5 25.Qe5 Ba7 26.Qg3 1-0**

After 12...b5

93) Fischer,R-Sherwin,J [9/2/57] New Jersey Open [7] B40/00
Sicilian/King's Indian Attack **1.e4 c5 2.Nf3 e6 3.d3 Nc6 4.g3 Nf6** [4...d5] **5.Bg2 Be7 6.0-0 0-0 7.Nbd2** [7.e5! +=] **Rb8 8.Re1 d6 9.c3 b6 10.d4 Qc7?** [10...cd 11.cd d5] **11.e5! Nd5 12.ed6 Bd6 13.Ne4! c4 14.Nd6 Qd6 15.Ng5! Nce7 16.Qc2! Ng6 17.h4! Nf6 [D] 18.Nh7! Nh7** [18...Kh7 19.Bf4] **19.h5 Nh4! 20.Bf4 Qd8 21.gh4 Rb7! 22.h6! Qh4 23.hg7 Kg7?** [23...Rd8] **24.Re4! Qh5 25.Re3! f5 26.Rh3 Qe8 27.Be5 Nf6** [27...Kg8 28.Rg3 Kf7 29.Rg7#] **28.Qd2! Kf7 29.Qg5 Qe7** [29...Ke7 30.Rh7!] **30.Bf6 Qf6 31.Rh7 Ke8 32.Qf6 Rh7 33.Bc6 1-0**

After 17...Nf6

94) Cardoso,R-Fischer,R [9/57] Match, New York [1] B98/00
Sicilian,Najdorf [E:Minor piece] **1.e4 c5 2.Nf3 d6 3.d4 cd4 4.Nd4 Nf6 5.Nc3 a6 6.Bg5 e6 7.f4 Be7 8.Qf3 h6 9.Bh4 g5 10.fg5 Nfd7 11.0-0-0** [11.Qh5 is better] **Ne5 12.Qe2 hg5 13.Bg3 Nbd7 =+/-+** [Black has a strong post at e5 and the c-file] **14.Qe1 b5 15.a3 Bb7 16.Nf3 Qc7 17.Qd2 Nf3 18.gf3 Ne5 19.Be5 de5 20.Na2 Rd8 21.Bd3 Qb6 22.Kb1 f6 23.Qg2 Kf7 24.Qe2 Bc6 25.c3 a5 26.Bc2 b4 27.ab4 ab4 28.Bb3 Bb5** [28...bc 29.Be6!] **29.c4 Bc6 30.Rd8 Rd8 31.h4 g4 32.fg4 [D] Rd2! 33.Qd2 Be4 34.Bc2 Bh1 35.Qh6 Qg1 36.Nc1 Qg4 37.Qh7 Qg7 38.Qh5 Kf8 39.Ba4 Be4 40.Ka1 Bg6 41.Qd1 Qh6 42.Qe1 Qf4 43.Bb3 Qe4 44.Qe4 Be4 45.Bd1 f5 46.Ka2 f4 47.Ne2 Bd3 48.Kb3 f3 49.Ng3 f2 50.Bc2 f1=Q 51.Nf1 Bf1 52.Be4 Kg7 0-1**

After 32.fg4

95) Fischer,R-Cardoso,R [9/57] Match, New York [2] B90/00
Sicilian **1.e4 c5 2.Nf3 d6 3.d4 cd4 4.Nd4 Nf6 5.Nc3 a6 6.Bc4 e6 7.0-0** [7.Bb3] **Be7** [7...b5!] **8.Be3 0-0 9.Bb3 Nc6 10.f4 Na5** [10...Nd4] **11.Qf3 Qc7 12.g4** [Also good is 12.f5] **Nb3 13.ab3 Rb8 14.g5 Nd7 15.f5 Ne5 16.Qg3 Kh8 17.Nf3 Nf3 18.Rf3 b5 19.Qh4 ef5 20.ef5 Qc6 21.Raf1 Bb7 22.Bd4 b4 [D] 23.Bg7!?** [23.Qh5!] **Kg7 24.Qh6 Kh8 25.g6 Qc5? [25...fg 26.fg Rf7] 26.R1f2 fg6 27.fg6 Qg5 28.Qg5 Bg5 29.Rf8 Rf8 30.Rf8 Kg7 31.gh7 1-0**

After 22...b4

96) Cardoso,R-Fischer,R [9/57] Match, New York [3] B91/07
Sicilian **1.e4 c5 2.Nf3 d6 3.d4 cd4 4.Nd4 Nf6 5.Nc3 a6 6.g3 e5 7.Nde2 Be7 8.Bg2 0-0 9.0-0 Nbd7 10.h3 b5 =** [Black has easily equalized] **11.a4 b4 12.Nd5 Nd5 13.Qd5 Qc7 14.c3 Bb7 15.Qd1 Nc5 16.f3 a5 17.Be3 Ba6 18.Rc1 Rab8 [D] 19.f4 bc3 20.Rc3 Rb2 21.Rf2 Qb6 22.Rc1 Qb3 23.Nc3 ef4 24.Rb2 Qb2 25.Bc5 dc5 26.gf4 c4 27.Nd5 Bc5 28.Kh2 Bb4 29.Rc2 Qb3 30.e5 Qa4 31.Be4 g6 32.Qg4 Bb7 33.Nf6 Kg7 34.Qh4 Rc8 35.Qh7 Kf8 36.e6 Rc7 37.Qg8 Ke7 38.Qf7 Kd8 39.Rd2 Bd5 40.Rd5 1-0**

After 18...Rab8

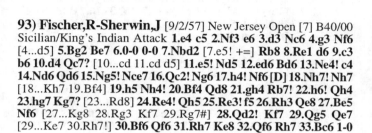

After 45...f5

97) Fischer,R-Cardoso,R [9/57] Match, New York [4] B90/00 Sicilian [E:Bishop + pawn] **1.e4 c5 2.Nf3 d6 3.d4 cd4 4.Nd4 Nf6 5.Nc3 a6 6.Bc4 e6 7.0-0 Bd7** [7...b5!] **8.Bb3 Nc6 9.Be3 Be7 10.f4 Qc7 11.f5 Nd4 12.Bd4 b5 13.a3 e5 14.Be3 Bc6 15.Nd5 Bd5 16.Bd5 Nd5 17.Qd5 +-** [White dominates d5] **Rc8 18.c3 Qc4 19.Qb7 Qc6 20.Qc6 Rc6 21.a4!** [Now the a-file is powerful] **Kd7 22.ab5 ab5 23.Ra7 Rc7 24.Rfa1 Rb8 25.Kf2 Rbb7 26.Rb7 Rb7 27.Ke2 Bd8 28.Kd3 h6 29.Ra8 h5 30.b4 Be7 31.Rg8 Bf6 32.Rf8 Kc6 33.c4!** [Outside passed pawn] **Rd7 34.Ra8 bc4 35.Kc4 Rc7 36.Ra7 Ra7 37.Ba7 Bd8 38.Be3 f6 39.b5 Kd7 40.Kd5 Ba5 41.Ba7 Bb4 42.Bb8 Bc5 43.g3 Ke7 44.Kc6 g6 45.fg6 f5 [D] 46.Bd6 1-0**

After 34.Ke4

98) Cardoso,R-Fischer,R [9/57] Match, New York [5] B55/03 Sicilian [E:Knight vs. Bishop; King + pawn] **1.e4 c5 2.Nf3 d6 3.d4 cd4 4.Nd4 Nf6 5.f3** [An old Russian move] **e5 6.Bb5 Nbd7 7.Nf5 d5!** [A strong pawn sacrifice for the initiative] **8.ed5 a6 9.Bd7?!** [9.Ba4 is better] **Qd7 10.Ne3 Bc5 11.c4 b5 12.Nc3 0-0 13.0-0 bc4 14.Kh1 Be3 15.Be3 Bb7 16.d6 Rac8 17.Bg5 Qe6 18.Qd2 Rfd8 19.Rad1 Rc6 20.Bf6 Rdd6 21.Qg5 Qf6 22.Qf6 gf6** [22...Rf6?? 23.Rd8#] **23.Rd6 Rd6 24.Rd1 Rd1 25.Nd1 Bd5 26.Kg1 f5 27.Kf2 f4 28.Nc3 Bc6 29.g3 fg3 30.hg3 Kg7 31.Ke3 h5 32.a3 Kg6 33.Ne4 Be4 34.Ke4 [D] f5! 35.Ke5 Kg5 36.a4 a5** [37.Kd5 f4 38.gf Kf4 39.Kc4 h4] **0-1**

After 9...Nbd7

99) Fischer,R-Cardoso,R [9/57] Match, New York [6] B90/00 Sicilian [E:Bishop vs. pawn] **1.e4 c5 2.Nf3 d6 3.d4 cd4 4.Nd4 Nf6 5.Nc3 a6 6.Bc4 e6 7.0-0 b5 8.Bb3 Bb7 9.Bg5** [9.Re1! and if 9...Be7 then 10.Be6! +-] **Nbd7 [D] 10.Be6 fe6 11.Ne6 Qc8 12.Nf8 Rf8 13.Qd6 Qc6 14.Rad1 Qd6 15.Rd6** [The ending is about even] **0-0-0 16.Rfd1 h6 17.Be3 Ne5 18.Rd8 Rd8 19.Rd8 Kd8 20.f3 Kd7 21.Kf2 Bc6 22.b3 Ke6 23.h3 Bb7 24.Ne2 Nc6 25.h4 Bc8 26.Nd4 Nd4 27.Bd4 g5 28.hg5 hg5 29.Bf6 Kf6 30.c3 Be6 31.Ke3 Ke5 32.g3 a5 33.f4 gf4 34.gf4 Kd6 35.f5 Bg8 36.Kd4 Bh7 37.c4 bc4 38.bc4 Kc6 39.a3 a4 40.Ke5 Bg8 41.Kf6 Bc4 42.Ke7 Kc5 43.e5 Kd4 44.Kd6 Ke4 45.f6 Kf5 46.Kc5 1/2-1/2**

After 24.Re4

100) Cardoso,R-Fischer,R [9/57] Match, New York [7] B91/07 Sicilian [E:Bishop + pawn; Queen + pawn] **1.e4 c5 2.Nf3 d6 3.d4 cd4 4.Nd4 Nf6 5.Nc3 a6 6.g3 e5 7.Nde2 Be7 8.Bg2 0-0 9.0-0 Nbd7 10.h3 b5 11.f4 Bb7 12.g4 b4 13.Nd5 Nd5 14.ed5 Qb6 15.Kh2 ef4 16.Bf4 Bf6** [Fischer again gets good play against the 6.g3 system] **17.c3 Rac8 18.Rc1 Rfe8 19.Qc2 Nf8 20.c4 Ng6 21.Bg3 Qe3 22.Rce1 Be5 23.Nf4 Qd4 24.Re4 [D] Qc5 25.Ng6 Bg3 26.Kg3 hg6 27.b3 Qc7 28.Rfe1 Qd7 29.Qe2 Kf8 30.Re8 Qe8 31.Qe8 Re8 32.Re8 Ke8 33.Kf4 Bc8 34.Be4 Ke7 35.h4 a5 36.Bf3 Kd8 37.Ke3 Kc7 38.Be2 Kb6 39.Kd4 Bd7 40.Bf3 Bc8 41.Be2 Bd7 42.c5 dc5 43.Ke5 Bb5 44.Bb5 Kb5 45.Kd6** [45.d6 Kc6] **c4 46.bc4 Kc4 47.Kc6 a4 48.d6 b3 49.ab3 ab3 50.d7 b2 51.d8=Q b1=Q 52.Qd5 Kc3 53.Qf7 Qe4 54.Kd6 Qg4 55.Qg7 Kd3 56.Qf6 Ke3 1/2-1/2**

101) Fischer,R-Cardoso,R [9/57] Match, New York [8] A07/05 King's Indian Attack **1.Nf3 Nf6 2.g3 d5 3.Bg2 Bf5 4.0-0 e6 5.d3 Bd6?!** [5...Be7; 5...h6; 5...c6] **6.Nbd2 h6? 7.e4!** Bg4 [7...de 8.de Ne4 9.Ne4 Be4 10.Qd4! Bf3 11.Bf3 ++-; b7 and g7 are attacked] **8.h3 Bf3 9.Nf3 Nbd7** [9...de 10.de Ne4 11.Nd4 Nc5 12.b4 ++-] **10.Qe2 de4 11.de4 Bc5 12.e5 Nd5 13.c4 Ne7 14.Bd2 Nf5 15.Kh2 c6 16.b4 Be7 17.Bc3 g5?** 18.Nd2 Qc7 19.Ne4 Rg8 20.c5 Kf8 21.Nd6 ++- [The d6 outpost is crushing] **b6 [D] 22.Nf5! ef5 23.e6! Bf6 24.Rad1 Ne5 25.Rfe1 Ng4 26.hg4 Bc3 27.Rd7 Qc8 28.Rf7 Ke8 29.Rd1 Rg7 30.Rg7 Bg7 31.gf5 Kf8 32.e7 1-0**

After 21...b6

102) Gardner,C-Fischer,R [11/29/57] North Central Open, Milwaukee [1] A49/07 King's Indian **1.d4 Nf6 2.Nf3 g6 3.g3 Bg7 4.Bg2 0-0 5.0-0 d6 6.c3** [Insipid, but playable] **Nbd7 7.Nbd2 e5 8.de5 de5 9.e4 b6 10.Qc2 Qe7 11.b3 Bb7 12.a4 Rfd8 13.Ba3 Qe6 14.Rfe1 Bf8 15.Bf8 Kf8 16.Nc4 Ne8 17.Rad1 f6 18.h4 Nc5 19.Nfd2 Qe7 20.Nb2 Bc8 21.Kh2 Bg4 22.f3 Be6 23.Bf1 Nd6 24.Nbc4 Qf7 25.Nd6 cd6!** [Preparing a central thrust] **26.Bc4** [26.c4 a5! followed eventually by ...f5] **d5 27.ed5 Bd5 28.Bd5 Rd5 29.Nc4 Rad8 30.Rd5 Qd5 -+ 31.Kg2 Qd3** [31...Na4 32.Ne5!] **32.Qb2 Rd7 33.Re2** [D] **Nb3! 34.Ne5 fe5 35.Re5 Qd2 36.Re2 Qb2 37.Rb2 Rd2 38.Rd2 Nd2 39.Kf2 Nb1 0-1**

After 33.Re2

103) Fischer,R-Sandrin,A [11/30/57] North Central Open, Milwaukee [2] A05/02 King's Indian Attack [E:Bishop + pawn] **1.Nf3 Nf6 2.g3 b6 3.Bg2 Bb7 4.0-0 c5 5.d3 d5** [5...g6] **6.Nbd2 Nc6 7.e4 e5? 8.ed5 Nd5 9.c4!** [With Black's King in the center, White opens up the position] **Ndb4 10.Ne5 Ne5 11.Bb7 Rb8 12.Bg2 Be7 13.Nf3 Nf3 14.Qf3 Qd3 15.Qd3 Nd3 16.Rd1 Rd8 17.Bc6 Kf8 18.Be4 Nc1 19.Rac1** [Despite opposite colored Bishops, White is much better - Black's Rh8 is out of play] **Rd4 20.Rd4 cd4 21.c5 bc5 22.b4 Ke8 23.bc5 Kd7 24.Rc4 Kc7 25.c6 Rd8 26.Kf1 g6 27.Ke2 a5 28.Kd3 f5 29.Bg2 Bb4 30.Rd4 Bc5 31.Rd8 Kd8 32.Ke2 Kc7 33.Bd5 h6 34.f4 g5 35.fg5 hg5 36.h4 gh4 37.gh4 Bd4 38.a4 Bf6 39.h5 Bg5 40.Kd3 Kb6 41.Kc4 Be3 42.Bf3 Kc7 43.Kd5** [D] **1-0**

Final position

104) Buerger,E-Fischer,R [11/30/57] North Central Open, Milwaukee [3] E86/09 King's Indian,Samisch [E:Rook + minor piece] **1.d4 Nf6 2.c4 g6 3.Nc3 Bg7 4.e4 d6 5.f3 e5** [5...0-0 is usual] **6.Nge2** [6.de5 de5 7.Qd8 Kd8 =] **0-0 7.Be3** [7.Bg5!] **c6 8.Qd2 ed4 9.Nd4 d5 10.cd5 cd5 11.e5 Ne8 12.f4 f6 13.Ndb5** [13.Bb5!] **fe5 14.Qd5 Qd5 15.Nd5 Nc6 16.Bc5 Rf7 17.Bc4 Be6 18.0-0** [18.Nbc7 Rc7!] **Na5 19.b3 Nc4 20.bc4 b6 21.Bb4 Bd5 22.cd5 ef4 23.Rae1 Rd8 24.Re4 a6 25.Nd4** [D] **Nf6 26.Ref4? Nd5 27.Ne6 Nf4 28.Rf4 0-1**

After 25.Nd4

After 30...Kf6

105) Fischer,R-Weinberger,T [11/30/57] North Central Open, Milwaukee [4] B77/00 Sicilian,Dragon **1.e4 c5 2.Nf3 d6 3.d4 cd4 4.Nd4 g6 5.Nc3 Bg7 6.Be3 Nf6 7.f3 0-0 8.Qd2 Nc6 9.Bc4 Bd7 10.h4** [10.0-0-0] **a6?!** [10...Rc8] **11.Bb3 Na5 12.Bh6 e5** [An unsound attempt to seize the initiative] **13.Nde2 Nb3 14.ab3 Bh6 15.Qh6 d5 16.ed5 b5 17.Ng3 e4** [17...b4 18.Nce4 Nd5 19.0-0-0 ++-] **18.Nce4 Rc8 19.0-0-0 Ne4 20.Ne4 f6 21.Qd2 a5 22.Kb1 b4 23.Qd4 a4 24.ba4 f5 25.Ng5 Ba4 26.b3 Qa5 27.ba4 Rc3 28.d6 Qa4 29.Qd5 Kg7 30.Ne6 Kf6** [D] **31.Qd4 Ke6 32.Rhe1 Kd7 33.Qg7 Kc6 34.Qc7 Kb5 35.Qb7 1-0**

After 36.a4!

106) Kalme,C-Fischer,R [12/1/57] North Central Open, Milwaukee [5] E66/15 King's Indian [E:Rook + pawn] **1.Nf3 Nf6 2.g3 g6 3.Bg2 Bg7 4.0-0 0-0 5.d4 d6 6.c4 Nc6 7.d5** [7.Nc3] **Na5 8.Nfd2 c5 9.Qc2 a6** [9...Bd7] **10.Nc3 Rb8 11.b3 b5 12.Bb2 e6 13.de6 Be6?** [13...fe] **14.cb5 ab5 15.Nce4 Bf5! 16.Rfd1! Nc6 17.Nf6 Bf6 18.Ne4 Be4 19.Be4 Nd4! 20.Bd4 Bd4?** [20...cd4! shields White's pressure on d5, while giving Black the c-file] **21.Rac1 Rb6 22.Qd3 Qe7 23.e3 Be5 24.h4 Qa7 25.Rc2 b4 26.Bd5 Ra6 27.h5! Kg7 28.f4 Bf6 29.Rdd2 Re8 30.Bc4 Rb6 31.g4 Qe7 32.g5 Bc3 33.Re2 Qe4 34.h6 Kf8 35.Qe4 Re4 36.a4!** [D] **Rc4 37.bc4 Bh8 38.Kf2 b3 39.Rc1 d5 40.cd5 c4 41.Rc4 b2 42.Re1 b1=Q 43.Rb1 Rb1 44.Rc8 Ke7 45.Rh8 1-0**

Final position

107) Fischer,R-Harrow,M [12/1/57] North Central Open, Milwaukee [6] A08/03 King's Indian Attack **1.Nf3 d5 2.g3 c5 3.Bg2 Nc6 4.0-0 Nf6 5.d3 e5 6.Nbd2 Be7 7.e4 d4** [7...0-0] **8.Nc4 Nd7 9.a4 0-0 10.Ne1** [10.Bh3! will eventually trade White's hampered KB for Black's better QB] **Nb6 11.b3 Be6 12.f4 ef4 13.gf4 f5 14.Bd2 Qd7 15.Qe2 Kh8 16.Nf3 Nc4 17.bc4 Rae8 18.Ng5 Bg5** [18...Bg8 19.Bh3] **19.fg5 Nb4 20.Bb4 cb4 21.a5 g6 22.Qd2 Qe7 23.Rab1 fe4 24.Rf8 Rf8 25.de4 Qc5 26.Qb4 Rc8 27.Qd2 Bc4 28.Rb7 Ba6 29.Rb1 d3 30.Kh1 Qc2 31.Qb4 Qc3 32.Qd6 d2 33.Rg1 Bb7 34.Rf1 Qc1 35.Qd4 Kg8 36.Bh3 Be4 37.Kg1 Bf5 38.Qd5 Kg7 39.Qd4 Kg8 40.Qd5 Kg7** [D] **1/2-1/2**

After 35...Nd4

108) Fischer,R-Feuerstein,A [12/17/57] US Championship [1] B40/00 King's Indian Attack **1.e4 c5 2.Nf3 e6 3.g3 Nf6 4.d3 d5 5.Nbd2 Be7 6.Bg2 0-0 7.0-0 Nc6 8.Re1 Qc7?!** [8...b5!] **9.Qe2 Rd8** [Better is 9...b5] **10.e5 Ne8** [10...Nd7] **11.c3?!** [Creates a target for b5-b4; 11.Nf1 is best] **b5 12.Nf1 b4 13.Bf4 Qa5** [13...bc3] **14.c4!** [Keeping the b-file shut] **Nc7 15.h4 Qb6 16.h5 b3 17.a3 dc4 18.dc4 Ba6 19.N1h2 Rac8 20.h6 g6 21.Bg5 Nd4 22.Qe3 Bg5 23.Qg5 Ne8 24.Ng4 Nf5 25.Rac1 Qc7 26.Nd2 Rd4 27.Nb3 Rc4 28.Rcd1 Ra4 29.Re4! Bb5 30.Rc1 Qb6 31.Nd2 Re4 32.Ne4 Bd3 33.Ngf6 Kh8 34.g4 Be4 35.Be4 Nd4** [D] **36.Ne8 Qd8 37.Qd8 Rd8 38.Nd6! Ne2 39.Kf1 Nc1 40.Nf7 Kg8 41.Nd8 Nb3 42.Ke2 Nd4 43.Kd3 Kf8 44.Nc6 1-0**

109) Seidman,H-Fischer,R [12/19/57] US Championship [2]
B98/08 Sicilian,Najdorf **1.e4 c5 2.Nf3 d6 3.d4 cd4 4.Nd4 Nf6
5.Nc3 a6 6.Bg5 e6 7.f4 Be7 8.Qf3 Qc7 9.0-0-0 h6** [More usual
nowadays is 9...Nbd7]**10.Bh4 Nc6 11.Nc6 Qc6 12.Bd3 Bd7 13.Qe2
Rc8 14.Kb1 b5 15.Rhf1 b4 [D] 16.Bf6 gf6 17.Nd5 ed5 18.ed5 Qc7
19.Ba6 Rb8 20.Rfe1 Bc8 21.Bc8 Rc8 22.Rd4 0-0 23.Re4 Rfe8
24.f5 Kh7 25.c3 bc3 26.Re7 Qb6 27.Rf7 Kg8 28.Qg4 Kf7 1/2-1/2**

After 15...b4

110) Fischer,R-Reshevsky,S [12/21/57] US Championship [3]
B41/09 Sicilian [E:Bishop + pawn] **1.e4 c5 2.Nf3 e6 3.d4 cd4 4.Nd4
a6 5.c4 Nf6 6.Nc3 Bb4 7.Bd3 Qb6?** [A terrible move, which only
loses time] **8.Be3 Bc3 9.bc3 Qa5 10.0-0! d6** [10...Qc3? 11.e5 is
crushing] **[D] 11.c5!** [Undoubling - now 11...Qc5 12.Ne6 ++-] **Qc7
12.cd6 Qd6 13.f4 Qe7 14.c4** [14.e5! +-/++-] **e5 15.Nb3 Nbd7
16.fe5?!** [16.f5 +=] **Ne5 17.Bc5 Qd8 18.Bd4 Qc7 19.Qd2 Be6
20.Qf4 Nfd7 21.Be2 f6 ∞ 22.Bh5 g6 23.Be2 0-0 24.Rac1 Rac8
25.c5 Nc6 26.Qe3 Nde5 27.Bb2 Rcd8 28.h3 Rd7 29.Kh1 Qd8
30.Rfd1 Rff7 31.a3 Rd1 32.Rd1 Rd7 33.Rd7 Qd7 34.Nd4 Nd4
35.Qd4 Qd4 36.Bd4 Kf7 37.Kg1 Bc4 38.Be5 Be2 39.Bd6 Bd3
40.e5 f5 41.Kf2 g5 42.g3 Be4 43.Ke3 Bd5 44.Bc7 Ke7 45.h4 f4
46.gf4 gh4 47.f5 h3 48.Bd6 Kf7 49.Kf2 Be4 50.Kg3 Bf5 51.Bc7
Bd7 52.Ba5 Ke6 53.Bb4 Ke5 54.Kh2 h5 55.Kg3 Kd4 56.Kh2 h4
57.Kg1 1/2-1/2**

After 10...d6

111) Bernstein,S-Fischer,R [12/22/57] US Championship [4]
B99/00 Sicilian,Najdorf [E:Rook + minor pieces] **1.e4 c5 2.Nf3 d6
3.d4 cd4 4.Nd4 Nf6 5.Nc3 a6 6.Bg5 e6 7.f4 Be7 8.Qf3 Nbd7
9.0-0-0 Qc7 10.g4 b5 11.Bg2 Bb7 12.Rhe1 b4 [D] 13.Nd5 ed5
14.ed5 Kf8 15.Nf5 Re8 16.Qe3 Bd8 17.Qd4 Bc8 18.Bh4 Nc5 19.Ng7
Kg7 20.g5 Bf5 21.gf6 Kh6 22.Qc4 Nd7 23.Qc7 Bc7 24.Bf3 Bd8
25.Bg5 Kg6 26.Rg1 Bf6 27.Bh4 Kh6 28.Bf6 Nf6 29.Rg5 Be4 30.Rf1
Bg6 31.Rfg1 Re3 32.Bd1 Ne4 33.R5g2 f5 34.Be2 a5 35.h4 Rh3 36.h5
Bh5 37.Bd3 Bg6 38.Rf1 Rf8 39.Kd1 Nf6 40.Re1 Nd5 41.Rf2 Re3
42.Rg1 Re7 43.Kd2 Kg7 44.Rf3 0-1**

After 12...b4

112) Fischer,R-Bisguier,A [12/23/57] US Championship [5]
C16/19 French,Winawer **1.e4 e6 2.d4 d5 3.Nc3 Bb4 4.e5 b6**
[Nimzowitsch's idea] **5.a3 Bc3 6.bc3 Qd7 7.Qg4 f5 8.Qg3 Ba6
9.Ba6 Na6 10.Ne2 0-0-0 11.a4 Kb7 12.0-0 Qf7 13.c4!** [13...dc4
14.Qc3] **Ne7 14.Bg5 dc4 15.Qc3 Nd5 16.Qc4 Ra8 17.Bd2 f4
18.Ra3! g5 19.a5 c6 20.ab6 ab6 21.Qb3! Nac7 22.c4 Ra3 23.Qa3
Ra8 24.Qb3 Ne7 25.Nc3 Qf5 26.Qb4! Nc8 27.Na4 f3 28.Nc5 Kb8
29.Nd7 Kb7 30.Qb3 Qg4 31.Nc5 Kb8 32.g3!! Qd4?** [32...Ra2
(best) 33.Bg5! Rb2! 34.Qc3 (34.Qb2? Qh3) 34...Rc2! 35.Qd3 Rc4
36.Bd8! ++-] **33.Be3! Qa1 [D] 34.Rb1 Ra3 35.Nd7 Kb7 36.Qd1!
Qa2 37.Nb6 Nb6 38.Rb6 Kc8 39.Qf3 Qc4! 40.Qf8 Kd7 41.Qa3
1-0**

After 33...Qa1

After 40...Nc5

113) Berliner,H-Fischer,R [12/26/57] US Championship [6]
E89/03 King's Indian,Samisch [E:Queen + pawn] **1.d4 Nf6 2.c4 g6
3.Nc3 Bg7 4.e4 d6 5.f3 e5 6.Nge2 0-0 7.Be3** [7.Bg5! +=] **c6 8.d5
cd5 9.cd5 Ne8 10.Qd2 f5 11.0-0-0 Nd7 12.Kb1 Nef6! 13.Nc1 fe4
14.fe4 Ng4 15.Bg1 Bh6 16.Qe1 Nc5 17.Nd3 Nd3 18.Bd3 Bd7
19.Bb5 Bb5 20.Nb5 a6 21.Na3?** [21.Nc3] **Rc8 22.h3 Nf6 23.Be3
Be3 24.Qe3 Qa5 25.Rhe1 b5 26.Rc1 Qa4 27.Nc2 Rf7! 28.a3 Rfc7
29.Nb4 Rc1 30.Rc1 Rc1 31.Qc1 a5 32.Qc8 Kg7 33.Qc7 Kh6
34.Qc1 g5 35.h4 Ne4 36.Nc6 b4 37.Qe1 ba3 38.hg5 Kg7 39.Na5
a2?** [39...ab2 -++] **40.Ka1 Nc5** [D] **41.b4 Nb3 42.Nb3 Qb3 43.Qe4
Kg8 44.g6 h6 45.Qf5 Qd5 46.Qd7! Kf8?** [46...Qd1]**47.b5 Qd1
48.Ka2 Qa4 49.Kb2 Qb4 50.Kc2 Qc5 51.Kb3 Qd5 52.Ka3 e4
53.Qh7 Qd3 54.Ka4 Qd4 55.Ka5 Qa1 56.Kb6 Qf6?** [56...Qg7 =]
57.Kc7? [57.g7 ++-] **Qg7! 1/2-1/2**

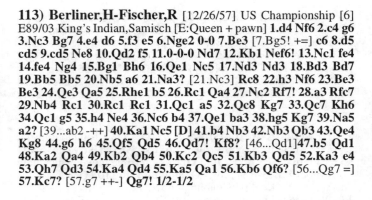

After 29...Rc3

114) Fischer,R-Sherwin,J [12/27/57] US Championship [7]
B87/00 Sicilian/Najdorf **1.e4 c5 2.Nf3 d6 3.d4 cd4 4.Nd4 Nf6
5.Nc3 a6 6.Bc4 e6 7.0-0 b5 8.Bb3 b4 9.Nb1** [9.Na4!] **Bd7** [9...Ne4
10.Qf3 gives White strong play] **10.Be3 Nc6 11.f3 Be7 12.c3 bc3
13.Nc6 Bc6 14.Nc3 0-0 15.Rc1 Qb8 16.Nd5! ed5 17.Rc6 de4
18.fe4 Qb5** [18...Ne4 19.Rf7 Rf7 20.Qd5 ++-] **19.Rb6 Qe5 20.Bd4
Qg5 21.Qf3 Nd7 22.Rb7 Ne5 23.Qe2 Bf6 24.Kh1 a5 25.Bd5 Rac8
26.Bc3 a4 27.Ra7 Ng4 28.Ra4 Bc3 29.bc3 Rc3** [D] **30.Rf7!!** **Rc1**
[30...Qd5 31.Rf8 Kf8 32.Qf1 Qf7 33.Ra8 Ke7 34.Ra7 ++-; 30...h5
31.Rf8 Kf8 32.Qf1 Nf6 ++-] **31.Qf1!!** **h5** [31...Rf1 32.Rf1 Rf7
33.Ra8 mates] **32.Qc1 Qh4 33.Rf8 Kh7 34.h3 Qg3 35.hg4 h4
36.Be6 1-0**

After 31.ab4

115) Kramer,G-Fischer,R [12/29/57] US Championship [8]
A04/16 King's Indian Attack **1.Nf3 Nf6 2.g3 g6 3.Bg2 Bg7 4.d3 d6
5.0-0 0-0 6.e4 c5 7.c3** [7.Nbd2; 7.Re1] **Nc6 8.Ne1?!** [8.Nbd2] **Rb8!
9.f4 Ne8 10.Be3 Bd7 11.Nd2 b5! 12.e5? de5 13.Bc5 ef4 14.Rf4
Nc7 15.Rf1 b4! 16.Qc2 bc3 17.bc3 Nb5 18.d4 Rc8! 19.Qb2 Nc3!
20.Qc3 Nd4 21.Qb4** [21.Qd4 Bd4 22.Bd4 Bb5! -++] **Ne2 22.Kh1
Rc5 23.Qc5 Ba1 24.Nef3 Bg7 25.Re1 Nc3 26.Qa7 Be6 27.a3 Qd6
28.Qa5 Bd5 29.Nb1? Ra8! 30.Qb4 Qb4 31.ab4** [D] **Bf3 32.Nc3**
[32.Bf3 Ra1] **Bg2 0-1**

After 31...fe6

116) Fischer,R-Mednis,E [12/30/57] US Championship [9]
B07/30 Pirc **1.e4 d6 2.d4 Nf6 3.Nc3 g6 4.Bg5 Bg7 5.Qd2 h6 6.Bf4
c6 7.0-0-0 Qa5 8.Kb1 g5 9.Bg3 Nh5 10.Bc4 b5? 11.Bb3?** [11.Nb5!
++-] **Nd7 12.f4! Ng3 13.hg3 g4 14.e5! d5 15.f5 ++-;** [The fifth-rank
pawn duo is too strong] **Nb6 16.Qf4 e6 17.Qg4 Bf8 18.fe6 Be6
19.Qf3 0-0-0 20.Nh3 Rg8 21.Qf2 Nc4 22.Bc4 bc4 23.Ka1 Rd7
24.Nb1 Rb7 25.c3 Rb6 26.Rd2 Kd7 27.Nf4 Be7 28.Rh6 Rf8
29.Qf3 Ra6 30.a3 Rb8 31.Ne6 fe6** [D] **32.Re6! Ba3** [32...Ke6
33.Qg4 Kf7 34.e6 Ke8 35.Qg8 Bf8 36.Qf7 Kd8 37.Qd7#] **33.Na3
Ke6 34.Qg4 Ke7 35.Rf2 Re8 36.Qg5 Kd7 37.Rf7 Kc8 38.Qf5 Kb8
39.Qd7 1-0**

117) Lombardy,W-Fischer,R [1/2/58] USA Championship [10] E60/06 King's Indian,Panno [E:Rook + minor piece] **1.d4 Nf6 2.c4 g6 3.Nf3 Bg7 4.g3 0-0 5.Bg2 d6 6.0-0 Nc6 7.d5 Na5 8.Nfd2 c5 9.a3?!** [9.Nc3] **b6! 10.b4 Nb7 11.Bb2 a5?! 12.b5 e5 13.de6 fe6 14.e4 e5 15.Nc3 Rb8 16.Nd5!** +- [strong point at d5. If 16...Nd5 then 17.cd5 and Nc4 is strong] **Be6 17.a4 Nd7 18.Ra3 Bh6 19.f4** [premature] **ef4! 20.Nf4 Bf7 21.Nd5 Bd5 22.cd5 Rf1 23.Bf1 Bg7 24.Bg7 Kg7 25.Nc4 Ne5 26.Ne5 de5 27.Qg4** [27.d6!?] **Qe7 28.Rd3 Nd6 29.Qe6 Re8 30.Bh3 Qc7 31.Qd7** [D] **Qd7 32.Bd7 Rd8 33.Bc6 Ne4! 34.Re3 Nd2?** [34...Ng5!] **35.Re2 Nc4 36.Re4 Nb2 37.Kf2 Nd1 38.Ke1 Nc3 39.Re5 Na4 40.Re7 Kh6 41.Kd2 c4! 42.Re4 Nc5 43.Re7 Na4 44.h4 Rf8 45.d6 c3 46.Kc2 Rf2 47.Kb3 Rb2 48.Ka4 c2 49.Re1 Rb4 50.Ka3 Rb1 51.Be4 Re1 52.Bc2 Re6 53.d7 Rd6 0-1**

After 31.Qd7

118) Fischer,R-di Camillo,A [1/4/58] US Championship [11] D02/06 Catalan [E:Rook vs. minor pieces] **1.Nf3 Nc6 2.d4 d5 3.g3 Nf6 4.Bg2 e6?** [Locks in the Bc8; 4...Bf5 was better] **5.0-0 Be7 6.c4 dc4 7.Qa4 Bd7 8.Qc4 Na5 9.Qc2 Rc8 10.Nc3 c5 11.dc5 Bc5 12.e4 Nc6 13.e5 Nb4 14.Qd2!** [Stops Black from occupying d5 effectively] **Nfd5** [D] **15.a3! Nc3 16.ab4 Bb4 17.bc3 Bc3 18.Qa2 Ba1 19.Qa1 0-0** [19...a6 20.Ba3!] **20.Qa7** +- [The minor pieces are too strong for Rook + pawns] **Bc6 21.Ba3 Re8 22.Bd6 Ra8 23.Qe3 Ra4 24.Nd2 Bg2 25.Kg2 Qa5 26.Rb1 Qd5 27.Nf3 Rc8 28.Qb6 h6 29.Qb7 Qb7 30.Rb7 Rc2 31.Rb5 Raa2 32.Bc5 Rab2 33.Ra5 Ra2 34.Rb5 Rab2 35.Ra5 Ra2 36.Ra2 Ra2 37.Bd6 Rb2 38.Nd4 Ra2 39.Nb3 Ra4 40.Nc5 Ra2 41.Nd7 Ra4 42.Nc5 Rc4 43.Kf3 Rc3 44.Ke4 Rc2 45.Nd3 Re2 46.Kf3 Rc2 47.h4 Rc3 48.Ke4 Rc6 49.Bc5 Ra6 50.h5 Ra4 51.Bd4 Ra2 52.g4 Re2 53.Be3 Ra2 54.f4 g6 55.hg6 fg6 56.Nc5 Kf7 57.f5! gf5 58.gf5 ef5 59.Kf5 h5 60.Ne4 Ra5 61.Bg5 Rd5** [D] **62.Nf6 Rd1 63.Nh5 Rd5 64.Nf6 Ra5 65.Ne4 Rd5 66.Nd6 Kf8 67.Ke6 Rd1 68.Be7 Kg7 69.Kd7 Ra1 1-0**

After 14...Nfd5

After 61...Rd5

119) Denker,A-Fischer,R [1/5/58] US Championship [12] E60/06 King's Indian,Panno [E:Rook + minor piece] **1.d4 Nf6 2.c4 g6 3.Nf3 Bg7 4.g3 0-0 5.Bg2 d6 6.0-0 Nc6 7.d5 Na5 8.Nfd2 c5 9.a3?!** [9.Nc3] **Nd7! 10.Ra2 Qc7** [10...Ne5 11.Qc2 Bf5 12.e4 Bd7 =+] **11.Qc2 Ne5 12.b4 cb4 13.ab4 Nac4 14.Na3 b5! 15.Nb5 Qb6 16.Nc4 Qb5 17.Ne5 Be5 18.Bh6 Re8 19.Qc6 Bd7 20.Qb5 Bb5 21.Rc1 a6 22.Bf1 f5 23.h4 Kf7 24.Rc7 Rec8 25.Rac2 Rc7 26.Rc7 Rb8 27.Bg5 Bf6 28.Bf6 Kf6 29.f4 Ba4 30.Rc4 Bb3 31.Rd4 Rc8 32.Kf2 Rc2 33.Bg2 Bc4 34.Bf3 Bb5 35.Ke1 Rb2 36.Kf2 Kf7 37.h5 Kf6 38.hg6 hg6 39.g4 fg4 40.Bg4 Rc2 41.Ke3 g5 42.fg5 Kg5 43.Bf3 Rc3 44.Kd2 Rc4 45.Rc4 Bc4 46.Kc3 Bb5 47.Kd4 Kf4 48.Bh5 Kg3 49.e4** [D] **1/2-1/2**

Final position

120) Fischer,R-Turner,A [1/7/58] US Championship [13] A05/03 King's Indian Attack **1.Nf3 Nf6 2.g3 d5 3.Bg2 e6 4.0-0 Be7 5.d3 0-0 6.Nbd2 b6** [6...c5 and Nc6] **7.e4 de4 8.de4 Bb7 9.Qe2 Qc8 10.e5 Nfd7 11.Ne4 Nc6 12.Bf4 Nc5 13.Nc5 Bc5 14.Rfd1 Ne7 15.Be3 Be3 16.Qe3 Nf5 17.Qe2 c5 18.c3 Qc7** [D] **1/2-1/2**

Final position

1958

After 30...Nc4

121) Fischer,R-Janosevic,D [7/58] Match, Belgrade [1]
B95/01 Ruy Lopez **1.e4 e5 2.Nf3 Nc6 3.Bb5 a6 4.Ba4 Nf6 5.0-0
Be7 6.Re1 b5 7.Bb3 d6 8.c3 0-0 9.h3 Na5 10.Bc2 c5 11.d4 Bb7
12.Nbd2** [12.d5! to block the Bb7] **cd4 13.cd4 Rc8 14.Nf1 Qc7
15.Bd3 d5 16.de5 Ne4 17.Ng3! f5 18.ef6 Bf6 19.Ne4 de4 20.Be4
Rcd8 21.Qe2 Rfe8 22.Nd2 Qe5 23.Qg4 Qg5 24.Kf1 Qg4 25.hg4
Bc8 26.f3 g6 27.Bc2 Be6 28.Ne4 Bd4 29.Be3 Bb2 30.Rab1 Nc4
[D] 31.Rb2 Nb2 32.Nf6 Kf7 33.Ne8 Re8 34.Bc1 Bc4 35.Kf2
Re1 36.Ke1 Nd3 37.Bd3 1/2-1/2**

After 16...Qb6

122) Janosevic,D-Fischer,R [7/58] Match, Belgrade [2]
B95/00 Sicilian **1.e4 c5 2.Nf3 d6 3.d4 cd4 4.Nd4 Nf6 5.Nc3 a6
6.Bg5 e6 7.Qd3 Bd7 8.f4 Nc6 9.0-0-0 Rc8 10.Kb1 Be7 11.Rg1 h6
12.Bh4 g5 13.fg5 Ng4 14.Nc6 Bc6 15.Qe2 hg5 16.Bg3 Qb6 [D]
17.Qg4 Qg1 18.Nd5 Bd5 19.Bb5 ab5 20.Rg1 Rc4 21.b3 Re4
22.Qd1 f5 23.h3 g4 24.Qd3 f4 25.Bf2 g3 26.Bd4 0-0 27.Kb2 Rf5
28.c3 Bc6 29.Rd1 Kf7 30.Rf1 e5 31.Bb6 Rh5 32.Qf3 Rh8 33.Qg4
Rh6 34.Kc1 Rg6 35.Qh5 Kg7 36.h4 Bd7 37.Qf3 Bc6 38.Qh5 Rh6
39.Qg4 Rg6 40.Qh5 1/2-1/2**

After 31...Kg6

123) Matulovic,M-Fischer,R [7/58] Match, Belgrade [1]
E80/05 King's Indian,Samisch [E:Minor piece] **1.c4 Nf6 2.Nc3 g6
3.e4 Bg7 4.d4 d6 5.f3 e5 6.d5 Nh5** [An old recommendation of
Lasker's] **7.Be3 f5 8.Qd2 Qh4 9.Bf2 Qe7 10.0-0-0 0-0 11.Nge2
Nd7 12.Ng3!** [Inducing the opening of the h-file] **Ng3 13.hg3 f4
14.g4 b6 15.Bd3 +-;** [Space advantage on both wings] **a5 16.Bc2
Ba6 17.b3 Rfb8 18.Qe2 Bf6 19.a3 Kg7 20.b4 ab4 21.ab4 b5?!**
[Desperation] **22.cb5 Bc8 23.Kb2 Nb6 24.Ra1 Ra1 25.Ra1 Bh4
26.Bg1 h5 27.gh5 gh5 28.Ra7 Rb7 29.Rb7 Bb7 30.Na4 Qd8
31.Qf1 Kg6 [D] 32.Bb6 cb6 33.Qg1 Qc7 34.Qb6 Qb6 35.Nb6 Be7
36.Nc4 Kg5 37.Na5 Bc8 38.b6 Kh4 39.Ba4 Kg3 40.Bd7 Bb7
41.Bh3 1-0** [This is the only recorded game of a four game match
between Fischer and Matulovic. Fischer won the match by a 2 1/2
- 1 1/2 score]

Final position

124) Fischer,R-Neikirch,O [8/5/58] Portoroz Interzonal [1]
C67/00 Ruy Lopez [E:Rook + Bishop] **1.e4 e5 2.Nf3 Nc6 3.Bb5
Nf6 4.0-0 Ne4** [The ancient Berlin Defense] **5.d4 Nd6 6.Bc6 dc6
7.de5 Nf5 8.Qe2 Nd4 9.Nd4 Qd4 10.Nc3** [10.Rd1 Bg4 =] **Bg4
11.Qe3 Qe3 12.Be3 Bb4 13.Ne4 Bf5 14.c3 Be4 15.cb4 a5 16.ba5 Ra5
[D] 1/2-1/2**

After 32.Rd3?

125) Fuster,G-Fischer,R [8/6/58] Portoroz Interzonal [2]
E86/02 King's Indian, Samisch [E:Rook + minor piece] **1.d4 Nf6
2.c4 g6 3.Nc3 Bg7 4.e4 d6 5.f3 e5 6.Nge2 0-0 7.Be3 c6 8.Qd2 Nbd7
9.d5 cd5 10.Nd5!** [Maintaining access to the backward d-pawn]
Nd5 11.Qd5 Nc5?! [Best is 11...Nb6 +=] **12.0-0-0 Qa5 13.Qd6 Ne6
14.a3 b5 15.Bd2 Qa4 16.Qb4 Rb8 17.Qa4 ba4 18.Bb4 Rd8
19.Rd8 Nd8 20.Nc3 Bd7 21.Bd6 Ra8 22.c5 Nb7 23.Bb5 Bb5
24.Nb5 Nc5 25.Bc5 Rc8 26.Na7? Rc5 27.Kb1 Bh6 28.Rd1 Kg7
29.g4 Be3 30.h4 h5 31.gh5 gh5 32.Rd3? [D] Rc1 33.Ka2 Ba7
34.Rd7 Bd4 35.f4 Rc2 36.Ka1 Rd2 0-1**

126) Fischer,R-Rossetto,H [8/8/58] Portoroz Interzonal [3]
C99/00 Ruy Lopez [E:Rook + minor piece] **1.e4 e5 2.Nf3 Nc6 3.Bb5
a6 4.Ba4 Nf6 5.0-0 b5 6.Bb3 Be7 7.Re1 0-0 8.h3 d6 9.c3 Na5
10.Bc2 c5 11.d4 Qc7 12.Nbd2 cd4 13.cd4 Bb7 14.Nf1 Rac8
15.Re2 Nc6** [15...Rfe8 or 15...d5!?] **16.Ng3 Rfe8 17.Bg5 g6 18.Rc1
Qb8 19.Qd2 a5?** [Weakens the pawns] **20.a3 ed4 21.Nd4 Nd4
22.Qd4 Rc4 23.Qd1 Nd7? 24.Be7 Re7 25.Rd2 Rc6 26.b4 Qc7
27.Ne2 ab4 28.Nd4 Rb6 29.ab4 Qc4 30.Bb3 Qb4 31.Rb2 Kg7
32.Rbb1 Be4 33.Bc2 Bc2 34.Rc2 Qa4 35.Ra1 Qb4 36.Nc6 Rc6
37.Rc6 Re6 38.Rb1 Qe4 39.Rcc1 Re5 40.Qc2 Qb7 41.Rb3 Nc5
42.Rb4 Ne6 43.Qc3 Kg8 44.Qc8 Qc8 45.Rc8 Kg7 46.g3 Rd5
47.Rb8 Nd4 48.Kg2 h5 49.Rb2 Kf6 50.Rd2 Ke5! 51.Rf8 Ne6
52.f4 Ke4 53.Rd5 Kd5** =; [Black's active King + Knight + outside
passed pawn] **54.Rf7 b4 55.f5 gf5 56.Rf5 Kc4 57.Rh5 b3 58.Rf5
b2 59.Rf1** [D] **Kd3 60.h4 Kc2 61.Rf2 Kc3 62.Rf1 Kc2 63.Kf3 d5
64.Rf2 Kc3 65.Rf1 Kc2 66.h5 b1=Q 67.Rb1 Kb1 68.h6 Kc2 69.h7
Ng5 70.Ke3 Nh7 71.Kd4 Nf6 72.g4 Ng4 73.Kd5** [D] **1/2-1/2**

After 59.Rf1

Final position

127) Benko,P-Fischer,R [8/10/58] Portoroz Interzonal [4]
E80/03 King's Indian,Samisch **1.d4 Nf6 2.c4 g6 3.Nc3 Bg7 4.e4
d6 5.f3 e5** [5...0-0] **6.Nge2 0-0 7.Bg5!** [More active than 7.Be3]
ed4 [7...c6] **8.Nd4 Nc6 9.Nc2** [White has a strong position] **Be6
10.Be2 h6 11.Bh4 g5** [Too weakening] **12.Bf2 Ne5 13.Ne3 c6
14.0-0 Qa5 15.Qd2 Rfd8 16.Rfd1 a6 17.a4!** [Stopping ...b5]
**Qc7 18.a5 c5 19.h4! Qe7 20.hg5 hg5 21.Nf5 Bf5 22.ef5 g4
23.Bh4 Qf8 24.fg4 Neg4 25.Bg4 Ng4 26.Qg5! Nf6 27.Rd3 Nh7
28.Qg4 f6 29.Nd5 Qf7 30.Re1 Re8 31.Rde3 Re5 32.Bg3 Re3
33.Re3 Re8** [D] **34.Re6 Ng5 35.Rd6 Re4 36.Rd8 Kh7 37.Bf4
Bh6 38.Rd7 Re1 39.Kf2 Ne4 40.Ke1 Qd7 41.Qg6 1-0**

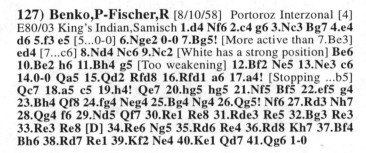

After 33...Re8

128) Fischer,R-Bronstein,D [8/13/58] Portoroz Interzonal [6]
C92/18 Ruy Lopez [E:Rook + Bishop] **1.e4 e5 2.Nf3 Nc6 3.Bb5 a6
4.Ba4 Nf6 5.0-0 Be7 6.Re1 b5 7.Bb3 d6 8.c3 0-0 9.h3 Nd7 10.d4
Nb6** [10...Bf6] **11.Be3 Rb8** [11...Na5 is usual] **12.Nbd2 Bf6 13.d5
Na5 14.Bc2 Nac4 15.Nc4 Nc4 16.Bc1 c6!** [Undermining White's
central pawns] **17.dc6 Qc7 18.Nh2 Qc6 19.Ng4 Be7 20.Ne3 Be6**
[Black has sufficient control of d5 - it is not a real weakness] **21.Qe2
Rfd8 22.Rd1 Ne3 23.Be3 a5 24.Bd3 a4 25.a3 Bf6 26.Bc2 d5
27.ed5 Bd5 28.Qg4 Be6 29.Qg3 Bc4 30.Bg5 Re8 31.Bf6 Qf6
32.Rd2 Rbd8 33.Rad1 Rd2 34.Rd2 h5 35.Qe3 Qf4 36.Qe1 h4
37.Rd4 Qf6 38.Qe4 g6 39.Rd2 Qf4 40.Rd1 Qe4 41.Be4 Kf8
42.Rd7 Rb8 43.g3 hg3 44.fg3 Be6 45.Rd2 Ke7 46.h4 f5 47.Bc2
Rh8 48.Kf2 Bc4 49.Ke3 Ke6 50.Rf2 Kd6 51.Rd2 Ke7 52.Rf2 Ke6
53.Rd2 g5 54.hg5 Rh3 55.Kf2 Rh2 56.Ke1 Rh1 57.Kf2 e4 58.Bd1
Rf1 59.Ke3 Re1 60.Kf2 Rf1 61.Ke3 Re1 62.Kf2** [D] **1/2-1/2**

Final position

129) Averbakh,Y-Fischer,R [8/15/58] Portoroz Interzonal [7]
E73/00 King's Indian **1.d4 Nf6 2.c4 g6 3.Nc3 Bg7 4.e4 d6 5.Be2
0-0 6.Bg5** [Averbakh's variation] **h6** [Not 6...e5? 7.de5 de5 8.Qd8
Rd8 9.Nd5 ++-] **7.Be3 c5 8.d5 e6 9.h3 ed5 10.ed5 Re8 11.Nf3 Bf5
12.g4 Be4! 13.Rg1 Nbd7 14.Nd2 a6 15.h4 b5! 16.g5 b4 17.gf6 bc3
18.Ne4 Re4 19.fg7 Qh4 20.Kf1 cb2 21.Rb1** [A very unclear
position] [D] **1/2-1/2**

Final position

After 21...Nh5

130) Fischer,R-Larsen,B [8/16/58] Portoroz Interzonal [8] B77/06 Sicilian **1.e4 c5 2.Nf3 d6 3.d4 cd4 4.Nd4 Nf6 5.Nc3 g6 6.Be3 Bg7 7.f3 0-0 8.Qd2 Nc6 9.Bc4 Nd4** [Popular at the time; nowadays 9...Bd7 is played] **10.Bd4 Be6 11.Bb3** [11.Be6? fe6 only helps Black] **Qa5 12.0-0-0 b5 13.Kb1 b4 14.Nd5 Bd5 15.Bd5 Rac8?** [15...Nd5!=] **16.Bb3! Rc7 17.h4 Qb5 18.h5! Rfc8 19.hg6 hg6 20.g4 a5 21.g5 Nh5 [D] 22.Rh5!** [Crashing through; note the strength of 16.Bb3!] **gh5 23.g6 e5 24.gf7 Kf8 25.Be3 d5 26.ed5! Rf7 27.d6 Rf6 28.Bg5 Qb7 29.Bf6 Bf6 30.d7 Rd8 31.Qd6 1-0**

After 22.ed5

131) Sanguinetti,R-Fischer,R [8/19/58] Portoroz Interzonal [9] B93/00 Sicilian **1.e4 c5 2.Nf3 d6 3.d4 cd4 4.Nd4 Nf6 5.Nc3 a6 6.f4 e5 7.Nf3 Qc7 8.Bd3 Nbd7 9.0-0 b5 10.Qe1 Bb7 11.Nh4 g6 12.Nf3 Bg7 13.Qh4 0-0 14.fe5 de5 15.Bh6 Nh5 16.Bg7 Kg7 17.Rad1 Nf4 18.Rf2 f6 19.Rfd2 Nc5 20.Bf1 b4 21.Nd5 Bd5 22.ed5 [D] Ne4 23.Qe1 Nd2 24.Qd2 Nd5 25.c4 bc3 0-1**

After 9.Bb3

132) Fischer,R-Panno,O [8/20/58] Portoroz Interzonal [10] B35/12 Sicilian **1.e4 c5 2.Nf3 Nc6 3.d4 cd4 4.Nd4 g6 5.Nc3 Bg7 6.Be3 Nf6 7.Bc4 0-0 8.f3?** [8.Bb3] **Qb6!** [Black equalizes easily] **9.Bb3 [D] Ne4 10.Nd5 Qa5 11.c3 Nc5 12.Nc6 dc6 13.Ne7 Kh8 14.Nc8 Rac8 15.0-0 Rcd8 16.Qc2 Qb5 17.Rfd1 Kg8 18.Rd8 Rd8 19.Rd1 Re8 20.Bf2 a5 21.Bc5 1/2-1/2**

After 20...fe6

133) Olafsson,F-Fischer,R [8/22/58] Portoroz Interzonal [11] D38/18 Queen's Gambit Declined [E:Rook + minor piece] **1.c4 Nf6 2.Nc3 e6 3.Nf3 d5 4.d4 Bb4 5.cd5 ed5 6.Bg5 h6 7.Bh4 c5 8.e3 Nc6 9.Rc1 c4 10.Be2 Be6 11.0-0 0-0 12.Nd2** [Black's d-pawn is a target] **Be7 13.b3! g5?! 14.Bg3 Ba3 15.Rc2 Nb4** [Wins the exchange, but White's strong center + Black's weak Kingside give him compensation] **16.bc4 Nc2 17.Qc2 dc4 18.Nb5 Bb4 19.Nc7 Bd2 20.Ne6 fe6 [D] 21.Bc4!** [21...Ba5 22.Qg6 Kh8 23.Qh6 Kg8 24.Be6 Rf7 25.Qg6 ++-] **22.Qd2 Ne4 23.Qd3 Ng3 24.hg3 Rf6 25.Qe4 Rc8 26.Bb3 Qd7 27.Rd1 Re8 28.f4 Qh7 29.Qe5 Qf5 30.g4 Qe5 31.de5 Rf7 32.f5 Rc7 33.Rd6 Rc5 34.Be6 Kf8 35.Bb3 Rce5 36.Rh6 Re3 37.Rg6! R8e4** [37...Rb3] **38.Rg5 Rg3? 39.Rg8 Ke7 40.g5 Re2 41.Bd5 Kd6 42.Bf3 Ra2 43.f6 Ke6 44.Re8 1-0**

Final position

134) Fischer,R-Tal,M [8/23/58] Portoroz Interzonal [12] C92/00 Ruy Lopez [E:Rook + minor piece] **1.e4 e5 2.Nf3 Nc6 3.Bb5 a6 4.Ba4 Nf6 5.0-0 Be7 6.Re1 b5 7.Bb3 0-0 8.h3 d6 9.c3 Nd7 10.d4 Nb6 11.de5** [Better was11.Nbd2 and on 11...Bf6 12.d5 +=] **Ne5 12.Ne5 de5 13.Qh5** [White's idea is pressure on the e-pawn, but Black has adequate defenses] **Qd6 14.Nd2 Be6 15.Nf3 Bb3 16.ab3 Nd7 17.b4 Rfd8 18.Bg5 f6 19.Be3 Qe6 20.Red1 c5 21.Nh4 Bf8 22.Nf5 g6 23.Qg4 Kf7 24.Nh6 Bh6 25.Qe6 Ke6 26.Bh6 cb4 27.cb4 Rdc8 28.Be3 Rc4 29.Rd2 Rb4 30.Rad1 Nf8 31.Rd6 Kf7 32.Rb6 Rb2 33.Rdd6 a5 34.Rb7 Kg8 35.Rf6 Re8 36.Rff7 Ne6 37.Rh7 a4 38.Ra7 Ra8 39.Rhg7 Kh8 40.Rh7 Kg8 41.Rhg7 [D] 1/2-1/2**

135) Petrosian,T-Fischer,R [8/27/58] Portoroz Interzonal [13] A16/04 English [E:Rook + pawn] **1.c4 Nf6 2.Nc3 g6 3.g3 Bg7 4.Bg2 0-0 5.Nf3 d6 6.0-0 Nc6 7.d3 Nh5** [Intending f5-f4 with Kingside possibilities] **8.d4 e5 9.d5 Ne7 10.e4 f5** [10...c5 is best] **11.ef5 gf5** [D] **12.Ne5! Ng3 13.hg3 Be5?** [13...de5!?] **14.f4 Bg7 15.Be3 Bd7 16.Bd4 Ng6 17.Re1 Rf7 18.Bf3!** [Stopping h5-h4] **Qf8 19.Kf2 Re8 20.Re8 Qe8 21.Bg7 Rg7 22.Qd4 b6 23.Rh1 a5 24.Nd1 Qf8 25.Ne3 Rf7 26.b3 Qg7 27.Qg7 Kg7 28.a3 Rf8 29.Be2 Ne7 30.Bd3 h6 31.Rh5 Be8 32.Rh2 Bd7 33.Rh1 Rh8 34.Nc2! Kf6 35.Nd4 Kg7 36.Be2 Ng8? 37.b4! Nf6 38.Bd3! ab4 39.ab4 Kg6 40.Ra1! Ng4 41.Ke2 Re8 42.Kd2 Nf6 43.Ra6 Rb8 44.Ra7 Rc8 45.c5 bc5 46.bc5 dc5 47.Nf3! Kf7 48.Ne5 Ke7! 49.Nd7 Nd7 50.Bf5 Rf8! 51.g4 Kd6? 52.Bd7! Kd7 53.Ke3 Re8 54.Kf3 Kd6 55.Ra6 Kd5 56.Rh6 c4 57.Rh1?** [57.Rh7] **c3 58.g5 c5** [D] **59.Rd1 Kc4 60.g6 c2 61.Rc1 Kd3 62.f5 Rg8! 63.Kf4 Kd2 64.Rc2 Kc2 65.Kg5 c4 66.f6 c3 67.f7 1/2-1/2**

After 11...gf5

After 58...c5

136) Fischer,R-Sherwin,J [8/28/58] Portoroz Interzonal [14] C92/01 Ruy Lopez [E:Rook + pawn] **1.e4 e5 2.Nf3 Nc6 3.Bb5 a6 4.Ba4 Nf6 5.0-0 b5 6.Bb3 Be7 7.Re1 d6 8.c3 0-0 9.h3 a5 10.d3** [Too passive. Best is the usual 10.d4] **Bb7 11.Nbd2 a4 12.Bc2 Nb8 13.Nf1 c5 14.d4 cd4 15.cd4 Nc6 16.Ng3 g6 17.Bd2 Re8 18.d5 Na5?** [Now the Knight is on a poor square] **19.b3** [D] **Bc8** [19...ab3 20.ab3 exposes the Na5 to an attack on the a-file] **20.ba4 ba4 21.Ba4 Bd7 22.Bd7 Nd7 23.Bb4 Qb6 24.a3 Nc5 25.Qe2 Reb8 26.Nd2 Nab3 27.Nb3 Nb3 28.Rab1 Nd4 29.Qd3 Qa6 30.Qa6 Ra6 31.Rb2 Rba8 32.Ra1 Ra4 33.Nf1 Nb5 34.Bd2 Ra3 35.Ra3 Na3 36.Rb7 Kf8 37.Ne3 Rc8 38.f3 h5 39.Bb4 Nc2 40.Nc2 Rc2** [D] **41.Rb6 Ke8** [41...Rb2 42.Rb8 Kg7 43.Bd6] **42.Bd6 Bd6 43.Rd6 h4 44.Ra6 Rc1 45.Kh2 g5 46.Ra2 Rf1 47.Ra6 Rd1 48.Rb6 Ke7 49.Rb2 Rf1 50.Rb3 Rd1 51.g4 Rd2 52.Kg1 Rd1 53.Kf2 Rd2 54.Ke3 Rh2 55.Rb7 Kf6 56.Rb6 Ke7 57.Rb7 Kf6 58.Rb6 Ke7 59.Rh6 Rh3 60.d6 Kd7 61.Rf6 Rh2 62.Rf7 Kd6 63.Rf6 Ke7 64.Rg6 h3 65.Rg5 Ke6 66.Rh5 Kf6 67.Kd3 Kg6 68.Rh8 Kg7 69.Rh4 Kg6 70.Rh5 Kf6 71.Ke3 Ke6 72.f4 ef4 73.Kf4 Rh1 74.Kg3 Re1 75.Kh3 Re4 76.Rf5 Ra4 77.Rf8 Ke7 78.Rf3 Ke6 79.Kh4 Ra8 80.g5 Rh8 81.Kg4 Ke7 82.g6 Rf8 83.Rf5 Rh8 84.Kg5 Rh1 85.Rf2 Rh3 86.g7 Rg3 87.Kh6 Rh3 88.Kg6 Rg3 89.Kh7 Rh3 90.Kg8 1-0**

After 19.b3

After 40...Rc2

137) de Greiff,B-Fischer,R [8/30/58] Portoroz Interzonal [15] B93/11 Sicilian **1.e4 c5 2.Nf3 d6 3.d4 cd4 4.Nd4 Nf6 5.Nc3 a6 6.f4** [A system which aims for a dangerous Kingside attack] **e5** [6...e6 transposes into the Scheveningen] **7.Nf3 Qc7** [Defending e5 and preventing Bc4] **8.Bd3 Nbd7 9.a4 b6 10.0-0 Bb7 11.Kh1 g6 12.Qe1 Bg7 13.fe5** [A key move, opening the f-file for pressure] **de5 14.Qh4 0-0 15.Ng5?** [15.Bh6] **h6 16.Nh3 g5! 17.Bg5? hg5 18.Ng5 Rfd8 19.Nd5 Bd5 20.ed5 Nf8 21.c4 Rd6 22.Rae1 Re8 23.h3 Qe7 24.Ne4 Ne4 25.Qe4 Rf6 26.Rf5 Rf5 27.Qf5 a5 28.b3 Rd8 29.Rf1 Rd6 30.Qg4 Rf6 31.Rf5 Rf5 32.Bf5 Qf6 33.Qe4 Ng6 34.g3 Ne7 35.Bh7** [D] **0-1** [Time]

Final position

After 17.Be3

138) Fischer,R-Szabo,L [8/31/58] Portoroz Interzonal [16] C88/04 Ruy Lopez [E:Queen vs. Rook + Bishop] **1.e4 e5 2.Nf3 Nc6 3.Bb5 a6 4.Ba4 Nf6 5.0-0 Be7 6.Re1 b5 7.Bb3 0-0 8.h3?!** [Better is 8.c3] **Bb7 9.c3 d5 10.ed5 Nd5 11.d3 Qd6 =+ 12.Nbd2 Rad8 13.Ne4 Qg6 14.Ng3 Bc5 15.d4 ed4 16.cd4 Ndb4 17.Be3 [D] Nd4 18.Nd4 Bd4 19.Bd4 c5 20.Bc5 Rd1 21.Rad1 Nd3 22.Bf8 Ne1 23.Rd8 h5 24.Bb4 Kh7 25.Rd6 Qb1 26.Rd1 Qg6 27.Rd6 Qb1 28.Rd1 Qg6 29.Re1 h4 30.Re3 hg3 31.Rg3 Qb1 32.Kh2 Qf5 33.Kg1 1/2-1/2**

Final position

139) Pachman,L-Fischer,R [9/3/58] Portoroz Interzonal [17] E81/03 King's Indian,Samisch **1.d4 Nf6 2.c4 g6 3.Nc3 Bg7 4.e4 d6 5.f3 e5 6.Nge2 0-0 7.Bg5 c6 8.Qd2 Qa5** [8...Nbd7 9.d5! +=] **9.d5** [9.0-0-0 is met by 9...b5!] **cd5 10.cd5 Na6 11.Nc1 Bd7 12.Be2** [12.a3! prevents ...Nc5 in view of 13.b4] **Nc5 13.0-0 Rfc8 14.Nd3 Na4 15.Na4 Qd2 16.Bd2 Ba4 17.Rfc1 Ne8 18.Be3 a6 19.b3 Bd7 20.Nb2 Bf6 21.Nc4 Bd8 22.g4 f5 23.gf5 gf5 24.ef5 Bf5 [D] 1/2-1/2**

Final position

140) Fischer,R-Matanovic,A [9/4/58] Portoroz Interzonal [18] C97/14 Ruy Lopez **1.e4 e5 2.Nf3 Nc6 3.Bb5 a6 4.Ba4 Nf6 5.0-0 Be7 6.Re1 b5 7.Bb3 0-0 8.c3 d6 9.h3 Na5 10.Bc2 c5 11.d4 Qc7 12.Nbd2 Bd7 13.Nf1 Rfe8 14.Ne3 g6 15.de5** [15.Bd2 Bf8 16.Rc1 +=] **de5 16.Nh2 Rad8 17.Qf3 Be6 18.Nhg4 Ng4 19.Ng4 Bg4** [Giving up the Bishop pair to eliminate the Ng4] **20.hg4 c4** [To have the option of sending the Knight to d3] **21.g3 Nb7 22.Kg2 Nc5 23.Rh1 f6 24.Be3 Rf8 25.Rad1 Rd1 26.Rd1 Rd8 27.Bc5 Qc5 28.Rd8 Bd8 29.Qd1 Bb6 30.Qd2 Kf8 31.a4 Ke7 32.g5 fg5 33.Qg5 Kf7 34.Qd2 Kf6 35.ab5 ab5 36.Bd1 [D] 1/2-1/2**

Final position

141) Filip,M-Fischer,R [9/6/58] Portoroz Interzonal [19] A49/02 King's Indian **1.Nf3 Nf6 2.g3 g6 3.b3** [A solid, drawish line typical of Filip's "stonewalling" style] **Bg7 4.Bb2 0-0 5.Bg2 d6 6.d4 e5 7.de5 Ng4 8.0-0 Nc6 9.Nbd2 Nge5 10.Ne5 Ne5 11.Kh1 d5!** [Stealing more central space] **12.Nf3 Nf3 13.Bg7 Kg7 14.Bf3 Be6 15.Qd4 Qf6 16.Rfd1 Rfd8 17.c3 c6 [D] 1/2-1/2**

After 19.b3

142) Fischer,R-Cardoso,R [9/7/58] Portoroz Interzonal [20] B10/17 Caro Kann,Two Knights [E:Bishop vs. Knight] **1.e4 c6 2.Nc3 d5 3.Nf3 de4** [3...Bg4 is =] **4.Ne4 Bg4 5.h3 Bf3 6.Qf3 Nd7 7.Ng5 Ngf6 8.Qb3?!** [Too greedy] **e6 9.Qb7 Nd5 10.Ne4 Nb4 11.Kd1 f5 12.c3 Rb8 13.Qa7 fe4 14.cb4 Bb4? 15.Qd4 0-0 16.Bc4 Nc5 17.Qd8 Rbd8 18.Rf1 Rd4 19.b3 [D] Bd2 20.Ke2 Bc1 21.Rac1 Rfd8 22.Rfd1 ++-** [B vs. N, outside passed pawn, better pawn structure, centralized King] **Kf8 23.Rd4 Rd4 24.Rd1 Rd1 25.Kd1 Ke7 26.Kd2 Kd6 27.Kc3 Nd7 28.Kd4 Nf6 29.a4 c5 30.Ke3 g5 31.Be2 Kc6 32.Bc4 e5 33.a5 h6 34.Kd2 h5 35.Ke3 h4 36.Be2 Kd6 37.Bc4 Kc6 38.Ke2 Kb7 39.Kd2 Kc6 40.Ke3 Kb7 41.Kd2 Kc7 42.g4 Kc6 43.Kc3 Ne8 44.b4 Nd6 45.Bf1 cb4 46.Kb4 Nc8 47.Bg2 Kd5 48.a6 Na7 49.Ka5 Kc5 50.Be4 Nb5 51.Bg2 Na7 52.Ka4 Nb5 53.Kb3 Kb6 54.Kc4 Ka6 55.Kd5 Kb6 56.Ke5 Kc7 57.Kf6 Nc3 58.Kg5 Nd1 59.f4 Kd6 60.Kh4 Ke6 61.Kg5 Kf7 62.f5 1-0**

143) Gligoric,S-Fischer,R [9/10/58] Portoroz Interzonal [21] B98/03 Sicilian **1.e4 c5 2.Nf3 d6 3.d4 cd4 4.Nd4 Nf6 5.Nc3 a6 6.Bg5 e6 7.f4 Be7 8.Qf3 h6 9.Bh4 g5** [The famous Goteberg variation] **10.fg5 Nfd7** [D] **11.Ne6** [11.Qh5! +=] **fe6 12.Qh5 Kf8 13.Bb5! Rh7! 14.Qg6?** [14.0-0 Kg8 15.g6 Rg7 16.Rf7 Bh4 17.Qh6 Rf7∞] **Rf7 15.Qh6 Kg8 16.Qg6 Rg7 17.Qe6 Kh8 18.Bd7 Nd7 19.0-0-0 Ne5 20.Qd5 Bg4 21.Rdf1 Bg5 22.Bg5 Qg5 23.Kb1 Qe7 24.Qd2 Be6 25.g3 Rd8 26.Rf4 Qg5 27.Qf2 Kg8 28.Rd1 Rf7 29.b3 Qe7 30.Qd4 Ng6 31.Rf7 Qf7 32.Qe3** 1/2-1/2

After 10...Nfd7

144) Lombardy,W-Fischer,R [12/58] US Championship [1] B90/00 Sicilian [E:Rook + minor piece] **1.e4 c5 2.Nf3 d6 3.d4 cd4 4.Nd4 Nf6 5.Nc3 a6 6.h3 e5?!** [Weakens d5 + f5; better is 6...g6 =] **7.Nde2 Be7 8.g4 0-0 9.Be3** [9.Ng3! g6 10.g5 Ne8 11.h4 +-] **Nbd7 10.a4 Nb6 11.Bg2 Be6 12.0-0 Nc4 13.Bc1 Rc8 14.b3 Nb6 15.a5 Nbd7 16.Be3 Re8 17.Nd5 Bd5 18.ed5 Nf8** [Clearing d7 for the Nf6] **19.Ng3 N6d7 20.Qd2 Ng6 21.Nf5 h6 22.c4 Nh4 23.Nh4 Bh4 24.Rfc1 Bg5 25.Bg5 hg5 26.Rc3 Qf6 27.Be4 Rc7 28.Re1 Rec8 29.Rf3 Qe7 30.Rf5 g6 31.Rf3 Nc5 32.Bc2 Nd7 33.h4 gh4 34.Qh6 Nf8 35.Rh3 Qf6 36.g5 Qh8 37.Qh8 Kh8 38.Rh4 Kg7 39.f4 ef4 40.Rf4 Nd7 41.Re7 Ne5 42.Rc7 Rc7 43.Rf6 Rd7 44.Kg2 Kf8 45.Kg3 Ke7 46.Rf1 Rc7 47.Ra1 f6** [D] 1/2-1/2

Final position

145) Fischer,R-Kalme,C [12/58] US Championship [2] C98/09 Ruy Lopez [E:Rook vs. pawn] **1.e4 e5 2.Nf3 Nc6 3.Bb5 a6 4.Ba4 Nf6 5.0-0 Be7 6.Re1 b5 7.Bb3 0-0 8.c3 d6 9.h3 Na5 10.Bc2 c5 11.d4 Qc7 12.Nbd2 Nc6 13.dc5** [The Rauzer Attack; the main idea is to put pressure on d5 and f5] **dc5 14.Nf1 Be6 15.Ne3 Rad8 16.Qe2 g6 17.Ng5 Bc8 18.a4** [Hoping to utilize the a-file later] **c4 19.ab5 ab5 20.b3 b4** [An attempt to gain counterplay by removing the c3-pawn's control of d4, but this attempt fails] **21.Qc4 h6 22.Nd5! Nd5** [22...Qb7 23.Qc6!] **23.ed5 hg5 24.Qc6 Qc6 25.dc6 bc3 26.Re5 Bf6 27.Rea5 Rfe8 28.Bg5 Bg5 29.Rg5 Rd2 30.Rc1 Ree2** [D] **31.Bg6! fg6 32.Rc3 Kh7 33.b4 Re1 34.Kh2 Rf2 35.b5 Rb2 36.Kg3 Kh6 37.Rcc5 Re3 38.Kf4 Reb3 39.Rgd5 Rg2 40.Rd8 Be6 41.Ke5 Bh3 42.Rh8 Kg7 43.Rh3! Rh3 44.c7 Rh8 45.Rd5 Re2 46.Kd6 Kf6 47.b6 Rb2 48.Kc6 Rc8 49.Rd8 Rc2 50.Kb7 R8c7 51.bc7 Kf5 52.c8=Q Rc8 53.Rc8 g5 54.Kc6 g4 55.Kd5 Kf4 56.Kd4 Kf3 57.Kd3** 1-0

After 30...Ree2

146) Sherwin,J-Fischer,R [12/58] US Championship [3] E94/22 King's Indian [E:Queen vs. Rook] **1.c4 Nf6 2.Nc3 g6 3.d4 Bg7 4.e4 d6 5.Nf3 0-0 6.Be2 e5 7.d5 Nbd7 8.0-0** [An old, but sound system] **Nc5 9.Qc2 a5 10.Ne1** [To dislodge the Nc5 with Nd3; if 10.Nd2 then 10...Bh6!] **Ne8** [10...Nfd7 =] **11.Be3 f5 12.ef5 gf5** [12...Bf5 =] **13.f4 e4 14.Qd2 Nf6 15.Nc2 Bd7 16.Bd4 Qe8 17.Ne3 Qg6 18.b3 h5 19.Ncd1 Ng4! 20.Bg7 Qg7 21.Nf2 Nf2 22.Kf2 h4 23.Kg1 Kf7 24.Rac1 Ke7! 25.Rc3 Rg8 26.Rf2 Nc2 Nb4 28.a3 Nc2 29.Rc2 c5 30.dc6 bc6 31.Rc1 Rgb8 32.Rd1 Qf6 33.Qe3 c5 34.Rd5 Be6 35.Rd2 a4 36.b4 cb4 37.c5 d5 38.c6** [D] **Qc3 39.Bd3 d4 40.Qh3 Rh8 41.Rd1 ed3 42.Rd3 Qc6 43.Rd4 b3 44.Re2 Kf7 45.Rd1 Rad8 46.Rde1 Qb6 47.Kh1 b2 48.Rb1 Rd1 49.Rd1 b1=Q 50.Rd2 Q1b3 51.Rd3 Rd8 52.Rd8 Qh3 53.gh3 Qe3 54.R8d3 Qf4 55.Kg2 Bc8 56.Kg1 Qe4 57.Kf2 Bb7 58.Rd7 Ke6**

After 38.c6

After 43...Rc6

Final position

After 9...Ne8?

After 18.h4

59.R1d6 Ke5 60.Rd3 Qg2 61.Ke1 Be4 62.Re3 Qg1 63.Ke2 Qh2 64.Ke1 Kf4 65.Rc3 Qb2 66.Rdc7 Bf3 67.R7c4 Kg3 68.Rc2 Qa3 69.R4c3 Qe7 70.Kf1 Qe4 71.Rg2 Kh3 72.Re3 Qb1 [Not 72...Qe3?? 73.Rg3! Kh2 74.Rh3! =] **0-1**

147) Fischer,R-Weinstein,R [12/58] US Championship [4] B88/06 Sicilian [E:Rook + minor piece] **1.e4 c5 2.Nf3 d6 3.d4 cd4 4.Nd4 Nf6 5.Nc3 Nc6 6.Bc4 e6 7.0-0 Be7 8.Bb3 0-0 9.f4 Bd7 10.Be3 Nd4 11.Bd4 Bc6** [11...Qa5!?] **12.Qe2 b5** [12...a6 13.f5! +-] **13.Nb5 Bb5 14.Qb5 Ne4 15.f5 Bf6** [15...e5!? 16.Be3 Bg5] **16.Qd3 d5 17.Bf6 Nf6 18.c4!** [Attacking Black's center] **dc4 19.Qd8 Rfd8 20.Bc4 e5 21.Rfe1 e4 22.Rad1 g6 23.fg6 hg6 24.h3 Kf8 25.Kf2 Ke7 26.Ke3 Rdc8 27.b3 Rc5 28.Rf1 Rac8 29.Rf2 R5c6 30.Rdf1 Rd6 31.Rf4 Rcd8 32.h4 Rh8 33.g3 Rh7 34.Ke2 Rh8 35.a3 Rg8 36.g4 g5 37.Rf5! gh4 38.g5 Nh5 39.Re5 Kd8 40.Rf7 Ng3 41.Ke3 h3 42.Ree7 h2 43.Ra7 Rc6** [D] **44.Rfd7 Kc8 45.Rh7 Kb8 46.Rab7 Kc8 47.Bg8 h1=Q 48.Rh1 Rc3 49.Kd2 Rd3 50.Kc2 Kb7 51.Re1 Rd8 52.Bc4 Rh8 53.g6 Rh2 54.Kc3 Rh3 55.Re3 Ne2 56.Kd2 Re3 57.Ke3 Ng3 58.Kf4 1-0**

148) Benko,P-Fischer,R [12/58] US Championship [5] E61/04 King's Indian [E:Rook + minor piece] **1.d4 Nf6 2.c4 g6 3.g3 Bg7 4.Bg2 0-0 5.Nc3 c5 6.e3** [Stodgy; 6.d5; 6.Nf3] **Nc6 7.Nge2** [7.dc Qa5] **d6 8.0-0 Bd7 9.b3 Rb8 10.Bb2 a6 11.dc5 dc5 12.Na4 b6 13.Nf4 Na5! 14.Be5 Rc8 15.Qc2** [15.Nc3?! Nc6] **Ba4 16.ba4 Nd7 17.Bg7 Kg7 18.Bh3 Qe8** [18...e6? 19.Be6!] **19.Qc3 Kg8 20.Rad1 Rd8 21.Nd5 e6 22.Nb6! Nb6 23.Rd8 Qd8 24.Qa5 Nc4 25.Qd8 Rd8 26.Rc1 Nb2 27.a5 c4 28.Rc2 Rb8 29.Bf1 Rb4** [D]**1/2-1/2**

149) Fischer,R-Reshevsky,S [12/58] US Championship [6] B35/00 Sicilian **1.e4 c5 2.Nf3 Nc6 3.d4 cd4 4.Nd4 g6 5.Be3 Nf6 6.Nc3 Bg7 7.Bc4 0-0** [7...Qa5!] **8.Bb3 Na5?** [A well-known mistake – a Russian chess magazine had recently given the following moves, known to Fischer, but not to Reshevsky!] **9.e5! Ne8?** [D] [9...Nb3 10.ef6 +-] **10.Bf7! Kf7** [10...Rf7 11.Ne6!] **11.Ne6! de6 12.Qd8 Nc6 13.Qd2 Be5 14.0-0 Nd6 15.Bf4 Nc4 16.Qe2 Bf4 17.Qc4 Kg7 18.Ne4 Bc7 19.Nc5 Rf6 20.c3 e5 21.Rad1 Nd8 22.Nd7! Rc6 23.Qh4 Re6 24.Nc5 Rf6 25.Ne4 Rf4 26.Qe7 Rf7 27.Qa3 Nc6 28.Nd6 Bd6 29.Rd6 Bf5 30.b4 Rff8 31.b5 Nd8 32.Rd5 Nf7 33.Rc5 a6 34.b6 Be4 35.Re1 Bc6 36.Rc6! bc6 37.b7 Rab8 38.Qa6 Nd8 39.Rb1 Rf7 40.h3 Rfb7 41.Rb7 Rb7 42.Qa8 1-0**

150) Byrne,D-Fischer,R [12/58] US Championship [7] A26/02 English [E:Rook + Bishop] **1.c4 Nf6 2.Nc3 g6 3.g3 Bg7 4.Bg2 0-0 5.d3 d6 6.Rb1 a5 7.e4** [7.Nf3; 7.e3] **e5 8.Nge2 Nc6 9.0-0 Nh5! 10.Be3 f5 11.f4 ef4 11.gf4 f5] f5 11.ef5 Bf5!** [11...gf5 12.f4 +-=] **12.h3 Be6 13.Nd5 Nd4 14.Nd4 ed4 15.Bd2 c6 16.Nf4 Nf4 17.Bf4 Qd7 18.h4** [D] **Rf4!?** [A nice positional exchange sacrifice to gain the initiative] **19.gf4 Rf8 20.Re1 Rf4 21.Qd2 Be5 22.c5 Rg4 23.f3 Rh4 24.cd6 Bh2 25.Kf1 Kf7 26.b4 a4 27.Qf2 g5 28.Re4 Re4 29.fe4 Ke8 30.Qd4 Qd6 31.Qd6 Bd6 32.a3 Be5 33.Bf3 g4 34.Bd1 b5 35.Rc1 Kd7 36.Rc2 Kd6 37.Rd2 Bf4 38.Rc2 g3 39.Bf3 Be5 40.Kg2 Bb3 41.Rc5 Bf7 42.d4 Bd4 43.e5! Be5 44.Rc6 Ke7 45.Rc5 Bb2 46.Rb5 Ba3 47.Rb7 Kf6 48.Rf7 1/2-1/2**

151) Fischer,R-Evans,L [12/58] US Championship [8] B99/00 Sicilian/Sozin **1.e4 c5 2.Nf3 d6 3.d4 cd4 4.Nd4 Nf6 5.Nc3 a6 6.Bc4 e6 7.Bb3 Be7 8.Be3 0-0 9.0-0 Nc6 10.f4 Na5 11.g4 d5** [The flank attack is met by a central counter] **12.e5 Nd7 13.Qf3 Qc7 14.h4 Nc4 15.Bc4 dc4 16.a4** [D] **b6 17.h5 Bb7 18.Qg3 h6 19.Rae1 Rad8 20.Re2 Kh8 21.Rh2 Ba8 22.Re1 Bc5 23.Qf2 Rde8 24.Nf3 Be3 25.Qe3 Qc5 26.Qc5 Nc5 27.Nd2 1/2-1/2**

After 16.a4

152) Mednis,E-Fischer,R [12/58] US Championship [9] A00/02 Sicilian **1.Nc3** [Rarely played] **c5 2.Nf3 Nf6 3.e4 d6 4.g3 g6 5.Bg2 Bg7 6.0-0 Nc6 7.d3 0-0 8.h3 Rb8 9.a4?!** [9.Be3] **a6 10.Be3 b5 11.ab5 ab5 12.e5 de5 13.Bc5 Qc7 14.Re1 b4 15.Na4 Rd8 16.Nd2 Nd4 17.Nc4 Nd5 18.Bd4 ed4 19.b3 Bb7 20.Qd2 e5 -++** [Bishop pair + strong center] **21.Nab2 Ra8 22.Kh2 h5!** [An excellent pawn sac] **23.Bd5 Bd5 24.Qb4 Ra1 25.Ra1 Qd7 26.Qe1 Qf5 27.Nd2 h4 28.Nbc4 hg3 29.fg3 Qe6 30.Ne4 f5 31.Qa5** [D] **Ra8 32.Qa8 Ba8 33.Ra8 Bf8 34.Ned6 Qd5 35.Re8 Qf3 36.h4 Qf2 37.Kh3 Qg1 0-1**

After 31.Qa5

153) Fischer,R-Bisguier,A [12/58] US Championship [10] C99/02 Ruy Lopez [E:Rook + pawn] **1.e4 e5 2.Nf3 Nc6 3.Bb5 a6 4.Ba4 Nf6 5.0-0 Be7 6.Re1 b5 7.Bb3 0-0 8.c3 d6** [8...d5!?; Marshall] **9.h3 Na5 10.Bc2 c5 11.d4 Qc7 12.Nbd2 cd4 13.cd4 Bd7** [Also possible is 13...Bb7] **14.Nf1 Rfc8** [14...Rfe8] **15.Ne3 Nc6 16.a3 a5 17.d5** [Gaining space while driving the Knight out of play] **Nd8 18.Bd2 a4 19.Bb4 Bf8 20.Bd3 Nb7 21.Qe2 Qb6 22.Nd2 Nc5 23.Kh2 g6 24.Rac1 Bh6 25.Bb1 Rc7 26.Qf3 Bg5 27.g3 h5 28.Kg2 Kg7 29.Rf1 h4 30.Qe2 Rh8 31.Rh1 Nh5 32.Nf3 hg3 33.fg3 Bf4 34.Be1 Qb8 35.Bf2 Qc8 36.h4 Bg4 37.Rc3 Bd7 38.Nf1 Bh6 39.N1d2 Nf6 40.Be3 Be3 41.Qe3 Ng4 42.Qe2 Nb3 43.Rc7 Qc7 44.Nb3 ab3 45.Nh2 Qc4 46.Bd3 Qd4 47.Ng4 Bg4 48.Qg4 Qd3 49.Rf1 Rf8 50.h5 Rh8** [D] **51.Qf3 Qf3 52.Rf3 gh5 53.Rb3 Rb8 54.Rb4 f5 55.ef5 Kf6 56.a4 Ra8 57.ab5 Kf5 58.b6 e4 59.Kf2 Ke5 60.Ke3 Kd5 61.Re4 Rb8 62.Rh4 Rb6 63.Rh5 Ke6 64.Rh2 Ke5 65.Kd3 Rb3 66.Kc4 Rg3 67.Re2 Kf5 68.Kd5 Rd3 69.Kc6 d5 70.b4 d4 71.Kd5 Rd1 72.Rf2 Kg4 73.Kc4 d3 74.Kc3 Rb1 75.Rd2 Kf4 76.Rd3 Ke4 77.Rd8 Rc1 78.Kb3 Ke5 79.Ka4 Ke6 80.Rd2 Rc7 81.b5 Rd7 82.Rd7 Kd7 83.Ka5 Kc7 84.Ka6 Kb8 85.Kb6 Kc8 86.Ka7** [D] **1-0**

After 50...Rh8

Final position

154) Byrne,R-Fischer,R [12/58] US Championship [11] E62/21 King's Indian **1.d4 Nf6 2.c4 g6 3.g3 Bg7 4.Bg2 0-0 5.Nc3 d6 6.Nf3 Nc6 7.0-0 e5 8.d5 Ne7 9.c5 Nd7** [9...dc5 10.Ne5 Nfd5 11.Nd5 Be5 12.Bg5 f6 13.Nf6! +-; best is 9...Ne8] **10.cd6 cd6 11.Nd2 f5 12.a4 e4 13.Nc4 +=** [Queenside initiative] **Ne5 14.Ne5 Be5 15.Be3 Bd7 16.a5 b5 17.ab6 ab6 18.Qb3 b5 19.f3 ef3 20.Bf3 Ra1 21.Ra1 f4 22.gf4 Bf4 23.Ne4 Be3 24.Qe3 Nf5 25.Qa7 Nh4 26.Rf1 Bh3 27.Rf2 Bf5 28.Ng3** [D] **1/2-1/2**

Final position

1959

Final position

Final position

After 55.Rc3

After 35.Nh3

155) Fischer,R-Emma,J [3/23/59] Mar del Plata [1] B00/08 Nimzowitsch [E:Rook + Bishop] **1.e4 Nc6 2.Nf3 d6 3.d4 Bg4 4.d5 Nb8 5.c4** +=/+- [More space + tempi gained] **e5 6.de6 fe6 7.Nc3 Nc6 8.Be2 Nf6 9.h3 Bh5 10.Be3 Be7 11.0-0 Qd7 12.Nd4 Bg6 13.Nc6 bc6 14.e5 de5 15.Qa4 0-0 16.Rad1 Qe8 17.Qa5 Bd6 18.c5 Be7 19.Qc7 Nd5 20.Nd5 ed5 21.Qe5 Bc5! 22.Qc3 Be3 23.Qe3 Qe3 24.fe3 Rae8 25.Rf8 Kf8 26.Kf2 Ke7 27.b4 Rb8 28.a3 Rf8 29.Bf3 a5 30.ba5 Ra8 31.e4 Ra5 32.ed5 cd5 33.Ra1 Bc2 34.Ke3 Kd6 35.Kd4 Bb3 36.Be2 Ra7 37.Kc3 Ba4 38.Kb4 d4 39.g3 Bc6 40.a4 Be4 41.Bb5 Rb7 42.Kc4 Ke5 43.a5 Rc7 44.Kb4 d3 45.a6 Kd4 46.a7 Rc8** [D] 1/2-1/2

156) Sanchez,L-Fischer,R [3/24/59] Mar del Plata [2] E93/03 King's Indian **1.Nf3 Nf6 2.d4 g6 3.c4 Bg7 4.Nc3 0-0 5.e4 d6 6.Be2 e5 7.d5 Nbd7** [7...a5!] **8.Bg5 h6 9.Bh4 a6** [9...g5!? 10.Bg3 Nh5 11.h4 g4 12.Nd2 f5 with equal chances] **10.0-0 Qe8 11.Ne1 Nh7 12.f3 f5 13.Nd3 f4 14.b4 g5 15.Bf2 h5 16.c5 Qg6 17.Rc1 Ndf6 18.Kh1 g4 19.Bh4 Bh6 20.cd6 cd6 21.Na4 Bg5 22.Qe1 Rb8 23.Nb6 Nd7 24.Nc4 Rf6 25.Rc2 b5 26.Na5 Nb6 27.Bf2 Bd7 28.Rc7 Rf7 29.Nb2 Rg7 30.Nc6 Bc6 31.Rg7 Qg7 32.dc6 Nf6 33.Qc3 Qc7 34.Rc1 h4 35.Qb3 Kg7 36.Qe6 g3 37.Bg1 gh2 38.Kh2 Nc8 39.Bd1 Ne7 40.Bb3 Ng6 41.Nd3** [D] 1/2-1/2

157) Fischer,R-Pachman,L [3/25/59] Mar del Plata [3] C75/12 Ruy Lopez [E:Rook + Bishop vs. Rook + pawns] **1.e4 e5 2.Nf3 Nc6 3.Bb5 a6 4.Ba4 d6 5.c3 Bd7 6.d4 Nge7 7.Bb3 h6 8.0-0** [8.h4!?; 8.Na3!?] **Ng6 9.Nbd2 Be7 10.Nc4 Bg5 11.Ne3 Be3 12.Be3 0-0 13.h3 Re8 14.Nh2 Qe7 15.de5 de5 16.Qh5 Na5!** [To answer 17.Qg6 with 17...Nb3] **17.Bc2 Nc4 18.Bc1 Nf4 19.Qf3 Rad8! 20.Bf4 ef4 21.Qf4 Bc6 22.Ng4 h5! 23.Ne3 Nb2 24.Nf5 Qf6 25.Qc7 Qc3 26.Rac1 Qf6 27.Rfe1 Nd3 28.Bd3 Rd3 29.Qf4 g6!** [Now on 30.Nh6 Kg7 31.Qf6 Kf6 -++] **30.Rc5 Re6 31.Qb8 Rd8 32.Qf4 gf5 33.Rf5 Qg7 34.Rh5 Rde8 35.f3 Re5 36.Rh4 Rg5 37.Rg4 Rg4 38.hg4 Qd4 39.Re3 Qe5 40.Qf5 Qf5 41.gf5 Rd8 42.Kf2 Bb5 43.Ke1 Kg7 44.e5 Rd4 45.g4 Kh6 46.e6 f6 47.Kf2 Rd2 48.Kg3 Kg7 49.Rc3 Bc6 50.a3 Re2 51.Kf4 a5 52.Rd3 a4 53.Rd8 Rf2 54.Rd3 b5 55.Rc3** [D] **Rf3! 56.Rf3 Bf3 0-1** [57.Kf3 b4]

158) Sousa Mendes,J-Fischer,R [3/26/59] Mar del Plata [4] E81/04 King's Indian,Samisch [E:Rook + minor pieces] **1.d4 Nf6 2.c4 g6 3.Nc3 Bg7 4.e4 d6 5.f3 e5 6.Nge2 0-0 7.Bg5!** [More aggressive than the usual 7.Be3, this is possible because of Black's early ...e5] **c6 8.Qd2 Qa5 9.d5 cd5 10.Nd5** [10.cd5] **Qd2 11.Kd2 Nd5 12.cd5 f6 13.Be3 Nd7 14.Nc3 a6 15.g4 f5 16.gf5 gf5 17.Bd3 fe4 18.fe4 Nf6 19.Na4 Ng4 20.Raf1 Rf1 21.Bf1 Ne3 22.Ke3 Bh6 23.Kd3 Bd7 24.Rg1 Kh8 25.Nc3 b5 26.Ne2 b4 27.Kc2 Rc8** -++ [Two Bishops and superior piece-pawn coordination] **28.Kb3 a5 29.Rg3 Rf8 30.Bh3 Bb5 31.Ng1 Bf4 32.Rg2 Bf1 33.Rf2 Bd3 34.Bf5 Rb8 35.Nh3** [D] **a4! 36.Ka4 b3! 37.ab3 Be3 38.Rf3 Ra8** [39.Kb4 Bd2 #] **0-1**

159) Fischer,R-Letelier,R [3/28/59] Mar del Plata [5] C97/13
Ruy Lopez [E:King + pawn] **1.e4 e5 2.Nf3 Nc6 3.Bb5 a6 4.Ba4 Nf6
5.0-0 Be7 6.Re1 b5 7.Bb3 d6 8.c3 0-0 9.h3 Na5 10.Bc2 c5 11.d4
Qc7 12.Nbd2 Re8 13.Nf1 Bd7 14.Ne3 Bf8 15.de5 de5 16.Nh2** [The
Knight goes to g4 to exchange off the Nf6. This indirectly weakens
d5 for the Ne3] **Rad8 17.Qf3 Be6 18.Nhg4 Nd7 19.Nd5 Qb8 20.h4
Nc4 21.h5 h6** [Otherwise h6, and f6 is critically weak] **22.b3 Nd6
23.Qg3 Kh8 24.f4! Bd5 25.ed5 e4 26.Ne5 Qb7** [D] **27.Re4! Ne4!
28.Nf7 Kg8 29.Nh6 Kh8 30.Nf7 Kg8 31.Nd8 Qd5 32.Qd3 Qd3
33.Bd3 Nc3 34.Bd2 Ne4 35.Re1 Ndf6 36.Be4 Ne4 37.Nc6 Bd6
38.Bc1 Kf7 39.Bb2 Ng3 40.Ne5 Be5 41.Re5 Re5 42.Be5 Nh5
43.Kf2 Nf6 44.Kf3 g6 45.Bf6 Kf6 46.Ke4 Ke6 47.a4 Kd6 48.a5**
[48. ab ab 49.g4 =] **Ke6 49.g3 Kd6 50.f5 gf5 51.Kf5 Kd5 52.g4
Kd4 53.g5 c4 54.bc4! b4 55.c5?** [55.g6] **b3 56.c6 b2 57.c7 b1=Q
58.Ke6 Qb7 59.Kd7 Kd5 60.g6 Qc6 61.Kd8 Qd6 0-1**

After 26...Qb7

160) Redolfi,R-Fischer,R [3/29/59] Mar del Plata [6] B52/00
Sicilian **1.e4 c5 2.Nf3 d6 3.Bb5 Bd7 4.Bd7** [4.a4!?] **Qd7 5.Nc3**
[5.c4 is a Maroczy Bind, but Black is = because of the exchange
of minor pieces] **Nc6 6.d4 cd4 7.Nd4 g6 8.0-0 Bg7 9.Be3 Nf6 10.f3
0-0 11.Qd2 Rac8 12.Rad1 Rfd8 13.Rf2 Nb8 14.b3 d5 15.Nd5 Nd5
16.ed5 Qd5 17.c4 Qc5 18.Rff1 a6 19.Qf2 Qa5 20.h3 Qc3 21.Rc1
Qa5 22.Rcd1 Rd6 23.f4 Nc6 24.Nc6 Rdc6 25.Rd7 R6c7 26.Rfd1**
[26.Bb6 Rd7! 27.Ba5 Bd4 -++] **Bf6 27.Rd8 Kg7 28.Bb6 Qb4
29.Bc7 Rc7 30.R8d7** [Playing too hard to win, Fischer slips into a
losing position] **Rc6 31.Kh2 b5 32.Rb7 Re6 33.Rd2 Qc3 34.cb5
Qa1 35.g3 Bc3 36.Rd3 Re1 37.ba6 Rb1 38.Rbd7 Bb4 39.a7** [D]
Bc5 40.Qc5?? [40.Qg2 ++-] **Rh1 0-1**

After 39.a7

161) Fischer,R-Shocron,G [3/30/59] Mar del Plata [7] C97/14
Ruy Lopez **1.e4 e5 2.Nf3 Nc6 3.Bb5 a6 4.Ba4 Nf6 5.0-0 Be7 6.Re1
b5 7.Bb3 d6 8.c3 0-0 9.h3 Na5 10.Bc2 c5 11.d4 Qc7 12.Nbd2 Bd7
13.Nf1 Rae8 14.Ne3 g6 15.de5 de5 16.Nh2 Rad8 17.Qf3 Be6
18.Nhg4 Ng4 19.hg4 Qc6 20.g5!?** [20.Qg3 +=] **Nc4 21.Ng4 Bg4
22.Qg4 Nb6! 23.g3 c4 24.Kg2 Nd7 25.Rh1 Nf8 26.b4 Qe6** [26...a5
=] **27.Qe2 a5 28.ba5 Qa6 29.Be3 Qa5 30.a4 Ra8 31.ab5 Qb5
32.Rhb1 Qc6 33.Rb6 Qc7 34.Rba6 Ra6 35.Ra6 Rc8 36.Qg4 Ne6
37.Ba4 Rb8 38.Rc6 Qd8?** [38...Qd7!] **39.Re6! Qc8** [D] **40.Bd7!!**
[A cute refutation - now 40...Qd7 41.Rg6 wins] **1-0**

After 39...Qc8

162) Najdorf,M-Fischer,R [3/31/59] Mar del Plata [8] E62/22
King's Indian [E:Rook + pawn] **1.Nf3 Nf6 2.c4 g6 3.g3 Bg7 4.Bg2
0-0 5.d4 d6 6.0-0 Nc6 7.Nc3 e5 8.d5 Ne7 9.e4** [9.c5!?] **Nd7 10.b4**
[White advances on the Queenside, Black on the Kingside] **f5**
[10...a5 11.Ba3 only helps White open lines on the Queenside]
**11.Ng5 Nf6 12.Ba3 fe4 13.Nce4 Nf5 14.Bb2 Ne4 15.Ne4 Nd4 16.f4
Bf5 17.Qd2 c5! 18.dc6** [18.bc5 Be4 19.Be4 dc5] **bc6 19.Kh1 Qd7
20.Rae1 Rad8 21.fe5 de5 22.c5 Qe6 23.Nd6 Nb5!!** [Now on
24.Bc6 Nd6 25.Bd5 Be4! 26.Re4 Rf1 27.Kg2 Rf2! or 26.Be4 Ne4
27.Rf8 Bf8! 28.Qd8 Qf7!] **24.Qe3! Nd6 25.cd6 Rd6 26.Be5 Be5
27.Qe5 Qe5 28.Re5 Be6 29.Rf8 Kf8 30.Bf3 Ba2 31.Ra5 Bd5
32.Bd5 cd5 33.Ra7 d4 34.Kg2 d3 35.Ra1** [D] **1/2-1/2**

Final Position

163) Fischer,R-Sanguinetti,R [4/2/59] Mar del Plata [9]
C97/07 Ruy Lopez [E:Rook vs. Bishop + pawns] **1.e4 e5 2.Nf3 Nc6 3.Bb5 a6 4.Ba4 Nf6 5.0-0 Be7 6.Re1 b5 7.Bb3 d6 8.c3 0-0 9.h3 Na5 10.Bc2 c5 11.d4 Qc7 12.Nbd2 Re8 13.Nf1 Bf8** [13...cd4 14.cd4 ed4] **14.Bg5 Nd7 15.Ne3 Nb6 16.Rc1 f6 17.Bh4 Be6 18.Nd5! Qb7 19.b4 Nac4 20.Nb6 Qb6 21.Bb3 cd4 22.cd4 a5 23.ba5 Na5 24.Be6 Ree6 25.Qd3 +-** [Better Bishop, more central control, and the Black b-pawn is a target] **Ree8 26.Rb1 b4 27.Re2 Reb8 28.Reb2 Qb5 29.Qb5 Rb5 30.d5 Rab8 31.Nd2 Kf7 32.f3 g6 33.Be1 Bh6 34.a4! Be3 35.Kf1 R5b7 36.Nb3 Nc4 37.Ra2 Ra8 38.Ke2 Na3 39.Rbb2 Bg1 40.a5 Raa7 41.Ra1 Bc5 42.Rc1 Rc7 43.Bd2 Nb5 44.Rbc2 Na3 45.Rb2 Nb5 46.Kd3 Na3 47.Nc5!** [Forcing Black's pawn duo to become vulnerable] **dc5 48.Be3 c4 49.Ke2 b3** [D] **50.Bb6! Rcb7 51.Ra1 Nc2 52.Rc1 Na3 53.Ra1 Nc2 54.Rc2! bc2 55.Rc1 Ra8 56.Rc2 Rc8 57.Kd2 Ke7 58.Kc3 Kd7 59.Kb4 Rbb8 60.Rc4 Rc4 61.Kc4 Rc8 62.Bc5 Rb8 63.a6 Rb2 64.a7 Ra2 65.Kb5 Kc7 66.d6 Kb7 67.d7 Rd2 68.a8=Q 1-0**

After 49...b3

164) Pilnik,H-Fischer,R [4/3/59] Mar del Plata [10] B92/12
Sicilian [E:Rook + Bishop] **1.e4 c5 2.Nf3 d6 3.d4 cd4 4.Nd4 Nf6 5.Nc3 a6 6.Be2 e5 7.Nb3 Be7 8.0-0 0-0 9.Be3 Be6 10.f3** [An old system, which shouldn't trouble Black. 10.a4; 10.f4] **Qc7 11.Qe1 Nbd7 12.Rd1 b5 13.Rd2 Nb6 14.Qf2** [14.Bb6 Qb6 = /=+] **Rab8** [14...Nc4!] **15.Bb6 Rb6 16.Nd5 Nd5 17.ed5 Bd7 18.f4 Bf6 19.c3 Rbb8 20.fe5 Be5 21.Nd4 g6 22.a3 a5 23.Kh1 b4 24.cb4 ab4 25.Rc2 Qb6 26.Nc6 ba3! 27.Qb6 Rb6 28.ba3 Ra8 29.Ne5?** [29.Ra2] **de5 30.Rc3 Rb2! 31.Rc7 Bf5 32.g4 Be4 33.Bf3 Bd3 34.d6 Rd8 35.Re1 Rd6 36.Re5 Rf6! 37.Re3** [D] **Rf3! 38.Rf3 Be4 39.Rf7 Rf2 40.Rf8 Kg7 0-1**

After 37.Re3

165) Fischer,R-Rossetto,H [4/5/59] Mar del Plata [12]
B41/05 Sicilian [E:Rook + minor piece] **1.e4 c5 2.Nf3 e6 3.d4 cd4 4.Nd4 a6 5.c4 Qc7** [5...Nf6 6.Nc3 Bb4] **6.Nc3 Nf6 7.Bd3** [7.a3!] **Nc6 8.Be3 Nd4?!** [8...Ne5] **9.Bd4 Bc5 10.Bc2 d6 11.0-0 Bd7 12.Na4 Bd4 13.Qd4 Rd8 14.Rfd1 0-0 15.Rac1 Qa5 16.Qb6 Qb6 17.Nb6 Bc6 18.f3 Nd7!** [D] **19.Nd5!** [Trying to mix it up positionally] **Bd5 20.ed5 e5 21.b4** [Now a well-timed c5 gives +=] **g6 22.Ba4 b6 23.Rd3 f5?** [23...a5] **24.Ra3! Nb8 25.c5! bc5 26.bc5 dc5 27.Rc5 Kg7 28.Rb3 Rf7 29.d6 Nd7 30.Rc7 Nf8 31.Rbb7 Rc7 32.dc7 Rc8 33.Bb3! a5 34.a4! h6 35.h3 g5 36.g4 fg4 37.hg4 1-0**

After 18...Nd7!

166) Wexler,B-Fischer,R [4/7/59] Mar del Plata [13] E61/15
King's Indian **1.c4 Nf6 2.d4 g6 3.Nc3 Bg7 4.Bg5** [Very solid; a Smyslov invention] **d6 5.Nf3 0-0 6.e3 c5 7.Be2 h6 8.Bh4 g5** [Gaining the Bishop pair at the expense of a slight pawn weakening] **9.Bg3 Nh5 10.0-0 Nc6 11.d5 Na5 12.Rc1 a6 13.Nd2 Ng3 14.fg3?** [Too ambitious; simply 14.hg3] **e6!15.Qc2 ed5 16.Nd5 Be6 17.Bd3 b5! 18.b3 Rb8 19.Rb1 Nc6 20.Be4 Kh8! 21.cb5 ab5 22.a4 f5! 23.Nf4 gf4 24.Bc6 fe3 25.Nf3 ba4 26.Ba4 Bd5! 27.Qe2 Bd4 28.Rbd1 Qf6 29.Nh4 Qe6 30.Nf3 Rb4 31.Kh1** [D] **Ra4 32.ba4 Bc4 33.Nd4 cd4 34.Qb2 e2 35.Qd4 Kh7 36.Rfe1 ed1=Q 37.Qd1 Qf6 38.Qc1 Bd3 0-1**

After 31.Kh1

167) Fischer,R-Bolbochan,,Julio [4/8/59] Mar del Plata [14] B45/09 Sicilian [E:Rook + Bishop] **1.e4 c5 2.Nf3 Nc6 3.d4 cd4 4.Nd4 Nf6 5.Nc3 e6 6.Ndb5 Bb4 7.a3 Bc3 8.Nc3 d5 9.Bd3** [9.ed5 ed5 10.Bd3 0-0 11.0-0 d4 12.Ne2 +=] **de4 10.Ne4 Ne4 11.Be4 Qd1 12.Kd1 Bd7 13.Be3 f5 14.Bf3 e5 15.b4 0-0-0 16.Kc1 Nd4 17.Bd4 ed4 18.Re1 Rhe8 19.Kd2 Bb5 20.Re8 Re8 21.a4 Bc4 22.Rc1 Kb8 23.c3 dc3 24.Rc3 Bf7 25.a5 Re7 26.Re3 Rd7 27.Rd3 Re7 28.Rd8 Kc7 29.Rh8 h6 30.Kc3 +-** [More active Rook, Bishop and King] **a6 31.Kd4 Be8 32.Rf8 Bd7 33.h4! Bc8 34.Bd5 Bd7 35.f4!** [Fixing pawns on the same color as his opponent's Bishop] **g6 36.Rf6 Be8 37.Be6 Bc6 38.g3 Rg7 39.Ke5 Be8 40.Bd5 h5 41.Rb6 Kc8 42.Be6 Kc7 43.Kf6 Rh7 44.Bd5 Kc8 45.Re6 Kd8 46.Rd6 Kc7 47.Rb6 Kc8 48.Bg8 Rc7 49.Be6 Kb8 50.Rd6 [D] 1-0**

Final position

168) Ivkov,B-Fischer,R [4/9/59] Mar del Plata [15] E80/05 King's Indian,Samisch [E:Rook + Bishop] **1.d4 Nf6 2.c4 g6 3.Nc3 Bg7 4.e4 d6 5.f3 e5 6.d5 Nh5 7.Be3 f5 8.Nge2 0-0 9.Qd2 a6 10.0-0-0 b5** [A thematic pawn sac for counterplay] **11.ef5 gf5 12.Ng3!** [Forcing play; now 12...Ng3 13.hg3 +-] **Nf6 13.Bg5 Qe8 14.h4 b4 15.Nb1 Nh5 16.Nh5 Qh5 17.Be2!** [17.Qb4? f4!] **f4 18.g4! Qf7** [18...fg3 19.Rdg1 h6 20.Rg3! hg5 21.Rg5 followed by 22.Rhg1 ++-] **19.Bd3 h6 20.Qc2 b3 21.ab3 a5 22.Qe2** [22.Bh7! Kh8 23.Nc3 +-] **hg5 23.hg5 Rd8 24.g6 Qe7 25.Nc3 Na6 26.Ne4 Nc5 27.Nc5 dc5 28.Rh5 a4 29.ba4** [29.Rdh1!] **Ra4 30.Kb1 Bd7 31.d6 cd6 32.Be4 Be6 33.Qd3 Qa7 34.Qdh1 Ra1 35.Kc2 Qa4 36.Qb3 Qb3 37.Kb3 Rb8 38.Kc3 Ra2 39.Rb1 Rb4 40.b3 Ra3 41.Kc2 Ra2 42.Kc3 Re2 43.Ra1! Re3 44.Kc2 Reb3 45.Ra8 Rb8 46.Ra7 Rb2 47.Kc1 R2b4 48.Rh7 Bf6 49.g7! Rc4 50.Kd1 Rd4 51.Kc1 Rc4 52.Kd1 Rd4 53.Kc1 [D] 1/2-1/2**

Final position

169) Fischer,R-Sanchez,L [4/59] Santiago [1] C92/18 Ruy Lopez [E:Rook + minor pieces] **1.e4 e5 2.Nf3 Nc6 3.Bb5 a6 4.Ba4 Nf6 5.0-0 Be7 6.Re1 b5 7.Bb3 d6 8.c3 0-0 9.h3 Nd7 10.d4 Nb6 11.de5?!** [11.Be3; 11.Nbd2] **Ne5 12.Ne5 de5 13.Qh5 Bf6 14.Nd2 g6** [14...Qe7] **15.Qf3 Qe7 16.Qg3 Bh4 17.Qh2 Bf6 18.Nf3 Be6 19.Bc2 Bd7 20.Bh6 Rfe8 21.h4 Bg7 22.Bg5 f6?!** [Weakens g6] **23.Bc1 Bf8 24.h5 g5 25.Qg3 Qg7 26.Nh2 h6 27.Ng4 Qf7 28.Qf3 Bg7 29.Ne3 Be6 30.Nf5 Bf8 31.b3 Rad8 32.Be3 Rd7 33.Qh3 Kh7 34.Bd1!** [Intending to trade Black's "good" Be6] **Nc8 35.Bg4 Nd6 36.Ng3 Bg4 37.Qg4 Qe6 38.Qe6 Re6 39.Red1 Rd8 40.a4 ba4 41.Ra4 Nb7 42.Rd5 Rc6 43.c4 Kg8 44.c5 Kf7 45.Rb4 Rb8 46.Rd7 Ke6 47.Rh7 Rb6 48.cb6 Bb4 49.bc7 Rc8 50.Nf5 Bf8 51.g4 Na5 52.b4 Bb4 [D] 53.Bd2! 1-0** [53...Bd2 54.Re7#; now the Knight will be lost]

After 52...Bb4

170) Sousa Mendes,J-Fischer,R [4/59] Santiago [2] E80/03 King's Indian,Samisch [E:Minor piece] **1.d4 Nf6 2.c4 g6 3.Nc3 Bg7 4.e4 d6 5.f3 e5 6.Nge2 Nfd7** [Intending to trade the "bad" Bg7 for White's Bc1, but this maneuver is artificial] **7.Be3 [D] Bh6 8.Qd2** [8.Bh6 Qh4; 8.Bf2! 0-0 9.h4 +=] **Be3 9.Qe3 c5! 10.d5 Na6 11.Qh6 Nc7 12.h4** [12.Qg7 Qf6] **Qf6 13.Ng3 Rb8 14.Bd3 b6 15.Kd2 Ba6 16.a4 Ke7 17.b3 Bc8 18.Nd1 Ne8 19.Nf2 Qg7 20.Qg7 Ng7 21.h5 Nf6 22.hg6 fg6 23.Kc3 a5 24.Ne2 Bd7 25.Rh2 h5 26.Rah1 g5 27.g4 Rh6 28.Nd1 Rbh8 29.Ne3 R6h7 30.Ng3 Kf7 31.gh5 Nfh5**

After 7.Be3

After 69.Kd2

32.Ngf5 Bf5 33.ef5 Nf6 34.Rh7 Rh7 35.Rh7 Nh7 36.Ng4 Nf6 37.Nh6 Ke7 38.Kd2 Ngh5 39.Ke3 Nf4 40.Bf1 N6h5 41.Kf2 Kf6 42.Ng8 Kf7 43.Nh6 Kf8 44.f6 Nf6 45.Nf5 Ne8 46.Kg3 Kf7 47.Kf2 Kf6 48.Ng3 Kg6 49.Ne4 Kh6 50.Ng3 Ng7 51.Ne4 Nf5 52.Nf6 Kg6 53.Nd7 Kf7 54.Nb6 Ke7 55.Nc8 Kd7 56.Na7 Nd4 57.Kg3 Nb3 58.Nc6 Kc7 59.Kf2 Kb6 60.Ke3 Nd4 61.Nd8 Nf5 62.Kf2 Nh6 63.Kg3 Nh5 64.Kf2 g4 65.fg4 Ng4 66.Ke1 Ne3 67.Nf7 Kc7 68.Bd3 e4 69.Kd2 [D] Nd5 70.cd5 ed3 71.Kd3 Nf6 72.Kc4 Nd7 73.Kb5 Nb6 74.Ka5 Nd5 75.Ng5 Nc3 76.Ne6 0-1

After 48.Kf4

171) Fischer,R-Ivkov,B [4/59] Santiago [3] C16/14 French [E:Rook + minor piece] **1.e4 e6 2.d4 d5 3.Nc3 Bb4 4.e5 Ne7 5.a3 Bc3 6.bc3 b6 7.Qg4 Ng6 8.Bg5** [8.h4! h5 9.Qd1 +-] **Qd7 9.h4 h6 10.Bd2 h5 11.Qf3 Qa4!** = [Blockading the light squares] **12.Bd3 Ba6 13.g4 hg4 14.Qg4 Bd3 15.cd3 Nc6 16.Qg5 Nce7 17.h5 Nf5 18.Ne2 Nge7 19.Ng3 0-0-0 20.Qg4 Rdf8 21.Rh3 Kb8 22.Bg5 Qc2 23.Rc1 Qb2 24.a4 Qa3 25.Qd1 Ng3 26.fg3 Nc6 27.h6 gh6 28.Bf6 Rhg8 29.Kf2 Rg6 30.Qc2 Rfg8 31.Rb1 Qf8 32.a5 Na5 33.Qa4 Ka8 34.Rb5 Qe8 35.c4 Nc6 36.Qa1 dc4 37.dc4 Qd7 38.c5 Qd4 39.Qd4 Nd4 40.Rb4 Nf5 41.c6 Rg4 42.Rg4 Rg4 43.Rh1 a5 44.Rg1 a4 45.Rd1 Rd4 46.Rg1 Rd2 47.Kf3 Rd3 48.Kf4** [D] **Rg3 49.Rc1 Rd3 50.Kg4 a3 51.Ra1 b5 52.Rb1 a2 0-1**

After 37...ed5

172) Sanguinetti,R-Fischer,R [4/59] Santiago [4] E81/04 King's Indian,Samisch [E:Queen vs. Rook] **1.d4 Nf6 2.c4 g6 3.Nc3 Bg7 4.e4 d6 5.f3 e5 6.Nge2 0-0 7.Bg5!** [Better than the routine Be3] **c6 8.Qd2 Qa5 9.d5 cd5 10.cd5 Bd7 11.g4 Na6 12.Ng3 Nc5** [Δ 13...Nb3] **13.Rb1 Qb4 14.Nb5 Qd2 15.Kd2 Bb5 16.Bb5 a6 17.Be2 Rfc8 18.Rbc1 Ne8 19.Rc2 Bf6** [Trading off the "bad" Bishop for White's "good" Bishop] **20.Bf6 Nf6 21.Rhc1 a5 22.Bb5 Kg7 23.h4 h5 24.gh5 Nh5 25.Nh5 gh5 26.Ke3 Rg8 27.Rg1 Kf6 28.Rcg2 Rg6 29.f4 Rag8 30.Rg5 ef4 31.Kf4 Rg5 32.hg5 Ke7 33.Rh1 Rh8 34.e5 Nd7 35.Bd7 Kd7 36.e6! fe6 37.g6 ed5** [D] **38.Rh5 Rh5 39.g7 Re5 40.g8=Q Kc7 41.Qh7 Kc6 42.Qc2 Kb6 43.Qb3 Kc7 44.Qc3 Kb6 45.Qa3 Re4 46.Kf5 Kb5 47.Qd6 Rc4 48.b3 Rc6 49.a4 Kb6 50.Qd8 Ka6 51.Qd5 Rb6 52.Ke5 Rb4 53.Kd6 Rb6 54.Kc7 Rb4 55.Kb8 1-0**

After 34...Bh4

173) Fischer,R-Stekel,M [4/59] Santiago [5] C76/02 Ruy Lopez **1.e4 e5 2.Nf3 Nc6 3.Bb5 a6 4.Ba4 d6 5.c3 Bd7 6.d4 g6 7.0-0 Bg7 8.Bg5 Nge7 9.de5 de5 10.Qe2 h6 11.Be3 Qc8 12.Rd1 Bg4 13.h3 Bf3 14.Qf3** += /+- [Bishop pair + better piece coordination] **0-0 15.Bc5 Qe6 16.Nd2 Rad8 17.Bc6 bc6 18.Qe2 Rb8 19.Qa6 Bf6 20.b4 Rfd8 21.a4 g5 22.Kh2 g4 23.Qc4 Qc8 24.Nf1 Ng6 25.Ne3 gh3 26.g3 Bg5 27.Nf5 h5 28.Kh3 Rd7 29.Kg2 Qd8 30.Qe2 h4 31.Rd7 Qd7 32.Qg4 Qd8 33.Rd1 Qf6 34.gh4 Bh4** [D] **35.Be7! 1-0**

174) Pachman,L-Fischer,R [4/59] Santiago [6] E40/03
Nimzo-Indian [E:Rook + minor piece] **1.Nf3 Nf6 2.c4 e6 3.d4 d5
4.e3 Nc6 5.Nc3 Bb4** [The Ragozin System] **6.Bd2 0-0 7.a3 Bc3
8.Bc3 Ne4 9.Qc2 a5** [Restraining b4] **10.b3** [To stop ...a4] **b6
11.Bb2 Ba6 12.Bd3 f5 13.Rc1 Rc8 14.0-0 Rf6?!** [Trying to force a
Kingside attack; 14...Ne7] **15.Rfd1 Rh6 16.Bf1 g5 17.cd5! g4!
18.Ba6 gf3 19.gf3 Qg5 20.Kf1?** [20.Kh1] **Rh2 21.fe4 Rf8 22.e5 f4
23.e4 f3 24.Ke1 Qg1?** [24...Ne7] **25.Kd2 Qf2 26.Kc3 Qg3 27.Qd3
ed5 28.Rg1 Rg2 29.Rg2 Qg2 30.Qf1 de4 31.Qg2 fg2 32.Rg1 Rf2
33.Bc4 Kf8 34.Bd5 Rf3 35.Kc4 b5 36.Kc5 Ne7 37.Rg2 Nd5
38.Kd5 Rb3 39.Ke4 b4 40.ab4** [D] **1-0**

Final position

175) Fischer,R-Letelier,R [4/59] Santiago [7] C97/13 Ruy
Lopez [E:Rook vs. minor piece] **1.e4 e5 2.Nf3 Nc6 3.Bb5 a6 4.Ba4
Nf6 5.0-0 Be7 6.Re1 b5 7.Bb3 d6 8.c3 0-0 9.h3 Na5 10.Bc2 c5
11.d4 Qc7 12.Nbd2 Re8 13.Nf1 Bd7 14.Ne3** [14.b3!] **Bf8 15.Bd2
Rab8 16.b4!** +- [Gaining more space] **Nc6 17.bc5 ed4 18.Nd5! Nd5
19.ed5 dc3 20.Bc3 Re1 21.Qe1 Ne7** [D] **22.cd6 Qd6 23.Be5 Qb6
24.Bb8 Qb8 25.Rd1 Nc8 26.Ne5 Qd6 27.Nd7 Qd7 28.Qa5 Qd6
29.Bb3 Ne7 30.Rc1 Nd5 31.Qd2 Qf4 32.Qf4 Nf4 33.Rc7 Ne6
34.Ra7 b4 35.Ra6 Nc7 36.Ra7 Bd6 37.Rb7 Kf8 38.Rb6 Ne8
39.Ba4! 1-0**

After 21...Ne7

176) Romo,J-Fischer,R [4/59] Santiago [8] E81/04 King's
Indian,Samisch [E:Rook + pawn] **1.d4 Nf6 2.c4 g6 3.Nc3 Bg7 4.e4
d6 5.f3 e5 6.Nge2 0-0 7.Bg5 c6 8.Qd2 Nbd7 9.d5 Nb6** [9...Qb6;
9...cd5 +=] **10.b3 cd5 11.Nd5?!** [11.cd5 +=] **Nbd5 12.cd5 Bd7
13.Nc3 a6 14.Bd3 b5 15.0-0 Qa5 16.Ne2 Qb6 17.Be3 Qb7 18.Qa5
Nh5 19.Rac1 Rac8 20.Qb6? Qb6 21.Bb6 Bh6! 22.Rc8 Rc8** =+/-+
[Control of the c-file; better placed minor pieces] **23.Rd1 f5 24.Kf2
fe4 25.Be4 Nf6 26.Bb1 Bf5 27.Bf5 gf5 28.Ng3** [D] **Rc2 29.Kg1 f4
30.Nf5 Bf8 31.a4 Rb2 32.Bd8 Kf7 33.ab5 ab5 34.g4 fg3 35.Ng3
Rb3 36.Bf6 Kf6 37.Rd2 b4 38.Kg2 Ke7 39.Kf2 Kd7 40.Nf5 Rc3
41.Ra2 Ra3 42.Rb2 b3 43.Ke3 Be7 44.Ne7 Ke7 45.Kd3 Kf6 46.Kc3
Kf5 47.Rg2 b2 48.Kb2 Rf3 49.h4 Ke4 50.Rg7 Kd5 51.Rh7 Rh3
52.h5 Kd4 53.h6 d5 54.Rh8 e4 55.h7 Ke3 56.Rd8 Rh7 57.Rd5 Rc7
58.Rd8 Ke2 59.Re8 e3 60.Rf8 Ke1 61.Re8 e2 62.Rf8 Rc5 63.Rf7
Kd2 64.Rd7 Ke3 65.Re7 Kd3 66.Re8 Rc4 0-1**

After 28.Ng3

177) Fischer,R-Flores,R [4/59] Santiago [9] C92/18 Ruy
Lopez [E:Minor piece] **1.e4 e5 2.Nf3 Nc6 3.Bb5 a6 4.Ba4 Nf6 5.0-0
Be7 6.Re1 b5 7.Bb3 d6 8.c3 0-0 9.h3 Nd7 10.d4 Nb6 11.de5**
[11.Be3; 11.Nbd2] **Ne5 12.Ne5 de5 13.Qh5 Qd6 14.Nd2 Be6
15.Nf3 Bb3 16.ab3 Nd7 17.b4 Qe6 18.Be3 Rfd8 19.Qf5 Qf5 20.ef5
f6 21.Red1 c5 22.bc5 Nc5 23.Bc5 Bc5 24.Kf1 b4 25.Nd2 bc3
26.bc3 a5 27.Ke2 a4 28.Ne4 Rdc8 29.Kd3 a3 30.Kc2 Ra7
31.Rdb1 Be7 32.Rb5 Kf7 33.Rab1 Rcc7 34.Rd1 g6 35.g4 Rcb7
36.Rb7 Rb7 37.Rb1 Ra7 38.Kb3 Rd7 39.Kc2 Ra7 40.Ra1 gf5
41.gf5 Rb7 42.Ra2 Rc7 43.Kb1 Rb7 44.Ka1 Rc7 45.Rd2 Ke8
46.Ka2 Rd7 47.Rd7 Kd7 48.c4 Kc6 49.Kb3 Kb6 50.h4 Kc6 51.h5
Kb6 52.Nc3 Kc5 53.Nd5 Bd8 54.Ne3 Kd4 55.Ka3 Ke4 56.Kb4
Kf3 57.c5 Kf2 58.Ng4 Kg3** [D] **59.Nf6 Bf6 60.c6 Bd8 61.f6 e4
62.f7 Be7 1/2-1/2**

After 58...Kg3

Final position

178) Jauregui,C-Fischer,R [5/59] Santiago [10] E81/09
King's Indian,Samisch **1.d4 Nf6 2.c4 g6 3.Nc3 Bg7 4.e4 d6 5.f3 0-0
6.Be3 Nbd7 7.Nge2 a6** [7...c5; 7...e5] **8.Qd2 c5 9.a3** [9.0-0-0; 9.Rd1
+=] **Rb8 10.b4 cd4 11.Nd4 Ne5 12.Rc1 Bd7 13.Be2 Rc8 14.Nd5
e6 15.Nf6 Qf6 16.0-0 Qe7 17.Rfe1 Rc7 18.f4 Nc6 19.Nf3 Bc8
20.Red1 +-** [White has more space, better piece coordination, and
the point d6 is weak] **Rd7 21.b5! Nd8 22.Qb4 Re8 23.Rd2 f5 24.c5!
d5 25.c6 bc6 26.Bc5 a5 27.Qb3 Qf7 28.Ng5 de4** [28...Qf6 29.e5
++-] **29.Nf7 Rd2 30.Nd6 Nb7 31.Nb7 Bb7 32.Qe3 Red8 33.Bc4
cb5 34.Bb5 e5 35.Bb6 ef4 36.Qf4 e3 37.Bd8 Bd4 38.Be2! Be4
39.Re1 Bd3 40.Qd4 [D] 1-0**

After 32...Qd5

179) Fischer,R-Pilnik,H [5/59] Santiago [12] B88/06 Sicilian
1.e4 c5 2.Nf3 Nc6 3.d4 cd4 4.Nd4 Nf6 5.Nc3 d6 6.Bc4 e6 7.Bb3
[7.Be3!? + Qe2 + 0-0-0 is Velimirovic's Attack] **Be7 8.0-0 0-0
9.Be3 Bd7 10.f4 Nd4 11.Bd4 Bc6 12.Qe2 Qa5** [12...b5! 13.Nb5
Bb5 14.Qb5 Ne4 =] **13.f5 e5 14.Bf2 Bd8 15.Rad1 Bb6 16.g4!**
[16.Rd6 Bf2 17.Rf2 Qc5 18.Rd2 Rad8 gives Black counterplay] **h6
17.h4 Nh7 18.Rd3 Kh8 19.g5! Bd4 20.Kh2 Bb5 21.Nb5 Qb5 22.c3
Bf2 23.Rf2 Qb6 24.Rg2 d5 25.Bd5 Rad8 26.Qh5 g6 27.Qh6 Rd5
28.ed5 e4 29.Rdg3 Qd6 30.h5 Rg8 31.hg6 fg6 32.f6 Qd5 [D]
33.Qh7!** [33...Kh7 34.Rh3#] **1-0**

After 18.Nf1

180) Ader,W-Fischer,R [5/6/59] Santiago [13] B99/01
Sicilian,Najdorf [E:Minor piece + pawn] **1.e4 c5 2.Nf3 d6 3.d4 cd4
4.Nd4 Nf6 5.Nc3 a6 6.Bg5 e6 7.f4 Be7 8.Qf3 Qc7 9.0-0-0 Nbd7 10.f5**
[10.Bd3; 10.g4] **e5 11.Nb3** [11.Nde2] **b5 12.a3 Bb7 13.h4 Rc8 14.Bd3
h5!** [Prevents g4, Bf6, g5] **15.Kb1 Nb6 16.Nd2 Ng4! 17.Be7 Qe7
18.Nf1 [D] Rc3!** [A typical exchange sac followed by central strike]
**19.bc3 d5 20.Qe2 0-0 21.Bb5 ab5 22.Qb5 Nc4 23.Qb4 Qb4 24.cb4
Nf2 25.Ng3 Na3 26.Kb2 Nc4 27.Kb3 Ne3 28.Rd2 Nh1 29.Nh1 de4
30.Ng3 Bd5 31.Ka4 Ra8 32.Kb5 Rb8 33.Kc5 Rc8 34.Kd6 Nc4
35.Kd7 Nd2 36.Kc8 Bc4 0-1**

After 16...e5

181) Walther,E-Fischer,R [5/19/59] Zurich [1] B99/15
Sicilian [E:Bishop + pawn] **1.e4 c5 2.Nf3 d6 3.d4 cd4 4.Nd4 Nf6
5.Nc3 a6 6.Bg5 e6 7.f4 Be7 8.Qf3 Nbd7 9.0-0-0 Qc7 10.Bd3 b5
11.Bf6 Nf6 12.Rhe1 Bb7 13.Kb1** [13.a3] **Rc8 14.g4** [14.a3] **Nd7?**
[14...b4!] **15.g5 Nb6 16.f5 e5 [D] 17.f6! gf6** [17...ed4 18.Nd5!]
18.gf6 Bf8 19.Nd5! Nd5 20.ed5 Kd8 21.Nc6! [Prying open lines]
**Bc6 22.dc6 Qc6 23.Be4 Qb6 24.Qh5 Kc7 25.Bf5 Rd8 26.Qf7 Kb8
27.Qe6 Qc7 28.Re3 Bh6 29.Rc3 Qb7 30.f7 Bg7 31.Rcd3 Bf8 32.Qe5
de5 33.Rd8 Ka7 34.R1d7 h5 35.Rb7 Kb7 36.c3 Kc7 37.Ra8 Kd6
38.Ra6 Ke7 39.Re6 Kf7 40.Re5 e4 41.cb4 Bb4 42.h3 Kf6 43.Rb5
Bd6 44.Be4 Re8 45.Rf5 Kg7 46.Bf3 Re1 47.Kc2 Rf1 48.Rd5 Rf2
49.Rd2 Rd2 50.Kd2 h4 51.Kd3 Kf6 52.Kc4 Ke5 53.Kb5! Kd4
54.a4?** [54.b4! ++-] **Kc7 55.b4 Kb8! 56.a5 Ka7 57.Kc4 Bg3 58.Kb3
Be1 59.Ka4 Bd2 60.Bh5 Be1 61.b5 Bf2! 62.Be2 Be3 63.Kb3 Bd2
64.b6 Kb7 65.Ka4 Kc6 66.Bb5 Kc5 67.Be8 Be1 1/2-1/2**

182) Fischer,R-Bhend,E [5/20/59] Zurich [2] B27/00 Sicilian [E:Rook + pawn] **1.e4 c5 2.Nf3 g6 3.d4 cd4 4.Nd4 Nf6 5.Nc3 Bg7? 6.e5! Ng8 7.Bf4 Nc6 8.Nc6 bc6 9.Bc4 f6 10.e6!** [Disrupting Black's development] **de6** [10...d6 11.Qd2 prevents Nh6 ++-] **11.Qf3 Qb6 12.0-0 Nh6 13.Na4 Qd4 14.Bh6 Bh6 15.Qc6 Kf7 16.Rae1 Rb8 17.Be6 Kg7 18.Bd5 Bg5 19.Re4 Qd2 20.Re7 Kh6 21.Ra7** [21.f4!] **Bf5 22.c4 Rbd8 23.Nc5 Rhe8!** [24.Ne6 Be6 25.Be6 Be3!** [Bhend fights hard - the threat is 26...Qf2!] **[D] 26.Rd7! Bf2 27.Rf2 Qe1 28.Rf1 Qe3 29.Kh1 Re6 30.Rh7! Kh7 31.Qc7 Kh6 32.Qd8 Qe2 33.Qd1 Qb2 34.Qc1 Qc1 35.Rc1 Re2 36.a3 Ra2 37.c5 Ra3 38.c6 Ra8 39.c7 Rc8 40.Kg1 Kg5 1-0**

After 25...Be3!

183) Olafsson,F-Fischer,R [5/59] Zurich [3] E93/00 King's Indian **1.c4 Nf6 2.Nc3 g6 3.d4 Bg7 4.e4 d6 5.Be2 0-0 6.Nf3 e5 7.d5 Nbd7 8.Bg5 h6 9.Bh4 a6 10.Nd2 Qe8 11.g4 Nh7 12.Qc2 Ng5 13.h3 Nc5 14.0-0-0 Bd7 15.f3 Na4 16.Na4 Ba4 17.b3 Bd7 18.Bf2 c5 19.h4 Nh7 20.Be3 b5 21.Nb1 f5 22.gf5 gf5 23.ef5 Bf5 24.Qd2** [D] **e4 25.Rdg1 ef3 26.Bh6** [26.Rg7! +-] **Ra7 27.Bg7 Rg7 28.Rg7 Kg7 29.Bd3 bc4 30.Rg1 Kh8 31.Qc3 Qe5 32.Qe5 de5 33.Bf5 Rf5 34.bc4 Nf6 35.Nd2 f2 36.Rh1 e4 37.Kd1 e3 38.Nf1 Re5 39.Ke2 Nh5 40.Kf3 e2 0-1**

After 24.Qd2

184) Fischer,R-Kupper,J [5/59] Zurich [4] B88/00 **1.e4 c5 2.Nf3 Nc6 3.d4 cd4 4.Nd4 Nf6 5.Nc3 d6 6.Bc4 e6 7.Bb3 Be7 8.0-0 Nd4?!** [8...a6; 8...Bd7] **9.Qd4 0-0 10.Kh1 b6 11.f4 Bb7 12.f5 e5 13.Qd3 h6?** [Weakens the Kingside; 13...Rc8] **14.Rf3! Rc8 15.Rh3 Kh7 16.Be3 Qd7 17.Nd5 Bd5 18.Bd5 Nd5 19.ed5 Bf6?** [19...f6] **[D] 20.Bh6! gh6 21.Qe3 Bg7 22.f6! Rh8 23.Rf1 Qb5 24.Qf3 Rc4 25.Qf5 1-0**

After 19...Bf6?

185) Blau,M-Fischer,R [5/59] Zurich [5] B52/02 Sicilian **1.e4 c5 2.Nf3 d6 3.Bb5 Bd7 4.Bd7 Qd7 5.c4 Nc6 6.0-0 g6 7.d4 cd4 8.Nd4 Bg7 9.Be3 Nf6 10.f3 0-0 11.Nc3 Rac8 12.b3 e6 13.Rc1 Rfd8 14.Qd2 d5 15.cd5** [Better is 15.ed5 ed5 16.c5 +=; Queenside majority + isolani] **ed5 16.Nc6 bc6 17.Rfd1 Qe7 18.ed5 Nd5 19.Nd5 Rd5 20.Qf2 Qd7 21.Rd5 cd5 22.Rc8 Qc8 23.Qd2** [D] **1/2-1/2**

Final position

186) Fischer,R-Larsen,B [5/59] Zurich [6] B11/08 Caro Kann,Two Knights [E:Bishops vs. Knights] **1.e4 c6 2.Nf3 d5 3.Nc3 Bg4 4.h3 Bf3 5.Qf3 Nf6 6.d3 e6 7.a3 Bc5 8.Be2 0-0 9.0-0 Nbd7 10.Qg3 Bd4 11.Bh6 Ne8 12.Bg5 Ndf6 13.Bf3 Qd6 14.Bf4 Qc5 15.Rab1 de4 16.de4 e5 17.Bg5 Bc3 18.bc3 b5** [D] **19.c4 a6 20.Bd2 Qe7 21.Bb4 Nd6 22.Rfd1 Rfd8 23.cb5 cb5 24.Rd3 Qe6 25.Rbd1 Nb7 26.Bc3 Rd3 27.cd3 Re8 28.Kh2 h6 29.d4 Nd6 30.Re1 Nc4 31.de5 Ne5 32.Bd1 Ng6 33.e5 Nd5 34.Bb3 Qc6 35.Bb2 Ndf4 36.Rd1 a5 37.Rd6 Qe4 38.Rd7 Ne6 39.Bd5 += [Bishop pair] Qe2 40.Bc3 b4 41.ab4 ab4 42.Bb4 Qe5 43.Ba5 Qg3 44.Kg3 Re7 45.Rd6 Nef4 46.Bf3 Ne6 47.Bb6 Ne5 48.Bd5 Rd7 49.Rd7 Nd7 50.Be3 Nf6 51.Bc6 g5 52.Kf3 Kg7 53.Ba4 Nd5 54.Bc1 h5 55.Bb2 Kh6 56.Bb3 Ndf4 57.Bc2 Ng6 58.Kg3 Nef4 59.Be4 Nh4 60.Bf6 Nhg6 61.Kf3 Nh4 62.Kg3 Nhg6 63.Kh2 h4 64.Kg1 Nh5 65.Bc3 Ngf4 66.Kf1 Ng7 67.Bf6 Nfh5 68.Be5 f6 69.Bd6 f5 70.Bf3 Nf4 71.Ke1 Kg6 72.Kd2 Nge6 73.Be5 Nc5 74.Ke3 Nce6 75.Bc6 Kf7 76.Kf3 Ke7 77.Bb7 Ng6 78.Bc3 Ngf4 79.Ba6 Nd5 80.Be5 Nf6 81.Bd3 g4 82.Ke2 Nd7 83.Bh2 gh3 84.gh3 Kf6 85.Ke3 Ne5 86.Be2 Ng6 87.Bf1 f4 88.Kf3 Ne5 89.Ke4 Ng5 90.Kf4 Nef3 91.Bg3 hg3 92.fg3 1/2-1/2**

After 18...b5

Final position

187) Duckstein,A-Fischer,R [5/59] Zurich [7] B53/06 Sicilian
1.e4 c5 2.Nf3 d6 3.d4 cd4 4.Qd4 Nc6 5.Bb5 Bd7 6.Bc6 Bc6 7.Nc3
[7.c4] **Nf6 8.Bg5 e6 9.0-0 Be7** [Black has easy play due to his Bishop
pair and White's simplifying 6.Bc6] **10.Rad1 0-0 11.Rfe1 Qa5**
12.Bh4 Rfd8 13.Qd3 Qh5 14.Re3? [14.Bg3] **Rac8 15.Bf6 Bf6**
16.Nd4 g6 17.Nce2 d5 18.Ng3 Qe5 19.c3 [19.Nc6] **de4 20.Qe2**
Qd6 21.Rd2 Bg5 22.Nb3 Qe5 [D] 0-1

After 64...Kc6

188) Fischer,R-Unzicker,W [5/59] Zurich [8] C97/14 Ruy
Lopez [E:Bishop vs. Knight] **1.e4 e5 2.Nf3 Nc6 3.Bb5 a6 4.Ba4**
Nf6 5.0-0 Be7 6.Re1 b5 7.Bb3 d6 8.c3 0-0 9.h3 Na5 10.Bc2 c5
11.d4 Qc7 12.Nbd2 Bd7 13.Nf1 Rfe8 14.Ne3 [14.b3!] **g6 15.de5**
de5 16.Nh2 Rad8 17.Qf3 Be6 18.Nhg4 Ng4 19.hg4 Qc6 [19...Nc4
=] **20.g5!?** [20.Qg3!] **Nc4** [20...Bg5 21.Nd5 Bc1 22.Nf6 Kh8
23.Rac1 Rf8∞] **21.Ng4 Bg4 22.Qg4 f6?** [Weakening; 22...Nb6]
23.gf6 Bf6 24.a4! +=/+-[Opening a second front] **Nb6 25.ab5 ab5**
26.Be3 Ra8 27.Red1 Kh8 28.b3 Bg7 29.Qh4 Bf6 30.Bg5! Bg5
31.Qg5 Ra1 32.Ra1 Nd7 33.Bd1! Nf6 34.Ra7 Qd6 35.Be2! Re7
36.Re7 Qe7 37.Bb5 Kg7 38.Be2 Qc7 39.Qe3 Qa5 40.g3 Qa3
41.Kg2 Qa5 42.Qd3 Qb6 43.Qc4 Qc6 44.Bd3 Qb6 45.b4 cb4
46.cb4 Ng4 47.Qc5 Qc5 48.bc5 Kf7 49.f4 Ke7 50.Kf3 Nf6 51.Bb5
Ke6 52.Bc4 Ke7 53.c6! Ne8 54.fe5 h6 55.Ke3 Nc7 56.Kd4 h5
57.Ke3! g5 58.Be2 h4 59.gh4 gh4 60.Bc4 Ne8 61.Kf4 Kd8 62.Kg4
Kc7 63.Bf7 Ng7 64.Kh4 Kc6 [D] 65.Kg5 1-0

After 49.Nc3

After 70.Ke3

189) Barcza,G-Fischer,R [5/59] Zurich [9] A49/12 King's
Indian [E:Rook + pawn; Queen + pawn] **1.Nf3 Nf6 2.g3 g6 3.b3**
Bg7 4.Bb2 0-0 5.Bg2 d6 6.d4 e5! 7.de5 Nfd7 8.0-0 Nc6 9.c4 de5!
[Maintaining a strong center pawn, with the possibility of expansion
via f5 + e4] **10.Ne1 Nd4 11.Nc3 c6 12.Nd3 f5 13.e3 Ne6 14.Na4**
Qe7 15.Qc1 Re8 16.f3 h5 17.Qe1 Ng5 18.f4 e4! 19.Bg7 Qg7
20.Ndc5 Nc5 21.Nc5 Nf7 22.Rd1 b6 23.Na4 Be6 24.Qc3 Rad8
25.Qc2 g5! 26.Rf2 h4 27.Rd8 Rd8 28.Qb2 Qg6 29.Bf1 gf4 30.ef4
Nh6 31.Rg2 Kf7 32.gh4 Qf6 33.Qf6 Kf6 34.Be2 Bf7 35.Nb2 Rd4
36.h3 Ng8 37.Kf1 Ne7 38.h5 Rd2 39.Bd1 Rd8 40.Ke1 c5!
[Preparing to use d4 as an outpost] **41.Rd2 Rd4 42.a3 Nc6 43.Rg2**
Nd8 44.Kf2 Ne6 45.Ke3 Rd8 46.Rg3 Rh8 47.Na4 Bh5 48.Bh5
Rh5 49.Nc3 [D] Nf4! 50.Ne4 [50.Kf4 Rh4 followed by ...f4] **fe4**
51.Kf4 Rh4 52.Ke3 Kf5 53.b4 a5! 54.bc5 bc5 55.a4 Rh7 56.Kf2
Rb7? [56...Kf4 -++] **57.h4 Kf4 58.Rh3 Kg4 59.Rh1 Kf4 60.Rh3**
Ke5 61.h5 Kd4 62.h6 Rh7 63.Rh1 Kd3 64.Rh5 e3 65.Ke1 Rb7
66.Rd5 Kc4 67.Rh5 Rh7 68.Ke2 Kb4 69.Rh4 c4 70.Ke3 [D] Kb3
71.Kd2 c3 72.Kc1 Rf7 73.Rd4 Rf6 74.Rd8 Rf1 75.Rd1 Rd1
76.Kd1 Kb2 77.h7 c2 78.Ke2 c1=Q 79.h8=Q Kb3 80.Qe8 Qc4
81.Kd2 Qd5 82.Ke2 Kc2 83.Qc8 Kb2 84.Qb8 Kc3 85.Qc8 Kd4
86.Qh8 Kc4 87.Qc8 Kb4 88.Qe8 Qc4 89.Kd2 Qd4 90.Ke2 Qb2
91.Kd3 Qc3 92.Ke2 Qc2 93.Ke3 Ka3 94.Qb5 Qa4 95.Qa4 Ka4
1/2-1/2

190) Fischer,R-Nievergelt,E [6/59] Zurich [10] B88/06
Sicilian 1.e4 c5 2.Nf3 Nc6 3.d4 cd4 4.Nd4 Nf6 5.Nc3 d6 6.Bc4 e6
7.Bb3 Be7 8.0-0 0-0 9.Be3 Bd7 10.f4 [10.Qe2 Nd4 11.Bd4 Bc6
12.Rad1 +=] Nd4 11.Bd4 Bc6 12.Qe2 b5! 13.Nb5 e5? [13...Bb5
14.Qb5 Ne4 15.f5 e5! =] 14.fe5 de5 15.Be3 a6 16.Nc3 Ne4 [D]
17.Rf7! Rf7 18.Bf7 Kh8 19.Qc4 Bg5 20.Ne4 Be3 21.Kh1 Qd7
22.Bh5 Bb5 23.Qb3 Qd4 24.Nd6! Qd6 25.Qe3 Bc6 26.Bf3 e4
27.Be2 Rd8 28.h3 h6 29.Rd1 Qf6 30.Rd8 Qd8 31.Ba6 Qd5 32.a3
h5 33.b4 Qd1 34.Kh2 h4 35.Qf4 Qe1 36.b5 Bd5 37.b6 e3 38.b7
Bb7 39.Qf8 [39.Bb7 e2!] Kh7 40.Bd3 g6 41.Qf7 Kh8 42.Qg6 1-0

After 16...Ne4

191) Gligoric,S-Fischer,R [6/59] Zurich [11] B99/20
Sicilian,Najdorf [E:Queen + minor piece] 1.e4 c5 2.Nf3 d6 3.d4 cd4
4.Nd4 Nf6 5.Nc3 a6 6.Bg5 e6 7.f4 Be7 8.Qf3 Nbd7 9.0-0-0 Qc7
10.g4!? b5 11.Bf6 gf6 [11...Nf6] 12.Bg2 [12.f5!?] Bb7 13.Rhe1
0-0-0! 14.a3 Nb6 = 15.Rd3 Kb8 16.Red1 d5 17.ed5 Nd5 18.Nd5
Bd5 19.Qf1 Bc5 20.Bd5 Rd5 21.Ne2 Rd3 22.Rd3 h5? [22...Qb7!]
23.gh5! Rh5 24.Qg2 Rh8 25.Rc3 Rc8 26.b4 Be3 27.Kb1 Qb6
28.Rc8 [The outside passed h-pawn is decisive] Kc8 29.Qf3 Kd8
30.h4 Ke7 31.h5 f5 32.h6 Bd4 33.Nd4 Qd4 34.Qh1! Qh8 35.h7
Kf8 36.Qa8 Kg7 37.Qh8 Kh8 38.c4 Kh7 39.c5 [D] 1-0

Final position

192) Fischer,R-Keres,P [6/59] Zurich [12] C99/15 Ruy Lopez
[E:Bishop + pawn] 1.e4 e5 2.Nf3 Nc6 3.Bb5 a6 4.Ba4 Nf6 5.0-0
Be7 6.Re1 b5 7.Bb3 0-0 8.c3 d6 9.h3 Na5 10.Bc2 c5 11.d4 Qc7
12.Nbd2 cd4 13.cd4 Bb7 14.Nf1 [14.d5! - to smother the Bb7]
Rac8 15.Bd3 [15.Bb1] Nc6 [15...d5!?∞] 16.Ne3! Rfe8 17.Nf5
[17.d5 +=] Bf8 18.Bg5 Nd7 19.Rc1 Qb8 20.Bb1 Nd4 21.N3d4
Rc1? [21...ed4! =] 22.Bc1 ed4 [D] 23.Nh6! gh6 24.Qg4 Kh8
25.Qd7 Bd5! 26.Qf5 Re5! 27.Qf3 f5! 28.Bf4 Re8 29.Qh5 Be4
30.f3 Bc6 31.Rc1! Bd7 32.Bh6 Re6 33.Bf8 Qf8 34.Qh4! [34.Bf5?
Rh6 -++] Qf6 35.Qf6 Rf6 36.Kf2? [36.Rc7! Rf7 37.Ra7 ++-] Kg7
37.Rc7 Rf7 38.Ke2 f4 39.Ra7 Kf6 40.Ra6 Re7 41.Kf2 Be6!
42.Rd6 Ke5 43.Rc6 Bd5 44.Rh6 Rc7 45.Rh5 Kd6 46.Rh6 Ke5
47.Rh5 Kd6 48.Rf5 Rc1 49.Bd3 Rd1 50.Ke2 Rg1 51.Kf2 Rd1
52.Ke2 Rg1 53.Rg5 Ba2 54.Bb5 Rb1 55.Kd3 h6? [55...Rb2 =]
56.Rh5 Rb2 57.Kd4 Rg2 58.Rh6 Ke7 59.Ke4 Rg5 60.Ba6?
[60.Bf1] Bf7? [60...Bb1 =] 61.Bc8! Rg6 62.Rh7 Kf8 63.Bg4 Rg7
64.Rh6 Rg6 65.Rg6! Bg6 66.Kf4 Kg7 67.Kg5! Bd3 68.f4 Be4
69.h4 Bd3 70.h5 Be4 71.h6 Kh8 72.Bf5 Bd5 73.Bg6 Be6 74.Kf6
Bc4 75.Kg5 Be6 76.Bh5 Kh7 77.Bg4 Bc4 78.f5 Bf7 79.Bh5 Bc4
80.Bg6 Kg8 81.f6 [D] 1-0

After 22...ed4

Final position

193) Donner,JH-Fischer,R [6/59] Zurich [13] E62/19 King's
Indian [E:Rook + minor piece] 1.d4 Nf6 2.c4 g6 3.g3 Bg7 4.Bg2
0-0 5.Nf3 d6 6.0-0 Nc6 7.Nc3 e5 [7...a6!] 8.de5 [Donner tries to
draw; sharpest is 8.d5] Ne5 9.Ne5 de5 10.Bg5! [10.Qd8 =] Qd1
11.Rad1 c6 12.b3 Be6 13.Na4? [13.Rd2] Nd7 14.Rd6? [14.Be7
=+] h6 15.Be3 Rfd8 16.Rc1? [16.Rfd1] Bf8 17.Rdd1 g5 18.Bd2?
Ba3 19.Ra1 f6 20.Bc1 Be7 21.Bb2 Kf7 22.Rd2 Nc5 23.Rd8 Rd8
24.Nc5 Bc5 25.Bc3 Bd4 26.Bd4 Rd4 27.Kf1 Rd2 28.Ke1 Rb2
29.Be4 f5 30.Bb1 [D] a5 31.Kd1 a4 32.ba4 e4 33.Bc2 Bc4 34.Kc1
Ra2 35.Rb1 b5 36.Rb4 Ra1 37.Kb2 Re1 38.a5 Re2 39.Kc1 e3
40.fe3 Re3 41.a6 Re8 42.Bb3 Bb3 43.Rb3 Ra8 44.Ra3 Ke6 0-1

After 30.Bb1

After 26.Nf3

Final position

After 12...Bb7

After 28.Rb1

194) Fischer,R-Keller,D [6/59] Zurich [14] C92/08 Ruy Lopez [E:Rook + minor piece] **1.e4 e5 2.Nf3 Nc6 3.Bb5 a6 4.Ba4 Nf6 5.0-0 Be7 6.Re1 b5 7.Bb3 d6 8.c3 0-0 9.h3 Nd7 10.d4 Nb6 11.de5** [11.Be3; 11.Nbd2] **Ne5 12.Ne5 de5 13.Qh5 Bf6 14.Nd2 Qe7 15.Nf1 Be6 16.Ne3 g6 17.Qf3 Bb3 18.ab3 Bg7 19.b4 c6 = 20.g3?!** [20.Bd2] **Qe6 21.h4 f5! 22.h5 f4 23.Nf1 g5 24.Qh5 Rf6 25.Nh2 Rg6 26.Nf3 [D] fg3 27.fg3 Rg3 28.Kh2 Qg4 29.Qg4 Rg4 30.Rg1 Rg1 31.Kg1 Na4! 32.Kf1 c5 33.b3 Nc3 34.bc5 Ne4 35.c6 Nc5 36.Be3 Nb3 37.Ra2 a5 38.Rg2 Kh8 39.Ng5 Rf8 40.Ke1 Nd4 41.Bd4 ed4 42.Ne6 Re8 43.c7 Be5!** [43...Re6? 44.Re2 Rc6 45.Re8 .++-] **44.Kd2 Rc8 45.Rg5 Bc7 46.Rb5 Bd6 47.Kd3 Ra8 48.Rb6 Bg3 49.Rb7 a4 50.Ng5 a3 51.Rh7 Kg8 52.Rh1 a2 53.Ra1 Be5 54.Ne6 Ra3 55.Ke4 Bf6 56.Kf5 Kf7 57.Ng5 Bg5 0-1**

195) Tal,M-Fischer,R [6/59] Zurich [15] B99/04 Sicilian,Najdorf [E:Minor piece] **1.e4 c5 2.Nf3 d6 3.d4 cd4 4.Nd4 Nf6 5.Nc3 a6 6.Bg5 e6 7.f4 Be7 8.Qf3 Qc7 9.0-0-0 Nbd7 10.Qg3 h6 11.Bh4 Rg8** [11...b5!? 12.Bf6 Nf6 13.Qg7 Rg8 14.Qh6 b4 ∞] **12.Be2** [12.Bf6 Bf6 13.f5 +=/+-] **g5 13.fg5 Ne5!** [13...Nh7 14.g6! Rg6 15.Qh3 +=/+-] **14.g6 Ng6 15.Rhf1 Nh4 16.Qh4 Rg6 17.Bd3 Ng4 18.Qh5 Ne5 19.Nf3 Qc5! 20.Ne5 Qe5 21.Qe5 de5 22.g3 Bd7 23.Be2 Bc6 24.Bh5 Rf6 25.a3 Rd8 26.Rd8 Bd8 27.Rf6 Bf6 28.Kd2 Bg5 29.Kd3 Bc1 30.Nd1 Bb5 31.c4 Ba4 32.Nc3 Bc6 33.Nd1 Kf8 34.h4 Ba4 35.Nc3 [D] 1/2-1/2**

196) Keres,P-Fischer,R [9/7/59] Yugoslavia Candidates Tournament [1] B99/08 Sicilian [E:Queen vs. Rook] **1.e4 c5 2.Nf3 d6 3.d4 cd4 4.Nd4 Nf6 5.Nc3 a6 6.Bg5 e6 7.f4 Be7 8.Qf3 Qc7 9.0-0-0 Nbd7 10.Be2 b5!** [Envisioning a Queen sacrifice for counterplay] **11.Bf6 Nf6 12.e5 Bb7 [D] 13.ef6!?** [To sneak the Rook into play] **Bf3 14.Bf3 Bf6 15.Ba8 d5 16.Bd5 Bd4 17.Rd4 ed5 18.Nd5 Qc5 19.Re1 Kf8 20.c3 h5 21.f5 Rh6 22.f6?** [gf6 23.Nf4 h4 24.Rd8?] [24.Re2] **Kg7 25.Ree8 Qg1 26.Kd2 Qf2 27.Ne2 Rg6 28.g3 f5** [To trade off the doubled pawns] **29.Rg8 Kf6 30.Rg6 fg6 31.gh4 Qh2!** [31...Qh4!] **32.Rd4 Qh1 33.Kc2 Ke5 34.a4 Qf1 35.Nc1 Qf2 36.Kb3?** [36.Kd1] **ba4 37.Ka3 Qc2 38.Nd3 Kf6 39.Nc5 Qc1! 40.Ra4 Qe3 41.Na6? f4 42.Rd4 Kf5! 43.Nb4 Qe7 44.Kb3 Qh4 45.Nd3 g5 46.c4 Qg3 47.c5 f3 48.Kc4 f2 49.Nf2 Qf2 50.c6 Qb2 51.Kc5 Qc3 52.Kd5 g4 53.Rc4 Qe5# 0-1**

197) Fischer,R-Petrosian,T [9/8/59] Yugoslavia Candidates Tournament [2] B11/07 Caro Kann,Two Knights **1.e4 c6 2.Nc3 d5 3.Nf3 Bg4 4.h3 Bf3** [4...Bh5] **5.Qf3 Nf6 6.d3 e6 7.g3** [7.a3 to prevent 7...Bb4 is better] **8.Bd2 d4 9.Nb1 Bd2 10.Nd2 c5 11.Bg2 c-0 12.0-0 Nc6 13.Qe2 g5** [13...Qe7] **14.Nf3 h6 15.h4 Rg8 16.a3 Qe7 17.hg5 hg5 18.Qd2 Nd7 19.c3 0-0-0 20.cd4 ed4!** [To use e5] **21.b4 Kb8 22.Rfc1 Nce5! 23.Ne5 Qe5 24.Rc4 Rc8 25.Rac1?** [25.Rb1!] **g4 26.Qb2 Rgd8 27.a4 Qe7! 28.Rb1 [D] Ne5 29.Rc5 Rc5 30.bc5 Nd3 31.Qd2 Nc5 32.Qf4 Qc7 33.Qg4 Na4 34.e5 Nc5 35.Qf3 d3! 36.Qe3 d2 37.Bf3 Na4 38.Qe4 Nc5 39.Qe2 a6 40.Kg2 Ka7 41.Qe3 Rd3! 42.Qf4 Qd7 43.Qc4 b6 44.Rd1 a5 45.Qf4 Rd4 46.Qh6 b5! 47.Qe3 Kb6 48.Qh6 Ne6 49.Qe3 Ka6 50.Be2 a4 51.Qc3 Kb6 52.Qe3 Nc5 53.Bf3 b4 54.Qh6 Ne6 55.Qh8 Qd8 56.Qh7 Qd7 57.Qh8 b3! 58.Qb8 Ka5 59.Qa8 Kb5 60.Qb8 Kc4 61.Qg8 Kc3 62.Bh5 Nd8 63.Bf3 a3 64.Qf8 Kb2 65.Qh8 Ne6 66.Qa8 a2 67.Qa5 Qa4! 68.Rd2 Ka3! 0-1**

198) Benko,P-Fischer,R [9/10/59] Yugoslavia Candidates Tournament [3] E61/14 King's Indian [E:Rook + Bishop] **1.c4 Nf6 2.Nc3 g6 3.d4 Bg7 4.Bg5 d6 5.e3** [A solid system, overprotecting the d-pawn to limit activity of the Bg7] **c5 6.Nf3 h6 7.Bh4 g5 8.Bg3 Nh5 9.dc5 Ng3** [Winning the Bishop pair at the cost of pawn structure] **10.hg3 dc5 11.Qd8 Kd8 12.0-0-0 Nd7 13.Be2 e6 14.Ne4 Ke7 15.Rd2 b6 16.Nd6 a6 17.Rhd1 Ra7 18.Nh2 Nf6 19.Ng4 Ng4 20.Bg4 f5 21.Bf3 Rc7 22.Nc8 Rhc8 23.g4 f4 24.ef4 gf4 25.Re2 Bd4 26.Rh1 Rh8 27.Bd5 e5 28.Rh5 Kf6 29.f3 Kg7 30.Re1 Rd7 31.Reh1 Rd6 32.Kc2 Rg6 33.Be4 Rd6 34.g5 Be3 35.gh6 Rdh6 36.Rg5 Kf6 37.Rh6 Rh6 38.Rg8 Ke7 39.Rg7 Kd8 40.Bd5 Bd4 41.b3 Rh1 42.Rg6 b5 43.a3 Ra1 44.Ra6 b4 45.a4 Re1 46.Be4 Bc3 47.Bd3 e4! 48.Be4 Re2 49.Kc1 Re1** [D] **1/2-1/2**

Final position

199) Fischer,R-Gligoric,S [9/11/59] Yugoslavia Candidates Tournament [4] B57/02 Sicilian **1.e4 c5 2.Nf3 Nc6 3.d4 cd4 4.Nd4 Nf6 5.Nc3 d6 6.Bc4 Bd7** [Initiating the Fischer-Sozin Attack] **7.Bb3 g6 8.f3** [Transposing into the Yugoslav attack vs. the Dragon] **Na5 9.Bg5 Bg7 10.Qd2 h6 11.Be3 Rc8 12.0-0-0 Nc4 13.Qe2!?** [A very original concept; usually White wants to preserve the dark-squared Bishop] **Ne3 14.Qe3 0-0** [14...Qb6] **15.g4 Qa5 16.h4 e6 17.Nde2! Rc6 18.g5 hg5 19.hg5 Nh5 20.f4 Rfc8 21.Kb1 Qb6 22.Qf3 Rc5 23.Qd3! Bc3 24.Nc3 Nf4 25.Qf3 Nh5** [D] **26.Rh5! gh5 27.Qh5 Be8 28.Qh6 Rc3 29.bc3 Rc3 30.g6! fg6 31.Rh1 Qd4 32.Qh7 1-0**

After 25...Nh5

200) Olafsson,F-Fischer,R [9/14/59] Yugoslavia Candidates Tournament [5] B86/02 Sicilian [E:Rook vs. Bishop] **1.e4 c5 2.Nf3 d6 3.d4 cd4 4.Nd4 Nf6 5.Nc3 a6 6.Bc4 e6 7.a3** [Waste of time; best is 7.Bb3] **Be7 8.0-0 0-0** [8...b5] **9.Ba2 b5 10.f4 Bb7 11.f5 e5 12.Nde2 Nbd7 13.Ng3 Rc8** [Black plays on the c-file + c4 for the outpost; White has the d5 square combined with Kingside pressure] **14.Bg5 Nb6 15.Nh5 Rc3?!** [Simply 15...Nc4 =] **16.bc3 Nh5 17.Be7 Qe7 18.Qh5 Be4 19.Qg4! d5 20.f6 Qc5 21.Kh1 g6 22.Rae1! Re8 23.Qh4 h5 24.Qg5 Nc4 25.Bc4 bc4 26.Re3! Qf8 27.Rb1 Rb8 28.Ree1 Rb1 29.Rb1 Bc2 30.Rb7 Bf5 31.Qe3 Be6 32.Qe5 Qa3 33.h3 Qc1 34.Kh2 g5 35.Ra7 h4 36.Ra6 Kh7** [D] **37.Ra1! Qf4 38.Qf4 gf4 39.Rf1 d4 40.cd4 Kg6 41.Rf4 Bf5 42.Rf3 Kf6 43.Re3 Kg5 44.g3 Bd3 45.d5 Bf5 1-0**

After 36...Kh7

201) Tal,M-Fischer,R [9/15/59] Yugoslavia Candidates Tournament [6] E93/03 King's Indian **1.d4 Nf6 2.c4 g6 3.Nc3 Bg7 4.e4 d6 5.Be2 0-0 6.Nf3 e5 7.d5 Nbd7** [7...a5 is preferred now] **8.Bg5 h6 9.Bh4 a6** [To play ...Qe8, unpinning without the possibility of Nb5] **10.Nd2 Qe8 11.0-0 Nh7 12.b4 Ng5 13.f3 f5 14.Bf2 Qe7 15.Rc1 Nf6 16.c5 Bd7 17.Qc2 Nh5 18.b5! fe4 19.Nde4 Ne4 20.fe4 Nf4 21.c6 Qg5 22.Bf3 bc6 23.dc6 Bg4 24.Bg4 Qg4 25.Be3 ab5 26.Bf4 ef4 27.Nb5 Rf7 28.Qc4 Rc8 29.Rf3! Be5 30.Rcf1 Kg7 31.a4 Ra8 32.Kh1 Qg5?** [32...g5 =] **33.g3 Raf8 34.gf4 Bf4 35.Nd4 Qh4** [D] **36.Rf4 Rf4 37.Ne6 Kh8 38.Qd4 R8f6 39.Nf4 Kh7 40.e5 de5 41.Qd7 1-0** [41...Kg8 42.Qd8 Kh7 43.Qc7]

After 35...Qh4

Final position

After 26.Bg4

After 16...Ng5

After 18...ef4

After 16...e5

202) Fischer,R-Smyslov,V [9/17/59] Yugoslavia Candidates Tournament [7] B11/03 Caro Kann,Two Knights [E:Rook + pawn] **1.e4 c6 2.Nc3 d5 3.Nf3 Bg4 4.h3 Bh5 5.ed5 cd5 6.Bb5 Nc6 7.g4 Bg6 8.Ne5 Rc8 9.h4** [9.d4 e6 10.Qe2 Bb4 11.h4 Ne7 12.h5 Be4 13.f3 0-0 with wild play and about even chances] **f6 10.Ng6 hg6 11.d4 e6 12.Qd3 Kf7 13.h5 gh5 14.gh5 Nge7 15.Be3 Nf5 16.Bc6 Rc6 17.Ne2 Qa5 18.c3 Qa6 19.Qc2 Bd6 20.Bf4 Bf4 21.Nf4 Rh6 22.Qe2 Qe2 23.Ke2 Rh8! 24.Kd3 b5 25.Rhe1 b4 26.cb4 Rc4 27.Ne6 Rh5 28.b3 Rh3 29.Kd2 Rcc3 30.Nf4 Rhf3 31.Re2 g5! 32.Nd5 Rcd3 33.Kc1 Rd4 34.Ne3 Ne3 35.fe3 Rb4 36.Kd2 g4 37.Rc1 Rb7 38.Rg1 Rd7 39.Kc2 f5 40.e4! Kf6 41.ef5 g3! 42.Re8 Rg7 43.Rf8 Ke7 44.Ra8 Kd6 45.Rf8! Rf2 46.Kd3 g2 47.f6 Rg3 48.Kc4! Ke6 49.Re1 Kf5 50.f7 Rg7 51.Rg1 Kf6 52.a4 Rf7 [D] 1/2-1/2**

203) Fischer,R-Keres,P [9/18/59] Yugoslavia Candidates Tournament [8] B11/07 Caro Kann,Two Knights **1.e4 c6 2.Nc3 d5 3.Nf3 Bg4 4.h3 Bf3 5.Qf3 Nf6 6.d3 e6 7.g3** [7.a3 to prevent 7...Bb4] **Bb4 8.Bd2 d4 9.Nb1 Qb6!** [Black pressures White's Queenside to force weaknesses there; perhaps even better is 9...Bd2] **10.b3 a5 11.a3 Be7 12.Bg2 a4 13.b4 Nbd7 14.0-0 c5! 15.Ra2 0-0 16.bc5 Bc5 17.Qe2 e5 18.f4 Rfc8 19.h4 Rc6 20.Bh3 Qc7 21.fe5 Ne5 22.Bf4 Bd6 23.h5 Ra5! 24.h6 Ng6 25.Qf3 Rh5! 26.Bg4 [D] Nf4 27.Bh5 N4h5 28.g4 Bh2 29.Kg2 Ng4 30.Nd2 Ne3 0-1**

204) Petrosian,T-Fischer,R [9/21/59] Yugoslavia Candidates Tournament [9] E51/02 Nimzo-Indian **1.d4 Nf6 2.c4 e6 3.Nc3 Bb4 4.e3 d5** [4...c5 is more popular] **5.a3 Bd6?!** [5...Be7] **6.Nf3 0-0 7.c5!** [Leaving Black severely cramped] **Be7 8.b4 Ne4 9.Bb2 Nd7 10.Bd3 f5 11.Ne2! Bf6 12.0-0 Qe7 13.Ne5 Ne5 14.de5 Bg5 15.Bd4 Bh6 16.f3 Ng5 [D] 17.c6! b6** [17...bc6 18.Bc5] **18.b5 a6 19.a4 ab5? 20.ab5 Ra1 21.Qa1 Nf7 22.Qc3 Qh4 23.Ra1 Ng5 24.Qe1 Qh5 25.Ra7 Qg6 26.Kh1 Qh5 27.f4 Ne4 28.Rc7 g5 29.Bb6 Kh8 30.Be4 fe4 31.Bc5 Rg8 1-0**

205) Fischer,R-Benko,P [9/22/59] Yugoslavia Candidates Tournament [10] B57/04 Sicilian **1.e4 c5 2.Nf3 Nc6 3.d4 cd4 4.Nd4 Nf6 5.Nc3 d6 6.Bc4 Qb6 7.Nde2** [7.Nb3 e6 8.0-0 Be7 9.Bg5 +=] **e6 8.0-0 Be7 9.Bb3 0-0 10.Kh1 Na5 11.Bg5 Qc5! 12.f4 b5 13.Ng3 b4?** [13...Bb7 =] **14.e5 de5 15.Bf6 gf6 16.Nce4 Qd4** [16...Qc7 17.Nh5!] **17.Qh5 Nb3 18.Qh6! ef4 [D] 19.Nh5 f5 20.Rad1! Qe5 21.Nef6 Bf6 22.Nf6 Qf6 23.Qf6 Nc5 24.Qg5 Kh8 25.Qe7! Ba6 26.Qc5 Bf1 27.Rf1 1-0**

206) Gligoric,S-Fischer,R [9/24/59] Yugoslavia Candidates Tournament [11] B99/27 Sicilian [E:Rook vs. minor pieces] **1.e4 c5 2.Nf3 d6 3.d4 cd4 4.Nd4 Nf6 5.Nc3 a6 6.Bg5 e6 7.f4 Be7 8.Qf3 Qc7 9.0-0-0 Nbd7 10.g4 b5 11.Bf6 Nf6** [Also possible is 11...gf6] **12.g5 Nd7 13.a3 Bb7?!** [13...Rb8!] **14.Bh3 0-0-0 15.f5! Bg5 16.Kb1 e5 [D] 17.Ndb5! ab5 18.Nb5 Qc5 19.Nd6 Kb8 20.Nf7? [20.Qb3] Qe7 21.Nh8 Rh8 22.Rhe1 Bf4? [22...Nc5!] 23.Qb3! Nc5 24.Qb5 Qc7 25.b4 Na6 26.Rd7 Qc8 27.Red1 Qc6 28.Qc6 Bc6 29.Rg7 Be4 30.f6 Bh6 31.Re7 Nc7 32.f7 Bc6 33.Bd7! Kb7 34.Rd6 Bd7 35.Rh6 Bb5 36.Rh7 Rf8 37.Rg7 Bc4 38.Re5 Be6 39.h4 Kc6 40.h5 Kd6 41.Re1 Bf7 42.h6 Ne6 43.Rg4 Rh8 1-0**

207) Fischer,R-Olafsson,F [9/25/59] Yugoslavia Candidates Tournament [12] C75/13 Ruy Lopez [E:Rook + Knight] **1.e4 e5 2.Nf3 Nc6 3.Bb5 a6 4.Ba4 d6 5.c3 Bd7 6.d4 Nge7 7.Bb3 h6 8.Nbd2 Ng6 9.Nc4 Be7 10.Ne3 0-0** [10...Bg5!?] **11.0-0 Kh7 12.g3 Bf6 13.Re1 Kh8 14.a3 Qe8 15.h4 Bd8 16.Nf5 Nge7 17.de5 de5 18.Qc2 Be6 19.Be6 fe6 20.Ne7 Be7 21.Qe2 Qg6 22.b4 Rf6 23.Nh2 Raf8 24.h5 Qe8 25.Be3 Bd6 26.a4 Nb8 27.Rec1 Qc6 28.f3 Qe8 29.g4 Nc6 30.b5 Na5 31.Rd1 Nb3 32.Rab1 Nc5 33.a5 Na4! 34.Rdc1 Bc5 35.Bc5 Nc5 36.Qe3 Qe7 37.Rd1 Rf4 38.Rb4 Ra8 39.Rdb1 Kh7 40.Kh1 Qd6 41.R4b2 ab5! 42.Rb5 Nd7 43.Rb7 Ra5 44.R7b2! Qe7! 45.Rg1 Qg5 46.c4 Rc5 47.Qc3 Rf8** [47...Nb6] **48.Rd1 Rf7 49.Rb5 Qf4 50.Kg2 Rc6 51.c5 Ra6 52.c6 Ra2 53.Rb2 Rb2 54.Qb2 Nf6 55.Qb3 Re7 56.Rd8 Qg5 57.Kh3 g6 58.Qb4 Rg7 59.hg6 Kg6 60.Qd2 Qd2 61.Rd2 Ng8 62.Rd7 Nf6 63.Rd3 Ng8 64.Rc3 Ne7 65.Nf1 Rg8 66.Ng3 Kg5 67.Nh5 Rd8 68.Rc5 Ng6 69.Kg3 Rd3** [D] **70.Ng7 Kf6 71.Ne8 Ke7 72.Nc7 Kd6 73.Na6 Ne7 74.c7 Nc8 75.Rc1 Rd2 76.Rh1 Ra2 77.Rd1 Ke7 78.Nb4 1-0**

After 69...Rd3

208) Fischer,R-Tal,M [9/28/59] Yugoslavia Candidates Tournament [13] B86/04 Sicilian **1.e4 c5 2.Nf3 d6 3.d4 cd4 4.Nd4 Nf6 5.Nc3 a6 6.Bc4 e6 7.Bb3 Be7 8.f4 0-0 9.Qf3** [9.f5 +=] **Qc7 10.0-0 b5 11.f5 b4! 12.Na4 e5 13.Ne2 Bb7 14.Ng3 Nbd7 15.Be3 Bc6! 16.Bf2 Qb7 17.Rfe1 d5! 18.ed5 Nd5 19.Ne4 Nf4 20.c4 g6!** [Opening up play] **21.fg6 f5 22.g7 Kg7 23.Qg3 Kh8 24.Nec5 Nc5 25.Bc5 Bc5! 26.Nc5 Qc7 27.Qe3 Rae8! 28.Re2 Ne2 29.Qe2** [D] **Bg2! 30.Na6 Qa7 31.Kg2 Rg8 32.Kh3 Qg7! 33.Bd1 Re6 0-1**

After 29.Qe2

209) Smyslov,V-Fischer,R [9/29/59] Yugoslavia Candidates Tournament [14] B50/04 Sicilian [E:Rook + minor piece] **1.e4 c5 2.Nf3 d6 3.c3 Nf6 4.Qc2** [4.d3] **Nc6 5.d4 cd4 6.cd4 d5! 7.e5 Ne4 8.Nc3 Bf5 9.Qb3** [9.Bd3? Nb4] **Nc3 10.bc3 Qd7 11.Ba3 Rc8!** =+ [Black has better pawns] **12.Nh4 Bg4 13.h3 Bh5 14.g4 Bg6 15.Ng6 hg6 16.Bg2 Na5 17.Qd5 Qd5 18.Bd5 e6! 19.Bf8 Rf8 20.Bg2 Rc3 21.Kd2 Ra3 22.Rhc1 f6 23.Ke2! Kd7 24.ef6 gf6 25.Rc2 Kd6 26.Rd1 f5 27.g5 f4 28.Bf3 Rh8 29.Bg4 Nc6 30.Rb2 b6 31.Kf1!** [D] **Rah3! [Sacrificing the exchange to strive for a win] 32.Bh3 Rh3 33.Ke2 Kd5 34.Rb3 Rb3 35.ab3 Nd4 36.Kd3 e5 37.b4 a5 38.ba5 ba5 39.Rb1 e4 40.Kc3 e3 41.fe3 fe3 42.Rb6 a4 43.Rg6! a3 44.Ra6 Nb3! 45.Ra3 e2 46.Ra1! 1/2-1/2**

After 31.Kf1!

210) Keres,P-Fischer,R [10/3/59] Yugoslavia Candidates Tournament [15] A48/05 King's Indian **1.d4 Nf6 2.Nf3 g6 3.Bf4** [Playable but no real problem for Black] **Bg7 4.Nbd2 c5! 5.c3 cd4 6.cd4 d5 7.Bb8?** [Going after a tainted pawn; 7.e3 =] **Rb8 8.Qa4 Bd7 9.Qa7 Ne4 10.e3 Nd2 11.Nd2 e5! 12.Nb3 0-0 13.Qc5 Rc8 14.Qb4 Re8 15.Be2 ed4 16.Nd4 Qh4 17.Qb7 Bd4 18.Qd7 Bb2 19.Rd1 Bc3 20.Kf1 d4! 21.ed4 Qe4 22.Qg4 Qc2 23.g3 Qa2 24.Bb5??** [24.Bd3 holds] **[D] Qd5 25.Be8 Qh1 26.Ke2 Re8 27.Kd3 Be1 0-1**

After 24.Bb5??

After 47.Kg3

211) Fischer,R-Petrosian,T [10/4/59] Yugoslavia Candidates Tournament [16] B11/07 Caro Kann,Two Knights **1.e4 c6 2.Nc3 d5 3.Nf3 Bg4 4.h3 Bf3 5.Qf3 Nf6 6.d3 e6 7.g3 Bb4 8.Bd2 d4 9.Nb1 Bd2** [Black trades off his dark-squared Bishop followed by placing pawns on dark squares] **10.Nd2 e5 11.Bg2 c5 12.0-0 Nc6 13.Qe2 Qe7 14.f4 0-0-0 15.a3 Ne8 16.b4 cb4 17.Nc4? f6! 18.fe5 fe5 19.ab4 Nc7 20.Na5 Nb5! 21.Nc6 bc6 22.Rf2 g6 23.h4 Kb7 24.h5 Qb4 25.Rf7 Kb6 26.Qf2 a5 27.c4 Nc3? 28.Rf1!** [28.Qf6] **a4 29.Qf6 Qc5 30.Rh7! Rdf8! 31.Qg6 Rf1 32.Bf1 Rh7 33.Qh7 a3 34.h6 a2 35.Qg8 a1=Q 36.h7 Qd6? 37.h8=Q Qa7 38.g4 Kc5 39.Qf8? Qae7 40.Qa8 Kb4 41.Qh2 Kb3! 42.Qa1 Qa3 43.Qa3 Ka3 44.Qh6 Qf7 45.Kg2 Kb3 46.Qd2 Qh7 47.Kg3** [D] **Qe4 48.Qf2 Qh1!** 1/2-1/2

Final position

212) Benko,P-Fischer,R [10/6/59] Yugoslavia Candidates Tournament [17] B90/06 Sicilian [E:Rook + pawn] **1.e4 c5 2.Nf3 d6 3.d4 cd4 4.Nd4 Nf6 5.Nc3 a6 6.Bc4 Nbd7** [6...e6 is normal] **7.a4 g6 8.0-0 Bg7 9.Bg5 0-0 10.Qd2 Nc5 11.f3 Bd7 12.a5 Rc8 13.b3 Ne6 14.Be3 Qc7 15.Nde2 Bc6 16.Ra2 Nd7 17.Nd5 Qd8 18.Nec3** += [More space + better pawns] **Nc7 19.Nb4 Ne5 20.Be2 Qe8 21.Na4 Ba4 22.Ra4 Nc6 23.Nd5 Nd5 24.ed5 Ne5 25.Bd4 Qd8 26.f4 Nd7 27.Bg7 Kg7 28.Bg4 Rc5 29.Bd7 Qd7 30.f5!** [30...gf5 31.Rh4!] **f6 31.fg6 hg6 32.Rh4 g5 33.Re4 Qc7 34.c4 Ra5 35.h4 gh4 36.Rfe1?** [36.Qe2!] **e5 37.de6 Rg5 38.Rh4 Qc5 39.Qf2 Re5 40.Rg4 Kh6 41.Qc5 Re1 42.Kf2 dc5 43.Ke1 Re8 44.Re4 Kg7 45.g4 Rg8 46.Rf4 b6 47.Kd2 Re8 48.Re4 Rh8 49.Rf4 Rh2 50.Kd3 Rh3 51.Kd2 a5 52.g5 fg5 53.e7 Rh8 54.Rf5 g4 55.Rg5 Kf7 56.Rg4 Ke7 57.Rg7 Kd6 58.Rg6 Kc7 59.Kc3 Kb7 60.Rf6 Ka6 61.Rg6 Rh3 62.Kb2 a4 63.ba4 Ka5 64.Rf6** [D] 1/2-1/2

Final position

213) Fischer,R-Gligoric,S [10/7/59] Yugoslavia Candidates Tournament [18] C87/13 Ruy Lopez [E:Rook + minor pieces] **1.e4 e5 2.Nf3 Nc6 3.Bb5 a6 4.Ba4 d6 5.c3 Nf6 6.0-0 Be7 7.d4 Bd7 8.Nbd2 0-0 9.Re1 Re8 10.a3 Bf8 11.b4 d5! 12.Bb3 Bg4 13.h3 Bh5 14.de5 Ne5 15.g4 Nf3 16.Nf3 de4 17.gh5 ef3 18.Re8 Qe8 19.Qf3 Qe1 20.Kg2 Re8 21.h6 c6 22.Bc2 Qe2 23.Qe2 Re2 24.Bd1 Re8 25.Be3 Nd5 26.Bd2 gh6 27.c4 Bg7 28.Rc1 Nc7 29.Be3 Ne6** [White has the Bishop pair, but Black's pieces are more active] **30.c5 Nd4 31.Bg4 f5 32.Bh5 Re4 33.Rd1 Kf8! 34.Rd3 Ke7 35.Bd1 Ne6 36.Kf3 Nd4 37.Kg3 Ne6 38.Kf3 Nd4 39.Kg2 Ne6 40.Kf3** [D] 1/2-1/2

Final position

214) Olafsson,F-Fischer,R [10/10/59] Yugoslavia Candidates Tournament [19] E66/04 King's Indian **1.d4 Nf6 2.c4 g6 3.g3 Bg7 4.Bg2 0-0 5.Nf3 d6 6.0-0 Nc6 7.d5 Na5 8.Nfd2 c5 9.Nc3 e5! 10.a3 b6 11.b4 Nb7 12.Rb1 Ne8 13.Nde4 f5 14.Ng5 e4 15.Qb3 Qf6 16.Nd1** [16.Bd2 e3!] **h6 17.Nh3 g5 18.f3 ef3 19.ef3 Bd7 20.f4 g4 21.Nhf2 Nc7 22.Nd3 Rae8 23.Bb2 Qf7 24.Qc2 Na6 25.Bc3 h5 26.N1b2 h4 27.Rfe1 h3 28.Bf1 Bf6 29.Re8 Re8 30.Re1 Re1 31.Be1 cb4 32.ab4 Bd4 33.Bf2 Bf2 34.Qf2 Qf6 35.Nd1 Qa1 36.Ne3 Qc3 37.Nd1! Qc4 38.Ne5 Qc1 39.Nd7 Qd1 40.Qb2 Qe1** [D] 1/2-1/2

215) Tal,M-Fischer,R [10/11/59] Yugoslavia Candidates Tournament [20] E93/03 King's Indian [E:Rook + minor piece] **1.d4 Nf6 2.c4 g6 3.Nc3 Bg7 4.e4 d6 5.Be2 0-0 6.Nf3 e5 7.d5 Nbd7** [7...a5] **8.Bg5 h6 9.Bh4 a6 10.0-0 Qe8 11.Nd2** [Preventing Nh5 and overprotecting e4] **Nh7 12.b4 Bf6 13.Bf6 Nhf6 14.Nb3 Qe7 15.Qd2 Kh7 16.Qe3 Ng8 17.c5 f5 18.ef5 gf5 19.f4! ef4 20.Qf4 dc5 21.Bd3!** [Working on Black's exposed King, a Tal specialty] **cb4 22.Rae1 Qf6 23.Re6 Qc3 24.Bf5 Rf5 25.Qf5 Kh8 26.Rf3! Qb2 27.Re8 Nf6 28.Qf6 Qf6 29.Rf6 Kg7 30.Rff8 Ne7 31.Na5 h5 32.h4 Rb8 33.Nc4 b5 34.Ne5 [D] 1-0**

Final position

216) Fischer,R-Smyslov,V [10/13/59] Yugoslavia Candidates Tournament [21] B87/14 Sicilian [E:Rook + pawn] **1.e4 c5 2.Nf3 e6 3.d4 cd4 4.Nd4 Nf6 5.Nc3 d6 6.Bc4 Be7** [6...a6 + b5] **7.0-0 a6 8.Bb3 b5 9.f4 0-0 10.f5 b4 11.Nce2 e5 12.Nf3 Bb7 13.Ng3 Ne4 14.Ne4 Be4 15.Qe1 Bf3 16.Rf3 Nc6 17.Qe4?** [17.c3, stopping Nd4 with equality] **Nd4 18.Rh3 Bf6 19.Bd5 Rc8 20.c3 bc3 21.bc3 Nb5 22.Bd2 Rc5 23.Kh1 Qd7 24.Bb3 d5 25.Qf3 Nd6 26.Rf1 Ne4 27.Qh5 h6 [D] 28.Bh6 gh6 29.Bc2 Bg5 30.f6 Rb8 31.Be4 de4 32.Rg3 Qf5 33.Kg1 Qg6 34.Qe2 Rc6 35.h4 Rf6 36.Rf6 Qf6 37.Qh5 Qf4 38.Kh2 Kg7 39.hg5 hg5 40.Qg5 Qg5 41.Rg5 Kf6 42.Rh5 Rb1! 43.Kg3 Rf1! 44.Rh4 Kf5 45.Rh5 Ke6 46.Rh6 f6 47.Rh4 e3 48.Re4 f5 0-1**

After 27...h6

217) Fischer,R-Keres,P [10/18/59] Yugoslavia Candidates Tournament [22] B11/07 Caro Kann,Two Knights [E:Rook + minor piece] **1.e4 c6 2.Nc3 d5 3.Nf3 Bg4 4.h3 Bf3 5.Qf3 Nf6 6.d3 e6 7.g3 Bb4 8.Bd2 d4 9.Nb1 Qb6 10.b3 Nbd7 11.Bg2 a5 12.a3 Bd2 13.Nd2 Qc5! 14.Qd1 h5 15.Nf3 Qc3 16.Ke2 Qc5 17.Qd2 Ne5 18.b4** [18.Ne5 =] **Nf3 19.Bf3 Qe5 20.Qf4 Nd7 21.Qe5 Ne5 22.ba5 Kd7 23.Rhb1 Kc7 24.Rb4 Ra5 25.Bg2 g5! 26.f4 gf4 27.gf4 Ng6 28.Kf3 Rg8 29.Bf1 e5 30.fe5 Ne5 31.Ke2 c5 32.Rb3 b6 33.Rab1 Rg6 34.h4 Ra6 35.Bh3 Rg3 36.Bf1 Rg4 37.Bh3 Rh4 38.Rh1 Ra8 39.Rbb1 Rg8 40.Rbf1 Rg3 41.Bf5 Rg2 42.Kd1 Rhh2 43.Rh2 Rh2 44.Rg1 c4! 45.dc4 Nc4 46.Rg7 Kd6 47.Rf7 Ne3 48.Kc1 Rc2 49.Kb1 Rh2 50.Rd7 Ke5 51.Re7 Kf4 52.Rd7 Nd1 53.Kc1 Nc3 54.Bh7 h4 55.Rf7 Ke3 [D] 0-1**

Final position

218) Petrosian,T-Fischer,R [10/19/59] Yugoslavia Candidates Tournament [23] D58/14 Queen's Gambit Declined **1.d4 d5 2.Nf3 e6 3.c4 Be7 4.Nc3 Nf6 5.Bg5 h6 6.Bh4 0-0 7.e3 b6 8.Bd3 Bb7 9.0-0 Nbd7 10.Rc1 c5 11.Qe2 dc4 12.Bc4 Ne4 13.Bg3! Ng3 14.hg3 Qc7 15.Rfd1 Rad8 16.d5 ed5 17.Nd5 Bd5 18.Rd5 Bf6 19.Rcd1 Ne5 20.b3 Nc4 21.bc4 Qc6 22.e4?** [22.Ne5! +-] **Qe6 23.Qc2 Rd5 24.cd5 Qd6 25.Qa4 Ra8! 26.Re1 Be5 27.Qa6 Qc7 28.Qc4 g5 29.Nh2 Qd7 30.Nf3 Qd6 [D] 1/2-1/2**

Final position

After 34...e5?

219) Fischer,R-Benko,P [10/21/59] Yugoslavia Candidates Tournament [24] B11/07 Caro Kann,Two Knights **1.e4 c6 2.Nc3 d5 3.Nf3 Bg4 4.h3 Bf3 5.Qf3 Nf6 6.d3 e6 7.g3 Bb4 8.Bd2 d4 9.Nb1 Qb6 10.b3 a5 11.a3 Bd2 12.Nd2 Qc5 13.Qd1 h5 14.h4 Nbd7 15.Bg2 Ng4 16.0-0 g5 17.b4 Qe7 18.Nf3 gh4 19.Nh4 Nde5 20.Qd2 Rg8 21.Qf4 f6 22.ba5 Ra5 23.Rfb1 b5 24.Nf3! Ra4 25.Bh3 Nf3 26.Qf3 Kd7 27.Kg2 Qg7 28.Rb4 Rga8 29.Ra4 Ra4 30.Bg4 hg4 31.Qf4 Ra8 32.Rh1 Rg8 33.a4!** [Opening lines to get at Black's exposed King] **ba4 34.Rb1 e5?** [D] **35.Rb7 Kd6 36.Rg7 ef4 37.Rg8 f3 38.Kh1 Kc5 39.Rb8!** 1-0

After 22.Rd6

220) Gligoric,S-Fischer,R [10/22/59] Yugoslavia Candidates Tournament [25] B99/20 Sicilian [E:Rook + pawn] **1.e4 c5 2.Nf3 d6 3.d4 cd4 4.Nd4 Nf6 5.Nc3 a6 6.Bg5 e6 7.f4 Be7 8.Qf3 Qc7 9.0-0-0 Nbd7 10.g4 b5 11.Bf6 gf6!?** [Sharper than the usual 11...Nf6] **12.f5 Ne5 13.Qh3 0-0! 14.Nce2! Kh8 15.Nf4 Rg8 16.Rg1 d5! 17.fe6 de4 18.Nd5 Qc5 19.Ne7 Qe7 20.Nf5 Qe6 21.Qh6 Bd7 22.Rd6** [D] **Ng4 23.Rg4 Qf5 24.Rg8?** [24.Rf4] **Rg8?** [24...Kg8] **25.Rf6 Qd5 26.Rd6! Qf5 27.Rf6 Qg5 28.Qg5 Rg5 29.Rf7 Bg4 30.Kd2 Bf3 31.Ke3 Rg1 32.Bh3 Re1 33.Kf4 Bd1 34.Ke5! e3 35.Bf5 Rg1 36.Rh7 Kg8 37.Rc7 Bg4 38.Bg4 Rg4 39.Rc3 e2 40.Re3 Rg2 41.Kd4 e1=Q! 42.Re1 Rc2 43.Rb1 Kf7! 44.a3 Ke6 45.b3 Rh2 46.Kc5 Kd7 47.Kb6 Ra2 48.Ka6 Ra3 49.Kb7 Kd6 50.Kb6 Kd7 51.b4 Rh3 52.Rc1 Rh8?** [52...Rh5] **53.Kb5?** [53.Rc7!] **Rb8 54.Ka4 Ra8 55.Kb3 Rc8 56.Rc8 Kc8 57.Kc4 Kb8** 1/2-1/2

After 35...g5

221) Fischer,R-Olafsson,F [10/25/59] Yugoslavia Candidates Tournament [26] B10/16 Caro Kann,Two Knights [E:Rook + pawn] **1.e4 c6 2.Nc3 d5 3.Nf3 Nf6 4.e5 Ne4?! 5.Ne2** [Avoiding exchanges while preparing to build a strong central position] **Qb6 6.d4 c5 7.dc5 Qc5 8.Ned4 Nc6 9.Bb5 a6 10.Bc6 bc6 11.0-0 Qb6 12.e6! fe6 13.Bf4! g6 14.Be5 Nf6 15.Ng5 Bh6 16.Nde6 Bg5 17.Ng5 0-0 18.Qd2 Bf5 19.Rae1 Rad8 20.Bc3 Rd7 21.Ne6 Be6 22.Re6 d4 23.Bb4 Nd5 24.Ba3 Rf7 25.g3 Nc7 26.Re5 Nd5 27.Qd3 Nf6 28.Qc4 Ng4 29.Re6 Qb5 30.Qb5 ab5 31.Rc6 Ne5 32.Rc8 Kg7 33.Bb4 Nf3 34.Kg2 e5 35.Rd1 g5** [D] **36.Bf8! Rf8 37.Rf8 Kf8 38.Kf3 Kf7 39.c3 Ke6 40.cd4 ed4 41.Ke4 Rf7 42.f3** 1-0

After 19.Bd6

222) Fischer,R-Tal,M [10/26/59] Yugoslavia Candidates Tournament [27] B87/05 Sicilian [E:Rook + minor piece] **1.e4 c5 2.Nf3 d6 3.d4 cd4 4.Nd4 Nf6 5.Nc3 a6 6.Bc4 e6 7.Bb3 b5 8.f4 b4?!** [A very dangerous pawn grab; correct is 8...Bb7] **9.Na4 Ne4 10.0-0 g6? 11.f5!** [Blasting open lines to get at the Black King] **gf5 12.Nf5! Rg8 13.Bd5! Ra7 14.Be4?** [14.Be3 ++-] **ef5 15.Bf5 Re7! 16.Bc8 Qc8 17.Bf4 Qc6 18.Qf3 Qa4! 19.Bd6** [D] **Qc6 20.Bb8 Qb6 21.Kh1 Qb8 22.Qc6 Rd7 23.Rae1 Be7 24.Rf7 Kf7 25.Qe6 Kf8! 26.Qd7 Qd6 27.Qb7 Rg6 28.c3! a5 29.Qc8 Kg7 30.Qc4 Bd8 31.cb4 ab4 32.g3** [32.Qe4 holds] **Qc6 33.Re4 Qc4 34.Rc4 Rb6 35.Kg2 Kf6 36.Kf3 Ke5 37.Ke3 Bg5 38.Ke2 Kd5 39.Kd3 Bf6 40.Rc2? Be5 41.Re2 Rf6 42.Rc2 Rf3 43.Ke2 Rf7 44.Kd3 Bd4! 45.a3 b3 46.Rc8 Bb2 47.Rd8 Kc6 48.Rb8 Rf3 49.Kc4 Rc3 50.Kb4 Kc7 51.Rb5 Ba1 52.a4 b2!** 0-1

223) Smyslov,V-Fischer,R [10/29/59] Yugoslavia Candidates Tournament [28] B99/22 Sicilian [E:Rook + minor piece] **1.e4 c5 2.Nf3 d6 3.d4 cd4 4.Nd4 Nf6 5.Nc3 a6 6.Bg5 e6 7.f4 Be7 8.Qf3 Qc7 9.0-0-0 Nbd7 10.g4 b5 11.Bf6 Nf6 12.g5 Nd7 13.Bh3?** [13.a3 to stop ...b4] **b4!** [Kicking the Knight weakens e4 and d5, allowing Black to strike in the center] **14.Nce2 Bb7 15.Kb1?!** [15.Ng3 - reinforcing e4 was necessary] **Nc5 16.Ng3 d5!** [D] **17.f5** [After 17.e5 g6, White is strategically lost, hence the text] **de4 18.Qg4 ef5 19.Ndf5 g6 20.Ne7 Qe7 21.Qf4 0-0 22.Rd6 Rad8 23.Rf6 Rd5 24.Bg4 Nd7 25.Rf1 e3** [25...Nf6?? 26.gf6 followed by 27.Qh6 ++-] **26.b3 Rd2 27.Bd7 Rd7 28.Re1 Re8 29.h4 Qc5 30.Qc4 Qc4 31.bc4 Rd4 32.c5 Rh4 33.c6 Bc8 34.Rd6 Rc4 35.Kb2 Kg7 36.Kb3 Rg4 37.Ne2 Re6! 38.Red1 Rg2 39.Nf4 Rd6 40.Rd6 Rd2 41.Rd3 Rf2 42.Rd4 e2 43.Nd3 Bf5 44.c7 Rf3 45.c8=Q Bc8 46.Re4 Bf5 47.Re2 Bd3 48.cd3 Rd3 49.Kb4 Rd5 50.Rg2 h6 51.gh6 Kh6 52.a4 g5 53.Rc2 Rd6 54.Kc5 Re6 0-1**

After 16...d5!

224) Fischer,R-Bisguier,A [12/18/59] US Championship [1] C42/11 Petroff [E:King + pawn] **1.e4 e5 2.Nf3 Nf6 3.Ne5 d6 4.Nf3 Ne4 5.Qe2** [5.Bd3] **Qe7 6.d3 Nf6 7.Bg5 Qe2 8.Be2 Be7 9.Nc3 Bd7 10.0-0-0 Nc6 11.d4 h6 12.Bh4 0-0-0 13.Bc4 Rdf8 14.Rde1 Bd8 15.d5 Nb8 16.Nd4 Re8 17.Ndb5 Bb5 18.Bb5 Re1 19.Re1 Nd5!** [A tactical struggle ensues with Fischer keeping an edge] **20.Nd5** [20.Bd8 Nc3] **Bh4 21.g3! Bg5 22.f4 c6! 23.fg5 hg5** [D] **24.Re7 cd5 25.Rf7 Rh2 26.Rg7 Nc6 27.Rg5 Ne5 28.Rg7 Rg2 29.Bd3 Nc4 30.Bc4 dc4 31.a4 d5 32.c3 Rg1 33.Kd2 Rg2 34.Kc1 Rg1 35.Kc2 Ra1 36.Rg5 Ra4 37.Rd5 Kc7 38.g4 Kc6 39.Rd2 Ra5 40.Kd1 Rd5 41.Ke2 Rd2 42.Kd2 Kd5 43.Ke3 Ke5 44.Kf3 a5 45.Ke3 a4 46.g5 Kf5 47.Kd4 Kg5 48.Kc4 Kf4 49.Kb4 Ke3 50.Ka4 Kd2 51.Kb3 Kd3 52.c4 Kd2 53.Ka4 Kc2 54.Ka3 Kd3 55.Kb3 b6 56.Kb4 Kc2 57.Ka3 Kd3 58.Kb3 Kd2 59.Ka4 Kc2 60.b4 1-0**

After 23...hg5

225) Byrne,R-Fischer,R [12/19/59] US Championship [2] D41/29 Queen pawn, Semi-Tarrasch Defence **1.d4 Nf6 2.c4 e6 3.Nc3 d5 4.cd5 Nd5** [The Semi-Tarrasch; 4...ed5] **5.Nf3 c5 6.e3 Nc6 7.Bc4 Nc3 8.bc3 Be7 9.0-0 0-0 10.Qe2 b6 11.Rd1 Qc7 12.e4 Bb7 13.Be3 Rac8 14.Bd3 cd4 15.cd4 Ba3?** [15...Nb4] **16.e5!** [Initiating a strong Kingside attack] **Nb4 17.Ng5** [Not 17.Bh7 Kh7 18.Ng5 Kg8 19.Qh5 Qc2 -++] **h6 18.Bh7 Kh8 19.Qh5 Nd5 20.Bd3 Qe7 21.Nh7! Ne3 22.fe3 Rfd8 23.Rf1 Rd7 24.h4! Rc3 25.Ng5?!** [25.Nf6! ++-] **Rd3! 26.Rf7 Rd2! 27.e4! Qf7 28.Nf7 Rf7! 29.Qf7 Be4 30.Re1** [30.Qe6 Bb2 31.Re1 Bg2 =] **Rg2 31.Kf1 Bd5! 32.Re2 Rg4?** [Simply 32...Re2 33.Ke2 Ba2 gives a problem-like positional draw] **33.Rc2 Kh7 34.h5 Rg5 35.Ke2** [35.Qa7 ++-] **Rg2 36.Kd3 Rg3 37.Ke2 Rg2 38.Ke3 Rg3 39.Kf2 Rg5 40.Ke2 Rg2** [D] **1/2-1/2**

Final position

Final position

After 34.Kb2

After 30...Ng6

After 18.Bg2

After 17.0-0

226) Fischer,R-Weinstein,R [12/20/59] US Championship [3] B11/07 Caro Kann,Two Knights [E:Rook + pawn] **1.e4 c6 2.Nc3 d5 3.Nf3 Bg4 4.h3 Bf3 5.Qf3 Nf6 6.d3 e6 7.g3** [7.a3] **Be7** [7...Bb4] **8.Bg2 de4 9.de4** [9.Ne4!?] **e5 10.0-0 Nbd7 11.Nd1** [Heading for f5] **0-0 12.Ne3 g6 13.Rd1 Qc7 14.Ng4 h5 15.Nf6 Nf6 16.Bg5 Nh7 17.Bh6 Rfd8** [It's dead even. The pawn structure permits no real play for either side and the Bishop pair is soon traded off] **18.Bf1 Bg5 19.Bg5 Ng5 20.Qe3 Qe7 21.h4 Ne6 22.Bc4 b5 23.Be6 Qe6 24.Qc5** [24.Rd8 Rd8 25.Qa7 Qc4] **Qc4 25.Qc4 bc4 26.b3 Rd4! 27.Rd4 ed4 28.Kf1** [28.bc4 Rb8 =] **Re8 29.f3 Re5 30.Rd1 c5 31.c3 dc3 32.Rc1 f5 33.ef5 Rf5 34.Rc3 cb3 35.Rb3 c4 36.Ra3 Rc5 37.Ke2 c3 38.Kd1 c2 39.Kc1 a5 40.Rb3 Kg7 41.Rb7 Kf6 42.Rb6 Kg7 43.g4 [D] 1/2-1/2**

227) Denker,A-Fischer,R [12/22/59] US Championship [4] D38/21 Queen's Gambit Declined **1.d4 Nf6 2.c4 e6 3.Nf3 d5 4.Nc3 Bb4 5.Bg5 h6 6.Bf6 Qf6 7.cd5 ed5 8.Rc1 0-0 9.a3 Bc3 10.Rc3 c6 11.e3** [The opening has transposed into a typical position from the QGD exchange variation; 11...a5 prevents b4 - the famous Minority Attack] **a5 12.Bd3?!** [12.Be2] **Bg4 13.h3 Bh5 14.g4?!** [Overambitious] **Bg6 15.Ne5 Bd3 16.Qd3 Qe7 17.Qf5** [To prevent ...Nd7] **Rd8!** [To play ...Nd7] **18.Rg1 Nd7 19.Nd7 Rd7 20.g5 Rd6 21.h4 h5! 22.Ke2 g6 23.Qf3 Re6 24.Kd2 Re4 25.Qh3 Qc7 26.Rgc1 Rae8 27.f3 R4e6 28.Re1 b6! 29.Kc2 c5 30.dc5 d4! 31.cb6 Qb6 32.Rd3 Rb8 33.b3 Rc6 34.Kb2 [D] Rc3 35.Rc3 dc3 36.Kc3 Qb3 37.Kd2 Qa2 38.Kd3 Rd8 39.Ke4 Qc4 40.Ke5 Rd5 0-1**

228) Fischer,R-Ault,R [12/23/59] US Championship [5] B07/29 Pirc **1.e4 d6 2.d4 Nf6 3.Nc3 g6 4.Bg5 Bg7 5.Qd2 Nbd7** [5...h6!? 6.Bh4 g5 7.Bg3 Nh5 ∞] **6.0-0-0 e5?!** [6...h6] **7.de5 de5 8.Nf3 h6 9.Bh4 g5 10.Bg3 Qe7 11.h4 g4 12.Nh2 c6 13.f3!** [Forcing open lines] **h5 14.Kb1 Bh6 15.Qf2 Nc5 16.Be2 b5 17.Bd3 Rb8 18.Ne2 Na4 19.Nc1 0-0 20.fg4 hg4? 21.h5! Nh5 22.Nf1 Qg5 23.Bh4 Qg6 24.Ne3 Nf4 25.Nf5 Bg5 26.Qg3 Bf5 27.ef5 Qg7 28.Bg5 Qg5 29.Rh4 Qg7 30.Rg4 Ng6 [D] 31.f6! Qh8 32.Rg6 1-0**

229) Sherwin,J-Fischer,R [12/26/59] US Championship [6] B99/27 Sicilian [E:Rook + pawn] **1.e4 c5 2.Nf3 d6 3.d4 cd4 4.Nd4 Nf6 5.Nc3 a6 6.Bg5 e6 7.f4 Be7 8.Qf3 Qc7 9.0-0-0 Nbd7 10.g4 b5 11.Bf6 Nf6 12.g5 Nd7 13.a3** [13.f5 is sharper] **Bb7** [13...Rb8] **14.h4** [14.Bh3] **d5!** [This central counterthrust equalizes easily] **15.ed5 Nb6 16.f5 Nd5 17.fe6 0-0-0 18.Bg2 [D] Nc3 19.Qb7 Qb7 20.Bb7 Kb7 21.bc3 Ba3 22.Kb1 fe6 23.Ne6 Rc8 24.Rh3 g6 25.c4! = Rhe8 26.Ra3 Re6 27.cb5 ab5 28.Rd7 Kb6 29.Rh7 Re2 30.Ra2 Rh2 31.Rha7 Rh4 32.R7a6 Kc5 33.Rg6 Rg4 34.Rg7 Kc4 1/2-1/2**

230) Fischer,R-Seidman,H [12/27/59] US Championship [7] B01/16 Center Counter **1.e4 d5 2.ed5 Qd5 3.Nc3 Qa5 4.d4 Nf6 5.Nf3 Nc6? 6.d5!** [Gaining time and space] **Nb4 7.Bb5 c6 8.dc6 bc6 9.Ba4 Ba6 10.a3! Rd8 11.Bd2 Rd6 12.ab4 Qf5 13.Bb3 Ne4 14.Ra6 Rd2 15.Qa1 Nc3 16.bc3 Rd6 17.0-0 [D] 1-0**

231) Fischer,R-Bernstein,S [12/28/59] US Championship [8]
C89/03 Ruy Lopez [E:Rook + minor piece] **1.e4 e5 2.Nf3 Nc6 3.Bb5
a6 4.Ba4 Nf6 5.0-0 Be7 6.Re1 b5 7.Bb3 0-0 8.c3 d5 9.ed5 e4?!
10.dc6** [10.Ng5 ∞] **ef3 11.Qf3** [11.d4! is best +=/+-] **Bg4 12.Qg3
Bd6 13.Qh4 Re8 14.f3 Bf5 15.d4 Bh2! 16.Kh2 Ng4 17.Kg3 Qh4
18.Kh4 Re1 19.fg4 Rc1 20.gf5 Rd8! 21.a4 b4 22.d5 Rb8** [22...bc3]
**23.d6! cd6 24.Bc4 Rc8 25.Ba6 Rc6 26.Bb5 Rb6 27.c4! d5 28.a5
g5 29.Kg5 h6 30.Kg4 Rb8 31.a6 dc4 32.a7 Ra8 33.Bc6 h5 34.Kg5
Rb1 35.Rb1 Ra7 36.Rc1 Ra2 37.Rc4 Rb2 38.f6 [D] 1-0**

Final position

232) Mednis,E-Fischer,R [12/29/59] US Championship [9]
B99/20 Sicilian **1.e4 c5 2.Nf3 d6 3.d4 cd4 4.Nd4 Nf6 5.Nc3 a6
6.Bg5 e6 7.f4 Be7 8.Qf3 Qc7 9.0-0-0 Nbd7 10.g4 b5 11.Bf6 gf6**
[11...Nf6 is usual but the text is playable] **12.a3 Bb7 13.f5 e5
14.Nde2 Nb6 15.Nd5 Bd5 16.ed5 Rc8 17.Nc3 Nc4 18.Bc4 bc4?!**
[18...Qc4] **19.Kb1 Rb8 20.Ka2 h5 21.gh5 Bf8 22.Rhg1 Ke7
23.Qe2 Bh6 24.Rg4 Rhc8 25.Qf2 Rb7 26.Rb1 Rcb8 27.Ne4! Rb6
28.Nf6! Qb7** [28...Kf6 29.Qh4] **29.Ng8 Kf8 30.c3?** [This loses, but
30.b4!! would have won: 30...cb3 31.cb3 Rb3 32.Rb4!] **[D] Bc1!**
[Now it is Black who wins] **31.Rg2 Rb2 32.Rb2 Bb2 33.Qc2 Qb5
34.f6 Qa5 35.Qb2 Rb2 36.Kb2 Qd5 37.Rg7 Qd2 38.Kb1 Qd1
39.Kb2 Qb3 40.Kc1 Qc3 0-1**

After 30.c3?

233) Fischer,R-Benko,P [12/30/59] US Championship [10]
B63/07 Sicilian [E:Rook + pawn] **1.e4 c5 2.Nf3 d6 3.d4 cd4 4.Nd4
Nf6 5.Nc3 Nc6 6.Bg5 e6 7.Qd2 Be7 8.0-0-0 0-0 9.Nb3 Qb6 10.f3
Rd8 11.Be3 Qc7 12.Qf2!** [Preventing 12...a6] **Nd7 13.Nb5 Qb8
14.g4 a6 15.N5d4 Nde5 16.g5 d5 17.ed5 ed5 18.h4 Nc4 19.Nc6
bc6 20.Bc5!** [Trading off Bishops accentuates dark-square
weaknesses] **Bc5 21.Qc5 Qf4 22.Kb1 Ne3 23.Re1 d4 24.Bd3 Be6
25.Be4 Nf5 26.Bf5 Bf5 27.Qe5 Qe5 28.Re5 g6 29.Rd1 d3 30.cd3
Bd3 31.Kc1 Bc4 32.Rd8 Rd8 33.Nc5 +-** [Good Knight vs. limited
Bishop and Black's a- and c-pawns are weak] **Bd5 34.f4 Kf8 35.b3
a5 36.Re3 f6 37.Ne6!** [Forcing a winning Rook + pawn ending]
**Be6 38.Re6 fg5 39.fg5 Rd4 [D] 40.Rc6 Rh4 41.Ra6 Rh1 42.Kb2
Rh2 43.Ka3 Rh3 44.Ra5 h6 45.Ra8 Kf7 46.gh6 Rh6 47.Kb4 g5
48.Ra7 Kf6 49.a4 g4 50.Rd7 g3 51.Rd6 Kf7 52.Rd7 Kf6 53.Rd1
g2 54.Rg1 Rg6 55.a5 Ke7 56.a6 Rb6 57.Ka5 Rb3 58.Rg2 Ra3
59.Kb6 Rb3 60.Kc5 Ra3 61.a7 Ke6 62.Rg7 Ra1 63.Kc6 Ra2
64.Kb7 Rb2 65.Kc8 Ra2 66.Kb8 Rb2 67.Rb7 Rh2 68.a8=Q Rh8
69.Ka7 1-0**

After 39...Rd4

234) Reshevsky,S-Fischer,R [1/1/60] US Championship [11]
D41/31 Queen's Gambit Declined [E:Rook + pawn] **1.d4 Nf6 2.c4
e6 3.Nc3 d5 4.cd5 Nd5** [The Semi-Tarrasch; 4...ed5 followed by c5
is the Tarrasch proper] **5.Nf3 c5 6.e3 Nc6 7.Bc4 cd4 8.ed4 Be7 9.0-0
0-0 10.Re1 a6 11.Bd3 Bd7 12.a3 Nc3 13.bc3 Rc8 14.Qc2 g6
15.Bh6 Re8 16.Re4 Bf8 17.Bg5 Qc7 18.h4 [D] e5!** [Countering the
Kingside attack with central counteraction] **19.de5 Bf5 20.Re2 Bg4
21.Rae1 Bf3 22.gf3 Re5!** [22...Ne5 23.Be4!] **23.a4 Be7 24.f4 Re2
25.Qe2 Bg5 26.fg5 Qa5 27.Bc4 Ne5! 28.Qe5 Qe5 29.Bf7 Kf7
30.Re5 Rc3 31.Re4 Rc6 32.Rb4 b6 33.Kg2 Ke6 34.Re4 Kd7
35.Kg3 b5 36.ab5 ab5 37.f4 Rb6 38.Rb4 Kd6 39.Kg4 Kc5 40.Rb1
1/2-1/2**

After 18.h4

1960

After 40.Qa3

235) Wexler,B-Fischer,R [3/29/60] Mar del Plata [1] E93/04 King's Indian **1.d4 Nf6 2.c4 g6 3.Nc3 Bg7 4.e4 d6 5.Nf3 0-0 6.Be2 e5 7.d5 Nbd7** [7...a5] **8.Bg5 h6 9.Bh4 g5 10.Bg3 Nh5** [10...a5!? and Nc5] **11.0-0** [11.h4!? +=] **Nf4 12.Ne1** [12.Nd2 ∞] **Ne2 13.Qe2 f5 14.ef5 Nf6 15.Nd3 Bf5 16.f3 Qe8 17.Nf2 Qg6 18.Nfe4?!** [18.Nce4 =] **g4! 19.Rfe1 gf3 20.gf3 Ne4 21.Ne4 Qh5 22.Rac1 b6 23.Rc3 a5 24.b3 Rf7 25.a3 Raf8 26.Rf1 Bg4! 27.fg4** [27.Nd2 Bh3] **Rf1 28.Kg2 Qg6 29.Bf2 Ra1 30.Re3 Rf4 31.h3 h5 32.g5 Ra3 33.Bg3 Re4 34.Re4 Rb3 35.h4 a4 36.Bf2 a3 37.c5 Rb2 38.Qf3 a2 39.Ra4 e4 40.Qa3 [D] Qf7 0-1**

After 28...Qh4

236) Spassky,B-Fischer,R [3/30/60] Mar del Plata [2] C39/20 King's Gambit **1.e4 e5 2.f4 ef4 3.Nf3 g5 4.h4 g4 5.Ne5 Nf6 6.d4** [6.Ng4 Ne4 7.d3 Ng3 =+] **d6 7.Nd3 Ne4 8.Bf4 Bg7 9.Nc3** [Better was 9.c3 and 10.Nd2 =] **Nc3 10.bc3 c5 11.Be2 cd4 12.0-0 Nc6 13.Bg4 0-0 14.Bc8 Rc8 15.Qg4 f5 16.Qg3 dc3 17.Rae1 Kh8?** [17...Qd7! - +] **18.Kh1? Rg8 19.Bd6 Bf8! 20.Be5 Ne5 21.Qe5 Rg7! 22.Rf5 Qh4 23.Kg1 Qg4** [23...Qg3! -+] **24.Rf2 Be7 25.Re4 Qg5 26.Qd4! Rf8?** [26...Bf8! =] **27.Re5 Rd8 28.Qe4 Qh4 [D] 29.Rf4 1-0**

After 22...Rb8??

237) Fischer,R-Gadia,O [3/31/60] Mar del Plata [3] B87/07 Sicilian **1.e4 c5 2.Nf3 d6 3.d4 cd4 4.Nd4 Nf6 5.Nc3 a6 6.Bc4 e6 7.Bb3 b5 8.0-0 Bb7 9.f4 Nc6?** [9...Nbd7] **10.Nc6 Bc6 11.f5 e5 12.Qd3 Be7 13.Bg5!** [Removing the Nf6 to dominate d5] **Qb6 14.Kh1 0-0 15.Bf6 Bf6 16.Bd5!** [Leaving Black the bad Bishop vs. the good Knight] **Rac8 17.Bc6 Rc6 18.Rad1 Rfc8 19.Nd5 Qd8 20.c3 Be7 21.Ra1!** [With the idea of opening the a-file] **f6 22.a4! Rb8?? [D] 23.Ne7 1-0** [23...Qe7 Qd5 ++-]

After 28.Qa4

238) Saadi,,J-Fischer,R [4/2/60] Mar del Plata [4] A39/04 King's Indian **1.c4 Nf6 2.Nc3 g6 3.d4 Bg7 4.g3 0-0 5.Bg2 c5 6.Nf3** [6.d5] **cd4 7.Nd4 Nc6 8.0-0 Ng4** [8...d6!? 9.Nc6 bc6 10.Bc6 Rb8 ∞] **9.e3?! d6! 10.Nc6 bc6 11.Bc6 Rb8** [Similar to a Benko Gambit!] **12.Bf3 Ne5 13.Be2 Ba6 14.b3 Nc4 15.Qc2 Qa5 16.Nd5 Qd5 17.bc4 Qb7 18.Ba3 Ba1 19.Ra1 Rfc8 20.e4 Rc7 21.Bd3 Qc6 22.Rc1 Rbc8 23.Qb3 Qd7 24.Bb2 Qe6 25.Qc3 f6 26.Qa5 Bc4 27.Bd4 Rc6 28.Qa4 [D] Bb5 29.Qb5 Rc1 30.Kg2 Rd1 31.Be3 Rd3 32.Qd3 Qa2 33.Qb5 Qe6 34.Qb7 a5 0-1**

After 31...ef4

239) Fischer,R-Eliskases,E [4/3/60] Mar del Plata [5] C98/07 Ruy Lopez [E: Rook + minor piece] **1.e4 e5 2.Nf3 Nc6 3.Bb5 a6 4.Ba4 Nf6 5.0-0 Be7 6.Re1 b5 7.Bb3 0-0 8.c3 d6 9.h3 Na5 10.Bc2 c5 11.d4 Qc7 12.Nbd2 Nc6 13.dc5** [Rauzer's attack - often used by Fischer] **dc5 14.Nf1 Rd8** [14...Be6] **15.Qe2 Nh5 16.a4 Rb8 17.ab5 ab5 18.g3! g6** [18...Bh3 19.Ng5! +-] **19.h4 Be6 20.Ne3 c4 21.Ng5 Bg5 22.hg5 Na5 23.Ng4 Bg4 24.Qg4 += / +- Nb3 25.Bb3 cb3 26.Be3 Ra8 27.Ra8 Ra8 28.Rd1 Qc6 29.Rd5 f5 30.Qd1 f4 31.gf4 ef4 [D] 32.Qb3 Qc4 33.Qc4 bc4 34.Bd4 f3 35.Be3 h6 36.gh6 Nf6 37.Rd6 Kf7 38.Rf6 Kf6 39.Bd4 Kg5 40.h7 Kf4 41.Kh2 g5 42.h8=Q Rh8 43.Bh8 g4 44.e5 1-0**

240) Foguelman,A-Fischer,R [4/4/60] Mar del Plata [6] B54/04 Sicilian [E:Rook vs. minor pieces] **1.e4 c5 2.Nf3 d6 3.d4 cd4 4.Nd4 Nf6 5.f3 Nc6** [5...e5 6.Bb5 Nbd7] **6.c4 e6 7.Nc3 Be7 8.Nc2** [The Maroczy bind - White avoids simplifying exchanges] **0-0 9.Ne3 d5!** [Sacrificing a pawn for strong counterplay] **10.cd5 ed5 11.ed5 Ne5 12.Qb3** [12.Qd4] **Bc5 13.Bd2 Re8 14.Be2 Ng6 15.Nc2 Nh4! 16.0-0-0 Ng2 17.Ne4 Ne4 18.fe4 Nh4 19.Qc4 Bb6 20.Bc3 Ng6 21.Bf3 Bh3 22.Rhe1 Rc8 23.Qe2 Ba5! 24.Ba5 Qa5 25.Kb1 Ne5 26.Rc1** [D] **Rc2! 27.Qc2 Nf3 28.Re3 Bg4 29.h3 Bh5 30.Qc7! Nd2?** [30...Qc7 31.Rc7 Bg6] **31.Ka1 Qc7 32.Rc7 f6 33.d6 Rd8 34.e5 fe5 35.Re5 Bg6 36.d7 Kf7 37.Rb7 Nc4 38.Rc5 Nb6 39.Ra7 Nd7 40.b4 Ke6 41.Ra6 Ke7 42.Rd5 Rf8 43.Rd1 Rf4! 44.a3 Bf5 45.Ra7 Bh3 46.b5 Bg4 47.Rd2 Rf1 48.Kb2 Bf5 49.a4 h5 50.Ka3 h4 51.Rb2 h3 52.b6 Ra1 53.Kb4 Rb1 54.Rb1 Bb1 55.b7 Kd6 56.Ra8 Kc7 57.Rh8 Bf5 58.Kc3 g5 59.Kd4 g4 60.Ke3 g3 61.Kf3 g2 62.Kf2 Kb7 63.Rh5 Bg4 64.Rg5 Nf6 65.Kg1 Bc8 66.Rg7 Kb8 67.a5 Nh5 68.Rg8 Kc7 69.Kh2 Nf4 70.a6 Ba6 71.Rg7 Kb6 0-1**

After 26.Rc1

241) Fischer,R-Olafsson,F [4/5/60] Mar del Plata [7] B52/06 Sicilian **1.e4 c5 2.Nf3 d6 3.Bb5 Bd7 4.Bd7 Qd7 5.0-0** [5.c4 =+] **Nc6 6.Qe2** [6.c3] **g6 7.c3 Bg7 8.Rd1 e5** [Otherwise d4] **9.Na3 Nge7 10.d4 cd4 11.cd4 ed4 12.Nb5 0-0 13.Nfd4 d5 14.Nb3! a6 15.Nc3 d4 16.Na4 Rae8 17.Bf4 Nd5 18.Bg3 Qe7 19.Nac5 Kh8 20.Re1 Nb6 21.Rac1 f5 22.Qd2 Qf7 23.ef5 gf5 24.Nd3 Nd5 25.Bd6 Rg8 26.Na5! Na5 27.Re8 Re8 28.Qa5 h6 29.g3 Kh7 30.Nf4 Nf4 31.Bf4 Qe6 32.Bd2 Rc8 33.Re1 Qf7?** [33...Qg6] **[D] 34.Re7! Qg6 35.Rb7 f4 36.Qd5 Re8** [36...fg3] **37.Bf4 Re1 38.Kg2 Qd3 39.Kh3 Qg6 40.Rd7 h5 41.Kg2 h4 42.Rd6 1-0**

After 33...Qf7?

242) Bazan,O-Fischer,R [4/7/60] Mar del Plata [8] D38/20 Queen's Gambit **1.Nf3 Nf6 2.c4 e6 3.Nc3 d5 4.d4 Bb4 5.cd5 ed5 6.Bg5 h6 7.Bh4 c5 8.e3 Nc6 9.Be2 g5** [Black "sacrifices" pawn structure for piece activity] **10.Bg3 Ne4 11.Rc1 Qa5 12.0-0 Bc3 13.bc3 Nc3 14.Qe1 Ne2 15.Qe2 c4 16.e4 Be6 17.Bc7! Qc7 18.ed5 g4 19.Nd2 Nd4 20.Qe4 Qf4! 21.Rc4 Qe4 22.Ne4 Ne2 23.Kh1 Bd7 24.Re1 Kf8 25.Nf6 Bb5 26.Rb4 Ba6 27.Nd7 Ke7 28.Nc5 Rhe8 29.Na6** [D] **Kd6 30.Rb7 Ng3 31.hg3 Re1 32.Kh2 Rc8 33.Rf7 Rcc1 0-1**

After 29.Na6

243) Fischer,R-Bielicki,C [4/8/60] Mar del Plata [9] B88/09 Sicilian **1.e4 c5 2.Nf3 d6 3.d4 cd4 4.Nd4 Nf6 5.Nc3 a6 6.Bc4 e6 7.Bb3 Nc6 8.f4 Na5** [Striving to eliminate the dangerous Bb3, but this costs time and development] **9.f5 Nb3 10.ab3 Be7 11.Qf3 0-0 12.Be3 Bd7** [12...e5 13.Nde2 d5!? +=] **13.g4 e5 14.Nde2 d5 15.ed5 e4 16.Qg2 Bb4 17.0-0-0 a5 18.g5 Ne8 19.f6 a4 20.Na2!** [Slowing up Black's attack] **Bd6 21.b4! Qc7 22.Kb1 Rc8 23.Nec3 a3 24.b3 Be5 25.Ne4 Bf5 26.fg7 Kg7 27.Bc5! Nd6 28.Nd6 Bd6 29.Qf2 b6 30.Bd4 Kg6 31.Rc1 Be5 32.Rhf1 Bd4 33.Qd4 Bc2 34.Ka1 f5 35.gf6 Qd6 36.Rg1 Kf7 37.Rg7 Ke8 38.Qe3** [D] **1-0**

Final position

After 28.f4

244) Redolfi,R-Fischer,R [4/9/60] Mar del Plata [10] B52/06
Sicilian [E:Queens + minor pieces] **1.e4 c5 2.Nf3 d6 3.Bb5 Bd7
4.Bd7 Qd7 5.0-0** [5.c4 +=] **Nc6 6.d3** [6.c3 with the idea of d4] **e6
7.Nbd2 g6 8.a4 Bg7 9.Nc4 Nge7 10.Bf4?!** [Losing time] **e5 11.Bg5
f6 12.Bd2 0-0 13.h3? Kh8 14.Qc1 f5 15.Bc3 fe4 16.de4 Nd4!
17.Nd4 ed4 18.Bd2 d5 19.ed5 Qd5 20.b3 Nf5 21.Qd1 Rae8
22.Re1 h5 23.Re8 Re8 24.Qf1 d3 25.c3 Nd6 26.Nd6 Qd6 27.Re1
Rd8 28.f4** [D] **Qb6 29.Re3 Qb3 30.Rd3 Rd3 31.Qd3 Qa4 32.f5
gf5 33.Qd8 Kh7 34.Qg5 Qd7 35.Qh5 Kg8 36.Qg5 b5 37.Bf4
Kf7 38.h4 Qd1 39.Kh2 Qg4 40.Qg4 fg4 0-1**

245) Fischer,R-Incutto,C [4/10/60] Mar del Plata [11] C99/15
Ruy Lopez [E:Bishop + pawn] **1.e4 e5 2.Nf3 Nc6 3.Bb5 a6 4.Ba4
Nf6 5.0-0 Be7 6.Re1 b5 7.Bb3 d6 8.c3 0-0 9.h3 Na5 10.Bc2 c5 11.d4
Qc7 12.Nbd2 cd4 13.cd4 Bb7 14.Nf1 Rac8 15.Bd3 Nd7 16.Ne3**
[16.d5! Nc5 17.Bb1 +=; more space] **ed4 17.Nd4 Bf6 18.Ndf5 g6
19.Nh6 Kh8 20.Neg4 Bg7 21.Bg5 Ne5 22.Ne5 de5 23.a4 Nc4 24.Qe2
f6 25.Bc1 Na5 26.ab5 ab5 27.Be3 Nb3 28.Ra7 Nd4 29.Qg4 Ra8
30.Ra8 Ba8 31.Rc1 Qd6 32.Rc8! Qe7** [32...Rc8 33.Nf7] **33.Bb5 Be4
34.Bc4 f5 35.Qg5 Bf6?!** [35...Nf3!!] [D] **36.Nf7 Kg8 37.Ne5 Ne6
38.Ng6 Bg5 39.Ne7 Be7 40.Bh6! Rc8 41.Be6 Kh8 42.Bc8 Bf6
43.b4 Bd4 44.b5 Bd3 45.Bd7 Kg8 46.Be8 Bc4 47.g3 Bd3 48.Be3
Be3 49.fe3 Kf8 50.b6 Be4 51.Bd7 Ke7 52.Bf5 1-0**

After 35...Bf6?!

Final position

246) Bronstein,D-Fischer,R [4/12/60] Mar del Plata [12]
D01/09 Queen's Pawn **1.d4 Nf6 2.Nc3 d5 3.Bg5** [Veresov's attack]
Bf5 4.e3 [4.f3] **e6 5.Bd3 Bd3 6.Qd3 c5 7.Bf6 gf6 8.dc5 Nd7 9.e4
de4 10.Qe4 Nc5 11.Qf3 Bg7 12.Nge2 0-0 13.g4!** [Preventing ...f5]
b5! 14.Ng3 Na4! 15.Na4 ba4 16.0-0 Rc8 17.Rac1 Qd4 18.b3?
[18.c3] **Qb2 19.ba4 Rc2 20.Rc2 Qc2 21.Qb3 Qg6 22.h3
Bh6! 23.Qf3 Rd8 24.Rd1 Rd1 25.Qd1 f5!** [Now the f-pawn can be
used aggressively] **26.Qd8 Bf8 27.gf5 ef5 28.Qb8 Qh6** [28...f4!
29.Qf4 Qb1] **29.Nf5 Qh3 30.Ne7 Kg7 31.Qe5! f6 32.Nf5 Kf7
33.Qd5 Kg6 34.Ne3 Qh5 35.Qg8 Bg7 36.Qe4 Kh6 37.Qd7 Qg6
38.Kf1 Bf8 39.Qa7 Qd3 40.Kg2 Qe4 41.Kg1 Qg6 42.Kf1 Qd3
43.Kg2 Qe4 44.f3 Qd3 45.Qd4 Qe2 46.Kg3 Qe1 47.Kg4 Qg1
48.Kf5 Qg6 49.Ke6 Qe8 50.Kd5 Qd8 51.Ke6 Qe8 52.Kf5 Qg6
53.Kf4 Qg5 54.Ke4 Kg6 55.f4 Qg1 56.Qd7 Qh1 57.Kd3 Qb1
58.Ke2 Qa2 59.Kf3 Qa1 60.Qg4 Kf7 61.Qh5 Kg7 62.a5 Qc3
63.Qg4 Kh8 64.Qe6 Bc5 65.Qe8 Kg7** [D] **1/2-1/2**

After 34...Kb6

247) Fischer,R-Alvarez,J [4/13/60] Mar del Plata [13] C85/02
Ruy Lopez [E:Rook vs. Bishop] **1.e4 e5 2.Nf3 Nc6 3.Bb5 a6 4.Ba4
Nf6 5.0-0 Be7 6.Bc6 dc6 7.Nc3** [7.d3] **Bg4 8.h3 Bh5 9.Qe2?!** [9.g4
Bg6 10.Ne5] **Nd7 10.Nd1 Nc5 11.d3 Ne6 12.Be3 Bf6 13.Nc3 Qe7
14.Nb1 g5 15.Nbd2 Rg8 16.g4 Bg6 17.Nc4 h5 18.Nce5 Nf4 19.Bf4
gf4 20.Ng6 Rg6 21.g5 0-0-0 22.c3 Bg5 23.Kh2 Qd6 24.d4 Re6
25.e5 Qe7 26.Qe4 Kb8 27.Qf5 Bh6 28.Rae1 c5 29.dc5 Qc5 30.Qf7
Rde8 31.a3 Ka7 32.Qd7 Qe7 33.Qe7 R8e7 34.Rg1 Kb6** [D]
35.Nd4 f3 36.Ne6 Re6 37.Kg3 1-0

248) Letelier,R-Fischer,R [4/14/60] Mar del Plata [14] A45/07
Queen's Pawn [E:Rook + minor pieces] **1.d4 Nf6 2.Bg5 c5 3.c3**
[3.d5] **Qb6! 4.Qb3 cd4 5.Qb6 ab6 6.Bf6 gf6 7.cd4 Nc6 8.Nf3 Nb4
9.Kd2 Ra2 10.Ra2 Na2 11.Na3 d5 12.e3 e6 13.Nc2 Nb4 14.Nb4
Bb4 15.Kc2 Bd7 16.Kb3 Bd6** =+/-+ [Extra pawn and the two
Bishops] **17.Bd3 Ke7 18.Ra1 Rc8 19.Ra7 Bc6 20.g3 h6 21.Ra1
Kd7 22.Ra7 Kc7 23.Ra1 b5 24.Rc1 Kb6 25.Ra1 Bd7 26.Nh4 Rc6!
27.Ra8 Rc1 28.Rh8 b4! 29.Rh6?** [29.Rd8! =] [D] **Ka5 30.Ka2 b3!
31.Kb3 Ba4 32.Ka2 Kb4 33.b3 Bb3 34.Kb2 Rd1 35.Bb1 Rd2
36.Ka1 Kc3 0-1**

After 29.Rh6?

249) Fischer,R-Marini,L [4/15/60] Mar del Plata [15] B57/02
Sicilian [E:Bishop vs. Knight] **1.e4 c5 2.Nf3 Nc6 3.d4 cd4 4.Nd4
Nf6 5.Nc3 d6 6.Bc4 Bd7 7.Bb3 g6 8.f3 Na5 9.Bg5 Bg7 10.Qd2 h6
11.Be3 Rc8 12.0-0-0 Nc4 13.Qe2! Ne3 14.Qe3 Qb6** [A suggested
improvement on Fischer-Gligoric,Yugoslavia 1959] **15.Qd2 Qc5
16.f4 Nc4 17.Nf3 Bh6 18.e5! Ng4 19.Rhe1 0-0 20.Ne4 Qb6 21.ed6
e5 22.Neg5 Bf5 23.Ne5 Be5 24.fg5 Nf2 25.d7 Rcd8** [D] **26.Nf7!
Rf7 27.Re8 Kh7 28.Rd8 Qd8 29.Bf7 Nd1 30.Be8 Bd7 31.Qd7
Qd7 32.Bd7 Ne3 33.Bc8 b6 34.Bb7 a5 35.Kd2 1-0**

After 25...Rcd8

250) Fischer,R-Foguelman,A [6/23/60] Buenos Aires [1]
B18/05 Caro Kann [E:Rook + pawn] **1.e4 c6 2.d4 d5 3.Nc3 de4
4.Ne4 Bf5 5.Ng3 Bg6 6.Nh3 Nf6 7.Nf4 e5 8.de5 Qd1?** [8...Qa5
=] **9.Kd1 Ng4 10.Ng6 hg6 11.Ne4 Ne5 12.Be2?!** [12.Bf4! +-] **f6
13.c3 Nbd7 14.Be3 0-0-0 15.Kc2 Nb6 16.h4?!** [16.a4 +=] **Nec4
17.Bf4 Nd5 18.Bg3 Nd6 19.Nd6 Rd6 20.Bd6 Rd6 21.g3 Kc7 22.c4
Nb4 23.Kc3 c5 24.a3 Re6 25.Bf1 Nc6 26.Bd3 Ne5 27.Be4 Ng4?**
[27...Rd4 -+] **28.Bg6 Re2 29.Rae1 Rf2 30.Re7 Kb6 31.Be4 Re2
32.Rb7 Ka6 33.Re7 Kb6 34.b4 Nf2 35.Rb7 Ka6 36.b5 Ka5
37.Ra7 Kb6 38.Ra6 Kc7** [D] **39.b6! Rb6 40.Rb6 Ne4 41.Kd3 Kb6
42.Rg1 Rd2?** [42...Ng3 =] **43.Ke4 Rd4 44.Kf5 Rc4 45.Re1! Rc3
46.g4 Rf3 47.Kg6 Ra3 48.Kg7 Rg3 49.Re4 f5 50.Re6 Kb5 51.g5
Rg4 52.g6 Rh4 53.Kf7 c4 54.g7 Rh7 55.Rg6 c3 56.Kf6 Rg7
57.Rg7 Kc4 58.Kf5 c2 1/2-1/2**

After 38...Kc7

251) Szabo,L-Fischer,R [6/24/60] Buenos Aires [2] A36/16
English **1.c4 Nf6 2.Nc3 g6 3.g3 Bg7 4.Bg2 0-0 5.e4** [Botvinnik's
idea - to blockade the light squares in the center and expand on the
Kingside and/or Queenside] **c5 6.Nge2 Nc6 7.d3 Rb8 8.h3 a6 9.Be3
d6 10.a4 Ne8 11.0-0 Nc7 12.d4 b6 13.Rb1 cd4 14.Nd4 Nd4 15.Bd4
Bd4 16.Qd4 b5 17.b4 ba4 18.Na4 e5!** [Blockading central dark
squares-now Black's Bc8 is better than the Bg2] **19.Qd3 Ne6
20.Rfd1 Nd4 21.Nc3 Be6 22.Ne2 Ne2 23.Qe2 Qc7 24.Bf1** [D]
1/2-1/2

Final position

After 29...Nb7

252) Fischer,R-Rossetto,H [6/25/60] Buenos Aires [3] B33/11
Sicilian [E:Rook + pawn] **1.e4 c5 2.Nf3 Nc6 3.d4 cd4 4.Nd4 Nf6
5.Nc3 e5 6.Ndb5 d6 7.Bg5 a6 8.Bf6 gf6 9.Na3 d5 10.Nd5 Ba3
11.ba3 Be6 12.Bc4 Qa5 13.Qd2 0-0-0?** [13...Qd2 +=] **14.Rd1 Qa3
15.0-0 Rhg8 16.Qe3 Qe3 17.fe3 +=** [The f-file] **Kb8 18.Bb3 Rg6
19.Nb6 Kc7 20.Rd8 Nd8 21.Nd5 Bd5 22.Bd5 Ne6 23.h4 h5 24.Rf5
Rh6 25.Rf3 Rg6 26.Kf2 b6 27.Rf5 Rh6 28.Bc4 Nc5 29.Kf3 Nb7**
[D] **30.Bf7 Nd6 31.Rh5 Nf7 32.Kg4 Rg6?** [32...Rh5 =] **33.Kf5
Rg2 34.Rh7 Rf2 35.Kg6 Rc2 36.Rf7 Kc6 37.a3 Rg2 38.Kf6 Ra2
39.Ke5 Ra3 40.Rf6 Kc5 41.Rf1 Re3 42.Rc1 Kb4 43.Rh1 a5
44.h5 1-0**

After 15.Be2?!

253) Fischer,R-Ivkov,B [6/26/60] Buenos Aires [4] B14/13
Caro Kann [E:Rook + pawn] **1.e4 c6 2.d4 d5 3.ed5 cd5 4.c4 Nf6
5.Nc3 e6 6.Nf3 Be7 7.c5 0-0 8.b4** [8.Bd3] **b6 9.Bd3 bc5?** [9...a5
10.Na4] **10.bc5 Nc6 11.0-0 Bd7 12.h3 Ne8 13.Bf4 Bf6 14.Bb5 Nc7
15.Be2?!** [15.Ba4! maintains the bind +-] [D] **Nd4! 16.Nd4 e5 17.c6
Be8 18.Bg3 ed4 19.Bc7 Qc7 20.Nd5 Qd6 21.Nf6 Qf6 22.c7 Rc8
23.Rc1 Bc6 24.Rc4 Rc7 25.Bd3?** [Better was 25.Rd4 =] **Rd7
26.Qc2 Bd5 27.Ra4 g6 28.Qc5 Rfd8 29.Bb5 Rd6 30.Rd1 Be6
31.Bd3 Rd5 32.Qa7 Bh3! 33.Be4** [33.gh3 Qf3 34.Rd2 Rg5 35. Kf1
Re8 -++] **R5d7 34.Qa6 Qa6 35.Ra6 Be6 36.a4 d3 37.Rd2 Rd4
38.f3 Bd5 39.Bd5 R8d5 40.Kf2 Rc4 41.a5 Ra4 42.Rc6 Ra3 43.Rc1
h5 44.Rcd1 Kg7 45.a6 g5 46.a7 Ra7 47.Rd3 Ra2 48.Kg1 Rd3
49.Rd3 Kg6 50.Kh2 Ra4 51.Rd5 g4 52.fg4 hg4 53.g3 Kf6 54.Rd7
Ke5 55.Kg2 f5 56.Rd2 Rc4 57.Re2 Kd4 58.Rf2 Rc5 59.Rf4 Ke3
60.Kg1 1/2-1/2**

After 54.f6

254) Eliskases,E-Fischer,R [6/28/60] Buenos Aires [5] E22/03
Queen's Gambit [E:Knight vs. Bishop] **1.c4 Nf6 2.Nc3 e6 3.Nf3 d5
4.d4 Bb4 5.Qb3 Nc6 6.Bg5 h6?!** [6...dc4] **7.Bf6 Qf6 8.e3 dc4 9.Bc4
0-0 10.0-0 Qe7 11.Qc2 Bd6 12.Rad1 Nb8 13.a3 e5 14.Nd5 Qe8
15.de5 Ne5 16.Ne5 Qe5 17.f4** [White utilizes the Kingside majority
and better development; Black has the Bishop pair and a Queenside
majority] **Qe8 18.e4 c6 19.Nc3 Bc7 20.Qe2 Be6 21.e5 Qe7 22.Ne4
Rad8 23.Kh1 Rfe8 24.Be6 Qe6 25.Nc5 Qc8 26.Qh5 Rd1 27.Rd1
Rd8 28.h3 Kg8 29.Rd8 Qd8 30.e6 Qe7 31.Qf5 b6 32.ef7 Qf7
33.Qc8 Kh7 34.Ne6 Bd6 35.g4 Qf6 36.Qd7 Qe7 37.Qe7 Be7
38.Nd4 c5 39.Nc6 Bd6 40.Na7 c4 41.Nc8 Bc5?** [41...Ba3!] **42.a4!
Kg6 43.Kg2 Kf6 44.Kf3 Ke6 45.Ke4 Bf2 46.f5 Kd7 47.Na7 Kd6
48.Nb5 Kc5 49.Nc7 Bh4 50.Ne8 Kb4 51.Kd5 Be7 52.Ng7 Bf6
53.Ne8! Bb2 54.f6** [D] **Bf6 55.Nf6 c3 56.Nh5! Ka4 57.Nf4 b5
58.Ne2 c2 1-0**

After 15...e4!

255) Fischer,R-Pachman,L [6/30/60] Buenos Aires [6]
B44/06 Sicilian **1.e4 c5 2.Nf3 Nc6 3.d4 cd4 4.Nd4 e6 5.Nb5 d6
6.Bf4 e5 7.Be3 Nf6 8.N1c3 a6 9.Na3 b5 10.Nd5 Nd5** [10...Rb8 =]
11.ed5 Ne7 12.c4 Nf5! 13.Bd2 [13.cb5 Ne3 14.fe3 Qh4 15.g3 Qe4
16.Qc2 Qe3 -++] **Be7! 14.cb5 Bf6 15.Be2 e4!** [D] **16.b6! 0-0 17.Nc4
Bd4! 18.0-0 Bb6 19.Nb6 Qb6 20.Bc3 Bb7 21.Bc4 Rac8 22.b3 Ne3
23.Bd4 Nd1 24.Bb6 Nc3 1/2-1/2**

256) Wexler,B-Fischer,R [7/1/60] Buenos Aires [7] A16/02
English **1.c4 Nf6 2.Nc3 g6 3.g3 Bg7 4.Bg2 0-0 5.d3 d6 6.Bd2 Nc6
7.Qc1 e6!?** [Fighting for d5; 7...e5] **8.Nf3 d5 9.0-0 d4 10.Ne4 Nd7?!**
[10...Ne4 11.de4 a5 stopping b4 is =] **11.b4 +=/+- f5 12.Neg5 Qe7
13.b5 Nd8 14.Rb1 a5 15.h4 e5 16.e3!** [Undermining the center]
**de3 17.Be3 h6 18.Nh3 Kh7 19.c5! Nf6 20.Re1! Ng4 21.Bf4! Nf7
22.Ne5! Nge5 23.d4 Be6 24.de5 Rab8 25.a4 Rfd8 26.Qe3 Bc4
27.b6 Rd3 28.Qc1 Be6 29.bc7 Qc7 30.Rb6 Bd5 31.e6 Ne5** [D]
**32.Rd6 Bg2 33.Rd3 Bh3 34.Be5 Qc6 35.f3 Rd8 36.Rd8 Qf3
37.Qd2 Be5 38.Qf2 1-0**

After 31...Ne5

257) Fischer,R-Uhlmann,W [7/2/60] Buenos Aires [8] C19/14
French [E:Queen vs. Rook + Bishop] **1.e4 e6 2.d4 d5 3.Nc3 Bb4 4.e5
Ne7 5.a3 Bc3 6.bc3 c5 7.a4 Nbc6 8.Nf3 Bd7 9.Qd2 Qa5 10.Bd3 c4
11.Be2 f6 12.Ba3 Ng6 13.0-0 0-0-0 14.Bd6 Nce7 ∞ 15.Nh4 Rde8
16.Ng6 hg6 17.ef6 gf6 18.h3 Nf5 19.Bh2 g5 20.f4 Nd6! 21.Bf3** [21.fg5
Ne4 22.Qf4 e5! ∞; or 22.Qe3 Qc3 ∞] **g4!!** [A positional sacrifice to
incarcerate the Bh2] **22.hg4** [22.Bg4 Ne4 -+] **f5 23.g5 Re7 24.Bg3 Be8
25.Qe3 Ne4 26.Be4 de4 27.Kf2** [27.d5! to prevent the blockade] **Reh7
28.Rfb1** [28.d5!] **Qd5 29.Qc1** [D] **Rh1! 30.Qh1 e3! 31.Kg1 Rh1
32.Kh1 e2 33.Rb5 Bb5 34.ab5 Qb5 35.Re1 a5! 36.Re2 a4 37.Re6 a3
38.g6 Qd7 39.Re5 b6 40.Bh4 a2 41.Re1 Qg7 42.Ra1 Qg6 0-1**

After 29.Qc1

258) Taimanov,M-Fischer,R [7/4/60] Buenos Aires [9]
E51/11 Nimzo-Indian [E:Bishop + pawn] **1.c4 Nf6 2.Nc3 e6 3.d4
Bb4 4.e3 0-0 5.Bd3 d5 6.Nf3 Nc6 7.0-0 dc4 8.Bc4 Bd6 9.Nb5 Be7**
[9...a6!?] **10.h3 a6 11.Nc3 Bd6** [11...b5] **12.e4 e5 13.Be3 ed4
14.Nd4** [White hopes the Kingside majority will give an advantage]
Bd7 15.Re1 Qe7?! [15...Ne5 16.Bb3 Ng6] **16.Bg5! Nd4 17.Nd5!
Qe5 18.f4 Nf3 19.Qf3 Qd4 20.Kh1 Ng4!** [Not 20...Qc4 21.Bf6 ++-]
**21.hg4 Qc4 22.b3 Qb5 23.a4 Qa5 24.Red1 Bc6 25.e5 Bb4 26.Qe4
Bd5 27.Rd5 Qb6 28.f5 Bc3 29.Rc1 Bb2 30.Rb1 Bc3 31.Rc1 Bb2
32.Rc4?!** [32.Rc2! Qb3 33.Rc7 ++-] **Rae8 33.f6** [D] **c6 34.fg7! cd5
35.gf8=Q Kf8 36.Qh7 Be5 37.Rf4! Qe6 38.Rf1 b5?** [38...Bg7]
39.ab5 ab5 [D] **40.Bd2 Ke7 41.Bb4 Kd8 42.Rf7 Rh8 43.Rf8 Rf8
44.Bf8 Qf6 45.Bc5 d4 46.Kg1 Qf4 47.Qe7 Kc8 48.Qf8 Qf8 49.Bf8
Bg3! 50.Kf1 d3 51.Bb4 Kd7 52.Be1 Bf4 53.Bc3 Bg3 54.g5 Ke6
55.g6 Ke7 56.Be1 Bf4 57.Bh4 Kf8 58.g3 Bd6 59.Kf2 Bc5 60.Kf3
Kg7 61.Bg5 Kg6 62.Bf4 Kh5 63.Ke4 Kg4 64.Kd3 Kf3 65.Bc7 Bf2
66.Bd6 Be1 67.Kd4 Kg4 68.Kc5 b4 69.Kb5 Kf5 70.Kc4 Ke6
71.Bc7 Kf5 72.Kd3 Kg4 73.Bd6 Bc3 74.Kc4 Be1 75.Bb4 Bg3
76.Bc3 Bd6 77.Kd5 Be7 78.Bd4 Bb4 79.Kc4 Ba5 80.Bc3 Bd8
81.b4 Kf4 82.b5 Ke4 83.Bd4 Bc7 84.Kc5 Kd3! 85.Kc6 Kc4
86.Bb6 Bf4 87.Ba7 Bc7 1/2-1/2**

After 33.f6

After 39...ab5

259) Fischer,R-Reshevsky,S [7/5/60] Buenos Aires [10]
B44/06 Sicilian **1.e4 c5 2.Nf3 Nc6 3.d4 cd4 4.Nd4 e6 5.Nb5 d6
6.Bf4 e5 7.Be3 a6 8.N5a3 b5 9.c4 b4 10.Nc2 Nf6 11.Be2 Be7 12.0-0
0-0 13.Nd2 Rb8 14.Re1 Be6 15.f3 Nd7 16.Bf2 Nc5 17.Ne3 Nd4
18.Nb3 Ndb3 19.ab3 a5 20.Qc2 g6 21.Red1 Qc7 22.h4 Rfc8 23.g3
Ra8 24.Kg2 Qd7 25.h5 a4 26.ba4 b3! 27.Qd2 Ra4 28.Ra4 Na4
29.Rh1 Bg5 30.hg6 fg6 31.Ra1 Nc5 32.Rd1 Rd8 33.Qa5 Qa4
34.Qc3 Qa2 35.Rd2 Kf7 36.Qb4 Qa4 37.Qb6 Qa6** [D] **1/2-1/2**

Final position

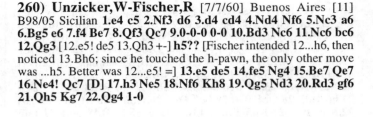

After 16...Qc7

260) Unzicker,W-Fischer,R [7/7/60] Buenos Aires [11] B98/05 Sicilian **1.e4 c5 2.Nf3 d6 3.d4 cd4 4.Nd4 Nf6 5.Nc3 a6 6.Bg5 e6 7.f4 Be7 8.Qf3 Qc7 9.0-0-0 0-0 10.Bd3 Nc6 11.Nc6 bc6 12.Qg3** [12.e5! de5 13.Qh3 +-] **h5??** [Fischer intended 12...h6, then noticed 13.Bh6; since he touched the h-pawn, the only other move was ...h5. Better was 12...e5! =] **13.e5 de5 14.fe5 Ng4 15.Be7 Qe7 16.Ne4!** Qc7 [D] **17.h3 Ne5 18.Nf6 Kh8 19.Qg5 Nd3 20.Rd3 gf6 21.Qh5 Kg7 22.Qg4 1-0**

Final position

261) Fischer,R-Olafsson,F [7/8/60] Buenos Aires [12] B87/20 Sicilian **1.e4 c5 2.Nf3 d6 3.d4 cd4 4.Nd4 Nf6 5.Nc3 a6 6.Bc4 e6 7.Bb3 b5 8.0-0** [8.f4] **Be7** [8...Bb7] **9.Qf3** [9.f4] **Qc7** [9...Qb6 10.Be3 Qb7 =] **10.Qg3 b4** [10...Nc6!?] **11.Nce2 g6 12.c3 Ne4 13.Qe3 Nf6 14.cb4 0-0 15.Bd2 e5 16.Nf3 Bb7 17.Rac1 Qd7 18.Nc3 Qf5 19.Bc2 Qh5 20.Ne4 Be4 21.Be4 d5 22.Bc2 e4 23.Nd4 Bd6 24.h3 Nbd7 25.Bd1 Qe5 26.g3 Rfc8 27.Be2 Qe8 28.a3 Be5 29.b5 ab5 30.Bb5 Rc1 31.Rc1 Qb8 32.Bc6 Ra6 33.Bd7 Nd7 34.Nc6 Qe8 35.Bb4 Bf6 36.Qf4 h5 37.b3 Qe6 38.Qc7 Kh7 39.Qc8 Rb6 40.Nd8 Qh3 41.Nf7 Rb8 42.Qc6 Qf5 43.Nd6 Qe6** [D] **1/2-1/2**

Final position

262) Evans,L-Fischer,R [7/9/60] Buenos Aires [13] C64/07 Ruy Lopez **1.e4 e5 2.Nf3 Nc6 3.Bb5 Bc5 4.0-0 Nge7** [4...d6] **5.c3 Bb6 6.d4 ed4 7.cd4 d5 8.ed5 Nd5 9.Re1 Be6 10.Ne5** [10.Bg5! Qd6 11.Nbd2 0-0 12.Nc4 +-] **Ne7 11.Be3 0-0 12.Bc5 Nc6 13.Nc6 bc6 14.Nc3 Qf6 15.Qa4 Bd5** [Black's two Bishops vs. White's better pawns equalize] **16.Rac1 Rae8 17.h3 Re6 18.Nd5 cd5 19.Qb4 Rfe8 20.a4 a5 21.Qd2 h6 22.b4 ab4 23.Qb4** [D] **1/2-1/2**

After 20...Bg4!

263) Fischer,R-Korchnoi,V [7/11/60] Buenos Aires [14] B28/03 Sicilian **1.e4 c5 2.Nf3 a6 3.d4 cd4 4.c3** [Tit for tat! Transposing into the Smith-Morra Gambit] **dc3 5.Nc3 Nc6 6.Bc4 d6 7.0-0 Nf6 8.Bg5 e6 9.Qe2 Be7 10.Rfd1 Qc7 11.Rac1 0-0 12.Bb3 h6 13.Bf4 e5 14.Be3 Qd8 15.Nd5 Nd5 16.Bd5 Bd7 17.Nd2 Nb4 18.Bb3 Bg5 19.Bg5 Qg5 20.Nf3 Bg4!** [D] **21.Rc7! Qd8 22.Rb7 Rb8 23.Rb8 Qb8 24.h3 Bf3 25.Qf3 Nc6 26.Qd3 Nd4 27.Bc4 a5 28.b3 Qb4 29.f4 Kh7 1/2-1/2**

After 25.Rd8

264) Guimard,C-Fischer,R [7/12/60] Buenos Aires [15] A48/14 King's Indian [E:Rook + pawn] **1.d4 Nf6 2.Nf3 g6 3.Bg5** [The Torre Attack] **Bg7 4.Nbd2 d6 5.e4 h6 6.Bf6** [Better was 6.Bh4] **Bf6 7.Bb5 c6 8.Bd3 0-0 9.e5!? Bg7 10.Qe2 c5!** [Striking back in the center] **11.h4 cd4 12.h5 g5 13.Qe4 f5 14.ef6 Rf6 15.Ng5 d5!** [15...hg5 16.Qh7 Kf8 17.h6 ++-] **16.Qh7 Kf8 17.0-0-0 Nc6 18.f4 Nb4!** [Trading the dangerous Bd3] **19.a3 Nd3 20.Qd3 hg5! 21.h6** [21.fg5 Bf5!] **Bh6 22.fg5 Bf5 23.Rh6 Bd3 24.Rh8 Kg7 25.Rd8** [D] **Rc6! 26.Ra8 Rc2 27.Kb1 Rd2 28.Kc1 Rc2 29.Kb1 Rc8 30.Rd3 Ra8 31.Rd4 Rd8 32.Kc2 Kg6 33.Rf4 Kg5 34.Rf7 Rd7 35.Kd3 Kg6 36.Rf8 Kg7 37.Ra8 b6 38.Kd4 Kf6 39.Rf8 Ke6 40.Rg8 Kd6 41.g4 e5 42.Kd3 Rh7 43.g5 Ke6 44.g6 Rh3 45.Kc2 Rh2 46.Kb3 Rg2 47.g7 Kf6 48.Rd8 Rg7 49.Rd5 Rc7! 50.a4 e4 51.Rh5 e3 52.Rh3 Re7 53.Rh1 e2 54.Re1 Kf5 55.Kc3 Kf4 56.Kd2 Kf3 57.Rh1 Rd7 58.Kc2 Kg2 0-1**

265) Fischer,R-Bazan,O [7/17/60] Buenos Aires [16] B44/07
Sicilian [E:Rook + minor piece] **1.e4 c5 2.Nf3 Nc6 3.d4 cd4 4.Nd4
e6 5.Nb5 d6 6.Bf4 e5 7.Be3 a6 8.N5c3 Nf6 9.Na3 Ng4?!** [Allowing
White a grip on d5] **10.Nc4 Ne3 11.Ne3 Be7 12.Bc4 0-0 13.0-0 Bg5
14.Nf5 Bf5 15.ef5 Nd4 16.Qd3 Rc8 17.Bb3 Qd7 18.g4 Rfd8
19.Rad1 Qc6 20.Bd5 Qb6 21.Ne4 Bf4 22.c3 Nb5 23.g5 Nc7 24.g6
Nd5 25.Qd5 Rc7 26.c4 Qc6 27.gf7 Kf8 28.Nd6 Qd5 29.Rd5 Rc4
30.Rfd1 [D] Rd4 31.R5d4 ed4 32.Nb7 Rd5 33.b4 Kf7 34.Nc5 a5
35.Nd3 Bd6 1/2-1/2**

After 30.Rfd1

266) Gligoric,S-Fischer,R [7/18/60] Buenos Aires [17] C64/10
Ruy Lopez **1.e4 e5 2.Nf3 Nc6 3.Bb5 Bc5 4.c3 Nf6** [4...f5!?] **5.d4
ed4 6.e5 Ne4 7.0-0 d5 8.Nd4 0-0 9.f3 Ng5 10.Bc6** [10.Be3 +-] **bc6
11.Be3 f6 12.Kh1 Bd4 13.Bd4 fe5 14.Be5 Ba6 15.Re1 Ne6 16.Na3
Qd7 17.Nc2 Rae8 18.b4 c5 19.Qd2 c6 20.Bg3 cb4 [D] 1/2-1/2**

Final position

267) Fischer,R-Wade,R [7/19/60] Buenos Aires [18] C92/04
Ruy Lopez [E:Queen vs. Rook + Knight] **1.e4 e5 2.Nf3 Nc6 3.Bb5
a6 4.Ba4 Nf6 5.0-0 Be7 6.Re1 b5 7.Bb3 0-0 8.c3 d6 9.h3 Qd7 10.d4
Re8 11.Nbd2 Bf8 12.d5** [12.a3 g6 13.Ba2 Bg7 14.b4 Nh5 15.Nf1
+=] **Ne7 13.Nf1 g6** [13...h6] **14.c4 Bg7 15.c5 Nh5 16.a4 dc5 17.ab5
Bb7 18.ba6 Ba6 19.Be3 c4 20.Ba4 Bb5 21.Bb5 Qb5 22.Qc2 f5
23.Ra8 Ra8 24.g4 fe4 25.Qe4 Nf6 26.Qe5 Qd5 27.Qe7 Qf3 28.Qe6
Kh8 29.Bd4 Rf8 30.Re3 Qb7 31.Qc4 Nd5 32.Rb3 Nb6 33.Bg7
Kg7 34.Qd4 Kg8 35.Ne3 Rf7 36.g5 h5 37.Rd3 Qf3 [D] 38.Ng4
hg4 39.Rf3 gf3 40.Qe4 Kg7 41.Qe5 Kg8 42.h4 Kh7 43.b4 Nc4
44.Qe6 Nd6 45.b5 1-0**

After 37...Qf3

268) Benko,P-Fischer,R [7/21/60] Buenos Aires [19] E62/18
King's Indian **1.d4 Nf6 2.c4 g6 3.g3 Bg7 4.Bg2 0-0 5.Nc3 d6 6.Nf3
Nc6 7.h3 e5** [7...Nd7] **8.0-0 ed4 9.Nd4 Nd4 10.Qd4 Be6 11.Qh4
Nd7 12.Bg5 f6 13.Be3 g5 14.Qd4 f5 15.Qd2 f4 16.gf4 gf4 17.Bf4
Nb6 18.Qe3 Qf6 19.Bg5 Qg6 20.Qg3 Nc4 21.Nd5! Qf7 22.Bh6!
c6 23.Bg7 Qg7 24.Qg7 Kg7 25.Nc7 Kf6 26.Na8 Ra8 27.b3 [D]
1-0**

Final position

269) Fischer,R-Johannsson,I [10/5/60] Reykjavik [1] C79/10
Ruy Lopez [E:Rooks + minor pieces] **1.e4 e5 2.Nf3 Nc6 3.Bb5 a6
4.Ba4 d6 5.c3 Bd7 6.d4 Nf6 7.0-0 Be7 8.d5 Nb8 9.Bc2 Bg4 10.c4
Nbd7 11.Re1! 0-0 12.Nbd2 c5!** 13.a4 Ne8 14.Nf1 Bf3 15.Qf3 Bg5
16.Ne3 g6 17.g3 Ng7 18.h4?!** [18.Ra3] **Be3 19.Be3 f5 20.Bh6 f4
[20...fe4 21.Qe4 Nf6 =+] **21.g4 Qh4 22.g5 Qh5 23.Bd1 Qf3 24.Bf3
Rfb8 25.Bg4 Nf8 26.b4 cb4 27.a5 Rc8?** [27...b6!] **28.Bc8 Rc8
29.Reb1 Nd7 30.Rb4 Nc5 31.Bg7 Kg7 32.Rb6 Rd8 33.f3 Rd7
34.Kf2 Kf7 35.Ke2 Kg8 36.Kd2 Kf8 37.Kc3 Ke8 38.Kb4! Nd3
39.Ka3 Nc5 40.Rh1 Kf8 41.Rd1 [D] 1-0**

Final position

After 17.Kh1

270) Gudmundsson,A-Fischer,R [10/6/60] Reykjavik [2] D95/02 Grunfeld **1.d4 Nf6 2.Nf3 d5 3.e3 g6 4.c4 Bg7 5.Nc3 0-0 6.Qb3** [6.Bd2; 6.Be2; 6.b4] **e6 7.Be2 Nc6 8.Qc2 dc4 9.Bc4 e5! 10.de5 Ng4 11.0-0** [11.e6!] **Nce5 12.Ne5 Ne5 13.Be2 c6 14.f4 Ng4! 15.h3 Bf5! 16.e4 Qd4 17.Kh1** [D] **Nf2 18.Rf2 Qf2 19.ef5 Bc3! 20.bc3 Rae8 21.Bd3 Re1 22.Kh2 Qg1 23.Kg3 Rfe8 24.Rb1? gf5! 25.Bd2 Rb1 26.Qb1 Qb1 27.Bb1 Re2 0-1**

271) Fischer,R-Olafsson,F [10/8/60] Reykjavik [3] B92/09 Sicilian **1.e4 c5 2.Nf3 d6 3.d4 cd4 4.Nd4 Nf6 5.Nc3 a6 6.Be2 e5 7.Nb3 Be7 8.Bg5 Nbd7** [8...Be6] **9.a4 0-0 10.0-0 h6! 11.Bh4 b6 12.Bc4 Bb7 13.Qe2 Qc7 14.Rfd1 Rfc8 15.Nd2** [15.Bf6!] **g5 16.Bg3 Nf8 17.f3 Ne6 18.Bf2 Kg7 19.Kh1 Nf4 20.Qe3?** [20.Qe1] **d5! 21.ed5 Bc5 22.Qe1 Bf2 23.Qf2 N6d5 24.Nce4 f5 25.Ng3 Rf8 26.Bb3 Rae8 27.Ndf1 h5** [27...e4] **28.Nh5 Kg6 29.Nf4 Nf4 30.Ng3 g4 31.Ne2 Ng2?** [31...Ne2] **32.Kg2 gf3 33.Kf1 e4 34.Qh4! f4 35.Qg4 Kh6** [D] **36.Rd7 fe2 37.Ke1 Qc5 38.Qg7 Kh5 39.Qh7 Kg5 40.Rg7 Kf6 41.Rg6 Ke5 42.Qg7 1-0**

After 35...Kh6

272) Thorbergsson,F-Fischer,R [10/10/60] Reykjavik [4] E58/00 Nimzo-Indian **1.d4 Nf6 2.c4 e6 3.Nf3 d5 4.Nc3 Bb4 5.a3 Bc3 6.bc3 c5 7.e3 0-0 8.Bd3 Nc6 9.0-0 Na5 10.Ne5 dc4 11.Nc4 Nc4 12.Bc4 Qc7 13.Qe2 e5** [13...b6] **14.Bb2 e4 15.h3 Bf5 16.Rfd1 Rac8 17.a4 cd4 18.Rd4 Rfd8 19.Rad1 Rd4 20.Rd4 Be6 21.Be6 fe6 22.Qd1 e5 23.Qb3 Qf7 24.Rb4 Qb3 25.Rb3 b6 26.Rb5** [D] **1/2-1/2**

Final position

273) Ghitescu,T-Fischer,R [10/17/60] Leipzig Olympiad Prelim E51/13 Nimzo-Indian **1.d4 Nf6 2.c4 e6 3.Nc3 Bb4 4.e3 0-0 5.Bd3 d5** [5...c5] **6.Nf3 Nc6** [Transposing into the Ragozin system] **7.0-0 dc4 8.Bc4 Bd6 9.Bb5 Bc6 10.Bc6 ed4 11.ed4 bc6 12.Bg5 Re8** [12...h6] **13.Qd3 c5 14.dc5??** [D] **Bh2 0-1**

After 14.dc5??

274) Fischer,R-Munoz,C [10/18/60] Leipzig Olympiad Prelim B77/02 Sicilian [E:Rook + pawn] **1.e4 c5 2.Nf3 d6 3.d4 cd4 4.Nd4 Nf6 5.Nc3 g6 6.Be3 Bg7 7.f3 0-0 8.Qd2 Nc6 9.Bc4 a6?!** [9...Bd7] **10.Bb3 Qa5 11.0-0-0 Bd7 12.Kb1** [12.h4!?] **Rac8 13.g4 Ne5 14.Bh6 Nc4 15.Bc4 Rc4 16.Nb3** [16.Nd5! +-] **Qe5! 17.h4 Rfc8 18.Bf4 Qe6 19.h5 b5 20.hg6 fg6 21.Bh6** [21.e5 was better] **Bh8 22.e5** [D] **b4! 23.ef6 bc3 24.Qh2 Qf6 25.Bg5 Qf7 26.Qe2 cb2 27.Qe7 Qe7 28.Be7 Rc2 29.Rd6 Ba4! -++ 30.Bg5 Rf2 31.Be3 Rf3 32.Bd4 Bb3 33.ab3 Bd4 34.Rd4 Rb3 35.Rd2 Rcb8 36.Rd7 Ra3 0-1**

After 22.e5

275) Jimenez,E-Fischer,R [10/19/60] Leipzig Olympiad Prelim C64/09 Ruy Lopez [E:Rook + Knight] **1.e4 e5 2.Nf3 Nc6 3.Bb5 Bc5 4.c3 Nf6 5.d4 ed4 6.e5 Ne4 7.cd4 Bb4 8.Bd2 Nd2 9.Nbd2 0-0 10.0-0 a6 11.Ba4 d6 12.a3 Bd2 13.Qd2 Ne7 14.Rac1 Be6 15.Qf4 Bd5 16.Bc2 f6 17.ed6 Qd6 18.Qd6 cd6 19.Nd2 Nc6** [Black has obtained comfortable equality, but no more] **20.Bb3 Bf7 21.Bf7 Rf7 22.Nf3 d5 23.Rfe1 g5 24.h3 h5 25.Kf1 Rd7 26.Red1 Re8 27.h4 g4 28.Ng1 Rde7 29.Rc5 Nd4 30.Rd5** [D] **1/2-1/2**

Final position

276) O'Kelly,A-Fischer,R [10/21/60] Leipzig Olympiad Prelim B99/27 Sicilian **1.e4 c5 2.Nf3 d6 3.d4 cd4 4.Nd4 Nf6 5.Nc3 a6 6.Bg5 e6 7.f4 Be7 8.Qf3 Qc7 9.0-0-0 Nbd7 10.g4 b5 11.Bf6 Nf6 12.g5 Nd7 13.a3 Bb7** [13...Rb8!] **14.Kb1** [14.Bh3 0-0-0 15.f5 +=] **d5! = 15.ed5 Nb6 16.Bg2 Nd5 17.Nd5 Bd5 18.Qg4 Bg2 19.Qg2 0-0 20.f5 ef5 [D] 1/2-1/2**

Final position

277) Perez,F-Fischer,R [10/23/60] Leipzig Olympiad Prelim B53/06 Sicilian **1.e4 c5 2.Nf3 d6 3.d4 cd4 4.Qd4 Nc6** [4...a6 and 5...Nc6] **5.Bb5 Bd7 6.Bc6 Bc6 7.Nc3 Nf6 8.Bg5 e6 9.0-0-0 Be7 10.e5** [10.Qd3 or 10.Qd2] **de5 11.Qe5 Qc8 12.Nd4 0-0 13.h4 h6 14.Kb1 Rd8! 15.f3 hg5! 16.hg5 Bd6 17.Qe1 Ne8 18.Qh4 Kf8 19.Nf5 ef5 20.Rde1 [D] Qe6!** [The refutation; Black gets more than enough for the Queen] **21.Re6 fe6 22.Re1 Ke7 23.b4 Nc7 24.Qh7 Rg8 25.b5? Bg3! 26.Qf5 Be1 27.Qc5 Kf7 28.bc6 bc6 29.Qc6 Rgb8 30.Kc1 Bg3 31.Ne2 Be5 32.f4 Bb2 33.Kd1 Nd5 34.Ke1 Ne7 35.g6 Kf6 36.Qc5 Ng6 37.c3 Rc8 38.Qd4 Kf7 39.f5 Nf8! 40.g4 Kg8 41.g5 Rc6 42.Qb4 Ba1! 43.f6 Rac8 44.fg7 Kg7 45.Qe7 Kg8 46.Nf4 Bc3 47.Ke2 Be5 48.Nh5 Rc2 49.Kd1 Rc1 50.Kd2 R1c7 0-1**

After 20.Rde1

278) Letelier,R-Fischer,R [10/24/60] Leipzig Olympiad Prelim E70/01 King's Indian **1.d4 Nf6 2.c4 g6 3.Nc3 Bg7 4.e4 0-0 5.e5 Ne8 6.f4 d6 7.Be3 c5! 8.dc5 Nc6 9.cd6 ed6 10.Ne4 Bf5! 11.Ng3?** [11.Nd6] **Be6 12.Nf3 Qc7 13.Qb1 de5 14.f5 e4! 15.fe6 ef3 16.gf3 f5! 17.f4 Nf6 18.Be2 Rfe8 19.Kf2 Re6 20.Re1 Rae8 21.Bf3 Re3 22.Re3 Re3 23.Ke3 [D] Qf4! 0-1** [24.Kf4 Bh6#]

After 23.Ke3

279) Fischer,R-Unzicker,W [10/26/60] Leipzig Olympiad Prelim C96/07 Ruy Lopez **1.e4 e5 2.Nf3 Nc6 3.Bb5 a6 4.Ba4 Nf6 5.0-0 Be7 6.Re1 b5 7.Bb3 d6 8.c3 0-0 9.h3 Na5 10.Bc2 c5 11.d4 cd4 12.cd4 Bb7 13.Nbd2 Nc6 14.d5 Nb4 15.Bb1 a5 16.Nf1** [16.Qe2! Qc7 17.Nf1 Rfc8 18.Bd2 +=] **Na6 17.Ng3 Bc8** [Relocating the Bishop, while watching f5] **18.Bd3 Bd7 19.Be3 Qb8** [19...Rc8 20.a4! +-] **20.Rc1 Bd8 21.Qe2 Qb7 22.Nh2 Nb4 23.Bb1 Bb6 24.Bg5 Bd8 25.Qf3 Ne8 26.Be3 Bb6 27.Bd2 Nf6 28.Ng4 Ng4 29.hg4 Rac8 30.Nf5 Bf5 31.Qf5 Bd4 32.a3 Na6 33.b4 ab4 34.ab4 Bb2 35.Rc8 Rc8 36.Qf3 Qb6 37.Rd1 Bd4 38.g3 Rc4 39.Bd3** +=/+- [Two Bishops and more space] **Rc7 40.Kg2 Bc3 41.Be3 Qb8 42.Rh1 Qc8 43.Bb5 Nb4 44.Qd1 Bd4 45.Bd4 ed4 46.g5 Qb8** [D] **47.Qh5 Qb5 48.Qh7 Kf8 49.Qh8 Ke7 50.Qg7 Nd5 51.Qd4 Nc3 52.Qf6 Kd7 53.g6 Ne4 54.Qf7 Kc8 55.g7! 1-0**

After 46...Qb8

280) Fischer,R-Ghitescu,T [10/28/60] Leipzig Olympiad Final B92/07 Sicilian [E:Rook + pawn] **1.e4 c5 2.Nf3 d6 3.d4 cd4 4.Nd4 Nf6 5.Nc3 a6 6.Be2 e5 7.Nb3 Be7 8.Bg5 0-0** [8...Be6] **9.Nd2 Ne4?!** [9...b5] **10.Be7 Nc3 11.Bd8 Nd1 12.Be7 Re8 [D] 13.Nc4 Nb2 14.Nb6 Re7 15.Na8 Na4 16.0-0-0 Nc6 17.Rd6 Be6 18.Bf3 g6 19.Bc6 bc6 20.Rc6 Ra7 21.Nc7 Bd7 22.Rc4 Nb6 23.Rb4 Rc7 24.Rb6 Bb5 25.Re1 Rc5 26.Re3 Kg7 27.Rb7 e4 28.Re4! Bc6 29.Rbe7 Be4 30.Re4 h5 31.c4 f5 32.Rd4 Kf6 33.f4 Ke6 34.Kc2 Rc8 35.Kc3 Rb8 36.c5 Rb1 37.Rd6 Kf7 38.Ra6 Rc1 39.Kd4 Rc2 40.g3 Rh2 41.Kd5 Rg2 42.c6 Ke7 43.Ra8 1-0**

After 12...Re8

After 16...Rc8

281) Penrose,,J-Fischer,R [10/29/60] Leipzig Olympiad Final B93/09 Sicilian [E:Rook + pawn] **1.e4 c5 2.Nf3 d6 3.d4 cd4 4.Nd4 Nf6 5.Nc3 a6 6.f4 e5 7.Nf3 Nbd7 8.a4 b6** [8...Be7 9. Bc4 0-0 10.0-0 Qb6!?] **9.Bc4 Qc7 10.Qe2 Be7 11.0-0 Bb7 12.fe5 de5 13.Bg5 h6 14.Bh4 Bb4 15.Bf6 Nf6 16.Nh4 Rc8** [D] **17.Bb5 Nd7 18.Bd7 Qd7 19.Rad1 Bc5 20.Kh1 Bd4 21.Nf5 g6 22.Nd4 ed4 23.Nd5 Bd5 24.ed5 Qe7 25.Qf2 0-0 26.Rd4 Qc5 27.Rd2 Qb4 28.c3 Qb3 29.Rd4 Rc4 30.Rc4 Qc4 31.Kg1 Qa4 32.Qb6 Qc4 33.Qb4 Qb4 34.cb4 Rb8 35.Rf4 Rd8 1/2-1/2**

Final position

282) Fischer,R-Bobotsov,M [10/30/60] Leipzig Olympiad Final C92/08 Ruy Lopez **1.e4 e5 2.Nf3 Nc6 3.Bb5 a6 4.Ba4 Nf6 5.0-0 Be7 6.Re1 b5 7.Bb3 d6 8.c3 0-0 9.h3 Be6 10.d4 Bb3 11.ab3 ed4 12.cd4 d5 13.e5 Ne4 14.Nc3 f5! 15.ef6 Bf6! 16.Ne4 de4 17.Re4 Qd5 18.Rg4! h5 19.Rf4 Nb4** [19...Rfd8! =] **20.Be3 Rad8 21.Rc1?** [21.Qd2!] **c5 22.Qd2 Nc6 23.Qc2 Nd4 24.Bd4 Bd4 25.Rf8 Rf8?** [25...Kf8] **26.b4! Rf3 27.gf3 Qf3 28.bc5 Qg3 29.Kf1 Qh3 30.Ke1 Qh1 31.Ke2 Qc6 32.Qb3 Kh8 33.Qf3 Qe6 34.Kf1 Qh6 35.Rd1** [D] **1-0**

After 27...Rf8

283) Gligoric,S-Fischer,R [10/31/60] Leipzig Olympiad Final E51/13 Nimzo-Indian **1.d4 Nf6 2.c4 e6 3.Nc3 Bb4 4.e3 Nc6 5.Nf3 0-0 6.Bd3 d5 7.0-0 dc4 8.Bc4 Bd6 9.Nb5** [9.Bb5 e5 ∞] **Be7 10.h3 a6 11.Nc3 b5** [Queenside space] **12.Bd3 Bb7 13.Qe2 Bd6 14.Rd1 Qe7 15.Bb1 e5 16.d5 Nd8 17.Ng5 h6 18.Nge4 Ne4 19.Ne4 f5 20.Nd6 cd6 21.a4 ba4 22.Ra4 Rf6 23.Rc4 e4 24.b4 Nf7 25.Bb2 Rg6?** [25...Ne5 =] **26.f4! ef3 27.Qf3 Rf8** [D] **28.Bf5 Ng5 29.Qh5 Rf5 30.Qg6 Nh3 31.Kh2 Rg5 32.Re4! Qf8 33.Qe8 1-0**

After 14.Bg5

284) Fischer,R-Tal,M [11/1/60] Leipzig Olympiad Final C17/18 French **1.e4 e6 2.d4 d5 3.Nc3 Bb4 4.e5 c5 5.a3 Ba5** [5...Bc3] **6.b4! cd4 7.Qg4 Ne7 8.ba5 dc3 9.Qg7 Rg8 10.Qh7 Nbc6! 11.Nf3 Qc7 12.Bb5! Bd7 13.0-0 0-0-0 14.Bg5** [14.Bc6! Bc6 15.Qf7 +-] [D] **Ne5! 15.Ne5! Bb5 16.Nf7 Bf1 17.Nd8 Rg5 18.Ne6 Rg2! 19.Kh1! Qe5 20.Rf1 Qe6 21.Kg2 Qg4 1/2-1/2**

After 19.b3

285) Szabo,L-Fischer,R [11/2/60] Leipzig Olympiad Final E70/17 King's Indian **1.d4 Nf6 2.c4 g6 3.Nc3 Bg7 4.e4 0-0 5.Bg5 d6 6.Qd2 c5! 7.d5 e6 8.Bd3** [8.f3 +=/=] **ed5 9.Nd5?!** [9.cd5 or 9.ed5] **Be6 10.Ne2 Bd5 11.ed5 Nbd7 12.0-0 Ne5 13.f4?** [Weakens e3 and e4] **Nd3 14.Qd3 h6 15.Bh4 Re8 16.Rae1 Qb6! 17.Bf6 Bf6 18.f5 g5 19.b3** [D] **Qa5! 20.Rc1?** [20.Qb1] **Qa2 21.Rc2 Re3 22.Qe3 Qc2 23.Kh1 a5 24.h4 a4 0-1**

286) Fischer,R-Euwe,M [11/3/60] Leipzig Olympiad Final
B13/08 Caro Kann [E:Rook + Bishop vs. Rook + Bishop] **1.e4 c6 2.d4
d5 3.ed5 cd5 4.c4** [The Panov Attack] **Nf6 5.Nc3 Nc6 6.Nf3 Bg4 7.cd5**
[**7.Bg5**] **Nd5 8.Qb3 Bf3 9.gf3 e6 10.Qb7 Nd4 11.Bb5 Nb5 12.Qc6
Ke7 13.Qb5 Nc3** [13...Qd7 14.Nd5 Qd5 =] **14.bc3 Qd7** [14...f6! ∞]
**15.Rb1! Rd8? 16.Be3 Qb5 17.Rb5 Rd7 18.Ke2 f6 19.Rd1! Rd1
20.Kd1 Kd7 21.Rb8 Kc6 22.Ba7 g5 23.a4 Bg7 24.Rb6 Kd5 25.Rb7
Bf8 26.Rb8 Bg7 27.Rb5 Kc6 28.Rb6 Kd5 29.a5 f5 30.Bb8! Rc8 31.a6
Rc3 32.Rb5 Kc4 33.Rb7** [33.Ra5? Bd4 34.a7 Ba7 35.Ra7 Rf3 =] **Bd4
34.Rc7 Kd3 35.Rc3 Kc3** [D] **36.Be5 1-0**

After 35...Kc3

287) Fischer,R-Najdorf,M [11/4/60] Leipzig Olympiad Final
B81/15 Sicilian [E:Rook + minor piece] **1.e4 c5 2.Nf3 d6 3.d4 cd4
4.Nd4 Nf6 5.Nc3 e6 6.g4** [The Keres Attack] **a6** [6...h6 or 6...Nc6]
7.g5 Nfd7 8.Be3 b5 [8...Be7 9.Qh5 +=] **9.a3 Bb7 10.Qd2 Be7 11.h4
Nc5 12.f3 Qc7 13.0-0-0 Nbd7** [13...Nc6 14.Nc6 +=] [D] **14.Bb5!**
[Three pawns and the initiative] **ab5 15.Ndb5 Qc6 16.Nd6 Bd6
17.Qd6 0-0-0?** [17...Qd6] **18.Qc6 Bc6 19.b4! Na4! 20.Rd6! Kc7
21.Rc6 Kc6 22.Na4 Ra8 23.Nc3 Ra3 24.Kb2 Rha8 25.f4 Nb6
26.Bb6 Kb6 27.Rd1 R3a7 28.Rd6 Kb7 29.h5 h6 30.gh6 gh6 31.f5
Re8 32.Nb5 Ra4 33.c3 ef5 34.Rf6 Re7! 35.Nd6 Kb8 36.ef5 Ra6
37.Rh6 Kc7 38.Nb5 Kb7 39.Nd6 Kc7 40.Nb5 Kb7 41.Rh7 Rf6
42.Nd4 Re4 43.Kc2 Re3 44.Kb3 Re4 45.Rh8 Rh4 46.Re8 Rh5
47.Re7 Kc8 48.Kc4 Rh3 49.b5 Rg3 50.Nc6 Rf5 51.Na7 Kd8
52.Nc6 Kc8 53.Re4 Kc7 54.Nd4 Rf1 55.Re7 Kb6 56.Rd7 Rc1
57.Rd6 Kb7 58.Ne2 Rg4 59.Nd4 Rg3 1/2-1/2**

After 13...Nbd7

288) Unzicker,W-Fischer,R [11/5/60] Leipzig Olympiad Final
C65/14 Ruy Lopez **1.e4 e5 2.Nf3 Nc6 3.Bb5 Bc5 4.c3 Nf6 5.d4 Bb6**
[5...ed4] **6.0-0** [6.Qe2! +-] **0-0 7.Re1 ed4 8.cd4 d5 9.e5 Ne4 10.Nc3
Bg4 11.Bc6 bc6 12.Ne4 de4 13.Re4 Bf3 14.Qf3 Bd4 15.Be3 Bb2
16.Rb1 f5 17.ef6** [D] **1/2-1/2**

Final position

289) Fischer,R-Pachman,L [11/6/60] Leipzig Olympiad Final
C11/20 French [E:Queen + Rook vs. Queen + Rook] **1.e4 e6 2.d4
d5 3.Nc3 Nf6 4.Bg5 de4 5.Ne4 Be7 6.Bf6 Bf6 7.Nf3 Nd7 8.Bc4**
[8.Qd2 b6 9.Bb5 +=] **0-0 9.0-0 c6 10.Qe2 b6 11.Rad1 Qc7 12.Nf6
Nf6 13.Qe5!** += **Qe7** [13...Qe5 14.de5 +-] **14.c3 Bb7 15.Rfe1 Rfd8
16.Ng5 h6 17.Ne4 Ne4 18.Re4 Qd6** [18...c5? 19.d5] **19.Qh5 c5
20.Rg4 Kf8 21.Rd3 cd4 22.Rgd4 Qc7 23.Qh4 Rd4 24.Qd4 Re8!
25.Bb5 Bc6 26.a4 Bb5 27.ab5 f6 28.c4 Rc8 29.b3 Re8 30.f4 Ke7
31.h3 Rc8 32.Kf1 Ra8 33.Kg1 a5 34.Qe4 Rd8 35.Rg3 Kf7** [D]
36.Qh7! Rg8 37.Qg6 Ke7?? [37...Kf8 =] **38.Qg7 Rg7 39.Rg7 Kd6
40.Rc7 Kc7 41.g4 Kd6 42.h4! e5 43.g5 1-0**

After 35...Kf7

Final position

290) Uhlmann,W-Fischer,R [11/8/60] Leipzig Olympiad Final E79/04 King's Indian [E:Bishop vs. Knight] **1.d4 Nf6 2.c4 g6 3.Nc3 Bg7 4.e4 0-0 5.Be2 d6 6.f4 c5 7.Nf3** [7.d5] **cd4 8.Nd4 Nc6 9.Be3 Ng4** [9...Nd4 or 9...e5] **10.Bg4 Bd4** [10...Bg4? 11.Nc6 Qd7 12.Ne7 +-] **11.Bd4 Bg4 12.Qd2** [12.Qg4 +=] **Nd4 13.Qd4 e5! 14.fe5 Qh4 15.Qf2** [15.g3 Qh3] **Qf2 16.Kf2 de5 17.Rac1 Rad8 18.Nd5 Be6 19.Rhd1 f5 20.ef5 gf5 21.Rd2 Kf7 22.Rcd1 Rd7 23.Nc3 Rfd8 24.Rd7 Rd7 25.Rd7 Bd7 26.b4 b6 27.a4 Be6 28.c5 bc5 29.bc5 Ke7 30.Kg3 Kd7 31.Kh4 Kc6 32.Kg5 e4 33.g4 fg4 34.Ne4 a5 35.Kf4 Bb3 36.Ke3 Ba4 37.Kd2 h6 38.Nf6 Kc5 39.Ng4 h5 40.Ne3 Kd4 41.Nf1 Ke5 42.Ke3 Bb3 43.Ng3 [D] 0-1**

After 32...e4?

291) Fischer,R-Weinstein,R [12/18/60] US Championship [1] C19/14 French **1.e4 e6 2.d4 d5 3.Nc3 Bb4 4.e5 Ne7 5.a3 Bc3 6.bc3 c5 7.a4 Nbc6 8.Nf3 Qa5 9.Qd2 Bd7 10.Bd3 c4 11.Be2 0-0-0 12.Ba3 f6 13.0-0 Nf5 14.Rfe1?!** [14.g4!] **Be8?** [14...h5 to stop g4] **15.g4 Nfe7 16.Bf1 Bd7 17.Bh3 h6 18.Bd6 Rdf8 19.Rab1 Rf7 20.ef6 gf6 21.Bg3 Ng6 22.Rb5 Qa6 23.Reb1 b6 24.Qc1?** [24.Nh4] **Qa4 25.R5b2 Qa3! 26.Qe3 Kb7 27.Nh4 Nh4 28.Bh4 e5?** [28...Ka8] **29.de5 fe5? 30.Rb6 Ka8 31.R6b5 Be6 32.Bg3 e4? [D] 33.Qh6 1-0** [33...Rh6 Rb8; 33...Re8 34.Qe6]

Final position

292) Lombardy,W-Fischer,R [12/19/60] US Championship [2] B54/04 Sicilian [E:King + pawn] **1.e4 c5 2.Nf3 d6 3.d4 cd4 4.Nd4 Nf6 5.f3 Nc6 6.c4 e6 7.Nc3 Be7 8.Be3 0-0 9.Nc2 d5!?** [Breaking the Maroczy bind with a pawn sacrifice for counterplay] **10.cd5 ed5 11.Nd5 Nd5 12.Qd5 Qc7!? 13.Qb5** [13.Be2 =] **Bd7 14.Rc1 Nb4! 15.Nb4 Qc1 16.Bc1 Bb5 17.Nd5 Bh4! 18.g3 Bf1 19.Kf1 Bd8 20.Bd2 Rc8 21.Bc3 f5! 22.e5 Rc5 23.Nb4 Ba5 24.a3 Bb4 25.ab4 Rd5 26.Ke2 Kf7 27.h4 Ke6 28.Ke3 Rc8 29.Rg1 Rc4 30.Re1?** [30.Ra1] **Rc3! ** [Entering a won King and pawn ending] **31.bc3 Re5 32.Kd2 Re1 33.Ke1 Kd5 34.Kd2 Kc4 35.h5 b6 36.Kc2 g5 37.h6 f4 38.g4 a5 39.ba5 ba5 40.Kb2 a4 41.Ka3 Kc3 42.Ka4 Kd4 43.Kb4 Ke3 [D] 0-1**

Final position

293) Fischer,R-Kalme,C [12/20/60] US Championship [3] C92/13 Ruy Lopez [E:Minor piece] **1.e4 e5 2.Nf3 Nc6 3.Bb5 a6 4.Ba4 Nf6 5.0-0 Be7 6.Re1 b5 7.Bb3 0-0 8.c3 d6 9.h3 Nd7 10.a4 Nc5?** [10...Bb7] **11.Bd5** [11.ab5! Nb3 12.Qb3 Rb8 13.Qc4 +-] **Bb7 12.ab5 ab5 13.Ra8 Qa8 14.d4 Nd7 15.Na3 b4 16.Nc4 ed4 17.cd4 Nf6 18.Bg5 Qd8 19.Qa4 Qa8 20.Qa8 Ra8 21.Bf6 Bf6 22.e5 de5 23.Nfe5 Ne5 24.Bb7 Nd3 25.Ba8 Ne1 26.Be4 b3 27.Nd2 [D] 1/2-1/2**

294) Reshevsky,S-Fischer,R [12/22/60] US Championship [4]
E97/02 King's Indian **1.d4 Nf6 2.c4 g6 3.Nc3 Bg7 4.e4 0-0 5.Nf3
d6 6.Be2 e5 7.0-0 Nc6 8.Be3 Ng4 9.Bg5 Bf6?!** [9...f6] **10.Bf6 Nf6
11.d5 Ne7 12.Ne1 Ne8 13.f4 ef4 14.Rf4 f5 15.ef5 Nf5 16.Qd2 Qe7
17.Nc2 Bd7 18.Raf1 Neg7 19.Re4 Qd8 20.g4 Nh4 21.Rf8 Qf8
22.Nd4** [22.Qg5!] **c5! = 23.dc6 Bc6 24.Nd5 Bd5 [D] 1/2-1/2**

Final position

295) Fischer,R-Berliner,H [12/23/60] US Championship [5]
B03/04 Alekhine's **1.e4 Nf6 2.e5 Nd5 3.d4 d6 4.c4 Nb6 5.ed6** [5.f4]
cd6 [5...ed6] **6.Nc3 g6 7.Bd3 Bg7 8.Nge2 Nc6 9.Be3 0-0 10.0-0
e5?!** [10...Bg4 =] **11.d5 Ne7 12.b3 Nd7 13.Ne4 Nf5 14.Bg5 f6
15.Bd2 Nc5 16.Nc5 dc5 17.Bf5! Bf5 18.f4 ef4 19.Nf4 Qd6 [D]
20.Nh5! Rae8 21.Ng7 Kg7 22.Bf4 Qd7 23.Qd2 Rf7 24.Bh6 Kg8
25.Rae1 Rfe7 26.Re7 Qe7 27.h3 Qe4 28.Qf2 Qe7 29.g4! Bd3
30.Rd1 Be4 31.d6 Qe5 32.Bf4 Qc3 33.d7 Rd8 34.Qe2 Qf3 35.Qf3
Bf3 36.Bc7! 1-0**

After 19...Qd6

296) Fischer,R-Seidman,H [12/26/60] US Championship [6]
C89/03 Ruy Lopez [E:Queen vs. Rooks] **1.e4 e5 2.Nf3 Nc6 3.Bb5
a6 4.Ba4 Nf6 5.0-0 Be7 6.Re1 b5 7.Bb3 0-0 8.c3 d5 9.ed5 e4 10.dc6
ef3 11.Qf3?!** [11.d4!] **Bg4 12.Qg3 Bd6 13.f4 g5?** [13...Re8] **14.d4
Kh8 [D] 15.Re5 gf4 16.Bf4 Nh5?** [16...Rg8] **17.Rh5 Bh5 18.Nd2
Re8 19.Rf1 Re2 20.Bd1! Rd2 21.Bh5 f6 22.Re1 Bf4 23.Qf4 Rb2
24.Re8 Qe8 25.Be8 Re8 26.h3 b4 27.cb4 Rb4 28.Qf6 Kg8 29.Qg5
Kh8 30.Qf4 Ra4 31.Qf7 Rg8 32.Qc7 Ra2 33.Qe5 Rg7 34.g4 h6
35.Qb8 Rg8 36.c7! 1-0**

After 14...Kh8

297) Byrne,R-Fischer,R [12/27/60] US Championship [7]
E62/20 King's Indian **1.d4 Nf6 2.c4 g6 3.g3 Bg7 4.Bg2 0-0 5.Nc3
d6 6.Nf3 Nc6 7.0-0 e5** [7...a6] **8.d5 Ne7 9.a4** [Planning a5, cramping
the Queenside] **a5 10.c5** [Opening up the Queenside] **e4**
[Counterattacking in the center] **11.Ng5 dc5 12.Nce4 Ne4 13.Ne4
b6 14.Nc3 Ba6! 15.d6 cd6 16.Ba8 Qa8 17.Qd6 Nf5 18.Qb6 Nd4
19.Re1 Rb8 20.Qc7 Rb7 21.Qd6 Nc2 22.Bf4 Na1 23.Ra1 Rb2
24.Qc5 [D] 1/2-1/2**

Final position

298) Fischer,R-Sherwin,J [12/28/60] US Championship [8]
C19/14 French **1.e4 e6 2.d4 d5 3.Nc3 Bb4 4.e5 c5 5.a3 Bc3 6.bc3
Ne7 7.a4 Nbc6 8.Nf3 Bd7 9.Bd3 Qa5 10.Qd2 c4 11.Be2 f6 12.Ba3
Ng6 13.0-0 0-0-0 14.Bd6 Rde8 15.Rfe1 ∞** [White has more space
and the two Bishops; Black has the better pawn structure] **h5 16.h4
Nd8 17.Bf1 Nf7 18.Bb4 Qc7 19.Qe2 a5 20.Ba3 Ba4 21.Bf8 Rhf8
22.Ra4 Nd8 23.g3 b5 24.Ra2 Nc6 25.ef6 gf6 26.Bh3 Kb8 27.Qd1
Ka7 28.Be6 Qd6 29.Bf5 Re1 30.Ne1 Nge7 31.Qh5 Nf5 32.Qf5
Re8 33.Ng2 ++- Qe6 34.Qh5 f5 35.Ra1 Qd7 36.Ne3 Rf8 37.Qf3
f4 38.Nd5 fg3 39.Qf8 gf2 40.Kf2 Qd5 [D] 1-0**

Final position

After 32.c6

299) Saidy,A-Fischer,R [12/29/60] US Championship [9] E46/32 Nimzo-Indian [E:Rook + pawn] **1.d4 Nf6 2.c4 e6 3.Nc3 Bb4 4.e3 0-0 5.Ne2 d5 6.a3 Bd6?!** [Allowing c5 with tempo; correct is 6...Be7] **7.c5 Be7 8.b4 b6 9.Nf4 bc5 10.bc5 Ba6 11.Ba6 Na6 12.0-0 Nb8 13.Bd2 Nc6 14.Qa4 Qd7 15.Nd3 a5** [Stopping Nb4, but weakening] **16.f3 Rfd8 17.Rfb1 Ne8 18.f4 Nf6 19.Rb7 Ne4 20.Be1 g5 21.Ne5 Ne5 22.fe5 Qa4 23.Na4 Rdc8 24.Rab1 Kf8 25.R1b5 Ke8 26.Nb2 a4 27.Kf1 f6 28.Nd3 fe5 29.Ne5 Bf6 30.Nc6 Kd7 31.Na7 Rf8 32.c6** [D] **Ke8 33.Ke2 Bd8 34.Ra5 Rf6 35.Nb5 Ra5 36.Ba5 Rf2 37.Ke1 Rb2 38.Rb8 Kf7 39.Rd8 Rb5 40.Bc7?** [40.Rd7 +-] **Rb1 41.Ke2 Rc1 42.Rd7 Kg6 43.Be5 Rc6 44.Rg7 Kh6 45.Ke1 Rc2 46.g4 Nf2 47.h3 Nd3 48.Kd1 Rc3! 49.Kd2 Ra3 50.Re7 Ne5 51.de5 Ra1 52.Re6 Kg7 53.Ra6 a3 54.Kc2 Kf7 55.Rh6 Re1 56.Rh7 Ke6 57.Kb3 Re3 58.Ka2 d4 59.Ra7 Rh3 0-1**

Final position

300) Fischer,R-Benko,P [1/2/61] US Championship [10] B36/00 Sicilian **1.e4 c5 2.Nf3 Nc6 3.d4 cd4 4.Nd4 g6 5.c4 Nf6 6.Nc3 Nd4 7.Qd4 d6 8.Be2** [8.Bg5 +=] **Bg7 9.Be3 0-0 10.Qd2 Be6 11.0-0 Qa5 12.f4 Rfc8** [A Grandmaster draw-extremely rare for Bobby Fischer] **[D] 1/2-1/2**

After 29.Rd1

301) Bisguier,A-Fischer,R [1/3/61] US Championship [11] E90/04 King's Indian [E:Queen vs. Rooks + Knight] **1.d4 Nf6 2.c4 g6 3.Nc3 Bg7 4.Nf3 0-0 5.Bf4** [Offbeat but playable] **c5 6.d5** [6.e3] **d6 7.e4 Qa5 8.Bd3 Bg4!** [Developing and controlling e5] **9.0-0 Nbd7 10.h3 Bf3 11.Qf3 Ne5 12.Qe2 Nd3 13.Qd3 a6 14.Bd2 Nd7 15.b3 Qc7 16.f4 b5! 17.cb5 Qb6 18.Kh2 ab5 19.Nb5 Ba1 20.Ra1 Rfc8 21.Qc4 Qa6 22.a4 Nb6 23.Qc2 c4 24.b4 c3! 25.Nc3** [25.Bc3 Na4] **Qc4 26.b5 Qd4 27.Be1 Nc4 28.Qf2 Ne3 29.Rd1** [D] **Qc3! -++ 30.Bc3 Nd1 31.Qd4 Nc3 32.b6 Rc5 33.e5 Ra4 34.b7 Rd4 35.b8=Q Kg7 36.ed6 ed6 37.Qd6 Rcd5 38.Qc7 Ne2 39.f5 Rf5 40.Qa7 Rfd5 41.Qa1 Nf4 0-1**

1961

302) Reshevsky,S-Fischer,R [7/16/61] Match, New York [1]
E97/02 King's Indian [E:Rook + pawn] **1.d4 Nf6 2.c4 g6 3.Nc3 Bg7
4.e4 d6 5.Be2 0-0 6.Nf3 e5 7.0-0 Nc6 8.Be3** [8.d5] **Ng4 9.Bg5 Bf6?!**
[To trade the "bad" Bishop, but it isn't "bad". Correct was
9...f6]**10.Bf6 Nf6 11.d5 Ne7 12.Ne1 Nd7 13.Nd3 f5 14.ef5 gf5 15.f4
Ng6 16.Qd2 Re8 17.fe5 Nde5** +=/+- [Isolated f-pawn and more
space] **18.Ne5 Re5 19.Nb5! Bd7 20.Bd3 Bb5 21.cb5 Qd7 22.Qf2
f4** [Conceding the f-pawn and hoping for drawing chances in a Rook
and pawn ending] **[D] 23.Bg6 hg6 24.Qf4 Rae8 25.Rad1 Qg7
26.h3 R5e7 27.Rd2 Re4 28.Qf2 b6 29.a3 R8e5 30.Qf5 Qf6 31.Rf6
Kg7 32.Rff2 Kh6 33.Kh2 Rc4 34.Rc2 Rc2 35.Rc2 Rd5 36.a4! Rd4
37.b3 Rd3 38.Rc7 Rb3 39.Ra7 d5 40.Rd7 Rd3 41.Rd6 Rd4
42.Rb6 Ra4 43.Kg3 Rb4 44.Rb8 d4 45.Kf3 Rb3 46.Ke4 d3
47.Ke3 g5 48.Rb6 Kg7 49.Kd2 Kf7 50.g3 Rb2? 51.Kd3 Rb3
52.Kc4 Rg3 53.Rh6 Kg7 54.Rc6 Rh3 55.b6 Rh1 56.Kb5 Rb1
57.Ka6 Ra1 58.Kb7 g4 59.Kc8 Ra6 60.Kc7 1-0**

After 22...f4

303) Fischer,R-Reshevsky,S [7/61] Match, New York [2]
B72/08 Sicilian **1.e4 c5 2.Nf3 Nc6 3.d4 cd4 4.Nd4 g6 5.Nc3 Bg7
6.Be3 Nf6 7.Be2 0-0 8.f4 d6 9.Nb3 Be6 10.g4 d5 11.f5 Bc8 12.ed5
Nb4 13.Bf3! gf5 14.a3 fg4 15.Bg2! Na6 16.Qd3! e6 17.0-0-0 Nd5
18.h3 g3** [Keeping lines closed] **19.Rhg1 Qd6! 20.Bd5 ed5
21.Nd5?** [21.Bd4!] **Kh8 22.Bf4 Qg6 23.Qd2 Bh3! 24.Rg3 Bg4
25.Rh1 Rfe8 26.Ne3 Qe4? [26...f5 ∞] 27.Qh2! Be6 [D] 28.Rg7!
Kg7 29.Qh6 Kg8 30.Rg1 Qg6 31.Rg6 fg6 32.Nd4 Rad8 33.Be5
Rd7 34.Ne6 Re6 35.Ng4 Rf7 36.Qg5 Rf1 37.Kd2 h5 38.Qd8 1-0**

After 27...Be6

304) Reshevsky,S-Fischer,R [7/61] Match, New York [3]
E49/09 Nimzo-Indian **1.d4 Nf6 2.c4 e6 3.Nc3 Bb4 4.e3 d5 5.a3 Bc3
6.bc3 0-0 7.cd5 ed5 8.Bd3 c5 9.Ne2 Nc6 10.0-0 Bg4 11.f3 Bh5
12.Rb1 b6 13.Nf4 Bg6 14.g4 cd4! 15.cd4 Rc8 16.Rb2 Bd3 17.Qd3
Ne7 18.g5 Ne8 19.e4 Ng6 20.Ne2 f6? [20...de4 21.fe4 Ne5 22.Qg3
Nc4] 21.gf6 Nf6 22.e5 Nh5 23.f4 Qh4 24.Qf3 Kh8 25.Be3! ∞**
[Agreed drawn in a very unclear position] **[D] 1/2-1/2**

Final position

305) Fischer,R-Reshevsky,S [7/61] Match, New York [4]
B35/13 Sicilian [E:Rook + minor piece] **1.e4 c5 2.Nf3 Nc6 3.d4 cd4
4.Nd4 g6 5.Be3 Bg7 6.Nc3 Nf6 7.Bc4 0-0 8.Bb3 Ng4 9.Qg4 Nd4
10.Qd1 Nb3 11.ab3 b6 12.Qd5** [12.Bd4 f6 13. Qd3 Bb7 14.0-0-0
Bc6 15.h4 +-] **Bc3! 13.bc3 Qc7 14.0-0-0 Qc3! 15.Bd4 Qc6 16.Qe5
f6 17.Qe7 Bb7 18.f3 a5 [D] 19.Bb6 Rac8 20.c4 Rfe8 21.Qd6 a4
22.Qc6 Bc6 23.b4 f5 24.ef5 gf5 25.Kb2 Re2 26.Kc3 Rg2 27.Rhg1
Rg1 28.Rg1 Kf7 29.f4 Bd5 30.Bc5 Be6 31.Rd1 a3 32.Kb3 a2
33.Ka2 Bc4 34.Kb2 Be6 35.Kc3 Rc6 36.Rd3 d6 37.Rd6 Rd6
38.Bd6 Bd5 39.b5 Ke6 40.Bb8 Be4 41.Kd4 Bh1 42.h4 h5 1/2-1/2**

After 18...a5

After 23.Kg2

306) Reshevsky,S-Fischer,R [7/27/61] Match,Los Angeles [5] D42/11 Queen's Gambit Declined [E:Rook + pawn] **1.d4 Nf6 2.c4 e6 3.Nc3 d5 4.cd5 Nd5 5.Nf3 c5 6.e3 Nc6 7.Bd3 Be7 8.0-0 0-0 9.a3 cd4 10.ed4 Nf6** [10...Bf6] **11.Bc2 b6 12.Qd3 Bb7 13.Bg5 g6 14.Rfe1 Re8 15.h4 Rc8 16.Rac1 Nd5 17.Ne4 f5 18.Nc3 Bg5 19.Ng5! Nf4 20.Qe3 Qd4 21.Nb5 Qe3 22.fe3 Ng2 23.Kg2** [D] **Nd4 24.Be4! Be4 25.Ne4 Nb5 26.Nf6 Kf7 27.Ne8 Re8 28.a4! Nd6 29.Rc7 Kf6 30.Rec1! h6 31.Ra7 Ne4 32.Ra6 Rd8! 33.Rc2?** [33.Rb6 +-] **Rd3 34.Rb6 Re3 35.a5 f4 36.Rf2?** [36.a6!] **Nf2 37.Kf2 Re5! 38.b4 Re3! 39.a6 Ra3 40.Rc6 g5 41.hg5 hg5 42.b5 g4 43.Rc8 Kf5 44.b6 g3 45.Ke1 Ra1 46.Ke2 g2 47.Rf8 Ke4 48.Rf4 Kf4 49.b7 g1=Q 50.b8=Q Kf5 51.Qf8 Ke4 52.Qa8 Kd4 53.Qd8 Kc4 54.Qd3 Kc5 55.Qc3 Kd6 56.Qd2 Ke5 57.Qb2 Kf5 0-1**

Final position

307) Fischer,R-Reshevsky,S [7/30/61] Match, Los Angeles [6] B35/13 Sicilian **1.e4 c5 2.Nf3 Nc6 3.d4 cd4 4.Nd4 g6 5.Nc3 Bg7 6.Be3 Nf6 7.Bc4 0-0 8.Bb3 Ng4 9.Qg4 Nd4 10.Qh4** [Best was 10.Qd1] **Qa5 11.0-0 Bf6!** 12.Qg4 [12.Qg3 Qc3! 13.bc3 Ne2] **d6 13.Qd1 Nc6 14.Qd3?!** [14.Bd2] **b6! 15.Qd2 Ba6 16.Rfd1 Bc3 17.bc3 Ne5 18.Bd4 Nc6 19.Qh6 Nd4 20.cd4 Rac8 21.Re1 e5 22.de5 Qe5 23.Rad1 Bc4 24.Qd2 Bb3 25.cb3 Rc6** [D] **1/2-1/2**

After 27...Qa3

308) Reshevsky,S-Fischer,R [8/1/61] Match, Los Angeles [7] E51/09 Queen's Gambit Declined **1.d4 d5 2.Nf3 Nf6 3.c4 e6 4.Nc3 Bb4 5.e3 0-0 6.Bd3 Nc6 7.a3 Bc3?** [7...dc4 =] **8.bc3 Na5 9.Nd2 c5 10.0-0 b6 11.cd5 ed5 12.f3** +=/+- [White will expand in the center] **Re8 13.Re1 Be6 14.Ra2 Rc8 15.Nf1 cd4 16.cd4 h5?** [16...Qd7] **17.h3 h4 18.Rf2 Qd7 19.e4! de4 20.fe4 Bb3 21.Qd2 Bc4 22.Bc2 Nb3 23.Bb3 Bb3 24.e5 Nd5 25.Qg5 Qe7 26.Qg4 Rc6 27.Bg5 Qa3** [D] **28.Qd7! 1-0**

After 26...Bc3?

309) Fischer,R-Reshevsky,S [8/3/61] Match, Los Angeles [8] B36/12 Sicilian [E:Rook + minor piece] **1.e4 c5 2.Nf3 Nc6 3.d4 cd4 4.Nd4 g6 5.c4 Nf6 6.Nc3 Nd4 7.Qd4 d6 8.Be2** [8.Bg5 Bg7 9.Qd2 Be6 10.Rc1 +=] **Bg7 9.Be3 0-0 10.Qd2 Be6 11.0-0 Qa5 12.Rac1 Rfc8 13.b3 a6 14.f4 Bg4 15.Bd3 Bd7 16.h3 Bc6 17.Qf2 Nd7 18.Nd5 Bd5 19.ed5 Bc3 20.Rfe1 Nc5 21.Bb1 bc4 22.Rc4 Nd7 23.Bd2 Qb6 24.Rc8 Rc8 25.Qb6 Nb6 26.Re7 Bc3?** [D] **27.Bc3 Nd5 28.Rd7 Nc3 29.Bd3 d5 30.Ba6 Ra8 31.Rd6 Na2 32.Bb7 Rb8 33.Bd5 Nc1 34.f5 gf5 35.Rf6 Nb3 36.Rf5 Kh8 37.Rf7 Nc5 38.Rc7 Na6 39.Rc4 Rd8 40.Be6 Rd6 41.Bf5 Rf6 42.Bd3 h6 43.Kh2 Kg7 44.Kg3 Nb8?** [44...Rd6] **45.Be4??** [45.Rd7 ++-] **Rf7 46.Bd5 Rd7 47.Bf3 Rf7 48.Bh5 Ra7 49.Rg4 Kh8 50.Re4 Kg7 51.Re6 Na6 52.Rg6 Kh7 53.Rd6 Nc5 54.Bg6 Kg7 55.Bf5 Ra6 56.Rd5 Ne6 57.Re5 Ra3 58.Kf2 Nf4 59.Re4 Nd5 60.Rg4 Kf6 61.Be4 Ne7 62.Rf4 Kg7 63.Bf3 Ra5 64.Rc4 Re5 65.Kg3 Re6 66.Rc7 Kf6 67.Kg4 Re5 68.h4 Rb5 69.Rc4 Rb6 70.Be4 Kf7 71.Rc7 Kf6 72.Kh5 Rb5! 73.Kg4 Rb4 74.Kf3 Rb3 75.Kf2 Rb4 76.Ke3 Rb3 77.Kf4 Ng6 78.Kg4 Rb4 79.Rc6 Kf7** [D] **1/2-1/2**

Final position

310) Reshevsky,S-Fischer,R [8/6/61] Match, Los Angeles [9] E97/01 King's Indian [E:Bishop + pawn] **1.c4 Nf6 2.d4 g6 3.Nc3 Bg7 4.e4 0-0 5.Be2 d6 6.Nf3 e5 7.0-0 Nc6 8.Be3** [8.d5] **Re8! 9.de5 de5 10.Qd8 Nd8! 11.Nb5 Ne6 12.Ng5 Re7! 13.Rfd1 c6** [13...b6 =] **14.Ne6 Be6 15.Nc3 Rd7 = 16.Rd7 Bd7 17.Rb1 Ng4 18.Bd2 Be6 19.f3 Nf6 20.Be3 Bf8 21.Rd1 Nd7!** [To trade the "bad" Bg7 for the "good" Be3 via c5] **22.Na4! f6 23.h4 Be7 24.g3 Kf8 25.Kg2 Ke8 26.Kf2 Bf7 27.Kg2 Rc8 28.f4 ef4 29.gf4 f5 30.ef5 gf5 31.b3 Ra8 32.Bd3 Be6 33.Nc3 Kf7 34.Ne2 Nc5 35.Bc2 Ne4 36.Kf3 Rg8! 37.Rg1 Rg1 38.Bg1 Bh4 39.Ba7 h5 40.Nd4! Nd6 41.Bb8! Bf6! 42.Ke3 Bd4 43.Kd4 Ne4 44.Be4 fe4 45.Ke4 Kg6** [D] **46.f5! Bf5 47.Kd4 Bb1 48.a3 Bc2 49.b4 b5 50.Kc5 Ba4 51.cb5 cb5 52.Kd4 1/2-1/2**

After 45...Kg6

311) Fischer,R-Reshevsky,S [8/8/61] Match, Los Angeles [10] B36/11 Sicilian [E:Rook + pawn] **1.e4 c5 2.Nf3 Nc6 3.d4 cd4 4.Nd4 g6 5.c4 Nf6 6.Nc3 Nd4 7.Qd4 d6 8.Be2 Bg7 9.Be3 0-0 10.Qd1 Bd7 11.0-0 Bc6 12.f3 Nd7 13.Qd2 Rc8 14.Rac1 a5!** [Securing c5 for the Knight] **15.Kh1 Nc5 16.b3 Qb6 17.Nd5 Bd5 18.cd5 Qb4! 19.Qb4 ab4 20.Bd2 Ra8 21.Rc2 Bc3 22.Bc3 bc3 23.b4 Na4 24.a3 f5 25.Bb5** [D] **fe4 26.fe4 Rf1 27.Bf1 Kg7 28.Bb5 Kf6! 29.Ba4 Ra4 30.Rc3 Ke5 31.Rc7 Kf6 32.Rc3 Ke5 33.Kg1 Ke4 34.Rc7 Kd5 35.Re7 b5! 36.Rh7 Ra3 37.Rg7 Rb3 38.Rg6 Rb4 39.Rg5 Ke6 40.Kf2 d5 1/2-1/2**

After 25.Bb5

312) Reshevsky,S-Fischer,R [8/10/61] Match, Los Angeles [11] E98/04 King's Indian [E:Rook + Bishop vs. Rooks] **1.c4 Nf6 2.d4 g6 3.Nc3 Bg7 4.e4 0-0 5.Be2 d6 6.Nf3 e5 7.0-0 Nc6 8.d5 Ne7 9.Ne1 Nd7 10.Nd3 f5 11.ef5 Nf5** [11...gf5] **12.f3 Nd4** [To obtain the two Bishops] **13.Ne4 b6 14.Bg5?** [Chases Black's Queen to a good square; Correct was 14.Bd2] **Qe8 15.Bd2 a5 16.Re1 Ne2 17.Qe2 h6 18.b3 g5 19.a3 Qg6 20.b4 Nf6 21.ba5?** [21.Ndf2] **g4! 22.Ndf2 gf3 23.Qf3 Nh5 24.Qe3 ba5 25.Rac1 Bf5 26.c5 Nf4 27.Qg3 Be4! 28.Re4** [28.Ne4] [D] **Qe4! 29.Ne4 Ne2 30.Kh1 Ng3 31.hg3 Ra6 32.cd6 cd6 33.a4 Rf7 34.g4 Bf8 35.Kh2 Kh7 36.Rc8 Rb6 37.Ra8 Rb3 38.Ba5 Rf4?** [38...Re3] **39.Bc7! Re4 40.Rf8 Rd3 41.Rf6 Rg4 42.Rd6 Rg7** [42...Rd2] **43.Rc6! Rd5 44.Rc2! e4 45.a5 Rd3 46.Bf4 Rf7 47.g3 e3 48.Rc1 Re7 49.Re1 Ra3 50.Re2 Kg6 51.Kg2 Ra5 52.Re3 Ra2 53.Kf3?** [53.Kh3] **Rb7?** [53...Re3] **54.Re6 Kf5 55.Re5 Kf6 56.Rd5 Rb3 57.Kg4 1/2-1/2**

After 28.Re4

313) Gligoric,S-Fischer,R [9/3/61] Bled [1] E98/04 King's Indian **1.d4 Nf6 2.c4 g6 3.Nc3 Bg7 4.e4 d6 5.Nf3 e5 6.Be2 e5 7.0-0 Nc6 8.d5 Ne7 9.Ne1 Nd7 10.Nd3 f5 11.ef5 Nf5** [11...gf5] **12.f3 Nf6 13.Nf2 Nd4** [13...c6!?] **14.Nfe4 Nh5 15.Bg5 Qd7** [15...Qe8 16.Nb5!] **16.g3 h6 17.Be3 c5 18.Bd4 ed4 19.Nb5 a6 20.Nbd6 d3 21.Qd3 Bd4 22.Kg2** [D] **Ng3! 23.Nc8! Nf1 24.Nb6! Qc7! 25.Rf1 Qb6 26.b4! Qb4 27.Rb1 Qa5 28.Nc5 Qc5 29.Qg6 Bg7 30.Rb7 Qd4 31.Bd3 Rf4 32.Qe6 Kh8 33.Qg6 1/2-1/2**

After 22.Kg2

After 22...e5

After 25...Nc7

After 32...Bh6

After 26.Qh7

After 8...Bg6

314) Fischer,R-Tal,M [9/4/61] Bled [2] B47/01 Sicilian [E:Queen vs.Rooks + pawns] **1.e4 c5 2.Nf3 Nc6 3.d4 cd4 4.Nd4 e6 5.Nc3 Qc7 6.g3 Nf6?** [6...a6] **7.Ndb5! Qb8 8.Bf4 Ne5 9.Be2! Bc5 10.Be5 Qe5 11.f4 Qb8 12.e5 a6 13.ef6 ab5 14.fg7 +- / ++- Rg8 15.Ne4 Be7 16.Qd4 Ra4 17.Nf6 Bf6 18.Qf6 Qc7 19.0-0-0! Ra2 20.Kb1 Ra6** [20...Qa5 21.b3 ++-] **21.Bb5 Rb6 22.Bd3 e5** [D] **23.fe5!! Rf6 24.ef6 Qc5 25.Bh7 Qg5 26.Bg8 Qf6 27.Rhf1 Qg7 28.Bf7 Kd8 29.Be6** [29.Bd5] **Qh6 30.Bd7 Bd7 31.Rf7 Qh2 32.Rdd7 Ke8 33.Rde7 Kd8 34.Rd7 Kc8 35.Rc7 Kd8 36.Rfd7 Ke8 37.Rd1 b5 38.Rb7 Qh5 39.g4 Qh3 40.g5 Qf3 41.Re1 Kf8 42.Rb5 Kg7 43.Rb6 Qg3 44.Rd1 Qc7 45.Rdd6 Qc8 46.b3 Kf7 47.Ra6 1-0**

315) Donner,J-Fischer,R [9/5/61] Bled [3] A35/06 King's Indian **1.d4 Nf6 2.c4 g6 3.g3 Bg7 4.Bg2 0-0 5.Nc3 c5 6.Nf3** [6.d5] **cd4 7.Nd4 Nc6 8.Nc2 Ng4 9.Bd2** [Black threatened 9...Bc3! smashing White's pawns] **a6 10.0-0 b5 11.h3 Nge5 12.cb5 ab5 13.b3 d5 14.Nb5 Ba6 15.a4 Bb5 16.ab5 Ra1 17.Na1 Na7 18.Bb4 d4 19.f4 Nd7 20.Qd3 Qb6 21.Rc1 Nb5 22.Rc6 Qb8 23.Nc2 Re8 24.e3 e5 25.Ra6 Nc7** [D] **26.Bd6 Nc5 27.Bc5 e4 28.Be4 Na6 29.ed4 Nc5 30.dc5 Qc8 31.c6 Qh3 32.b4 Bf8 33.Bg2 Qg4 34.Kf2 Qe6 35.Bd5 Qf6 36.Qd4 Qe7 37.Qc4 h5 38.b5 1/2-1/2**

316) Fischer,R-Olafsson,F [9/8/61] Bled [4] B35/08 Sicilian **1.e4 c5 2.Nf3 g6 3.d4 cd4 4.Nd4 Bg7 5.Nc3 Nc6 6.Be3 Nf6 7.Bc4 Qa5 8.0-0 d6 9.Nb3** [9.Bb5 Bd7 10.Nb3 Qd8 11.Be2 +=] **Qc7 10.Be2 0-0 11.f4 a5?!** [Weakens b5 and b6; 11...b6 12.Bf3 Bb7 +=] **12.a4 Nb4 13.Rf2!** [A clever means of activating the Rook] **e5 14.Bf3 Bd7 15.Rd2 Rfd8 16.Kh1! Bc6 17.Qg1 Nd7 18.f5! b6 19.Rad1 Nc5 20.Nb5 Qe7 21.Nd6 Nc2 22.Nc5 Ne3 23.Qe3 bc5 24.Be2 Ba4 25.b3 Be8 26.Bc4 a4 27.Bd5! Rd6 28.Ba8 Rd4 29.fg6 hg6 30.ba4 Ba4 31.Ra1 Qf8 32.Bd5! Bh6** [D] **33.Rd4! Be3 34.Rda4 Qh6 35.Rf1! Bf4 36.g3 Qh3 37.Raa1 Bg3 38.Ra8 1-0**

317) Parma,B-Fischer,R [9/9/61] Bled [5] B97/05 Sicilian **1.e4 c5 2.Nf3 d6 3.d4 cd4 4.Nd4 Nf6 5.Nc3 a6 6.Bg5 e6 7.f4 Qb6 8.Qd2 Qb2 9.Rb1 Qa3 10.Bf6 gf6 11.Be2 Nc6 12.Nb3 Bg7** [12...h5 13.0-0 Bd7 14.Rf3 Rc8 ∞] **13.f5 0-0 14.0-0 Ne5 15.Nd4 b5 16.Kh1 Bd7 17.Bh5 Rac8 18.Rb3 Qc5 19.Nce2** [White's strategy is to throw everything into the Kingside attack] **Nc4 20.Qc1 e5 21.Rg3! Kh8 22.Rg7!! Kg7 23.Rf3 Rg8 24.Rg3 Kf8 25.Qh6 Ke7 26.Qh7** [D] **ed4 27.Qf7** [27.Bf7!] **Kd8 28.Rg8 Kc7 29.Nf4 Qa3! 30.Nd5 Kb8 31.h3 Ne3 32.Rc8?** [32.Qd7 ++-] **Kc8 33.Ne3 Qe3 34.Bf3 Qc1 35.Kh2 Qf4 36.Kg1 Qc1 37.Kh2 Qf4 38.Kg1 Qc1 39.Kh2 Qf4 1/2-1/2**

318) Fischer,R-Geller,E [9/10/61] [6] Bled C72/04 Ruy Lopez **1.e4 e5 2.Nf3 Nc6 3.Bb5 a6 4.Ba4 d6 5.0-0 Bg4 6.h3! Bh5 7.c3 Qf6? 8.g4! Bg6** [D] **9.d4! Be4** [9...b5 10.Bg5 +-] **10.Nbd2 Bg6** [10...Bd3 11.Bc6 bc6 12.Re1 0-0-0 13.Re3 +-] **11.Bc6 bc6 12.de5 de5 13.Ne5! Bd6 14.Ng6! Qg6** [14...hg6 15.Ne4 Qe5 16.Nd6 Qd6 17.Qf3 +-] **15.Re1 Kf8 16.Nc4 h5 17.Nd6! cd6 18.Bf4 d5? 19.Qb3 hg4 20.Qb7 gh3 21.Bg3 Rd8 22.Qb4 1-0**

319) Darga,K-Fischer,R [9/13/61] Bled [7] E62/19 King's Indian **1.Nf3 Nf6 2.c4 g6 3.g3 Bg7 4.Bg2 0-0 5.0-0 d6 6.d4 Nc6 7.Nc3 e5 8.de5** [Darga forces play into drawish channels] **Ne5 9.Ne5 de5 10.Bg5 Qd1 11.Rad1 c6 12.Rd2 Be6 13.b3 Rfe8 14.Na4 Ng4 15.Nc5 h6 16.Ne6 Re6 17.h3 hg5 18.hg4** [D] 1/2-1/2

Final position

320) Fischer,R-Matanovic,A [9/14/61] Bled [8] C97/13 Ruy Lopez [E:Bishop + pawn] **1.e4 e5 2.Nf3 Nc6 3.Bb5 a6 4.Ba4 Nf6 5.0-0 Be7 6.Re1 b5 7.Bb3 d6 8.c3 0-0 9.h3 Na5 10.Bc2 c5 11.d4 Qc7 12.Nbd2 Bd7 13.Nf1 Rfe8 14.Ne3** [14.b3!] **g6 15.Bd2 Bf8 16.b4 cb4 17.cb4 Nc4 18.Nc4 bc4 19.Rc1 ed4 20.Nd4 d5 21.ed5 Re1** [21...Nd5 22.Be4] **22.Be1 Qd6 23.Ne2** [23.Nf3! Re8 24.Qd4 +=] **Re8 24.Nc3? Qe5!** [Threatens both 25...Bd6 and 25...Bb4] **25.Ba4 Ba4** [25...Bb4!] **26.Qa4? Bd6 27.g3 Qg5! 28.Qc2 Bb4 29.Bd2 Qh5 30.Qa4 Qh3! 31.Re1! Re1 32.Be1 Bc5 33.Qc4 Qg3 34.Kf1 Qh3 35.Ke2 Qh5 36.Kf1 Qh1 37.Ke2 Qh5 38.Kf1 Bf8 39.Qa6 Nd5 40.Nd5 Qd5 41.a4 f5 42.Bc3 f4 43.Qf6 Qh1 44.Ke2 Qe4 45.Kd2 f3 46.Qh8 Kf7 47.Qf6! Ke8 48.Qe5 Qe5 49.Be5 Bc5 50.Kd3 g5 51.Ke4 g4 52.Bg3 h5 53.a5 Kd7 54.Kd5 Ba7 55.Ke4 Kc8 56.Kf5! Bb8 57.Kg5** [D] 1/2-1/2

Final position

321) Bisguier,A-Fischer,R [9/15/61] Bled [9] D42/06 Queen's Gambit [E:Knight vs.Bishop] **1.d4 Nf6 2.Nf3 d5 3.c4 e6 4.e3 c5 5.Nc3 Nc6 6.cd5 Nd5** [Fischer prefers the Semi-Tarrasch over the regular Tarrasch-6...ed5] **7.Bd3 Be7 8.0-0 0-0 9.a3 cd4 10.ed4 Nf6** [10...Bf6!?] **11.Be3 b6 12.Rc1 Bb7 13.Qe2 Ng4** [Going after the two Bishops] **14.Bf4? Nd4 15.Nd4 Qd4 16.Qg4 Qd3 17.Rfd1 Qg6 18.Qg6 fg6! 19.Rd7 Bc5 20.Be3 Bc6 21.Rc7 Rfc8 22.Rc8 Rc8 23.Nb5!?** Bd7 [23...Bb5 24.b4 with opposite colored Bishops] **24.b4 Be3 25.Rc8 Bc8 26.fe3 Bd7 27.Nd6** [27.Na7 b5] **Kf8 28.e4 e5 29.Kf2 Bc6 30.Nc4 Be4 31.Ne5 Ke7 32.Nc4 Ke6 33.Ne3 Ke5 34.Ke2 Kd4 35.Kd2 Bc6 36.g3 Bd7 37.Nd1 Ke4 38.Ne3 Kf3 39.Kd3 g5 40.Kd4 Be6 41.Ke5 Ke3 42.Ke6 Kf3 43.Kf5 Kg2 44.Kg5 Kh2 45.g4 b5 46.Kf5 Kg3 47.g5 g6** [D] 0-1

Final position

322) Fischer,R-Bertok,M [9/18/61] Bled [10] B35/01 Sicilian [E:Rooks + minor pieces] **1.e4 c5 2.Nf3 Nc6 3.d4 cd4 4.Nd4 Nf6 5.Nc3 g6 6.Be3 Bg7 7.Bc4 Na5 8.Be2 0-0 9.0-0 d5** [Too aggressive; Correct was 9...d6 =] **10.ed5 Nd5 11.Nd5 Qd5 12.Nb5! Qd1 13.Rad1 Nc6** [13...Bb2 14.Nc7 Rb8 15.Ba7] **14.c3 a6 15.Nc7 Rb8 16.Bc5 Be5 17.Nd5 Be6 18.Bf3 Bd5 19.Rd5 Bf6 20.Rfd1 Rfc8 21.Bb6 Ne5 22.Be2 e6 23.R5d2 Rc6 24.Bd4 Kg7 25.b3 h5 26.h3 Rcc8 27.c4 Nc6 28.Bb6 h4 29.Bf3 Bc3 30.Rd7 Ne5** [D] **31.Bb7! Nd7 32.Rd7 Rg8 33.c5 a5 34.c6 e5 35.Ba7 Rbe8 36.c7 Bd4 37.Bd4 ed4 38.Rd4 Rc8 39.Rc4 Kf6 40.Kf1 Ke6 41.Bc8 Rc8 42.Ke2 Kd7 43.Kf3 Re8 44.c8=Q** 1-0

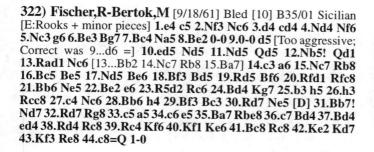

After 30...Ne5

After 35.Kh2

323) Germek,M-Fischer,R [9/19/61] Bled [11] E81/09 King's Indian **1.d4 Nf6 2.c4 g6 3.Nc3 Bg7 4.e4 0-0 5.Be3 d6 6.f3 Nbd7 7.Nh3 c5** [7...e5] **8.d5 Ne5 9.Nf2 e6 10.Be2 ed5 11.cd5 a6 12.f4 Ned7 13.a4** [Black has lost time and has an inferior Benoni] **Qe7 14.Qd2 Ne8 15.0-0 Rb8 16.Rfe1 f5 17.Bd3 Qf6 18.Rab1 Kh8 19.Rec1 Qe7 20.b4 cb4 21.Rb4 fe4 22.Nfe4 Nef6 23.Nf6 Nf6 24.Ba6 ++- Bf5 25.Bf1 Rbc8 26.Bd4 Qc7 27.Re1 Kg8 28.h3 Rfe8 29.Re8 Re8 30.Bb6 Qe7 31.Bf2 Rc8 32.Rc4 Rc4 33.Bc4 Qc7 34.Bb3 h5 35.Kh2** [D] **Ng4 36.hg4 Bc3 37.Qc1 hg4 38.Qe3 1/2-1/2**

After 23...Rd6

Final position

324) Fischer,R-Trifunovic,P [9/20/61] Bled [12] C80/05 Ruy Lopez [E:Rook + pawn] **1.e4 e5 2.Nf3 Nc6 3.Bb5 a6 4.Ba4 Nf6 5.0-0 Ne4 6.d4 b5 7.Bb3 ed4?** [7...d5] **8.Re1 d5 9.Nc3! Be6** [9...dc3 10.Bd5 Bd7 11.Be4!] **10.Ne4 de4 11.Re4 Be7 12.Be6 fe6 13.Nd4! 0-0 14.Qg4 Nd4 15.Rd4 Qc8 16.Re4 Rf6 17.Be3** [17.Bg5 Rg6 18.h4 h6 19.Qh5 Qe8 -++] **Qd7 18.Rd1 Qc6 19.Bd4 Rg6 20.Qe2 Rd8 21.g3 Qd5 22.Re1! c5 23.Bc3 Rd6** [D] **24.Be5 Rd8 25.Bf4! c4 26.Re6 Re6 27.Qe6 Qe6 28.Re6 Bf6 29.Ra6 Rd1 30.Kg2 Bb2?** [30...Rb1] **31.Rb6 Ra1 32.Rb5 Ra2 33.Rc5 Ra4 34.Be5 Be5 35.Re5 Ra2 36.Re2 Kf7 37.Kf3 Kf6 38.Ke4 g5 39.Kd4 Kf5 40.f3 c3 41.Rf2 Ra3 42.Kc4 h5 43.Kb4 Ra8 44.f4 Ke4! 45.fg5 Ke3 46.Rg2 Kd4 47.Re2 Rb8 48.Ka4 Rg8 49.h4 Rf8 50.Re7 Rf3 51.Rd7 Kc4 52.Rc7 Kd4 53.Rd7 Kc4 54.Rc7 Kd4 55.Kb3 Rg3 56.Rd7 Ke4 57.Rh7 Kd4 58.Rh5 Rg1 59.Rh8 Rb1 60.Ka4 Ra1 61.Kb5 Rb1 62.Kc6 Rg1 63.Rd8 Kc4 64.Re8 Kb4 65.Kd5 Rd1 66.Ke6 Re1 67.Kf7 Rf1 68.Kg6 Rf2 69.h5 Rc2 70.h6 Rh2 71.h7 c2 72.Rc8 Kb3 73.Kg7** [D] **1-0**

After 16.Nd5

325) Pachman,L-Fischer,R [9/23/61] Bled [13] E62/19 King's Indian **1.c4 Nf6 2.Nf3 g6 3.g3 Bg7 4.Bg2 0-0 5.0-0 d6 6.Nc3 Nc6 7.d4 e5 8.de5 de5** [8...Ne5] **9.Nd5** [9.Bg5] **Be6 10.Ng5 Bf5 11.h3 h6 12.g4 Bc8 13.Nf6 Qf6 14.Ne4 Qh4 15.Nc3 f5 16.Nd5** [D] **fg4 17.Nc7 gh3 18.Bd5 Kh8 19.Na8 Ne7 20.Be3 h2 21.Kh1 Bh3 22.Nc7 Nf5 23.Ne6 Rf6 24.Ng7 Ne3 25.fe3 Rf1 26.Qf1 Bf1 27.Rf1 Kg7 28.Rf7 1/2-1/2**

Final position

326) Fischer,R-Udovcic,M [9/24/61] Bled [14] B09/10 Pirc [E:Rook + minor piece] **1.e4 d6 2.d4 g6 3.Nc3 Bg7 4.f4 Nf6 5.Nf3 0-0 6.Be2** [6.Bd3 or 6.Be3] **c6** [Passive; 6...c5 7.dc5 Qa5 8.0-0 Qc5 ∞] **7.0-0 Nbd7 8.e5! Ne8 9.Be3 Qb6 10.Qd3 Qa5 11.Ng5 f6 12.Nh7** [12.Ne6 Ne5] **Kh7 13.e6 f5 14.ed7 Bd7 15.d5 Nf6 16.Bf3 Rac8 17.Rfe1 cd5 18.Nd5 Bb5 19.Qd1 Ba4 20.Nc3 e5 21.Na4 Qa4 22.c3 Qa6 23.Qb3 b6 24.a4 Ng4 25.Bg4 fg4 26.fe5 Be5 27.Qe6 Qc4 28.Qc4 Rc4 29.a5 ba5 30.Ra5 Rb8 31.Ra7 Kg8 32.Bc1 g3 33.hg3 Bg3 34.Re6 Rg4 35.b4 Be5 36.Bd2 Kf8 37.b5 g5 38.Rg6 Rb5 39.Bg5 Rb1 40.Kf2 Rb2** [D] **1/2-1/2**

327) Portisch,L-Fischer,R [9/25/61] Bled [15] D38/20 Queen's Gambit [E:Rooks + minor piece] **1.d4 Nf6 2.c4 e6 3.Nf3 d5 4.Nc3 Bb4 5.cd5 ed5 6.Bg5 h6 7.Bh4 c5 8.e3 Nc6 9.Bb5 Qa5 10.Bc6 bc6 11.Bf6 Bc3 12.bc3 Qc3 13.Nd2 gf6 14.Rc1 Qd3 15.Rc5 Rg8!** 16.Qc2 [16.g3 Bg4! or 16.Rg1 Bg4!] **Qc2 17.Rc2 Rg2 18.Rc6 Rb8 19.h4 Be6** =+ [Active Rook and Bishop vs.Knight with pawns on both sides of the board] **20.Kf1 Rg6 21.Nb3 Rb4 22.f3 a5! 23.Rc2 Bf5 24.Rch2 a4 25.Nc5 a3 26.e4 de4 27.fe4 Bg4 28.Kf2 Rd4 29.Ke3 Rc4 30.Nd3 Be6 31.Rf1 Rg3 32.Rf3 Rf3 33.Kf3 Rc3 34.Ke3 f5! 35.Rf2 fe4 36.Ke4 Rc4 37.Ke5 Ke7 38.h5 Ra4! 39.Nc5 Rh4 40.Ne6 Rh5 41.Kd4 Ke6 42.Rf3 Rh4 43.Kc3 f5 44.Kb3 f4 45.Kc4 Ke5 46.Ra3 f3 47.Kd3 Rf4** [D] 0-1

Final position

328) Fischer,R-Keres,P [9/28/61] Bled [16] B11/11 Caro Kann **1.e4 c6 2.Nc3 d5 3.Nf3 Bg4 4.h3 Bf3** [4...Bh5] **5.Qf3 Nf6 6.d4** [6.d3] **de4 7.Qe3! Nbd7 8.Ne4 Ne4 9.Qe4 Nf6 10.Qd3 Qd5 11.c4! Qd6 12.Be2 e5 13.d5! e4 14.Qc2 Be7 15.dc6 Qc6 16.0-0 0-0 17.Be3 Bc5 18.Qc3 b6 19.Rfd1 Rfd8 20.b4 Be3 21.fe3** +- [Queenside majority, and Bishop vs.Knight] **Qc7 22.Rd4 a5 23.a3 ab4 24.ab4 h5 25.Rad1 Rd4 26.Qd4 Qg3 27.Qb6 Ra2 28.Bf1 h4 29.Qc5 Qf2 30.Kh1 g6 31.Qe5! Kg7 32.c5! Qe3 33.c6 Rc2 34.b5 Rc1 35.Rc1 Qc1 36.Kg1 e3 37.c7 e2 38.Qe2 Qc7 39.Qf2 g5 40.b6?** [40.Qd4!] **Qe5 41.b7 Nd7 42.Qd2 Nb8 43.Be2 Kf6 44.Bf3 Ke6 45.Bg4 f5 46.Bd1 Kf6 47.Qd8 Kg6 48.Qg8 Kh6 49.Qf8 Kg6 50.Qg8 Kh6 51.Qf8 Kg6 52.Qb4 Nc6 53.Qd2 Nd8! 54.Bf3** [D] **Nb7! 55.Bb7 Qa1 56.Kh2 Qe5** 1/2-1/2

After 54.Bf3

329) Najdorf,M-Fischer,R [9/29/61] Bled [17] E81/09 King's Indian **1.d4 Nf6 2.c4 g6 3.Nc3 Bg7 4.e4 d6 5.f3 0-0 6.Be3 Nbd7 7.Bd3 e5 8.d5 Nh5 9.Nge2 f5 10.Qd2 Nc5 11.Bc2 fe4 12.Ne4 Ne4 13.Be4 Nf6 14.0-0** [14.Nc3] **Bf5 15.Nc3 Be4 16.fe4 Ng4 17.Rf8 Bf8 18.Bg5 Be7 19.Be7 Qe7 20.Rf1 a6 21.Rf3 Rf8 22.Rf8 Qf8 23.h3 Nf6** [D] 1/2-1/2

Final position

330) Fischer,R-Petrosian,T [9/30/61] Bled [18] B17/10 Caro Kann [E:Rooks + minor pieces] **1.e4 c6 2.d4 d5 3.Nc3 de4 4.Ne4 Nd7 5.Nf3** [5.Bc4] **Ngf6 6.Nf6 Nf6 7.Bc4 Bf5 8.Qe2 e6 9.Bg5 Bg4!** [Removing any real chance of initiative] **10.0-0-0 Be7 11.h3 Bf3 12.Qf3 Nd5 13.Be7 Qe7 14.Kb1 Rd8 15.Qe4 b5! 16.Bd3 a5 17.c3 Qd6 18.g3 b4 19.c4 Nf6 20.Qe5 c5 21.Qg5 h6! 22.Qc5 Qc5 23.dc5 Ke7 24.c6 Rd6 25.Rhe1 Rc6 26.Re5 Ra8 27.Be4 Rd6??** [27...Ne4 28. Re4 Rd6 29. Red4 Rad8 =] [D] **28.Ba8 Rd1 29.Kc2 Rf1 30.Ra5 Rf2 31.Kb3 Rh2 32.c5 Kd8 33.Rb5! Rh3 34.Rb8 Kc7 35.Rb7 Kc6 36.Kc4** 1-0

After 27...Rd6??

331) Ivkov,B-Fischer,R [10/3/61] Bled [19] D35/15 Queen's Gambit Declined [E:Knight + pawn] **1.d4 Nf6 2.c4 e6 3.Nf3 d5 4.cd5 ed5 5.Nc3 c6 6.Bg5 h6 7.Bh4 Be7 8.Qc2** [Stopping ...Bf5] **0-0 9.e3 Ne4 10.Ne4 Bh4 11.Nc3 Re8 12.0-0-0** [12.Bd3 Re3] **Bg4 13.h3 Bh5 14.Bd3 Qf6 15.Qe2 Nd7 16.Rhg1 Nf8 17.g4 Bg6 18.Bf5 Qe7 19.Ne5 Bf6 20.f4 Be5 21.de5 Rad8 22.Qf2 Ne6 23.h4 b5 24.h5 Bh7 25.Qc2 Nf8 26.Rg3 Kh8 27.Rdg1 d4 28.ed4 Rd4 29.g5 Bf5 30.Qf5 Qe6 31.Qc2 Rf4 32.Qd2 Qe5 33.gh6 g6 34.hg6 Ng6 35.Nd1 Rd4 36.Qg2 Qf4 37.Kb1 Rd2 38.Qc6 Qf5 39.Ka1 Rc8 40.Ne3 Rc6 41.Nf5 Rf6 42.Ne3 Rd3 43.a3 a6 44.Kb1 Re6 45.Nf5 Rd5 46.Ne3 Rde5 47.Ng4 Rg5 48.Rc1 Ne7 49.Rd1 f5 50.Rd8 Rg8 51.Rg8 Ng8 52.Re3 Rd6 53.Ne5 Nh6 54.Rg3 Kh7 55.Rc3 Kg7 56.Rc6 Rc6 57.Nc6 Nf7 58.Kc2 Kf6 59.Nb4 a5 60.Nc6 a4 61.Nd4 Nd6 62.b3 Ke5** [D] **63.Nf5 Nf5 64.ba4 ba4 65.Kc3** 1/2-1/2

After 62...Ke5

1962

After 14.Rc1

332) Teschner,R-Fischer,R [1/27/62] Stockholm Interzonal [1] E92/04 King's Indian [E:Rook + minor piece] **1.d4 Nf6 2.c4 g6 3.Nc3 Bg7 4.e4 0-0 5.Nf3 d6 6.Be2 e5 7.de5** [A patent attempt to draw] **de5 8.Qd8 Rd8 9.Bg5 Re8** [9...c6] **10.Nd5 Nd5 11.cd5 c6 12.Bc4 cd5 13.Bd5 Nd7 14.Rc1** [D] **h6 15.Be3 Nf6 16.Bb3 Ne4 17.Rc7 Be6 18.Be6 Re6 19.Rb7 Ra6 20.a3 Nd6 21.Rb4** [Equal, but Fischer outplays Teschner] **Rc6 22.0-0 f5 23.g3 g5 24.Rd1 a5 25.Ra4 Nc4 26.Rc1 Nb2 27.Rc6 Na4 28.h4 f4 29.Bd2 e4 30.Ne1 fg3 31.Rc4 gf2 32.Kf2 e3 33.Ke3 Nb6 34.Re4 Nd5 35.Ke2 Nf6 36.Ra4 gh4 37.Rh4 Kh7 38.Ra4 Re8 39.Kf3 Nd7 40.Ra5 Ne5 41.Kf2 1/2-1/2**

Final position

333) Fischer,R-Benko,P [1/28/62] Stockholm Interzonal [2] B33/01 Sicilian [E:Bishop vs. Knight] **1.e4 c5 2.Nf3 Nc6 3.d4 cd4 4.Nd4 Qb6 5.Nb3 Nf6 6.Nc3 e6 7.Be2** [7.a3] **Bb4 8.0-0 0-0 9.Qd3 Bc3 10.bc3 d5 11.ed5 ed5 12.Bf4 Re8 13.Rab1 Ne5 14.Qd4 Qd4 15.Nd4** ∞ [The Bishop pair vs. weaker pawns] **b6 16.Nb5 Ng6 17.Be3 Ba6 18.Rfe1 Re7 19.Bf1 Ne4 20.Bd4 Rd8 21.Rbd1 Bb5 22.Bb5 Rc7 23.Re3 Nd6 24.Bf1 Nf5 25.Rf3 Nd4 26.Rd4 Ne5 27.Re3 f6 28.f4 Nc6 29.Rd1 Kf8 30.g3 Na5 31.Rd5 Nc4 32.Bg2 Rc5 33.Rd5 Rcd5 34.Rd5 Rd5 35.Bd5 Ne3 36.Be4 f5 37.Bd3 g6 38.c4 Ke7 39.Kf2 Ng4 40.Kg2 Kd6 41.h3 Nf6 42.Kf3 h5 43.c3 Kc5 44.Bc2 Ne8 45.g4 hg4 46.hg4 Kc4 47.gf5 gf5 48.Bf5 Nd6 49.Be6 Kc3 50.Kg4 b5 51.Kg5 a5 52.Kf6 b4 53.Bb3 Ne4 54.Ke7 Ng3 55.Kd6 Nh5 56.f5 Ng7** [D] **1/2-1/2**

After 29.Rd2??

334) Aaron,M-Fischer,R [1/30/62] Stockholm Interzonal [3] E81/11 King's Indian **1.d4 Nf6 2.c4 g6 3.Nc3 Bg7 4.e4 d6 5.f3 0-0 6.Be3 Nbd7 7.Qd2 c5 8.Nge2 a6 9.Ng3?!** [9.0-0-0 +=] **cd4 10.Bd4 Ne5 11.Be2** [11.Be5?! de5 =+; the two Bishops and the hole at d4] **Be6 12.Nd5 b5! 13.cb5 ab5 14.Bb5 Nd5 15.ed5 Bd5 16.a4 e6 17.0-0 Qh4 18.Ne2 Rfc8 19.Be3 Nc4 20.Bc4 Qc4 21.Rfc1 Qa6 22.Rc8 Rc8 23.Nc3 Bc4 24.f4 d5 25.Bd4 Bd4 26.Qd4 Qb7 27.Qf2 Ba6 28.Rd1 Rc4 29.Rd2??** [D] **Rc3! 0-1**

After 67...Ke7

335) Fischer,R-Portisch,L [1/31/62] Stockholm Interzonal [4] B17/11 Caro Kann [E:Rook + pawn] **1.e4 c6 2.Nc3 d5 3.Nf3 de4 4.Ne4 Nd7 5.Bc4 Ngf6 6.Neg5 Nd5** [6...e6] **7.d4 h6 8.Ne4 N7b6 9.Bb3 Bf5 10.Ng3 Bh7 11.0-0 e6 12.Ne5 Nd7 13.c4 N5f6 14.Bf4 Ne5 15.Be5 Bd6 16.Qe2 0-0 17.Rad1 Qe7 18.Bd6 Qd6 19.f4 c5 20.Qe5!** [Forcing a favorable ending] **Qe5** [20...Qe7 21.d5!] **21.de5 Ne4 22.Rd7 Ng3 23.hg3 Be4 24.Ba4** [Stopping ...Bc6] **Rad8 25.Rfd1 Rd7 26.Rd7 g5! 27.Bd1!** [To trade off Black's Bishop which defends b7] **Bc6 28.Rd6 Rc8 29.Kf2 Kf8 30.Bf3! Bf3 31.gf3 gf4?** [31...Ke7] **32.gf4 Ke7 33.f5! ef5 34.Rh6 Rd8 35.Ke2 Rg8 36.Kf2 Rd8 37.Ke3 Rd1 38.b3 Re1 39.Kf4 Re2 40.Kf5 Ra2 41.f4 Re2 42.Rh3 Re1 43.Rd3 Rb1 44.Re3 Rb2 45.e6 a6 46.ef7 Kf7 47.Ke5 Rd2 48.Rc3 b6 49.f5 Rd1 50.Rh3 b5 51.Rh7 Kg8 52.Rb7 bc4 53.bc4 Rd4 54.Ke6! Re4 55.Kd5 Rf4 56.Kc5 Rf5 57.Kd6 Rf6 58.Ke5 Rf7 59.Rb6 Rc7 60.Kd5 Kf7 61.Ra6 Ke7 62.Re6 Kd8 63.Rd6! Ke7 64.c5 Rc8 65.c6 Rc7 66.Rh6 Kd8 67.Rh8 Ke7** [D] **68.Ra8 1-0**

336) Bilek,I-Fischer,R [2/3/62] Stockholm Interzonal [5] B97/11 Sicilian **1.e4 c5 2.Nf3 d6 3.d4 cd4 4.Nd4 Nf6 5.Nc3 a6 6.Bg5 e6 7.f4 Qb6 8.Qd2 Qb2 9.Rb1** [9.Nb3] **Qa3 10.e5** [10.f5] **de5 11.fe5 Nfd7 12.Bc4 Be7** [D] **13.Be6 0-0 14.0-0 Bg5 15.Qg5 h6 16.Qh4** [Better was 16.Qh5 fe6 17.Ne6 Rf1 18.Rf1 +=] **Qc3! 17.Rf7 Rf7 18.Qd8 Nf8 19.Bf7 Kf7 20.Rf1 Kg6! 21.Rf8 Bd7! 22.Nf3 Qe3 23.Kh1 Qc1 24.Ng1 Qc2 25.Rg8?** [25.Qe7] **Qf2 26.Rf8 Qa2 27.Rf3 Kh7 0-1** [Time]

After 12...Be7

337) Fischer,R-Barcza,G [2/4/62] Stockholm Interzonal [6] B15/07 Caro Kann [E:Rook + minor piece] **1.e4 c6 2.Nc3 d5 3.Nf3 de4 4.Ne4 Nf6 5.Nf6 ef6** [5...gf6] **6.d4 +=** [Queenside majority - Black's Kingside majority is not as mobile because of the doubled pawns] **Bd6 7.Bc4 0-0 8.0-0 Re8 9.Bb3 Nd7?** [9...Bg4] **10.Nh4 Nf8 11.Qd3! Bc7 12.Be3 Qe7 13.Nf5 Qe4 14.Qe4 Re4 15.Ng3 Re8 16.d5! cd5 17.Bd5 Bb6 18.Bb6 ab6 19.a3 Ra5 20.Rad1 Rc5 21.c3 Rc7 22.Bf3! Rd7 23.Rd7 Nd7** [D] **24.Nf5 Nc5 25.Nd6 Rd8 26.Nc8 Rc8 27.Rd1 Kf8 28.Rd4! Rc7 29.h3 f5 30.Rb4 Nd7 31.Kf1 Ke7 32.Ke2 Kd8 33.Rb5 g6 34.Ke3 Kc8 35.Kd4 Kb8 36.Kd5? [36.Bd5] Rc6 37.Kd4 Re6 38.a4 Kc7 39.a5 Rd6 40.Bd5 Kc8 41.ab6 f6? 42.Ke3 Nb6 43.Bg8 Kc7 44.Rc5 Kb8 45.Bh7 Nd5 46.Kf3 Ne7 47.h4! b6 48.Rb5 Kb7 49.h5 Ka6 50.c4 gh5 51.Bf5 Rd4 52.b3 Nc6 53.Ke3 Rd8 54.Be4 Na5 55.Bc2 h4 56.Rh5 Re8 57.Kd2 Rg8 58.Rh4 b5 59.Rf4 bc4 60.bc4 Rg2 61.Rf6 Ka7 62.Kc3 Rg4 63.f4 Nb7 64.Kb4 1-0**

After 23...Nd7

338) Bisguier,A-Fischer,R [2/6/62] Stockholm Interzonal [7] B22/00 Sicilian [E:Rooks + Knight vs. Queen + Bishop] **1.e4 c5 2.c3 Nf6 3.e5 Nd5 4.Nf3 Nc6 5.Na3!? g6 6.g3 Bg7 7.Bg2 Nc7 8.Qe2 0-0 9.0-0 d6 10.d4 cd4 11.cd4 Bg4 12.Rd1 Ne6 13.Qe4 Bf5 14.Qe1 Bg4 15.Qe4 Bf3 16.Bf3 d5! 17.Qe3** [17.Qd5 Ned4] **Rc8 18.Bg4 Nb6 19.Be6 fe6 20.b3 g5 21.Bb2 Rf5 22.Rd2 Rcf8 23.Nc2 h6 24.Qe2 Rf2! 25.Qf2 Rf2 26.Rf2 g4 27.Bc1 Qb5 28.Bf4 Qd3 29.Rd2 Qg6 30.Ne1 h5 31.Ng2 Kh7 32.Re1 Nd8 33.Nh4 Qe8 34.h3 gh3 35.Kh2 Nf7 36.Kh3 Bh6 37.Rc2 Qg8 38.Rf1 Qg4 39.Kh2 Ng5 40.Bg5 Bg5 41.Nf3 Be3 42.Re2 Bh6 43.Ref2 Kg8 44.Nh4? Qd4 45.Rf7 Qg4 46.R1f3 Qg5 47.R3f4 d4 48.Nf3 Qg6 49.Nh4** [D] **Qf7! 50.Rf7 Kf7 51.Kg2 d3 52.Kf2 Bg7 53.Nf3 Kg6 54.Ke3 Kf5 0-1**

After 49.Nh4

339) Fischer,R-Pomar,A [2/10/62] Stockholm Interzonal [9] B29/01 Sicilian [E:Bishop vs. Knight] **1.e4 c5 2.Nf3 Nf6 3.Nc3 d5 4.Bb5** [Better was 4.ed5 Nd5 5.Bb5 Bd7 6.Qe2 +-] **Bd7 5.e5 d4 6.ef6 dc3 7.fg7 cd2 8.Qd2 Bg7 9.Qg5 Bf6 10.Bd7** [10.Qc5? Qa5] **Nd7 11.Qh5 Qa5 12.Nd2 Qa6 13.Ne4 0-0-0 14.Qe2** [14.Qf7? would be too dangerous with the King in the center] **Qe6 15.Nf6 Qe2 16.Ke2 Nf6 17.Be3 b6 18.Rad1 Rd1 19.Rd1 Rd8 20.Rd8 Kd8 21.Kf3 +=** [Bishop vs. Knight with pawns on both sides and an isolated h-pawn] **Kd7 22.Kf4 Ng8 23.c4 f6 24.Ke4 e6 25.Bd2 Ne7 26.Bc3 Ng8 27.g4 Ke7 28.f4 h6** [D] **29.f5 ef5 30.gf5 h5 31.Bd2 Kd7 32.a4 Ne7 33.Bc3 Ng8 34.Kf4 Ke7 35.b4 cb4 36.Bb4 Kd7 37.Bf8 Ke8 38.Bd6 Kd7 39.c5 bc5 40.Bc5 a6 41.Ke4 Kc6 42.Bf8 Kd7 43.h3 Ke8 44.Bc5 Kd7 45.Bd4 Kd6 46.Bb2 Kc6 47.Bc3 Kd6**

After 28...h6

Final position

48.Bb4 Kd7 49.a5 Nh6 50.Bc3 Ng8 51.Bb4 Nh6 52.Bc3 Ng8 53.Kd5 Ne7 54.Kc5 Nf5 55.Bf6 Ke6 56.Bg5 Nd6 57.Kb6 Kd5 58.Ka6 Kc6 59.Bd2 Ne4 60.Bb4 Nf6 61.Ka7 Nd7 62.a6 Kc7 63.Ba5 Kc6 64.Be1 Nc5 65.Bf2 Nd7 66.Bh4 Nc5 67.Be7 Nd7 68.Ba3 Kc7 69.Bb2 Kc6 70.Bd4 Kc7 71.Bg7 Kc6 72.Ba1 Nc5 73.Bd4 Nd7 74.Be3 Kc7 75.Bf4 Kc6 76.Ka8 Kb6 77.a7 Kc6 [D] 1/2-1/2

After 21.Rd5

340) Gligoric,S-Fischer,R [2/11/62] Stockholm Interzonal [10] E92/10 King's Indian [E:Rook + pawn] **1.d4 Nf6 2.c4 g6 3.Nc3 Bg7 4.e4 d6 5.Nf3 0-0 6.Be2 e5 7.Be3 ed4 8.Nd4 Re8 9.f3 c6 10.Qd2 d5 11.ed5 cd5 12.0-0 dc4 13.Rad1 a6 14.Bc4 b5 15.Bb3 Bb7 16.Qf2** [16.a4 +=] **Nbd7 17.Nc2 Qc7 18.Nb4 Bf8 19.Nbd5 Nd5 20.Nd5 Bd5 21.Rd5** [D] **Re3 22.Qe3 Bc5 23.Rc5 Qc5 24.Qc5 Nc5 =** 25.Bc2 Na4 26.Ba4 ba4 27.Rc1 Rd8 28.a3 Rd2 29.Rc6 Rb2 30.Ra6 Ra2 31.Ra4 g5 32.h4 gh4 33.Kh2 Kh8 34.Kh3 h6 35.Rf4 Ra3 36.Rf7 Ra4 37.Re7 Ra2 38.Re4 Ra6 39.Rh4 Kg7 40.Rg4 Kf6 41.Kh4 Ra5 42.Rb4 Kg6 43.Rb6 Kg7 44.g3 Ra4 45.f4 Rc4 46.Rb3 Rc5 47.Kg4 Kf6 48.Kf3 Rc1 49.Rb6 Kg7 50.g4 Rg1 51.Re6 Kh7 52.Re7 Kg6 53.f5 Kf6 54.Re6 Kg7 55.Kf4 Ra1 56.Rg6 Kh7 57.Rd6 Kg7 58.Ke5 Re1 59.Kf4 Ra1 60.Rg6 Kh7 61.Rc6 Kg7 62.Ke5 Re1 63.Kd5 Rd1 64.Ke6 Re1 65.Kd7 Re4 66.Rg6 Kf7 67.Kd6 Rd4 68.Ke5 Ra4 69.Rh6 Rg4 70.Rh7 Kg8 71.Re7 Rg1 72.Kf6 Rf1 73.Rg7 Kf8 74.Rd7 Kg8 75.Rd8 Kh7 76.Rf8 Ra1 77.Re8 Rf1 78.Re4 Kg8 79.Rd4 Rf2 80.Rd1 Rf3 81.Rd8 Kh7** [D] **1/2-1/2**

Final position

After 39...Rb8

341) Fischer,R-Schweber,S [2/13/62] Stockholm Interzonal [11] B92/00 Sicilian **1.e4 c5 2.Nf3 d6 3.d4 cd4 4.Nd4 Nf6 5.Nc3 a6 6.Be2 g6 7.0-0 Bg7 8.Be3 0-0 9.Nb3 Be6 10.f4 Qc8 11.Nd5 Nd5 12.ed5 Bf5 13.c3 Nd7 14.Bd4 Bd4 15.Qd4 Bc2! 16.Kh1! Bb3 17.ab3 Qc5 18.Qd2 a5 19.Ra4! b5 20.Rd4 Nf6 21.f5 b4 22.Bc4 Kh8 23.Qe2** [23.fg6 fg6 +=] **Qc7 24.cb4 ab4 25.h3 g5 26.Rd3 Ra7?** [26...g4!] **27.Re3 Rb8 28.Re1 Qc8 29.Qd2 Rbb7 30.Rg3 Qf5 31.Rg5 Qd7 32.Qd4! Ra8 33.Rg3 Qf5 34.Rge3 Raa7 35.Rf1 Qg5 36.Rfe1 Qg7? 37.Qh4! Ng8 38.Rg3 Qf6 39.Qg4 Rb8** [D] **40.Rf1 Qb2 41.Rf7 Qa1 42.Kh2 e6 1-0**

After 25.Ra3

342) Yanofsky,A-Fischer,R [2/14/62] Stockholm Interzonal [12] B92/11 Sicilian [E:Rook + minor piece] **1.e4 c5 2.Nf3 d6 3.d4 cd4 4.Nd4 Nf6 5.Nc3 a6 6.Be2 e5 7.Nb3 Be7 8.0-0 0-0 9.Be3 Qc7 10.a4 Be6 11.f4 ef4** [Preventing f5 and clearing e5 for a Knight] **12.Rf4 Nbd7 13.Nd5** [13.Nd4!?] **Bd5 14.ed5 Ne5 15.a5 Rfe8 16.Bb6 Qc8 17.Bd3 Bd8!** [Trading off the "bad" Bishop] **18.Bd8 Qd8 19.c4 b6 20.Bf1 Rb8 21.Qd4 Ng6 22.Rf2 Ne4 23.Re2 Nc5 24.Re8 Qe8 25.Ra3** [D] **Nb3 26.Rb3 ba5 =+/-+** [Black grips the dark squares] **27.Ra3 Qd8 28.c5 Rb4 29.Qc3 dc5 30.Qc5 Rb2 31.d6 Nf8 32.Qc7 Qc7 33.dc7 Rc2 34.Ra5 Rc7 35.Ra6 g6 36.Be2 Kg7 37.Bf3 Nd7 38.Kf2 Ne5 39.Ra3 Rc2 40.Kg3 Kf6 41.Be4 Rc4 42.Bf3 Kg5 43.Re3 f6 44.Re4 Rc3 45.Rf4 f5 46.h4 Kf6 47.Ra4 Nd3 48.Rd4 Nc5 49.Rd6 Ke5 50.Rd5 Ke6 51.Rd4 h6 52.Kf2 Nd3 53.Ke2 Nc5 54.Kf2 g5 55.hg5 hg5 56.Ke2 Nb3 57.Rd8 Rc2 58.Kd1 Rc1 59.Ke2 Ke5 60.Re8 Kf6 61.Rf8 Kg6 62.Rg8**

Kh6 63.Bd5 Rc2 64.Ke3 Rc3 65.Kf2 Nc5 66.Bf3 Nd7 67.Rd8 Nf6
68.Rd6 Kg7 69.Ke2 [D] g4 70.Bb7 Nh5 71.Ke1 Re3 72.Kf2 Rc3
73.Ke1 Re3 74.Kf2 Rb3 75.Ba8 Ng3 76.Ke1 Re3 77.Kd1 Ra3
78.Bb7 Ra2 79.Rd4 Nh1 80.Ke1 Ra1 81.Ke2 Rg1 82.Rd6 Rb1
83.Ba8 Rb3 84.Rd3 Rb2 85.Ke1 Rb8 86.Bc6 Rb6 87.Ba8 f4
88.Rd4 Rf6 89.Bb7 Kg6 90.Rd8 Re6 91.Kd2 Nf2 92.Rd4 Kg5
93.Ba8 Rf6 94.Ke1 Nh1 95.Rd8 Rb6 96.Rd4 Ng3 97.Kd2 Nf1
98.Ke2 Ne3 99.Rd2 Kh4 100.Kf2 Rb3 101.Be4 Ra3 102.Bc6 Nf5
103.Rb2 Ra1 104.Rb4 Ra2 105.Ke1 Kg3 106.Rb3 Ne3 107.Be4
Kh2 108.Rb4 Ng2 109.Bg2 Kg2 110.Rf4 g3 111.Rg4 Kf3 112.Rg8
Ra1 0-1

After 69.Ke2

343) Fischer,R-German,E [2/17/62] Stockholm Interzonal
[13] C43/14 Petroff **1.e4 e5 2.Nf3 Nf6 3.d4 ed4 4.e5 Ne4 5.Qe2
Nc5** [5...Bb4 6.Kd1 d5 7.ed6 f5 ∞] **6.Nd4 Nc6 7.Nc6 bc6 8.Nc3
Rb8 9.f4 Be7 10.Qf2! d5 11.Be3! Nd7 12.0-0-0 0-0 13.g4 Bb4
14.Ne2 Nb6 15.Nd4 Qe8** [D] **16.c3 Be7 17.f5 c5 18.Nb5 d4!** 19.Bf4
dc3** [19...Bb7] **20.Nc3 Na4 21.Bb5! Rb5 22.Na4 Rb4 23.Nc3 Bb7
24.Rhe1 Kh8 25.f6! Bd8 26.Bg5! Rd4 27.fg7 Kg7 28.Bf6 Kg8
29.Qh4 Rd1 30.Nd1 1-0**

After 15...Qe8

344) Cuellar,M-Fischer,R [2/18/62] Stockholm Interzonal
[14] E62/ King's Indian **1.d4 Nf6 2.c4 g6 3.g3 Bg7 4.Bg2 0-0 5.Nf3
d6 6.0-0 Nc6 7.Nc3 Bf5 8.d5** [8.Re1 Ne4 9.Nd5 +=] **Na5 9.Nd4**
[9.Nd2 +=] **Bd7** [9...Nc4? 10.Nf5 gf5 11.Qd3 +-] **10.Qd3 c5 11.Nb3
Ng4** [11...b5!?] **12.f4! b5 13.Na5 Qa5 14.Nb5** [14.cb5 a6] **Bb5
15.cb5 Rfb8 16.Bf3 Nf6 17.a4 a6** [17...Rb5? 18.Bd2 +-] **18.ba6
Qa6 19.Ra3 Qd3 20.ed3 Rb4 21.a5 Rb5 22.Bd2 Rb2 23.Bc3 Rb7
24.Re1 Ne8 25.Bd2 Kf8 26.Bd1 Rb2 27.Bc1 Bd4 28.Kh1 Rf2!
29.Bg4 Nf6 30.Bh3 Rc2 31.a6 Ra7 32.Bc8 Nd5 33.Rb3 Nb4 34.f5
gf5 35.Bg5 e6 36.Bd8 Ra8 37.Bb6 Rc8** [D] **0-1**

Final position

345) Fischer,R-Olafsson,F [2/20/62] Stockholm Interzonal
[15] B88/02 Sicilian [E:Rook + pawn] **1.e4 c5 2.Nf3 d6 3.d4 cd4
4.Nd4 Nf6 5.Nc3 Nc6 6.Bc4 e6 7.Bb3 Be7 8.f4 0-0 9.Be3 Nd4
10.Bd4 b5 11.e5 de5 12.fe5 Nd7 13.0-0 b4?!** [13...Bc5! =] **14.Ne4
Bb7 15.Nd6 Bd6 16.ed6 Qg5 17.Qe2 Bd5 18.Rad1 Bb3 19.ab3 e5**
[D] **20.Qb5! a6 21.Qd7 ed4 22.Qf5 Qf5 23.Rf5 Rfd8 24.Rd4 Rac8
25.Rf2 a5 26.Rfd2 f6 27.Rc4 Kf7 28.Rc7 Kg6 29.Re7 h5 30.d7
Rc7 31.c4 Kh7 32.h4 Kg6 33.Rd5 1-0**

After 19...e5

346) Stein,L-Fischer,R [2/21/62] Stockholm Interzonal [16]
D35/17 Queen's Gambit Declined [E:Rook + Bishop] **1.d4 d5 2.c4
e6 3.Nf3 Nf6 4.cd5 ed5 5.Bg5 c6 6.Nc3 Bf5?** [Allows a weakening
of pawns; 6...Be7 was correct] **7.Qb3! Qb6 8.Bf6 gf6 9.e3 Na6
10.Qb6 ab6 11.Kd2 Kd7 12.g3?!** [12.Nh4! +=/+-] **b5 13.a3 Nc7
14.Nh4 Be6 15.Bd3 Ne8 16.Nf5 Nd6 17.Nd6 Bd6 18.e4 b4 19.ab4
Bb4 20.ed5 Bd5 21.Ra8 Ra8 22.Re1 h6 23.Kc2 Ra5 24.Re3 Be6
25.Re4 Bc3 26.Kc3 Rh5** [D] **1/2-1/2**

Final position

Final position

347) Fischer,R-Petrosian,T [2/24/62] Stockholm Interzonal [17] C11/13 French [E:Rook + Bishop vs. Rook + Knight] **1.e4 e6 2.d4 d5 3.Nc3 Nf6 4.Bg5 de4 5.Ne4 Nbd7 6.Nf3 Be7 7.Nf6 Bf6 8.Qd2** [Better was 8.Bf6 Qf6 9.Bd3 +=] **Bg5 9.Ng5 Nf6 10.Be2 0-0 11.Rd1 Qd6 12.0-0 Bd7 13.Nf3 Rfd8 14.c4 Bc6 =** [Simplification has neutralized White's spatial plus] **15.Ne5 Nd7 16.Nc6 Qc6 17.Bf3 Qa6 18.Qc3 Nf6 19.b4 c6 20.a4 Rac8 21.a5 b5! 22.Rc1 h6 23.h3 bc4 24.Qc4 Qc4 25.Rc4 Nd5 26.Rfc1 Rb8! 27.Rc6 Rb4 28.Rc8 Rc8 29.Rc8 Kh7 30.Ra8 Rb7 31.a6 Rd7 32.Rb8 Rd6! 33.Be2 Nc7 34.Rb7 Na6 35.Rf7 Nb4 36.Ra7 Rd4 37.Bg4 Rd6 38.Re7 Nd5! 39.Re6 Re6 40.Be6 Nf6 [D] 1/2-1/2**

After 19.N1a2

348) Geller,E-Fischer,R [2/25/62] Stockholm Interzonal [18] B92/11 Sicilian [E:Bishop vs. Knight] **1.e4 c5 2.Nf3 d6 3.d4 cd4 4.Nd4 Nf6 5.Nc3 a6 6.Be2 e5 7.Nb3 Be7 8.0-0 0-0 9.Be3 Qc7** [Better was 9...Be6 and ...Nbd7] **10.a4 b6?!** [10...Be6] **11.Qd2 Bb7 12.f3 Bc6 13.Rfd1 Nbd7 14.Qe1! h6 15.Qf1 Qb7 16.Bc4 Rfc8 17.Rd2 Nf8 18.Nc1** [Planning N1a2 and Nb4 with pressure on a6 and d5] **Ng6 19.N1a2 [D] b5 20.ab5 ab5 21.Bb5 Bb5 22.Qb5 Qb5 23.Nb5 Ra5 24.Nbc3 Rca8 25.Rdd1 Nf4 26.b3? [26.b4] Rc8 27.b4 Ra3 28.b5 Ne2 29.Ne2 Re3 30.Kf2 Ra3 31.Nb4 Ra1 32.Ra1 d5 33.Nd5 Nd5 34.ed5 Rc2 35.Rb1 Bc5 36.Ke1 Bb6 37.Rc1 Rb2 38.Rc8 Kh7 39.Kd1 Rb5 40.Nc3 Rb4 41.Kc2 Rd4 42.Ra8 Bc5 43.Ra4 Kg6 44.Rd4 Bd4 45.Nb5 Bb6 46.Kd3 f5 47.Nd6 Kf6 48.Kc4 Bg1 49.h3 Bh2 50.Nb7 e4 51.fe4 fe4 52.Kd4 Kf5 1/2-1/2**

After 38...Rbe8

349) Fischer,R-Korchnoi,V [2/27/62] Stockholm Interzonal [19] C91/06 Ruy Lopez **1.e4 e5 2.Nf3 Nc6 3.Bb5 a6 4.Ba4 Nf6 5.0-0 Be7 6.Re1 b5 7.Bb3 0-0 8.c3 d6 9.d4 [9.h3] Bg4 10.Be3 ed4 11.cd4 Na5 12.Bc2 Nc4 13.Bc1 c5 14.b3 Na5 15.d5! Nd7 16.Nbd2 Bf6 17.Rb1 c4 18.h3 Bf3 [18...Bh5 19.g4!] 19.Nf3 cb3 20.ab3 Qc7 21.Be3 [21.Bd2 +-] Bc3! 22.Re2 b4 23.Nd4 Rfe8 [23...g6] 24.Nf5 Nb7 25.Bd4 g6 26.Nh6 Kf8 27.Rc1! Rac8 28.Bd3 [28.Re3 +-] Qa5 29.Rec2 Ne5 30.Bf1 Nc5 31.Bc3 bc3 32.Rc3 Kg7 33.Ng4 Ng4 34.Qg4 Rb8 35.Rf3 Ne4 36.Qf4 f5 37.Re3 Re5 38.Rc6 Rbe8 [D] 39.Rd6! Qa1? 40.Ra6 Qd4 41.Rd3 Qb2 42.d6 g5 43.Qe3 f4 44.Qa7 1-0**

Final position

350) Filip,M-Fischer,R [2/28/62] Stockholm Interzonal A49/07 [20] King's Indian **1.d4 Nf6 2.Nf3 g6 3.g3 Bg7 4.Bg2 0-0 5.0-0 d6 6.Nbd2** [One of the world's most safe and solid grandmasters, Filip picks a drawing line] **Nc6 7.e4 e5 8.de5 Ne5 9.Ne5 de5 10.Qe2 b6 11.Rd1 Qe7 12.b3 a5 13.a4 Ba6 14.Qe1 Rfd8 15.Ba3 Qe6 16.Nf1 Bf8 17.Bf8 Kf8 18.Ne3 Bb7 19.Qc3 Be4 20.Qc7 Rd4 21.Be4 Ne4 22.Rd4 ed4 23.Nc4 Rc8 24.Qb7 Qc6 [D] 1/2-1/2**

351) Fischer,R-Bolbochan,Jacobo [3/3/62] Stockholm Interzonal [21] B90/02 Sicilian **1.e4 c5 2.Nf3 d6 3.d4 cd4 4.Nd4 Nf6 5.Nc3 a6 6.h3 Nc6** [6...g6 or 6...b5 =] **7.g4 Nd4? 8.Qd4 e5?** [Weakens d5] **9.Qd3 Be7 10.g5! Nd7 11.Be3 Nc5?** [11...Bg5] **12.Qd2 Be6 13.0-0-0 0-0 14.f3 Rc8 15.Kb1 Nd7 16.h4 b5 17.Bh3 Bh3 18.Rh3 Nb6 19.Bb6 Qb6 20.Nd5 Qd8 21.f4!** [Opening lines to increase the pressure] **ef4 22.Qf4 Qd7 23.Qf5 Rcd8 24.Ra3! Qa7 25.Rc3 g6! 26.Qg4 Qd7 27.Qf3 Qe6 28.Rc7 Rde8 29.Nf4 Qe5 30.Rd5 Qh8 31.a3 h6 32.gh6 Qh6 33.h5 Bg5 34.hg6! fg6 [D] 35.Qb3! Rf4 36.Re5 Kf8 37.Re8 1-0**

After 34...fg6

352) Bertok,M-Fischer,R [3/4/62] Stockholm Interzonal [22] D59/04 Queen's Gambit Declined **1.d4 d5 2.c4 e6 3.Nc3 Be7 4.Nf3 Nf6 5.Bg5 0-0 6.e3 h6 7.Bh4 b6 8.cd5 Nd5 9.Be7 Qe7 10.Nd5 ed5 11.Be2 Be6!** [Better than 11...Bb7. Black foresees opening the b-file and ...Bb7 would block it] **12.0-0 c5 13.dc5?** [13.Ne5] **bc5 14.Qa4 Qb7 15.Qa3 Nd7 16.Ne1 a5 17.Nd3 c4!** [Now b2 is the target] **18.Nf4 Rfb8 19.Rab1?** [19.Ne6 was the only chance] **Bf5 20.Rbd1 Nf6 21.Rd2 g5! 22.Nd5 Nd5 23.Bc4 Be6 24.Rfd1 [D] Ne3! 25.Qe3 Bc4 26.h4 Re8 27.Qg3 Qe7 28.b3 Be6 29.f4 g4 30.h5 Qc5 31.Rf2 Bf5 0-1**

After 24.Rfd1

353) Fischer,R-Uhlmann,W [3/6/62] [23] Stockholm Interzonal C19/15 French **1.e4 e6 2.d4 d5 3.Nc3 Bb4 4.e5 c5 5.a3 Bc3 6.bc3 Ne7 7.Nf3 Nbc6 8.a4 Qa5 9.Qd2 Bd7** [9...cd4 10.cd4 Qd2 11.Bd2 +=] **10.Bd3 f6** [Opening the f-file and weakening White's e pawn] **11.0-0 fe5 12.Ne5 Ne5 13.de5 0-0 14.c4 Qd2 15.Bd2 Bc6 16.a5 Rad8 17.Be3 d4 18.Bd2 Ng6 19.f4 Nh4 20.Rf2 Rd7 21.Re2 Rdf7 22.Rb1 g5 23.fg5 [D] Bg2 24.Rg2 Ng2 25.Kg2 Rf2 26.Kg3 Rd2 27.Rb7 Rf7 28.Rb8 Kg7 29.Re8 Rdf2 30.Re6 R7f3 31.Kg4 Rf4 32.Kg3 ½-½**

After 23.fg5

354) Benko,P-Fischer,R [5/2/62] Curacao Candidates [1] B07/08 King's Indian **1.g3 Nf6 2.Bg2 g6 3.e4 d6 4.d4 Bg7 5.Ne2** [Benko beat both Tal and Fischer with this setup] **0-0 6.0-0 e5 7.Nbc3 c6?!** [7...Nc6 =] **8.a4!** [Restraining b5] **Nbd7 9.a5 ed4** [9...Qc7 +=/+-] **10.Nd4 Nc5 11.h3 Re8 12.Re1 Nfd7 13.Be3 Qc7 14.f4 Rb8 15.Qd2 b5 16.ab6 ab6 17.b4!** [To gain control of d5] **Ne6 18.b5! Nd4 19.Bd4 Bd4 20.Qd4 c5 21.Qd2 Bb7 22.Rad1 Re6 23.e5! Bg2 24.Kg2 Qb7 25.Kf2 Rd8 26.ed6 Nf6 27.Re6 fe6 28.Qe3 Kf7 29.Qf3 Qb8 30.Ne4! Ne4 31.Qe4 Rd7 32.Qc6 Qd8 33.Kf3 Kg7 34.g4 e5 35.fe5 Rf7 36.Kg2 Qh4 37.Rf1 Rf1 38.Kf1 Qh3 39.Qg2 Qe3 40.Qe2 Qh3 [D] 1-0**

Final position

355) Geller,E-Fischer,R [5/3/62] Curacao Candidates [2] B92/12 Sicilian [E:Bishop + pawn] **1.e4 c5 2.Nf3 d6 3.d4 cd4 4.Nd4 Nf6 5.Nc3 a6 6.Be2 e5 7.Nb3 Be7 8.0-0 0-0 9.Be3 Qc7?!** [9...Be6 followed by Nbd7 and Rc8] **10.a4 Be6 11.a5 Nbd7 12.Nd5 Nd5 13.ed5 Bf5 14.c4 Bg6?** [14...Rc8] **15.Rc1 Nc5? 16.Nc5 dc5 17.b4! Rac8 18.Qb3 Bd6 19.Rfd1 Qe7 20.bc5 Bc5 21.Bc5 Rc5 22.Ra1 Rd8 23.Ra4! Bf5 24.Rb4 Bc8 25.Rb6 Rd6 26.Qb4 Qc7 27.Rd6 Qd6 28.Rb1 Qc7 29.Qa4! Bd7 30.Qa3 Ra5 31.Rb7 Qb7 32.Qa5 g6 33.h3 Qb1 34.Kh2 Bf5 35.Qc3! Qe4 36.Bf3 Qd4 37.Qd4 ed4 38.g4 Bc8 39.c5 a5 40.c6 Kf8 41.d6 [D] 1-0**

Final position

356) Fischer,R-Filip,M [5/5/62] Curacao Candidates [3]
C98/06 Ruy Lopez [E:Queen + minor pieces] **1.e4 e5 2.Nf3 Nc6 3.Bb5 a6 4.Ba4 Nf6 5.0-0 Be7 6.Re1 b5 7.Bb3 d6 8.c3 0-0 9.h3 Na5 10.Bc2 c5 11.d4 Qc7 12.Nbd2 Nc6 13.dc5 dc5 14.Nf1 Bd6** [Botvinnik's regrouping] **15.Nh4** [White's strategy is to pressure d5 and f5] **Ne7 16.Qf3 Rd8 17.Ne3 Qb7 18.Ng4 Ng4 19.hg4 Ng6 20.Nf5 Be6 21.g5!?** [21.Be3!] **Bc7! 22.Be3 c4 23.Red1 Rd1 24.Rd1 Rd8 25.g3 Rd1 26.Qd1 Qc6 27.a4 Kf8? 28.Qa1!?** [28.Qh5! wins a pawn, since 28...Kg8 allows 29.Qg6] **Bc8 29.Qa3 Kg8 30.ab5 ab5 31.Qa7 Bb7 32.Kh2 Qa6 33.Qc5 Qc6 34.Qb4 Bc8 35.Bc5 Bd8 36.Be3 Bc7 37.Kg1 Be6 38.Qa3 Bc8 39.Kh2 Be6 40.Qa1 Bc8 41.Qb1 Be6 42.Kg1 Bc8 43.b3 Be6 44.bc4 Bc4 45.Bd3 Bd3 46.Qd3 Kf8 47.Qb1 Qc4 48.Qd1 Qc6 49.Qb3 Kg8 50.Qb4 Qd7 51.Kh2 Qe8?** [51...Nf8 =] **52.Qc5 Qd7 53.Kg2 Bb8 54.Qb6 Bc7 55.Qc5 Bb8 56.Qb6 Bc7 57.Qb7 Nf8 58.Bb6 Bb6 59.Qb6 Ne6 60.Qb8 Qd8 61.Qb5 Ng5 62.Qe5 Ne6 63.Nd4 Nf8 64.c4 Ng6 65.Qd5 Qc8 66.Nf5 [D] 1-0**

Final position

357) Tal,M-Fischer,R [5/6/62] Curacao Candidates [4] B92/00 Sicilian [E:Rook vs. Bishop] **1.e4 c5 2.Nf3 d6 3.d4 cd4 4.Nd4 Nf6 5.Nc3 a6 6.Be2 e5 7.Nb3 Be6 8.0-0 Nbd7 9.a4 Be7 10.f4 Qc7 11.Be3 0-0 12.a5 b5! 13.ab6 Nb6 14.f5 Bc4 15.Bb6?** [15.Kh1 =] **Qb6 16.Kh1 Bb5 17.Bb5 ab5 18.Nd5 Nd5 19.Qd5 Ra4! -+** [Clever use of the file] **20.c3 Qa6 21.Rad1 Rc8 22.Nc1 b4 23.Nd3 bc3 24.bc3 Ra5! 25.Qb3 Ra3 26.Qb1 Rac3 27.Nb4 Qa7 28.Nd5 R3c6 29.Qb3 Bf8 30.h3 Ra6 31.Rb1 Ra3 32.Qb5 Qd4 33.Rfe1 Rg3 34.Qe2 Qd3 35.Qh5 Qc2 36.Qe2 Qe2 37.Re2 h5 38.Ra2 Rd3 39.Ra7 h4 40.f6 g6?** [40...gf6] **41.Kh2 [D] Rd5!!** [A positional exchange sacrifice which draws] **42.ed5 Bh6 43.Re7 Bg5 44.Rf1 Bf4 45.Kg1 g5 46.Rb1 e4! 47.Re4 Kh7 48.Re7 Kg6 49.Rbb7 Kf6 50.Rf7 Ke5 51.Rfc7 Ra8 52.Rb1 Kd5 53.Rd1 Ke6 54.Rc2 Ra3 55.Kf2 Rb3 56.Re2 Kf5 57.Rd5 Kf6 58.Re4 1/2-1/2**

After 41.Kh2

358) Fischer,R-Korchnoi,V [5/9/62] Curacao Candidates [5] B09/10 Pirc **1.e4 d6 2.d4 Nf6 3.Nc3 g6 4.f4 Bg7 5.Nf3 0-0 6.Be2** [6.Bd3 or 6.Be3] **c5 7.dc5** [7.d5] **Qa5 8.0-0 Qc5 9.Kh1 Nc6 10.Nd2** [10.Qe1 Bg4 11.Bd3 Bf3 12. Rf3 +=] **a5 11.Nb3 Qb6 12.a4 Nb4 13.g4?** [13.Ra3 ∞] **Bg4! 14.Bg4 Ng4 15.Qg4 Nc2 16.Nb5 Na1 17.Na1 Qc6 18.f5 Qc4 19.Qf3 Qa4 20.Nc7 Qa1 21.Nd5 Rae8 22.Bg5 Qb2 23.Be7 Be5! 24.Rf2 Qc1 25.Rf1 Qh6 26.h3 gf5 27.Bf8 Rf8 28.Ne7 Kh8 29.Nf5 Qe6 30.Rg1 a4 31.Rg4 Qb3 32.Qf1 a3 33.Rg3 [D] Qg3 0-1**

After 33.Rg3

359) Petrosian,T-Fischer,R [5/10/62] Curacao Candidates [6] E84/07 King's Indian **1.d4 Nf6 2.c4 g6 3.Nc3 Bg7 4.e4 d6 5.f3 0-0 6.Nge2 Nc6 7.Be3 a6 8.Qd2 Rb8 9.Nc1 e5 10.Nb3 ed4 11.Nd4 Bd7** [11...Nd4 12.Bd4 Be6 =] **12.Be2 Nh5 13.Nc6 bc6 14.0-0 +=** **c5 15.Rab1 Bc6 16.Nd5 a5 17.b3 Ra8 18.Rfe1 Re8 19.a4 Qd7 20.Bd3 Nf6 21.Bg5 Nd5 22.ed5 Bb7 23.Re8 Qe8 24.Re1 Qf8 25.h4 h6 [D] 1/2-1/2**

Final position

360) Fischer,R-Keres,P [5/12/62] Curacao Candidates [7]
C96/10 Ruy Lopez [E:Rook + pawn] **1.e4 e5 2.Nf3 Nc6 3.Bb5 a6
4.Ba4 Nf6 5.0-0 Be7 6.Re1 b5 7.Bb3 d6 8.c3 0-0 9.h3 Na5 10.Bc2
c5 11.d4 Nd7** [Keres' patent] **12.dc5!** [12.Nbd2 cd4 13.cd4 Bf6
14.Nf1 +=] **dc5 13.Nbd2 Qc7?** [13...f6 =] **14.Nf1 Nb6 15.Ne3 Rd8
16.Qe2 Be6 17.Nd5! Nd5 18.ed5 Bd5 19.Ne5 Ra7 20.Bf4! +- Qb6
21.Rad1! g6 22.Ng4 Nc4 23.Bh6 Be6 24.Bb3! Qb8 25.Rd8 Bd8?**
[25...Qd8] **26.Bc4 bc4** [D] **27.Qc4! Qd6 28.Qa4 Qe7 29.Nf6 Kh8
30.Nd5 Qd7 31.Qe4! Qd6 32.Nf4 Re7 33.Bg5 Re8 34.Bd8 Rd8
35.Ne6 Qe6 36.Qe6 fe6 37.Re6 Rd1 38.Kh2 Rd2 39.Rb6 Rf2
40.Rb7! Rf6 41.Kg3 Kg8 1-0**

After 26...bc4

361) Fischer,R-Benko,P [5/13/62] Curacao Candidates [8]
C11/22 French [E:Rook + pawn] **1.e4 e6 2.d4 d5 3.Nc3 Nf6 4.Bg5
de4 5.Ne4 Be7 6.Bf6 Bf6 7.Nf3 Nd7 8.Qd2 Be7 9.0-0-0 Nf6 10.Bd3
0-0 11.Nf6 Bf6 12.Qf4 c5 13.dc5** [Better was 13.g4] **Qa5 14.Qc4
Be7 15.h4?** [15.Rhe1] **Qc5 16.Qe4 f5 17.Qe2 b5! 18.Ng5 Bf6
19.Ne6 Be6?** [19...Bb2 draws] **20.Qe6 Kh8 21.Kb1 Qf2 22.Qf5
Qf5 23.Bf5 g6 24.Bd3 Rad8 25.h5 Kg7 26.hg6 hg6 27.Bb5 Rd1
28.Rd1 Rb8 29.a4 a6 30.Rd7 Kh6 31.Rd6 Bb2 32.Kb2 ab5 33.a5
Ra8 34.a6 Kh5 35.Kb3 g5 36.Kb4 Kg4 37.Kb5 Kg3 38.Rd7 g4
39.a7** [D] **1-0**

Final position

362) Fischer,R-Geller,E [5/16/62] Curacao Candidates [9]
B88/02 Sicilian [E:Rook + pawn] **1.e4 c5 2.Nf3 d6 3.d4 cd4 4.Nd4
Nf6 5.Nc3 Nc6 6.Bc4 e6 7.Bb3 Be7 8.f4** [8.0-0] **0-0 9.Be3 Nd4
10.Bd4 b5! 11.e5 de5 12.fe5 Nd7 13.0-0 Bc5 14.Bc5 Nc5 15.Qd8
Rd8 16.Nb5 Ba6 17.Bc4 Rab8 18.a4 Na4 = 19.Nd6?** [19.Ra4 =]
Bc4 20.Nc4 Nb2 21.Nd6 Rd7 22.Rfb1 Rc7 23.h3? [23.c4] **Rb6!
24.c4 h6 25.Nb5 Rc5! 26.Rb2 a6 27.Rf2 ab5 28.Ra7 Re5 29.Rff7
Rg5 30.Rfb7 Rb7 31.Rb7 bc4 32.Rc7 Rf5 33.Rc4 Kf7 34.g4 Rf3
35.Kg2 Rd3 36.Rc7 Kf6 37.h4 Ra3 38.Rb7 Rc3 39.g5 hg5 40.hg5
Kg6 41.Re7 Re3 42.Kf2 Re5 43.Kf3 Rf5 44.Ke3 e5 45.Ke4 Rg5
46.Re8 Rg1 47.Kf3 Rf1 48.Kg3 Rf5 49.Rb8 Kg5 50.Re8 Kf6
51.Rf8 Ke6 52.Re8 Kf6 53.Rf8 Ke6 54.Re8 Kd5 55.Ra8 Rf7
56.Kg4 Re7 57.Ra5 Ke6 58.Ra6 Kf7 59.Kf3 Re6 60.Ra8 e4
61.Ke3 g5 62.Ra1 Kg6 63.Rb1 Re5 64.Kd4 Kf6 65.Re1 Ra5
66.Re4 Kf5 67.Re8 Kg4 68.Ke3 Kg3** [D] **0-1**

Final position

363) Filip,M-Fischer,R [5/17/62] Curacao Candidates [10]
E22/04 Nimzo-Indian [E:Rook vs. minor pieces] **1.d4 Nf6 2.c4 e6
3.Nc3 Bb4 4.Nf3 0-0 5.Qb3 c5 6.dc5 Na6 7.Bd2 Qe7 8.e3 Nc5
9.Qc2 b6 10.Be2 Bb7 11.0-0 Rac8 12.Rac1 =** [Both sides are well
developed with no weaknesses] **Nce4 13.Ne4 Ne4 14.Bb4 Qb4
15.Bd3 d5 16.Qb1 Nf6 17.cd5 Bd5 18.a3 Qd6 19.Rfd1 Rc1
20.Qc1 Qb8 21.Qd2 h6 22.Qe2 Ng4 23.e4 Bb7 24.Bb1 Rc8 25.h3
Nf6 26.Qe3 Qc7 27.Re1 Nd7 28.Qd2 Nc5 29.Rc1 Qd8 30.Qe3 Rc7
31.Qf4 Rd7 32.Bc2 Qf6! 33.Qf6 gf6 34.Re1** [D] **Nd3 35.Rd1! Be4
36.Ne1 Ne1 37.Rd7 Nc2 38.Ra7 Bd5 39.a4 Nb4 40.Rc7 Kg7
41.Rc8 Nd3 42.b4! Nb4 43.Rb8 Nc6 44.Rb6 f5 1/2-1/2**

After 34.Re1

After 49...Rf3

After 44.Kg2

After 28.Rd1

After 65.Kg2!

364) Fischer,R-Tal,M [5/19/62] Curacao Candidates [11] B32/16 Sicilian [E:Rook + Bishop vs. Rook + Knight] **1.e4 c5 2.Nf3 Nc6 3.d4 cd4 4.Nd4 e5 5.Nb5 a6 6.Nd6 Bd6 7.Qd6 Qf6 8.Qd1 Qg6 9.Nc3 Nge7 10.h4 h5 11.Bg5 d5!? 12.Be7** [12.ed5 Nb4 13.Be7 Ke7 14.d6 +-] **d4! 13.Bg5 dc3 14.bc3 Qe4 15.Be2 f6 16.Be3 Bg4 = 17.Qd3 Qd3 18.cd3 Be2 19.Ke2 0-0-0 20.Rad1 Ne7 21.d4?! Nd5** [Better was 21...ed4] **22.Rc1 Rhe8 23.Rhd1 f5 24.Bg5 Rd7 25.de5 Re5 26.Kf3 Re4 27.Rd3 Rc4 28.Rcd1! Rc3 29.Rc3 Nc3 30.Rc1 Rc7 31.Bf4 Rc6 32.Be5 Nd5 33.Rd1 Nf6? [33...Rc5] 34.Kf4 g6 35.f3! Nd7 36.Bd6 Rc2 37.g3! Re2 38.Kg5 Re6 39.Bf4! Nf8 40.Rd6 a5 41.Kh6 Re2 42.Rd2 Re7 43.Bd6 Rh7 44.Kg5 Rf7 45.Rb2 f4 46.Bf4 Rf5 47.Kh6 b5 48.Bd6 b4 49.g4 Rf3** [D] **50.g5! Ne6 51.Kg6 Rd3 52.Be5 Re3 53.Kf5 Nf8 54.Rg2 Rf3 55.Bf4 Kd7 56.g6 Ne6 57.g7 Rf4 58.Ke5 Rf8 59.gf8=Q Nf8 60.Kd5 a4 61.Rg7 Ke8 62.Kd6 b3 63.a3 1-0**

365) Korchnoi,V-Fischer,R [5/20/62] Curacao Candidates [12] E62/20 King's Indian [E:Rook + minor pieces] **1.d4 Nf6 2.c4 g6 3.g3 Bg7 4.Bg2 0-0 5.Nc3 d6 6.Nf3 Nc6 7.0-0 e5 8.d5 Ne7 9.c5 Nd7?!** [9...Ne8 10.b4 f5 11.Ng5 +=] **10.cd6 cd6 11.a4** [Stealing Queenside space] **Nc5 12.Nd2 b6 13.b4 Nb7 14.Qb3 Bd7 15.Ba3 a6 16.Nc4 +- b5 17.Nd2 Qb6 18.Bb2 f5 19.Ra3!** [Seizing a file] **Bh6 20.e3 Rac8 21.ab5 ab5 22.Qa2 Bg7 23.Ra1 e4 24.Bf1 Nd8 25.Ra6 Qb8 26.Ra7 Rc7 27.Rc7 Qc7 28.Nb5 Bb5 29.Bb5 Nf7 30.Bg7 Kg7 31.Bc6?** [31.Qb2] **Nc6 32.Rc1? [32.Qc2] Qa7! 33.Qa7 Na7 34.Rc7 Nb5 35.Rb7 Nc3 36.Nc4 Kf6 37.b5 Ne5 38.Nd6 Rd8 39.Rb6 Kg5 40.Ra6 Nd5 41.b6 Nb4 42.Ra4 Rd6 43.Rb4 Rd1 44.Kg2** [D] **Nf3 0-1**

366) Fischer,R-Petrosian,T [5/23/62] Curacao Candidates [13] C12/12 French [E:Rook + pawn] **1.e4 e6 2.d4 d5 3.Nc3 Nf6 4.Bg5 Bb4 5.e5 h6 6.Bd2 Bc3 7.Bc3 Ne4 8.Ba5?!** [8.Bb4 =] **0-0 9.Bd3 Nc6! 10.Bc3 Nc3 11.bc3 f6 12.f4 fe5 13.fe5 Ne7 14.Nf3 c5 15.0-0 Qa5 16.Qe1 Bd7 17.c4 Qe1 18.Rfe1 dc4 19.Be4 cd4 20.Bb7 Rab8 21.Ba6 Rb4 22.Rad1 d3 23.cd3 cd3 24.Rd3 Bc6 25.Rd4 Rd4 26.Nd4 Bd5 27.a4?** [27.Bf1] **Rf4 28.Rd1** [D] **Ng6 29.Bc8 Kf7 30.a5 Ne5 31.a6 Rg4 32.Rd2 Nc4 33.Rf2 Ke7 34.Nb5 Nd6 35.Nd6 Kd6 36.Bb7 Bb7 37.ab7 Kc7 38.h3 Rg5 39.Rb2 Kb8 40.Kf2 Rd5 41.Ke3 Rd7 42.Ke4 Rb7 43.Rf2 0-1**

367) Keres,P-Fischer,R [5/24/62] Curacao Candidates [14] B20/09 Sicilian [E:Queen + minor pieces] **1.e4 c5 2.Ne2 d6 3.g3 g6 4.Bg2 Bg7 5.0-0 Nc6 6.c3 e5! 7.d3 Nge7 8.a3 0-0 9.b4 b6 10.f4 ef4! 11.gf4 d5! 12.e5 Bg4 13.h3 Be2 14.Qe2 f6 15.b5 Na5 16.Nd2 fe5 17.fe5 Rf1 18.Nf1 Nb3 19.Rb1 Nc1 20.Rc1 Qc7! 21.Re1 Rd8 22.Nh2 d4 23.cd4 cd4 24.Nf3** [24.Ng4] **Bh6 25.Qa2 Kh8 26.Qe6 Nd5? [26...Nf5] 27.Nh2! Ne3 28.Bc6! Rf8 29.Nf3 Bf4 30.Nd4 Be5 31.Nf3 Bd4! 32.Re3 Be3 33.Qe3 Qg3 34.Kf1 Qh3 35.Ke1 Qf5 36.d4 Kg7 37.Kf2! h5 38.Kg3 Qg4 39.Kh2 Rf4 40.Qe7 Kh6 41.Qe2 Qf5 42.Qe3 g5 43.Kg2 Rg4 44.Kf2 Rf4 45.Kg2 Qc2 46.Kh1 Qb1 47.Kh2 Qa2 48.Kh3 Qf7 49.Kh2 Qf6 50.Kg2 Kg7 51.Kg3 h4 52.Kg2 Rg4 53.Kh1 Rg3 54.Qe4 g4 55.Nh2 Qg5 56.Nf1? [56.Qe5 =] Rh3? [56...Ra3 -++] 57.Kg1 Ra3 58.d5 g3 59.Bd7! Ra1 60.Bf5! Qf6 61.Qf4 Re1 62.d6 Re5 63.Qg4! Kf8 64.d7 Rd5 65.Kg2!** [D] **Rd7 66.Bd7! Qf2**

67.Kh3 Qf1 68.Kh4 g2 69.Qb4 Kf7! 70.Qb3 Kg7 71.Qg3 Kh7!
72.Qe5! Qh1 73.Bh3 Qh3 74.Kh3 g1=Q 75.Qe7 Kh8 76.Qf8 Kh7
77.Qf7 1/2-1/2

368) Benko,P-Fischer,R [6/1/62] Curacao Candidates [15]
A00/07 Flank [E:Bishop vs. Knight] **1.g3 g6 2.Bg2 Bg7 3.d4 c5 4.c3**
[Unusual, but super solid] **Qb6 5.Nf3 Nf6 6.0-0 0-0 7.d5 d6 8.c4 e6
9.Nc3 ed5 10.cd5 Nbd7 11.Nd2 Ne5** [Play has transposed into a
Benoni] **12.h3 Qa6 13.Qb3 Rb8 14.a4 Ne8 15.Ra3 f5 16.f4 Nf7
17.e4 Qa5 18.Nc4 Qd8 19.Re1 fe4 20.Ne4 Nc7 21.Bd2 Bf5 22.Nc3
Re8 23.Raa1 b6 24.Nb5 Nb5 25.ab5 Rb7 26.Bc3 Re1 27.Re1 Re7
28.Re7 Qe7 29.Bg7 Qe1 30.Kh2 Kg7 31.Qc3 Qc3 32.bc3 Bd3
33.Na3 g5 34.Kg1 gf4 35.gf4 Kg6 36.Kf2 Kh5 37.Kg3 Nh6 38.Bf3
Kg6 39.Kf2 Nf5 40.Bd1 Be4 41.Bf3 Bd3 42.Bd1 Ne7 43.c4 Kf5
44.Ke3 Bf1 45.Bc2 Kf6 46.Bh7 Nf5 47.Kf2 Bh3 48.Nc2 Kg7
49.Bf5 Bf5 [D] 50.Ne3 Bc8 51.Kf3 Kg6 52.Kg3 a6 53.ba6 Ba6
54.Kg4 b5 55.cb5 Bb5 56.Kf3 1/2-1/2**

After 49...Bf5

369) Geller,E-Fischer,R [6/2/62] Curacao Candidates [16]
B92/17 Sicilian [E:Rook + Bishop] **1.e4 c5 2.Nf3 d6 3.d4 cd4 4.Nd4
Nf6 5.Nc3 a6 6.Be2 e5 7.Nb3 Be6 8.0-0 Nbd7 9.a4 Be7 10.f4 Qc7
11.f5 Bc4 12.a5 0-0 13.Be3 b5 14.ab6 Nb6 15.Kh1 Rfc8 16.Bb6!
Qb6 17.Bc4 Rc4 18.Qe2 Rb4?!** [18...Rac8! =] **19.Ra2 Qb7 20.Na5
Qc7 21.Nd5 Nd5 22.ed5 Rb5 23.Qd2 Qc5 24.c4 Rb6 25.Qe2?!**
[25.Ra4! Rab8 26.Nc6 R8b7 27.Ra5! Qc4 28.Ne7 Re7 29.Rc1 ++-]
**Bg5 26.Rf3 Bf6 27.Nc6 e4! 28.Rf4 e3 [D] 29.b4 Rb4 30.Nb4 Qb4
31.Qd3 a5 32.Rf1 Qc3 33.Qc3 Bc3 34.Rb1 h5 35.Kg1 Rc8 36.Kf1
Rc4 37.Ke2 Bb4 38.Ke3 Kh7 39.Rf1 Kh6 40.Rf3 Kg5 41.Kd3
Rc3 42.Ke4 Rc1 43.f6 g6 44.Kd4 h4 45.h3 1/2-1/2**

After 28...e3

370) Fischer,R-Filip,M [6/4/62] Curacao Candidates [17]
C76/02 Ruy Lopez [E:Rooks + minor pieces] **1.e4 e5 2.Nf3 Nc6
3.Bb5 a6 4.Ba4 d6 5.c3 Bd7 6.d4 g6 7.0-0 Bg7 8.d5 Nce7 9.Bd7
Qd7 10.c4 h6 11.Nc3 f5 12.ef5 gf5** [The Ruy Lopez has essentially
transposed into a King's Indian] **13.Nh4 Nf6 14.f4 e4 15.Be3 0-0
16.h3** [White prepares for the g4 break] **c5 17.dc6 bc6 18.Qe2 Qe6
19.Rad1 Kh7 20.Kh2 Rg8 21.Rd2 Ne8 22.g3 a5 23.Rfd1 Ng6
24.Ng2 Rb8 25.Bd4 Rb7 26.g4 Re7 27.Bg7 Rgg7 28.Rd4 fg4
29.Qg4 Ne5 30.Qe6 Nf3 31.Kh1 Re6 [D] 32.f5 Re5 33.Re4 Rf5
34.Re8 Rg3 35.Nf4 Rf4 36.Ne2 Rh3 37.Kg2 Rfh4 38.Rd6 Ne1
39.Kf1 Rh1 40.Kf2 R4h2 41.Ke3 Rh3 42.Ke4 Kg7 1-0**

After 31...Re6

371) Tal,M-Fischer,R [6/5/62] Curacao Candidates [18]
C64/07 Ruy Lopez **1.e4 e5 2.Nf3 Nc6 3.Bb5 Bc5 4.c3 Nge7 5.d4**
[5.0-0 Bb6 6.d4 ed4 7.cd4 d5 8.ed5 +-] **ed4 6.cd4 Bb4 7.Bd2 Bd2
8.Qd2 a6 9.Ba4 d5 10.ed5 Qd5 11.Nc3 Qe6 12.Kf1 Qc4 13.Kg1
0-0 14.d5 Na7 15.Re1 Nf5 16.h3 Nb5 17.Nb5 ab5 18.Bb3 Qc5
19.Rc1 Qd6 20.Qc3 Bd7! 21.g4 [D] Ng3! 22.fg3 Qg3 23.Kf1 f5
24.g5 f4 25.d6 Kh8 26.dc7 Rae8 27.Bd5 Bh3 28.Rh3 Qh3 29.Kf2!
1/2-1/2**

After 21.g4

After 11...Ne8

372) Fischer,R-Korchnoi,V [6/8/62] Curacao Candidates [19] B88/05 Sicilian [E:Rook + Bishop vs. Rook + pawns] **1.e4 c5 2.Nf3 Nc6 3.d4 cd4 4.Nd4 Nf6 5.Nc3 d6 6.Bc4 e6 7.Bb3 Be7 8.0-0 0-0 9.Be3 Na5 10.f4 b6 11.e5 Ne8** [D] **12.f5 de5 13.fe6 Nb3 14.Nc6! Qd6 15.Qd6! Bd6** += [Black's b-pawn is weak and White's pieces are more coordinated] **16.ab3 Be6 17.Na7 Rb8 18.Ra6** [Better was 18.Ne4!] **Nf6 19.Rb6 Rb6 20.Bb6 Rb8 21.Bf2 Ng4 22.Nab5 Bb4 23.Ba7 Rb7 24.h3 Bc3 25.bc3 Rb5 26.hg4 Bg4 27.c4 Rb7 28.Ra1 Bf5 29.c5?** [29.Ra2!] **Bc2 30.c6 Rb3! 31.g4??** [31.c7 =] **Rg3 32.Kf2 Rg4 33.c7 Bf5 34.Be3 h5 35.Ra8 Kh7 36.c8=Q Bc8 37.Rc8 h4 38.Kf3 f5 39.Rf8 Kg6 40.Rh8 Rg3 41.Kf2 f4 42.Ba7 h3 43.Bb8 Kf5 44.Rf8 Ke4 45.Re8 Rg5 0-1**

Final position

373) Petrosian,T-Fischer,R [6/9/62] Curacao Candidates [20] D54/03 Queen's Gambit Declined **1.c4 Nf6 2.Nc3 e6 3.d4 d5 4.Bg5 Be7 5.e3 h6 6.Bh4 b6** [The Tartakower Defense] **7.cd5 Nd5 8.Be7 Qe7 9.Nd5 ed5 10.Ne2 0-0 11.Nf4 Bb7 12.Be2 Nd7 13.Rc1 Nf6 14.Qa4 c5 15.0-0 Rfc8 16.Qa3 Qf8 17.dc5 Rc5! 18.Rc5 Qc5 19.Qc5 bc5 20.Rc1 c4 21.Kf1 Rb8 22.Rc2 Bc6 23.f3** [D] **1/2-1/2**

After 30...Kh8

374) Fischer,R-Benko,P [6/14/62] Curacao Candidates [22] C11/07 French **1.e4 e6 2.d4 d5 3.Nc3 Nf6 4.e5 Nfd7 5.f4 c5 6.dc5?!** [Better was 6.Nf3] **Bc5?** [6...Nc6 =+] **7.Qg4 0-0 8.Bd3?!** [8.Nf3] **f5 9.Qh3 Bg1! 10.Rg1 Nc5 11.Bd2 Nc6 12.Nb5?! Qb6 13.0-0-0 Bd7 14.Nd6 Na4! 15.Bb5 Nd4 16.Be3 Ne2! 17.Be2 Qb2 18.Kd2 Qb4 19.Kc1 Nc3 20.Rde1 Na2 21.Kd1 Nc3 22.Kc1 d4?** [22...a5 23.Bd3 a4 24.Kd2 a3 -+] **23.Bf2 Rfc8 24.Bd3 Na2 25.Kd1 Nc3 26.Kc1 Rc5 27.Qh4! Ra5 28.Kd2 h6 29.g4 fg4 30.Rg4 Kh8** [D] **31.Qh6 1-0**

After 70.Rf2

375) Fischer,R-Keres,P [6/15/62] Curacao Candidates [21] C96/10 Ruy Lopez [E:Rook + minor pieces] **1.e4 e5 2.Nf3 Nc6 3.Bb5 a6 4.Ba4 Nf6 5.0-0 Be7 6.Re1 b5 7.Bb3 d6 8.c3 0-0 9.h3 Na5 10.Bc2 c5 11.d4 Nd7 12.d5?!** [Better was 12.Nbd2] **Nb6 13.g4?!** [Preventing ...f5, but too weakening] **h5 14.Nh2 hg4 15.hg4 Bg5!** [Trading off the bad Bishop for White's good Bishop] **16.Nd2 g6 17.Ndf3 Bc1 18.Qc1 Kg7 19.Qg5 Nb7 20.Qd8 Rd8 21.a4 ba4 22.Ba4 Na4 23.Ra4 Bd7 24.Ra2 c4 25.Nd2 Bb5 26.Nhf1 Rh8 27.Ne3 Rh4 28.Kg2 Rah8 29.Nf3 Rh3 30.Nf1 Nc5 31.Ng3 Bd7 32.g5 f6 33.gf6 Kf6 34.Re3 Ke7 35.Nd2 Rh2 36.Kg1 Bb5 37.Ra1 R2h4 38.Kg2 Rf8 39.Rf3 Rb8 40.Kg1 Ra8 41.Ra5 Rc8 42.Ra3 Ra8 43.Ra5 Ra7 44.Kg2 Nb7 45.Ra1 a5 46.Ngf1 Nc5 47.Ne3 a4 48.Rh3 Rh3 49.Kh3 Nd3 50.Ra2 Nf2 51.Kg3 Nd3 52.Nec4 Ra8 53.Nb6 Ra6 54.Nbc4 Nc5 55.Kf3 Ra8 56.b4 Nb3 57.Na3 Bd7 58.Kg2 Bg4 59.Nac4 Rc8 60.Ne3 Bd7 61.c4 Rb8 62.b5 Nc5 63.Nd1 Kd8 64.Nc3 Ra8 65.Nf3 Kc7 66.Ng5 Kb6 67.Nf7??** [67.Nf3 =] **Rf8 68.Rf2 a3 69.Rf3 Bg4 70.Rf2** [D] **a2 71.Na2 Ne4 72.Rf1 Bf5 73.c5 dc5 0-1**

376) Fischer,R-Geller,E [6/16/62] Curacao Candidates [23]
B88/01 Sicilian [E:Queen vs. Rooks] **1.e4 c5 2.Nf3 Nc6 3.d4 cd4
4.Nd4 Nf6 5.Nc3 d6 6.Bc4 e6 7.Bb3 Be7 8.0-0 Nd4 9.Qd4 0-0 10.f4
b6 11.Kh1** [Better was 11.Qd3, stopping 11...Ba6] **Ba6! 12.Rf3 d5!
13.ed5 Bc5 14.Qa4 Bb7 15.Be3 ed5 16.Bd4 Re8?** [Better was
16...a6 17.Bf6 gf6! -+] **17.Rd1 Ng4?** [17...Ne4] **18.h3 Qh4 19.Rdf1
Bd4 20.Qd4 Rad8 21.Nd5 Bd5 22.Bd5 Nf6 23.c4 Rd7 24.Re3
Red8 25.Qe5 h6 26.Bf3 Rd2 27.b4 Rf2 28.Ree1** [D] **Rf3 29.Rf3
Re8 30.Qe8 Ne8 31.Re8 Kh7 32.c5 Qf6 33.Re1 bc5 34.bc5 Qb2
35.Rff1 Qa2 36.c6 Qa5 37.Rc1 Qc7 38.Rfd1 g5 39.fg5 Kg6 40.gh6
Kh6 41.Rd6 Kg7 42.Rd4 Kg6 43.Ra4 1-0**

After 28.Ree1

377) Filip,M-Fischer,R [6/17/62] Curacao Candidates [24]
D58/10 Queen's Gambit Declined **1.d4 d5 2.c4 e6 3.Nc3 Nf6 4.Bg5
Be7 5.e3 0-0 6.Nf3 h6 7.Bh4 b6 8.Rc1** [8.Bf6 Bf6 9.cd5 ed5 +=]
**Bb7 9.cd5 Nd5 10.Be7 Qe7 11.Be2 Nf6 = 12.0-0 Nbd7 13.Qa4 c5
14.Qa3 Rfc8 15.Rfd1 Qf8 16.Ba6 Ba6 17.Qa6 cd4 18.Nd4 Qb4
19.a3 Qc4 20.Qc4 Rc4 21.Nce2 Rac8 22.Rc4 Rc4 23.Rc1** [D]
1/2-1/2

Final position

378) Korchnoi,V-Fischer,R [6/21/62] Curacao Candidates
[26] E60/04 Benoni **1.g3 g6 2.Nf3 Nf6 3.Bg2 Bg7 4.d4 c5 5.d5 d6
6.c4 b5!?** [An early example of the Benko Gambit] **7.cb5 Qa5?!**
[7...a6!] **8.Nfd2 Qb5 9.0-0 0-0 10.Na3 Qa6 11.Re1 Nbd7 12.e4**
[Strategies: White plays for e4-e5; Black plays on the a1-h8 diagonal
and the b-file] **Ne5 13.Bf1 Qb7 14.h3 a5 15.f4 Ned7 16.Ndc4 Nb6
17.Bd2 Nc4 18.Nc4 Qc7 19.Bc3** [Better was 19.a4! stopping ...a4]
Nd7 20.e5 a4! 21.h4 Nb6! 22.h5 Ba6 23.Nb6 Qb6 24.Ba6 [Better
was 24.Bg2] **Ra6 25.Kg2 de5 26.fe5 a3 27.b3 Qb7 28.Qf3 e6
29.Rad1 ed5 30.hg6 Rg6 31.Rd5 Qc8 32.Red1 Re6 33.Qg4 Rfe8
34.Kg1 Kh8 35.Qf5 Rf8 36.Rd7 Kg8 37.R1d5 Rg6 38.g4 Qa6
39.Kf2 Rh6 40.Qf4 Rh1 41.Rd3 Rb1** [D] **1/2-1/2**

Final position

379) Fischer,R-Petrosian,T [6/23/62] Curacao Candidates
[27] B47/06 Sicilian [E:Rook + minor piece] **1.e4 c5 2.Nf3 Nc6 3.d4
cd4 4.Nd4 e6 5.Nc3 Qc7 6.g3 a6 7.Bg2 Nf6 8.0-0 Be7 9.b3 0-0
10.Bb2 Nd4 11.Qd4 d6 12.Rac1 b5 13.Nd1 Bb7 14.Ne3 Rfd8
15.c4 b4 16.c5! += dc5 17.Qb4 Bc6 18.Qc3 Qb7 19.f3 a5** [A sort
of minority attack] **20.Nc4 a4 21.Na5 Qb6 22.Nc6 Qc6 23.b4 Qb6
24.bc5 Bc5 25.Qc5 Qb2 26.Rc2 Qd4 27.Qd4 Rd4 28.Rfc1 g5
29.Rc8 Rc8 30.Rc8 Kg7 31.Rc2 g4** [D] **32.Kf2 gf3 33.Bf3 Rd3
34.Ke2 Ra3 35.Rd2 h5 1/2-1/2**

After 31...g4

380) Keres,P-Fischer,R [6/26/62] Curacao Candidates [28]
D35/11 Queen's Gambit Declined **1.d4 d5 2.c4 e6 3.Nc3 Nf6 4.Nf3
Be7 5.cd5 ed5 6.Bf4 c6 7.Qc2 g6 8.e3 Bf5 9.Bd3 Bd3 10.Qd3 Nbd7
11.0-0 0-0 12.h3 Nh5** [Better was 12...Re8] **13.Bh6 Re8 14.Rab1
a5 15.Rfe1 f5 16.g4! fg4 17.hg4 Nhf6 18.Nh2 Kh8 19.Bf4 Bf8
20.Kg2 Ne4 21.Nf3 Bg7 22.Rh1 Qf6 23.Qc2?** [Better was 23.Rh4
+-] **Kg8 24.Be5 Qe6 25.Ne4 de4 26.Qe4 Be5 27.de5 Nf6 28.Qf4
Qg4 29.Qg4 Ng4 30.Rbd1 Ne5** [D] **1/2-1/2**

Final position

After 23.Re2

381) Sliwa,B-Fischer,R [9/62] Warsaw Team Tournament D36/01 Queen's Gambit Declined **1.d4 d5 2.c4 e6 3.Nc3 Nf6 4.cd5 ed5 5.Bg5 c6 6.Qc2 Na6** [Unusual, but plausible; the Knight can maneuver to e6 via c7] **7.e3 Nc7 8.Bd3 Be7 9.Nge2 Nh5 10.Be7 Qe7 11.0-0-0** [11.Bh7 g6 12.Bg6 fg6 13.Qg6 Qf7-the piece is better than three pawns] **g6 12.h3 Bd7 13.Kb1 0-0-0 14.Na4 Kb8 15.Nc5 Bc8 16.Nc1 Ng7 17.N1b3 b6 18.Na4 Bb7 19.Rhe1 Nge6 20.Rc1 Rhe8 21.a3 f5 22.f4?** [Too weakening] **Qh4 23.Re2** [D] **g5! 24.Nd2 gf4 25.Nf3 Qf6 26.Bf5 fe3 27.Be6 Ne6 28.Qc3 c5 29.Rd1 cd4 30.Nd4 Nd4 31.Qd4 Qg6 32.Rc2 Re4 33.Qc3 Rc8 34.Qb3 Rc2 0-1**

After 20...e4

382) Fischer,R-Purevzhav [9/16/62] Varna Olympiad Preliminaries [1] B77/10 Sicilian **1.e4 c5 2.Nf3 d6 3.d4 cd4 4.Nd4 Nf6 5.Nc3 g6 6.Be3 Bg7 7.f3 Nc6 8.Qd2 0-0 9.Bc4! Nd7 10.0-0-0** [Better was 10.h4 Na5 11.Bb3 Ne5 12.Qe2 Bd7 13.h5 +=] **Nb6 11.Bb3 Na5 12.Qd3! Bd7 13.h4 Rc8 14.h5 Nbc4 15.hg6 hg6?** [15...fg6! ∞] **16.Bh6 e6?** [16...e5] **17.f4 e5 18.Nf5! Bf5 19.ef5 Nb2 20.Kb2 e4** [D] **21.Bg7! Kg7** [21...ed3 22.f6 ++-] **22.Ne4 1-0**

Final position

383) Fischer,R-Padevsky,N [9/17/62] Varna Olympiad Preliminaries [3] C19/16 French **1.e4 e6 2.d4 d5 3.Nc3 Bb4 4.e5 Ne7 5.a3 Bc3 6.bc3 c5 7.Nf3 Nbc6 8.a4 Qa5 9.Bd2 Bd7 10.Be2 c4** [10...f6!?] **11.h4?!** [11.0-0 f6∞] **f6 12.h5 fe5 13.h6 gh6! 14.Ne5 Ne5 15.de5 0-0-0 16.Rh6 Ng6 17.Bg5 Qc3 18.Kf1 Rdf8 19.Bf6 Rf6!** [A nice exchange sac to seize the initiative] **20.ef6 Qf6 21.Ra3 Bc6?** [21...Qg7!] **22.Rah3 Qg7 23.Bg4 Kb8 24.g3 Rf8 25.Rh7 Qf6 26.Qe1 d4 27.R3h6 d3 28.cd3 cd3 29.Rg6! Qg6 30.Qe5 Ka8 31.Rh8 Qe8 32.Rf8 Qf8 33.Qd4 a6 34.Qd3** [D] **1/2-1/2**

After 29.Rf1

384) Blau,M-Fischer,R [9/19/62] Varna Olympiad Preliminaries [4] B53/07 Sicilian **1.e4 c5 2.Nf3 d6 3.d4 cd4 4.Qd4 Nc6 5.Bb5 Bd7 6.Bc6 Bc6 7.c4 Nf6 8.Nc3 g6 9.Bg5** [9.0-0 Bg7 10.Qd3] **Bg7 10.Nd5?** [10.0-0] **0-0 11.Qd3** [11.Nf6 ef6! -+] **Bd5 12.ed5 Nd7 13.Qd2 Rc8 14.Rc1 b5 15.b3 bc4 16.bc4 Nc5 -+** [White's c-pawn is backward and vulnerable] **17.0-0 Ne4 18.Qe3 Ng5 19.Qg5 Rc5 20.Qe3 Qc7 21.Nd4 Bd4 22.Qd4 Rc8 23.Rc2 Rc4 24.Rc4 Qc4 25.Qa7 Qe4 26.h3 Rc4 27.Rd1 Kg7 28.Qb7 Qe2 29.Rf1** [D] **Ra4 30.Qb3 Ra2 31.Qc3 f6 32.Qe1 Qe5 33.f4 Qd5 34.Qe7 Kh6 35.Qf8 Kh5 36.g4 Kh4 37.Qf6 Kh3 38.Qc3 Kg4 39.Qc8 Kh4 40.Qd8 Kh5 0-1**

Final position

385) Fischer,R-Aloni,I [9/20/62] Varna Olympiad Preliminaries [5] C10/24 French [E:Rook + Knight] **1.e4 e6 2.d4 d5 3.Nc3 Nf6 4.Bg5 de4 5.Ne4 Nbd7 6.Nf6 Nf6 7.Nf3 Be7 8.Bd3 h6 9.Bh4 0-0 10.Qe2 Nd5 11.Bg3 Bb4 12.Nd2** [12.c3 Nc3] **f5?!** [Permanently weakening e5 and e6] **13.Be5 Bd6 14.c3 Be5 15.Qe5 Qf6 16.Nf3 Bd7 17.Bc4 Nb6 18.Bb3 Rac8 19.0-0 Qe5 20.Ne5 Rfe8 21.Rfe1 Ba4 22.Nd3 Bb3 23.ab3 a6 24.Nc5 Rb8 25.Ne6 Be7 26.Nc5 Rf7 27.Re5 c6 28.Rae1 Kf8 29.c4 Na8 30.d5 cd5 31.Rd5 Re8 32.Re8 Ke8 33.Kf1 Nb6 34.Re5 Kd8 35.Re6 Nc8 36.Rg6 Ke8 37.Ne6 Re7 38.Nf4 Kf7 39.Rg3** [D] **1-0** [Time]

386) Fischer,R-Ciocaltea,V [9/23/62] Varna Olympiad Preliminaries [8] C75/09 Ruy Lopez **1.e4 e5 2.Nf3 Nc6 3.Bb5 a6 4.Ba4 d6 5.c3 Bd7 6.d4 Nge7 7.Bb3 h6 8.Qe2 Ng6 9.Qc4 Qf6** [Better was 9...Qe7] **10.d5 b5 11.Qe2 Na5 12.Bd1 Be7 13.g3 0-0** [13...Bh3] **14.h4 Rfc8?? [D] 15.Bg5! hg5 16.hg5 Qg5 17.Ng5 Bg5 18.Na3 c6 19.dc6 Be6 20.Qh5 Bh6 21.Bg4 Bg4 22.Qg4 Nc6 23.Rd1 b4 24.Nc4 bc3 25.bc3 Nd4 26.Nb6 1-0**

After 14...Rfc8??

387) Rivera,D-Fischer,R [9/25/62] Varna Olympiad Preliminaries [9] E26/01 Nimzo-Indian **1.d4 Nf6 2.c4 e6 3.Nc3 Bb4 4.e3 d5 5.a3 Bc3 6.bc3 c5 7.Bd3 dc4 8.Bc4 Qc7 9.Bb3 b6 10.Ne2 0-0 11.Bb2 Nc6 12.0-0 Na5 13.Ng3 Bb7 14.Rc1 [D] Qc6!** [Winning a piece "in broad daylight"] **15.f3 Qb5 16.Ba4 Qb2 0-1**

After 14.Rc1

388) Uhlmann,W-Fischer,R [9/27/62] Varna Olympiad Final [1] E79/07 King's Indian **1.d4 Nf6 2.c4 g6 3.Nc3 Bg7 4.e4 d6 5.Be2 0-0 6.f4** [The Four pawns Attack can be used as a drawing weapon as in this game] **c5 7.Nf3 cd4 8.Nd4 Nc6 9.Be3 e5 10.Nc6 bc6 11.fe5 de5 12.Bc5** [12.0-0 Qc7 13.Qe1 Be6 =] **Re8 13.Qd8 Rd8 14.0-0 [D] Rd2 15.Rad1 Rd1 16.Rd1 Be6 17.Bd6 Ng4 18.Bc5 Nf6 19.Bd6 1/2-1/2**

After 14.0-0

389) Fischer,R-Najdorf,M [9/28/62] Varna Olympiad Final [2] B90/02 Sicilian **1.e4 c5 2.Nf3 d6 3.d4 cd4 4.Nd4 Nf6 5.Nc3 a6 6.h3 b5 7.Nd5 Bb7?** [7...Ne4! 8.Qf3 Nc5 9.b4 ∞; or 9.Nf6 gf6 10.Qa8 Bb7 =+] **8.Nf6 gf6 9.c4! bc4 10.Bc4 Be4 11.0-0 d5 12.Re1! e5 13.Qa4! Nd7 [D] 14.Re4!** [An exchange sac to get at Black's uncastled King] **de4 15.Nf5! Bc5 16.Ng7! Ke7 17.Nf5 Ke8 18.Be3 Be3 19.fe3 Qb6 20.Rd1 Ra7 21.Rd6! Qd8 22.Qb3 Qc7 23.Bf7 Kd8 24.Be6 1-0**

After 13...Nd7

390) Filip,M-Fischer,R [9/29/62] Varna Olympiad Final [3] D79/10 Grunfeld [E:Bishop vs. Knight] **1.d4 Nf6 2.c4 g6 3.g3 c6 4.Nc3 d5 5.cd5 cd5 6.Bg2 Bg7 7.Nf3 0-0 8.0-0 Ne4!** [Equalizing easily] **9.Ne4 de4 10.Ng5 Qd4 11.Qd4 Bd4 12.Ne4 Nc6 13.Nc3 Be6 14.Bg5 f6 15.Bd2 Rfd8 16.Rfd1 Bc4 17.Be1** [With no pawn majorities and identical minor pieces, the draw is certain] **Kf7 18.e3 Be5 19.f4 Bd6 20.b3 Be6 21.Kf2 Rac8 22.Rac1 Bg4 23.Bf3 Bf3 24.Kf3 a6 25.Ke2 f5 26.Na4 Ba3 27.Rd8 Rd8 28.Rd1 Rd1 29.Kd1 e5 30.Nc3 Ke6 31.Bd2 Bb4 32.Ne2 Be7 33.Kc2 Nb4 34.Bb4 Bb4 35.fe5 Ke5 36.Kd3 g5 37.Nd4 Be7 38.Nf3 Kd5 39.Nd4 Ke5 40.Nf3 Kf6 41.Kd4 Ke6 42.e4 g4 43.ef5 Kf5 44.Nd2 Ke6 45.Ke4 Kd6 46.Kf5 [D] 1/2-1/2**

Final position

391) Fischer,R-Robatsch,K [9/30/62] Varna Olympiad Final [4] B01/10 Center Counter **1.e4 d5 2.ed5 Qd5 3.Nc3 Qd8** [3...Qa5] **4.d4 g6 5.Bf4! Bg7 6.Qd2!!** [Now if 6...Qd4, then 7.Qd4 Bd4 8.Nb5 +- or 6...Bd4 7.0-0-0 c5 8.Nb5 ++-] **Nf6 7.0-0-0 c6 8.Bh6 0-0 9.h4 Qa5 10.h5! gh5 11.Bd3 Nbd7 12.Nge2 Rd8 [D] 13.g4! Nf8 14.gh5 Ne6 15.Rdg1 Kh8 16.Bg7 Ng7 17.Qh6 Rg8 18.Rg5 Qd8 19.Rhg1 Nf5 20.Bf5 1-0**

After 12...Rd8

After 23...Rac8

After 23...Qa7

After 26.Kf1

Final position

After 9.bc3

392) Ciocaltea,V-Fischer,R [10/1/62] Varna Olympiad Final [5] A04/14 King's Indian Attack [E:Rook + minor piece] **1.e4 c5 2.Nf3 d6 3.d3 Nc6 4.g3 g6 5.Bg2 Bg7 6.0-0 e5** [Botvinnik's system] **7.c3 Nge7 8.Nh4 0-0 9.f4 ef4 10.gf4 f5 11.Nd2 Kh8 12.Ndf3 fe4?** [12...d5 =] **13.de4 d5 14.ed5 Qd5** [14...Nd5 15.Ng5 +=] **15.Qd5 Nd5 16.Ng5! Nb6 17.Be3 Na4 18.Rae1** +- [White has a big lead in development and Black has many weakened interior squares] **Bd7 19.Bc1 Bf6 20.Nhf3 Bf5 21.Ne5 Ne7 22.Ne4 Bh4 23.Rd1 Rac8** [D] **24.Nd6 Rc7 25.Nb5 Rcc8 26.Na7 Ra8 27.Nb5 Ra5 28.c4 Nb6 29.Nc3 Na4 30.Nb5 Nb6 31.Na3 Bf6 32.Rfe1 Na4 33.Nb5 Nb6 34.Nc3 Nc6 35.Bc6 bc6 36.b3 Nd7 37.Na4 Ne5 38.fe5 Bh4 39.Rf1 Kg7 40.Rd6 Raa8 41.Be3 Bh3 42.Rf8 Rf8 43.Rd1 Rf5 44.Nc5 Rf3 45.Bd4 Rf4 46.e6 Kf8 47.Be5 Bf2 48.Kh1 Rg4 49.Nd7 Ke7 50.Bg3 Ke6 51.Rd6 Ke7 52.Rd2 Bg3 53.hg3 Rg3 54.Ne5 c5 55.Kh2 Re3 56.Nd3 Bf5 57.Nc5 h5 58.a4 h4 59.a5 g5 60.a6 Kf6 61.a7 Re8 62.Ra2 Ra8 63.b4 g4 64.b5 g3 65.Kg2 Kg5 66.b6 Kg4 67.b7 h3 68.Kf1 g2 69.Rg2 1-0**

393) Fischer,R-Donner,J [10/3/62] Varna Olympiad Final [6] B19/01 Caro Kann **1.e4 c6 2.d4 d5 3.Nc3 de4 4.Ne4 Bf5 5.Ng3 Bg6 6.h4 h6 7.Nf3 Nd7 8.Bd3** [8.h5 Bh7 9.Bd3] **Bd3 9.Qd3 e6 10.Bf4 Qa5 11.Bd2 Qc7 12.c4** [12.0-0-0] **Ngf6 13.Bc3 a5 14.0-0 Bd6?!** [14...Bb4 =] **15.Ne4 Ne4 16.Qe4 0-0 17.d5 Rfe8 18.dc6 bc6 19.Rad1 Bf8 20.Nd4 Ra6** [20...Rc8 21.Nc6] **21.Nf5 Nc5 22.Qe3 Na4 23.Be5 Qa7** [D] **24.Nh6?** [Unsound] **gh6 25.Rd4 f5! 26.Rfd1 Nc5 27.Rd8 Qf7 28.Re8 Qe8 29.Bd4 Ne4 30.f3 e5!** [Perhaps overlooked by Fischer] **31.fe4 ed4 32.Qg3 Bg7 33.ef5 Qe3 34.Qe3 de3 35.Rd8 Kf7 36.Rd7 Kf6 37.g4 Bf8 38.Kg2 Bc5 39.Rh7 Ke5 40.Kf3 Kd4 41.Rh6 Rb6 42.b3 a4 43.Re6 ab3 44.ab3 Kd3 45.g5 0-1**

394) Unzicker,W-Fischer,R [10/4/62] Varna Olympiad Final [7] B92/00 Sicilian **1.e4 c5 2.Nf3 d6 3.d4 cd4 4.Nd4 Nf6 5.Nc3 a6 6.Be2 e5 7.Nb3 Be6 8.0-0 Nbd7 9.f4 Qc7 10.f5 Bc4 11.a4 Be7 12.Be3 0-0 13.a5 b5 14.ab6 Nb6 15.Bb6?!** [15.Kh1 =] **Qb6 16.Kh1 Bb5! 17.Bb5 ab5 18.Nd5 Nd5 19.Qd5 Ra4! 20.c3 Qa6 21.h3 Rc8 22.Rfe1 h6!? 23.Kh2 Bg5 24.g3 Qa7! 25.Kg2 Ra2 26.Kf1** [D] **Rc3! 0-1** [27.bc3 Qf2# or 27.Ra2 Rf3 28.Ke2 Rf2 29.Kd3 Qa2 -++]

395) Padevsky,N-Fischer,R [10/5/62] Varna Olympiad Final [8] B23/11 Sicilian **1.e4 c5 2.Nc3 Nc6 3.f4 e6** [3...g6] **4.Nf3 Nf6 5.g3 d5 6.e5 Ne4 7.Bg2 Nc3 8.bc3 Qa5 9.0-0 c4 10.Kh1 Be7 11.a4 b6 12.Ba3 Ba3 13.Ra3 Bb7 14.Qe2 Qc5 15.Raa1 0-0 16.Rab1 Rad8 17.h4 h6 18.Kh2 Rd7 19.Qe3 Qe3 20.de3** [White is somewhat better, but allows the draw] [D] **1/2-1/2**

396) Fischer,R-Portisch,L [10/6/62] Varna Olympiad Final [9] B41/05 Sicilian [E:Rook + pawn] **1.e4 c5 2.Nf3 e6 3.d4 cd4 4.Nd4 a6 5.c4 Nf6 6.Nc3 Qc7** [6...Bb4!?] **7.Be2** [7.a3!] **Bb4 8.Nc2! Bc3 9.bc3** [D] **Nc6** [9...Ne4 10.Qd4 Nf6 11.Bf4 with initiative] **10.f3 0-0 11.Ba3 Rd8 12.Bd6 Qa5 13.Nb4 Ne8 14.0-0 Nd6 15.Qd6 Qa3 16.c5 a5! 17.Nc6 bc6 18.Qd4 d5!** [Breaking the bind on d6] **19.cd6 Rd6 20.Qb6 h6 21.Rad1 Rd1 22.Rd1 Qc3 23.h3 Qb4 24.Qc7 Qb7 25.Rd8 Kh7 26.Qb7 Bb7 27.Rd7**

Ba6 28.Ba6 Ra6 29.Rf7 Kg6 30.Rb7 a4 31.a3 Ra5 32.Kf2 Kf6 33.g4 h5! 34.gh5 Rh5 35.Kg3 Rg5 36.Kf4 Rh5 37.Rc7 Rh3 38.e5 Kg6 39.Rc6 Rh4 40.Kg3 Rd4 41.Re6 Kf5 1/2-1/2

397) Botvinnik,M-Fischer,R [10/7/62] Varna Olympiad Final [10] D98/13 Grunfeld [E:Rook + pawn] 1.c4 g6 2.d4 Nf6 3.Nc3 d5 4.Nf3 Bg7 5.Qb3 dc4 6.Qc4 0-0 7.e4 Bg4 8.Be3 Nfd7 9.Be2 Nc6 10.Rd1 Nb6 [10...Bf3 =] 11.Qc5 Qd6 12.h3 Bf3 13.gf3 Rfd8 [13...e6] 14.d5 Ne5 15.Nb5 Qf6! 16.f4 Ned7 17.e5 [D] Qf4! [Botvinnik analyzed this position years earlier for his match with Smyslov, but he and his team had overlooked this shot!] 18.Bf4 Nc5 19.Nc7 Rac8 20.d6 ed6 21.ed6 Bb2 22.0-0 Nbd7 23.Rd5 b6 24.Bf3?! [24.Bc4 =] Ne6! 25.Ne6? [25.Be3] fe6 26.Rd3 Nc5 27.Re3 e5 28.Be5 Be5 29.Re5 Rd6 30.Re7 Rd7 31.Rd7 Nd7 32.Bg4 Rc7 33.Re1 Kf7 34.Kg2 Nc5 35.Re3 Re7 36.Rf3 Kg7 37.Rc3 Re4 38.Bd1 Rd4 39.Bc2 Kf6 40.Kf3 Kg5 41.Kg3 Ne4 42.Be4 Re4 43.Ra3 Re7 44.Rf3 Rc7 45.a4 Rc5 46.Rf7 Ra5 47.Rh7! Ra4 48.h4! Kf5 49.Rf7 Ke5 50.Rg7 Ra1 51.Kf3 b5? 52.h5! Ra3 53.Kg2 gh5 54.Rg5 Kd6 55.Rb5 h4 56.f4 Kc6 57.Rb8! h3 58.Kh2 a5 59.f5 Kc7 60.Rb5 Kd6 61.f6 Ke6 62.Rb6 Kf7 63.Ra6 Kg6 64.Rc6 a4 65.Ra6 Kf7 66.Rc6 Rd3 67.Ra6 a3 68.Kg1 [D] 1/2-1/2

After 17.e5

Final position

398) Fischer,R-Gligoric,S [10/9/62] Varna Olympiad Final [11] B80/03 Sicilian 1.e4 c5 2.Nf3 d6 3.d4 cd4 4.Nd4 Nf6 5.Nc3 a6 6.g3 e6 [6...e5!] 7.Bg2 Be7?! [7...Bd7] 8.0-0 0-0 9.f4 Qc7 10.g4! Nc6 11.Nc6 bc6 12.g5 Nd7 13.f5 Re8 14.Kh1 Bf8 15.Bf4 Ne5! 16.f6 g6 17.h4 a5 18.h5 Ba6 19.Re1 Qb6 20.hg6 fg6 21.Be5 de5 22.Qf3 Ra7 23.Bf1 Rf7 24.Ba6 Qa6 25.Qg3? [Better was 25.Nd1 to maneuver the Knight to c4 +=/+-] Qb6 26.Qe5 Qb2 27.Rad1 h6 28.Re3 Bb4 29.gh6 Qc2 30.Rg1 Kh7 31.Qg3 Rg8 32.e5 Bc3 33.Rc3 Qe4 34.Rg2 Rd8 35.Re3 Rd1 36.Kh2? [36.Re1] Qb1 37.Qg4 Rh1 38.Kg3 Qc1 39.Re4 Rd7! 40.Qe2 Qg5 41.Qg4 Rd3 42.Kf2 Rd2 43.Kg3? Rg2 44.Kg2 [D] Qc1 0-1

After 44.Kg2

399) Fischer,R-Mednis,E [12/16/62] US Championship [1] C19/03 French [E:Rook + minor pieces] 1.e4 e6 2.d4 d5 3.Nc3 Bb4 4.e5 c5 5.a3 Bc3 6.bc3 Qc7 7.Nf3 Bd7 8.a4 Ne7 9.Bd3 Nbc6 10.0-0 c4 11.Be2 f6 12.Ba3 [Better was 12.Re1! +=] 0-0 13.Re1 Rf7 14.ef6 gf6 15.Bf1 Re8 16.Nh4 Ng6 17.Qh5 Rg7 18.g3 Qa5 19.Bb2 Nd8 20.Re3 Nf7 21.Kh1 Nd6 22.Ng6 hg6 23.Qe2 Rh7 24.Kg1 Kf7 25.h4 f5 26.Qf3 Ne4 27.Qf4 Rc8 28.Bg2 Qc7 29.Qc7 Rc7 30.a5 Rc6?! [30...Kf6 =+] 31.Ba3 Ra6 32.Bb4 Rh8 33.Ree1 Bc6 34.Bf3 Nd2 35.Be2 Ne4 36.Kg2 Nf6 37.Rh1 Be8 38.Kf3 Ne4 39.Ke3 Nf6 40.f3 Bd7 41.g4 Be8 42.Kf4 Bb5 43.h5 gh5 44.Rag1 Be8 45.Ke3 b6 46.ab6 Rb6 47.Ra1 Rb7 48.Bd6 Rh7 49.gf5? [49.g5 ∞] ef5 50.Rh4 [Better was 50.Bf4] Ke6 51.Bh2 Rb2 52.Kd2 Rhb7 [D] 53.Kc1 R2b6 54.Bf1 Ng8! 55.Bf4 a5 56.Rh2 a4 57.Bh3 Ne7 58.Bg5 Kf7 59.Re2 Re6 60.Re6 Ke6 61.Kd1 Nc8 62.Kd2 Bd7! 63.Bg2 Ra7 64.Re1 Kd6 65.Bh6 a3 66.Bf8 Kc6 67.Bc5 Ra8 68.Ra1 a2 69.Ke3 Nd6 70.Kf4 Nb5 71.Bb4 h4 72.Bh3 Nc7 73.Be7 [D] 0-1

After 52...Rhb7

Final position

Final position

400) Rossolimo,N-Fischer,R [12/17/62] US Championship [2] B52/06 Sicilian [E:King + pawn] **1.e4 c5 2.Nf3 d6 3.Bb5 Bd7 4.Bd7 Qd7 5.0-0 Nc6 6.Qe2** [6.c3] **g6 7.c3 Bg7 8.Rd1 e5! 9.d4 ed4 10.cd4 Nd4 11.Nd4 cd4 12.Na3 Ne7 13.Nb5 Nc6 14.Bf4 Be5 15.Bh6 0-0-0!** =+ **16.f4 Bf6 17.Bg5 Bg5 18.fg5 Qe7 19.Qg4 Qe6 20.Qe6 fe6 21.Nd4 Nd4 22.Rd4 e5 23.Rd3 Rhf8 24.Rf3 Kd7 25.Rc1 Rf3 26.gf3 Ke6 27.Rc7 Rd7 28.Rd7 Kd7 29.Kf2 Kc6 30.Ke3 Kc5 31.Kd3 Kb5 32.Kd2 Kc5 33.Kc2 Kd4 34.Kd2 Kc5 35.Kc2 Kd4 36.Kd2 b5 37.Ke2 a5 38.Kd2 a4 39.Ke2 a3 40.ba3 Kc3 41.a4 ba4 [D] 1/2-1/2**

After 29...f4?

401) Fischer,R-Berliner,H [12/19/62] US Championship [3] B03/04 Alekhine's [E:Rook + minor piece] **1.e4 Nf6 2.e5 Nd5 3.d4 d6 4.c4 Nb6 5.ed6 cd6 6.Nc3 g6 7.Bd3 Bg7 8.Nge2 Nc6 9.Be3 0-0 10.0-0 e5?!** [10...Bg4 =] **11.d5 Nb4 12.b3 Nd3 13.Qd3** [Black has won the two Bishops, but at the cost of several tempi] **Nd7 14.Qd2 f5 15.f4 b6 16.Rad1 Nf6 17.fe5 de5 18.Bg5 Bd7 19.Kh1 Rf7 20.Ng1 Qf8 21.d6 Bc6 22.b4** +=/+- [Utilizing the Queenside majority] **h6 23.Bf6 Bf6 24.c5 bc5 25.bc5 Re8 26.Nd5 Bd8 27.Qe2 Ba8 28.Qb5 Kg7 29.Qc4 f4?** [D] **30.c6! Qd6 31.Nf4 Qc6 32.Nh5!** ++- **Kh8 33.Qc6 Bc6 34.Rf7 gh5 35.Rd6 Be4 36.Rh6 Kg8 37.Ra7 Bg5 38.Rh5 Be3 39.Rd7 Bd4 40.Ne2 Rf8 41.Rg5 Kh8 42.h4 Ba1 43.Ng3 Ba8 44.Rd6 Kh7 45.Nf5 1-0**

After 17.Qb7

402) Evans,L-Fischer,R [12/20/62] US Championship [4] D98/11 Grunfeld [E:Rook + pawn] **1.d4 Nf6 2.c4 g6 3.Nc3 d5 4.Nf3 Bg7 5.Qb3 dc4 6.Qc4 0-0 7.e4 Bg4 8.Be3 Nfd7 9.Rd1 Nc6 10.Qb3 e5! 11.de5 Bf3** [11...Nce5 12.Be2 Be6 =] **12.gf3 Nce5 13.Bh3 Nf3 14.Ke2 Nfe5 15.Bd7** [15.f4 Qh4!] **Nd7 16.Qb5 c6 17.Qb7** [D] **Rb8 18.Qd7 Rb2 19.Kf1 Qd7 20.Rd7 Bc3 21.Ra7 Re8 22.Ra4 Bb4 23.Bd4 Rc2 24.Rb4 c5 25.Bc5 Rc5 26.Kg2 Rc2 27.a4 Rd8 28.Kg3 Ra2 29.Rc1 Rdd2 30.Rf1 Rd3 31.f3 Rda3 32.Rd1 Ra4 33.Rd8 Kg7 1/2-1/2**

After 33...Ke6

403) Fischer,R-Reshevsky,S [12/22/62] US Championship [5] B90/02 Sicilian [E:Rook + minor piece] **1.e4 c5 2.Nf3 d6 3.d4 cd4 4.Nd4 Nf6 5.Nc3 a6 6.h3** [Playing for g4 and a Kingside attack, but Black has counterchances] **g6 7.g4 Bg7 8.g5 Nh5!** [Observing the new weakness at f4] **9.Be2 e5 10.Nb3 Nf4 11.Nd5 Nd5 12.Qd5 Nc6 13.Bg4 Bg4 14.hg4 Qc8! 15.Qd1 Nd4?** [15...Qe6! =] **16.c3! Nb3 17.ab3 Qe6 18.Ra5! f6 19.Qd5!** [White has a favorable ending] **Qd5 20.Rd5 Kd7 21.gf6 Bf6 22.g5 Be7 23.Ke2 Raf8 24.Be3 Rc8 25.b4 b5** [Otherwise White plays b5] **26.Rdd1 Ke6 27.Ra1 Rc6 28.Rh3 Bf8 29.Rah1 Rc7 30.Rh4! d5 31.Ra1! Rc6 32.ed5 Kd5 33.Rd1 Ke6** [D] **34.Rd8 Kf5 35.Ra8 Re6 36.Rh3! Bg7 37.Rh8 Bh8 38.Rh7 Re8 39.Rf7 Kg4 40.f3 Kg3 41.Kd3?!** [41.Kf1! mates soon] **e4 42.fe4 Rd8 43.Bd4 Kg4 44.Rf1 Be5 45.Ke3 Bc7 46.Rg1 Kh5 47.Kf3 Rd7 48.e5 Rf7 49.Ke4 Rf5 50.e6 Bd8 51.Bf6! Bf6 52.gf6 Rf6 53.Ke5 Rf2 54.Re1 1-0**

After 10.Qb3

404) Benko,P-Fischer,R [12/23/62] US Championship [6] D79/12 Grunfeld **1.Nf3 Nf6 2.g3 g6 3.Bg2 Bg7 4.0-0 0-0 5.c4 c6 6.d4 d5 7.cd5 cd5 8.Ne5 Bf5** [8...Ng4 and 8...e6 also equalize] **9.Nc3 Ne4 10.Qb3** [D] **Nc6 11.Qd5 Nc3 12.bc3 Qd5 13.Bd5 Ne5 14.de5 Be5 15.Bh6 Rfd8 16.Bb7 Rab8 17.Rad1 Bc3 18.Rd8 Rd8 19.Kg2 1/2-1/2**

405) Fischer,R-Addison,W [12/26/62] US Championship [7]
B45/10 Sicilian [E:Rook + minor piece] **1.e4 c5 2.Nf3 Nc6 3.d4 cd4
4.Nd4 Nf6 5.Nc3 e6 6.Ndb5 Bb4 7.a3 Bc3 8.Nc3 d5 9.ed5 Nd5?**
[Correct is 9...ed5 +=] **10.Bd2 Nc3 11.Bc3 Qd1 12.Rd1** +- [The two
Bishops, better development and a Queenside majority] **f6 13.f4!
Bd7 14.Bc4 0-0-0 15.0-0 Kc7 16.Rde1 Rhe8 17.Rf3 Bc8 18.Rg3
Re7 19.Rge3 Rd6 20.b4! Nd8 21.b5 Red7 22.Bd3 h6 23.Rg3 b6
24.Bb4 Rd4 25.Rf1 Nb7** [D] **26.Bf8! Nc5 27.Bg7 Nd3 28.cd3 Rf7
29.Rg6 Kd6 30.Bf6 Rd3 31.Rh6 Bb7 32.Be5 Kd5 33.a4 Rd2 34.h3
Kc4 35.Rf2 Rfd7 36.Rd2 Rd2 37.Rg6 Kb4 38.h4 Be4 39.Rg7 Ka4
40.h5 Kb5 41.h6 Rd1 42.Kh2 a5 43.h7 Bh7 44.Rh7 a4 45.Ra7 Kb4
46.g4 1-0**

After 25...Nb7

406) Steinmeyer,R-Fischer,R [12/27/62] US Championship [8]
D73/05 Grunfeld [E:Rook + minor pieces] **1.Nf3 Nf6 2.g3 g6 3.Bg2
d5 4.d4 Bg7 5.c4 dc4** [Avoiding the drawish 5...c6] **6.Qa4 Nfd7
7.0-0 Nc6 8.Qc4 0-0 9.Rd1 Nb6 10.Qb3 Be6 11.Qc2 Bf5 12.Qb3
a5 13.Nc3 a4 14.Qa3 Ra5!** =+/-+ **15.Nb1 Bc2! 16.Re1 Nd4 17.Nd4
Bd4 18.Qb4 Ra8 19.e3 Bg7 20.Na3 Bf5 21.Bb7 Rb8 22.Bg2 Qd6
23.Qa5 Be6 24.e4 Qe5 25.Qa6 Rfd8 26.Rb1 Ra8 27.Qe2 Ba2
28.Bf4 Qd4 29.Bc7 Bb1 30.Bd8 Rd8 31.Rb1** [D] **Qd2 32.Qd2 Rd2
33.b3 Bd4 34.ba4 Rf2 35.Kh1 Na4 36.Nb5 Be5 37.Kg1 Rd2
38.Kh1 Nb2 39.Na3 h5 40.Bf1 h4 41.Nc4 0-1**

After 31.Rb1

407) Fischer,R-Sherwin,J [12/29/62] US Championship [9]
B29/01 Sicilian **1.e4 c5 2.Nf3 Nf6 3.Nc3** [3.e5] **d5 4.Bb5** [Better was
4.ed5 Nd5 5.Bb5 Bd7 6.Qe2 +-] **Bd7 5.e5! d4 6.ef6 dc3 7.fg7 cd2
8.Qd2 Bg7 9.Bd3 Qc7** [Better was 9...Qb6] **10.0-0! c4 11.Be4 Nc6
12.Qe2 c3 13.bc3 Bc3 14.Rb1 0-0-0 15.Qc4! f5 16.Qc3 fe4 17.Ng5
Rhg8 18.Ne4 Nd4 19.Qc7 Kc7 20.Ng3 Bc6 21.Re1 Nc2 22.Re7 Rd7
23.Bf4 Kc8 24.Rd7 Kd7 25.Rd1 Kc8** [D] **26.Nf5 Rg2 27.Kf1 b6
28.Ne7 Kb7 29.Nc6 Rg4 1-0**

After 25...Kc8

408) Byrne,R-Fischer,R [12/30/62] US Championship E60/02
[10] King's Indian **1.d4 Nf6 2.c4 g6 3.g3 c6 4.d5 b5?!** [4...cd5 5.cd5
d6 ∞] **5.dc6 bc4 6.cd7 Nbd7 7.Bg2 Rb8 8.Nf3 Bg7 9.0-0** += **0-0
10.Nc3 Bb7 11.Qc2 Nd5 12.Rd1 Nc3 13.bc3** [D] **Qa5! 14.Rd7 Bf3
15.Be3** [15.Bf3 Qc3] **Bg2 16.Kg2 Bc3 17.Rc1 Bb2 18.Rb1 c3 19.Ra7
Qd5 20.Kg1 Qf5 21.Qf5 gf5 22.Rc7 Rfd8 23.a4 Ra8 24.Rc4 Rd6
25.Kf1 Rda6 26.Bc1 Ra4 27.Ra4 Ra4 28.Bb2 Rb4 29.Ke1 Rb2
30.Rc1 1/2-1/2**

After 13.bc3

409) Fischer,R-Bisguier,A [1/3/63] US Championship [11]
C67/07 Ruy Lopez **1.e4 e5 2.Nf3 Nc6 3.Bb5 Nf6 4.0-0 Ne4 5.d4 Nd6
6.Bc6 dc6 7.de5 Nf5 8.Qd8 Kd8 9.Nc3 Ke8 10.Ne2 Be6 11.Nf4 Bd5
12.Nd5 cd5 13.g4** += [White's Kingside majority is more active than
Black's majority on the Queenside] **Ne7 14.Bf4 c6 15.Rfe1 Ng6 16.Bg3
Bc5 17.c3 Nf8 18.b4 Bb6 19.Kg2 Ne6 20.Nh4 h5 21.h3 hg4 22.hg4
g6 23.Rh1 Bd8?** [23...Kd7] [D] **24.Nf5 Rh1 25.Nd6 Kf8 26.Rh1 b5
27.f4 Kg8 28.f5 Nf8 29.e6! f6 30.Nf7 Be7 31.Bf4 g5 32.Bd6 Re8
33.Be7 Re7 34.Nd8 Re8 35.Nc6 Ne6 36.fe6 Re6 37.Na7 1-0**

After 23...Bd8?

1963

After 15...Rd4

410) Fischer,R-Fuller,J [7/4/63] Western Open, Bay City [1] C67/06 Ruy Lopez **1.e4 e5 2.Nf3 Nc6 3.Bb5 Nf6 4.0-0 Ne4 5.d4 Nd6 6.Bg5!?** [6.Bc6] **Be7 7.Be7 Qe7 8.Bc6 dc6 9.de5 Nf5 10.Nc3 Be6 11.Qd2 Rd8 12.Qf4 0-0 13.Ne4 h6 14.h4 Nd4??** [14...c5 +=] **15.Nd4 Rd4** [D] **16.Nf6 Qf6 17.Qd4 Rd8 18.Qe4 Bd5? 19.Qd5 1-0**

After 19.Bg5

411) Reinhard,A-Fischer,R [7/4/63] Western Open, Bay City [2] A04/15 King's Indian Attack **1.Nf3 Nf6 2.g3 g6 3.Bg2 Bg7 4.0-0 0-0 5.d3 d6 6.e4 c5** [6...e5!?] **7.Nc3 Nc6 8.h3** [8.Nh4] **Rb8 9.Be3 b5 10.e5?!** de5 **11.Bc5 b4 12.Ne4 Ne4 13.de4 Qa5 -+** [Development] **14.Be3 Ba6 15.Re1 Rfd8 16.Qc1 Nd4 17.Kh2 Rbc8 18.Nd4 ed4 19.Bg5** [D] **d3 20.a3 Rc2 21.ab4 Qb6 22.Qe3 Bd4 23.Qf3 Rf2 24.Qg4 d2 0-1**

After 25...Qc8

412) Fischer,R-Leopoldi,N [7/5/63] Western Open, Bay City [3] B35/01 Sicilian **1.e4 c5 2.Nf3 Nc6 3.d4 cd4 4.Nd4 g6 5.Nc3 Bg7 6.Be3 Nf6 7.Bc4 Na5 8.Bb3 Nb3 9.ab3 d6** [9...0-0 10.0-0 d5! =] **10.f3 Bd7 11.g4 a6 12.h4 h6 13.Qd2 +-** [Black's King is caught in the center] **Rc8 14.h5 e5 15.Nde2 gh5 16.gh5 Be6 17.0-0-0 Rc6 18.Kb1 b5 19.Nd5 a5 20.Rhg1! Nh5 21.Nec3 b4 22.Nb5 Bf8 23.Na7! Ra6 24.Qd3 Bc8 25.Nc8 Qc8** [D] **26.Qa6 Qa6 27.Nc7 Kd7 28.Na6 Kc6 29.Rd5 1-0**

After 8.Nd1

413) Poschel,P-Fischer,R [7/5/63] Western Open, Bay City [4] A19/01 English **1.c4 Nf6 2.Nc3 e6 3.e4 c5 4.g3 Nc6 5.Bg2 d5! 6.d3** [6.ed5 ed5 7.cd5 Nb4 -+] **dc4 7.dc4 Qd1 8.Nd1** [D] **Ne5 9.Ne3 Nd3 10.Ke2 Nc1 11.Rc1 Bd6 12.f4 e5 13.f5 Bd7** [Black has the Bishop pair, but he cannot open the position] **14.Nh3 Bc6 15.Nf2 Ke7 16.g4 g5 17.h4 h6 18.Bf3 b5 19.b3 b4 20.Nd5 Bd5 21.ed5 a5 22.hg5 hg5 23.Rh8 Rh8 24.Rh1 Ra8 25.Ne4 Ne4 26.Be4 a4 27.Bc2 1/2-1/2**

After 48...Bg4

414) Fischer,R-Finegold,R [7/6/63] Western Open, Bay City [5] C15/18 French [E: Bishop + pawn] **1.e4 e6 2.d4 d5 3.Nc3 Bb4 4.a3** [4.e5] **Bc3 5.bc3 de4 6.Qg4 Nf6 7.Qg7 Rg8 8.Qh6 Rg6 9.Qe3?!** [9.Qd2 =] **b6 10.Bb2 Bb7? 11.0-0-0 Nbd7 12.h3 Qe7 13.Ne2 0-0-0 14.c4 e5 15.de5 Ne5 16.Rd8 Kd8 17.Nf4 Rg8 18.Be2 Kc8 19.Rd1 Rd8 20.Rd8 Kd8 21.Qg3 Ng6 22.h4 Nf4 23.Qf4 Ne8 24.h5 Bc8 25.h6 Qd6 26.Qg5 Qe7 27.Qd5 Qd6 28.Qg5 Qe7 29.Qg3 Bf5 30.Qf4 Qe6 31.g4 Bg6 32.Qg5 Qe7 33.Qd5 Qd6 34.Be5 Qd5 35.cd5 f6 36.Bg3 Ke7 37.Kd2 Nd6 38.Ke3 b5 39.Bd6 Kd6 40.Kd4 a6 41.c4 bc4 42.Bc4 a5 43.Ba2 f5 44.gf5 Bf5 45.Bb3 Bg6 46.Ba4 Bf5 47.Be8 Ke7 48.Ke5 Bg4** [D] **49.Bg6! Bd7 50.Bh7 c5 51.dc6 Bc6 52.Be4 Be4 53.Ke4 Kf6 54.f4 1-0**

415) Bisguier,A-Fischer,R [7/6/63] Western Open, Bay City [6] E61/13 King's Indian **1.d4 Nf6 2.c4 g6 3.Nc3 Bg7 4.Nf3 0-0 5.e3 d6 6.Be2 Nbd7 7.0-0 e5 8.b4 Re8 9.Bb2?!** [9.a4] **e4 10.Nd2 Nf8 11.Qc2 Bf5** [The overprotected e4 square will form the basis of a later Kingside attack] **12.d5 h5 13.Nb5 h4 14.Nd4 Bd7 15.a3?** [15.a4] **h3 16.g3 Qe7 17.Rfc1 Bg4 18.Bf1 N8h7 19.a4 Ng5 20.a5 a6 21.Rab1 Nd7 22.c5 Bd4! 23.Bd4 Ne5 24.Be5 Qe5 25.Nc4 Qe7 26.b5 ab5 27.Rb5 dc5 28.Rb7 Qd8 29.Qc3 Bc8 30.Rb5 Qd5 31.Qa3 Qd8 32.Qc5 Nf3 33.Kh1 Qf6 34.Qc7?** [D] **Nh2! 35.Kh2 Qf2 36.Kh1 Bg4 0-1**

After 34.Qc7?

416) Fischer,R-Byrne,D [7/7/63] Western Open, Bay City [7] B77/03 Sicilian [E: Queen vs. Rooks] **1.e4 c5 2.Nf3 d6 3.d4 cd4 4.Nd4 Nf6 5.Nc3 g6 6.Be3 Bg7 7.f3 Nc6 8.Qd2 0-0 9.Bc4 a5** [D. Byrne's patent] **10.h4!?** [Better was 10.Bb3 Bd7 11.a4 +-] **Ne5 11.Be2 d5 12.Bf4?! Nc4?!** [12...Nh5 =+] **13.Bc4 dc4 14.0-0-0 e5 15.Be5 Ne4 16.Qf4 Nc3 17.Bg7 Kg7 18.bc3 Qf6 19.Qc7 Re8 20.h5 Qe5 21.Qc4 Be6 22.h6 Kg8 23.Ne6 Re6** [D] **24.Rhe1 Qe1 25.Re1 Re1 26.Kb2 Rh1 27.Qf4 Rf8 28.c4 f6 29.c5 Rh5 30.Qc7 Rh6 31.Qb7 Rh5 32.c6 Re5 33.c7 Ree8 34.Kb3 g5 35.Ka4 Ra8 36.c4 h5 37.c5 h4 38.Kb5 Kh8 39.a4 Kg8 40.Kb6 f5 41.Qd5 Kg7 42.Kb7 Kg6 43.Qe6 Kg7 44.Qe7 Kg6 45.f4! gf4 46.Qh4 1-0**

After 23...Re6

417) Berliner,H-Fischer,R [7/7/63] Western Open, Bay City [8] D41/21 Queen's Gambit Declined [E: Rook + pawn] **1.d4 Nf6 2.c4 e6 3.Nc3 d5 4.cd5 Nd5 5.e4 Nc3 6.bc3 c5 7.Nf3 cd4 8.cd4 Bb4 9.Bd2 Bd2 10.Qd2 0-0 11.Bd3** [11.Bc4 was better] **b6 12.0-0 Bb7 13.Rfd1 Nc6 14.Qb2?!** [14.Qe3] **Qf6 15.Rac1 Rfd8 16.Bb5 Rac8 17.Ne5? Ne5 18.de5 Qf4 19.Rc8 Rc8 20.Qd4 g5!!** [Protecting the back rank and starting an inspired counterattack] **21.f3 g4! 22.Be2 gf3 23.gf3 Kh8! 24.Kh1** [D] **Ba6! 25.Qf2 Be2 26.Qe2 Qe5 27.Rg1 f5 28.Qd3 fe4 29.fe4 Rf8 30.Qc2 Qf6 31.Rg2 Qd4 32.h3 Qa1 33.Rg1 Qe5 34.Qe2 b5 35.Qc2 b4 36.Qd3 a5 37.Qc2 Qf6 38.Qc4 Qf3 39.Kh2 Rd8 40.Qc2 Qc3 41.Qc3 bc3 42.Rc1 Rd3 43.Rb1 Kg7 44.Rb5 a4 45.Rc5 a3 46.Kg2 Re3 47.Rc4 Kf6 48.h4 Ke5 49.Kf2 Rh3 50.Kg2 Rd3 51.h5 Kf4 52.h6 Ke3 53.Rc7 Kd2 0-1**

After 24.Kh1

418) Oster,R-Fischer,R [9/63] New York State Open, Poughkeepsie D97/02 Grunfeld **1.d4 Nf6 2.Nf3 g6 3.c4 Bg7 4.Nc3 d5 5.Qb3 dc4 6.Qc4 0-0 7.e4 c6** [7...Bg4 and ...Nfd7] **8.Qb3 e5! 9.Be3?** [9.de5] **Ng4 10.Rd1 Ne3 11.fe3 ed4 12.ed4 c5! 13.d5 Bg4** [To trade off the Nf3, further undermining the dark squares] **14.Be2 Bf3 15.Bf3 Bd4 16.Ne2 Qa5 17.Rd2 Bg7 18.Nc3 Nd7 19.0-0 b5 20.Rdd1 b4 21.Qa4 Qd8 22.Nb5 Qb6 23.d6 c4 24.Kh1 Nc5 25.Qb4 a6 26.Rd5** [D] **Nd3 27.Qc4 Nf2 28.Rf2 Qf2 29.Rd1 ab5 30.Qb5 Qb2 31.Qc6 Ra2 32.d7 Ra1 33.Qc8 Rd1 34.Bd1 Qd2 0-1**

After 26.Rd5

After 23.ed5

419) Greenwald-Fischer,R [9/63] New York State Open, Poughkeepsie D86/10 Grunfeld **1.d4 Nf6 2.c4 g6 3.Nc3 d5 4.cd5 Nd5 5.e4 Nc3 6.bc3 Bg7 7.Bc4 Nc6** [7...0-0 and ...c5] **8.a4 Na5 9.Ba2 c5 10.Ne2 cd4 11.cd4 b6 12.Qd3** [To stop 12...Ba6] **0-0 13.Bd2 Bb7 14.0-0 e6 15.Rfd1 Qd7 16.Ba5 ba5 17.Bc4 Rab8 18.Ra2 Bc6 19.Nc3 Rb4! 20.d5 Bb7 21.Bb5 Qd6 22.Ne2 ed5 23.ed5 [D] Qd5! 24.Qd5 Bd5 25.Rd5 Rb1 26.Nc1 Rc1 27.Bf1 Re8 28.f4 Ree1 29.Rf2 Bf8 0-1**

After 20...cd5

420) Fischer,R-Beach [9/63] New York State Open, Poughkeepsie B06/13 Pirc **1.e4 g6 2.d4 Bg7 3.Nc3 d6 4.f4 c6 5.Nf3 Bg4 6.Be3 Nd7 7.h3 Bf3 8.Qf3 e6 9.0-0-0 +-** [More space, two Bishops, and a lead in development] **Ne7 10.g4 Qa5 11.Kb1 Rb8 12.e5 de5 13.de5 Nd5 14.Ne4 Bf8 15.Bc1 b5 16.f5 b4 17.fe6 fe6 18.Bc4 Ne5 19.Qg3 Bg7 20.Bd5 cd5 [D] 21.Bh6! Qc7** [21...Bh6 22.Qe5] **22.Nd6! Kd8 23.Bg7 Qd6 24.Qe5 1-0**

After 22.Rgf1

421) Richman,,J-Fischer,R [9/63] New York State Open, Poughkeepsie C68/04 Ruy Lopez **1.e4 e5** [A rare example of Fischer defending the Ruy Lopez] **2.Nf3 Nc6 3.Bb5 a6 4.Bc6 dc6 5.d4 ed4 6.Qd4 Qd4 7.Nd4 Bd7 8.Be3 0-0-0 9.Nd2 Ne7 10.0-0-0 Ng6 11.h3 Re8 12.Rhe1 Bd6 13.Ne2 Nh4 14.Rg1** [14.g3 Ng2 -+] **f5 15.Nc4 Bf8 16.ef5 b5 17.Nd2 Nf5 18.Nf1 Ne3 19.Ne3 Bc5 20.Nd4 Rhf8 21.Nb3 Bb6 22.Rgf1 [D] Rf2 23.Rf2 Be3 24.Rfd2 Be6 25.Re1 Bb3 26.Kd1 Bf7 27.Rd3 Bg5 28.b3 Re1 0-1**

After 26...Rb2

422) Fischer,R-Bisguier,A [9/1/63] New York State Open, [5] Poughkeepsie C59/02 Two Knights **1.e4 e5 2.Nf3 Nc6 3.Bc4 Nf6 4.Ng5 d5 5.ed5 Na5 6.Bb5 c6 7.dc6 bc6 8.Be2 h6 9.Nh3 Bc5 10.0-0-0 0-0 11.d3 Bh3** [Better was 11...Nb7, bringing the Knight back into play] **12.gh3 Qd7 13.Bf3 Qh3 14.Nd2 Rad8 15.Bg2 Qf5 16.Qe1 Rfe8 17.Ne4 Bb6 18.Nf6 Qf6 19.Kh1 c5 20.Qc3 Nc6 21.f4 Nd4 22.Qc4 Qg6 23.c3 Nf5** [23...Nc2 24.Rb1 Qd3 25.Qd3 Rd3 26.Be4 c4 ∞] **24.fe5 Re5 25.Bf4 Re2 26.Be4 Rb2 [D] 27.Be5 Re8 28.Rf5 Re5 29.Re5 1-0**

After 11...Re8

423) Fischer,R-Radoicic,M [9/2/63] New York State Open, Poughkeepsie [7] C59/02 Two Knights **1.e4 e5 2.Nf3 Nc6 3.Bc4 Nf6 4.Ng5 d5 5.ed5 Na5 6.Bb5 c6 7.dc6 bc6 8.Be2 h6 9.Nh3 Bc5 10.d3 0-0 11.Nc3 Re8 [D] 12.0-0 Bh3 13.gh3 +=** [Two Bishops] **Qd7 14.Bg4 Ng4 15.hg4** and the rest of the game score is not available **1-0**

424) Mednis,E-Fischer,R [12/15/63] US Championship [1]
C54/14 Giuoco Piano [E: Knight + pawn] **1.e4 e5 2.Nf3 Nc6 3.Bc4
Bc5 4.c3 Nf6 5.d4 ed4 6.cd4 Bb4 7.Bd2 Bd2 8.Nbd2 Ne4!**
[Equalizing] **9.Qe2 d5 10.Ne4 0-0 11.0-0-0 Bg4 12.h3 Bf3 13.gf3
dc4 14.Qc4 Qh4 15.Kb1 Qf4 16.d5 Ne5 17.Qc7 Rac8 18.Qd6
Rcd8 19.Qc7 Rc8 20.Qd6 Rfd8 21.Qe7 Nf3 22.d6 Ne5 23.Rhe1
Rd7 24.Qg5?** [24.Nc5!! Re7 25.de7 Re8 26.Rd8 f6 27.Re8 Kf7
28.Rg8 +=] **Qg5 25.Ng5 f6 26.Ne4 Ng6 27.Rc1 Rc1 28.Rc1 b6
29.Rc7 Nf8 30.Kc2 Kf7 31.Kc3 Ke6 32.Rc8 Ng6 33.Kd4 h6
34.Re8 Kf7 35.Rc8 Nf4 36.h4 g6 37.Rh8 f5** [D] **38.Rh7 Ke6
39.Rd7 Kd7 40.Nc3 Kd6 41.Nb5 Kd7 42.Na7 Ng2 43.Ke5 Nh4
44.Kf4 g5 45.Kg3 Ng6 46.a4 f4 47.Kg2 g4 48.Nb5 Ne5 49.Nc3
Ke6 50.b4 Nc6 51.f3 h5 52.b5 Ne5 53.fg4 hg4 54.Kf2 Nd3 55.Kg2
Nc5 56.Kf1 Kf5 57.Kg2 Ke5 58.Kf2 Nd3 59.Ke2 g3! 60.Kf3 Ne1
61.Ke2 g2 62.Kf2 f3 0-1**

After 37...f5

425) Fischer,R-Evans,L [12/16/63] US Championship [2]
C33/15 King's Gambit **1.e4 e5 2.f4 ef4 3.Bc4 Qh4 4.Kf1 d6** [4...d5;
4...c6] **5.Nc3 Be6 6.Qe2 c6 7.Nf3 Qe7 8.d4 Bc4 9.Qc4 g5 10.e5 d5
11.Qd3 Na6 12.Ne2 Nb4 13.Qd1 0-0-0 14.c3 Na6 15.h4 g4 16.Nh2
h5** [16...f3] **17.Nf4 += Qh4? 18.Kg1 Nh6 19.Nf1 Qe7 20.Nh5 Rg8
21.Nfg3 Rg6 22.Nf4 Rg5 23.Be3 Nc7 24.Qd2 Rg8** [D] **25.Nfe2 f6
26.ef6 Qf6 27.Bh6 Bd6 28.Rf1 Qe6 29.Bf4 Rde8 30.Rh6 Bf4
31.Qf4 Qe7 32.Rf6 Ne6 33.Qe5 Ng5 34.Qe7 Re7 35.Rf8 Rf8
36.Rf8 1-0**

After 24...Rg8

426) Byrne,R-Fischer,R [12/18/63] US Championship [3]
D71/01 Grunfeld **1.d4 Nf6 2.c4 g6 3.g3 c6 4.Bg2 d5 5.cd5 cd5
6.Nc3 Bg7 7.e3 0-0 8.Nge2 Nc6 9.0-0 b6 10.b3 Ba6 11.Ba3 Re8
12.Qd2 e5!!** [Opening the center. Black's piece activity offsets the
resulting isolani] **13.de5 Ne5 14.Rfd1?** [The wrong Rook] **Nd3
15.Qc2 Nf2! 16.Kf2 Ng4 17.Kg1 Ne3 18.Qd2 Ng2!!** [A brilliant
attack follows] **19.Kg2 d4! 20.Nd4 Bb7 21.Kf1** [D] **Qd7!! 0-1**
[Splendid! Now 22.Qf2 Qh3 23.Kg1 Re1!! -++, or 22.Ndb5 Qh3
23.Kg1 Bh6! -++]

After 21.Kf1

427) Fischer,R-Bisguier,A [12/19/63] US Championship [4]
C98/07 Ruy Lopez **1.e4 e5 2.Nf3 Nc6 3.Bb5 a6 4.Ba4 Nf6 5.0-0
Be7 6.Re1 b5 7.Bb3 0-0 8.c3 d6 9.h3 Na5 10.Bc2 c5 11.d4 Qc7
12.Nbd2 Nc6 13.dc5 dc5 14.Nf1 Rd8 15.Qe2 Nh5 16.g3** [16.a4 is
more accurate] **g6** [16...Bh3 17.Ng5 Bg5 18.Bg5 Nf6 (18...Bf1
19.Bd8) 19.Bf6 gf6 20.Ne3 +-. Black's Kingside is too weak] **17.h4
Be6 18.Ne3 f6 19.Nd5! Qb7 20.Ne7 Qe7 21.Nh2 Ng7 22.Ng4 c4
23.Qf3 Bg4 24.Qg4 Ne6 25.h5?!** [25.Be3] **Kh8 26.Kg2 g5 27.Be3
Nf4!? 28.Kh2! Nd3 29.Bd3 cd3 30.Red1 Rd7 31.Rd2 Na5 32.b3
Qd6 33.Rad1 Re8** [D] **34.Rd3 Qd3 35.Qd7 1-0**

After 33...Re8

After 36.Nd5

428) Reshevsky,S-Fischer,R [12/21/63] US Championship [5]
D32/16 English **1.c4 c5 2.Nf3 Nc6 3.d4 cd4 4.Nd4 Nf6 5.Nc3 e6
6.e3 d5 7.cd5 ed5 8.Be2 Bd6 9.0-0 0-0 10.Nf3** [10.Bf3 was better]
Bg4 11.g3?! [Passive. 11.Nb5] **Bb4! 12.Bd2 Ne4! 13.a3 Bc3 14.Bc3
Nc3 15.bc3** [Now the c-pawn is a target] **Rc8 16.Rb1 b6 17.Rb5
Qe7 18.a4 Be6 19.Qa1 Qf6 20.Kg2 Na5 21.Nd4 Nb7 22.Rb4 Nd6
23.a5 Ne4 24.ab6 ab6 25.Qb2 Nc3 26.Ba6 Rc5 27.Kg1** [Better was
27.Rc1] **Bh3 28.Ra1 b5 29.Bb5 Nb5 30.Rb5 Rb5 31.Qb5 Qe5
32.Re1 h5 33.Nc6 Qc3 34.Rb1 Qc2 35.Ne7?** [35.Re1] **Kh8 36.Nd5
[D] Rc8 37.Nc3 Rc3 38.Qh5 Kg8 39.Rb8 Rc8 40.Rc8 Bc8 41.Kf1
Ba6 42.Ke1 Qc3 43.Kd1 Qd3 44.Kc1 Qc3 45.Kd1 Bc4 46.Qf3
Bb3 47.Ke2 Qc4 0-1**

After 15...Nce4

429) Fischer,R-Steinmeyer,R [12/22/63] US Championship [6]
B19/01 Caro Kann **1.e4 c6 2.d4 d5 3.Nc3 de4 4.Ne4 Bf5 5.Ng3 Bg6
6.Nf3 Nf6 7.h4 h6 8.Bd3 Bd3 9.Qd3 e6 10.Bd2 Nbd7 11.0-0-0 Qc7
12.c4 0-0-0?!** [12...Bd6 =] **13.Bc3 Qf4? 14.Kb1 Nc5 15.Qc2 Nce4
[D] 16.Ne5! Nf2 17.Rdf1 1-0** [17...Qg3 18.Rf2 Qe3 19.Re2 Qf4
20.Nf7 ++-]

After 27.Re4

430) Addison,W-Fischer,R [12/26/63] US Championship [7]
C70/06 Ruy Lopez [E: Rook + minor piece] **1.e4 e5 2.Nf3 Nc6
3.Bb5 a6 4.Ba4 b5 5.Bb3 Na5 6.d4** [6.0-0 d6 7.d4 was better] **ed4
7.Qd4 Ne7 8.c3?** [8.0-0 +=] **Nb3 9.ab3 Bb7 10.Bf4 d5 11.e5 c5!**
=+ [Two Bishops and a Queenside majority. Now 12.Qc5? Nf5!]
**12.Qd3 Ng6 13.Bg3 Be7 14.Nbd2 Nf8 15.0-0 Ne6 16.Rad1 g5
17.h3 h5 18.Rfe1 Qb6 19.Nf1 d4 20.N3d2 g4 21.h4 Qc6 22.Qe4
0-0-0 23.Qc6 Bc6 24.c4 Kd7 25.Ra1 Ra8 26.Ne4 Be4 27.Re4 [D]
Ng7 28.Nd2 Nf5 29.Rf4 Ke6 30.Ne4 bc4 31.bc4 Rhb8 32.Ra2 Rb4
33.Nd2 Nh4 34.Bh4 Bh4 35.Re4 Bg5 36.f4 gf3 37.Nf3 Be3 38.Kh2
Rc4 0-1**

After 35...Qb6

431) Fischer,R-Weinstein,R [12/28/63] US Championship [8]
C96/08 Ruy Lopez **1.e4 e5 2.Nf3 Nc6 3.Bb5 a6 4.Ba4 Nf6 5.0-0
Be7 6.Re1 b5 7.Bb3 d6 8.c3 0-0 9.h3 Na5 10.Bc2 c5 11.d4 cd4
12.cd4 Bb7 13.d5** [Blocking the Bb7, but more promising is 13.Nc3
Qc7 14.Qe2 Rac8 15.Bd3 +=] **Bc8 14.Nbd2 Nd7 15.b4 Nb7 16.a4
Bd7 17.ab5 ab5?** [17...Bb5 =] **18.Ra8 Qa8 19.Re3 Qc8 20.Ra3
Qc7 21.Nb3 Nh5 22.Bd3 Rc8 23.Qf1 Nf6 24.Bg5 Rb8 25.Ra7 Qd8
26.Qa1 Qe8 27.Qa6 Qc8 28.Ne5! de5 29.Bf6 Bf6 30.Qf6 Qc3
31.Nc5! Nc5 32.bc5 Be8 33.Bf1 Qc5 34.Re7 b4 35.d6 Qb6 [D]
36.Bc4 1-0**

432) Byrne,D-Fischer,R [12/29/63] US Championship [9] B20/05 Sicilian [E: Rook + minor pieces] **1.g3 c5 2.Bg2 Nc6 3.d3 g6 4.e4 Bg7 5.f4 e6 6.Nf3 Nge7 7.0-0 Rb8 8.Nbd2 d6 9.a4?!** [Only helping Black's Queenside play] **0-0 10.c3 a6 11.g4 b5 12.ab5 ab5 13.Nh4 b4 14.c4 Nd4 15.g5 Bd7 16.Nb3 Qc7 17.Nd4 Bd4 18.Kh1 Bg7 19.Rb1 Ra8 20.Be3 Ra2 21.Qd2 Re8!** [Preparing central action] **22.Qf2 Bc6 23.d4 cd4 24.Bd4 Bd4 25.Qd4 Ba8 26.Ra1 e5! 27.Qd2 Ra1 28.Ra1 ef4 29.b3 Nc6 30.Qf4 Nd4 31.Qe3** [31.Rb1 Ne2 and 32...Nc3 -++] **Nc2 32.Qa7 Qa7 33.Ra7 Nd4 34.Rd7 Nb3 35.Rd6 Nc5 36.Rb6 b3 37.Kg1 Be4 38.Nf3 Ra8 39.Rb5** [D] **b2 40.Rb2 Ra1 41.Kf2 Nd3 42.Ke3 Nb2 43.Ke4 Nc4 44.Kf4 Ra2 45.Kg3 Ne3 46.Bh3 0-1**

After 39.Rb5

433) Fischer,R-Benko,P [12/30/63] US Championship [10] B09/30 Pirc **1.e4 g6 2.d4 Bg7 3.Nc3 d6 4.f4 Nf6 5.Nf3 0-0 6.Bd3 Bg4 7.h3 Bf3 8.Qf3 Nc6 9.Be3 e5 10.de5 de5 11.f5 gf5?!** [11...Nd4 12.Qf2 b5 13.0-0 c5 +=] **12.Qf5 Nd4 13.Qf2 Ne8 14.0-0 Nd6 15.Qg3! Kh8 16.Qg4 c6?** [16...c5] **17.Qh5 Qe8 18.Bd4 ed4** [D] **19.Rf6!! Kg8** [19...Bf6 20.e5] **20.e5 h6 21.Ne2** [Not 21.Rd6 Qe5!. Now 21...Bf6 22.Qh6] **1-0**

After 18...ed4

434) Saidy,A-Fischer,R [1/2/64] US Championship [11] A33/05 English [E: Bishop vs. Knight] **1.c4 c5 2.Nf3 Nc6 3.d4 cd4 4.Nd4 Nf6 5.Nc3 e6 6.Ndb5 Bb4 7.a3 Bc3 8.Nc3 d5 9.e3 0-0 10.cd5 ed5 11.Be2 Bf5 12.Nb5 Qb6** [After White's passive opening Black has easy play] **13.0-0 a6 14.Nd4 Nd4 15.Qd4 Qd4 16.ed4 Rac8 17.Bd1 Bc2 18.Be3 Bd1 19.Rfd1 Rc2 20.Rd2 Rfc8 21.Rc2 Rc2 22.Rc1 Rc1 23.Bc1** =+/-+ [Good Knight vs. bad Bishop] **Nd7 24.Kf1 Nf8 25.Ke2 Ne6 26.Kd3 h5 27.Be3 Kh7 28.f3 Kg6 29.a4 Kf5 30.Ke2 g5 31.Kf2 Nd8 32.Bd2 Kg6 33.Ke3 Ne6 34.Kd3 Kf5 35.Be3 f6 36.Ke2 Kg6 37.Kd3 f5 38.Ke2 f4 39.Bf2 Ng7 40.h3 Nf5 41.Kd3 g4 42.hg4 hg4 43.fg4 Nh6 44.Be1?** [44.Ke2 was better] **Ng4 45.Bd2 Kf5 46.Be1 Nf6 47.Bh4 Nh5 48.Be1 Kg4 49.Ke2 Ng3 50.Kd3** [D] **Nf5 51.Bf2 Nh4 52.a5 Ng2 53.Kc3 Kf3 54.Bg1 Ke2 55.Bh2 f3 56.Bg3 Ne3 0-1**

After 50.Kd3

(No. 434 is the only tournament game Bobby played in 1964).

1965

After 31.bc4

435) Lehmann,H-Fischer,R [8/25/65] Capablanca Memorial [1] B84/08 Sicilian **1.e4 c5 2.Nf3 d6 3.d4 cd4 4.Nd4 Nf6 5.Nc3 a6 6.Be2 Nbd7 7.0-0 e6 8.f4 b5 9.Bf3 Bb7 10.e5 Bf3 11.Nf3 de5 12.fe5 Ng4** [Better is 12...b4 +=] **13.Qe2** [Better is 13.Qe1] **b4 14.Ne4 Nge5 15.Ne5 Ne5 16.Ng5** [16.Bg5!?] **Qb6 17.Kh1 Qb5! 18.Qe1 Be7 19.b3 0-0 20.a4 Qc5 21.Qe2 Rac8 22.c4 bc3 23.Ba3 Qc7 24.Be7 Qe7 25.Qe5 Rc5 26.Qe2 Rg5 27.Qa6 Qb4 28.Rfb1 Rd8 29.a5 h6 30.Qc4 Qc4 31.bc4 [D] c2 32.Rc1 Ra5 0-1**

Final position

436) Fischer,R-Smyslov,V [8/26/65] Capablanca Memorial [2] C77/04 Ruy Lopez [E:Rook + minor pieces] **1.e4 e5 2.Nf3 Nc6 3.Bb5 a6 4.Ba4 Nf6 5.d3 d6 6.c3 Be7 7.Nbd2 0-0 8.Nf1 b5 9.Bb3 d5** [9...Na5 =] **10.Qe2 de4 11.de4 Be6 12.Be6 fe6 13.Ng3 Qd7 14.0-0 Rad8 15.a4 Qd3 16.Qd3 Rd3 17.ab5 ab5 18.Ra6 Rd6 19.Kh1 Nd7** [19...b4! ∞] **20.Be3 Rd8 21.h3 h6 22.Rfa1 Ndb8 23.Ra8 Rd1 24.Kh2 Ra1 25.Ra1 Nd7 26.b4!** [Blockading the target b-pawn] **Kf7 27.Nf1 Bd6 28.g3 Nf6 29.N1d2 Ke7 30.Ra6 Nb8 31.Ra5 c6 32.Kg2 Nbd7 33.Kf1 Rc8? [33...Ne8] 34.Ne1 Ne8 35.Nd3 Nc7 36.c4! bc4 37.Nc4 Nb5 38.Ra6 Kf6 39.Bc1 Bb8 40.Bb2 c5 41.Nb6 Nb6 42.Rb6 c4 43.Nc5 c3 [D] 1-0**

After 43.Kc2

437) Ciocaltea,V-Fischer,R [8/29/65] Capablanca Memorial [3] B03/04 Alekhine's [E:Rook vs. Bishop + pawn] **1.e4 Nf6 2.e5 Nd5 3.d4 d6 4.c4 Nb6 5.ed6 cd6 6.Nc3 g6 7.h4 h6?!** [7...h5!] **8.Be3 Bg7 9.Qd2 Nc6 10.d5 Ne5 11.b3 Nbd7 12.f3 Nc5 13.Nh3 Bf5 14.Nf2 b5** [After a bad opening, Fischer sacrifices a pawn to confuse the issue] **15.cb5 Qa5 16.Rc1 0-0 17.Na4 Qd8 18.Nc5 dc5 19.f4 Ng4 20.Ng4 Bg4 21.Rc5 e5 22.f5 gf5 23.Bh6 f4 24.Bg7 Kg7 25.Be2 Bd7 26.Qc3 Qf6 27.b4 Rg8 28.Bf3 e4 29.Be2 Qc3 30.Rc3 Kf6 31.Rh2 Rac8 32.Rc5 Ke5 33.h5 Kd4 34.h6 Rc5 35.bc5 Kc5 36.Rh4?** [36.Rh5 +-] **f5 37.h7 Rh8 38.Rh6 Kd5 39.Kd2 Kc5 40.a4 Kb4 41.Ra6 Rh7 42.Ra7 e3 43.Kc2 [D] Bb5 44.Rh7 Be2 45.Rf7 f3 46.gf3 Bf3 47.Kd3 Be4 48.Ke3 Ka4 1/2-1/2**

Final position

438) Fischer,R-O'Kelly,A [8/30/65] Capablanca Memorial [4] C89/22 Ruy Lopez [E:Queen + pawn] **1.e4 e5 2.Nf3 Nc6 3.Bb5 a6 4.Ba4 Nf6 5.0-0 Be7 6.Re1 b5 7.Bb3 0-0 8.c3 d5 9.ed5 Nd5 10.Ne5 Ne5 11.Re5 c6 12.g3 Bf6** [12...Bd6] **13.Re1 Ra7 14.d4 Re7 15.Re7 Qe7 16.Bd5** [Better is 16.Na3! +-] **cd5 17.Be3 Re8 18.Nd2 Bh3 19.Qf3 Qe6 20.Re1 Bg4 21.Qg2 Bh3 22.Qf3 Bg4 23.Qh1** [Fischer avoids repetition, but now Black has good chances] **h5 24.h4 Qf5** [24...b4!] **25.Qg2 Qd3 26.Nf1 Qc4 27.a3 Qa2 28.f3 Bf5 29.Qd2 Re6 30.Bf2 Re1 31.Be1 Qb1 32.Ne3 Be6 33.Ng2 Be7 34.Nf4 g6 35.Kg2 Bd6 36.Ne6 fe6 37.Bf2 Kf7 38.Be3 Ke8 39.Bh6 Kd7 40.Bg7 Qf5 41.Bh8 Qf8 42.Be5 Be5 43.de5 Qf5 44.Qe3 Kc6 45.b4 Kb7 46.Kh2 Ka8 47.Qe2 Kb7 48.Kg2 Kb8 49.g4 Qf4 50.Qf2 Kb7 51.Qd4 Qc1 52.Qd3 Qe1 53.gh5 gh5 54.f4 [D] 1/2-1/2**

439) Tringov,G-Fischer,R [8/31/65] Capablanca Memorial [5]
B97/13 Sicilian **1.e4 c5 2.Nf3 d6 3.d4 cd4 4.Nd4 Nf6 5.Nc3 a6
6.Bg5 e6 7.f4 Qb6 8.Qd2 Qb2 9.Rb1 Qa3 10.e5 de5 11.fe5 Nfd7
12.Bc4 Bb4 13.Rb3 Qa5 14.0-0 0-0 15.Ne6?** [15.Bf6! Nf6 16.ef6
Rd8 17.Rb4 Qb4 18.Qg5 g6 ∞] **fe6 16.Be6 Kh8 17.Rf8 Bf8 18.Qf4
Nc6 19.Qf7 Qc5 20.Kh1 Nf6 21.Bc8 Ne5 22.Qe6 [D] Neg4 0-1**

After 22.Qe6

440) Fischer,R-Wade,R [9/1/65] Capablanca Memorial [6]
C89/26 Ruy Lopez [E:Rook + minor piece] **1.e4 e5 2.Nf3 Nc6 3.Bb5
a6 4.Ba4 Nf6 5.0-0 Be7 6.Re1 b5 7.Bb3 0-0 8.c3 d5 9.ed5 Nd5
10.Ne5 Ne5 11.Re5 c6 12.d4 Bd6 13.Re1 Qh4 14.g3 Qh3 15.Be3
h5 16.Qf3 h4 17.Bd5 cd5 18.Nd2 Be6 19.Bf4 Bg4 20.Qg2 Qg2
21.Kg2 h3 22.Kg1 Bf4 23.gf4 Rfd8 24.f3 Be6 25.Nb3** += [Extra
pawn plus good Knight vs. bad Bishop, but Black's position is still
hard to crack] **Rab8 26.a3 Rb6 27.Kf2 g6 28.Re5 Kg7 29.Rae1
Kf6 30.Na5 Rh8 31.b4 Rc8 32.R5e3 Rg8 33.Nb3 Ra8!** [To answer
Nc5 with ...a5, thus activating the Rooks] **34.Rd1 g5 35.fg5 Kg5
36.Rg1 Kf6 37.Ree1 Rc6 38.Rc1 Bf5 39.Rge1 Rg8 40.Rg1 Ra8
41.Nc5 a5 42.Ra1 Rcc8 43.Ra2 Rg8 44.Rg3 ab4 45.cb4 Rh8
46.Rg1 Rhg8 47.Rg8 Rg8 48.Ke3 Re8 49.Kf4 Rg8 50.Re2 Rg2
51.Ke3 Rg1 52.a4 ba4 53.Na4 Rd1 54.Rb2 Rd3 55.Kf2 Rd4
56.Nc3 Rd3 57.Ne2 d4 58.b5 Bc8 59.Nc1 Rd1 60.Nb3 Rh1 61.Kg3
Rg1 62.Kf4 Rg2 [D] 63.Rd2 Bb7 64.b6 Ba8 65.Rd4 Rh2 66.Rd6
Ke7 67.Rh6 Rb2 68.Nd4 h2 69.Kg3 1/2-1/2**

After 62...Rg2

440a) Parma,B-Fischer,R (9/2/65) Capablanca Memorial [7]
B97/06 Sicilian [E:Rook + minor piece] **1.e4 c5 2.Nf3 d6 3.d4 cd4
4.Nd4 Nf6 5.Nc3 a6 6.Bg5 e6 7.f4 Qb6 8.Qd2 Qb2 9.Rb1 Qa3
10.Bf6 gf6 11.Be2 Bg7 12.0-0 f5 13.Rfd1 Nc6 14.Nc6 Bc3 15.Qe3
bc6 16.Rb3 Qc5 17.Qc5 dc5 18.Rc3 fe4 19.Rc5 Bd7 20.Re5 f5
21.g4 Rg8 22.Kf2 fg4 23.Re4 h5 24.Kg3 Ke7 25.Re5 h4 26.Kh4
Rh8 27.Rh5 Rh5 28.Kh5 Rh8 29.Kg4 Rh2 30.Rd2 a5 31.Kg3 Rh1
32.Bc4 Re1 33.Re2 Re2 34.Be2 (D) 1/2-1/2**

Final position

441) Fischer,R-Szabo,L [9/5/65] Capablanca Memorial [8]
C92/08 Ruy Lopez **1.e4 e5 2.Nf3 Nc6 3.Bb5 a6 4.Ba4 Nf6 5.0-0
Be7 6.Re1 b5 7.Bb3 0-0 8.c3 d6 9.h3 Be6 10.d4 Bb3 11.ab3 ed4**
[Better is 11...Qd7 +=] **12.cd4 Nb4 13.d5 Nd7** [13...c5 14.dc6 d5
15.e5 Ne4 +-] **14.Na3!** [Preparing to oust the strong Nb4] **Bf6
15.Nc2 c5 16.Nb4 cb4 17.Nd4 Bd4 18.Qd4 a5 19.Bf4 Nc5 20.Re3
f6 21.Rae1 Qc7 22.Bg3 Nd7 23.Kh2 Rfd8 24.R3e2 Nc5 25.Re3
Nd7 26.Qd3 Rab8 27.Qe2 Rb7 28.Kh1 Nc5 29.f4 Rf8 30.e5 f5
31.Bh4 de5 32.fe5 f4 33.Rf3 Qd7 34.Qd2 Qf5 35.e6 Ne4 [D] 1-0**

Final position

442) Garcia,G-Fischer,R [9/6/65] Capablanca Memorial [9]
D86/02 Grunfeld **1.d4 Nf6 2.c4 g6 3.Nc3 d5 4.cd5 Nd5 5.e4 Nc3
6.bc3 Bg7 7.Be3** [7.Bc4; 7.Nf3] **c5 8.Bc4 Qa5 9.Qd2 c4 10.Rb1
cd4 11.cd4 Qd2 12.Kd2 Nc6 13.Nf3 e6** [Restraining the d-pawn]
14.Ke2 b6 15.Rhc1 Bb7 16.Bd3 Rac8 17.Rc2 Rcd8 18.Rc4 f5!
[D] [Punching holes in White's once proud center] **19.e5 Na5** =+/-+
[White's 2 to 1 center pawn majority is crippled - and the outpost
on d5] **20.Ra4 Rd7 21.Ng5 Bd5 22.Bd2 Nc6 23.Bb5 Rc8 24.Ke1
h6 25.Nh3 g5 26.f3 Bf8 27.Nf2 Rdc7 28.Ba6 Rd8 29.Rc1 Rdd7
30.Bb5 a5 31.Nd3 Rf7 32.h4 Na7 33.Bc4 f4 34.Ke2 Rc6 35.Nf2**

After 18...f5!

Rfc7 36.Bd5 ed5 37.Rb1 Be7 38.hg5 hg5 39.Kd3 Rd7 40.Nd1 Kf7
41.Nc3 Bb4 42.a3 Be7 43.Nd5 [A desperate sacrifice] Rd5 44.Ke4 Rb5
45.Rh1 Kg6 46.Rh8 Rb2 47.Bb4 Bb4 48.ab4 Nb5 49.Ra1 Rb4
50.Kd5 Nd4 51.Rah1 Rc5 52.Kd6 Nf5 0-1

After 33.Rfe1

443) Robatsch,K-Fischer,R [9/9/65] Capablanca Memorial [11]
*(Round 11 actually preceded round 10 due to telex communication
problems caused by a hurricane)* B86/02 Sicilian 1.e4 c5 2.Nf3 d6 3.d4
cd4 4.Nd4 Nf6 5.Nc3 a6 6.Bc4 e6 7.a3 Be7 8.Ba2 [White loses time
assuring Black good play] 0-0 9.0-0 b5 10.f4 [Better is 10.Qe1] Bb7
11.f5 e5 12.Nde2 Nbd7 13.Ng3 Rc8 14.Be3 Nb6 15.Bb6 Qb6 16.Kh1
Qe3! [Immediately invading on the weakened dark squares] 17.Nd5
Bd5 18.Bd5 Bd8 19.a4 Bb6 20.ab5 ab5! 21.Ra6 b4 22.Nh5 Nd5
23.Qg4 g6 24.ed5 Rc2 25.fg6 hg6 26.Nf6 Kg7 27.Nh5 Kh6 28.Nf6
Rf2 29.Raa1 Ra8! 30.Qb4 Kg7 31.Qd6 Qe2! 32.Ne8 Re8 33.Rfe1 [D]
Qg4 0-1

After 41.Kh1

444) Fischer,R-Ivkov,B [9/10/65] Capablanca Memorial [10]
C96/12 Ruy Lopez [E:Knight vs. pawns] 1.e4 e5 2.Nf3 Nc6 3.Bb5 a6
4.Ba4 Nf6 5.0-0 Be7 6.Re1 b5 7.Bb3 0-0 8.c3 d6 9.h3 Na5 10.Bc2 c5
11.d4 Nd7 12.dc5 dc5 13.Nbd2 f6 [Better than ...Qc7, but White is still
slightly on top] 14.Nh4! [Taking advantage of the weakened f5] Nb6
15.Nf5 Rf7 16.Ne7?! [Correct was 16.Qg4! Kh8 17.h4 g6 18.Nh6 Rg7
19.Qf3 with an edge] Re7 17.Qf3 Be6 18.Nf1 Rd7! [Concentrating on
d3] 19.Ne3 c4 20.Nf5 Na4! 21.Ba4 ba4 22.Be3 Rd3 23.Qg4 Qd7 24.Bc5
Rc8 25.Be7 Bf5 26.Qf5 Nc6 27.Bc5 Nd8 28.Qd7 Rd7 29.Rad1 Rd3
30.Ba3 Nc6 31.Rd3 cd3 32.Rd1 Rd8 33.Kf1 g6 34.g4 f5 35.gf5 gf5 36.ef5
e4 37.Ke1 Ne5 38.Bc5 Nf3 39.Kf1 Kf7 40.Kg2 Rg8 41.Kh1 [D] Rg1
42.Rg1 Ng1 43.Be3 Nf3 44.Kg2 d2 45.Bd2 Nd2 46.Kg3 Kf6 47.Kf4 h5
48.Ke3 Nf3 49.Ke4 Ng5 50.Kf4 Nh3 51.Kg3 Ng5 52.Kh4 Kf5 53.Kh5
Ne4 0-1

After 17...f6

445) Fischer,R-Bilek,I [9/12/65] Capablanca Memorial [12] C11/15
French [E:Queen vs. Rooks] 1.e4 e6 2.d4 d5 3.Nc3 Nf6 4.Bg5 de4 5.Ne4
Nbd7 6.Nf3 Be7 7.Nf6 Bf6 8.h4 h6 9.Bf6 Qf6 10.Qd2 0-0 11.0-0-0 b6?
[Better would have been 11...c5 12.Bb5 cd4 13.Qd4 +=] 12.Bb5 Qe7
13.Rh3 Bb7 14.Rg3 Kh8? [14...Kh7] 15.Bd7 Bf3 16.gf3 Qd7 17.Rdg1
f6 [D] 18.Rg7 Qg7 19.Rg7 Kg7 20.Qf4 Rac8 21.h5 c5 22.Qg4 Kf7
23.Qg6 Ke7 24.dc5 Rc5 25.Qh6 Rg5 26.b3 e5 27.Kb2 Rf7 28.a4 Ke6
29.Qh8 Re7 30.h6 Kf7 31.Qh7 Kf8 32.Qd3 Kf7 33.h7 Rh5 34.Qd5
Re6 35.f4 f5 36.fe5 Rh7 37.Qd7 Re7 38.Qf5 Ke8 39.f4 Kd8 40.e6 1-0

After 28...Be8

446) Pachman,L-Fischer,R [9/13/65] Capablanca Memorial [13]
E65/07 King's Indian [E:Bishop + pawn] 1.Nf3 Nf6 2.c4 g6 3.g3 Bg7
4.Bg2 0-0 5.0-0 c5 6.d4 d6 7.dc5 [Although seemingly drawish, this
symmetrical position holds dangers if Black isn't accurate] dc5 8.Nc3 Nc6
9.Bf4 Qa5 [9...Be6 is the most reliable] 10.Bd2 Bf5 11.Qc1 [11.Nd5 Qd8
12.Nh4 Bg4 13.h3 Bd7 =] Nd4 [Threatening 12...Qc3] 12.Nd4 cd4
13.Nd5 Qd8 14.Bh6 Bh6 15.Qh6 Nd5 16.cd5 Rc8 17.Qd2 Qb6
18.Rac1 a5 19.a3 Rc1 20.Rc1 Rc8 21.Rc8 Bc8 22.h3 Qc5 23.Qf4 Kg7
24.Qb8 a4 25.Qf4 f6 26.h4 h6 27.Bf3 Bd7 28.Qe4 Be8 [D] 29.d6 Qd6
30.Qb7 Bf7 31.Qc6 Qc6 32.Bc6 Bb3 33.f4 e5 34.fe5 fe5 35.Kf2 Kf6
36.Be4 g5 37.hg5 Kg5 38.e3 Kg4 39.ed4 ed4 40.Bd3 Bd1 1/2-1/2

447) Fischer,R-Cobo,E [9/14/65] Capablanca Memorial [14]
B75/04 Sicilian [E:Rook + Bishop] **1.e4 c5 2.Nf3 g6 3.d4 Bg7 4.Nc3
cd4 5.Nd4 Nc6 6.Be3 Nf6 7.Bc4 d6 8.f3 Qb6 9.Nf5 Qb2 10.Ng7
Kf8 11.Nd5 Nd5 12.Bd5 Kg7 13.0-0 Qc3 14.Re1 Qa5 15.Qc1 h5
16.Qb2 +=** [White has pressure for the pawn] **f6 17.Rad1 Qc7 18.f4
h4 19.h3 Bd7 20.Rb1 Rab8 21.e5 de5 22.fe5 Ne5 23.Ba7 Ra8
24.Bd4 Nc6 25.Bc6 Bc6 26.Re6 Raf8?** [Better is 26...Rhf8 ∞]
27.Rbe1 Rf7 [D] **28.Re7! Qg3 29.Bf6 Kh6 30.Qc1 g5 31.Qg5 Qg5
32.Bg5 Kg7 33.Rf1 Re7 34.Be7 Ra8 35.a3 Ra4 36.Bb4 Kg6
37.Rf4 Kg5 38.Rd4 Kh5 39.c4 1-0**

After 27...Rf7

448) Jimenez,E-Fischer,R [9/15/65] Capablanca Memorial
[15] E82/04 King's Indian **1.d4 Nf6 2.c4 g6 3.Nc3 Bg7 4.e4 d6 5.f3
0-0 6.Be3 b6 7.Bd3 Bb7 8.Nge2 c5 9.d5 e6 10.0-0 ed5 11.ed5**
[11.cd5 +=] **Nbd7 12.Qd2 Ne5 13.Rae1 Re8 14.b3 a6 15.a4 Nd3
16.Qd3 Nh5** [In order to play ...f5, contesting e4 and gaining space]
**17.Ng3 Ng3 18.hg3 f5 19.Bf2 Qf6 20.Re8 Re8 21.Re1 Re1 22.Be1
Bc8 23.Kf2 Bd7 24.Bd2 =** [The two Bishops vs. more space] **Kf7
25.Kf1 h5 26.Be1 Qe5 27.Qe2 Qf6 28.Qd3 Ke7 29.Qe2 Kf8
30.Qa2 Kg8 31.Qd2 Kh7 32.Qd3 Bh6 33.Bd2 Bf8 34.Be1 Bg7
35.Qe2 Qf8 36.Qd3 Be5 37.Ne2 b5 38.ab5 ab5 39.f4 Bf6 40.Bc3
bc4 41.bc4 Bd8 42.Ba1 Bc8 43.Qc3 Ba6 44.Kf2 Be7 45.Ng1 g5
46.Nf3 gf4 47.gf4 h4 48.Qc2 Kg6 49.Qa2 Qc8 50.Qb2** [D] **1/2-1/2**

Final position

449) Fischer,R-Donner,J [9/16/65] Capablanca Memorial [16]
C89/27 Ruy Lopez **1.e4 e5 2.Nf3 Nc6 3.Bb5 a6 4.Ba4 Nf6 5.0-0
Be7 6.Re1 b5 7.Bb3 0-0 8.c3 d5 9.ed5 Nd5 10.Ne5 Ne5 11.Re5 c6
12.d4 Bd6 13.Re1 Qh4 14.g3 Qh3 15.Be3 Bg4 16.Qd3 Ne3 17.Re3
c5 18.Bd5** [Better is 18.Qf1 +-] **Rad8 19.Nd2 Bb8** [Better is
19...Bc7! =] **20.Bg2 Qh6 21.d5 c4 22.Qd4** [If Black had played
19...Bc7!, then now 22.Qd4 would meet 22...Bb6] **Bf5 23.b3 Rc8
24.bc4 Bd6 25.Qb6 Bf4 26.Qh6 Bh6 27.f4 g5 28.Re5 Bd3 29.c5
Rc5 30.d6 Rc3 31.d7 gf4 32.Rae1 Bg7 33.Re8 Bd4 34.Kh1 Bf6
35.gf4** [D] **1-0**

Final position

450) Geller,E-Fischer,R [9/19/65] Capablanca Memorial [17]
E80/11 King's Indian [E:Queen + minor piece] **1.c4 g6 2.Nc3 Bg7
3.d4 Nf6 4.e4 d6 5.f3 c6 6.Be3 a6 7.Bd3** [7.a4 a5! =] **b5** [Better is
7...Nbd7] **8.cb5** [8.e5! +=/+-] **ab5 9.Nge2 0-0 10.b4 Nbd7 11.0-0
Bb7** [11...Nb6 =] **12.Qd2 e5 13.Rfd1 ed4 14.Nd4 Ne5 15.Bf1 Nfd7
16.a4 Nb6 17.Qc2 ba4 18.Na4 Na4 19.Ra4 Ra4 20.Qa4 Qe7
21.Qb3 Ra8 22.Nc2 Bc8 23.Nd4 Bd7 24.h3 Rb8 25.Qa3 d5 26.ed5
cd5 27.Nc2 Bh3 28.Bc5 Qg5 29.f4 Qh5 30.Rd5 Bf5 31.Ne3 Ng4
32.Ng4 Qg4 33.Qa7 Re8 34.Qc7 h5 35.Rd8 Rd8 36.Qd8 Kh7
37.Be3 Bh6 38.Qf6 Bg7 39.Qf7 Qd1 40.Qc4 h4 41.Qe2 Qa1
42.Kh2 Bd4 43.Bf2 Bf2 44.Qf2 Kg7 45.b5 Be4 46.b6 Bb7 47.Qe2
Kf6 48.Qd3 Ke7 49.Qc4 Kf6 50.Qd3 Ke7 51.Qe3 Kd6 52.Be2
Qb2 53.Bf3 Bf3** [D] **54.Qe5 Qe5 55.fe5 Ke5 56.gf3 Kd6 57.f4 1-0**

After 53...Bf3

After 19.b4?

After 36.Rhf5

After 22...b4

After 23.Bd4

After 18.Bf3

451) Fischer,R-Kholmov,R [9/20/65] Capablanca Memorial [18] C98/10 Ruy Lopez [E:Rook + Bishop] **1.e4 e5 2.Nf3 Nc6 3.Bb5 a6 4.Ba4 Nf6 5.0-0 Be7 6.Re1 b5 7.Bb3 0-0 8.c3 d6 9.h3 Na5 10.Bc2 c5 11.d4 Qc7 12.Nbd2 Nc6 13.dc5 dc5 14.Nf1 Be6 15.Ne3 Rad8 16.Qe2 c4 17.Ng5 h6!** [A remarkable move, allowing White to double and isolate the e-pawns while winning the two B's. However, the f-file plus reinforcement of d5 + f5 and loss of time by the Knight fully compensates] **18.Ne6 fe6 19.b4?** [19.b3 or 19.a4 =] **[D] Nd4 20.cd4 ed4 21.a3 d3 22.Bd3 Rd3 23.Ng4 Kh7 24.e5 Ng4 25.Qe4 g6 26.Qg4 Rf5 27.Qe4 Qd7 28.Be3 Qd5 29.Qd5 Rd5 30.f4 g5 31.g3 gf4 32.gf4 Rf8 33.Kg2 Kg6 34.Rg1 Rd3 35.Kf3 Kf5 36.Rg7 Bd8 37.Rb7 Rg8 38.Rb8 Rg7 39.a4 h5 40.ab5 ab5 41.Rb5 Bh4 42.Ke2 Rg2 43.Kf1 Rh2 44.Kg1 Re2 45.Bb6 c3 46.Kf1 Rh2 0-1**

452) Doda,Z-Fischer,R [9/22/65] Capablanca Memorial [19] A37/13 English **1.Nf3 c5 2.g3 g6 3.Bg2 Bg7 4.0-0 Nc6 5.c4 e6 6.Nc3 Nge7 7.e3 0-0 8.d4 cd4 9.Nd4 Nd4 10.ed4 d6** [10...d5 =; Fischer takes risks to beat a weaker player] **11.d5 e5 12.b3 e4 13.Bb2 f5 14.Qd2 h6 15.Nb5! Bb2 16.Qb2 +=** a6 **17.Nd4 g5 18.f3** [Otherwise g4 shuts in the Bg2] **ef3 19.Bf3 Ng6 20.Ne6! Be6 21.de6 Qe7 22.Bd5 f4 23.Qg2 Rf6 24.Bb7 Raf8 25.Bd5 Kh8 26.Kh1 Ne5 27.gf4 gf4 28.Qh3 f3 29.Rad1 Qh7 30.Rd4 f2 31.Rh4?** [31.e7!] **Rg8 32.Be4 Qg7 33.Bg2 Nf3 34.Rh5 Nd2! 35.Rf2 Rg6 36.Rhf5 [D] Qa1 0-1**

453) Fischer,R-Perez,F [9/23/65] Capablanca Memorial [20] B09/35 Pirc **1.e4 d6 2.d4 Nf6 3.Nc3 g6 4.f4 Bg7 5.Nf3 0-0 6.Bd3 Nc6 7.e5 de5 8.fe5 Nd5 9.Nd5 Qd5 10.c3 Bg4?** [10...Be6 =] **11.Qe2 Rad8 12.Be4 Qd7 13.h3 Be6 14.0-0 Bd5 15.Bd5 Qd5 16.Bf4 b5 17.Rad1 a6 18.b3 Na5? 19.e6! Rc8 20.ef7 Rf7 21.Ng5 Rf6 22.Rde1 b4 [D] 23.Ne6 bc3 24.Ng7 Qd4 25.Kh2 1-0**

454) Pietzsch,W-Fischer,R [9/26/65] Capablanca Memorial [21] E67/03 King's Indian **1.Nf3 Nf6 2.c4 g6 3.g3 Bg7 4.Bg2 0-0 5.0-0 d6 6.d4 Nbd7 7.Nc3 e5 8.de5** [Probably trying to draw] **de5 9.Qc2 c6 10.Rd1 Qe7 11.Ng5 Ne8!** [Preparing the advance of the f-pawn] **12.e4 Nc7 13.Be3 h6 14.Nf3 Ne6 15.Rab1 f5 16.Nh4 Qf7 17.ef5 gf5 18.Bh3 f4! 19.Qg6 Ng5! 20.Bd7 Bd7 21.Qf7 Rf7 22.gf4 ef4 23.Bd4 [D] Bg4 24.Rd2 Rd7 0-1**

455) Addison,W-Fischer,R [12/12/65] US Championship [1] E45/08 Nimzo-Indian [E:Rook + Bishop] **1.d4 Nf6 2.c4 e6 3.Nc3 Bb4 4.e3 b6 5.Ne2 Ba6 6.a3 Bc3 7.Nc3 d5 8.b3 0-0 9.a4 Nc6 10.Bb2 dc4 11.bc4 Na5 12.Nb5 c6 13.Na3 Qe7 14.Qc2 c5 15.Be2 cd4 16.ed4 =** [White has hanging pawns, but the two Bishops compensate] **Rfc8 17.0-0 Rc6! 18.Bf3 [D] Nd5! 19.Bd5 ed5 20.Rfe1 Qf8 21.Qf5 dc4 22.d5 Rg6 23.Nc2 Nb3 24.Ba3 Qd8 25.Be7 Qc8 26.Qc8 Bc8 27.Ra3 Bd7 28.Ne3 Nd4 29.Rd1 Nf5 30.Nf5 Bf5 31.d6 Bd7 32.Rc1 Rg4 33.f3 Rd4 34.Kf2 Rc8 35.Rac3 f6 36.Ke3 Rh4 37.g3!** [White's active Rook insures a draw] **Rh2 38.Rc4 Rc4 39.Rc4 Kf7 40.Rc7 Ke6 41.Ra7 Rb2 42.f4 Rb3 43.Kf2 f5 44.g4 g6 45.gf5 gf5 46.a5 b5 47.a6 Rb4 48.Kg3 Ra4 49.Bf8 h5 50.Be7 Bc6 51.Bf8 h4 52.Kh3 Bd7 53.Bh6 Kd6 54.Kh4 Bc8 55.Kg5 Ba6 56.Ra8 Kc7 57.Bg7 b4 58.Be5 Kd7 59.Kf6 1/2-1/2**

456) Fischer,R-Suttles,D [12/65] US Championship [2]
B06/10 Pirc **1.e4 g6 2.d4 Bg7 3.Nc3 d6 4.Be3 c6 5.Qd2 Nd7 6.f4
Ngf6 7.Nf3 0-0 8.h3 b5 9.Bd3 Nb6 10.b3 a5 11.0-0 b4 12.Ne2**
+=/+- [White retains an imposing classical center formation] **d5
13.e5 Ne4 14.Qe1 f5 15.a3! ba3 16.Ra3 a4 17.Qa1 Ba6 18.Ba6
Ra6 19.Nc3 Qc7 20.Ne1 Rfa8 21.Nd3 R6a7 22.Qb2 e6 23.Nc5
Bf8 24.Rfa1 Kf7 25.N3a4 Na4 26.ba4 Bc5 27.dc5 Kg8 28.Rb3
Qa5 29.Kh2 h5 30.Rb8 Rb8 31.Qb8 Kh7 32.Rb1 Qa4 33.Qf8 Rg7
34.Rb8 g5 35.Qh8 Kg6 36.Qe8 Rf7** [D] **37.Rb7 1-0**

After 36...Rf7

457) Evans,L-Fischer,R [12/65] US Championship [3]
E45/08 Nimzo-Indian [E:Queen + pawn] **1.d4 Nf6 2.c4 e6 3.Nc3
Bb4 4.e3 b6 5.Ne2 Ba6 6.a3 Bc3 7.Nc3 d5 8.b3 Nc6 9.Be2 0-0
10.a4 dc4 11.Ba3 Re8 12.b4?!** [12.bc4] **Ne7 13.0-0** [13.b5] **Ned5
14.Rc1 c6 15.Bf3 b5 16.a5 Qc7 17.Qc2 Rad8 18.Rfd1 Bb7
19.Rd2 Nc3 20.Qc3 c5!!** [Giving back the pawn to obtain
dominance on the light squares] **21.dc5** [21.Bb7 cd4] **Bf3 22.gf3
Rd2 23.Qd2 Rd8 24.Qe1 Rd3 25.Bb2 Nd5 26.Bc3 f6 27.Ba1 e5
28.Kg2 Qd7 29.Rc2** [D] **e4 30.Rc1 ef3 31.Kh1 Nb4 32.Qg1 Kf7
33.Bd4 Nc6 34.Qg3 Nd4 35.ed4 Rd4 36.Rg1 g5 37.c6 Qc6
38.Qb8 Rd7 39.h3 Qe6 40.Rg3 c3 41.Qh8 Qf5 42.Kh2 Rd2
43.Rf3 Rf2 44.Rf2 Qf2 45.Kh1 Qf3 46.Kh2 Qf4 47.Kg1 Qe3
48.Kf1 Qh3 49.Ke2 g4 50.a6 Qf3 51.Ke1 Qe3 52.Kf1 Qd3
53.Kf2 g3 54.Kg2 Qe4 55.Kg3 Qg6 0-1**

After 29.Rc2

458) Fischer,R-Benko,P [12/65] US Championship [4] C95/02
Ruy Lopez **1.e4 e5 2.Nf3 Nc6 3.Bb5 a6 4.Ba4 Nf6 5.0-0 Be7 6.Re1
b5 7.Bb3 d6 8.c3 0-0 9.h3 Nb8 10.d4 Nbd7 11.Nh4 Nb6 12.Nd2
c5 13.dc5 dc5 14.Nf5 Bf5** [14...c4!?] **15.ef5 Qc7?!** [15...Nbd7]
16.g4 h6 17.h4 c4 18.Bc2 Nh7 19.Nf3 f6 20.Nd2! [Aiming for the
strong outpost e4] **Rad8 21.Qf3 h5 22.gh5 Nd5 23.Ne4 Nf4 24.Bf4
ef4 25.Kh1 Kh8 26.Rg1 Rf7 27.Rg6 Bd6 28.Rag1 Bf8 29.h6 Qe5
30.Qg4 Rdd7 31.f3 Bc5 32.Nc5 Qc5 33.Rg7 Rg7 34.hg7 Kg8
35.Qg6 Rd8 36.Be4 Qc8?** [D] **37.Qe8!! 1-0**

After 36...Qc8?

459) Bisguier,A-Fischer,R [12/65] US Championship [5]
A48/12 King's Indian **1.d4 Nf6 2.Nf3 g6 3.Bg5 Bg7 4.Nbd2 c5 5.c3**
[5.Bf6 Bf6 6.Ne4 Bd4 =] **cd4 6.cd4 Nc6 7.e3 0-0 8.a3 h6 9.Bh4**
[9.Bxf6 Bxf6 10.Ne4 =] **d6 10.Bc4 Bf5 11.h3 Rc8 12.0-0 e5!**
[Active play in the center] **13.e4 Bd7 14.de5 de5 15.Ba2 g5!**
[Neutralizing the activity of White's Bishop and preparing Kingside
action] **16.Bg3 Qe7 17.Re1 Rcd8 18.Nh2 Be6 19.Be6 Qe6 20.Nhf1
Rd3 21.Re3 Rd7 22.Qb3 Qc7 23.Nf3 Rfd8 24.Rae1 Nh5 25.Rc3
Qf6 26.Ne3 Nd4! 27.Nd4 ed4 28.Ng4 Qg6 29.Rd3 Ng3 30.fg3 Rc7
31.Nf2 Rdc8 32.Re2 Rc1 33.Kh2 h5 34.Qb7 Be5 35.Qd5 R1c5
36.Qd7 h4 37.Nh1 Rc1 38.Rf3 g4 39.Qg4 Qg4 40.hg4 Kg7!
41.Rf5** [D] **Rh1! 0-1** [42.Kh1 Rc1 43.Kh2 Bg3 44.Kh3 Rh1#]

After 41.Rf5

460) Fischer,R-Zuckerman,B [12/65] US Championship [6]
B87/06 Sicilian **1.e4 c5 2.Nf3 d6 3.d4 cd4 4.Nd4 Nf6 5.Nc3 a6
6.Bc4 e6 7.Bb3 b5 8.f4 Bb7 9.f5 e5 10.Nde2 Nbd7** [10...Ne4 11.Ne4
Be4 12.0-0 followed by Ng3 gives excellent attacking chances] **11.Bg5
Be7 12.Bf6?!** [Better is 12.Ng3 =] **Nf6 13.Qd3 Rc8 14.0-0 0-0 15.Ng3
Rc5!** =+ [But Fischer now outplays Zuckerman] **16.Nd5 Bd5 17.ed5
a5 18.a4 b4 19.Ne4 Ne4 20.Qe4 Qb6 21.Kh1 Bf6 22.g3 Rfc8 23.Kg2
Kf8 24.Rae1 Ke7 25.Qd3 Kd8 26.Re4 Kc7 27.Bc4 Kb8 28.Rf2 Ka7
29.h4 Qd8 30.Ba6 Rb8 31.Bb5 Rbc8 32.Rd2 Qb6 33.Kh2 h6 34.Bc6
Be7 35.Qe2 R8c6 36.dc6 Qc6 37.b3 f6 38.Qg4 Bf8 39.Rc4 d5 40.Rc5
Qc5 41.Qg6 d4 42.Qe8 Kb7 43.Kh3 Qc3 44.Qf7 Kb6 45.Rg2 Qc5
46.Re2 Qd6 47.Qe8 Qc5 48.Kg4 Be7 49.Kh5 Bd6 50.Kg6 Bc7
51.Kg7 Qc3 52.Qb5 Ka7 53.Qd3 Qc6 54.Kh6 Qe8** [D] **55.Qd4 Bb6
56.Qd5 1-0**

After 54...Qe8

461) Saidy,A-Fischer,R [12/65] US Championship [7] E45/06
Nimzo-Indian [E:Rook vs. Bishop + pawns] **1.c4 Nf6 2.Nc3 e6 3.d4
Bb4 4.e3 b6 5.Ne2 Ba6 6.Ng3 Bc3 7.bc3 d5 8.Qf3 0-0 9.e4** [9.cd5
ed5 10.Ba6 Na6 11.Qe2 +=] **dc4?!** [9...de4 10.Ne4 Ne4 11.Qe4
Qd7! =] **10.Bg5 h6 11.Bd2** [11.h4! +=] **Nbd7 12.e5 Nd5 13.Nf5 ef5
14.Qd5 Re8 15.Bc4** [D] **Ne5!!** [An exchange sacrifice which soon
regains the material with interest] **16.Qd8 Nc4 17.Qe8 Re8 18.Kd1
Nd2 19.Kd2 Re2 20.Kc1 Rf2 21.g3 Bb7 22.Re1 Be4 23.Re3 Rh2
24.a4 h5 25.Ra3 g5 26.Rb3 f6 27.a5 h4 28.ab6 ab6 29.gh4 Rh4
30.Ra3 Rh7 31.Ra7 Re7 32.d5 Kf7 33.Kd2 f4 34.Re1 f5 35.c4 g4
36.Rb7 g3 37.d6 cd6 38.Rb6 f3 0-1**

After 15.Bc4

462) Fischer,R-Byrne,R [12/65] US Championship [8] C03/09
French **1.e4 e6 2.d4 d5 3.Nd2 Nc6 4.c3** [Better is 4.Ngf3 +=] **e5!
5.ed5 Qd5 6.Ngf3 ed4 7.Bc4 Qh5 8.0-0 Nf6 9.Qe1? Be7 10.Nd4
0-0! 11.Be2** [11.Nc6 Bd6!] **Bg4 12.Nc6?? Bd6 13.h3 Be2 14.Nd4
Bf1 15.Qf1 Rfe8 16.N2f3 a6 17.Bg5 Qg6 18.Rd1 Re4 19.Be3 Nd5
20.Bc1 Rae8 21.Nd2 R4e7 22.Nc4 Bf4 23.Nf3 c6 24.Nb6 Bc1
25.Nd5 cd5 26.Rc1 Re2 27.Rb1 Qc2 28.Rc1 Qb2 29.Rb1 Qc3
30.Rb7 Ra2 31.Kh2 h6 32.Qb1 Rf2 33.Qf5** [D] **Qf3 34.Qf3 Rf3
35.gf3 Rd8 36.Rb6 d4 0-1**

After 33.Qf5

463) Reshevsky,S-Fischer,R [12/65] US Championship [9]
E43/07 Nimzo-Indian [E:Queen vs. Rook + pawns] **1.d4 Nf6 2.c4
e6 3.Nc3 Bb4 4.e3 b6 5.Bd3 Bb7 6.Nf3 0-0 7.0-0 Bc3** [7...d5!] **8.bc3
Be4 9.Qc2 Bd3?!** [9...d5 to keep a hold on e4] **10.Qd3 d6 11.e4 e5
12.Bg5 Nbd7 13.Nh4! h6 14.Bd2 Re8 15.Rae1 Nf8 16.Nf5 Ng6
17.f4!** +- [More space plus a powerful Kingside buildup] **ed4 18.cd4
c6 19.d5 cd5 20.cd5 Ne7 21.Ng3 Rc8 22.Bc3 Ng6 23.Bd4 Kh7
24.Nf5 Rc7 25.Kh1 Rg8 26.Re3 Nh5 27.Ref3 Nf6 28.Rh3 b5
29.g4! Ng4 30.Qg3 Qe8** [30...Nf6 31.Qg5!] **31.Nd6 Qe7 32.e5 Nf6
33.f5 Nd5 34.fg6 fg6** [D] **35.Nf7 Qf7 36.Rf7 Rf7 37.e6 Rf1 38.Kg2
Rf5 39.Rh4 Re8 40.Qd6 Ref8 41.h3 Rc8 42.Re4 Rc2 43.Kg3 Rd2
44.e7 Rg5 45.Rg4 Ne7 46.Rg5 hg5 47.Qe7 Rd4 48.Qa7 Rf4
49.Qe7 Rf5 50.Qe8 Rc5 51.Kf3 Rc2 52.Qe6 Rc1 53.Qb3 Rc5
54.Ke4 Rf5 55.Kd4 Kh8 56.Kc3 Kh7 57.Kb4 Re5 58.a3 Kh6
59.Qg8 g4 60.h4 g5** [D] **61.h5 1-0**

After 34...fg6

After 60...g5

464) Fischer,R-Rossolimo,N [12/65] US Championship [10]
C12/19 French **1.e4 e6 2.d4 d5 3.Nc3 Nf6 4.Bg5 Bb4 5.e5 h6 6.Bd2
Bc3 7.bc3 Ne4 8.Qg4 g6 9.Bd3 Nd2 10.Kd2 c5 11.Nf3 Nc6**
[11...Qc7!?] **12.Qf4 Qc7 13.h4** [Better is 13.Qf6! Rg8 14.h4 +=/+-]
f5 14.g4 cd4 15.cd4 Ne7? 16.gf5 ef5 17.Bb5! Kf8 [17...Kd8! +=/+-]
18.Bd3 Be6 19.Ng1 Kf7 20.Nh3 Rac8 21.Rhg1 b6 [D] **22.h5! Qc3
23.Ke2 Nc6 24.hg6 Kg7 25.Rad1 Nd4 26.Kf1 Rhe8 27.Rg3 Nc6
28.Qh4 Ne5 29.Nf4 Ng4 30.Ne6 Re6 31.Bf5 Qc4 32.Kg1 1-0**

After 21...b6

465) Burger,K-Fischer,R [12/30/65] US Championship [11]
E61/03 English **1.c4 g6 2.Nc3 Bg7 3.g3 e5 4.Bg2 d6 5.e3 Nf6
6.Nge2 0-0 7.0-0 c6 8.d4 Qe7** [8...Re8] **9.Qc2?!** [9.b3] **Re8 10.e4?!**
[Transposing to a King's Indian formation, minus a tempo] **Nbd7
11.d5 a5 12.h3 cd5** [12...Nc5!?] **13.cd5 b6 14.Nb5 Ba6 15.Nec3
Rec8 16.a4 Ne8 17.Re1 Bb5 18.ab5 Qf8 19.h4!** [Activating the
Bg2] **Nc5 20.Bh3 Rcb8 21.Ra3 Bh6 22.Bg5 Bg5 23.hg5** [D] **h6
24.gh6 Qh6 25.Kg2 Nf6 26.Nb1 Kg7 27.Nd2 Rh8 28.Rh1 Rh7
29.b4 Nb7 30.Nf1 Rah8 31.Rf3 ab4 32.Qc7 Nc5 33.Rf6?** [33.Qd6
+=] **Kf6 34.Qd6 Kg7 35.Qe5 Kg8 36.Ne3 Qg7 37.Qb8 Qf8
38.Qb6 Ne4 39.Qd4 f5 40.d6 Qd6 41.Qc4 Kg7 42.Rd1 Qe7
43.Nd5 Qc5 44.Qa2 Rh3 45.Qb2 Kf7 0-1**

After 23.hg5

1966

466) Reshevsky,S-Fischer,R [7/17/66] Piatigorsky Cup, Santa Monica [1] E97/01 King's Indian [E:Rooks + minor pieces] **1.d4 Nf6 2.c4 g6 3.Nc3 Bg7 4.e4 d6 5.Be2 0-0 6.Nf3 e5 7.Be3 Nc6 8.0-0 Re8!** [Now on 9.d5 Nd4! =] **9.de5 de5 10.Qd8 Nd8 11.Nb5 Ne6 12.Ng5 Re7 13.Ne6 Be6 14.f3 c6 15.Nc3 Rd7 16.Rfd1 Bf8 17.Kf2 b6 18.b3 Rb7** [Trying to obtain play with ...b5] **19.Na4 Nd7 20.Nb2 b5 21.cb5 cb5 22.Rdc1 a5 23.Nd3 Ba3 24.Rc6 b4 25.Rb1 a4 26.Nc5 Nc5 27.Rc5 ab3 28.ab3 f6 29.Bc4 Bc4 30.bc4 b3 31.Rb5 Rb5 32.cb5 b2 33.b6 Kf7 34.Ke2 Ke6 35.Kd3 Rc8 36.Bd2 Rc6 37.Ba5 Rc5 38.Bc3 Rb5 39.Kc2 Rb6 40.Bb2 Rb2 41.Rb2 Bb2 42.Kb2 Kd6 [D] 1/2-1/2**

Final position

467) Fischer,R-Portisch,L [7/19/66] Piatigorsky Cup, Santa Monica [2] C95/08 Ruy Lopez [E:Rook vs. Knight + pawn] **1.e4 e5 2.Nf3 Nc6 3.Bb5 a6 4.Ba4 Nf6 5.0-0 Be7 6.Re1 b5 7.Bb3 d6 8.c3 0-0 9.h3 Nb8 10.d4 Nbd7 11.c4 c6 12.c5 Qc7 13.cd6 Bd6 14.Bg5 ed4!** [Allowing the weakening of his pawn structure in return for active piece play] **15.Bf6 gf6 16.Qd4** [16.Nd4 Nc5 ∞] **Ne5 17.Nbd2 Rd8 18.Qe3** [Preparing an exchange sacrifice] **Nd3 [D] 19.Qh6 Bf4! 20.Qf6 Rd6 21.Qc3 Ne1 22.Re1 Qd8 23.Re2 Rg6 24.Kh1 Be6 25.Be6 fe6 26.g3 Bh6 27.Kg2?!** [27.Nb3] **Rc8 28.e5 Qd5 29.Ne4 Bg7 30.b3 Rf8 31.Qc2 Rf4 32.Ned2 c5 33.Re3 Qc6 34.Ne4 c4 35.bc4 bc4 36.Ned2 Bh6 37.Rc3 Rg7 38.Rd3 Qa8 39.Nc4 Qc6 40.Na3 Qc2 41.Nc2 Ra4 42.Rd8 Kf7 43.a3 Rg6 44.h4 Bf8 45.Ng5 Ke7 46.Ra8 h6 47.Nh7 Bg7 48.Ra7 Ke8 49.h5 Rgg4 50.f3?!** [50.Ne3! Be5 51.Ng4 Rg4 52.f4 Bb2 53.Ng5!! trapping the Rg4 ++-] **Rgc4 51.Rg7 Rc2 52.Kh3 Ra3 53.f4 Rcc3 54.Nf6 Kf8 55.Rg4 a5 56.Ne4 Rc2 57.Rg6 Re3 58.Nd6 Rcc3 59.Re6 Rg3 60.Kh4 Rg1 61.f5 Rc2 62.Re8 Kg7 63.f6 Kh7 64.Re7 Kg8 65.Kh3 Rc3 66.Kh4 Rc2 67.Kh3 Rc3 68.Kh2 Rcg3 69.f7 Kg7 [D] 70.Nf5 Kf8 71.Ng3 Rg3 1/2-1/2**

After 18...Nd3

After 69...Kg7

468) Ivkov,B-Fischer,R [7/20/66] Piatigorsky Cup, Santa Monica [3] A49/08 Queen's pawn [E:Rooks + minor pieces] **1.d4 Nf6 2.Nf3 g6 3.g3 Bg7 4.Bg2 0-0 5.0-0 d6 6.Nc3 d5** [To stop e4] **7.Ne5 c6 8.e4 Be6** [Simply 8...de4 =, but Fischer often avoids simplicity to try for the win] **9.ed5 cd5 10.Ne2 Nc6 11.Nf4 Bf5 12.c3 Be4 13.Bh3 Qc7 14.Nfd3** [14.f3! +-] **Bd3 15.Nd3 e6 16.Bf4 Qd8 17.Re1 Re8 18.Bg2 Nd7 19.h4 h5 20.Bf3 b5!** [The Minority Attack] **21.a3 a5 22.Qe2 Rc8 23.Bd6 Qb6 24.Be5 Nde5 25.Ne5 Ne5 26.de5 [D] b4 27.ab4 ab4 28.Qe3 Qe3 29.Re3 bc3 30.bc3 Rc5 31.Be2 Rec8 32.Ra3 Bf8 33.Rb3 Be7 34.Kg2 Bd8 35.Ba6 Ra8 36.Rf3 Bc7 37.Rb5 Rc4 38.Bb7 Ra3 39.Re3 Kg7 40.Bc8 Rac3 41.Re1 Rc2 42.Bd7 0-1**

After 26.de5

469) Fischer,R-Donner,J [7/21/66] Piatigorsky Cup, Santa Monica [4] C89/27 Ruy Lopez **1.e4 e5 2.Nf3 Nc6 3.Bb5 a6 4.Ba4 Nf6 5.0-0 Be7 6.Re1 b5 7.Bb3 0-0 8.c3 d5 9.ed5 Nd5 10.Ne5 Ne5 11.Re5 c6 12.d4 Bd6 13.Re1 Qh4 14.g3 Qh3 15.Be3 Bg4 16.Qd3 Ne3 17.Re3 c5 18.Qf1 Qh6 19.Nd2 Rad8 20.Nf3 Bf3 21.Rf3 cd4 22.cd4 Qd2 23.Rd3** [23.Rd1!] **Qg5 24.Rc1 Rc8 25.Rdc3 Rc3 26.bc3 Ba3 27.Rc2 Rc8 28.c4 bc4 29.Bc4 Qf5 30.Bd3?** [Better is 30.Qb1] **[D] Rc2 31.Bf5 Rc1 32.Qc1 Bc1 33.Kf1 Kf8 1/2-1/2**

After 30.Bd3?

470) Unzicker,W-Fischer,R [7/24/66] Piatigorsky Cup, Santa Monica [5] B92/07 Sicilian **1.e4 c5 2.Nf3 d6 3.d4 cd4 4.Nd4 Nf6 5.Nc3 a6 6.Be2 e5 7.Nb3 Be7 8.Bg5 Be6 9.Bf6 Bf6 10.Nd5 Nd7 11.0-0 0-0 12.Qd3 Rc8 13.c3 Bg5!** [Activating the bad Bishop] **14.Rad1 g6 15.Kh1 Bh6 16.Ne3 Nf6 17.Bf3 Rc6 18.Qe2 Qb6 19.Nd5 Bd5 20.ed5 Rcc8 21.Qc2 Nd7 22.Be2 f5** =+ [Black has an active Kingside Majority] **23.f3 Kg7 24.Nd2 Qc7 25.a4 Bg5 26.Nc4 h5 27.Qb3 Rcd8 28.Qa3 Nf6 29.Qb4 h4 30.Qb6 Qe7 31.Na5 Rd7 32.Nc4 Nh5 33.Rfe1 Bf4 34.Nd2 Qg5 35.Nf1 Rh8 36.Bd3 Rf7 37.Re2 Qf6 38.Kg1 Re8 39.Bc2 Bh6 40.Ree1 Nf4 41.Kh1 Rc8?** [41...h3! 42.g3 Ng2! 43.Re2 e4 -+] **42.Qf2 Nh5 43.Kg1 Bf4 44.Bb3 Rc5 45.Ba2 Qg5 46.Qc2 Rc8 47.Bb1 Re8 48.Re2 Qd8 49.Ree1**

After 49.Ree1

[D] b5 50.ab5 ab5 51.Qf2 Bg5 52.Bd3 Qb8 53.Ra1 Nf4 54.Bc2 Qb7 55.Rad1 Bd8 56.Qd2 Bb6 57.Kh1 Rh8?! 58.Ne3 Nh5 59.h3 Ba7 60.Kh2 Qb6 61.Bd3 Ng3 62.b4 Rhf8 63.c4 f4 64.Ng4 [64.Nc2] **bc4 65.Bc4 Rb8 66.Rb1 Rc7 67.Ba2 Rbc8 68.Rec1 Rc1 69.Rc1 [D] Ne2 70.Re1 Nc3 71.Bb1 Nb1 72.Rb1 Rc4 73.Qe1 g5 74.Rc1 Qc7 75.Rc4 Qc4 76.Ne5 Qd5 77.Ng4 Kf7 1/2-1/2**

After 69.Rc1

471) Fischer,R-Larsen,B [7/25/66] Piatigorsky Cup, Santa Monica [6] C82/17 Ruy Lopez **1.e4 e5 2.Nf3 Nc6 3.Bb5 a6 4.Ba4 Nf6 5.0-0 Ne4 6.d4 b5 7.Bb3 d5 8.de5 Be6 9.c3 Bc5 10.Nbd2 0-0 11.Bc2 Bf5 12.Nb3 Bg4 13.Nc5 Nc5 14.Re1** [14.Be3!] **Re8 15.Be3 Ne6 16.Qd3 g6 17.Bh6 Ne7?!** [17...Bf5] **18.Nd4 Bf5 19.Nf5 Nf5 20.Bd2 Qh4 21.Qf1?** [21.Qf3! +=] **Nc5 22.g3 Qc4 23.Qg2 Nd3 24.Bd3 Qd3 25.Bg5 c6 26.g4 Ng7 27.Re3 Qd2 28.b3? b4 29.Qh3? bc3 30.Qh6 [D] Ne6 0-1**

After 30.Qh6

472) Najdorf,M-Fischer,R [7/27/66] Piatigorsky Cup, Santa Monica [7] E74/08 King's Indian **1.d4 Nf6 2.c4 g6 3.Nc3 Bg7 4.e4 d6 5.Be2 0-0 6.Bg5 c5 7.d5 e6 8.Nf3 h6 9.Bh4 ed5 10.cd5 g5 11.Bg3 b5?!** [11...Nh5!] **12.Nd2 a6 13.0-0 Re8 14.Qc2 Qe7 15.Rae1 Nbd7 16.a4 b4 17.Nd1 Ne5 18.Ne3 Ng6 19.Nec4 Nf4 20.Bf4 gf4 21.e5!** [A crushing breakthrough] **de5 22.Bf3 Qf8 23.Ne5 Bb7 24.Ndc4 Rad8 25.Nc6 Re1 26.Re1 Re8 27.Rd1 Rc8 28.h3 Ne8** [28...Nd5? 29.N6a5 ++-] **29.N6a5 Rb8 30.Qf5 Nd6 [D] 31.Nd6 1-0**

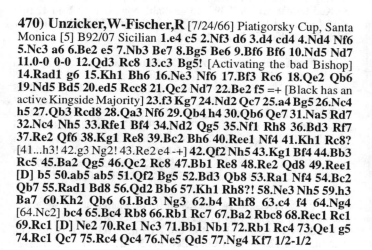

After 30...Nd6

After 25...Qf6

After 21...Kb7

After 36...Kh6

After 28.h4

After 28...Rdg8

473) Spassky,B-Fischer,R [7/28/66] Piatigorsky Cup, Santa Monica [8] D87/11 Grunfeld [E:Bishop vs. Knight] **1.d4 Nf6 2.c4 g6 3.Nc3 d5 4.cd5 Nd5 5.e4 Nc3 6.bc3 Bg7 7.Bc4 c5 8.Ne2 Nc6 9.Be3 0-0 10.0-0 Qc7 11.Rc1 Rd8 12.Qe1 e6 13.f4 Na5 14.Bd3 f5 15.Rd1 b6 16.Qf2 cd4 17.Bd4 Bd4** [17...Bb7! =] **18.cd4 Bb7 19.Ng3 Qf7 20.d5! fe4 21.de6 Qe6 22.f5! +=/+- Qf7 23.Be4 Rd1 24.Rd1 Rf8 25.Bb1 Qf6 [D] 26.Qc2 Kh8 27.fg6 hg6 28.Qd2 Kg7 29.Rf1 Qe7 30.Qd4 Rf6 31.Ne4 Be4 32.Be4 Qc5 33.Qc5 Rf1 34.Kf1 bc5 35.h4!** [Fixing the g-pawn as a target for the Bishop] **++- Nc4 36.Ke2 Ne5 37.Ke3 Kf6 38.Kf4 Nf7 39.Ke3 g5 40.h5 Nh6 41.Kd3 Ke6 42.Ba8 Kd6 43.Kc4 g4 44.a4 Ng8 45.a5 Nh6 46.Be4 g3 47.Kb5 Ng8 48.Bb1 Nh6 49.Ka6 Kc6 50.Ba2 1-0**

474) Fischer,R-Petrosian,T [7/31/66] Piatigorsky Cup, Santa Monica [9] B48/07 Sicilian [E:Rook + minor pieces] **1.e4 c5 2.Nf3 Nc6 3.d4 cd4 4.Nd4 e6 5.Nc3 Qc7 6.Be3 Nf6 7.Bd3 a6 8.0-0 Ne5 9.h3 b5 10.f4 Nc4 11.Bc4 Qc4 12.Qd3** [12.e5 Nd5 13.Nd5 Qd5 14.Qe2 Bb7 15.Nb3 +=] **d5 13.e5 Nd7 14.Qc4 dc4 15.f5!?** [Trying to take advantage of his lead in development] **Ne5! 16.fe6 Be6 17.Rae1 Nd7 18.Ne6 fe6 19.Bd4 0-0-0 20.Re6?! Nc5 21.Rc6 Kb7 [D] 22.Rc5 Rd4 23.Rcf5 Bd6 24.Rf7 Kc6 25.Rg7 b4 26.Na4 Rd5 27.b3 Be5 28.Re7 c3 29.Re6 Bd6 30.Re4 Rf8 31.Rf8 Bf8 32.Kf2 Bd6 33.Re2 Rf5 34.Ke3 a5 35.Rf2 Re5 36.Kf3 Rf5 37.Ke2 Re5 38.Kf1 h5 39.Re2 Rf5 40.Rf2 ½-½**

475) Fischer,R-Reshevsky,S [8/1/66] Piatigorsky Cup, Santa Monica [10] C92/21 Ruy Lopez **1.e4 e5 2.Nf3 Nc6 3.Bb5 a6 4.Ba4 Nf6 5.0-0 Be7 6.Re1 b5 7.Bb3 0-0 8.c3 d6 9.h3 Nd7 10.d4 Nb6 11.Nbd2 ed4 12.cd4 d5 13.Bc2 Be6 14.e5 Qd7 15.Nb3 Bf5 16.Bg5 Rfe8? [16...Bb4] 17.Be7 Re7 18.Rc1 Nb4 19.Nc5!** [Occupying the weakened dark squares] **Bc2 20.Qd2!!** [The unexpected tactical point] **Qe8 21.Qb4 a5 22.Qc3 Bg6 23.Nh4 Na4 24.Qb3 Nc5 25.Rc5 c6 26.Rec1 ++-** [The backward c-pawn] **Re6 27.f4 f5 28.a4 ba4 29.Qa4 Rb8 30.Qa3 Qd8 31.Ng6 hg6 32.Rc6 Rc6 33.Rc6 Qh4 34.Rg6 Kh7 35.Rg5 Rb4 36.Qf3 Kh6 [D] 37.g3 Qh3 38.Qd5 1-0**

476) Portisch,L-Fischer,R [8/3/66] Piatigorsky Cup, Santa Monica [11] E45/06 Nimzo-Indian **1.d4 Nf6 2.c4 e6 3.Nc3 Bb4 4.e3 b6 5.Ne2 Ba6 6.Ng3 Bc3 7.bc3 d5 8.Qf3** [8.Ba3!?] **0-0 9.e4 de4 10.Ne4 Ne4 11.Qe4 Qd7!** [Fischer's innovation of giving up two Rooks for the Queen] **12.Ba3 Re8 13.Bd3 f5 14.Qa8 Nc6 15.Qe8 Qe8 16.0-0 Na5 17.Rae1 Bc4 18.Bc4 Nc4 19.Bc1 c5 20.dc5 bc5 21.Bf4 h6 22.Re2 g5 23.Be5 Qd8 24.Rfe1 Kf7 25.h3 f4 26.Kh2 a6 27.Re4 Qd5 28.h4 [D] Ne3! 29.R1e3 fe3 30.Re3 Qa2 31.Rf3 Ke8 32.Bg7 Qc4 33.hg5 hg5 34.Rf8 Kd7 35.Ra8 Kc6 0-1**

477) Fischer,R-Ivkov,B [8/4/66] Piatigorsky Cup, Santa Monica [12] A08/06 Sicilian **1.e4 c5 2.Nf3 e6 3.d3 Nc6 4.g3 d5 5.Nbd2 Bd6 6.Bg2 Nge7 7.0-0 0-0 8.Nh4** [Intending f4, gaining a Kingside space advantage] **b6 [8...Qc7] 9.f4 de4 10.de4 Ba6 11.Re1 c4 12.c3!** [Otherwise the pawn sacrifice c3! gives Black play] **Na5 13.e5 Bc5 14.Kh1 Nd5 15.Ne4 Bb7 16.Qh5 Ne7 17.g4!** +-/++ [A powerful attack is in progress] **Be4 18.Be4 g6 19.Qh6 Nd5 20.f5 Re8 21.fg6 fg6 22.Ng6! Qd7** [22...hg6 23.Qg6 Kf8 24.Bh6 Ke7 25.Qg7] **23.Nf4 Rad8 24.Nh5 Kh8 25.Nf6 Nf6 26.ef6 Rg8 27.Bf4 Rg4 28.Rad1 Rdg8 [D] 29.f7 1-0**

478) Donner,J-Fischer,R [8/7/66] Piatigorsky Cup, Santa Monica [13] E68/18 King's Indian **1.d4 Nf6 2.c4 g6 3.g3 Bg7 4.Bg2 0-0 5.Nc3 d6 6.Nf3 Nbd7 7.0-0 e5 8.e4 c6 9.Rb1 a6 10.b4?** [Weakening c4, which Fischer soon exploits; 10.Qc2 + Rd1] **ed4 11.Nd4 Re8 12.h3 Ne5 13.Qe2 b5!** [Securing an outpost at c4] **14.cb5 cb5 15.Rd1 Bb7 16.f4 Nc4 17.Qd3 Rc8 18.Kh2 Qc7 19.Rb3 Re7 20.Re1 Rce8 21.Nc2 Qc8 22.Ne3? Ne3 23.Re3 Ne4 24.Be4 Be4 25.Qd6 [D] Rd7 26.Qc5 Rc7 27.Ne4 Rc5 28.Nc5 Bd4 0-1**

After 25.Qd6

479) Fischer,R-Unzicker,W [8/8/66] Piatigorsky Cup, Santa Monica [14] C83/06 Ruy Lopez [E:Bishop + pawn] **1.e4 e5 2.Nf3 Nc6 3.Bb5 a6 4.Ba4 Nf6 5.0-0 Ne4 6.d4 b5 7.Bb3 d5 8.de5 Be6 9.c3 Be7 10.Bc2 0-0 11.Nbd2 f5 12.Nb3 Qd7 13.Nbd4** [Better is 13.Nfd4 Nd4 14.Nd4 c5 15.Ne6 Qe6 +- with two Bishops and better pawns] **Nd4 14.Nd4 c5 15.Ne2?!** [15.Ne6! transposes to above note] **Rad8 16.Nf4 Qc6 17.a4 Bc8 18.ab5 ab5 19.Qh5 g6 20.Qh6 Rf7 21.f3 Bf8 22.Qh3 Ng5 23.Qg3 Ne6 24.h4 Nf4 25.Bf4 h5 26.Bg5 Re8 27.f4 Kh7 28.Bd1 Be6 29.Kh2 Ra8 30.Bf3 Rfa7 31.Ra7 Ra7 32.Qf2 Rd7 33.Ra1 c4 34.Ra5** [Better is 34.Bf6] **Bc5 35.Qe2 Bf7 36.Kh3 Ra7 37.Ra7 Ba7 38.Be7 Qb6 39.Bg5 Qe3 40.Qd1 Qg1 41.Qg1 Bg1 42.Be7 Be3 43.g3 Bc1 44.Ba3 Kg7 45.Kg2 [D] d4 46.cd4 c3 47.bc3 Ba3 48.d5 Kf8 49.Kf2 Ke7 50.Ke2 Bc5 51.Ke1 Kd8 52.d6 Kd7 53.Bb7 Bc4 54.Bg2 Bb6 55.Bb7 Ba5 56.Kd2 Bb6 57.Ke1 Be3 58.Bf3 Ke6 59.Bb7 Kd7 60.Bf3 Bf7 61.Ke2 Ba7 62.Ba8 Bc4 63.Ke1 Be3 1/2-1/2**

After 45.Kg2

480) Larsen,B-Fischer,R [8/10/66] Piatigorsky Cup, Santa Monica [15] E74/08 Benoni **1.d4 Nf6 2.c4 g6 3.Nc3 Bg7 4.e4 d6 5.Be2 0-0 6.Bg5 c5 7.d5 e6 8.Nf3 h6 9.Bh4 ed5 10.cd5 g5 11.Bg3 Nh5!** [Improving on 11...b5?! as played against Najdorf earlier] **12.Nd2 Ng3 13.hg3 Nd7 14.Nc4 Qe7 15.Ne3 Nf6 16.Qc2 Re8 17.Bb5 Rd8 18.Be2 Re8 19.f3 Nh7! 20.g4 Nf8 21.a4 Ng6 22.Kf1 Rb8 23.Bb5 Rd8 24.Nf5 Bf5 25.ef5 Ne5 26.Ne4 a6 27.Be2 Nd7 28.Re1 Nf6 29.Nc3 Qd7 30.a5 Re8 31.Kf2 Qc7 32.Ra1 c4 33.Kg3** [33.Ne4 b5! 34.ab6 Qb6 -+] **Re3 34.Qd2 Rbe8 35.Rhe1 h5! 36.Bf1 [D] Ng4! 37.Re3 Re3 38.Kh3 Qe7 39.g3 Bc3 40.bc3 Rf3 41.Re1 Re3 42.Re3 Qe3 43.Qe3 Ne3 0-1**

After 36.Bf1

481) Fischer,R-Najdorf,M [8/11/66] Piatigorsky Cup, Santa Monica [16] B44/03 Sicilian [E:Rook + minor pieces] **1.e4 c5 2.Nf3 Nc6 3.d4 cd4 4.Nd4 e6 5.Nb5 d6 6.Bf4 e5 7.Be3 Nf6 8.Bg5 Be6 9.N1c3 a6 10.Bf6 gf6 11.Na3 Nd4** [Better is 11...d5! 12.Nd5 Ba3 13.ba3 Qa5 14.Qd2 Qd2 =] **12.Bc4 b5 13.Be6 fe6 14.Ne2 Nc6** [Better is 14...Ne2] **15.Ng3 Qd7 16.c4 Nd4 17.0-0 b4 18.Nc2 Nc2 19.Qc2 h5 20.Rfd1 h4 21.Nf1 Rg8 22.a3 h3 23.g3 ba3 24.Ra3 Qc6 25.Qe2 f5 26.c5! Qe4 27.Qe4 fe4 28.cd6 Bh6 29.Ra5 Kd7 30.Re5 Bg7 31.Re4 Bb2 32.Ne3 a5 33.Nc4 Rgb8 34.Rh4 Kc6 35.Rh7 Bd4 36.Rc7 Kd5 37.d7 a4 38.Nb6** [38.Rc8] **Rb6 39.Rc8 Rd6 40.Ra8 Rd7 41.Ra4 e5 42.Kf1 Rb7 43.f4 Ke6 44.fe5 Rf7 45.Ke2 Rf2 46.Kd3 Be5 [D] 47.Re1 1-0**

After 46...Be5

Final position

482) Fischer,R-Spassky,B [8/14/66] Piatigorsky Cup, Santa Monica [17] C89/22 Ruy Lopez [E:Rook + minor piece] **1.e4 e5 2.Nf3 Nc6 3.Bb5 a6 4.Ba4 Nf6 5.0-0 Be7 6.Re1 b5 7.Bb3 0-0 8.c3 d5 9.ed5 Nd5 10.Ne5 Ne5 11.Re5 c6 12.g3 Nf6** [12...Bf6!?] **13.d4 Bd6 14.Re1 Bg4 15.Qd3 c5 16.dc5 Bc5** [Black has sufficient play for the pawn] **17.Qd8 Rad8 18.Bf4 h6 19.Na3 g5 20.Be3 Be3 21.Re3 Rd2 22.Nc2 Re8 23.Re8 Ne8 24.Ne3 Bf3 25.Bc2 Nd6 26.b3 Kf8 27.a4 Ne4 28.Be4 Be4 29.ab5 ab5 30.b4 Rb2 31.g4 Kg7 32.Kf1 Kf6 33.Ra5 Rb1 34.Ke2 Rb2 35.Kf1 [D] 1/2-1/2**

After 16.Rc1

483) Petrosian,T-Fischer,R [8/15/66] Piatigorsky Cup, Santa Monica [18] E62/26 King's Indian **1.d4 Nf6 2.Nf3 g6 3.g3 Bg7 4.Bg2 0-0 5.0-0 d6 6.c4 Nc6 7.Nc3 Bf5 8.h3 e5 9.d5 Ne7 10.Ne1 Bc8!** [Better than 10...Bd7] **11.e4 Nd7 12.Nd3 f5 13.Bd2 Nf6 14.Kh2 c6 15.f3 Kh8 16.Rc1 [D] b5 17.cb5** [17.b3 allows 17...bc4 18.bc4 cd5 19.cd5 Ba6 - a point behind 10...Bc8] **cd5 18.ed5 Nfd5 19.Nd5 Nd5 20.Nb4 Be6 21.Nd5 Bd5 22.Bb4 Ba2 23.Rc6 Bg8 24.Bd6 Re8 25.Re1 Rc8 26.Bb4 Rb8 27.Qd8 Red8 28.Bc3 e4 1/2-1/2**

After 21.Re1

484) Yepez,O-Fischer,R [10/26/66] Havana Olympiad Prelim [1] E91/03 King's Indian [E:Rook + pawn] **1.d4 Nf6 2.c4 g6 3.Nc3 Bg7 4.e4 d6 5.Nf3 0-0 6.Be2 Nbd7 7.Bg5 h6 8.Bh4 g5 9.Bg3 Nh5** [To gain the two Bishops] **10.Qd2 e6!** [Planning ... f5 ...f4] **11.d5 ed5 12.cd5 Re8 13.Nd4 Ng3 14.hg3 Nf6 15.f3 c6! 16.0-0-0 cd5 17.ed5 Qb6 18.Bb5 Re5 19.Rhe1 Nh5 20.g4 Re1 21.Re1 [D] Bg4! 22.fg4 Bd4 23.gh5 Bc3 24.Qc3 Qb5 25.Qf3 Re8 26.Rf1 Qd7 27.Qf6 Qe7 28.Qe7 Re7 29.Rf6 Rd7 30.Kd2 Kg7 31.Rf2 Re7 32.Kd3 Re5 33.Kd4 f5 34.Rc2 Kf6 35.Rc7 Re7 36.Rc8 Re4 37.Kd3 Ke5 38.Rh8 Rg4 39.Rh6 Rg2 40.Kc3 Kd5 41.Rh7 Rg3 0-1**

After 32...Bf8

485) Fischer,R-Durao,J [10/28/66] Havana Olympiad Prelim [3] A04/11 King's Indian Attack [E:Rook + minor pieces] **1.e4 e6 2.d3 c5 3.Nf3 Nc6 4.g3 g6 5.Bg2 Bg7 6.0-0 Nge7 7.c3 0-0 8.d4 d6 9.dc5!** [Preparing to maneuver against the weak squares - d6, e5, f6] **dc5 10.Qe2 b6 11.e5 a5?!** [Weakening b6 + b5] **12.Re1 Ba6 13.Qe4 Ra7 14.Nbd2 Bd3 15.Qh4 Nd5 16.Qd8 Rd8 17.a4!** [Nailing down the weaknesses at b5 and b6] **Rad7 18.Bf1 Bf1 19.Kf1 Nde7 20.Nc4 Nc8 21.Bg5 N6e7 22.Nfd2 h6 23.Be7 Re7 24.Ra3 Rc7 25.Rb3 Rc6 26.Ne4 Bf8 27.Ke2 Be7 28.f4 Kf8 29.g4 Ke8 30.Rf1 Rd5 31.Rf3 Rd8 32.Rh3! Bf8 [D] 33.Na5!** [The decisive breakthrough] **Rc7** [33...ba5 34.Nf6 ++-] **34.Nc4 Ra7 35.Nb6 Nb6 36.Rb6 Rda8 37.Nf6 Kd8 38.Rc6 Rc7 39.Rd3 Kc8 40.Rc7 Kc7 41.Rd7 Kc6 42.Rf7 c4 43.Nd7 Bc5 44.Nc5 Kc5 45.Rc7 Kd5 46.b4 1-0**

After 20...Ne6

486) Fischer,R-Bednarsky,J [10/30/66] Havana Olympiad Prelim [5] B86/06 Sicilian **1.e4 c5 2.Nf3 d6 3.d4 cd4 4.Nd4 Nf6 5.Nc3 a6 6.Bc4 e6 7.Bb3 Nbd7** [7...b5] **8.f4 Nc5 9.f5 Nfe4?** [Too risky. Now White has a strong attack; correct was 9...Be7] **10.fe6 Qh4 11.g3 Ng3 12.Nf3 Qh5 13.ef7 Kd8 14.Rg1 Nf5 15.Nd5! Qf7 16.Bg5 Ke8 17.Qe2 Be6 18.Nf4 Kd7 19.0-0-0 Qe8 20.Be6 Ne6 [D] 21.Qe4! g6 22.Ne6 1-0**

487) Garcia Soruco,J-Fischer,R [10/31/66] Havana Olympiad Prelim [6] B87/01 Sicilian **1.e4 c5 2.Nf3 d6 3.d4 cd4 4.Nd4 Nf6 5.Nc3 a6 6.Bc4 e6 7.Bb3 b5 8.a3 Be7 9.Be3 0-0 10.0-0 Bb7 11.f3** [A rather passive formation] **Nbd7 12.Qd2 Ne5 13.Qf2 Qc7 14.Rac1 Kh8!** [Very original play] **15.Nce2 Rg8 16.Kh1 g5! 17.h3 Rg6 18.Ng3 Rag8 19.Ne6? fe6 20.Be6** [D] **Ne4 21.Ne4 Re6 0-1**

After 20.Be6

488) Fischer,R-Johannessen,S [11/3/66] Havana Olympiad Prelim [7] C70/09 Ruy Lopez **1.e4 e5 2.Nf3 Nc6 3.Bb5 a6 4.Ba4 b5 5.Bb3 Na5 6.0-0 d6 7.d4 Nb3 8.ab3 f6 9.c4!** [Strengthening his grip on the center] **Bb7 10.Nc3 Ne7 11.Qe2 c6** [11...b4 12.Nd5] **12.Rd1 Qc7 13.Be3 Ng6 14.Rac1 b4 15.Na4 c5** [Necessary to stop c5] **16.dc5 dc5 17.Qd3 Rb8** [D] **18.Nb6** [Cute. The Knight gets to d5 since 18...Qb6 allows mate] **Be7 19.Nd5 Qc6 20.Qe2 Bd6 21.Rd3 Rc8 22.Rcd1 Bb8 23.Nd2 Qe6 24.Nf1 0-0 25.Ng3 Nf4 26.Bf4 ef4 27.Nh5 Rce8 28.Nhf4 Bf4 29.Nf4 Qe4 30.Re3 Qc6 31.Re6 Qc8 32.h4 g6 33.Re7 Re7 34.Qe7 Rf7 35.Rd8 Kg7 36.Ne6 1-0**

After 17...Rb8

489) Pomar,A-Fischer,R [11/6/66] Havana Olympiad Final [3] A69/08 Benoni **1.d4 Nf6 2.c4 c5 3.d5 e6 4.Nc3 ed5 5.cd5 g6 6.e4 d6 7.Be2 Bg7 8.f4 0-0 9.Nf3 Re8 10.Nd2 c4** [Better is 10...Ng4!?] **11.Bf3** [Better is 11.a4! - stopping ...b5] **Nbd7 12.0-0 b5! 13.Kh1** [13.Nb5? Qb6] **a6 14.a4 Rb8 15.ab5 ab5 16.e5** [Otherwise ...Nc5 and ...b4 undermines the e-pawn anyway] **de5 17.Nde4 Ne4 18.Ne4 Nf6 19.d6 Be6 20.Nc5 e4!** -+/-++ **21.Ne4 Ne4 22.Be4 Qb6 23.f5 gf5 24.Bc2** [24.Bf5? Bf5 25.Rf5 Qd6!] **Qd4 25.Qh5** [D] **Qg4 26.Qg4 fg4 27.Bg5 Bb2 28.Rad1 b4 29.d7 Red8 30.Ba4 b3 31.Rfe1 Kg7 32.Bd8 Rd8 33.Rd6 Bf6 34.Red1 Bg5 35.Rb6 h6 36.Rc6 Ra8 37.Bb5 Bd7 38.h4 Bc6 39.Bc6 c3 40.hg5 c2 41.gh6 Kh8 0-1**

After 25.Qh5

490) Fischer,R-Olafsson,F [11/7/66] Havana Olympiad Final [4] C83/06 Ruy Lopez **1.e4 e5 2.Nf3 Nc6 3.Bb5 a6 4.Ba4 Nf6 5.0-0 Ne4 6.d4 b5 7.Bb3 d5 8.de5 Be6 9.c3 Be7 10.Bc2** [10.Be3 +=] **Bg4?!** [10...0-0 11.Qe2 Nc5 12.Nd4 Qd7 =] **11.h3 Bh5 12.g4!** [Cornering the Bishop and winning the d-pawn] **Bg6** [D] **13.Bb3 Na5 14.Bd5 c6 15.Be4 Be4 16.Qd8 Rd8 17.Nbd2 Bd5 18.Re1 h5 19.Ne4 hg4 20.hg4 Nc4 21.Kg2 Be6 22.b3 Nb6 23.Be3 Nd5 24.Kg3 f6 25.Bc5 f5 26.Nd6 Bd6 27.ed6 Kd7 28.Ne5 Kc8 29.Nc6 f4 30.Kg2 Ne3 31.Kg1 Bd5 32.Ne7 Kd7 33.fe3 Rh1 34.Kf2 Rh2 35.Kf1 Bf3 36.Ng6 Be4 37.Ne5 1-0**

After 12...Bg6

491) Uhlmann,W-Fischer,R [11/8/66] Havana Olympiad Final [5] E90/05 King's Indian [E:Rook + minor pieces] **1.d4 Nf6 2.c4 g6 3.Nc3 Bg7 4.e4 d6 5.Nf3 0-0 6.Bg5 h6 7.Bh4 g5!** [Going after the dark-squared Bishop] **8.Bg3 Nh5 9.Be2 e6!** [With the idea of ...f5-f4] **10.d5 f5 11.Nd4 Ng3 12.hg3 fe4 13.Ne6 Be6 14.de6 Bc3 15.bc3 Qf6 16.e7!** [16...Qf2 17.Kd2 Re8 18.Rh6 +-] **Re8 17.Rb1 Na6 18.Qd4 Kg7 19.Rb7 Re7 20.Qf6 Kf6 21.Rh6 Kg7 22.Rh5 Kg6 23.g4 =** [The extra doubled and isolated c-pawns are no better than one pawn] **Nc5 24.Rb1 Rf8 25.Kf1 Ref7 26.f3 ef3 27.gf3** [D] **Rf3 28.Bf3 Rf3 29.Ke2 Rg3 30.Rh8 Rg4 31.Rc8 Re4 32.Kd2 Re7 33.Re1 Rh7 34.Re2 Kf5 35.Rf8 Kg4 36.Kc2 Nd7 37.Rf1 Rg7 38.Re4 Kh3 39.Re3 Kg4 40.Re4 Kh5**

After 27.gf3

After 69.Re6

41.Rh1 Kg6 42.Rhe1 Ne5 43.c5 Kf5 44.cd6 cd6 45.Rd4 Rg6 46.Rf1 Ke6 47.Rfd1 Kd7 48.Ra4 Nc6 49.Rg1 Ke6 50.Ra6 Kd7 51.Kd3 d5 52.Ke3 Kd6 53.Ra4 Ke5 54.Kf3 Kf5 55.Kg3 a5 56.Rd1 Ke6 57.Ra3 Kd6 58.Rb3 Kc5 59.a4 Kc4 60.Rb5 Rd6 61.Rc1 Re6 62.Kg4 Re2 63.Rd1 Ra2 64.Rdd5 Ra4 65.Rdc5 Kd3 66.Kg5 Rc4 67.Rc4 Kc4 68.Rb6 Ne7 69.Re6 [D] Kc3 70.Re7 a4 71.Ra7 Kb3 72.Kf4 a3 73.Ke3 a2 74.Kd2 Kb2 75.Rb7 Ka1 1/2-1/2

After 33...Kg5

492) Fischer,R-Portisch,L [11/10/66] Havana Olympiad Final [6] C69/04 Ruy Lopez **1.e4 e5 2.Nf3 Nc6 3.Bb5 a6 4.Bc6** [Fischer's secret weapon, this was used to take several Grandmasters by surprise] **dc6 5.0-0!** [Better than the old 5.d4] **f6 6.d4 ed4 7.Nd4 c5 8.Nb3 Qd1 9.Rd1 Bd6** [Better is 9...Bg4 10.f3 Be6 11.Nc3 Bd6 =] **10.Na5! b5 11.c4!** [Fixing a target at c5] **Ne7 12.Be3 f5 13.Nc3 f4 14.e5 Be5 15.Bc5 Bc3 16.bc3 Ng6 17.Nc6 Be6? 18.cb5 ab5 19.Na7! Rb8 20.Rdb1 Kf7 21.Nb5 Rhd8 22.Rb4 Ba2 23.Nc7 Rbc8 24.h4 Rd2 25.Bb6 f3 26.Be3 Re2 27.Nb5 Ra8 28.h5 Ne5 29.Rf4 Ke7 30.Rd1 Rc8 31.Re4 Kf6 32.Rd6 Kf5 33.Rf4 Kg5 [D] 34.Rf3 1-0**

After 26.Nf4

493) Johannessen,S-Fischer,R [11/11/66] Havana Olympiad Final [7] A57/06 Queen's pawn **1.d4 Nf6 2.Nf3 c5 3.d5 b5** [Sharp and risky. No doubt played to enhance winning chances against a much weaker player] **4.c4 Bb7 5.g3** [Better is 5.Nbd2 bc4 6.e4 +=; the c4 square will be useful] **g6 6.Bg2 bc4 7.Nc3 Bg7 8.0-0 0-0 9.Ne5 d6 10.Nc4 Nbd7 11.Re1 Ba6 12.Qa4 Qc8?!** [Better would be 12...Bc4, getting rid of the dangerous Nc4] **13.Na5! Nb6 14.Qh4 Re8 15.Bg5 Qc7 16.Nc6 Bb7 17.e4 Nbd7 18.f4 Kh8 19.e5 de5 20.fe5?** [20.Ne5 +-] **Nd5 21.Nd5 Qc6 22.e6 Ne5 23.Re5 Be5 24.ef7 Rf8 25.h3 Rf7 26.Nf4 [D] Rf4 0-1**

After 17...Ka7?

494) Fischer,R-Gligoric,S [11/12/66] Havana Olympiad Final [8] C69/07 Ruy Lopez **1.e4 e5 2.Nf3 Nc6 3.Bb5 a6 4.Bc6 dc6 5.0-0 f6 6.d4 Bg4 7.c3 ed4 8.cd4 Qd7 9.h3 Be6 10.Nc3 0-0-0 11.Bf4 Ne7?** [Better is 11...Bd6] **12.Rc1 Ng6 13.Bg3 Bd6 14.Na4!** [Threat-15.d5, and if 15...cd5 16.Nb6] **Bg3 15.fg3 Kb8 16.Nc5 Qd6 17.Qa4 Ka7?** [D] **18.Na6!** [18...ba6 19.Rc6 ++-] **Bh3 19.e5 Ne5 20.de5 fe5 21.Nc5 Kb8 22.gh3 e4 23.Ne4 Qe7 24.Rc3 b5 25.Qc2 1-0**

After 53.Bd1

495) Najdorf,M-Fischer,R [11/13/66] Havana Olympiad Final A79/03 Benoni **1.d4 Nf6 2.c4 c5 3.d5 g6 4.Nc3 Bg7 5.e4 d6 6.Nf3 0-0 7.Be2 e6 8.0-0 ed5 9.cd5 Re8** [9...Bg4!?] **10.Nd2 Na6 11.f3 Nc7 12.a4 b6 13.Kh1!? Nd7 14.Nc4 Ne5 15.Ne3 f5 16.f4 Nf7 17.ef5 gf5 18.Bd3 Qf6 19.Ne2 Nh6 20.Ng3 Qg6 21.Qc2 Rf8 22.Bd2 Bd7 23.Rae1** [Better is 23.Rf3!] **Rae8 24.Be2** [Better is 24.Bc3 =] **Re7 25.Bd3 Bd4 26.b4 Be3 27.Be3 Rfe8 28.bc5 bc5 29.Bd2 Re1 30.Re1 Re1 31.Be1 Nd5!** [Nabbing the pawn without fear of the pin] **32.Bc4 Qe6 33.Bc3 Bc6 34.Qb3 Kf7 35.Qb8 Ng8 36.h3 Nge7 37.Qh8 Qh6 38.Ne2 Ba4 39.Qa8 Bc6 40.Qa7 Qe6 41.Qa2 Qe4 42.Bd2 Ke8 43.Ng3 Qd4 44.Kh2 Ne3 45.Be3 Qe3 46.Bg8 Qf4 47.Qf7 Kd7 48.Bh7 Be4 49.Bg6 Qe5 50.Bh5 Bd5 51.Qe8 Kc7 52.Kg1 Qg7 53.Bd1 [D] Bc6 0-1**

496) Fischer,R-Spassky,B [11/14/66] Havana Olympiad Final [2]
C93/13 Ruy Lopez [E:Rook + minor pieces] **1.e4 e5 2.Nf3 Nc6 3.Bb5
a6 4.Ba4 Nf6 5.0-0 Be7 6.Re1 b5 7.Bb3 0-0 8.c3 d6 9.h3 h6 10.d4 Re8
11.Nbd2 Bf8 12.Nf1 Bd7 13.Ng3 Na5 14.Bc2 c5 15.b3!** [Preventing
...Nc4] **cd4** [Better is 15...Nc6 =] **16.cd4 Nc6 17.Bb2 g6 18.Qd2 Bg7
19.Rad1 +-=/+-** [A strong pawn center, lead in development, and
harmonious piece arrangement] **Qb6 20.Nf1 Rad8 21.Ne3 Qb8 22.Bb1
Qb7 23.Rc1 Kh7 24.a3 Bc8 25.Bc3! Bd7 26.Qb2 Qb8 27.b4 Kg8
28.Rcd1 Nh7 29.Ba2 Ng5 30.Ng5 hg5 31.de5 de5 32.Nd5 Ne7 33.Ne7
Re7 34.Qd2 Bf6 [D] 35.Qd6 Kg7 36.Qa6?** [Giving Black strong
counterplay. Better is 36.Qb8 Rb8 37.Rd6! Bc8 38.Re3! threatening Rf3
+-/++-] **Rc8 37.Rd6 Rc3 38.Rf6 Be6 39.Re6 fe6 40.Rd1 Qb7 41.Qb7
Rb7 42.Be6 Ra3 43.Kh2 Ra4 44.Rb1 Rc7 45.f3 Ra6 46.Bb3 Ra3
47.Rb2 Ra1 48.Kg3 Kf6 49.Kg4 Rc3 50.Bd5 Raa3 51.h4 gh4 52.Kh4
Ra1 53.Rd2 Raa3 54.Kg4 Rd3 55.Re2 Rac3 56.Ra2 Ra3 57.Rb2
1/2-1/2**

After 34...Bf6

497) Fischer,R-Minev,N [11/15/66] Havana Olympiad Final [10]
C11/16 French **1.e4 e6 2.d4 d5 3.Nc3 Nf6 4.Bg5 de4 5.Ne4 Be7 6.Bf6
gf6 7.g3 Bd7** [Better is 7...f5! 8.Nc3 Bf6] **8.Nf3 Bc6 9.Qe2 f5 10.Ned2
Bf6 11.c3 Qe7 12.Bg2 Nd7 13.0-0 0-0 14.Rfe1 Rfe8? 15.b4!** [Gaining
Queenside space and harassing the Bc6] **a6 16.a4 b6 17.Nc4 Be4
18.Rad1 Red8 19.g4!** [Again taking advantage of the Bishop's
position] **Kh8 20.Ncd2 fg4 21.Ne4 gf3 22.Bf3 Rg8 23.Kh1 c6 24.Nf6
Nf6 25.Bc6 Rac8 26.b5 ab5 27.ab5 Rg5 28.d5 Qc5 29.de6 Rc6 30.bc6
Ng4 31.Rd4 Qc6 32.f3 Re5 [D] 33.ef7 Qf6 34.Rg4! 1-0**

After 32...Re5

498) Pachman,L-Fischer,R [11/16/66] Havana Olympiad Final
[11] A33/02 English [E:Rook + Bishop] **1.d4 Nf6 2.Nf3 c5 3.c4 cd4
4.Nd4 e6 5.e3 Nc6 6.Be2 d5 7.Nc3 Bc5 8.0-0 Bd4! 9.ed4 dc4 10.Be3
Na5 11.Bc4 Nc4 12.Qa4 Bd7 13.Qc4 Bc6** =/=+ [Black has traded off
two minor pieces and left White with the isolani] **14.Bg5 Qa5 15.Qc5
Qc5 16.dc5 a5!** [Preventing ...b4 and thereby artificially isolating the
c-pawn] **17.Rfd1 h5 18.h4 Nd7 19.Be3 Ne5 20.Bd4 Nd7 21.b3 Rg8
22.Be3 Ne5 23.f3 Ng6 24.Bf2 Nf4 25.Be3 Nd5! 26.Nd5 Bd5 27.Rd4
Kd7 28.Rc1 Kc6 29.Rc3 f6 30.f4 Rgd8 31.Kf2 [D] a4! 32.Ra4 Ra4
33.ba4 Ba2 34.Rc2 Bd5 35.Rb2 Ra8 36.Rb4 Ra5 37.g3 Kc7 38.Bd4
Bc6 39.Be3 Ba4 40.Rd4 Bd7 41.Rd2 Ra8 42.Rb2 Rb8 43.Rd2 0-1**

After 31.Kf2

499) Gheorghiu,F-Fischer,R [11/17/66] Havana Olympiad Final
[12] E27/07 Nimzo-Indian [E:Rook + minor piece] **1.d4 Nf6 2.c4 e6
3.Nc3 Bb4 4.f3 d5** [4...c5!] **5.a3 Bc3** [5...Be7] **6.bc3 0-0 7.cd5 ed5 8.e3
Nh5 9.Qc2 Re8 10.g4!** [Very sophisticated strategy follows. White
conducts a general Kingside pawn advance and his pieces then position
themselves on favorable squares] **Nf4 11.h4 c5 12.Kf2! Ng6 13.Bd3
Nc6 14.Ne2 Be6 15.g5 Rc8 16.h5 Nf8 17.g6! fg6 18.hg6 h6 19.Qb1
Na5 20.Nf4 c4 21.Bc2 Rc6 22.Ra2 Nd7 23.a4 Nf6 24.Ba3 Qd7
25.Rb2 b6 26.Rb5 Nb7 27.e4!** [A powerful central expansion] **de4
28.Be4 Rcc8! 29.Re5! [D] Bg4 30.Nd5! Re5 31.Nf6 gf6 32.de5 Nc5
33.Bc5 Qd2 34.Kg3 Bf3 35.Bf3 Rc5 36.Qc1 Qc1 37.Rc1 Re5 38.Kf4
Kg7 39.Be4 h5 40.Rd1 Re7 41.Rd5 Kh6 42.Rd6 Kg7 43.Rc6 h4
44.Rc4 h3 45.Kg3 Kh6 46.Bb1 Re3 47.Kh2 Re1 48.Bd3 Re3
49.Rh4 Kg5 50.g7 1-0**

After 29.Re5!

After 9...Bh5

500) Fischer,R-Jimenez,E [11/20/66] Havana Olympiad Final [13] C69/07 Ruy Lopez [E:Rook + minor piece] **1.e4 e5 2.Nf3 Nc6 3.Bb5 a6 4.Bc6 dc6 5.0-0 f6 6.d4 Bg4 7.c3** [7.de5 Qd1 8.Rd1 fe5 9.Rd3 +=] **ed4?!** [7...Bd6 =] **8.cd4 Qd7 9.h3 Bh5** [9...Be6 10.Nc3 0-0-0 11.Bf4 Ne7 12.Rc1 +-] **[D] 10.Ne5!** [Exploiting the unprotected Bh5] **Bd1 11.Nd7 Kd7 12.Rd1 Re8 13.f3 Ne7 14.Nc3 Kc8 15.Be3 f5 16.Rac1 fe4 17.fe4 g6 18.Bf4 Bg7 19.d5 Rd8 20.Na4 Rhf8 21.g3 g5 22.Bg5 Rf7 23.Kg2 cd5 24.ed5 Kb8 25.Re1 Bf8 26.Rf1 Rg7 27.Bf6 Rg8 28.Rce1 Re8 29.d6 cd6 30.Be7 Be7 31.Rf7 1-0**

After 25.Na8

501) Benko,P-Fischer,R [12/66] US Championship [1] E72/05 King's Indian **1.g3 g6 2.Bg2 Bg7 3.d4 Nf6 4.e4 d6 5.Ne2 0-0 6.0-0 Nbd7** [6...Nc6 + e5] **7.c4** [7.Nbc3] **e5 8.Nbc3 c6 9.d5 cd5 10.Nd5** [Maintaining access to the backward d-pawn] **Nd5 11.Qd5 Nc5 12.Rd1 Bg4! 13.f3 Be6 14.Qd6 Bc4 15.Nc3 Qa5 16.Bg5** [16.Be3 Nd3! and if 17.Rd3 Rad8! -+] **Ne6 17.Be7 Rfe8 18.Nd5 Be2?!** [Bold, but unsound; 18...Nd4 =] **19.Rdc1 Nd4 20.Qb4 Qb4 21.Bb4 Nf3 22.Kf2 Nd4 23.Nc7 Bh6 24.Re1? Rec8 25.Na8 [D] Rc2 26.Re2 Re2 27.Kf1 Rb2 28.Bc3 Rc2 29.Bd4 ed4 30.e5 Be3 31.Bb7 Rf2 32.Ke1 d3 33.Ba6 Re2 34.Kd1 Rh2 35.Bd3 Rd2 36.Ke1 Rd3 37.Ke2 Ra3 38.Nc7 Bd4 39.Nb5 Ba1 40.Na3 Be5 41.g4 Kg7 42.Nc4 Kf6 0-1**

After 24...e5

502) Fischer,R-Saidy,A [12/13/66] US Championship [2] B57/10 Sicilian **1.e4 c5 2.Nf3 Nc6 3.d4 cd4 4.Nd4 Nf6 5.Nc3 d6 6.Bc4 Qb6 7.Nb3 e6 8.0-0 Be7 9.Be3 Qc7 10.f4 0-0 11.Bd3 a6 12.g4 b5** [12...d5!?] **13.g5 Ne8** [13...Nd7] **14.Qh5 g6 15.Qh6 f5 16.ef5 gf5** [16...ef5 17.Nd5] **17.Nd4 Nd8 18.Rae1 Ng7 19.Rf3 Nf7 20.Qh4 Nh8 21.Rh3 h5 22.Be2 Ng6 23.Qf2 b4 24.Nd1 e5 [D] 25.Bh5! [Breaking in] Nh5 26.Rh5 ed4 27.Bd4 Bb7 28.Rh6 Kf7 29.Qe2 Be4 30.Qh5 Rg8 31.Rg6! Rg6 32.Qh7 Ke8 33.Qg6 Kd7 34.Nf2 Qc4 35.Ne4 Qd4 36.Nf2 Qf4 37.Qe6 Kc6 38.Qe7 Rg8 39.Qe3 Rg5 40.Kh1 1-0**

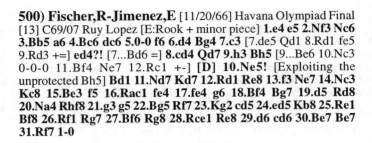

503) Rossolimo,N-Fischer,R [12/66] US Championship [3] B90/04 Sicilian [E:Rook + minor pieces] **1.e4 c5 2.Nf3 d6 3.d4 cd4 4.Nd4 Nf6 5.Nc3 a6 6.Be3 e5 7.Nde2 Be7 8.h3 Be6 9.Ng3 g6!** [Limiting the scope of the Ng3] **10.Bd3 Nbd7 11.0-0 0-0 12.Qf3 Kh8 13.Rad1 b5 14.Qe2 Qa5 15.a3 Rab8 16.Rfe1 Qc7 17.Nf1 Nb6 18.Bb6** [Otherwise ...Nc4, but now Black has the two Bishops =+] **Rb6 19.Ne3 b4 20.Na4 Rb4 22.Na1 Qc6 23.Nc3 Rb2 24.Ned1 Rb6 25.Ra6 Bd8 26.Rb6 Bb6 27.Nb5 Nh5! 28.Qd2 Nf4 29.Bf1 Bc5 30.c4 f5 31.g3 Nh5 32.ef5 gf5 33.Qh6 Ng7 34.Qd2 f4 35.Kh2 Nf5 36.Bg2 Qd7 37.g4 [D] Bc4 38.Re5 Nd4 39.Re4 Bb5 40.Rd4 Qg7 41.Rd5 Bc4 42.Rh5 f3 43.Bh1 Bd4 44.Ne3 Be2 45.h4 Qa7 46.Bg2 Be5 47.Re5 de5 48.Qd6 Qb8 49.Qb8 Rb8 50.Bh3 h6! 51.Kg3 Kg7 52.Nf5 Kg6 53.Ne7 Kf7 54.Nf5 Rb6 55.h5 Ra6 56.Kh4 Bd3 57.Ne3 Ra2 58.Kg3 Be4! 59.Bf1 Re2 60.Nc4 Kf6 61.Nd6 Bc6 62.Bh3 Bd5 63.Nf5 Kg5 64.Ne3 Bc6 65.Bf1 Re1 66.Bh3 e4 67.Nf5 Bd7 68.Nh6 Kh6 69.g5 Kg5 70.h6 0-1**

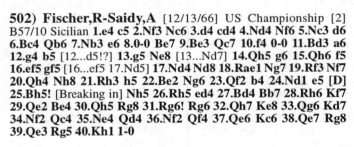

After 37.g4

504) Fischer,R-Byrne,R [12/66] US Championship [4] C15/15
French **1.e4 e6 2.d4 d5 3.Nc3 Bb4 4.a3 Bc3 5.bc3 de4 6.Qg4 Nf6
7.Qg7 Rg8 8.Qh6 Nbd7** [Better is 8...Rg6 9.Qd2 b6 10.Bb2 Bb7 =]
9.Ne2 c5 10.Ng3 Qc7 11.Qe3 [Better is 11.Bb5 +=] **Qc6 12.a4 a6
13.dc5 Qc5 14.Qc5 Nc5 15.Be3 Ncd7 16.a5** [16.Be2] **Nd5 17.Ne4
Ne3 18.fe3 Ke7 19.Be2 f5 20.Ng3 Ne5 21.0-0 Bd7 22.e4 fe4 23.Ne4
Bc6 24.Ng3 Rad8 25.Rad1 Rd1 26.Rd1 Rg5 27.Re1 h6 28.Ra1 Ng4
29.Bf3 Ne3 30.Kf2 Ng4 31.Kg1 Ne3** [D] **1/2-1/2**

Final position

505) Byrne,D-Fischer,R [12/66] US Championship [5] A21/11
English **1.c4 g6 2.g3 Bg7 3.Bg2 e5 4.Nc3 d6 5.e4 f5** [Very sharp;
5...Ne7 =] **6.ef5 gf5 7.Qh5 Kf8 8.d3 Nf6 9.Qe2 Kf7 10.Bg5 c6 11.Nf3
Rf8 12.Qd2 Kg8 13.d4 ed4** [13...e4 14.Nh4 +=/+-] **14.Nd4 Qe8
15.Nde2 Nbd7! 16.0-0** [16.Qd6 Ne5! 17.b3 Ne4! -+] **Ne5 17.Qd6 Nc4
18.Qf4 Ne5** [18...Nb2 19.Rb1 Nd3 20.Qc4 ++-] **19.Bh6** [19.Rad1] **Nd3
20.Qd2 Bh6 21.Qh6 Nb2 22.Nf4 Qf7 23.Rfe1 Nc4 24.Rad1 Bd7
25.Bh3 Rae8 26.Re8 Re8 27.Nce2 Ne5 28.Nd4 Nfg4 29.Qg5 Qg7
30.Qg7 Kg7 31.f3 Ne3 32.Re1 c5 33.Re3 cd4 34.Rb3 b6 35.Kf2 Rc8
36.Rb2 d3 37.Rb1 d2 38.Rd1 Nc4 39.Ke2** [D] **Ba4 40.Rd2 Re8
41.Kd3 Nd2 42.Kd2 Re5 43.Ne2 Bd7 44.Nc3 0-1**

After 39.Ke2

506) Fischer,R-Zuckerman,B [12/66] US Championship [6]
B75/10 Sicilian **1.e4 c5 2.Nf3 Nc6 3.Nc3 g6 4.d4 cd4 5.Nd4 Bg7 6.Be3
Nf6 7.Bc4 d6 8.f3 Bd7 9.Qd2 Rc8 10.Bb3 Ne5 11.0-0-0** [Better is
11.Bh6 +=] **Nc4 12.Bc4 Rc4 13.Nb3 Qc7 14.Bd4 Be6** [D] **15.e5 de5
16.Be5 Qc8 17.Na5 Rc7?** [17...Rb4! ∞] **18.Bc7 Qc7 19.Nb5 Qb6
20.Nd4 Bd7 21.Rhe1 ++-** [Black has no compensation] **0-0 22.Re7
Qd6 23.Ree1 Qh2 24.Kb1 Qc7 25.Nab3 Rc8 26.g4 b6 27.Re7 Qd6
28.Re2 Nd5 29.c3 a5 30.Nc2 a4 31.Qd5 Qd5 32.Rd5 Be6 33.Rb5
ab3 34.ab3 Rc6 35.Rd2 Bf6 36.Nb4 1-0**

After 14...Be6

507) Evans,L-Fischer,R [12/66] US Championship [7] A36/17
English [E:Rook + minor pieces] **1.c4 Nf6 2.g3 g6 3.Bg2 Bg7 4.Nc3
0-0 5.e4 c5 6.Nge2 Nc6 7.0-0 d6 8.a3 Ne8 9.Rb1 a5 10.d3 Nc7 11.Be3
Nd4 12.b4 ab4 13.ab4 b6 14.bc5 bc5** [A very drawish position, but
both players persist] **15.Qc1 Re8 16.Bh6 Ne2 17.Ne2 Bh8 18.Bd2 Ne6
19.Bc3 Bc3 20.Qc3 Ra2 21.Rb2 Qa5 22.Qa5 Ra5 23.Rfb1 Nd8
24.Bf1 Nc6 25.Nc3 Kg7 26.Kg2 Be6 27.Rb7 Nb4 28.Nb5 Kf8 29.d4
Ra2 30.Nc7 Rd8 31.Nd5 Bc8 32.Rb6 Na6 33.dc5 Nc5 34.Nb4 Rd2
35.Kf3 Na4 36.Rc6 Nc3 37.Rc1 Na2 38.Na2 Ra2 39.Ke3 Be6 40.Rb1
Ra3 41.Bd3 Rda8 42.Rb2 R8a4 43.Kd2 Ra1 44.c5 dc5 45.Rc5 Rh1
46.h4 Raa1 47.Ke3 Ra3 48.Rbc2 Raa1 49.Rc7 h6 50.Rb2 Rhe1
51.Re2 Rec1** [D] **1/2-1/2**

Final position

508) Fischer,R-Addison,W [12/66] US Championship [8]
C80/13 Ruy Lopez [E:Rook + Bishop] **1.e4 e5 2.Nf3 Nc6 3.Bb5 a6
4.Ba4 Nf6 5.0-0 Ne4 6.d4 b5 7.Bb3 d5 8.Ne5** [Usual is 8.de5] **Ne5
9.de5 c6 10.Be3 Be7 11.Nd2 Nd2 12.Qd2 0-0 13.Qc3 Bb7 14.f4**
[Worth consideration was 14.Bc5 to trade Black's better Bishop] **a5
15.a3 b4 16.Qd2 a4 17.Ba2 ba3 18.ba3 Ba3 19.Rfb1 Bc8 20.Bd5
Qd5 21.Ra3 Qd2 22.Bd2 Bf5** [Opposite colored Bishops] **= 23.Rb2
Rfd8 24.Be3 h5 25.h3 Rdb8 26.Rb8 Rb8 27.Ra4 Bc2 28.Rc4 Rb1
29.Kf2 Rb2 30.Kg3 Bf5 31.Rc6** [D] **Rg2 1/2-1/2**

After 31.Rc6

After 38.Nc3

After 88.Ra6

After 23...Rac8

After 60.Kh2

After 69.Kg1

509) Sherwin,J-Fischer,R [12/66] US Championship [9] E69/13 King's Indian [E:Rooks + minor pieces / Rook + pawn] **1.Nf3 Nf6 2.g3 g6 3.Bg2 Bg7 4.0-0 0-0 5.d4 d6 6.c4 Nbd7 7.Nc3 e5 8.e4 c6 9.h3 Qb6 10.Re1 Re8** [10...ed4!? 11.Nd4 Re8 ∞]**11.d5 c5 12.a3 a6 13.Rb1 Qc7 14.Be3 b6 15.Bf1 Nf8 16.b4** += [White has more space and Queenside operations are already underway] **Bd7 17.Kh2 Reb8 18.Qc2 Ne8 19.Rb2 f5 20.Reb1 Qc8 21.bc5 bc5 22.Rb6 Rb6 23.Rb6 Bf6!** [In order to chase the Rb6] **24.Rb2 Ng7 25.Bd2 Bd8 26.Qb3 Bc7 27.Qb7 Ba5! 28.Qc8 Bc8 29.Bd3 Nd7 30.Na4 Bc7** [Carefully guarding all entry points on the b-file] **31.Nh4 fe4 32.Be4 Nf6 33.f3 Ne4 34.fe4 Ne8 35.Nc3 Ba5 36.g4 Nf6 37.Nb1 Bd8 38.Nc3** [D] **Ng4 39.hg4 Bh4 40.g5 Bg4 41.Be3 Rf8 42.Nb1 Rf3 43.Rb3 Bg3 44.Kg2 Bf4 45.Rb8 Kf7 46.Bf4 ef4 47.Rb7 Ke8 48.Rb8 Kd7 49.Rb7 Kd8 50.Rf7 Ke8 51.Rf6 Ke7 52.Re6 Kd7 53.Rf6 Bh5 54.Nd2 Rg3 55.Kf2 Rd3 56.Nf1 Rf3 57.Kg2 Ra3 58.Rf4 Be2 59.Ng3 Bc4 60.Rf7 Ke8 61.Rh7 Bd3 62.Rh8 Ke7 63.Rh7 Kf8 64.Rh8 Kg7 65.Rc8 Kf7 66.Rc7 Ke8 67.e5 de5 68.Rc5 Kd7 69.Rc6 Ra5 70.Kf3 Rd5 71.Rf6 Rd6 72.Rf7 Ke6 73.Ra7 Kd5 74.Ke3 Ke6 75.Ra8 Bb5 76.Rf8 Ke7 77.Rg8 Kf7 78.Rb8 Rd3 79.Kf2 Bc6 80.Rb6 Rf3 81.Kg2 Rc3 82.Kf2 a5 83.Ra6 a4 84.Ne2 Rc4 85.Ng3 Ke6 86.Ra7 Rc2 87.Kf1 Rc3 88.Ra6** [D] **Rg3 89.Rc6 Kf5 90.Ra6 Ra3 91.Ra5 Ra2 92.Kg1 a3 93.Kf1 Kf4 94.Kg1 e4 95.Kf1 Kf3 96.Kg1 e3 97.Re5 Rg2 98.Kh1 a2 99.Ra5 Rb2 100.Re5 a1=Q# 0-1**

510) Fischer,R-Reshevsky,S [12/66] US Championship [10] B81/01 Sicilian **1.e4 c5 2.Nf3 d6 3.d4 cd4 4.Nd4 Nf6 5.Nc3 e6 6.g4 d5?** [A known opening error - an example of Reshevsky's occasional ignorance of theory] **7.ed5 Nd5 8.Bb5 Bd7 9.Nd5 ed5 10.Qe2 Qe7 11.Be3 g6 12.Bd7 Nd7 13.Nb5 Ne5 14.0-0-0** +-/++- [The rest is virtually a matter of technique for Bobby] **Bg7 15.Rd5 0-0 16.Rhd1 a6 17.Nd6 Qh4 18.f3 b5 19.Bd4 Nc4 20.Bg7 Kg7 21.Nc4 bc4 22.Qc4 Qh2 23.Rd7 Rac8** [D] **24.Rf7 Rf7 25.Qc8 Qf4 26.Kb1 Qf3 27.Rc1 g5 28.b3 Qe2 29.Qc3 Kg6 30.Qh3 h6 31.Rh1 Rh7 32.a3 Rh8 33.a4 Rh7 34.Rh2 Qe1 35.Ka2 Qe4 36.Qh5 Kg7 37.Rd2 Qe7 38.Qh3 Kg8 39.Qf3 Rf7 40.Qa8 Kg7 41.Qa6 Qe4 42.Qe2 Qf4 43.Rd5 1-0**

511) Bisguier,A-Fischer,R [12/66] US Championship [11] B50/05 Sicilian [E:Minor piece] **1.e4 c5 2.Nf3 d6 3.c3 Nf6 4.Bd3 Nc6 5.Bc2 Bg4** [This pin restrains d4] **6.d3 g6 7.Nbd2 Bg7 8.h3 Bd7 9.0-0 0-0 10.Nh2** [Clearing a way for the f-pawn] **b5 11.f4 b4 12.Nc4 d5!** [Opening up central play] **13.Ne5 bc3 14.bc3 de4 15.de4 Ne5 16.fe5 Ne8 17.Nf3 Nc7 18.Rf2 Bb5** =+ [Black plays against White's weakened pawns] **19.Bg5 Qd1 20.Rd1 Rfe8 21.Bb3 c4 22.Bc2 Ne6 23.Be3 Reb8 24.Rb1 a6 25.Rff1 Be8 26.Kf2 Nd8 27.Rb8 Rb8 28.Rb1 Rb5 29.Rb5 ab5 30.Ke2 h6 31.Kd2 g5 32.h4 g4 33.Nd4 e6 34.Bf4 h5 35.Bg5 Nb7 36.Bf6 Bh6 37.Bg5 Bg5 38.hg5 Kg7 39.Ke3 Kg6 40.Kf4 Nc5 41.g3 Bd7 42.a3 Be8 43.Bb1 Na4 44.Ne2 Nb2 45.Nd4 Nd1 46.Ne2 Nf2 47.Ke3 Nh3 48.Nf4 Kg5 49.Ng2 f6 50.ef6 Kf6 51.Nh4 e5 52.Bc2 Bd7 53.Bb1 Ng5 54.Bc2 Nf7 55.Bb1 Nh8 56.Bc2 Ng6 57.Ng6 Kg6 58.Kf2 Kg5 59.Kg2 h4 60.Kh2** [D] **h3 61.Kg1 Kf6 62.Kh2 Ke7 63.Kg1 Kd6 64.Kf2 Kc5 65.Kg1 Kb6 66.Kh1 Ka5 67.Kg1 Bc6 68.Kh1 Bb7 69.Kg1** [D] **Be4!** [Now Black's King can invade. This, in conjunction with the passed pawns, is decisive] **70.Be4 Ka4 71.Bf5 Kb3 72.Bg4 e4 73.Bh3 Kc3 74.g4 Kd2 0-1**

1967

512) Lombardy,W-Fischer,R [3/24/67] Monaco [1] A15/14
King's Indian **1.Nf3 Nf6 2.c4 g6 3.b3 Bg7 4.Bb2 0-0 5.g3 d6 6.Bg2
e5 7.0-0 Nc6 8.Nc3 Nh5 9.e3 f5** [Planning 10...f4 =]**10.d3 g5?!**
[Better would be 10...f4] **11.Ne1 g4 12.f3 Nf6 13.f4 += Ne7 14.Qd2
Ng6 15.Nd5 Ne8 16.Rd1 c6 17.Nc3 ef4 18.ef4 h5 19.Nc2 h4
20.Rfe1 Nf6 21.Ne2 Bd7 22.Bd4 +=** [White's Queenside play vs.
Black's stalled Kingside action] **Rf7 23.Bf2 h3 24.Bh1 Qc7 25.Nc3
a6 26.Nd4 Nf8 27.b4 Rd8 28.Nb3 Re8 29.Re8 Be8 30.a4 Kh7
31.Ne2?** [31.b5 +=] **Re7 32.a5 Kg6 33.Nc3 Bf7 34.Re1 Rd7
35.Qc2 d5 36.Bb6 Qc8 37.Ne2 dc4 38.dc4 Re7 39.Bc5 Re8 40.Bf2
Ne4 41.Bd4 Bd4 42.Ned4 Nd6 43.Re5 Re5 44.fe5 [D] Qe8 45.Qe2
Bc4 46.Qe3 Bb3 47.Nb3 Nc4 48.Qe2 Ne5 49.Nc5 Qe7 50.Nb7
Nfd7 51.Qd2 Nc4 52.Qc3 Qe2 53.Bc6 Nd2 54.Qc1 Ne5 0-1**

After 44.fe5

513) Fischer,R-Forintos,G [3/25/67] Monaco [2] C95/05 Ruy
Lopez [E: Rook + Bishop] **1.e4 e5 2.Nf3 Nc6 3.Bb5 a6 4.Ba4 Nf6
5.0-0 Be7 6.Re1 b5 7.Bb3 d6 8.c3 0-0 9.h3 Nb8 10.d4 Nbd7
11.Nh4 ed4** [11...g6] **12.cd4 Nb6 13.Nd2 Nfd5 14.Nhf3 Nb4 15.d5
c5 16.dc6 Nc6 17.Nf1 Bf6** [Better is 17...Na5 =] **18.Be3 Na5 19.Bd4
Bb7 20.Ng3 += Nbc4 21.Bc4 Nc4 22.Nh5 Ne5 23.Ne5 de5
[23...Be5 24.Be5 de5 25.Qg4 g6 26.Rad1 Qe7 27.Rd7 ++-]24.Be5
Qd1 25.Rad1 Rfd8 26.Nf6 gf6 27.Rd8 Rd8 28.Be7 Rd4 29.Re3!
Be4 30.Bf6 Kf8 31.a3 Bc6 32.Re5 Rd5 33.Re3 Rf5 34.Be5 h5 35.f3
a5 36.Kf2 a4 37.g4 hg4 38.hg4 Rg5 39.Bf6 Rd5 40.f4 Rd2 41.Kg3
Rg2 42.Kh4 Rd2 43.f5 Bd5 44.Kg5 Rd1 45.Rc3 Re1 [D] 46.Rh3
Ke8 47.Rd3 1-0**

After 45...Re1

514) Mazzoni,G-Fischer,R [3/26/67] Monaco [3] B97/12
Sicilian [E: Rook + Bishop] **1.e4 c5 2.Nf3 d6 3.d4 cd4 4.Nd4 Nf6
5.Nc3 a6 6.Bg5 e6 7.f4 Qb6 8.Qd2 Qb2 9.Rb1 Qa3 10.e5 de5
11.fe5 Nfd7 12.Bc4 Qa5 13.Ne6?** [Unsound; 13.0-0 ∞] **fe6 14.Be6
Qe5 15.Qe3 Qe3 16.Be3 Nc6 17.Nd5 Bd6 18.0-0 Nf6 19.Nf6 gf6
20.Rf6 Ke7 21.Rf8 Kf6 22.Bb7? [D] Ne5 23.Ba8 Ra8 24.Rb7 Rc8
25.Ra7 Rc6 26.Bd4 Kf5 27.c3 Rc3 28.Ra6 Rc1 29.Kf2 Ng4
30.Ke2 Bh2 31.Kd3 Rd1 32.Kc4 Rd2 33.a4 Rg2 34.Ra8 Ke4
35.Re8 Ne5 36.Be5 Be5 37.a5 Rc2 38.Kb5 Kd5 39.Rd8 Bd6
40.Rh8 Rc7 41.Kb6 Rd7 42.Rc8 Be5 43.Rc5 Ke4 44.Rc4 Bd4
45.Kb5 h5 0-1**

After 22.Bb7

515) Fischer,R-Bergraser,C [3/27/67] Monaco [4] B01/02
Center Counter **1.e4 d5 2.ed5 Nf6 3.Bb5 Bd7 4.Bc4 Bg4 5.f3 Bf5
6.g4 Bc8 7.Nc3 Nbd7** [7...a6!?; 7...c6] **8.g5 Nb6 9.Bb5 Nfd7 10.f4
Nd5 11.Nd5 c6 12.Bc4 cd5 13.Bd5 Ne5? 14.Be4 Bg4 15.Nf3 Nc6
16.d4 e6 17.c3 Qc7 18.Qa4 f6 19.Rg1 Bf3 20.Bf3 0-0-0 21.Qc4
Kb8 22.Be3 Bd6 23.gf6 gf6 24.Bc6 bc6 25.Rf1 e5 26.fe5 fe5
27.0-0-0 Rhf8 [D] 28.Rf8 Rf8 29.de5 Be5? 30.Qb4 1-0**

After 27...Rhf8

After 30.h4

516) Larsen,B-Fischer,R [3/28/67] Monaco [5] E97/01 King's Indian [E: Rook + minor piece] **1.d4 Nf6 2.c4 g6 3.Nc3 Bg7 4.e4 d6 5.Be2 0-0 6.Nf3 e5 7.0-0 Nc6 8.Be3 Re8 9.de5 de5 10.Qd8 Nd8! 11.Nb5 Ne6 12.Ng5 Re7 13.Rfd1 b6 = 14.c5 Nc5 15.Rd8 Bf8 16.Na7 Ra7 17.Rc8 Kg7! 18.f3 Ne8 19.a3?! Nd6 20.Rd8 h6 21.Nh3 Ne6 22.Rb8 Re8 23.Re8 Ne8 24.Bb5** [24.Nf2] **Nd6 25.Bf1 Nb7 26.Nf2 Bc5 27.Bc5 Nbc5 28.Rd1 h5 29.Rd5 Kf6 30.h4** [D] **Ke7 31.Bc4 c6 32.Rd2 Nd4 33.Kf1 f5 34.b4** [34.ef5 Nf5 -++] **b5 35.Bg8 fe4 36.fe4 Nd7 37.Rd3 Ra6 38.Rc3 c5! 39.g4? c4 40.gh5 gh5 41.Bd5 Nf6 42.Rg3 Nd5 43.ed5 Rf6 44.Kg2 Nf5 45.Rh3 Rg6 46.Kf3 Nd4 47.Ke3 Rg2 48.Rh1 Kd6 49.Ne4 Kd5 50.Nc3 Ke6 51.Rc1 Rh2 52.a4 Rh3 53.Kf2 Nb3 54.Kg2 Nc1 55.Kh3 ba4 56.Na4 Ne2 57.b5 c3 58.b6 c2 59.Nc5 Kd5 60.Nb3 Kc6 61.Kg2 Kb6 0-1**

Final position

517) Fischer,R-Smyslov,V [3/30/67] Monaco [7] C69/13 Ruy Lopez [E: Rook + pawn] **1.e4 e5 2.Nf3 Nc6 3.Bb5 a6 4.Bc6 dc6 5.0-0 f6 6.d4 Bg4 7.de5 Qd1 8.Rd1 fe5 9.Rd3!** += **Bf3 10.Rf3 Nf6 11.Nc3 Bb4 12.Bg5 Bc3 13.bc3 Rf8 14.Bf6 Rf6 15.Rf6 gf6 16.Rd1 Ke7** [Better is 16...a5! =] **17.Rd3 Rf8 18.Kf1 a5 19.g4? Rg8! 20.h3 b5 21.Ke2 Ke6 22.Kf3 Rb8 23.Ke3 c5 24.c4 bc4 25.Ra3 Rb5 26.Kd2 Kd6 27.Rf3 Ke6 28.Kc1 Rb8 29.Ra3 Rb5 30.Rc3 Kd6 31.a3** [31.Rc4 Rb4 -+] **Rb8 32.Rc4 h5 33.f3 Kc6 34.Rc3 Rd8 35.Rd3 Rh8 36.Kd2 c4 37.Re3 Kc5 38.Re2 hg4 39.hg4 Rh1 40.Rg2** [D] **1/2-1/2**

Final position

518) Matanovic,A-Fischer,R [3/31/67] Monaco [8] B91/01 Sicilian **1.e4 c5 2.Nf3 d6 3.d4 cd4 4.Nd4 Nf6 5.Nc3 a6 6.g3** [Very solid, trying to avoid Fischer's deep preparations] **g6 7.Bg2 Bg7 8.0-0 0-0 9.Nde2 Nc6 10.h3 Bd7 = 11.Nf4 Rc8 12.Ncd5 Nd5 13.Nd5 Ne5 14.Bg5 Be6 15.b3 h6 16.Be3 Be6 17.Nf4 Bd7 18.Nd5 Be6 19.Nf4 Bd7 20.Nd5 Bc6 21.Nb6 Rb8 22.Rc1 Nd7 23.Nd7 Qd7 24.Qd2 Kh7 25.c4 b6 26.Rfe1 Qb7 27.Bd4 Bd4 28.Qd4 a5 29.h4 h5 30.Bh3 Qc7 31.a3 Bb7 32.b4 ab4 33.ab4 Ra8 34.c5 bc5 35.bc5 Ra6 36.cd6 Qd6 37.Qd6 Rd6 38.Rc7 Rb6 39.Bg2 Rb4 40.e5 Bg2 41.Kg2 Kg7 42.Kf3 Kf8 43.Rec1** [D] **1/2-1/2**

After 41...g5

519) Gligoric,S-Fischer,R [4/3/67] Monaco [10] E92/08 King's Indian **1.d4 Nf6 2.c4 g6 3.Nc3 Bg7 4.e4 d6 5.Nf3 0-0 6.Be2 e5 7.Be3 Qe7 8.d5 Ne8?!** [Better is 8...Ng4 9.Bg5 f6 10.Bh4 Nh6 11.Nd2 a5 =] **9.h4! f5 10.h5 f4 11.Bd2 g5 12.h6 Bf6 13.Nh2 Kh8 14.Bg4!** +- [Trading off his bad Bishop for Black's good Bishop] **Bg4 15.Ng4 Nd7 16.Qf3** [16.Qe2!] **Rg8 17.0-0-0 Rg6 18.g3 c5 19.Rdg1 Nc7 20.Nd1 b5 21.Qe2 bc4 22.Qc4 Nb6 23.Qe2 Rag8 24.f3 Qe8 25.Nc3 a6 26.Rg2 Bd8 27.Rhg1 Nd7 28.Qf1 Rf8 29.Rh2 Nf6 30.gf4 gf4 31.Nf6 Bf6 32.Rg6 hg6 33.b3 Kh7 34.Nd1 Nb5 35.Nb2 Be7 36.Nc4 Qd7 37.Ba5 Nd4 38.Bc3 Nb5 39.Bb2 Bd8 40.a4 Na7 41.Bc3 g5** [D] **42.Be5? de5 43.Ne5 Qd6! -++ 44.Nc4 Qg6 45.Rg2 Nc8 46.Qf2 Nd6 47.Qc5 Be7 48.Qd4 Nc4 49.bc4 Qh6 50.Kc2 Qh3 51.Qg1 Qd7 52.Rh2 Kg7 53.Kd3 Qa4 54.Rc2 Rb8 55.Rc3 Rb3 56.Qd4 Kg6 57.e5 Rc3 0-1**

520) Fischer,R-Geller,E [4/4/67] Monaco [11] B97/14
Sicilian **1.e4 c5 2.Nf3 d6 3.d4 cd4 4.Nd4 Nf6 5.Nc3 a6 6.Bg5 e6
7.f4 Qb6 8.Qd2 Qb2 9.Rb1 Qa3 10.f5 Nc6 11.fe6 fe6 12.Nc6 bc6
13.e5 Nd5 14.Nd5 cd5 15.Be2 de5 16.0-0 Bc5 17.Kh1 Rf8 18.c4
Rf1 19.Rf1 Bb7 20.Bg4?** [20.Qc2! and White is better] **dc4 21.Be6
Qd3 22.Qe1 Be4!** -++ **23.Bg4 Rb8 24.Bd1 Kd7 25.Rf7 Ke6 [D]
0-1**

Final position

521) Ilievsky,B-Fischer,R [8/67] Skopje [1] D77/07 Grunfeld
1.Nf3 g6 2.g3 Bg7 3.d4 Nf6 4.Bg2 0-0 5.0-0 d5 6.c4 dc4 7.Na3 Nc6
[7...Na6 8.Nc4 c5 =] **8.Nc4 Be6 9.b3 a5 10.Bb2 a4 11.Ng5 Bd5
12.e4 Bc4 13.bc4** += [strong center and two Bishops] **h6 14.Nh3
a3 15.Bc3 Nd7 16.e5 Nb6 17.Rb1 Na4 18.Ba1 Nb2 19.Bb2 ab2
20.Bc6 bc6 21.Rb2 Qd7 22.Nf4 Rad8 23.e6 Qd4 24.ef7 Rf7
25.Qd4 Rd4 26.Rc2 g5 27.Ne6 Re4 28.Ng7 Kg7 29.Rb1 Rf5 30.c5
Ree5 31.Rbc1 Re4 32.Rb1 Ree5 33.Rbc1 [D] 1/2-1/2**

Final position

522) Fischer,R-Geller,E [8/67] Skopje [2] B89/10 Sicilian **1.e4
c5 2.Nf3 d6 3.d4 cd4 4.Nd4 Nf6 5.Nc3 Nc6 6.Bc4 e6 7.Be3 Be7
8.Bb3 0-0 9.Qe2 Qa5 10.0-0-0 Nd4 11.Bd4 Bd7 12.Kb1 Bc6 13.f4
Rad8 14.Rhf1** [14.f5! +=] **b5 15.f5!? b4 16.fe6 bc3 17.ef7 Kh8
18.Rf5 Qb4 19.Qf1 Ne4 20.a3 Qb7 21.Qf4 [D] Ba4 22.Qg4 Bf6
23.Rf6 Bb3!** [24.cb3 Nf6 -++] **0-1**

After 21.Qf4

523) Damjanovic,M-Fischer,R [8/67] Skopje [3] B90/02
Sicilian [E: Rook + minor piece] **1.e4 c5 2.Nf3 d6 3.d4 cd4 4.Nd4
Nf6 5.Nc3 a6 6.h3 g6** = **7.g4 Bg7 8.g5 Nh5 9.Be2 e5 10.Nb3 Nf4
11.Bg4 Nc6 12.Nd5 0-0 13.h4 Bg4 14.Qg4 Nd5 15.ed5 Ne7 16.Qe4
Rc8 17.Be3 b5 18.0-0-0 Rc4** =+ [c-file and the d-pawn weakness]
**19.Qd3 Qc7 20.Nd2 e4 21.Qb3 Ra4 22.Kb1 Nf5 23.c3 Rc8 24.Rc1
Qb7 25.a3 Be5 26.h5 Ne7 27.hg6 hg6 28.c4 Qd7 29.cb5 Rc1 30.Rc1
Qb5 31.Qb5 ab5 32.Rc7 Nd5 33.Rb7 Bf4 34.Bf4 Nf4 35.Rb5 d5
36.Nb3 Kf8 37.Nc5 Ra7 38.a4 Nh3 39.a5 Nf2 40.a6 e3 41.Rb8 Kg7
42.Re8 d4 43.Nb3 [D] d3 0-1**

After 43.Nb3

524) Fischer,R-Dely,P [8/67] Skopje [4] B88/09 Sicilian **1.e4
c5 2.Nf3 d6 3.d4 cd4 4.Nd4 Nf6 5.Nc3 Nc6 6.Bc4 e6 7.Bb3 a6
8.f4 Qa5 9.0-0 Nd4 10.Qd4 d5** [Premature, especially with the
King left in the center] **11.Be3** [11...Bc5 is threatened] **Ne4 12.Ne4
de4 13.f5! Qb4 14.fe6 Be6 15.Be6 fe6 [D] 16.Rf8! Qf8 17.Qa4
1-0** [17...b5 18.Qe4 Rd8 19.Qc6 Rd7 20.Rd1 Qe7 21.Rd3 ++-]

After 15...fe6

After 15.Qg3

525) Minic,D-Fischer,R [8/67] Skopje [5] B96/25 Sicilian [E: Rook + Bishop] **1.e4 c5 2.Nf3 d6 3.d4 cd4 4.Nd4 Nf6 5.Nc3 a6 6.Bg5 e6 7.f4 b5 8.e5 de5 9.fe5 Qc7** [A favorite line of Polugaevsky's with mind-boggling complexities] **10.ef6 Qe5 11.Be2 Qg5 12.Qd3 Ra7 13.Ne4 Qe5 14.0-0-0 Rd7 15.Qg3 [D] gf6!** [A deep exchange sacrifice for the two Bishops, passed center pawns and an active King] **16.Qe5 fe5 17.Nf6 Ke7 18.Nd7 Bd7 19.Nb3 Bc6 20.Bf3 e4 21.Be2 Nd7 22.Na5 Ba8 23.Rhf1 f5 24.Kb1 Bh6 25.a4 ba4 26.Rd4 a3 27.Rfd1 Nf6 28.Bc4 Bf4 29.Bb3 ab2 30.Rb4 Rb8 31.Rc4 Rb6 32.Rc8 Bd5 33.c4 Bb7 34.Nb7 Rb7 35.Kb2 a5 36.Ka3 Rc7 37.Ra8 Bd6 38.Ka2 Bb4 39.c5 Nd7 40.Rh8 Nf8 41.Rf8 Kf8 42.Rd6 Bc5 43.Re6 Re7 44.Kb2 a4 45.Bc4 Kg7 46.Rc6 Rb7 47.Kc3 Be7 48.Kd4 Ra7 49.g4 a3 50.Ba2 Bf6 51.Ke3 Bg5 52.Kd4 Rd7 53.Ke5 e3 54.Rc2 Re7 55.Be6 f4 0-1**

After 27...Qh7

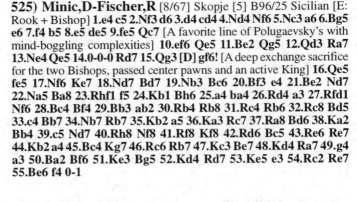

526) Fischer,R-Panov,V [8/67] Skopje [6] B15/00 Caro Kann **1.e4 c6 2.Nc3 d5 3.Nf3 de4 4.Ne4 Nf6 5.Nf6 ef6 6.Bc4 Bd6 7.0-0 0-0 8.d4 Be6 9.Be6 fe6 +=** [Black's e6 is a permanent target] **10.Re1 Re8 11.c4 Na6 12.Bd2 Qd7 13.Bc3 Bb4 14.Qb3 Bc3 15.bc3 Nc7 16.a4 b6 17.h3 Rab8 18.Re4 a6 19.Qc2 b5 20.ab5 ab5 21.cb5 cb5 22.Nd2 Ra8 23.Rae1 Qd5 24.Rh4 Qf5 25.Ne4 e5 26.Re3 h6 27.Rf3 Qh7 [D] 28.Nf6 gf6 29.Rg3 Kh8 30.Rg6 1-0**

After 28.h4

527) Maric,R-Fischer,R [8/67] Skopje [7] B21/06 Bird's [E: Rook + Bishop] **1.f4 Nf6 2.Nf3 g6 3.d3 Bg7 4.e4 0-0 5.Be2 c5 6.0-0 Nc6 7.a4 d6 8.Qe1 c4 9.Na3 cd3 10.Bd3 Nd7 11.c3 Nc5 12.Bc2 Nb3!** [Winning the Bishop pair] **13.Bb3 Qb6 14.Kh1 Qb3 15.Nb5 Bd7 16.f5** [An unsound pawn sacrifice; characteristically, Fischer accepts] **gf5 17.ef5 Bf5 18.Nfd4 Bd4 19.Nd4 Nd4 20.cd4 Qe6 21.Qh4 f6 22.Bh6 Rf7 23.Rae1 Qd5 24.Re3 Bg6 25.Rg3 Rc8 26.Qg4 f5 27.Qg5 Qd4 28.h4 [D] f4 29.Rg4 Rc5 30.Qf4 Rf4 31.Rgf4 Rf5 32.Rd4 Rf1 33.Kh2 Kf7 34.Rb4 b6 35.a5 ba5 36.Rb7 Rf2 37.Ra7 Rb2 38.Ra5 e5 39.Ra6 d5 40.Ra7 Ke6 41.Ra6 Kf5 42.Bg7 d4 43.Rf6 Kg4 44.Rf3 Re2 45.Rg3 Kf4 46.Rf3 Ke4 47.Kg1 Bh5 0-1**

After 22.gf3

528) Danov,K-Fischer,R [8/67] Skopje [8] A35/04 English **1.Nf3 g6 2.c4 Bg7 3.Nc3 c5 4.d4 cd4 5.Nd4 Nc6 6.e3 Nf6 7.Be2 0-0 8.0-0 Nd4** [8...b6 =] **9.Qd4** [9.ed4 d5] **d6 10.Qd2 Be6 11.Qc2** [11.b3 Ne4] **a6 12.Bd2 Rc8 13.Qa4 [13.b3 b5! -+] Nd7 14.Qb4 a5 15.Qb3 Ne5 16.Nd5 b5 17.Qb5 Rb8 18.Qa5 Rb2 19.Bf3 Qd7 20.Rac1 Rc8 21.Bc3 Nf3 22.gf3 [D] Bd5 23.Qd5 Bc3 24.Rc3 Rc5 25.Qa8 Kg7 26.f4 Rb7 27.Rfc1 Qg4 28.Kf1 Rb2 29.Qg2 Qe2 30.Kg1 Ra2 31.Qf1 Qg4 32.Qg2 Qh5 33.e4 Re2 34.f5 Qh4 35.Re3 Re3 36.fe3 Re5 37.Rf1 Qe4 0-1**

529) Fischer,R-Bukic,E [8/67] Skopje [9] B81/18 Sicilian [E: Rook + minor piece] **1.e4 c5 2.Nf3 d6 3.d4 cd4 4.Nd4 Nf6 5.Nc3 e6 6.g4 Nc6 7.g5 Nd7 8.Ndb5** [8.Be3 +=] **Nb6 9.Bf4 Ne5 10.Qh5 Ng6 11.Be3 a6 12.Nd4 Ne5** [12...d5 ∞] **13.Rd1 g6 14.Qe2 Bd7 15.h4 h6 16.Bg2 hg5 17.Bg5 Be7 18.f4 Nc6 19.Be7 Qe7 20.Qf2 Nc8 21.Nf3 Qd8 22.b3 Qa5 23.Qe3 N8a7 24.0-0 Qc5 25.Qc5 dc5 26.Na4 Nd4 27.Nc5 Nf3 28.Rf3 Bc6 29.Rh3 Rc8 30.c4 Ke7 31.Kf2 b5 32.Bf1 bc4 33.bc4 a5 34.e5 Rb8 35.Rd2 Rb4 36.Be2 Nc8 37.Nb3 a4 38.Nd4 Be8 39.a3 Rb1 40.Bd3 Ra1 41.Be4 Rc1 42.Rc2 Rc2 43.Nc2 f6 44.ef6 Kf6 45.Ne3 Nd6 46.Bd3 Nb7 47.Ng4 Kg7 48.Ne5 Nc5 49.Bc2 Bf7 50.Ke3 Rd8 51.Rg3 Kf6 [D] 52.Bg6 Bg6 53.Rg6 Kf5 54.Rg5 1-0**

After 51...Kf6

530) Knezevic,M-Fischer,R [8/67] Skopje [10] B52/06 Sicilian [E: Rook + pawn] **1.e4 c5 2.Nf3 d6 3.Bb5 Bd7 4.Bd7 Qd7 5.0-0 Nc6 6.c3 Nf6 7.Re1 e6 8.d4 cd4 9.cd4 d5 10.e5 Ne4 11.Nbd2** [White plays a known drawing variation] **Nd2 12.Bd2 Be7 13.Bg5 Bb4 14.Bd2** [D] **a5 15.Bb4 ab4 16.a3 ba3 17.Qb3 Qe7 18.Re3 0-0 19.Ra3 Ra3 20.Qa3 Qa3 21.Ra3 f6 22.Kf1 fe5 23.de5 h6 24.Rb3 Rf7 25.h4 = Kf8 26.h5 Ke8 27.Ra3 Nd7 28.Ra4 Re7 29.Ra8 Kc7 30.Ke2 Kb6 31.Kd3 Kc5 32.Ra4 Rf7 33.Ke3 b5 34.Rg4 Rf5 35.Rg7 Ne5 36.Ne5 Re5 37.Kd3 Rh5 38.f4 Rf5 39.g3 h5 40.Rc7 Kd6 41.Rh7 e5 42.b4 Ke6 43.Rh6 Kf7 44.fe5 Re5 45.Kd4 Rg5 46.Rd6 Rg4 47.Kc5 1/2-1/2**

After 14.Bd2

531) Fischer,R-Popov,L [8/67] Skopje [11] B40/01 Sicilian **1.e4 c5 2.Nf3 e6 3.d3 d6 4.g3 Ne7 5.Bg2 g6 6.d4! Bg7 7.dc5 Qa5 8.Nc3?!** [8.c3 +=] **dc5 9.0-0 0-0 10.Qd6 Nec6 11.Be3 Na6 12.Rfd1 e5 13.Nd5 Be6 14.Ng5 Rfd8 15.Ne7 Ne7** [15...Kh8 16.Qe6!! fe6 17.Nf7#] **16.Qe7 Re8 17.Qb7 Reb8 18.Qc6 Rc8 19.Qd6 Rd8 20.Qc6 Rdc8 21.Bd2 Nb4** [D] **22.Qa8** [In order to avoid a draw by repetition, Fischer sacrifices his Queen - it's just enough to draw] **Ra8 23.Ne6 Qb6 24.c3 Nc2 25.Rac1 Qb2 26.Nc7 Rb8 27.a4 Qa2 28.a5 Qa5 29.Rc2 Qc7 30.Ra1 Bf8 31.Rca2 Rb7 32.Be3 Kg7 33.Ra6 Qb8 34.Bf1 Rb1 35.Ra7 Ra1 36.Ra1 Qb2 37.Rc1 Be7 38.c4 h6 39.Rd1 Qb6 40.Rd5 Bd6 41.g4 1/2-1/2**

After 21...Nb4

532) Janosevic,D-Fischer,R [8/67] Skopje [12] B93/04 Sicilian [E: Rook + minor piece] **1.e4 c5 2.Nf3 d6 3.d4 cd4 4.Nd4 Nf6 5.Nc3 a6 6.f4 Nc6** [6...e5; 6...Qc7] **7.Nf3 Bg4 8.h3 Bf3 9.Qf3 +=** [Two Bishops] **g6 10.Be3 Bg7 11.Bc4 0-0 12.0-0 Qc7 13.Bb3 b5 14.g4?!** [14.Rad1] **b4 15.Na4 Nd7 16.Raf1 Na5 17.e5!? Nb3** [17...de5 18.Bf7!] **18.ed6 ed6 19.cb3 Rae8 20.Rc1 Qb8 21.Rfd1 Re6 22.Bf2 Rfe8 23.g5 h6 24.h4 R8e7 25.Qd5 Qe8 26.Rc2 Re4 27.Qd6 Bf8 28.Qa6 Qb8 29.Qd6 Re1 30.Kg2 Rd1 31.Qd1 Qf4 32.Qf3 hg5 33.Qf4 gf4 34.Rc8 f6 35.Nb6 Kf7 36.Nd5 Re5?!** [36...Re2] **37.Nf4 g5? 38.Rc7 Ke8 39.Ng6 Re2 40.Nf8 Nf8** [D] **41.h5 Rb2 42.Kg3 f5 43.Bc5 Nd7 44.h6 f4 45.Kh3 Ra2 46.Bd4 g4 47.Kg4 Rd2 48.Bg7 Nb6 49.Rb7 Nd5 50.Rb5 Ne7 51.Rb4 Ng6 52.Rb6 Rg2 53.Kf3 Rg3 54.Ke4 Re3 55.Kd4 Kf7 56.Rf6 Kg8 57.b4 Kh7 58.b5 Rb3 59.Kc4 Rb1 60.Rf7 Kg8 61.Rb7 Rc1 62.Kd3 Rf1 63.b6 f3 64.Ke3 Nh4 65.Rb8 Kh7 66.b7 Re1 67.Kf2 Re2 68.Kg3 f2 69.Rf8 1-0**

After 40...Nf8

After 40...Kg5

533) Fischer,R-Matulovic,M [8/67] Skopje [13] B48/01
Sicilian [E: Rook + pawn] **1.e4 c5 2.Nc3 Nc6 3.Nge2 e6 4.d4 cd4
5.Nd4 Qc7 6.f4 a6 7.Be3 Bb4 8.Nc6 Qc6 9.Qd4 Bc3 10.bc3 Nf6
11.Bd3 b5** = [White has the two Bishops and more space, Black has
the better pawn structure. In addition, two pieces have been
exchanged, thus reducing White's attacking chances] **12.a4 Bb7
13.Rb1 0-0 14.Rb4 d5 15.ab5 ab5 16.Bb5 Qc7 17.0-0 Ne4 18.Bd3
Ba6 19.c4 Nf6 20.c5 Ng4 21.h3 Ne3 22.Qe3 Rfc8 23.Ra1 Bd3
24.Ra8 Ra8 25.cd3 h5 26.Rb6 Ra1 27.Kh2 d4 28.Qd4 Rc1
29.Rb5 Qc6 30.Ra5 Rc2 31.Qd8 Kh7 32.Qg5 Qd5 33.Qd5 ed5
34.f5 Kh6 35.h4 d4 36.Kg3 Rc3 37.Kf4 Rd3 38.Ke4 Rd1 39.Ra3
g5 40.hg5 Kg5** [D] **41.Rd3 Rc1 1-0**

After 34.Qg4

534) Nicevski,R-Fischer,R [8/67] Skopje [14] B93/07 Sicilian
**1.e4 c5 2.Nf3 d6 3.d4 cd4 4.Nd4 Nf6 5.Nc3 a6 6.f4 Qc7 7.Nf3
Nbd7 8.Bd3 b5 9.a3 g6 10.0-0 Bg7 11.Qe1 Bb7 12.Kh1 e5 13.Qh4
h6!** [Preventing White from playing Bh6] **14.fe5 de5 15.Bd2 Nc5
16.Rae1 g5! 17.Qg3 Nh5!** =+ [Black uses f4 to seize the initiative]
**18.Qg4 Nf4 19.Bf4 ef4 20.Nd5 Bd5 21.ed5 Kf8 22.b4 Nd3 23.cd3
Qc8 24.Qh5 Qf5 25.d6 Rd8 26.Re7 Rd6 27.Rfe1 Kg8 28.Nh4 Qf6
29.Nf3 Rd3 30.h4 Bf8 31.Re8 Ra3 32.Ne5 Kg7 33.Nd7 Qc6
34.Qg4** [D] **Rg3 35.Qe2 Qd7 0-1**

After 38...Ke8

535) Fischer,R-Soos,B [8/67] Skopje [15] B43/09 Sicilian **1.e4
c5 2.Nf3 e6 3.d4 cd4 4.Nd4 a6 5.Nc3 Qc7 6.Bd3 Nc6 7.Nb3 Nf6
8.Be3 d6 9.f4 b5 10.Qf3 Bb7 11.g4** [The sharpest line] **Be7 12.0-0-0
Nb4** [12...b4] **13.g5 Nd7 14.Kb1 Rc8 15.a3 Nd3 16.cd3 Nc5
17.Nd4 Ba8 18.f5! e5 19.Nde2 Bd8 20.Rhg1 Qb8 21.g6! hg6
22.fg6 Rc7 23.d4** ++- [Black is hopelessly placed] **ed4 24.Rd4 Rd7
25.Nd5 Ne6 26.Rd2 fg6 27.Rg6 Nf8 28.Rg4 Rf7 29.Qg2 Qb7
30.Bg5 Bg5 31.Rg5 Rh6 32.Nd4 Ne6 33.Ne6 Re6 34.Qg4 Rh6
35.Rc2 Kd8 36.Rf5 Rf5 37.Qf5 Rh8 38.Qg5 Ke8** [D] **39.Rc8 1-0**

After 27.Nc5

536) Kholmov,R-Fischer,R [8/67] Skopje [16] A49/08 King's
Indian **1.d4 Nf6 2.Nf3 g6 3.g3 Bg7 4.Bg2 0-0 5.0-0 d6 6.Nc3 Nbd7
7.b3 e5 8.de5** [Trying to draw, which would have allowed his
countryman, Geller, to tie for 1st] **de5 9.e4 Re8 10.Ba3** [Better is
10.a4] **c6 11.Bd6?!** [Very tempting but unsound] **Qa5 12.Qd3 Re6!
13.b4** [13.Ng5 Rd6 14.Qd6 h6! -++] **Qa3! 14.Bc7 Qb4 15.Rab1
Qe7 16.Rfd1 Ne8 17.Ba5 Rd6 18.Qe2 Rd1 19.Qd1 Bf8 20.Nd2
Qa3 21.Nc4 Qc5 22.Bf1 b5 23.Nd2 Qa3 24.Nb3 Nc5 25.Bb5 cb5
26.Nb5 Qa4 27.Nc5** [D] **Qa5 28.Qd5 Rb8 29.a4 Bh3 30.Qe5 Rc8
31.Nd3 Qa4 32.Ne1 a6 0-1**

After 14...gf6

537) Fischer,R-Sofrevsky,J [8/67] Skopje [17] B89/10
Sicilian **1.e4 c5 2.Nf3 d6 3.d4 cd4 4.Nd4 Nf6 5.Nc3 Nc6 6.Bc4 e6
7.Bb3 Be7 8.Be3 0-0 9.Qe2 Qa5 10.0-0-0 Nd4 11.Bd4 Bd7 12.Kb1
Rad8 13.Qe3! b6?** [13...b5] **14.Bf6 gf6** [D] **15.Nd5!** [15...ed5
16.Rd5 Qa6 17.Rh5 ++-] **Rfe8 16.Ne7 Re7 17.Rd6 Rc8 18.Qd4
Be8 19.Qf6 1-0**

538) Fischer,R-Barczay,L [10/16/67] Sousse Interzonal [1]
C95/05 Ruy Lopez **1.e4 e5 2.Nf3 Nc6 3.Bb5 a6 4.Ba4 Nf6 5.0-0
Be7 6.Re1 b5 7.Bb3 d6 8.c3 0-0 9.h3 Nb8 10.d4 Nbd7 11.Nh4 ed4
12.cd4 Nb6 13.Nf3 d5?!** [13...c5=] **14.e5 Ne4 15.Nbd2 Nd2
16.Bd2 Bf5 17.Bc2 Bc2 18.Qc2 Rc8 19.b3 Nd7 20.e6! fe6 21.Re6
c5 22.Ba5! Qa5 23.Re7 Qd8** [D] **24.Ng5 1-0**

After 23...Qd8

539) Portisch,L-Fischer,R [10/17/67] Sousse Interzonal [2]
E69/13 King's Indian **1.Nf3 Nf6 2.g3 g6 3.Bg2 Bg7 4.c4 d6 5.d4
0-0 6.Nc3 Nbd7 7.0-0 e5 8.e4 c6 9.h3 Qb6 10.Re1 Re8 11.d5 Nc5
12.Rb1 a5 13.Be3 Qc7 14.Bc5?!** [Better is 14.Nd2 Bd7 15.Bf1 +=]
dc5 15.dc6 bc6! [The doubled pawns are not weak; in fact they help
control d4] **16.Na4 Bf8 17.Qb3 Nh5** [Heading for d4 via g7 and
e6] **18.Qe3 Qa7 19.h4! Ng7 20.Kh2 f6 21.Bh3 Bh3 22.Kh3 Ne6
23.h5 gh5! 24.Rh1 Rad8 25.Kg2 Qg7 26.Kf1 Qg4 27.Rh4 Qg6
28.Qe2 Bh6 29.b3 Rd7?!** [29...Bg5] **30.Rd1 Rd1 31.Qd1 Rd8
32.Qe2 Bg5 33.Ng5 fg5 34.Rh5 Rd2 35.Qg4 h6 36.Rh2 Kg7
37.Nc3 Rd3 38.Nd1 Qf7 39.Kg2 Qd7 40.Qf5 Rd1 41.Qe5 Kg8
42.Rh6 Ng7 43.Rg6 g4** [D] **44.Rg7 Qg7 45.Qe8 Kh7 46.Qh5 Kg8
1/2-1/2**

After 43...g4

540) Fischer,R-Miagmarsuren,L [10/18/67] Sousse Interzonal
[3] A08/10 French **1.e4 e6 2.d3 d5 3.Nd2 Nf6 4.g3 c5 5.Bg2 Nc6
6.Ngf3 Be7 7.0-0 0-0 8.e5 Nd7 9.Re1 b5 10.Nf1 b4 11.h4 a5 12.Bf4
a4 13.a3 ba3 14.ba3 Na5 15.Ne3 Ba6 16.Bh3!** [Restraining f6 or f5]
**d4 17.Nf1 Nb6 18.Ng5 Nd5 19.Bd2 Bg5 20.Bg5 Qd7 21.Qh5! Rfc8
22.Nd2 Nc3 23.Bf6! Qe8** [23...gf6 24.ef6 Kh8 25.Nf3 Rg8 26.Ne5 ++-]
**24.Ne4 g6 25.Qg5 Ne4 26.Re4 c4 27.h5 cd3 28.Rh4 Ra7 29.Bg2!!
dc2 30.Qh6 Qf8** [D] **31.Qh7! 1-0**

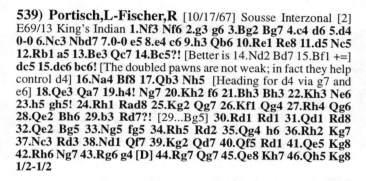

After 30...Qf8

541) Cuellar,M-Fischer,R [10/19/67] Sousse Interzonal [4]
A71/01 Benoni **1.d4 Nf6 2.c4 c5 3.d5 e6 4.Nc3 ed5 5.cd5 d6 6.Nf3
g6 7.e4 Bg7 8.Bg5 h6 9.Bf4 g5 10.Bc1 0-0 11.Nd2 Nbd7 12.Be2
Ne5 13.Nf1 b5! 14.Bb5 Qa5 15.Ng3 c4! 16.0-0 Rb8 17.Qa4 Qa4
18.Ba4 Nd3** [Black has excellent play for the pawn] **19.Bb5 Ng4
20.Nge2 Nc1 21.Rac1 Ne5 22.b3 cb3 23.ab3 a6 24.Ba4 Nd3
25.Rc2 f5 26.Ng3 f4 27.Nge2 f3 28.Ng3 fg2 29.Kg2 Bg4 30.Nf5
Nf4! 31.Kg3 Bf5 32.ef5** [D] **Bc3 33.Kf3 Be5 34.Ke4 Rb4 35.Rc4
Rfb8 36.f6 Kf7 37.Kf5 Rc4 38.bc4 Ne2 39.Re1 Nd4 40.Kg4 h5
41.Kh3 Kf6 0-1**

After 32.ef5

542) Fischer,R-Sarapu,O [10/21/67] Sousse Interzonal [5]
C10/19 French **1.e4 e6 2.d4 d5 3.Nc3 Nf6 4.Bg5 de4 5.Ne4 Nbd7
6.Nf6 Nf6 7.Nf3 c5 8.Bb5 Bd7 9.Bd7 Qd7 10.Qe2 cd4 11.0-0-0
Bc5 12.Qe5 Be7 13.Nd4 Rc8 14.f4?** [14.Kb1 +=] **0-0** [14...h6]
**15.Nf5 Qc7 16.Ne7 Qe7 17.Rd2 Rc5 18.Bf6 gf6 19.Qe3 Rfc8
20.Rhd1 Qc7 21.c3 Rf5? 22.g3 Ra5 23.a3 Qc4 24.Qf3 Qb3
25.Qg4 Kf8 26.Rd8 Rd8 27.Rd8 Ke7 28.Qg8 f5** [D] **29.Qg5 1-0**

After 28...f5

Final position

After 34...Rf6

After 19.Rd3

After 24...Kh7

After 26.Qh3

543) Kavalek,L-Fischer,R [10/22/67] Sousse Interzonal [6]
B97/16 Sicilian **1.e4 c5 2.Nf3 d6 3.d4 cd4 4.Nd4 Nf6 5.Nc3 a6 6.Bg5 e6 7.f4 Qb6 8.Qd2 Qb2 9.Rb1 Qa3 10.f5 Nc6 11.fe6 fe6 12.Nc6 bc6 13.e5 de5 14.Bf6 gf6 15.Ne4 Be7** [15...Qa2!? ∞] **16.Be2 h5 17.c4 f5 18.Rb3 Qa4 19.0-0?** fe4 **20.Qc3 Qa2?** [Better is 20...Bc5 21.Kh1 Rf8!] **21.Bd1 Rf8 22.Bh5 Kd8 23.Rd1 Bd7 24.Qe3 Qa5 25.Rb7 Bc5 26.Rdd7 Kc8 27.Rdc7 Kd8 28.Rd7** [D] **1/2-1/2**

544) Fischer,R-Stein,L [10/24/67] Sousse Interzonal [7] C92/27
Ruy Lopez **1.e4 e5 2.Nf3 Nc6 3.Bb5 a6 4.Ba4 Nf6 5.0-0 Be7 6.Re1 b5 7.Bb3 d6 8.c3 0-0 9.h3 Bb7 10.d4 Na5 11.Bc2 Nc4 12.b3 Nb6 13.Nbd2 Nbd7 14.b4!** ed4 **15.cd4 a5 16.ba5 c5 17.e5!** += [Indicating Kingside attacking intentions] **de5 18.de5 Nd5 19.Ne4 Nb4 20.Bb1 Ra5 21.Qe2 Nb6 22.Nfg5 Be4 23.Qe4 g6 24.Qh4 h5 25.Qg3 Nc4 26.Nf3 Kg7 27.Qf4 Rh8 28.e6!** f5 [28...Bf6 29.Ng5!] **29.Bf5! Qf8 30.Be4 Qf4 31.Bf4 Re8 32.Rad1 Ra6 33.Rd7 Re6 34.Ng5 Rf6** [D] **35.Bf3!** Rf4 **36.Ne6 Kf6 37.Nf4 Ne5 38.Rb7 Bd6 39.Kf1 Nc2 40.Re4 Nd4 41.Rb6 Rd8 42.Nd5 Kf5 43.Ne3 Ke6 44.Be2 Kd7 45.Bb5 Nb5 46.Rb5 Kc6 47.a4 Bc7 48.Ke2 g5 49.g3 Ra8 50.Rb2 Rf8 51.f4 gf4 52.gf4 Nf7 53.Re6 Nd6 54.f5 Ra8 55.Rd2 Ra4 56.f6 1-0**

545) Korchnoi,V-Fischer,R [10/25/67] Sousse Interzonal [8]
A35/12 English [E: Rooks + minor piece] **1.Nf3 c5 2.c4 Nc6 3.Nc3 g6 4.e3 Bg7 5.d4 d6 6.d5 Ne5 7.Nd2 f5 8.Be2 Nf6 9.h3** [9.b3] **0-0 10.f4 Nf7 11.g4 e5 12.de6 Be6 13.g5 Ne8 14.Bf3 Rb8** [14...Nc7!] **15.a4 Nc7 16.Ra3 d5 17.Nd5 Nd5 18.cd5 Bd5 19.Rd3** [D] **Bf3 20.Rd8 Bd1 21.Rb8 Ba4?!** [21...Rb8 =+] **22.Rf8 Kf8 23.Rh2 Bc6 24.b3 Ke7 25.Kd1 b5 26.Re2 Ke6 27.Kc2** [27.h4 h5!] **Nd6 28.Bb2 Bf8 29.Re1 a6 30.Ra1 Bb7 31.h4 Nc8 32.Kd3 Bd6 33.e4 Nb6 34.ef5?** [34.Be5 +-] **Kf5 35.Be5 Bf8 36.Re1 a5 37.Bc7 Nd5 38.Re5 Kg4 39.Re8 Nc7 40.Rf8 Ne6 41.Rf7 Nf4 42.Ke3 Ng2 43.Kf2 Bd5 44.Rh7 Nf4 45.Ra7 Kh4 46.Ra5 b4 47.Ke3 Ng2 48.Ke2 Nf4 49.Ke3 Ng2 50.Ke2 1/2-1/2**

546) Fischer,R-Reshevsky,S [10/29/67] Sousse Interzonal [11]
C93/14 Ruy Lopez **1.e4 e5 2.Nf3 Nc6 3.Bb5 a6 4.Ba4 Nf6 5.0-0 Be7 6.Re1 b5 7.Bb3 0-0 8.c3 d6 9.h3 h6 10.d4 Re8 11.Nbd2 Bf8 12.Nf1 Bd7 13.Ng3 Na5 14.Bc2 c5 15.b3 Nc6 16.Be3 cd4 17.cd4 Nb4?** [17...ed4 18.Nd4 d5 =] **18.Bb1 a5 19.a3 Na6 20.Bd3 Qc7 21.Qe2 Qb7 22.Rad1 g6 23.Qb2!** [White has achieved an ideal position] **Qb8 24.Bb1 Kh7** [D] **25.de5 de5 26.Ne5!** ++- **Re5? 27.Bf4 Qb7 28.Be5 Ne8 29.Ne2 Nc5 30.Nf4 b4 31.a4 Bc6 32.Nd5 Nd7 33.Bd4 Ng7 34.Bd3 Ne6 35.Bc4 Re8 36.Bf6 Nec5 37.Qc2 Ne6 38.Ba1 Qa7 39.Kh1 Bg7 40.Bg7 Ng7 41.Bb5 Bb5 42.ab5 Rb8 43.Qc6 Ne8 44.e5 Nf8 45.Nf6 Nf6 46.ef6 Rb6 1-0**

547) Byrne,R-Fischer,R [10/31/67] Sousse Interzonal [12]
B87/06 Sicilian **1.e4 c5 2.Nf3 d6 3.d4 cd4 4.Nd4 Nf6 5.Nc3 a6 6.Bc4 e6 7.Bb3 b5 8.f4 Bb7 9.f5 e5 10.Nde2 Nbd7 11.Bg5 Be7 12.Ng3 Rc8 13.0-0?!** [A subtle inaccuracy. Correct was 13.Nh5 =] **h5!** [Threatening ...h4, winning the e-pawn] **14.h4 b4 15.Bf6 Bf6 16.Nd5 Bh4 17.Nh5 Qg5 18.f6 g6 19.Ng7 Kd8 20.Rf3 Bg3 21.Qd3 Bh2 22.Kf1 Nc5 23.Rh3 Rh4 24.Qf3 Nb3 25.ab3 Rh3 26.Qh3** [D] **Bd5 27.ed5 Qf6 28.Ke1 Qf4 0-1**

1968

548) Fischer,R-Hamann,S [6/17/68] Netanya [1] B88/14
Sicilian **1.e4 c5 2.Nf3 Nc6 3.d4 cd4 4.Nd4 Nf6 5.Nc3 d6 6.Bc4 e6
7.Bb3 Be7 8.Be3 a6 9.f4 Qc7 10.0-0 Na5?!** [Neglecting Kingside
development] **11.Qf3 0-0 12.f5 e5 13.Nde2 Nb3 14.ab3 b5 15.g4!
b4 16.g5 bc3 17.gf6 Bf6 18.bc3!** [Δ 19.c4] **Bb7 19.c4 d5?!** [D]
**20.ed5 e4 21.Qg3 Qg3 22.Ng3 Ba1 23.Ra1 f6 24.Kf2 Rfe8 25.Rd1
a5 26.c5 Red8 27.c4 a4 28.b4 a3 29.b5 a2 30.Ra1 Ra4 31.c6 Bc8
32.Bb6 1-0**

After 19...d5?!

549) Kraidman,Y-Fischer,R [6/18/68] Netanya [2] A79/02
Benoni [E:Rooks + minor piece] **1.d4 Nf6 2.c4 e6 3.Nf3 c5 4.d5 ed5
5.cd5 d6 6.Nc3 g6 7.e4 Bg7 8.Be2 0-0 9.0-0 Re8 10.Nd2 Na6 11.f3
Nc7 12.a4 Nd7 13.Nc4 Ne3 14.Ne3 b6 15.Re1 Rb8 16.f4 Nd7 17.Nc4
Nf6** [17...Bd4 18.Kh1 Nf6 ∞] **18.Bf3 Ba6 19.Na3 Nd7 20.Nab5 Bb5
21.ab5 +=/+** [Space, Bishop pair, and a central majority] **Ra8 22.e5!**
[D] **de5 23.d6 Ne6 24.Ba8 Qa8 25.fe5 Ne5 26.Qd5 Qd5 27.Nd5 Rd8
28.Ra7 Nd3 29.Rd1 Nc1 30.Ne7 Kf8 31.Rc1 Rd6 32.Nc8 Rd2 33.Rf1
f5 34.Nb6 Rb2 35.g4 f4 36.Ra8 Kf7 37.Nd5 g5 38.Ra7 Kf8 39.Ra8
Kf7 40.Ra7 Kf8 41.b6 c4 42.Re7 Bd4 43.Kh1** [D] **Rb6 44.Nb6 Ke7
45.Nc4 Kf6 46.Nd2 Kg6 47.Nf3 Bf6 48.Rc1 h5 49.h3 hg4 50.hg4 Nd8
51.Kg1 Nf7 52.Rc6 Kg7 53.Ra6 Nh6 54.Kh2 Nf7 55.Nd2 Ne5 56.Ne4
Be7 57.Nc4 Nf7 58.Kg2 Nd6 59.Kf3 Nf7 60.Rd5 Bf6 61.Nf2 Ne5
62.Ke4 Nc4 63.Rc5 Nd6 64.Kd5 Nf7 65.Ne4 Be7 66.Rc7 Kf8 67.Ke6
Nd8 68.Kf5 Nf7 69.Rc8 Kg7 70.Ke6 Bd8 71.Ra8 Bb6 72.Rb8 Bc7
73.Re8 Bd8 74.Nd2 Bf6 75.Ne4 Bd8 76.Nd6 Nd6 77.Rd8 Nc4 78.Kf5
f3 79.Rd3 f2 80.Rf3 1/2-1/2**

After 22.e5!

After 43.Kh1

550) Fischer,R-Czerniak,M [6/19/68] Netanya [3] B13/02
Caro Kann [E:Bishop vs. Knight] **1.e4 c6 2.d4 d5 3.ed5 cd5 4.Bd3
Nc6 5.c3 Nf6 6.Bf4 g6 7.Nf3 Bg7 8.Nbd2 Nh5 9.Be3 0-0 10.0-0 f5?!**
[Weakening e5 and e6] **11.Nb3 Qd6 12.Re1 f4 13.Bd2 Bg4 14.Be2
Rae8 15.Nc1 Bf3 16.Bf3 e5 17.Qb3!** [17.de5 Ne5 18.Bh5 gh5
19.Qh5 f3!] **ed4 17...e4 18.Re4! Na5 19.Re8! Nb3 20.Rf8 Bf8
21.ab3 +-] 18.Nd3! Rd8 19.c4! dc4 20.Qc4 Kh8 21.Re6 Qb8
22.Rae1 Rc8 23.Bc6 Rc6 24.Rc6 bc6 25.Qc6 Qc8 26.Qc8 Rc8
27.Kf1 Bh6 28.Rc1 Rc1 29.Bc1 g5 30.b4 Kg8 31.b5 Kf7 32.Ba3
Bf8 33.Ne5 Ke6 34.Bf8 Ke5** [D] **35.Bc5 Nf6 36.Ba7 Ne4 37.f3 Nd2
38.Ke2 Nc4 39.b6 Na5 40.b7 Nb7 41.Kd3 h5 42.Bd4 Kd5 43.h3
Nd8 44.a4 Ne6 45.Bb6 g4 46.hg4 hg4 47.fg4 Ng5 1-0**

After 34...Ke5

551) Troianescu,O-Fischer,R [6/20/68] Netanya [4] B99/01
Sicilian [E:Minor piece] **1.e4 c5 2.Nf3 d6 3.Nc3 a6 4.d4 cd4 5.Nd4
Nf6 6.Bg5 e6 7.f4 Be7 8.Qf3 Qc7 9.0-0-0 Nbd7 10.Kb1?** [Loss of
time] **b5 11.Bd3 b4 12.Nce2 Bb7 13.Rhe1 h6 14.Bf6 Bf6 =+** [Two
Bishops and the initiative] **15.Qe3 Qc5 16.Qg1 g5 17.Nb3 Qg1 18.Rg1
Bd8 19.g3 Ke7 20.c3 a5 21.cb4 ab4 22.Bc2 Bb6 23.Rge1 Rhg8 24.f5
Rgc8 25.Nec1 Ne5 26.Nd3 Nf3 27.Re2 Ba6 28.Rg2 Rc4 29.Ne1 Nc5
30.Rgd2 Rd8 31.f6 Kf6 32.Rd6 Rd6 33.Rd6 Rc6 34.Rc6 Nc6
35.Bd3 Bb7 36.Nd2 g4 37.Be2 h5 38.Nc4 Bg1 39.Nd3 Nd4 40.e5
Ke7 41.Bf1** [D] **0-1**

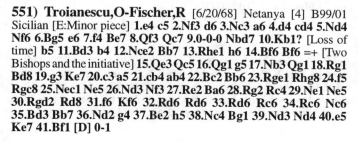

Final position

After 30...Nb4

552) Fischer,R-Cagan,S [6/22/68] Netanya [5] B11/08 Caro
Kann **1.e4 c6 2.Nc3 d5 3.Nf3 Bg4 4.h3 Bf3 5.Qf3 Nf6 6.d3 e6 7.a3
Nbd7** [7...Be7] **8.g4!** += [Kingside space] **Bd6 9.g5 Ng8 10.h4 Ne7
11.h5 Qb6 12.Bh3 0-0-0 13.a4! a5 14.0-0** [14.Qf7? Rhf8 -++] **Rhf8
15.Kh1 f5 16.Qg2 g6 17.h6 Kb8 18.f4 Rfe8 19.e5 Bc5 20.Qf3 Nc8
21.Bg2 Kc7 22.Ne2 Nb8 23.c3!** [Preparing b4] **Kd7 24.Bd2 Na6
25.Rfb1 Bf8 26.b4! ++- ab4 27.cb4 Bb4 28.a5 Qc5 29.d4 Qf8
30.Bb4 Nb4 [D] 31.Qc3 Na6 32.Rb7 Nc7 33.Nc1 Re7 34.a6 1-0**

After 21.Rfc1

553) Porath,J-Fischer,R [6/23/68] Netanya [6] E62/25 King's
Indian **1.d4 Nf6 2.c4 g6 3.g3 Bg7 4.Bg2 0-0 5.Nc3 d6 6.Nf3 Nc6
7.0-0 Bg4!? 8.d5 Na5 9.b3 c5 10.Bb2 Qd7** [10...a6] **11.Qd3 a6
12.e4 b5 13.cb5 c4 14.bc4 Bf3** [To stop White from playing Nd2 in
response to ...Rfc8] **15.Bf3 Rfc8 16.c5 Rc5 17.Na4 Rb5 = /∞
18.Bd4 Rab8 19.Nc3 Rb4 20.Rab1 Qc8 21.Rfc1 [D] Ne4 22.Bg7
Nc5 23.Qe3 Kg7 24.Rb4 Rb4 25.Ne4 Rc4 26.Be2 Rc1 27.Qc1
Nab7 28.Ba6 Qf5 29.Qb2 f6 30.Nc5 Nc5 31.Qe2 Kf8 32.Bc4 g5
33.Kg2 Qb1 34.h3 h6 35.Kh2 Qb4 36.Qc2 Ke8 37.Bf1 Qd4
38.Bg2 h5 39.Bf3 g4 40.hg4 hg4 41.Bg2 Kd8 42.Qe2 Nd7 43.f4
gf3 44.Qf3 Qb2 45.Qg4 Kc7 46.Qa4 Qb7 47.Qc2 Kb8 48.Qa4
Kc7 49.Qc2 Nc5 50.Qc2 Kd8 51.Qg4 Qa7 52.Qg8 Kc7 53.Qe8
Kb6 54.a3 Qb7 55.Qg6 Kb5 56.Qc2 Ka5 57.Qc3 Kb6 58.Qe3
Qd7 59.Qe1 Qa7 60.Qe3 Qb7 61.Qe1 Qa7 62.Qe3 Qd7 63.Qe1
Nb7 64.Qe3 1/2-1/2**

After 16...Na5?

554) Fischer,R-Ree,H [6/24/68] Netanya [7] C81/14 Ruy Lopez
**1.e4 e5 2.Nf3 Nc6 3.Bb5 a6 4.Ba4 Nf6 5.0-0 Ne4 6.d4 b5 7.Bb3
d5 8.de5 Be6 9.Qe2 Be7 10.Rd1 0-0** [10...Ne5 was better] **11.c4
bc4 12.Bc4 Qd7 13.Nc3 Nc3 14.bc3 f6 15.ef6 Bf6 16.Bg5 Na5?**
[16...Bc3] **[D] 17.Qe6 ++- Qe6 18.Bd5 Qd5 19.Rd5 Bc3 20.Rc1
Bb4 21.Rc7 Rac8 22.Ra7 Rc2 23.Rdd7 Bc3 24.Rac7 h6 25.Be3
1-0**

After 25.Bd4

555) Bernstein,Y-Fischer,R [6/25/68] Netanya [8] B25/05
Sicilian **1.e4 c5 2.Nc3 d6 3.g3 Nc6 4.Bg2 g6 5.d3 Bg7 6.f4 b6 7.Nf3
Bb7 8.0-0 Qd7 9.Be3 f5!** [Stopping White's chance to play f5]
10.Qd2 Nf6 11.Kh1 0-0-0 12.Rae1?! [12.a3 to follow with b4] **Kb8
13.Bg1? fe4 -++ 14.de4 Ba6 15.Ng5 Bf1 16.Bf1 Rhe8 17.Bb5 e5
18.fe5 Re5 19.Bc6 Qc6 20.Nf7 Rde8 21.Ne5 Re5 22.Qf4 b5 23.a3
b4 24.ab4 cb4 25.Bd4 [D] Rf5 0-1**

After 20...Qf6

556) Fischer,R-Domnitz,Z [6/26/68] Netanya [9] B09/24 Pirc
**1.e4 g6 2.d4 Bg7 3.Nc3 d6 4.f4 Nf6 5.Nf3 0-0 6.Bd3 Nfd7?! 7.0-0
c5 8.d5 e6 9.de6 fe6 10.Ng5! Nb6 11.a4! Nc6 12.a5 h6 13.ab6 hg5
14.Qg4! ++- c4 15.Bc4 d5 16.Bd3 de4 17.Be4 Bd4 18.Kh1 e5 19.f5
gf5 20.Bf5 Qf6 [D] 21.Ne4 Qg6 22.Ng3 Ne7 23.Bc8 1-0**

557) Ciocaltea,V-Fischer,R [6/27/68] Netanya [10] B99/24 Sicilian **1.e4 c5 2.Nf3 d6 3.d4 cd4 4.Nd4 Nf6 5.Nc3 a6 6.Bg5 e6 7.f4 Be7 8.Qf3 Qc7 9.0-0-0 Nbd7 10.g4 b5 11.Bf6 Nf6 12.g5 Nd7 13.f5 Nc5 14.f6 gf6 15.gf6 Bf8 16.Bh3** [16.Qh5!?] **b4 17.Nd5 ed5 18.ed5 Bh3 19.Rhe1 Kd8 20.Nc6 Kc8 21.Qh3 Kb7 22.Nb4?!** [22.Re2 ∞] **Qd7 23.Qh5 Rg8 24.Nc6? a5 25.Qh7 Rg6 26.Kb1 Rh6 27.Qg8 Rf6 28.Qg2 Kb6 29.Rd4 Qf5 30.b4 ab4 31.Rb4 Kc7 [D] 0-1**

Final position

558) Fischer,R-Geller,U [6/29/68] Netanya [11] A08/09 French **1.e4 e6 2.d3 d5 3.Nd2 c5 4.g3 Nf6 5.Bg2 Be7 6.Ngf3 0-0 7.0-0 Nc6 8.Re1 Qc7?!** [8...b5] **9.e5 Nd7 10.Qe2 b5 11.h4 a5 12.Nf1 Nd4 13.Nd4 cd4 14.Bf4 Ra6 15.Nh2 Rc6 16.Rac1 Ba6 [D] 17.Bd5! ed5 18.e6 Qd8 19.ed7 Re6 20.Qg4 f5 21.Qh5 Qd7 22.Nf3 g6 23.Qh6 Bf6 24.Re6 Qe6 25.Be5!** [25.Re1? Qe1!! 26.Ne1 Bg7! 27.Qg5 Bf6 28.Qh6 Bg7=] **Be5 26.Re1 f4 27.Re5 Qd7 28.h5 fg3 29.hg6 gf2 30.Kf2 hg6 31.Qg6 Qg7 32.Rg5 1-0**

After 16...Ba6

559) Fischer,R-Yanofsky,D [6/30/68] Netanya [12] B14/08 Caro Kann [E:Rook + pawn] **1.e4 c6 2.d4 d5 3.ed5 cd5 4.c4 Nf6 5.Nc3 g6 6.Qb3 Bg7 7.cd5 0-0 8.Be2 Na6 9.Bg5** [9.Bf3 +=] **Qb6 10.Qb6 ab6 11.a3 Rd8 12.Bf6 Bf6 13.Rd1 Bf5 14.Bc4 Rac8 15.Bb3 b5!** [To undouble the pawns and activate the Na6] **16.Nf3 b4 17.ab4 Nb4 18.Ke2 Bc2! 19.Bc2 Nc2 20.Kd3 Nb4 21.Ke4 Rd6 =** [White's extra pawn is useless] **22.Ne5 Bg7 23.g4 f5 24.gf5 gf5 25.Kf4 Rf8 26.Rhg1 Nd5 27.Nd5 Rd5 28.Nf3 Kh8 29.Rge1 Bf6 30.Ne5 e6 [D] 31.h4 Rc8 32.Nf7 Kg7 33.Ng5 Bg5 34.Kg5 Rc6 35.Re5 Rcd6 36.Rd5 Rd5 37.f4 Rb5 38.Rd2 Rb3 39.d5 h6 40.Kh5 ed5 41.Rd5 Rb2 42.Rd7 Kf6 43.Rd6 Kf7 44.Rh6 Rg2 45.Rb6 Rg4 46.Rb7 Kf6 1/2-1/2**

After 30...e6

560) Aloni,I-Fischer,R [7/1/68] Netanya [13] E43/04 Nimzo-Indian [E:Rook + minor piece] **1.d4 Nf6 2.c4 e6 3.Nc3 Bb4 4.e3 b6 5.Bd3 Bb7 6.Nf3 Ne4 7.Qc2 f5** [The strategic battle over e4 is typical of the Nimzo-Indian defense] **8.0-0 Bc3 9.bc3 0-0 10.Nd2** [10.Ne1 c5 11.f3 Nd6 =] **Qh4! 11.f3 Nd2 12.Bd2 Nc6 =** [Two Bishops vs. doubled c-pawns] **13.Rae1 Na5 14.Rb1** [Clearly a loss of time] **d6 15.Be1 Qg5 16.Qe2 e5 17.e4 fe4 18.fe4 Rf1 19.Kf1 c5!** [Permanently blockading the doubled pawns] **20.Kg1 Ba6 21.Bg3 cd4 22.cd4 ed4! 23.Bd6 Qe3 24.Qe3 de3 25.Re1 Bc4 26.Re3 Ba2 27.e5 Be6 28.Re1 Nb3 29.Ba6 Nc5 30.Be2 a5 31.Bc7 a4! 32.Bb6 Nb3 33.Bd1 Rc8 34.Kf2 Nc1 35.Re3 Rb8 36.Bc5 Rb2 37.Kg3 Nb3 38.Bd6 Nd4 39.Bg4 Bg4 40.Kg4 Rg2 41.Kh3 Rg1 42.e6 Nf5 43.Rd3 [D] g5! 44.Bg3 h5 0-1**

After 43.Rd3

561) Fischer,R-Wade,R [9/7/68] Vinkovci [1] C30/02 King's Gambit [E:Rook + minor piece] **1.e4 e5 2.f4 Nf6 3.fe5 Ne4 4.Nf3 Ng5 5.d4 Nf3 6.Qf3 Qh4 7.Qf2 Qf2 8.Kf2 Nc6 9.c3 d6 10.ed6 Bd6 11.Nd2 +=** [Better ending, with the center pawn and a more active King] **Be6 12.Ne4 Be7 13.Ng5 Bg5 14.Bg5 h6 15.Bh4 g5 16.Bg3 0-0-0 17.Bb5! f5 18.Bc6 bc6 19.Be5 Rhg8 20.h4! g4 21.h5 g3 22.Bg3 Rg4 23.Rh4 Rdg8 24.Rg4 Rg4 25.Re1 Kd7 26.Re5 f4 27.Bh2 Rh4 28.Bg1 Bd5 29.g3 Rg4 30.Bh2 f3 31.b3 a6 [D] 32.c4 Rd4 33.cd5 Rd2 34.Kf3 Rh2 35.dc6 Kc6 36.Re6 Kd7 37.Rh6 Ra2 38.Rg6 1-0**

After 31...a6

After 22...ba6

562) Fischer,R-Jovanovac,I [9/8/68] Vinkovci [2] B09/24 Pirc
1.e4 d6 2.d4 Nf6 3.Nc3 g6 4.f4 Bg7 5.Nf3 0-0 6.Bd3 Nfd7?!
[6...Nc6] 7.0-0 e5 8.de5 de5 9.f5! c6 10.Ng5! Nb6 [10...h6 11.fg6!
hg5 12.Qh5 Nf6 (12...fg6 13.Bc4) 13.Rf6 ++-] 11.a4 a5 12.Be3 Bh6
13.Qd2 f6 14.Qf2! Bg5 15.Bb6 Qd7 16.Bc5 Re8 17.h4 Bf4 18.g3
gf5 19.gf4 fe4 20.Ne4 Kh8 21.f5 Na6 22.Ba6 ba6 [D] 23.Kh2 1-0

Final position

563) Matulovic,M-Fischer,R [9/9/68] Vinkovci [3] B91/06
Sicilian [E:Rook + pawn] 1.e4 c5 2.Nf3 d6 3.d4 cd4 4.Nd4 Nf6 5.Nc3
a6 6.g3 e5 7.Nde2 Be7 8.Bg5 [8.a4] Nbd7 9.Bh3?! b5! 10.a4 b4
11.Nd5 Nd5 12.Qd5 Rb8 13.Be7 Ke7 [Allowing the Queen to be
deployed on the Queenside] 14.Qd2 Nf6 15.Bg2 [15.Bc8 Qc8 16.f3
Qc5! =+] Bb7 16.Qd3 Qb6 17.0-0 a5 18.Rfd1 Ba6 19.Qd2 Rhc8
20.h3 h5 21.b3 Be2 22.Qe2 Rc3 23.Rd3 Rbc8 24.Rc3 Rc3 25.Kh2
Qc5 26.Ra2 [26.Rc1 Rb3] g6 27.Bf1 Qd4 28.f3 Re3 29.Qg2 Qd1
30.Bc4 Qf3 31.Qf3 Rf3 32.Kg2 Re3 33.Bd3 Ne4 34.Be4 Re4 35.Kf2
d5 36.Ra1 d4 37.Rd1 Re3 38.h4 Rc3 39.Rd2 Ke6 40.Kg2 f5 [D] 0-1

After 26...Qb8

564) Fischer,R-Hort,V [9/11/68] Vinkovci [4] B13/01 Caro
Kann [E:Rook + minor piece] 1.e4 c6 2.d4 d5 3.ed5 cd5 4.Nf3 Nf6
5.c3 Bf5 6.Bb5 Nbd7 7.Nh4 Bg6 8.Bf4 e6 9.Nd2 Nh5 10.Ng6 hg6
11.Be3 Bd6 12.g3 a6 13.Bd3 += [Bishop pair] Rc8 14.0-0 Nb6
15.a4 Rc7 16.Qb3 Nc8 17.c4! [Opening up the position for the two
Bishops] dc4 18.Nc4 Nf6 19.Rac1 0-0 20.Bd2 Nd5 21.Be4 Be7
22.Na5 Ncb6 23.Bd5 Nd5 24.Nb7 [Winning a pawn, but Hort gains
strong counterplay] Qb8 25.Rc7 Qc7 26.Rc1 Qb8 [D] 27.Rc4 Rd8
28.Bc3 Rd7 29.Na5 Qb3 30.Rc8 Kh7 31.Nb3 Nb6 32.Rc6 Na4
33.Ra6 Nc3 34.bc3 Rc7 35.Nd2 Rc3 36.Ra7 Rd3 37.Nf1 Bf6
38.Rf7 Rd4 39.Kg2 g5 [Now it's clearly drawish] 40.h3 Kg6
41.Rc7 Ra4 42.Nd2 Rd4 43.Nb3 Rd6 44.Nc5 Kf5 45.Kf3 Rb6
46.Rd7 Rc6 47.Ne4 Ra6 48.Rd3 Be7 49.Rb3 Ra3 50.Ra3 Ba3
51.g4 Kg6 52.Ke3 Bc1 53.Kd4 Bf4 54.Kc5 Kf7 55.Kb6 Ke8
56.Kc6 Ke7 1/2-1/2

After 35...Re7

After 57.f4

565) Ivkov,B-Fischer,R [9/12/68] Vinkovci [5] A32/07 English
[E:Rook + pawn] 1.d4 Nf6 2.c4 c5 3.Nf3 cd4 4.Nd4 e6 5.Nc3 Bb4
6.Nc2 Bc3 7.bc3 Qa5 8.Qd3 Nc6 9.Ba3 b6 [9...d5!] 10.Bd6 Ba6
11.e4 b5?! [11...Ne5] 12.Be2? [12.c5!, with a strong bind on the
dark squares] bc4 13.Qe3 Qb6 14.f3 0-0-0 15.0-0 Qe3 16.Ne3 Ne8
17.Bg3 d5 18.ed5 ed5 -+ /-++ [With a pawn up the rest is purely
technique] 19.Rfd1 Ne7 20.Rd2 Nc7 21.Rad1 Bb7 22.Be5 f6
23.Bd4 Nc6 24.Bc5 Rhe8 25.Kf2 Ne6! 26.Ba3 Nf4 27.Bf1 Ne5!
28.Nf5 Kc7 29.Ng7 Rg8 30.g3 Nh3! 31.Bh3 Rg7 32.Bf1 Ba6
33.Bc5 [33.Rd5 Nd3] Nd3 34.Bd3 cd3 35.Ba7 Re7 [D] 36.Rd3 Bd3
37.Rd3 Ra8 38.Be3 Ra2 39.Bd2 Kc6 40.g4 f5 41.gf5 Rf7 42.Kg3
Rf5 43.Kg4 Rf7 44.h4 Ra1 45.Be3 Rf1 46.Bd4 Kb5 47.Be3 Rg7
48.Kh5 Rd7 49.Bd4 Kc4 50.Re3 Rf7 51.Kh6 Rh1 52.h5 Rf5
53.Kh7 Rhh5 54.Kg6 Rhg5 55.Kh6 Rg2 56.Be5 Rf2 57.f4 [D]
R2f4 58.Bf4 Rf4 59.Kg5 Rf1 60.Kg4 Rc1 61.Kf4 Rc3 62.Re8 d4
63.Rc8 Kd3 64.Ra8 Rc7 65.Ra3 Kc2 66.Ke4 d3 67.Ra2 Kb3
68.Rd2 Kc4 69.Rh2 Re7 70.Kf3 Kc3 71.Rh8 d2 72.Rc8 Kd3
73.Rd8 Kc2 74.Rc8 Kd1 75.Kf2 Rf7 0-1

566) Fischer,R-Minic,D [9/14/68] Vinkovci [6] C33/08 King's Gambit **1.e4 e5 2.f4 ef4 3.Bc4 Ne7 4.Nc3 c6 5.Nf3 d5 6.Bb3 de4 7.Ne4 Nd5 8.Qe2** [Better was 8.c4 Nf6 9.Nf6 Qf6 10.0-0 +-] **Be7 9.c4 Nc7 10.d4 0-0 11.Bf4 Ne6 12.Be3 Bb4 13.Kf2! Nd7 14.c5!** [pressuring f7] **Nf6 15.Nf6 Qf6 16.Rhf1 Nf4 17.Bf4 Qf4 18.g3 Qh6 19.Kg1 Bh3?** [19...Be6] **[D] 20.Ne5!!** [A brilliant exchange sacrifice, targeting f7] **Bf1 21.Rf1 Bd2 22.Rf3 Rad8** [22...Rae8 23.Nf7 ++-] **23.Nf7 Rf7 24.Qe7 1-0**

After 19.Bh3?

567) Matov,M-Fischer,R [9/15/68] Vinkovci [7] B97/08 Sicilian **1.e4 c5 2.Nf3 d6 3.d4 cd4 4.Nd4 Nf6 5.Nc3 a6 6.Bg5 e6 7.f4 Be7 8.Be2 Qb6 9.Qd2 Qb2 10.Rb1 Qa3 11.0-0 Nbd7 12.f5 Ne5 13.Kh1 0-0 14.Rb3 Qc5 15.Bf6 Bf6 16.Na4?** [D] **Nc4!** [Winning material] **17.Qf4 Qd4 18.Rd3 Qe5 19.Qg4 ef5 20.ef5 Ne3 0-1**

After 16.Na4?

568) Fischer,R-Matanovic,A [9/16/68] Vinkovci [8] C92/16 Ruy Lopez **1.e4 e5 2.Nf3 Nc6 3.Bb5 a6 4.Ba4 Nf6 5.0-0 Be7 6.Re1 b5 7.Bb3 d6 8.c3 0-0 9.h3 Nd7 10.d4 Bf6 11.a4 Na5 12.Bc2 Nb6 13.b4** [Better was 13.ab5 ab5 14.b4 +=] **Nac4 14.a5 Nd7 15.Bb3 ed4 16.cd4 c5 17.Bf4** [17.bc5 Nc5! ∞] **cb4 18.Nbd2 d5 19.ed5 Na5 20.Bd6 Nb3 21.Qb3 Re8** [D] **22.Bc7 Re1 23.Re1 Qc7** [23...Qf8 =] **24.Re8 Nf8 25.Qb4 Be7 26.Re7 Qd8 27.Ne5 Ng6 28.Nc6 Qf8 29.Qc5 a5 30.Rc7 Qe8 31.d6 Bd7 32.Ne7 Kh8 33.d5 a4 34.Nb1 Nf8 35.Na3 f6 36.Rb7 Qh5 37.Nb5 a3 38.Na3 Qd1 39.Kh2 Qd2 40.Qe3 Qa5 41.Nc4 Qa6 42.Qb3 Ba4 43.Qb4 Nd7 44.Nb2 1-0**

After 21...Re8

569) Nikolic,E-Fischer,R [9/18/68] Vinkovci [9] A24/01 English **1.c4 g6 2.Nc3 Bg7 3.g3 e5 4.Bg2 d6 5.e3 Nf6 6.Nge2 0-0 7.0-0 c6 8.d4 Re8 9.Rb1** [9.de5 de5 10.Qd8 Rd8, and the point d3 is weak =/=+] **e4 10.b4 Bf5 11.h3 h5 12.Nf4 Nbd7 13.a4 Nf8 14.c5?** **d5 15.b5 N8h7 16.Bd2 Ng5 17.Rb2 Qd7 18.Kh2 Bh6! 19.a5 [D] Bg4!!** [A deep sacrifice to dominate f3 and suffocate White's King defenses] **20.hg4 hg4 21.Rh1 Nf3 22.Bf3 gf3 23.Kg1 Bf4 24.ef4 Kg7 25.f5 Rh8 26.Bh6** [Despair] **Rh6 27.Rh6 Kh6 28.Qd2 g5 29.bc6 Qf5 30.Nd1 Qh3 31.Ne3 Kg6 0-1** [32...Ng4 will mate quickly]

After 19.a5

570) Fischer,R-Robatsch,K [9/19/68] Vinkovci [10] C95/05 Ruy Lopez [E:Rook vs. Knight + pawn] **1.e4 e5 2.Nf3 Nc6 3.Bb5 a6 4.Ba4 Nf6 5.0-0 Be7 6.Re1 b5 7.Bb3 d6 8.c3 0-0 9.h3 Nb8 10.d4 Nbd7 11.Nh4 ed4 12.cd4 Nb6 13.Nf3 c5 14.Bf4 Bb7 15.dc5 dc5 16.Qd8 Bd8 17.Bd6 Re8 = 18.Bc5 Nbd7 19.Bd4 Ne4 20.Nc3 Bf6 21.Bd5! Bd5 22.Nd5 Bd4 23.Nd4 Nef6 24.Re8 Ne8 25.a4!** +-[Bobby misses the way later and Robatsch manages a draw] **ba4 26.Ra4 Nc5 27.Rc4 Nd3 28.Nc6 a5 29.b3 Nb2 30.Rc2 Nd3 31.Ra2 Kf8 32.b4 Rc8** [D] **33.ba5 Rc6 34.a6 Rc1 35.Kh2 Nc7 36.Nc7 Rc7 37.a7 Ra7 38.Ra7 Nf2 39.Kg3 Ne4 40.Kf4 Nf6 41.Ke5 h5 42.Kd6 g6 43.Ke5 Kg7 44.Ra4 Nd7 45.Kd6 Nf6 46.Rf4 Ng8 47.Ke5 Nh6 48.Rf1 Kf8 49.Ra1 Kg7 50.Ra7 Ng8 51.Ra6 Nh6 52.Rc6 Ng8 53.g4 hg4 54.hg4 Nh6 55.g5 Nf5 56.Rc7 Ng3 57.Ra7 Nh5 1/2-1/2**

After 32...Rc8

After 27...Rca8

571) Byrne,D-Fischer,R [9/20/68] Vinkovci [11] A11/12 Catalan [E:Rook + pawn] **1.g3 Nf6 2.Bg2 d5 3.Nf3 Bf5 4.c4** [4.d3, 0-0, Nbd2 is the King's Indian Attack] **e6 5.0-0 c6 6.Qb3 Qc8 7.d4 Be7 8.Nc3 h6 9.Bf4 dc4?!** [No need to give up the center. 9...Nbd7] **10.Qc4 Nbd7 11.Qb3 0-0 12.Rac1 Nd5 13.Bd2 a5 14.Rfe1 Nc3 15.bc3!** [With pressure on the b-file] **a4 16.Qb2 Be4 17.c4 c5 18.Bc3 cd4 19.Bd4 Bf6 20.Red1** += **Ra5 21.Qb4 Qc7 22.Ne5 Be5 23.Be4 Bd4 24.Rd4 Nc5 25.Bf3 a3 26.Rb1 Rc8 27.Qd2 Rca8** [D] **28.Bb7! Nb7 29.Rd7 Qc4 30.Rbb7 Rd5 31.Rd5 ed5 32.Rd7 Re8 33.e3 Rb8 34.Qd5 Rb1 35.Kg2 Qf1 36.Kf3 Qh1 37.Kg4 Qd5 38.Rd5 Rb2 39.Ra5 Rf2 40.Ra3 Rh2 41.Kf3 h5 42.e4 h4 43.Ra8 Kh7 44.gh4 Rh4 45.Ra7 f6 46.a4 Kh6 47.Ra6 Kh5 48.Ra8 Rh3 49.Kf4 Kg6 50.e5** 1/2-1/2

After 34...Kf6

After 56...h3

572) Fischer,R-Gheorghiu,F [9/21/68] Vinkovci [12] C93/14 Ruy Lopez [E:Rook + minor piece] **1.e4 e5 2.Nf3 Nc6 3.Bb5 a6 4.Ba4 Nf6 5.0-0 Be7 6.Re1 b5 7.Bb3 d6 8.c3 0-0 9.h3 h6 10.d4 Re8 11.Nbd2 Bf8 12.Nf1 Bd7 13.Ng3 Na5 14.Bc2 c5 15.b3 Nc6 16.Be3 cd4 17.cd4 ed4 18.Bc1 Nb4 19.Bb2** [19.Bb1 d3] **d5 20.e5 Nc2 21.Qc2 Ne4** = [Black has played very accurately to achieve a viable position] **22.Ne4 Bf5! 23.Nf6 Qf6 24.ef6 Bc2 25.fg7 Bg7 26.Bd4 Re1 27.Re1 Be4 28.Bg7 Kg7 29.Nd4 Rc8! 30.f3 Bg6 31.Re5 Rc1 32.Kh2 Ra1 33.Rd5 Ra2 34.Kg3 Kf6** [D] **35.Kf4 Rg2 36.Rd6 Kg7 37.Ra6 Rh2 38.Kg3 Rb2 39.Rb6 Bd3 40.Rc6 Kh7 41.h4 Bf1 42.Kf4 Bd3 43.Rc3 Bf1 44.Rc1 Bd3 45.Rc3 Bf1 46.Ke3 Rh2 47.Rc1 Bh3 48.Nb5 Be6 49.Nd4 Rh4 50.b4 Rh2 51.b5 Rb2 52.Kf4 Rb4 53.Ke5 h5 54.Rc7 Kg6 55.f4 h4 56.Rc1 h3** [D] **57.f5 Bf5!** [With White's pawns gone it's a draw] **58.Rg1 Kh5 59.Nf5 Rb5 60.Kf4 Rb4 61.Kf3 h2 62.Rh1 Kg5 63.Ne3 Rh4 64.Nf1 Rf4 65.Ke3 Rh4 66.Nh2** [There was really no need to play this out] **Kf5 67.Rf1 Ke6 68.Nf3 Rg4 69.Nd4 Ke7 70.Nc6 Ke6 71.Nd8 Ke7 72.Nf7 Ke6 73.Nd8 Ke7 74.Nc6 Ke6 75.Nd4 Ke7 76.Kd3 Kd6 77.Rf6 Ke5 78.Rf5 Kd6 79.Rh5 Rg1 80.Nb5 Ke6 81.Nc3 Rg4 82.Ne4 Rg1 83.Nc5** 1/2-1/2

After 17.Bb5

573) Bertok,M-Fischer,R [9/23/68] Vinkovci [13] A32/00 Queen's Gambit Declined [E:Rook + minor piece] **1.d4 Nf6 2.Nf3 c5 3.c4 cd4 4.Nd4 e6 5.e3 Nc6 6.Be2 Bb4 7.Bd2 Bc5 8.Nb3 Bb6 9.Nc3 d5 10.cd5 ed5** [Black has no problems with White's unambitious opening] **11.Nb5 0-0 12.0-0 Ne4 13.Rc1 Qg5 14.Bc3 Re8 15.Bd4 Nd4 16.N5d4 a5 17.Bb5** [D] **Bh3! 18.Qf3 Bg4 19.h4** [19.Qf4 Qf4 20.ef4 a4! -+] **Qh4 20.Qf4 g5! 21.Qh2 Qh2 22.Kh2 Red8 23.f3 a4! -++ 24.fe4 ab3 25.ab3 Ra5 26.Bd3 de4 27.Be4 Bd4 28.ed4 Rd4 29.Bb7 Be6 30.Bc8 Bb3 31.Rc3 Rb5 32.Rf2 Rdb4 33.Ba6 Rb6 34.Bc8 Kg7 35.Bf5 Rf6 36.Kg1 Be6 37.Rcf3 Rf5 38.Rf5 Bf5 39.Rf5 Kg6 40.Rf2 h5 41.Rc2** 0-1

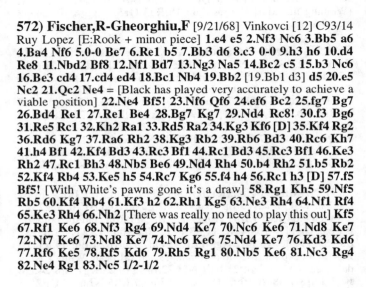

1969

574) Saidy,A-Fischer,R [1969] New York Metropolitan
League A25/09 English **1.c4 e5 2.Nc3 Nc6 3.g3 f5 4.Bg2 Nf6
5.d3 Bc5 6.e3 f4?!** [A rare example of speculative play in the
opening by Fischer] **7.ef4 0-0 8.Nge2?** [8.fe5 Re8 9.f4 d6
10.Bc6! bc6 11.d4 +-] **Qe8 9.0-0 d6 10.Na4 Bd4! 11.Nd4 ed4!**
[Leaving the Na4 out of play] **12.h3 h5 13.a3 a5 14.b3 Qg6
15.Nb2 Bf5 16.Qc2 Nd7 17.Re1 Nc5 18.Bf1 Ra6! 19.Bd2 Rb6
20.Ba5 Rb3 21.Bd2 Ra8 22.a4 Ra6 23.a5 Kh7 24.Red1 b6
25.Be1 ba5 26.Na4 Rd3 27.Bd3 Bd3 28.Qa2 Nb4 29.Qa3 Nc2
30.Qb2 Na1 31.Ra1 Na4 32.Ra4 Qe4 33.Ba5 [D] Ra5 34.Ra5
Qe1 35.Kh2 Qa5 0-1** [Fischer's only game of 1969 was voted
second-best game in the first half of 1969 by the *Chess Informant*
judges].

After 33.Ba5

1970

After 33...Qc6

575) Fischer,R-Petrosian,T [3/29/70] USSR vs. the Rest of the World [1] B13/04 Caro Kann **1.e4 c6 2.d4 d5 3.ed5 cd5 4.Bd3** [The ancient exchange variation, specially prepared by Fischer] **Nc6 5.c3 Nf6 6.Bf4 Bg4** [6...g6] **7.Qb3 Na5 8.Qa4 Bd7 9.Qc2 e6 10.Nf3 Qb6 11.a4!** [A star move, preventing 11...Bb5 and the exchange of Bishops] **Rc8 12.Nbd2 Nc6 13.Qb1 Nh5 14.Be3 h6 15.Ne5 Nf6 16.h3 Bd6 17.0-0 Kf8 18.f4 Be8 19.Bf2 Qc7 20.Bh4 Ng8 21.f5! Ne5 22.de5 Be5 23.fe6 Bf6 24.ef7 Bf7 25.Nf3 Bh4 26.Nh4 Nf6 27.Ng6 Bg6 28.Bg6 Ke7 29.Qf5 Kd8 30.Rae1 Qc5 31.Kh1 Rf8 32.Qe5 Rc7 33.b4! Qc6 [D] 34.c4! dc4 35.Bf5 Rff7 36.Rd1 Rfd7 37.Bd7 Rd7 38.Qb8 Ke7 39.Rde1 1-0**

After 21.Ned3

576) Petrosian,T-Fischer,R [3/31/70] USSR vs. the Rest of the World [2] A37/18 English [E:Minor piece] **1.c4 g6 2.Nc3 c5 3.g3 Bg7 4.Bg2 Nc6 5.Nf3 e6 6.0-0 Nge7 7.d3 0-0 8.Bd2 d5 9.a3 b6 10.Rb1 Bb7 11.b4 cb4 12.ab4 dc4 13.dc4 Rc8 14.c5 bc5 15.bc5 Na5 16.Na4** [16.Nb5] **Bc6 17.Qc2 Nb7! 18.Rfc1 Qd7 19.Ne1 Nd5 20.Nb2 Bb5 21.Ned3** [D] **Bd4 22.Qb3 Nc5 23.Nc5 Rc5 24.Rc5 Bc5 25.Nd3 Bd3 26.Qd3 Rd8 27.Bf3 Qc7 28.Bg5** [28.Rc1] **Be7 29.Be7 Qe7 30.Qd4? e5 31.Qc4 Nb6 32.Qc2 Rc8 33.Qd3 Rc4 34.Bg2 Qc7 35.Qa3 Rc3 36.Qa5 Rc5 37.Qa3 a5 38.h4 Nc4 39.Qd3 Nd6 40.Kh2 Kg7 41.Rd1 Ne8 42.Qd7 Qd7 43.Rd7 Nf6 44.Ra7 Ng4 45.Kg1 Rc1 46.Bf1 Ra1 47.e4 a4 48.Kg2 Ra2** [D] **49.Rf7 Kf7 50.Bc4 Ke7 51.Ba2 a3 52.Kf3 Nf6 53.Ke3 Kd6 54.f4 Nd7 55.Bb1 Nc5 56.f5 Na6 57.g4 Nb4 58.fg6 hg6 59.h5 gh5 60.gh5 Ke6 61.Kd2 Kf6 62.Kc3 a2 63.Ba2 Na2 64.Kb2 Nb4 65.Kc3 Nc6 66.Kc4 Nd4 0-1**

After 48...Ra2

Final position

577) Fischer,R-Petrosian,T [4/2/70] USSR vs. the Rest of the World [3] B15/02 Caro Kann **1.e4 c6 2.d4 d5 3.Nc3** [3.Nd2 would reserve the option of c2-c3 against 3...g6] **g6 4.e5 Bg7 5.f4 h5 6.Nf3** [6.Be3] **Bg4 7.h3 Bf3 8.Qf3 e6 9.g3 Qb6 10.Qf2 Ne7 11.Bd3 Nd7 12.Ne2 0-0-0 13.c3 f6! 14.b3 Nf5 15.Rg1 c5 16.Bf5 gf5 17.Be3 Qa6 18.Kf1 cd4** [18...Kb8] **19.cd4 Nb8** [19...Bf8] **20.Kg2 Nc6 21.Nc1 Rd7 22.Qd2 Qa5 23.Qa5 Na5 24.Nd3 Nc6 25.Rac1 Rc7 26.Rc3 b6 27.Rgc1 Kb7 28.Nb4 Rhc8 29.Rc6 Rc6 30.Rc6 Rc6 31.Nc6 Kc6 32.Kf3** [D] **1/2-1/2**

Final position

578) Petrosian,T-Fischer,R [4/4/70] USSR vs. the Rest of the World [4] D90/09 Grunfeld [E:Rook + pawn] **1.c4 g6 2.d4 Nf6 3.Nc3 d5 4.Nf3 Bg7 5.cd5 Nd5 6.Bd2 c5! 7.Rc1 Nc3 8.Bc3 cd4 9.Nd4 0-0 10.e3 Qd5! 11.Nb5 Qd1 12.Rd1 Nc6 13.Bg7 Kg7 14.Be2 Bf5 15.g4 a6! 16.Nc3 Be6 17.f4 Rfd8 18.Kf2 Nb4! 19.a3 Nd5 20.Ne4 Nf6 21.Nf6 ef6 22.Bf3 Rac8 23.Rd8 Rd8 24.Rd1 Rc8 25.Rd2 Rc7 26.h4 h6 27.Kg3 b5 28.Rd6 Rc2 29.b4 Rc3 30.Ra6 Bc4 31.f5 g5 32.hg5 hg5 33.Kf2 Rc2 34.Kg1 Rc1 35.Kg2 Rc2 36.Kg3 Rc3 37.Kf2 Rc2 38.Ke1 Rc3 39.Ra5 Re3 40.Kf2 Rd3 41.Bc6 Kf8 42.Bb5 Bb5 43.Rb5 Ra3 44.Rd5 Rb3 45.Rd4 Ke7 46.Ke2 Ra3 47.Kd2 Rb3 48.Kc2 Re3 49.Kb2 Ke8 50.Kc1 Re2 51.Kd1 Ra2 52.Ke1 Rb2** [D] **1/2-1/2**

579) Parma,B-Fischer,R [4/12/70] Rovinj/Zagreb [1] B97/06 Sicilian [E:Rook + Bishop] **1.e4 c5 2.Nf3 d6 3.d4 cd4 4.Nd4 Nf6 5.Nc3 a6 6.Bg5 e6 7.f4 Qb6** [Fischer and Parma have contested the Poisoned pawn variation on several occasions] **8.Qd2 Qb2 9.Rb1 Qa3 10.Bf6 gf6 11.Be2 Bg7 12.0-0 f5 13.Rfd1 0-0** [Better was 13...Nc6 14.Nc6 bc6 =] **14.ef5 ef5 15.Nd5 Nc6 16.Nc6 bc6 17.Ne7 Kh8 18.Nc8 Rfc8 19.Qd3** [19.Qd6 was better] **Qc5 20.Kh1 Re8 21.Qc4 Qc4 22.Bc4 Re4 23.Bf7 Rf8 24.Bh5 Rf4 25.Rb6 Be5** =+/-+ [The presence of Rooks and Bishops of opposite color make the extra pawn difficult to convert] **26.Ra6** [D] **Rh4 27.Bf3 Rh2 28.Kg1 c5 29.Ra8 Ra8 30.Ba8 Rh4 31.Bc6 Rb4 32.a4 Rb2 33.c4 Kg7 34.Rd3 Ra2 35.Kf1 Kg6 36.Re3 h5 37.Re2 Ra3 38.Rd2 h4 39.Ke2 Bf4 40.Rd3 Ra2 41.Kd1 Kf6 42.Rf3 Be5 43.Rd3 Ke7 44.Rd2 Ra3 45.Ke2 Bc3 46.Rd3 Ra2 47.Kd1 Bd4 48.Rh3 Bf6 49.Re3 Be5 50.Rd3 Kd8 51.Rd2 Ra1 52.Ke2 Kc7 53.Bb5 Bf4 54.Rc2 Ra3 55.Rb2 Be5 56.Rd2 Rg3 57.Kd1 f4 0-1**

After 26.Ra6

580) Fischer,R-Nicevski,R [4/13/70] Rovinj/Zagreb [2] B80/08 Sicilian **1.e4 e6 2.d4 c5 3.Nf3** [3.d5 +=; more space] **cd4 4.Nd4 a6 5.Nc3 Qc7 6.g3 Nf6 7.Bg2 Nc6 8.0-0 d6 9.Re1 Bd7 10.Nc6 bc6** [10...Bc6 11.Nd5! +=] **11.b3 Be7 12.e5!** [Wrecking Black's pawns - the sacrifice is only temporary] **de5 13.Bb2 0-0 14.Qe2 Nd5 15.Nd5 ed5 16.Be5 Bd6 17.Bd6 Qd6 18.c4! Be6 19.Rad1 a5 20.cd5 cd5 21.Rd4 a4 22.b4 a3 23.Qd2 Rab8 24.Re3 Rfc8 25.Ra3 Qe5 26.Rad3 h6 27.Bd5 Bd5 28.Rd5 Qa1 29.Kg2 Kh7 30.R3d4 Rc1 31.Qd3 g6 32.Rd7 Rg1 33.Kh3 Qa2** [D] **34.R4d6 1-0**

After 33...Qa2

581) Minic,D-Fischer,R [4/14/70] Rovinj/Zagreb [3] B99/30 Sicilian **1.e4 c5 2.Nf3 d6 3.d4 cd4 4.Nd4 Nf6 5.Nc3 a6 6.Bg5 e6 7.f4 Be7 8.Qf3 Qc7 9.0-0-0 Nbd7 10.g4 b5 11.Bf6 Nf6 12.g5 Nd7 13.a3** [13.f5] **Rb8 14.h4 b4 15.ab4 Rb4 16.Bh3 0-0?!** [16...Nc5; 16...Qb6] **17.Nf5 ef5** [Better was 17.Ne6! fe6 18.Be6 Kh8 19.Nd5 +-] **Nc5 18.Ne7 Qe7 19.h5?** [19.Qe3 +-] **Bb7 20.h6 Be4 21.Ne4 Ne4 22.hg7 Rc8 23.Rh2 Ra4 24.Kb1 d5 25.c4 Rac4 26.Bf1 Rb4 27.Qh3 Nc3 28.Kc1 Na4 29.Kb1** [D] **Rb2 30.Rb2 Nc3 31.Kc1 Qa3 32.Bd3 Qa1 33.Kd2 Qb2 34.Ke1 Ne4 0-1**

After 29.Kb1

582) Fischer,R-Marovic,D [4/15/70] Rovinj/Zagreb [4] B10/10 Caro Kann [E:Rook + pawn] **1.e4 c6 2.d3 d5 3.Nd2 Nd7 4.Ngf3 Qc7 5.ed5 cd5 6.d4!** [Transposing to a favorable exchange variation: the Bc8 is locked in] **g6 7.Bd3 Bg7 8.0-0 e6 9.Re1 Ne7 10.Nf1 Nc6 11.c3 0-0 12.Bg5 e5 13.Ne3!** +- **Nb6** [13...e4 14.Nd5 Qd6 15.Be4 f5 16.Bc2 Qd5 17.Bb3 ++-] **14.de5 Ne5 15.Bf4 f6 16.a4 Qf7 17.a5 Nbc4 18.Bc4 dc4 19.Be5 fe5** [D] **20.Qe2 h6 21.Nc4 Bg4 22.Nce5 Be5 23.Ne5 Be2 24.Nf7 Rf7 25.Re2 Rd8 26.Rae1 Rd5 27.b4 Rc7 28.Re3 Kf7 29.h4 Rd2 30.Rf3 Kg7 31.Re6 Rf7 32.Rf7 Kf7 33.Re5 Rd1 34.Kh2 Kg6 35.ab6 ab6 36.f3 Rd3 37.Rb5 Rc3 38.Rb6 h5 39.Rb7 Kf6 40.Rb5 Rb3 41.b6 Rb4 42.Kg3 Rb2 43.Rb8 Kg7 44.f4 Rb3 45.Kf2 Kf6 46.Ke2 Kg7 47.Kd2 Rg3 48.Rc8 1-0**

After 19...fe5

After 40...Re6

Final position

After 24...Rg2

After 25.b3

After 30.Qe3

583) Ivkov,B-Fischer,R [4/16/70] Rovinj/Zagreb [5] D40/12 Queen's Gambit Declined [E:Rook + Bishop] **1.d4 Nf6 2.c4 e6 3.Nf3 c5 4.e3** [Preferring a solid setup. 4.d5 with a Benoni is more ambitious] **d5 5.Nc3 Nc6 6.a3 cd4 7.ed4 Be7 8.c5** [Forming a Queenside pawn majority] **Ne4 9.Qc2** [Better was 9.Bb5] **f5 10.Bb5 0-0 11.0-0 g5!? 12.Bc6 bc6 13.Ne5 Bf6 14.Nc6?! Qc7 15.Ne4 fe4 16.Ne5 Ba6 17.Re1 Be5 18.de5 Qe5 19.Qc3 Qf5** =+ [Center pawns and active pieces] **20.Qg3 g4 21.b4 d4 22.h3 h5 23.a4 Bd3 24.b5 e5 25.c6 a6?!** [25...Rf6!?] **26.b6 Rf6 27.Bb2! Rc6 28.Bd4! h4** [28...ed4 29.b7 ++-] **29.Qe5 Qe5 30.Be5 Rb6 31.hg4 Rg6 32.f3 Re8 33.Bd4 Rf8 34.Re3 Rd8 35.Bc3 ef3 36.gf3 Bc4 37.Rae1 Rf8 38.Re8 Bd5 39.Rf8 Kf8 40.Re3 Re6 [D]** 41.Re5? [41.Re6 +-] **Kg8 42.f4 Rg6 43.g5 Rc6 44.Rh3 Rc1 45.Kf2 Rh1 46.Rd3 Rh2 47.Ke1 Be4 48.Rd6 Rg2 49.Rh6 Rg4 50.Ra6 h3 51.Rh6 Rg1 52.Kf2 Rg2 53.Ke3 Bf5 54.a5 Kf7 55.a6 Ra2 56.Kd4 h2 57.a7 Ra7 58.Rh2 Rd7 59.Kc5 Re7 60.Bd6 Re8 61.Ra2 Kg6 62.Ra7 Kh5 63.Rf7 Kg4 64.Rf6 Rc8 65.Kd5 Re8 66.Rh6 Be4 67.Kc5 Bf5 68.Be5 Rc8 69.Kd6 Ra8 70.Kd5 Rd8 71.Bd6 Re8 72.Bc7 Be4 73.Kd4 [D]** 1/2-1/2

584) Fischer,R-Uhlmann,W [4/19/70] Rovinj/Zagreb [6] C15/18 French **1.e4 e6 2.Nc3 d5 3.d4 Bb4 4.a3 Bc3 5.bc3 de4 6.Qg4 Nf6 7.Qg7 Rg8 8.Qh6 Rg6 9.Qe3** [Better was 9.Qd2 =] **Nc6 10.Bb2 Qd6** [10...Ne7 =+ was better] **11.f3 ef3?** [11...e5 ∞] **12.Nf3 Bd7 13.0-0-0 0-0-0 14.c4 Ng4 15.Qd2 f5 16.d5! Nb8 17.h3 Nf6 18.Ne5 Ne4 19.Qd4 Rg3 20.Nf7 Qf4 21.Kb1 c5 22.Qe5! Qe5 23.Be5 Rdg8 24.Bd3 Rg2 [D] 25.Be4 fe4 26.Nd6 Kc7 27.Ne4 Kb6 28.Nf6 Ba4 29.Ng8 Bc2 30.Kc1 Nd7 31.Rdg1** 1-0

585) Ghitescu,T-Fischer,R [4/20/70] Rovinj/Zagreb [7] E82/04 King's Indian [E:Rook + minor piece] **1.d4 Nf6 2.c4 g6 3.Nc3 Bg7 4.e4 d6 5.f3 0-0 6.Be3 b6 7.Bd3 Bb7** [7...c5? 8.e5! Δ 9.Be4] **8.Nge2 c5 9.d5** [9.0-0] **e6 10.0-0 ed5 11.ed5 Nbd7 12.Bg5 h6 13.Bh4 Ne5 14.f4 Nd3 15.Qd3 Qd7 16.Bf6 Bf6 17.f5 g5 18.Qh3** [18.Ne4 Be5! ∞] **Be5!** [A positional pawn sacrifice to obtain the Bishop pair and quell White's attacking ideas] **19.Qh6 f6 20.Rf3 Qh7 21.Qh7 Kh7 22.h4 g4 23.Rd3 Rae8 24.Ng3 Ba6! 25.b3 [D] b5 26.cb5 Bb5 27.Nb5 Ba1 28.Nd6 Bd4 29.Kf1 Re5 30.Nc4 Rd5 31.Ne3 Rd7 32.Ng4 Rg7 33.Nf2 Rfg8 34.Nfe4 Kh6 35.h5? Rg4 36.Ke2 Be5 37.Kf2 R4g7 38.Rf3 Rg4 39.Rd3 a6 40.Rf3 Bd4 41.Kf1 Be5 42.Kf2 a5 43.a4 Rd8 44.Ke3 Rb8 45.Kf2 c4 46.bc4 Rb2 47.Kf1 Rb4** 0-1

586) Fischer,R-Kovacevic,V [4/21/70] Rovinj/Zagreb [8] C15/15 French **1.e4 e6 2.d4 d5 3.Nc3 Bb4 4.a3 Bc3 5.bc3 de4 6.Qg4 Nf6 7.Qg7 Rg8 8.Qh6 Nbd7 9.Ne2 b6 10.Bg5?!** [10.Ng3 Bb7 11.Bb2 +=] **Qe7 11.Qh4 Bb7 12.Ng3 h6 13.Bd2 0-0-0 14.Be2 Nf8 15.0-0 Ng6 16.Qh6 Rh8 17.Qg5 Rdg8 18.f3 e3!** [Obtaining an overwhelming Kingside attack] **19.Be3 Nf8 20.Qb5 Nd5 21.Kf2 a6 22.Qd3 Rh2 23.Rh1 Qh4 24.Rh2 Qh2 25.Nf1 Rg2 26.Ke1 Qh4 27.Kd2 Ng6 28.Re1 Ngf4 29.Bf4 Nf4 30.Qe3 [D] Rf2!** 0-1

587) Smyslov,V-Fischer,R [4/22/70] Rovinj/Zagreb [9]
B26/04 Sicilian **1.e4 c5 2.Nc3 d6 3.g3 g6 4.Bg2 Bg7 5.d3 Nc6 6.Be3**
[6.f4] **Rb8!** [Immediately staking out Queenside space] **7.Qd2 b5**
8.Nf3 b4 9.Nd1 Bg4 10.h3 Bf3 11.Bf3 Nf6 12.Bg2 0-0 13.0-0 Re8
14.Bh6 Bh8 15.Ne3 Nd7 16.Rab1 Rb6! [Very original play]
17.Nc4 Ra6 18.a3 Nb6 19.ab4 cb4 20.Be3 Nc4 21.dc4 Ra2 22.f4
Bb2 23.e5! [Vigorous counterplay] **Bc3 24.Qd5 Ra6 25.e6 fe6**
26.Qe6 Kh8 27.f5 Nd4 28.Bd4 Bd4 29.Kh1 g5 30.Rb4 Bf6
31.Rfb1 Rb6 32.Rb6 ab6 33.Bd5 Rf8 34.Qe3 Qc8 35.g4 Qc5 [D]
1/2-1/2

Final position

588) Fischer,R-Gligoric,S [4/23/70] Rovinj/Zagreb [10]
C93/24 Ruy Lopez **1.e4 e5 2.Nf3 Nc6 3.Bb5 a6 4.Ba4 Nf6 5.0-0**
Be7 6.Re1 b5 7.Bb3 d6 8.c3 0-0 9.h3 h6 10.d4 Re8 11.Nbd2 Bf8
12.Nf1 Bb7 [12...Bd7] **13.Ng3 Na5 14.Bc2 Nc4 15.b3 Nb6 16.a4**
c5? [16...ba4 17.ba4 a5! =] **17.d5 c4 18.b4 Bc8 19.Be3 Bd7 20.a5**
+- [White has a strong spatial grip which transforms into a strong
Kingside attack] **Nc8 21.Qd2 Nh7 22.Kh2 Be7 23.Nf5 Bg5 24.Ng5**
hg5 25.g4 g6 26.Ng3 f6 27.Rh1 Rf8 28.Kg2 Rf7 29.f3 Nf8 30.h4
gh4 31.Rh4 Rh7 32.Rah1 Rh4 33.Rh4 g5 34.Rh6 Kg7? [D]
35.Rf6! 1-0

After 34...Kg7?

589) Kurajica,B-Fischer,R [4/24/70] Rovinj/Zagreb [11]
B50/08 Sicilian [E:Bishop vs. Knight] **1.e4 c5 2.Nf3 d6 3.Nc3 a6**
4.g3 Nc6 5.Bg2 g6 6.d4 Bg4!? 7.dc5 dc5 8.Be3 Qa5 9.0-0 Bg7
10.Bd2 Rd8 11.Nd5 Qa4 [A pawn grabbing expedition with his
King uncastled- only a Fischer can engage in such hair-raising
tactics] **12.Qc1 Qe4 13.Ng5 Qe5 14.Bf4 Qb2 15.Qb2 Bb2 16.Rab1**
Be5 17.Rb7? [17.Ne4 ∞] **Bf4 18.Nf4 Nd4 19.c3 h6 20.cd4 hg5**
21.Nd5 cd4 22.Re1 Kf8 23.Rb4 e6 24.Rd4 Bf5 25.g4 [D] **Rh4**
26.Red1 Rg4 27.Rg4 Bg4 28.f3 Rd5 29.Rd5 ed5 30.fg4 Nf6 31.h3
Ke7 32.Kf2 Kd6 33.Ke3 Ke5 34.Bf1 a5 35.Ba6 Ne4 0-1

After 25.g4

590) Fischer,R-Udovcic,M [4/28/70] Rovinj/Zagreb [12]
B06/12 Pirc **1.e4 g6 2.d4 Bg7 3.Nc3 d6 4.f4 Nc6 5.Be3 Nf6 6.h3**
0-0 [6...e5!?] **7.g4 e5 8.de5 de5 9.f5 gf5 10.gf5** [10.ef5 += was
better] **Nd4 11.Nf3 c5 12.Bg5 Qb6 13.Bf6 Qf6 14.Nd5 Nf3** [Better
was 14...Qd6] **15.Qf3 Qh4 16.Ke2** [D] **Be6?** [Tempting but
ineffective. 16...Bf6 was to be preferred] **17.Ne3 Rad8 18.Rg1 Kh8**
19.fe6 fe6 20.Qg3 Qf6 21.Qg7! ++ - Qg7 **22.Rg7 Kg7 23.Ng4 Rf4**
24.Ke3 Rdf8 25.Be2 h5 26.Ne5 Rh4 27.Rg1 Kh7 28.Rh1 Rhf4
29.Nd3 R4f7 30.Nc5 Rc8 31.Ne6 1-0

After 16.Ke2

591) Hort,V-Fischer,R [4/29/70] Rovinj/Zagreb [13] B26/04
Sicilian [E:Rook + minor piece] **1.e4 c5 2.Nc3 d6 3.g3 Nc6 4.d3 g6**
5.Bg2 Bg7 6.Be3 Rb8! 7.a4 e6 8.Qd2 Nd4 9.Nf3 Ne7 10.0-0 0-0 =
11.Bh6 e5! [Since the dark-squared Bishops are being exchanged
it's alright to place center pawns on dark squares to allow scope for
the Bc8] **12.Bg7 Kg7 13.Nd4 cd4 14.Ne2 Be6 15.f4 f6 16.c3 Qa5**
17.Qe1 dc3 18.bc3 f5! 19.c4 Qc5 20.Qf2 fe4 21.Be4 Bg4 22.Qc5
dc5 23.Rae1 Be2 24.Re2 ef4 25.Rf4 Rf4 26.gf4 b6 27.Rb2 Rf8
28.a5 Rf6 29.ab6 ab6 30.Kg2 Rd6 31.Ra2 Kf6 32.Ra8 Nc6 33.Kf2
Ne7 [D] **1/2-1/2**

Final position

After 30...Kg7

After 42.Ra1

After 81.Kb6

Final position

Final position

592) Fischer,R-Bertok,M [4/30/70] Rovinj/Zagreb [14] B24/02
Sicilian **1.e4 c5 2.Nc3 Nc6 3.Nge2 e6 4.g3 d5 5.ed5 ed5 6.Bg2 Nf6 7.d4 cd4 8.Nd4 Bg4** [8...Bb4 was better] **9.Qd3 Be7 10.h3 Be6 11.Ne6!** +=
[White has the Bishop pair, while Black's center pawns are exposed on open files] **fe6 12.0-0 0-0 13.Bg5 h6 14.Bd2 Qd7 15.Rae1 Bc5 16.Kh1 Rfe8 17.a3 a6 18.f4 Rad8 19.g4 Qf7 20.g5 Ne4 21.Ne4 de4 22.Qc3** [Better was 22.Qc4] **Bd4 23.Qb3 Bb2 24.Qb2 Rd2 25.gh6 Re7?!** [25...Qg6=] **26.Be4 Qh5 27.Qc3 Red7 28.Qe3 Ne7 29.hg7 Nf5 30.Qb3 Kg7** [D] **31.Bf5 ef5 32.Rg1 1-0**

593) Browne,W-Fischer,R [5/3/70] Rovinj/Zagreb [15] B04/09
Alekhine's [E:Rook + minor piece] **1.e4 Nf6 2.e5 Nd5 3.d4 d6 4.Nf3 g6 5.Be2 Bg7 6.c4 Nb6 7.ed6 cd6 8.Nc3 O-O 9.O-O Nc6 10.Be3 Bg4 11.b3 d5!** [Fixing the d-pawn to pressure it] **12.c5 Nc8 13.h3 Bf3 14.Bf3 e6 15.Qd2 N8e7 16.Nb5?** [16.Ne2 =] **Nf5 17.Bg4 a6 18.Bf5 ab5 19.Bc2 Ra3=+ 20.b4 f5 21.Bb3 Qf6 22.Qd3 f4 23.Bc1 Ra6 24.Bb2 f3 25.g3 Qf5 26.Qf5 gf5 27.Rad1 Nb4 28.Rfe1 f4 29.a3 Nc6 30.Re6 fg3 31.Bd5 gf2 32.Kf2 Kh8 33.Re3 b4 34.ab4 Nb4 35.Bf3 Ra2 36.Rb3 Nc6 37.Kg3 Rg8 38.Kf4 Rf8 39.Ke4 Rf7 40.Bg4 Re7 41.Kd3 Ra4 42.Ra1** [D] **Rd4 43.Bd4 Bd4 44.Ra8 Kg7 45.Rb5 Bf2 46.Bf5 Ne5 47.Kc3 Be1 48.Kd4 Nc6 49.Kc4 Bh4 50.Bc8 Nd8 51.Ra2 Rc7 52.Bg4 Be7 53.Kd5 Nc6 54.Rab2 Nd8 55.Rb1 Bf8 56.R1b2 Be7 57.Rg2 Kh8 58.Ra2 Kg7 59.Ra8 Bh4 60.Rb8 Rf7 61.Rb2 Kh6 62.Rb6 Kg7 63.Rb3 h5 64.Bc8 Be7 65.Rb5 Rf3 66.Bb7 Rh3 67.c6 Rc3 68.Ra8 h4 69.Ra4 h3 70.Rc4 h2 71.Rb1 Rc4 72.Kc4 Bd6 73.Kd5 Bg3 74.Bc8 Kf7 75.Bh3 Ke7 76.Rc1 Kf6 77.Ra1 Ke7 78.Rf1 Nf7 79.Bg2 Ng5 80.Kc5 Ne6 81.Kb6** [D] **Bc7 82.Kb7 Bd6 83.Bd5 Nc5 84.Kb6 Na4 85.Ka5 Nc5 86.Kb5 Kd8 87.Rf7 Kc8 88.c7 Nd7 89.Kc6 h1=Q 90.Bh1 Ne5 91.Kb6 Bc5 92.Kc5 Nf7 93.Kb6 Nd6 94.Bd5 Kd7 95.Bc6 Kc8 96.Bd5 Kd7 97.Bb3 Nc8 98.Kb7 Ne7 1/2-1/2**

594) Fischer,R-Korchnoi,V [5/4/70] Rovinj/Zagreb [16] B88/04
Sicilian [E:Rook + minor piece] **1.e4 c5 2.Nf3 e6 3.d4 cd4 4.Nd4 Nc6 5.Nc3 d6 6.Bc4 Nf6 7.Bb3 Be7 8.Be3 0-0 9.0-0 Nd4 10.Bd4 b5 11.Nb5 Ba6 12.c4 Bb5 13.cb5 Ne4 14.Qg4 Nf6 15.Qe2 Nd7?!** [15...d5!?]
16.Qe3?! [16.Rac1 +=] **Bf6 17.Ba7 Qa5 18.b6 Bd8 19.Rad1 Nb6** [19...d5 was better] **20.Bb6 Bb6 21.Qd2 d5 22.Qa5 Ra5 23.Rc1 Bd4 24.Rc2 g5 25.Rd1 Be5 26.Re1 Bd6 27.Rc6 Rd8 28.Rec1 Be5 29.R1c2 Rb8 30.g3 Rab5 31.Kf1 R5b6 32.R6c5 Kg7 33.Re2 Kf6 34.Rcc2 h5 35.Re3 h4 36.Rce2 Bd6 37.Rf3 Kg7 38.Rc3 Rb4 39.Kg2 R8b7 40.Rc6 R4b6 41.Rb6 Rb6 42.Bd1 Kf6 43.Rd2 Bc5 44.b3 Ke7 45.g4 Kd6 46.Rc2 Rb8 47.h3 Bd4 48.Be2 Bc5 49.Rc3 Bb4 50.Rc2 Ba5 51.Kf1 Rb4 52.Rc8 Bb6 53.Rc3 Rf4 54.Rf3 Rf3 55.Bf3 Kc5 56.Bd1 Kd4 57.Bc2 Bc5 58.Ke2 Ba3 59.Bh7 Kc3 60.Bb1 Bc5 61.Bh7 e5 62.f3** [D] **1/2-1/2**

595) Petrosian,T-Fischer,R [5/6/70] Rovinj/Zagreb [17] A40/09
Sicilian [E:Rook + pawn] **1.c4 c5 2.Nf3 g6 3.e4 Bg7 4.d4 Nc6 5.dc5 Qa5 6.Nfd2 Qc5 7.Nb3 Qb6 8.Be2 d6 9.0-0 Nf6 10.Nc3 0-0 11.Be3 Qd8 12.Rc1 Be6 13.Nd4** [13.f4 +=] **Nd4 14.Bd4 Qa5 15.f4 a6 16.f5 Bd7 17.c5! +- Bc6 18.cd6 ed6 19.fg6 fg6 20.Bc4 Kh8 21.Bd5 Rae8 22.h3 Bd5 23.Nd5 Nd5 24.Rf8 Rf8 25.ed5 Qb4 26.Bg7?! Kg7 27.b3 Qf4 28.Rc3 Qf2 29.Kh2 Rf7 30.a4 h5 31.Rc4 Re7 32.Qa1 Qf6 33.Qc3 Qc3 34.Rc3 Kf6 35.Rf3 Kg5 36.Rf8 Re3 37.g3 Re2 38.Kg1 Rb2 39.h4 Kg4 40.Rf6 Kg3 41.Rg6 Kh4 42.Rd6 Rb3 43.Rg6 Rb4 44.Rg7** [D] **1/2-1/2**

596) Fischer,R-Tukmakov,V [7/19/70] Buenos Aires [1]
A01/16 Nimzowitsch/Larsen **1.b3 e5 2.Bb2 Nc6 3.c4 Nf6 4.e3 Be7
5.a3 0-0 6.d3 d5 7.cd5 Qd5** [Better was 7...Nd5] **8.Nc3 Qd6 9.Nf3
Bf5 10.Qc2 Rfd8 11.Rd1 h6 12.h3 Qe6 13.Nd2 Nd7 14.Be2 Kh8?!**
[14...Qg6] **15.0-0 Bg6 16.b4 a6 17.Rc1 Rac8 18.Rfd1 f5 19.Na4
Na7 20.Nb3 b6 21.d4!** +- [This central reaction seizes the initiative]
f4 22.e4 Nb5? [22...Be4] **23.Bg4 Qf6 [D] 24.de5 Ne5 25.Bc8 Rc8
26.Rd5 1-0**

After 23...Qf6

597) Damjanovic,M-Fischer,R [7/20/70] Buenos Aires [2]
B36/12 Maroczy Bind [E:Bishop vs. Knight] **1.d4 Nf6 2.c4 c5 3.Nf3
cd4 4.Nd4 Nc6 5.Nc3 g6 6.e4 d6 7.Be2 Nd4 8.Qd4 Bg7 9.Be3 0-0
10.Qd2 Be6 11.f3 Rc8 12.Nd5 Nd7 13.0-0 Nc5 14.Rac1 a5 15.b3
Bd5 16.cd5** = [White has two Bishops and more space, but Black
has the strong Nc5 and Bg7] **Qb6 17.Rc4 Qa7 18.Rc2 [D] Bh6!
19.f4** [19.Bh6 Ne4!] **Rc7 20.g3 b6 21.Rfc1 Bg7 22.Bb5 Qa8
23.Qe2 e5!** 24.de6 fe6 25.Rd1 Rd8 26.Bd4 Bd4 27.Rd4 e5 28.fe5
de5 29.Rd8 Qd8 30.Bc4 Kg7 31.Bd5 Nd7 32.Qf2 Rc2 33.Qc2 b5
34.Kg2 b4 35.Qc6 Nf6 36.Kf3 Qd7 37.Qd7 Nd7 38.Ke3 Kf6
39.Kd3 Nb6 40.Bc6 Ke7 41.h4 h6 42.Ke3 Nc8 43.Kd3 Nd6
44.Ke3 Kd8 45.Kd3 Kc7 46.Ba4 Kb6 47.Ke3 Kc5 48.Bd7 Kb6
49.Ba4 Kc7 50.Kd3 Kd8 51.Bc6 Ke7 52.Ke3 Ke6 53.Kf3 Kf6
54.g4 g5 55.h5 Ke7 56.Ke3 Kd8 57.Kd3 Kc7 58.Ba4 Kb6 59.Bd7
Kc5 60.Ba4 Nc8 61.Be8 Ne7 62.Ke3 [D] Ng8 63.Bd7 Nf6 64.Bf5
Kb5 65.Kd3 a4 66.ba4 Ka4 67.Kc4 Ka3 68.Kc5 Ka2 69.Kb4 Kb2
70.Kc5 Kc3 71.Kd6 Kd4 72.Ke6 Ne4 73.Kf7 Nf2 74.Kg6 e4
75.Kh6 e3 76.Kg7 e2 77.h6 e1=Q 78.h7 Qe7 79.Kg8 Ne4 0-1**

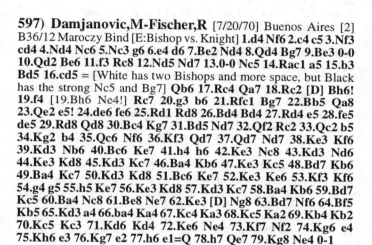
After 18.Rc2

After 62.Ke3

598) Fischer,R-Gheorghiu,F [7/21/70] Buenos Aires [3]
C42/12 Petroff **1.e4 e5 2.Nf3 Nf6 3.Ne5 d6 4.Nf3 Ne4 5.d4 Be7
6.Bd3 Nf6?!** [Passive and a tempo loss; 6...d5] **7.h3!** [Taking away
squares from the Bc8] **0-0 8.0-0 Re8 9.c4 Nc6 10.Nc3 h6 11.Re1
Bf8 12.Re8 Qe8 13.Bf4 Bd7 14.Qd2 Qc8** [Hoping to play 15...Bf5]
15.d5 Nb4 16.Ne4! Ne4 17.Be4 Na6 18.Nd4! Nc5 19.Bc2 +- [More
space and more active minor pieces] **a5 20.Re1 Qd8 21.Re3 b6
22.Rg3 Kh8 23.Nf3 Qe7 [D] 24.Qd4 Qf6 25.Qf6! gf6 26.Nd4 Re8
27.Re3 Rb8 28.b3 b5 29.cb5 Bb5 30.Nf5 Bd7 31.Nh6 Rb4 32.Rg3
Bh6 33.Bh6 Ne4 34.Bg7 Kh7 35.f3 1-0**

After 23...Qe7

599) Fischer,R-Schweber,S [7/23/70] Buenos Aires [4]
C19/04 French [E:Rook + minor piece] **1.e4 e6 2.d4 d5 3.Nc3 Bb4
4.e5 c5 5.a3 Bc3 6.bc3 Qc7 7.Nf3 Nc6 8.Be2 Bd7 9.0-0 Nge7 10.a4
Na5 11.Re1 cd4 12.cd4 Nc4 13.Bd3 h6 14.Nd2!** [Challenging the
Nc4 and preparing a Queen sortie] **Nd2 15.Bd2 Nc6 16.Qg4! g6
17.Re3** +- [Two Bishops, more space, and attacking chances] **0-0-0
18.Rg3 Kb8? 19.Rf3 f5 20.ef6 e5 21.Qg3 Nd4 22.Re3 e4 [D]
23.Re4!! Qg3 24.Rd4! Qg4** [24...Qc7 25.Bf4] **25.Rg4 Bg4 26.Bg6
Rhg8 27.Bh7 Rh8 28.Bd3 Rde8 29.f7 Re7 30.f8=Q! Rf8 31.Bb4
Rff7 32.Be7 Re7 33.f3 Bd7 34.a5 Kc7 35.Kf2 Rf7 36.Ke3 Kd6
37.g3 Kc5 38.f4 Bg4 39.Rb1 Re7 40.Kd2 b6 41.ab6 ab6 42.h3
Bd7 43.g4 d4 44.f5 Re3 45.f6 Rf3 46.Rf1 Rf1 47.Bf1 Be6 1-0**

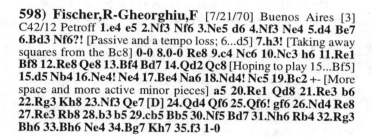

After 22...e4

After 27.Rc1

After 34...Kf7?

Final position

After 28...Qe7

After 28.Ra2

600) Quinteros,M-Fischer,R [7/25/70] Buenos Aires [5] A35/07
English **1.c4 g6 2.Nc3 Bg7 3.Nf3 c5 4.d4 cd4 5.Nd4 Nc6 6.Nc2 Bc3!**
[The sharpest strategy: giving up the strong Bg7 to permanently weaken White's c-pawns] **7.bc3 Nf6 8.f3 d6 9.e4 Be6 10.Be2 Rc8 11.Ne3 Qa5 12.Bd2 Ne5 13.Qb3 Nfd7 14.f4 Nc5 15.Qc2 Nc6 16.0-0** [16.f5!?] **Qa4 17.Qb1 Na5 18.e5 de5 19.fe5 0-0 20.Rf4 Nd7** [20...Nc6!?] **21.Nd5 Rfe8 22.Qe4 b5** [22...Nf8] **23.Rf7!!? Kf7** [23...Bf7 24.e6 +-] **24.Qh4 Kg7 25.Ne7 Qc2?!** [25...Rc4! -+] **26.Qh6** [26.Bh6 +- was better] **Kh8! 27.Rc1** [D] **Qc1 28.Bc1 Re7 29.cb5 Nc4 30.Qh4 Rf7 31.Qd4 Kg8 32.Bf4 Rc5 33.Bf3 Rb5 34.h3 Nce5 35.Ba8 Rf8 36.Be5 Ne5 37.Qa7 Bd5 38.Bd5 Rd5 39.Qe3 Ra5 40.Qe2 Rfa8 41.a4 Nf7 42.h4 Ra4 0-1**

601) Fischer,R-O'Kelly,A [7/26/70] Buenos Aires [6] C98/13
Ruy Lopez **1.e4 e5 2.Nf3 Nc6 3.Bb5 a6 4.Ba4 Nf6 5.0-0 Be7 6.Re1 b5 7.Bb3 d6 8.c3 0-0 9.h3 Na5 10.Bc2 c5 11.d4 Nc6 12.Nbd2 Qc7 13.dc5 dc5 14.Nf1 Be6 15.Ne3 Rad8 16.Qe2 c4 17.Nf5 Rfe8 18.Bg5 Nd7 19.Be7 Ne7 20.Ng5 h6** [20...Nf8] **21.Ne6 fe6 22.Ne3 Ng6 23.g3 Nf6 24.Red1 Rd1 25.Rd1 Rd8 26.Rd8 Qd8 27.b3!** [Activating the Bc2] **cb3 28.Bb3 Nf8 29.c4 Qd7 30.Qc2 Qb7 31.cb5 ab5 32.Ng4 N6d7 33.Qd3 Qc6 34.Qe3 Kf7?** [D] **35.Ne5 Ne5 36.Qf4 1-0**

602) Najdorf,M-Fischer,R [7/28/70] Buenos Aires [7] D41/31
Queen's Gambit Declined [E:Rook + minor piece] **1.d4 Nf6 2.c4 e6 3.Nf3 d5 4.Nc3 c5 5.cd5 Nd5 6.e3 Nc6 7.Bc4** [7.Bd3] **cd4 8.ed4 Be7 9.0-0 a6 10.Re1 0-0 11.a3 b5 12.Bd3 Bb7 13.Nd5 Qd5 14.Be4 Qd7 15.Bf4** = [Isolated d-pawn vs. freer development] **Rfd8 16.Qc2 g6 17.Rad1 Rac8 18.Qe2 Bf6 19.Ne5 Be5 20.de5 Nd4! 21.Qe3 Be4 22.Qe4 Qd5 23.Qd5 Rd5** [Threat: 24...Ne2] **24.Kf1 Rc2 25.Rd3 Nc6 26.Rd5 ed5 27.Bh6 d4 28.Rd1 a5 29.Rd2 Rc4 30.f4 a4 31.Ke2 Na5 32.Kd3 Nb3 33.Rc2 Nc5 34.Kd2 f5 35.ef6 Kf7 36.Bg5 d3 37.Rc4 bc4 38.Ke3 Ne6 39.g4 Ng5 40.fg5 [D] ½-½**

603) Fischer,R-Panno,O [7/30/70] Buenos Aires [8] A04/12
Sicilian **1.e4 c5 2.Nf3 e6 3.d3 Nc6 4.g3 g6 5.Bg2 Bg7 6.0-0 Nge7 7.Re1 d6** [7...d5!?, ...b6, ...a5, ...Ba6 and delayed castling was another plan] **8.c3 0-0 9.d4 cd4** [9...b6!?] **10.cd4 d5 11.e5 +=** [More space and Kingside attacking chances] **Bd7 12.Nc3 Rc8 13.Bf4 Na5 14.Rc1 b5 15.b3 b4 16.Ne2 Bb5 17.Qd2 Nac6** [Better was 17...Be2] **18.g4! a5 19.Ng3 Qb6 20.h4 Nb8 21.Bh6 Nd7 22.Qg5 Rc1 23.Rc1 Bh6 24.Qh6 Rc8 25.Rc8 Nc8 26.h5 Qd8 27.Ng5 Nf8 28.Be4!!** [28...de4 29.N3e4 and 30.Nf6 ++-] **Qe7** [D] **29.Nh7 Nh7 30.hg6 fg6 31.Bg6 Ng5 32.Nh5 Nf3 33.Kg2 Nh4 34.Kg3 Ng6 35.Nf6 Kf7 36.Qh7 1-0**

604) Agdamus,J-Fischer,R [8/1/70] Buenos Aires [9] A50/05
Queen's Indian **1.d4 Nf6 2.c4 b6?! 3.Nc3 Bb7 4.f3 d5 5.cd5 Nd5 6.Nd5?!** [6.e4] **Qd5 7.e4 Qd7 8.Bc4 g6 9.Qb3 e6 10.Ne2 Bg7 11.Be3 Nc6 12.Rd1 Na5 13.Qc2 Qc6!** [Forcing a favorable ending] **14.Bd3 Qc2 15.Bc2 0-0-0 16.Kf2 Rd6 17.b3 Nc6 18.Rd2 Rhd8 19.Rhd1 Nb4 20.Bb1 Ba6 21.a3 Nc6 22.Bd3 Bd3 23.Rd3 f5! 24.R3d2 Na5 25.e5 R6d7 26.Nc1 Bf8 27.b4 Nc4 28.Ra2** [D] **Ne5 29.Rc2 b5 30.Ne2 Nc4 31.Rc3 e5 32.f4 ed4 33.Rd4 Ne3 34.Ke3 Rd4 35.Nd4 Rd4 0-1**

605) Fischer,R-Rossetto,H [8/3/70] Buenos Aires [10] C99/10
Ruy Lopez [E:Bishop vs. Knight] **1.e4 e5 2.Nf3 Nc6 3.Bb5 a6 4.Ba4
Nf6 5.0-0 b5 6.Bb3 Be7 7.Re1 d6 8.c3 Na5 9.Bc2 c5 10.d4 Qc7
11.Nbd2 0-0 12.h3 cd4 13.cd4 Bb7 14.d5** [Slightly better is 14.Nf1]
Rfc8 15.Bd3 Nc4? [Creating a fatally weak c-pawn] **[D] 16.Bc4
bc4 17.Re3 a5 18.Rc3 Qd7 19.Qc2 Ba6 20.Nc4 Rc4 21.Rc4 Bc4
22.Qc4 ++- Rc8 23.Qd3 Qa4 24.Bg5 h6 25.b3 Qa3 26.Bf6 Bf6
27.Qd2 Bd8 28.Rb1 Bb6 29.Rb2 Qc5 30.Ne1 Qc1 31.Qc1 Rc1
32.Kf1 f5 33.ef5 Rd1 34.Ke2 Rd5 35.Nc2 Kf7 36.Ne3 Rb5 37.a4
Rc5 38.b4 ab4 39.Rb4 Bc7 40.Rc4 Rc4 41.Nc4 Ke7 42.Ne3 Kd7
43.Nd5 Ba5 44.Kd3 Kc6 45.Kc4 Be1 46.f3 Bd2 47.g3 Be1 48.g4
Ba5 49.Ne7 Kd7 50.Kb5 1-0**

After 15...Nc4?

606) Szabo,L-Fischer,R [8/4/70] Buenos Aires [11] E61/04
English **1.c4 g6 2.g3 Bg7 3.Bg2 c5 4.Nc3 Nc6 5.e3 Nf6 6.d4 0-0
7.Nge2 d6 8.0-0 Bf5 9.d5?!** [9.b3] **Na5 10.e4 Bd7 11.b3 a6 12.Rb1
b5 13.cb5 ab5 =+** [Queenside initiative] **14.b4 cb4 15.Rb4 Qc7!
16.Nb5 Qc5 17.Qd4 [D] Nd5! 18.Qc5 dc5 19.Rb1 Nb4 20.Nc7
Ra7 21.a3 Rc7 22.ab4 cb4 23.Rb4 Rc2 24.Nd4** [24.Nf4 was better]
**Bd4 25.Rd4 Bb5 26.Re1 Nb3 27.Rb4 Nc1 28.Rb5 Ne2 29.Kf1 Nc3
30.Rc5 Rd8 31.Bh3 Rdd2 -++ 32.Rc8 Kg7 33.Re3 Nd1 34.Rf3
Rf2 35.Rf2 Rf2 36.Kg1 Re2 37.Bg4 Re4 0-1**

After 17.Qd4

607) Fischer,R-Bisguier,A [8/6/70] Buenos Aires [12] C78/14
Ruy Lopez **1.e4 e5 2.Nf3 Nc6 3.Bb5 a6 4.Ba4 Nf6 5.0-0 b5 6.Bb3
Bb7 7.d4** [Not bad, but 7.d3! is +-] **Nd4 8.Nd4 ed4 9.c3 Ne4?**
[9...Be7 ∞] **10.Re1 Bd6 11.Nd2 Bh2 12.Kf1 d5 13.Qh5! 0-0
14.Qh2 dc3 15.Ne4 de4 16.bc3 c5 17.Re3! c4 18.Bc2 Qf6 19.Rf3
Qe6 20.Rh3 Qf5 21.Be3 Rad8 22.Re1 Rd7 23.Bd4 Re8 24.Rh5
g5 [D] 25.g4 1-0**

After 24...g5

608) Mecking,H-Fischer,R [8/8/70] Buenos Aires [13] D80/06
Grunfeld **1.d4 Nf6 2.c4 g6 3.Nc3 d5 4.Bg5 Ne4 5.Bh4 Nc3 6.bc3
dc4 7.e3 Be6 8.Rb1 b6 9.Nf3 Bg7 10.Nd2 0-0 11.Nc4 Bd5 12.Qd2
Qd7 13.Na3 c5 14.f3 Qa4 15.Nb5 Nc6 16.Nc7 [D] Qa2 17.Qc1
Rac8 18.Ra1 Qb3 19.Ra3 Rc7! 20.Rb3 Bb3 21.Qa3 Na5 22.Bg3
e5 23.Be5 Be5 24.de5 Rd8 25.Be2 Rcd7 26.Qc1 Bc4 27.Qc2 Bb3
28.Qc1 Bc4 29.Qc2 Bb3 30.Qc1 1/2-1/2** [30...Nc4! -+]

After 16.Nc7

609) Fischer,R-Rubinetti,J [8/9/70] Buenos Aires [14] C69/12
Ruy Lopez [E:Rook + minor piece] **1.e4 e5 2.Nf3 Nc6 3.Bb5 a6
4.Bc6 dc6 5.0-0 f6 6.d4 Bg4 7.de5 Qd1 8.Rd1 Bf3 9.gf3 fe5 10.Be3
Bd6 11.Nd2 Ne7 12.Nc4 0-0-0 13.Rd3 b5 14.Na5 Bb4 15.Nb3 Rd3
16.cd3 Ng6 17.Kf1 Rf8 18.Ke2 Nf4 19.Bf4 Rf4 20.Rg1 Rh4
21.Rg7 Rh2 22.a3 Bd6 23.f4!!** [Starting a pawn-roller in the center]
ef4 24.d4 Kd8 25.Na5 c5 26.e5 Bf8 [D] 27.Nc6 Ke8 28.Rc7 1-0

After 26...Bf8

After 39.Ke1

After 21.Ba3

After 35...Qg4

After 27.Bb2

After 15...Bc6?

610) Reshevsky,S-Fischer,R [8/11/70] Buenos Aires [15] E43/07 Nimzo-Indian **1.d4 Nf6 2.c4 e6 3.Nc3 Bb4 4.e3 b6 5.Bd3 Bb7 6.Nf3 0-0 7.0-0 Bc3 8.bc3 Be4 9.Be2 c5 10.Nd2 Bg6!? 11.Bf3 Nc6 12.Ba3 Rc8! 13.dc5 Qe7 14.Nb3 Ne5 15.Be2 Ne4 16.Rc1 Nc5 17.Bc5 bc5 18.f4 Nc6 19.Bf3 a5 20.e4 f6! = 21.Qe2 a4 22.Nd2 Rb8 23.Rb1 Qd6! 24.g3 e5 25.f5 Bf7 26.Rfd1 Na5 27.Nf1 Qc7 28.Ne3 Rb1 29.Rb1 Rb8 30.Rd1 Qc6 31.Qd3 Rb7 32.a3 h6?!** [32...Kf8! =+] **33.Be2 Rb3 34.Kf2 Ra3 35.Qd7 Qd7 36.Rd7 Ra2 37.Rd8 Kh7 38.Rf8 Bg8 39.Ke1** [D] **Ra1 40.Kf2 Ra2 41.Ke1 Ra1 1/2-1/2**

611) Smyslov,V-Fischer,R [8/13/70] Buenos Aires [16] A37/09 English [E:Rook + minor piece] **1.Nf3 c5 2.g3 g6 3.Bg2 Bg7 4.c4 Nc6 5.Nc3 e6 6.b3 Nge7 7.Bb2 0-0 8.Na4?! e5** [Better was 8...Bb2 =+/-+] **9.0-0 d6 10.e3 f5 11.d3 h6 12.Ne1 f4 13.Nc2 g5 14.Re1 Bf5 15.Nc3 Qd7 16.Ne4 Bh3 17.Bh1 Rf7** =+/-+ **18.b4!** [The only chance for counterplay] **cb4 19.a3 fe3 20.Ne3 ba3 21.Ba3** [D] **Nf5 22.Nf5 Qf5 23.Ra2 Nd4 24.Nd6 Nf3 25.Bf3 Qf3 26.Qf3 Rf3 27.Re3 Re3 28.fe3 b6 29.Ne4 Rd8 30.Nf2 Be6 31.Bb2 a5 32.e4 Rb8 33.Bc3 b5 34.Ra5 bc4 35.dc4 Bc4 36.Ng4 Be6 37.Ne5 Rc8 38.Bd4 Bh3 39.Kf2 Rc2 40.Ke3 Be5 1/2-1/2**

612) Fischer,R-Garcia,R [8/15/70] Buenos Aires [17] B24/02 Sicilian **1.e4 c5 2.Nc3 e6 3.Nge2 d6 4.g3 Nf6 5.Bg2 Nc6 6.0-0 a6?!** [6...Be7] **7.d3 Be7 8.h3 Qc7 9.Be3 b5 10.a3 Bb7 11.f4 b4 12.ab4 Nb4 13.f5!** [Beginning a pawn wave attack against Black's Kingside] **e5 14.Na4 0-0 15.c3 Nc6 16.Qd2 Rad8 17.g4 h6 18.Ng3 Nh7 19.b4! cb4 20.Bb6 ++- Qd7 21.Bd8 Qd8 22.cb4 Bg5 23.Qe1 Bh4 24.Kh2 h5 25.Qd1 Bg5 26.Rb1 Bf4 27.Rf4 ef4 28.Nh5 Qg5 29.Qf3 Ne5 30.Qf4 Nd3 31.Qd6 Nf2 32.Nc5 g6 33.Qf4 gh5 34.Qf2 Bc6 35.h4 Qg4** [D] **36.Bh3 1-0**

613) Miyasaka-Fischer,R [9/6/70] Siegen Olympiad Prelim [2] B92/07 Sicilian **1.e4 c5 2.Nf3 d6 3.d4 cd4 4.Nd4 Nf6 5.Nc3 a6 6.Be3 e5 7.Nb3 Be7 8.Be2 Be6 9.0-0 Nbd7 10.f4 Rc8 11.h3?** [Weakening and loss of time] **b5 12.a3 0-0 13.Qe1? Nb6 14.fe5 de5 15.Qg3 Na4! 16.Rad1 Nc3 17.bc3 Qc7 18.Bh6 Ne8 19.Rd3 Kh8 20.Bc1 Bc4 21.Rd2 Nf6 22.Qf3 Qc6 23.Bd3 Bd3 24.Rd3 Ne4 25.Na5 Qg6 26.Kh2 f5 27.Bb2** [D] **Bg5 28.Rfd1 Bf4 29.Kh1 Ng3 30.Kh2 Nh5 0-1**

614) Fischer,R-Camara,R [9/7/70] Siegen Olympiad Prelim [3] B75/08 Sicilian **1.e4 c5 2.Nf3 d6 3.d4 Nf6 4.Nc3 cd4 5.Nd4 g6 6.Be3 Bg7 7.f3 Nc6 8.Qd2 Bd7 9.Bc4 Rc8 10.Bb3 Qa5 11.0-0-0 Ne5 12.h4 Nc4 13.Bc4 Rc4 14.Nb3 Qc7 15.Bd4 Bc6?** [15...Be6 +=] [D] **16.e5! de5 17.Be5 Qc8 18.Qe2 Bd7 19.Rd7! Kd7 20.Nb5 Qc6** [20...a6 21.Rd1 Ke8 22.Bf6 Bf6 23.Nd6 ++-] **21.Rd1 Ke8 22.Nc7 Qc7 23.Bc7 Rc7 24.Qb5 1-0**

615) Acevedo,A-Fischer,R [9/8/70] Siegen Olympiad Prelim [4] A46/04 Queen's pawn [E:Rook + minor piece] **1.d4 Nf6 2.Nf3 c5 3.c3 g6 4.g3** [4.Bg5; 4.Bf4] **b6 5.Bg2 Bb7 6.0-0 Bg7 7.Nbd2 0-0 8.Re1 d5** =+ [White is passive and the Bc1 is locked in] **9.Ne5 Nc6 10.Ndf3 Rc8 11.Nc6 Bc6 12.Bh3 Bd7 13.Bf1 Bc6 14.Ne5 Bb7 15.a4 Ne4 16.f3 Nd6 17.e3 Qc7 18.a5 f6! 19.ab6 ab6 20.Nd3 e5** +- [Dominating center] **21.Nf2 e4 22.f4 Ra8 23.Bd2 Ra1 24.Qa1 Ra8 25.Qb1 Qc6 26.b3 Ba6! 27.Qb2 Bf1 28.Rf1 c4 29.b4 Qa4 30.Rb1 Bf8 31.Kf1 Nb5 32.Ke2 f5 33.Nd1 Kf7 34.Nf2 Qa2 35.Nd1 Ke6 36.Qa2 Ra2 37.Rb2 Ra1 38.Be1 Kd7!** [Heading for b5] **39.Bd2 Kc6 40.Be1 Na3 41.Kd2 Kb5 42.Bf2 Ka4 43.Be1 Be7 44.Bf2 Nb5 45.Kc2 Ka3 46.Rb1 Ra2 47.Rb2** [D] **Nc3! 48.Kc3 Ra1 0-1**

After 47.Rb2

616) Fischer,R-Hook,W [9/9/70] Siegen Olympiad Prelim [5] C18/01 French **1.e4 e6 2.d4 d5 3.Nc3 Bb4 4.e5 c5 5.a3 Bc3 6.bc3 Qa5? 7.Bd2 Qa4 8.Qg4! Kf8 9.Qd1 b6 10.h4! Ne7 11.h5 h6 12.Rh4! Ba6 13.Ba6 Na6 14.Rf4 Qd7 15.Qf3 Nc6 16.Nh3! Rc8 17.g4 Qe8 18.g5 Ne7 19.gh6 gh6 20.Rf6 Nf5 21.Nf4 Ke7 22.Nd5 ++- [A crush] Kd8 23.Ne3 Ne3 24.Be3 Rc7 25.dc5 Nc5 26.Rd1 Ke7 27.Bc5 bc5** [D] **28.Re6 1-0**

After 27...bc5

617) Fischer,R-Ibrahimoglu,I [9/10/70] Siegen Olympiad Prelim [6] B10/12 King's Indian Attack **1.e4 c6 2.d3 d5 3.Nd2 g6 4.Ngf3 Bg7 5.g3 Nf6** [5...e5] **6.Bg2 0-0 7.0-0 Bg4 8.h3 Bf3 9.Qf3 += [Two Bishops] Nbd7 10.Qe2 de4 11.de4 Qc7 12.a4!** [Probing the Queenside] **Rad8 13.Nb3 bc6 14.Be3 c5 15.a5 e5 16.Nd2 Ne8 17.ab6 ab6 18.Nb1! Qb7 19.Nc3 Nc7 20.Nb5 Qc6 21.Nc7 Qc7 22.Qb5 Ra8 23.c3 Ra1 24.Ra1 Rb8 25.Ra6 Bf8 26.Bf1! Kg7 27.Qa4 Rb7 28.Bb5 Nb8 29.Ra8 Bd6 30.Qd1 Nc6 31.Qd2 h5 32.Bh6 Kh7 33.Bg5 Rb8 34.Rb8 Nb8 35.Bf6 Nc6 36.Qd5 Na7 37.Be8 Kg8** [D] **38.Bf7 Qf7 39.Qd6 1-0**

After 37...Kg8

618) Uhlmann,W-Fischer,R [9/13/70] Siegen Olympiad Prelim [9] E74/15 King's Indian [E:Bishop + pawn] **1.d4 Nf6 2.c4 g6 3.Nc3 Bg7 4.e4 d6 5.Be2 0-0 6.Bg5 h6 7.Be3 c5 8.d5 e6 9.Qd2 ed5 10.ed5 Kh7 11.h3 Na6** [11...Bf5?! 12.g4! +-] **12.Nf3 Bf5 13.Bd3 Qd7! 14.0-0 Rfe8 15.Rfe1 Nb4 16.Bf5 Qf5 17.a3 Nc2 18.Nh4! Qh5 19.Qc2 Qh4 20.b3 Re5 21.Re2 Nh5 22.Rae1 f5 23.Bd2 Rae8 24.Re5 Be5?!!** [24...Re5 was safe, but Fischer provokes] **25.Nb5 a6 26.Nd6** [D] **Bd4! 27.Ne8** [27.Be3 Re3! 28.Re3 Be3 29.fe3 Qe1 30.Kh2 Qg3 -++] **Qf2 28.Kh2** [28.Kh1 Qf1! 29.Rf1 Ng3 with perpetual check!] **Nf4 29.Bf4!! Qe1 30.Qc1 Qe8 31.Bh6 +-/++- Qe4 32.Bf4 Kg8 33.Qf1 Kf7 34.h4** [34.a4! +-/++-] **b5 35.Bg3 bc4 36.bc4 Bf6 37.Qf4 Qf4 38.Bf4 Bh4 39.Be3 Be7 40.Kg3 g5 41.Kf3 Kf6 42.Bd2 Bd6 1/2-1/2**

After 26.Nd6

After 45...Nc6

619) Gheorghiu,F-Fischer,R [9/16/70] Siegen Olympiad Final [2] E80/01 King's Indian [E:Minor piece] **1.d4 Nf6 2.c4 g6 3.Nc3 Bg7 4.e4 d6 5.f3 c5 6.dc5 dc5 7.Qd8 Kd8 8.Be3 Nfd7 9.Nge2 Nc6 10.0-0-0 b6 11.f4! Bb7 12.g3 Na5 13.Bh3** [13.b3 += space advantage] **e6 14.b3 Ke7 15.Rd2 Rhd8 16.Rhd1 Nf6 17.e5 Ne4! 18.Ne4 Be4 19.Rd8 Rd8 20.Rd8 Kd8 21.Nc3 Bh1! 22.Bf1 f6 23.ef6 Bf6 24.Kd2 Nc6 25.Bd3 Nb4 26.Bb1 Bg7 27.Nd1 Ke7 28.Nf2 Bf3 29.a3 Nc6 30.Be4 Be4 31.Ne4 Bb2 32.a4 e5 33.fe5 Be5 34.Ng5 h5 35.Nf3 Ke6 36.Kd3 Bf6 37.h3 Kf5 38.Bf4 g5 39.Bc7 g4 40.hg4 hg4 41.Nd2 Bg5 42.Nb1 Bh6 43.Nc3 Nb4 44.Ke2 Bg7 45.Nb5 Nc6 [D] 46.Na7 Na7 47.Bb6 Nc6 48.a5 Nb4 49.Bc5 Na6 50.Bd6 Ke6 51.Bf4 Bf8 52.Bd2 Bd6 53.Kd3 Bg3 54.b4 Bd6 55.Ke4 Bf8 56.c5 Nc5 57.bc5 Bc5** 1/2-1/2

After 44...Rc8

620) Fischer,R-Najdorf,M [9/17/70] Siegen Olympiad Final [3] B42/07 Sicilian [E:Rook + minor piece] **1.e4 c5 2.Nf3 e6 3.d4 cd4 4.Nd4 a6 5.Bd3 Nf6 6.0-0 d6 7.c4 Bd7 8.Nc3 Nc6 9.Be3 Be7 10.h3 Ne5 11.Be2 Rc8 12.Qb3** [12.b3? b5] **Qc7 13.Rac1 0-0 14.f4 Nc6 15.Nf3 Qb8 16.Qd1 Be8 17.Qd2 Na5 18.b3 b6 19.Bd3 Nc6 20.Qf2 b5 21.Rfd1** [21.cb5 ab5 22.Bb5 Ne4!] **Nb4 22.Bf1 bc4 23.bc4!** [Keeping pawn control of d5. 23.Bc4 Ne4! and 24...d5] **a5 24.Nd4 Qa8 25.Qf3 Na6 26.Ndb5 Nc5 27.e5! de5 28.Qa8 Ra8 29.fe5 Nfe4 30.Nd6 Bc6 31.Nce4 Ne4 32.c5!** ++- [The outpost at d6 radiates power] **Ng3 33.Bc4 h5 34.Bf2 h4 35.Bg3 hg3 36.Bb5 Bb5 37.Nb5 f6 38.Rd7 Bd8 39.Rc3 fe5 40.Rg3 Rf7 41.Rf7 Kf7 42.c6 Bb6** [42...Rc8 43.Nd6] **43.Kf1 Kf8 44.c7 Rc8 [D] 45.a4 e4 46.Ke2 e5 47.Rg6 Bd4 48.h4 Bb2** 1-0

After 38...Kf7

621) Spassky,B-Fischer,R [9/20/70] Siegen Olympiad Final [6] D87/09 Grunfeld **1.d4 Nf6 2.c4 g6 3.Nc3 d5 4.cd5 Nd5 5.e4 Nc3 6.bc3 Bg7 7.Bc4 c5 8.Ne2 Nc6 9.Be3 0-0 10.0-0 Qc7 11.Rc1 Rd8 12.h3** [12.Bf4!? +=] **b6 13.f4 e6 14.Qe1 Na5 15.Bd3 f5 16.g4 fe4 17.Be4 Bb7 18.Ng3 Nc4 19.Bb7 Qb7 20.Bf2 Qc6 21.Qe2 cd4 22.cd4 b5 23.Ne4 Bd4?!** [Too materialistic; sound was 23...Re8 and ...Rad8] **24.Ng5 Bf2 25.Rf2 Rd6 26.Re1 Qb6 27.Ne4 Rd4?** [27...Rc6 =] **28.Nf6 Kh8 29.Qe6 Rd6 30.Qe4 Rf8 31.g5 Rd2 32.Rf1 Qc7 33.Rd2 Nd2 34.Qd4 Rd8 35.Nd5 Kg8 36.Rf2 Nc4 37.Re2 Rd6 38.Re8 Kf7 [D] 39.Rf8!** 1-0

After 21...c5

622) Fischer,R-Unzicker,W [9/21/70] Siegen Olympiad Final [7] C69/02 Ruy Lopez [E:Bishop vs. Knight] **1.e4 e5 2.Nf3 Nc6 3.Bb5 a6 4.Bc6 dc6 5.0-0 f6 6.d4 ed4 7.Nd4 Ne7?!** [7...c5] **8.Be3 Ng6 9.Nd2 Bd6 10.Nc4 0-0 11.Qd3 Ne5 12.Ne5 Be5 13.f4 +-** [Mobile Kingside majority and better development] **Bd6 14.f5!** [Cramping Black's Kingside and the Bc8] **Qe7 15.Bf4 Bf4 16.Rf4 Bd7 17.Re1 Qc5 18.c3 Rae8 19.g4 Qd6 20.Qg3 Re7?!** [20...c5] **21.Nf3** [Controlling e5] **c5 [D] 22.e5! fe5 23.Rfe4 Bc6 24.Re5 Rfe8 25.Re7 Re7 26.Ne5 h6 27.h4 Bd7 28.Qf4 Qf6 29.Re2 Bc8 30.Qc4 Kh7 31.Ng6! Re2 32.Qe2 Bd7 33.Qe7! Qe7 34.Ne7 g5 35.hg5 hg5 36.Nd5 Bc6 37.Nc7 Bf3 38.Ne8 Kh6 39.Nf6 Kg7 40.Kf2 Bd1 41.Nd7 c4 42.Kg3** 1-0

623) Gligoric,S-Fischer,R [9/22/70] Siegen Olympiad Final [8]
E94/31 King's Indian [E:Rook + minor piece] **1.d4 Nf6 2.c4 g6 3.Nc3
Bg7 4.e4 d6 5.Nf3 0-0 6.Be2 e5 7.d5 Nbd7 8.0-0 Nc5 9.Qc2 a5 10.Bg5
h6 11.Be3 Ng4 12.Bc5 dc5 13.h3 Nf6 14.Ne5 Nd5 15.cd5** [15.Nf7
Nb4 -++] **Be5** =/ ∞ [Bishop pair vs. central pawns] **16.f4 Bd4 17.Kh1?**
[17.Kh2 g5 18.e5 ∞] **Qh4 18.Qd3 c6! 19.Qf3 h5 20.f5 Bd7 21.Bc4
g5! 22.Rad1 Rae8 23.dc6 Bc6 24.Bd5 Re5 25.Bc6 bc6 26.Rd3 Rfe8
27.Qg3 Qg3 28.Rg3 f6 29.Rd3 h4 30.b3 Rb8 31.g3 hg3 32.Kg2 Rb4**
-+/-++ [The powerful Bd4, active Rooks, and weakened e4, h3] **33.Rc1
Kf7 34.Kg3 Ke7 35.Re1 Kd6 36.Rh1 Re7 37.h4 Rh7 38.h5 Rh6
39.Kf3 Ke5 40.Ne2 a4 41.Ng3 c4! 42.bc4 Rb2 43.Nf1 [D] Rh5!
44.Rh5 Rf2 45.Kg3 Rf1 46.Rh8 Ke4 47.Ra3 Rg1 48.Kh2 Rc1
49.Ra4 Rc2 50.Kh1 c5 51.Ra3 Kf5** -++ **52.Rh2 Rc1 53.Kg2 g4
54.Rh1 Rc2 55.Kf1 Kg5 56.Rh8 f5 57.Rg8 Kh4 58.Ke1 f4 59.Kd1
Rg2 60.Ra6 f3 61.Rh6 Kg3 62.Rhg6 Kf4 63.a4 Rg1 64.Kd2 f2 65.Rf8
Kg3 0-1**

After 43.Nf1

624) Fischer,R-Hort,V [9/23/70] Siegen Olympiad Final [9] B10/13
King's Indian Attack [E:Minor piece] **1.e4 c6 2.d3 d5 3.Nd2 g6 4.g3
Bg7 5.Bg2 e5 6.Ngf3 Ne7 7.0-0 0-0 8.Re1 Nd7 9.b3** [9.c3 a5 10.a4 =]
d4 10.Bb2 b5! [Staking out Queenside space and stopping Nc4] **11.c3
c5 12.Rc1 Bb7 13.cd4 cd4 14.Bh3 Nc6 15.a3 Re8 16.Qe2 Rc8 17.Rc2
Ne7 18.Rec1 Rc2 19.Rc2 Nc6 20.Qd1 Nb6 21.Qc1 Qf6** [Drawish: a
lack of pawn majorities while the remaining pieces are identical] **22.Bg2
Rc8 23.h4 Bf8 24.Bh3 Rc7 25.Nh2 Bc8 26.Bf1 Bd7 27.h5 Rc8 28.Be2
Nd8 29.Rc8 Bc8 30.Ndf3 Nc6 31.Nh4 b4 32.ab4** [32.a4 Na5] **Nb4
33.N4f3 a5 34.Qc7 Qd6 35.Qa7 Ba6 36.Ba3 Nc8 37.Qa8 Qb6 38.Bb4
Bb4 [D] 39.Qd5 Qc5 40.Qc5 Qe5 41.Ne5 Nd6 42.hg6 hg6 43.Kf1 Bb5
44.Nhf3 Bc3 45.Ne1 Nb7 46.Bd1 Nc5 47.f3 Kg7 48.Bc2 Kf6 49.Ng4
Ke7 50.Nf2 Bd7 51.Nd1 Bb4 52.Nb2 Be6 53.Nc4 Bc4 54.dc4 Be1
55.Ke1 g5 56.Ke2 Kd6 57.f4 gf4 58.gf4 f6 59.Kf3 Ke6 60.Ke2 Kd6**
1/2-1/2

After 38...Bb4

625) Portisch,L-Fischer,R [9/24/70] Siegen Olympiad Final
[10] E45/04 Nimzo-Indian [E:Rook + Knight / Knight + pawn] **1.d4
Nf6 2.c4 e6 3.Nc3 Bb4 4.e3 b6 5.Ne2 Ba6 6.Ng3 Bc3 7.bc3 d5 8.Ba3**
[8.Qf3!?] **dc4 9.e4 Qd7 10.Be2 Nc6 11.Qc2 0-0-0 12.0-0 h5 13.Rfd1
h4 14.Nf1 Nh5?** [14...Nb8, 15...Qc6] **15.d5! Ne5** [15...ed5 16.Rd5
++-] **16.de6 Qe8** [16...Qe6 17.Rd8 Kd8 18.Bh5 Rh5 19.Qd1 ++-, or
17...Rd8 18.Bh5 ++-] **17.Rd8 Qd8 18.Bh5 Rh5 19.f4 Nd3 20.ef7 c5
21.Qe2** [21.e5 was better] **Rh8 22.e5 Kb8 23.e6 Qf6 24.Re1 Bb5
25.Bc5!!** [25...Nc5 26.Qe5 Qe5 27.Re5 ++-] **bc5 26.Rb1 a6 27.a4
Nf4 28.Qf3** [28.Qe4!] **Ne6 29.Qf6 gf6 30.ab5 ab5 31.Rb5 Kc7
32.Ne3 Rf8 33.Ra5 Kb7 34.Nc4 Rf7 [D] 35.Rc5 Nc5 36.Nd6 Kc6
37.Nf7 Ne4 38.Nh6 Kd5 39.Nf5 h3 1/2-1/2**

After 34...Rf7

After 17...Nb4

626) Fischer,R-Hubner,R [11/9/70] Palma de Mallorca [1] B10/13 King's Indian Attack **1.e4 c6 2.d3 d5 3.Nd2 g6 4.g3 Bg7 5.Bg2 e5 6.Ngf3 Ne7 7.0-0 0-0 8.Re1** [Better was 8.b4 a5 9.ba5 Qa5 10.a4 =] **d4 9.a4 c5 10.Nc4 Nbc6 11.c3 Be6 12.cd4 Bc4 13.dc4 ed4 14.e5 Qd7 15.h4 d3! 16.Bd2 Rad8 17.Bc3 Nb4 [D] 18.Nd4!** =/∞ **Rfe8 19.e6 fe6 20.Ne6 Bc3 21.bc3 Nc2 22.Nd8 Rd8 23.Qd2 Na1 24.Ra1 Kg7! 25.Re1 Ng8 26.Bd5 Qa4 27.Qd3 Re8 28.Re8 Qe8 29.Bb7 Nf6 30.Qd6 Qd7 31.Qa6 Qf7 32.Qa7** [32.Bf3 was better] **Ne4 33.f3 Nd6 34.Qc5 Nb7 35.Qd4 Kg8 36.Kf2 Qe7 37.Qd5 Kf8 38.h5 gh5 39.Qh5 Nc5 40.Qd5 Kg7 41.Qd4 Kf7 42.Qd5 Kg7 43.Qd4 Kf7 44.Qd5 1/2-1/2**

After 14.Nc4

627) Smyslov,V-Fischer,R [11/10/70] Palma de Mallorca [2] A36/01 English [E:Rook + minor piece] **1.c4 g6 2.Nc3 Bg7 3.g3 c5 4.Bg2 Nc6 5.b3 e6 6.Bb2 Nge7 7.Na4 Bb2!** [Misplacing the Na4 to b2] **8.Nb2 0-0 9.e3 d5 10.cd5 Nd5 11.Ne2 b6 12.d4 Ba6! 13.dc5 Qf6!** [Shifting to attack mode] **14.Nc4 [D] Nc3 15.Nc3 Qc3 16.Kf1 Rfd8 17.Qc1 Bc4 18.bc4 Qd3 19.Kg1 Rac8! 20.cb6 ab6 21.Qb2 Na5 22.h4 Nc4 23.Qf6 Qf5!** [Entering a very favorable ending] **24.Qf5 gf5 25.h5 Rd2 26.Rc1 Rc5 27.Rh4 Ne5 28.Rc5 bc5 29.Ra4 c4 30.h6 Kf8 31.Ra8 Ke7 32.Rc8 Ra2 33.Bf1 Rc2 34.Kg2 Ng4 35.Kg1 Rf2 36.Bc4 Rf3 37.Kg2 Re3 38.Rh8 Nh6 39.Rh7 Ng4 40.Bb5 Rb3 41.Bc6 Rb2 42.Kg1 Ne5 43.Ba8 Rb8 44.Bh1 0-1**

After 20...Qb6

628) Fischer,R-Addison,W [11/11/70] Palma de Mallorca [3] B01/11 Center Counter **1.e4 d5 2.ed5 Qd5 3.Nc3 Qd8 4.d4 Nf6 5.Bc4 Bf5 6.Qf3 Qc8 7.Bg5!** [Sacrificing the c-pawn for a powerful initiative] **Bc2 8.Rc1 Bg6 9.Nge2 Nbd7 10.0-0 e6 11.Bf6 gf6 12.d5! e5** [Now f5 is critically weak] **13.Bb5 Be7 14.Ng3 a6 15.Bd3 Qd8 16.h4 h5 17.Bf5 Nb6 18.Nce4 Nd5 19.Rfd1 c6 20.Nc3 Qb6 [D] 21.Rd5 cd5 22.Nd5 Qb2 23.Rb1 Qa2 24.Rb7 1-0**

After 39...Kh6

629) Fischer,R-Filip,M [11/13/70] Palma de Mallorca [4] A14/04 Nimzowitsch/Larsen **1.b3 d5 2.Bb2 Nf6 3.Nf3 e6 4.g3 Be7 5.Bg2 0-0 6.0-0 c5 7.c4 Nc6 8.cd5 Nd5 9.Nc3 Bf6 10.Qc1 b6 11.Nd5 ed5 12.d4 Ba6 13.Re1 Nd4 14.Bd4 cd4 15.Qa3 Bb7?** [15...Qc8! =] **16.Rad1 Be7 17.Qa4 Qe8 18.Qd4 Rc8 19.Qf4 Bf6 20.Nd4 Be5 21.Qe3 g6 22.Nb5! Qb5 23.Qe5 Rfe8 24.Qb2 Rc5 25.h4 Rec8 26.Rd2 Rc3 27.Red1 Qc5 28.b4 Qe7 29.e3 h5 30.a3 Kh7 31.Bd5 Bd5 32.Rd5 Qe4 33.Rd8 Qf3 34.Kh2 R8c4 35.R1d7 g5 36.Rf8 Kg6 37.Rg8 Kh7 38.Rg5 Rc8 39.Rdd5 Kh6 [D] 40.Rdf5 1-0**

630) Hort,V-Fischer,R [11/14/70] Palma de Mallorca [5]
B50/08 Sicilian [E:Rook + Bishop] **1.e4 c5 2.Nc3 d6 3.Nf3 a6 4.g3
Nc6 5.Bg2 Bg4!? 6.h3 Bf3 7.Bf3 g6 8.d3 Bg7 9.a4 e6 10.Bg2 Nge7
11.0-0 0-0 12.Be3 Qa5 13.Bd2 Qc7 14.Qb1 Nd4 15.a5 Nec6
16.Nd1 c4! 17.dc4 Ne5! 18.Be3 Nc4 19.Ra4 Rac8 20.Bd4 Bd4
21.Qa2 Bf6 22.c3 Bd8!** [Forcing the weakening of c3] **23.b4 Bf6
24.Re1 Rfd8 25.Qe2 Kg7 26.Ra2 h5 27.h4 Qd7 28.Kh2 Ne5
29.Rc2 Ng4 30.Kh1 Rc7 31.Bh3 Ne5 32.Ne3 Qa4 33.Rb1? Nc4!
34.Ra2 Qc6 35.Nc4 Qc4 36.Qc4 Rc4 37.b5** [D] **Bc3 38.ba6 ba6
39.Rb6 Re4 40.Ra6 Re1 41.Kh2 d5 42.Rc6 Ra1 43.Ra1 Ba1 44.a6
Bd4 45.Rc2 Kf6 46.f4 Rb8 47.Ra2 Ba7 48.Bf1 Ke7 49.Kg2 Kd6
50.Bd3 Rb3 51.Be2 f6 52.Rd2 Ra3 53.Bd3 Bb6 54.Rd1 Ra2
55.Kf3 Bd4 56.g4 Ra3 57.Kg2 Be3 58.Kf3 Bc5 59.Kg3 e5 60.fe5
fe5 61.Kg2 hg4 62.Bg6 Ra6 63.Kg3 Ke6 64.h5 Be3 65.Kg4 Ra4
66.Kf3 Bh6 67.Rb1 e4 68.Kg3 Ra3 69.Kg4 Ke5 70.Rb8 Ra1
71.Re8 Kd4 72.Kf5 Rf1 0-1**

After 37.b5

631) Reshevsky,S-Fischer,R [11/15/70] Palma de Mallorca
[6] A32/09 English **1.d4 Nf6 2.c4 c5 3.Nf3 cd4 4.Nd4 e6 5.Nc3 Bb4
6.e3 Ne4 7.Qc2 Nc3 8.bc3 Be7 9.Be2 0-0 10.0-0 a6 11.f4 d6 12.f5
ef5 13.Nf5 Bf5 14.Qf5 Nd7** [Black has very satisfactory play due
to the weak White pawns, but the Bishop pair compensates] **15.Bf3
Qc7 16.Rb1 Rab8 17.Bd5 Nf6 18.Ba3 Rfe8 19.Qd3 Nd5 20.cd5
b5 21.e4 Bf8 22.Rb4 Re5 23.c4 Rbe8 24.cb5 ab5 25.Kh1 Qe7
26.Qb5 Re4 27.Re4 Qe4 28.Qd7** [D] **Qf4 29.Kg1?? Qd4! 30.Kh1
Qf2 0-1**

After 28.Qd7

632) Fischer,R-Matulovic,M [11/18/70] Palma de Mallorca
[7] B31/01 Sicilian [E:Rook + pawn] **1.e4 c5 2.Nf3 Nc6 3.Bb5 g6
4.c3 Nf6 5.Qe2 Bg7 6.e5 Nd5 7.Qc4** [Fischer likes to grab pawns,
but this is too risky] **Nc7 8.Bc6 dc6 9.Qc5 Qd3! 10.Qe3 Bf5 11.Qd3
Bd3 12.Kd1 Ne6 13.Ne1 Nf4 14.Nd3 Nd3 15.f4! Bh6 16.Kc2 Nc1
17.Re1 0-0-0 18.Kc1 Bf4 19.g3 Bh6 20.Kc2 Rd5 21.b4 b6 22.a4
a5 23.ba5 ba5 24.Re4 Rhd8 25.d4 c5 26.Kd3 cd4 27.cd4 Bg7
28.Ke3 Bh6?** [28...f5! -+] **29.Kd3 Bg7 30.Kc4 f5 31.Nc3 e6 32.Rh4
g5 33.Rh7 Rd4 34.Kb5 Be5 35.Rc1 Rb4 36.Ka5 Rc4 37.Ne2 Rd5
38.Kb6 Rdc5 39.Rc4 Rc4 40.h4!** [D] **Rc2 41.hg5 Re2 42.g6 Rb2
43.Ka6 Rb4 44.g7 Bg7 45.Rg7 Ra4 46.Kb5 Rd4 47.Re7 Re4
48.Kc5 Kd8 49.Ra7 Ke8 50.Kd6 Kf8 51.Rb7 Re3 52.Ra7 Re1
53.Rb7 Re4 54.Ra7 Re2 55.Rb7 Re3 56.Ra7 Kg8 57.Rb7 Re1
58.Re7 Re3 59.Re6 Rg3 60.Ke5 1/2-1/2**

After 40...Rc2

633) Naranja,R-Fischer,R [11/19/70] Palma de Mallorca [8]
A35/04 English [E:Rook + pawn] **1.c4 c5 2.Nc3 g6 3.Nf3 Bg7 4.d4
cd4 5.Nd4 Nc6 6.e3 Nf6 7.Be2 0-0 8.0-0 Nd4 9.Qd4 d6 10.Qh4
Be6 11.Rd1 Qb6 12.Rb1 Qc5 13.b4 Qf5?** [13...Qe5] **14.e4 Qe5
15.Rb3! Bd7 16.f4 Qe6 17.f5! gf5 18.ef5 Qf5 19.Bg5?** [19.Nd5!
Nd5 20.Bd3 ++-] [D] **h6 20.Bh6 Qh7 21.Bg5 Qh4 22.Bh4 Be6
23.Bf6 ef6 24.Nd5 Rfd8 25.Rf3 Kf8 26.Nf6 Rac8 27.Nh7 Kg8
28.Nf6 Bf6 29.Rf6 Bc4 30.Bc4 Rc4 31.Rfd6 Rd6 32.Rd6 Rb4
33.Rd2 b5 34.Kf2 Ra4 35.Ke3 Kg7 36.Kd3 Ra3 37.Kd4 a5
38.Kc5 b4 39.Kb5 f5 40.g3 Kf6 41.Re2 Kg5 42.Rf2 Kg6 43.Rd2
Kf7 44.Re2 Kf6 45.Kc4 Kg5 46.Kb5 Kg4 47.Rf2 Kh3 48.Rd2
1/2-1/2**

After 19.Bg5?

After 26.Ne6

Final position

After 26...Rad8

After 36.hg4

After 72.f5

634) Fischer,R-Larsen,B [11/20/70] Palma de Mallorca [9] B89/18 Sicilian [E:Rook + minor piece] **1.e4 c5 2.Nf3 d6 3.d4 cd4 4.Nd4 Nf6 5.Nc3 Nc6 6.Bc4 e6 7.Bb3 Be7 8.Be3 0-0 9.Qe2 a6 10.0-0-0 Qc7 11.g4 Nd7 12.h4?** [12.g5 +=] **Nc5 13.g5 b5 14.f3 Bd7 15.Qg2 b4 16.Nce2 Nb3** [Eliminating the dangerous Bb3] **17.ab3 a5 18.g6 fg6 19.h5 Nd4 20.Nd4 g5!** [Keeping Kingside lines closed] **21.Bg5 Bg5 22.Qg5 h6 23.Qg4 Rf7 24.Rhg1 a4 25.ba4 e5!** -++ **26.Ne6** [D] **Qc4 27.b3 Qe6 28.Qe6 Be6 29.Rd6 Re8 30.Rb6 Rf3 31.Rb4 Rc8! 32.Kb2 Rf2 33.Rc1 Bf7 34.a5 Ra8 35.Rb5 Bh5 36.Re5 Be2 37.Rc5 h5 38.e5 Bf3 39.Kc3 h4 40.Kd3 Re2 41.Rf1 Rd8 42.Kc3 Be4 43.Kb4 Rb8 44.Ka3 h3 45.e6 Bc2 46.b4 Re3 47.Kb2 Bd3 48.Ra1 Ba6 49.Rc6 Rb4 50.Kc2 Bb7 51.Rc3 Re2 52.Kd1 Rg2 0-1**

635) Portisch,L-Fischer,R [11/22/70] Palma de Mallorca [10] A70/04 Benoni **1.d4 Nf6 2.c4 c5 3.d5 e6 4.Nc3 ed5 5.cd5 d6 6.Nf3 g6 7.Bf4 Bg7 8.Qa4 Bd7 9.Qb3 Qc7 10.e4 0-0 11.Be2 a6 12.e5!** **de5 13.Be5 +=** **Qc8 14.0-0 Bg4 15.h3 Bf3 16.Bf3 Nbd7 17.Bd6 Re8 18.a4 Ne5 19.Be5 Re5 20.Rad1** [Better was 20.Rfd1 +=/+-] **Rb8 21.d6 b5 22.ab5 ab5 23.Rfe1 Re1 24.Re1 Bf8 25.Nb5 Qd7 26.Be2 Bd6 27.Bc4 Bf8 28.Rd1 Qe7 29.Qd3** [D] **1/2-1/2**

636) Fischer,R-Polugaevsky,L [11/23/70] Palma de Mallorca [11] A11/11 Reti [E:Rook + minor piece] **1.c4 Nf6 2.g3** [A very rare example of Fischer playing a Reti setup] **c6 3.Bg2 d5 4.Nf3 Bf5 5.Qb3 Qb6 6.cd5 Qb3 7.ab3 cd5 8.Nc3 Nc6 9.d3 e6 10.0-0 Be7 11.Be3 Ng4 12.Bf4 0-0 13.e4 de4 14.de4 Bg6 15.e5 Bd3 16.Rfd1 Bc2 17.Rdc1 Bb3 18.h3 g5!** [A sharp counter, giving Black fully adequate chances] **19.hg4 gf4 20.Nd2 f3 21.Bf3 Ne5 22.Bg2 Bd5 23.Nd5 ed5 24.Rc7 Bd8 25.Rb7 Bb6 26.Bd5 Rad8** [D] **27.Ne4 Ng4 28.Rd1 Kg7 29.Rd2 Nf6 30.Nf6 Kf6 31.Rd3 Kg7 32.Kg2 Rb8 33.Rd7 Rbd8 34.Bc4 Rd7 35.Rd7 Kg6 36.g4 Rd8 37.Bf7 Kg5 38.Rd8 Bd8 1/2-1/2**

637) Geller,E-Fischer,R [11/24/70] Palma de Mallorca [12] D79/12 Grunfeld [E:Rook + pawn] **1.Nf3 Nf6 2.c4 g6 3.g3 Bg7 4.Bg2 0-0 5.0-0 c6 6.d4 d5 7.cd5 cd5 8.Ne5 Bf5 9.Nc3 Ne4 10.Be3?!** [10.Ne4] **Nc3 11.bc3 Nc6 12.Nc6 bc6 13.Qa4 Qb6 14.Rac1 Rab8 15.c4 Bd4 16.Bd4 Qd4 17.e3 Qe5 18.cd5 cd5 19.Rfd1 e6 20.Qa7 Ra8 21.Qd4 Qd4 22.Rd4 Ra2** [Black is much better, but it is very difficult to win with all pawns on one side of the board] **23.e4 de4 24.Be4 Be4 25.Re4 Rb8 26.Re3 g5 27.h3 Kg7 28.Rc7 Kg6 29.Rf3 f6 30.Re7 Re2 31.g4 Rb1 32.Kg2 Ree1 33.Ra3 h5 34.Raa7 Rg1 35.Kf3 hg4 36.hg4** [D] **Rb3 37.Ke2 Rg4 38.Re6 Rb1 39.Raa6 Rf4 40.Ra2 Rh1 41.Rea6 Rb4 42.R6a4 Rbb1 43.Ra8 Rhg1 44.Kf3 Rb5! 45.R8a5 Rb3 46.Ke2 Rbb1?** [46...g4! -++] **47.Ra8 Kf5 48.R2a5 Kg4 49.Raa4 Kh5 50.Rh8 Kg6 51.Rg8 Kf7 52.Rd8 Rbe1 53.Kf3 Rec5 54.Rd2 Rf5 55.Ke2 Re5 56.Kf3 Kg6 57.Re4 Rf5 58.Ke2 Ra5 59.Re3 Kh5 60.Red3 Raa1 61.Rd8 f5 62.Kf3 Ra3 63.R2d3 g4 64.Kf4 Rd3 65.Rd3 Rf1 66.Rd2 Kh4 67.Kf5 g3 68.f4 Kh3 69.Rd3 Kh4 70.Rd2 Ra1 71.Ke5??** [A horrific blunder. 71.Rd8 draws] **Kg4 72.f5** [D] **Ra5 0-1**

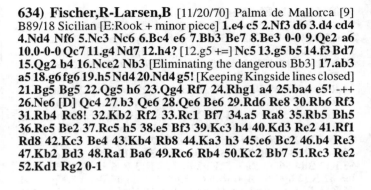

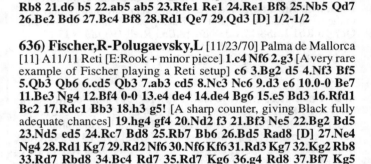

638) Fischer,R-Ivkov,B [11/27/70] Palma de Mallorca [13] C93/03 Ruy Lopez **1.e4 e5 2.Nf3 Nc6 3.Bb5 a6 4.Ba4 Nf6 5.0-0 Be7 6.Re1 b5 7.Bb3 d6 8.c3 0-0 9.h3 h6 10.d4 Re8 11.Be3 Bf8 12.Nbd2 Bb7 13.Qb1 Qb8?! 14.a3!** [Preparing to gain space with b4 and a4] **Nd8 15.Bc2 c6 16.b4 Qc7 17.Bd3 Ne6 18.Qc2 Rac8 19.a4 Nd7 20.Qb3?!** [20.Rec1] **Nf4 21.Bf4 ef4 22.c4 bc4 23.Bc4 d5 24.Bd3 Rb8 25.Qc3 Qb6 26.Reb1 Ba8 27.a5 Qa7 28.e5 Rb7 29.Qc6! Bb4 30.Qa6 Qb8 31.Be2 Re6 32.Qd3 Nf8 33.Qf5 Ra6 34.Nb3! g6 35.Qf4 Bc3 36.Nc5 Ra5 37.Nb7 Ra1 38.Ra1 Ne6 39.Qf6 Ba1 40.Nd6 Qc7** [D] **41.Bg6 Qc1 42.Ne1! Qe1 43.Kh2 Ng5 44.Bf7 1-0**

After 40...Qc7

639) Minic,D-Fischer,R [11/28/70] Palma de Mallorca [14] B03/04 Alekhine's [E:Rook + pawn] **1.e4 Nf6 2.e5 Nd5 3.d4 d6 4.c4 Nb6 5.ed6 cd6 6.Nc3 g6 7.Bd3 Bg7 8.Nge2 0-0 9.b3 Nc6 10.Be3 d5!** [Fixing the d-pawn as a target] **11.c5 Nd7 12.Bb5 e5! 13.0-0 Nc5! 14.de5 d4 15.Nd4 Ne5 16.h3 Ne6 17.Ne6 Be6 18.f4?** [18.Qd8 =] **Qa5! 19.fe5 Qc3 20.Qd4 Qa5 21.a4 Bb3 22.Bf4 a6 23.Be2 Rae8 24.Ra3 Bd5 25.Rb1** [D] **Bc6 26.Bf3 Be5 27.Be5 Re5 28.Bc6 bc6 29.Rc3 Re2 30.Rc6 Qg5 31.Qg4 Qg4 32.hg4 Rd8 33.g5 Rd5 34.Kf1 Ree5 35.Ra6 Rg5 36.Rb2 Rd1 37.Kf2 Rf5 38.Kg3 Rd3 39.Kh2 Ra3 40.Ra7 h5 41.Kg1 Kg7 42.Rb1 Kh6 43.Rf1 Rf1 44.Kf1 f5 45.Ra8 0-1**

After 25.Rb1

640) Fischer,R-Jimenez,E [11/29/70] Palma de Mallorca [15] C87/07 Ruy Lopez [E:Rook + minor piece] **1.e4 e5 2.Nf3 Nc6 3.Bb5 a6 4.Ba4 Nf6 5.0-0 Be7 6.Re1 d6 7.c3 0-0 8.d4 ed4 9.cd4 d5 10.e5 Ne4 11.Nc3?** [There was no need to weaken these pawns. 11.Nbd2 was better] **Nc3 12.bc3 Bf5 13.Bc6 bc6 14.Qa4 c5 15.dc5 Bc5 16.Ba3 Qe7 17.Bc5 Qc5 18.Nd4 Bg6 19.Qc6 Qc6 20.Nc6 Rfe8** [D] **21.Nb4 c6!** [Resourceful defence] **22.Nc6 Rac8 23.Nb4 Rc3 24.Nd5 Ra3 25.f4 h5 26.Ne3 Bd3 27.Rad1 Rb8 28.Rd2 Rb1 29.Kf2 Re1 30.Ke1 Bb1 31.Rd8 Kh7 32.Kf2 Ba2 33.f5 Ra5 34.Re8 Rb5 35.Kf3 a5 36.Kf4 a4 37.Ra8 Rb4 38.Kf3 Bb3 39.h3 Rb5 40.Kf4 Rb4 41.Kf3 Rb5 1/2-1/2**

After 20...Rfe8

641) Uitumen,T-Fischer,R [12/1/70] Palma de Mallorca [16] B03/05 Alekhine's [E:Knight + pawn] **1.e4 Nf6 2.e5 Nd5 3.d4 d6 4.c4 Nb6 5.f4 Bf5 6.Nc3 e6 7.Be3 Be7 8.Nf3 0-0 9.ed6** [Better was 9.Bd3 Bd3 10.Qd3 d5 11.b3! +=] **cd6 10.b3 d5 11.c5 Nd7 12.Bd3 Bd3 13.Qd3 b6 14.cb6 Qb6 15.0-0 Qa6 16.Qd1 Nc6 17.Ne5 Nce5 18.fe5 Rac8 19.Rc1 f6 20.ef6 Nf6 21.h3 Bb4 22.Na4 Rc1 23.Bc1 Ne4** [Black has a comfortable position, but Uitumen hangs on well] **24.Rf8 Bf8 25.Bf4 Bd6 26.Qg4 Bf4 27.Qf4 Qd6 28.Qd6 Nd6 29.Nc3 Nf5 30.Ne2 Ne3 31.Kf2 Nc2 32.Kf3 Kf7 33.Kf4 Kf6 34.h4 h6 35.h5 Ne1 36.g3 Nc2 37.Kg4 e5 38.de5 Ke5 39.Kf3 Nb4 40.Nc1 Kd4 41.g4 a5 42.Ne2 Ke5 43.Nc1** [D] **1/2-1/2**

Final position

642) Fischer,R-Rubinetti,J [12/2/70] Palma de Mallorca [17] B87/08 Sicilian **1.e4 c5 2.Nf3 d6 3.d4 cd4 4.Nd4 Nf6 5.Nc3 e6 6.Bc4 a6 7.Bb3 b5 8.0-0 Bb7 9.Re1 Nbd7 10.Bg5 h6 11.Bh4 Nc5?** [11...g5 must be tried] [D] **12.Bd5!** [The start of a terrific attack] **ed5 13.ed5 Kd7 14.b4 Na4 15.Na4 ba4 16.c4 Kc8 17.Qa4 Qd7 18.Qb3 g5 19.Bg3 Nh5 20.c5!** [Crushing] **dc5 21.bc5 Qd5 22.Re8 Kd7 23.Qa4 Bc6 24.Nc6 1-0**

After 11...Nc5?

After 12.h3?

643) Uhlmann,W-Fischer,R [12/3/70] Palma de Mallorca [18] A75/09 Benoni [E:Rook + minor piece] **1.d4 Nf6 2.c4 c5 3.d5 e6 4.Nc3 ed5 5.cd5 d6 6.e4 g6 7.Bf4 a6 8.a4 Bg7 9.Nf3 0-0 10.Be2 Bg4 11.0-0 Re8 12.h3?** [A known blunder] [D] **Ne4 13.Ne4 Re4 14.Bg5 Qe8 15.Bd3 Bf3 16.Qf3 Rb4** -++ [A pawn plus the famous Fischer technique] **17.Rae1 Be5 18.Qd1 Qa4 19.Qa4 Ra4 20.f4 Bd4 21.Kh1 Nd7 22.Re7 Nf6 23.Rb7 Nh5! 24.Kh2 Be3 25.Be2 Bf4 26.Bf4 Rf4 27.Rb6 Rf1 28.Bf1 Rd8 29.Ba6 Kg7 30.Bb5 Kf6 31.Bc6 Ke5 32.Rb7 Rf8 33.Re7 Kd4 34.Rd7 Nf6 0-1**

644) Fischer,R-Taimanov,M [12/6/70] Palma de Mallorca [19] B44/12 Sicilian [E:Rook + minor piece] **1.e4 c5 2.Nf3 Nc6 3.d4 cd4 4.Nd4 e6 5.Nb5 d6 6.c4 a6 7.N5c3 Nf6 8.Be2 Be7 9.0-0 0-0 10.Na3 b6 11.Be3 Bd7 12.Rc1 Qb8 13.f3 Ra7 14.Nc2 Rd8 15.Qe1 Be8 16.Qf2 Rb7 17.a4 a5!** [To create a Knight outpost at c5] **18.Nd4 Nd4 19.Bd4 Nd7 20.Qg3 Bf6!** [Active play] **21.Bf6 Nf6 22.Rfd1 e5 23.Qh4 h6 24.Rd2 Nd7 25.Bd1 Nc5 26.f4 ef4 27.Qf4 Ne6?!** [27...Re7] **28.Qg3 Qc7 29.Nd5 Qc5 30.Kh1 Bc6 31.Rc3! Ng5 32.Bc2 Bd5 33.Rd5 Qc7 34.e5 de5 35.Qe5 Rdb8 36.Bf5 Qe5 37.Re5 g6** [D] **38.h4 Nh7 39.Bg4 Nf6 40.Bf3 Rd7 41.Rb5 Rd4 42.c5 Rh4 43.Kg1 Rb4 44.Rb4! ab4 45.Rc4 bc5 46.Rc5 Kg7 47.a5 Re8 48.Rc1 Re5 49.Ra1 Re7 50.Kf2 Ne8 51.a6 Ra7 52.Ke3 Nc7 53.Bb7 Ne6 54.Ra5 Kf6 55.Kd3 Ke7 56.Kc4 Kd6 57.Rd5 Kc7 58.Kb4 1-0**

After 37...g6

645) Suttles,D-Fischer,R [12/7/70] Palma de Mallorca [20] B03/04 Alekhine's [E:Rook + minor piece] **1.e4 Nf6 2.e5 Nd5 3.d4 d6 4.c4 Nb6 5.ed6 cd6 6.Be3 g6 7.d5** [A prepared variation by Suttles, but it leads to nothing] **Bg7 8.Bd4 Bd4 9.Qd4** [The idea is that with the Bg7 traded White can attack the Kingside] **0-0 10.Nc3 e5!** =+ [Central counterpunch] **11.Qd2 f5 12.Nf3 N8d7 13.0-0-0 Qf6 14.Qh6 Qe7 15.Re1 e4 16.Nd2 Ne5 17.h3? Nbd7 18.Qe3 Qh4 19.g3 Qf6 20.Kb1 Nc5 21.f4 ef3 22.Nf3 f4! 23.gf4 Nf3 24.Qf3 Qh4 25.Be2 Bf5 26.Ka1 Rae8 27.Rc1 Be4 28.Ne4 Re4 29.Rh2 Rff4 30.Qc3 Qe7 31.Bf1 Re3 32.Qd2 Ref3 33.Re2 Qf6 34.Bg2 Rf2 35.Rce1** [D] **Re2 36.Re2 Rc4 37.Qe3 Qe5! 38.Kb1 Qe3 39.Re3 Rf4 40.Bf3 h5 41.Kc2 Kf7 42.Kd2 Rb4 43.Kc3 Rh4 44.b4 Nd7 45.Be2 Nf6 46.Rf3 Kg7 47.Rd3 g5 48.a3 g4 49.Bf1 Ne4 50.Kc2 Nf2 51.Re3 gh3 52.Re7 Kf8 0-1**

After 35.Rce1

646) Fischer,R-Mecking,H [12/8/70] Palma de Mallorca [21] A06/06 Nimzowitsch/Larsen [E:Rook + minor piece] **1.b3 d5 2.Bb2 c5 3.Nf3 Nc6?!** [Better avoided to prevent a pinning Bb5] **4.e3 Nf6 5.Bb5 Bd7 6.0-0 e6 7.d3 Be7 8.Bc6 Bc6 9.Ne5 Rc8 10.Nd2 0-0 11.f4** +=/+- [Control of e5 and the a1-h8 diagonal] **Nd7 12.Qg4 Ne5 13.Be5 Bf6 14.Rf3 Qe7 15.Raf1 a5 16.Rg3 Be5 17.fe5 f5 18.ef6 Rf6** [D] **19.Qg7** [Cleverly winning a pawn] **Qg7 20.Rf6 Qg3 21.hg3 Re8 22.g4 a4 23.Nf3 ab3 24.ab3 Kg7 25.g5 e5 26.Nh4 Bd7 27.Rd6 Be6 28.Kf2 Kf7 29.Rb6 Re7 30.e4 de4 31.de4 c4 32.b4 Bg4 33.Ke3 Rd7 34.g6 Kf8 35.gh7 Rh7 36.Ng6 Ke8 37.Ne5 Bc8 38.Nc4 Kd8 39.Nd6 Rg7 40.Kf2 Kc7 41.Nc8 Kc8 42.Rd6 1-0**

After 18...Rf6

647) Gligoric,S-Fischer,R [12/10/70] Palma de Mallorca [22]
A77/05 Benoni **1.d4 Nf6 2.c4 e6 3.Nc3 c5 4.d5 ed5 5.cd5 d6 6.Nf3
g6 7.e4 Bg7 8.Be2 0-0 9.0-0 Re8 10.Nd2 Nbd7 11.a4 Ne5 12.Qc2
g5 13.Nf3 Nf3 14.Bf3 h6** [14...Nd7 was better] **15.Bd2 a6 16.Be2
Qe7 17.Rae1** +=/+- **Qe5 18.Kh1 Qd4 19.f3 Nh5** [D] **20.Nb5?** [A
bad blunder] **ab5 21.Bb5 Qe5!** -++ **22.Bc3 Qe7 23.Be8 Qe8 24.Bg7
Kg7 25.b4 cb4 26.Qb2 Qe5 27.Qb4 Nf4 28.Rd1 b6 29.Rf2 Nd3
30.Qb6 Nf2 31.Qf2 Ra4 32.Kg1 Ra1 33.Qe1 Ra2 34.Qg3 Qb2
35.h4 Ra1 0-1**

After 19...Nh5

648) Fischer,R-Panno,O [12/12/70] Palma de Mallorca [23]
A30/00 English **1.c4** [It was rumored that Panno had intended to
withdraw from the tournament, but he came to the board before the
one hour limit had expired and resigned] **1-0**

After 1.c4

1971

649) Taimanov,M-Fischer,R [5/16/71] Candidates Match, Vancouver [1] E97/05 King's Indian **1.d4 Nf6 2.c4 g6 3.Nc3 Bg7 4.e4 d6 5.Nf3 0-0 6.Be2 e5 7.0-0 Nc6 8.d5 Ne7 9.Bd2 Ne8** [9...Nh5!?] **10.Rc1 f5** [10...c5!?] **11.ef5 gf5 12.Ng5 h6 13.Ne6 Be6 14.de6 Qc8 15.Qb3 c6! 16.Bh5 Qe6 17.Qb7 Nf6 18.Be2 Rfb8 19.Qa6 Rb2 20.Rfd1 =** [White's two Bishops are balanced by Black's extra pawn] **e4 21.Qa3 Rb7 22.Bf4 d5 23.cd5 cd5?!** [23...Ned5 ∞] **24.Nb5 Ng6 25.Nd4** [25.Nc7 Qf7 26.Na8 Nf4 =+] **Qd7 26.Qe3** [26.Qg3! +-] **Kh7 27.h3 Rf8 28.Ba6 Rb6 29.Rc7 Qa4** [D] **30.Rg7 Kg7 31.Bh6 Kf7! 32.Be2 Rfb8 33.Nf5 Rb1 34.Rb1 Rb1 35.Kh2 Qd7! 36.Nd4 Qd6 37.g3 Qb4 38.Nc6 Qb6 39.Na7 Qe3 40.Be3 Re1! 0-1**

After 29...Qa4

650) Fischer,R-Taimanov,M [5/18/71] Candidates Match, Vancouver [2] B44/05 Sicilian/Taimanov variation [E:Bishop vs. Knight] **1.e4 c5 2.Nf3 Nc6 3.d4 cd4 4.Nd4 e6 5.Nb5 d6 6.Bf4 e5 7.Be3 Nf6 8.Bg5 Qa5 9.Qd2** [Avoiding 9.Bd2 Qd8 10.Bg5 Qa5 with a draw by repetition] **Ne4 10.Qa5 Na5 11.Be3 Kd7! 12.N1c3 Nc3** [12...a6 =] **13.Nc3 Kd8 14.Nb5 Be6 15.0-0-0 b6 16.f4!** [Not 16.Na7 Kc7! 17.Nb5 Kc6] **ef4 17.Bf4 Nb7 18.Be2 Bd7 19.Rd2 Be7 20.Rhd1 Bb5 21.Bb5 Kc7 22.Re2 Bf6 23.Rde1 Rac8 24.Bc4 Rhf8 25.b4!** [Restricting the Nb7] **a5 26.Bd5 Kb8 27.a3 Rfd8 28.Bf7 Bc3 29.Bd2 d5 30.Rd1 d4 31.Bc3 Rc3 32.Kb2 [D] d3 33.Kc3 de2 34.Re1 Nd6 35.Bh5 Nb5 36.Kb2 ab4 37.ab4 Rd4 38.c3 Rh4 39.Be2 Nd6 40.Rd1 Kc7 41.h3 ++- Rf4 42.Rf1 Re4 43.Bd3 Re5 44.Rf2 h5 45.c4 Rg5 46.Kc3 Kd7 47.Ra2 Kc8 48.Kd4 Kc7 49.Ra7 Kd8 50.c5 bc5 51.bc5 Ne8 52.Ra2 Nc7 53.Bc4 Kd7 54.Rb2 Kc6 55.Bb3 Nb5 56.Ke3 Kc5 57.Kf4 Rg6 58.Bd1 h4 59.Kf5 Rh6 60.Kg5 Nd6 61.Bc2 Nf7 62.Kg4 Ne5 63.Kf4 Kd4 64.Rb4 Kc3 65.Rb5 Nf7 66.Rc5 Kd4 67.Rf5 g5 68.Kg4 Ne5 69.Kg5 Rg6 70.Kh4 Rg2 71.Bd1 Rg8 72.Bg4 Ke4 73.Kg3 Rg7 74.Rf4 Kd5 75.Ra4 Ng6 76.Ra6 Ne5 77.Kf4 Rf7 78.Kg5 Rg7 79.Kf5 Rf7 [D] 80.Rf6 Rf6 81.Kf6 Ke4 82.Bc8 Kf4 83.h4 Nf3 84.h5 Ng5 85.Bf5 Nf3 86.h6 Ng5 87.Kg6 Nf3 88.h7 Ne5 89.Kf6 1-0**

After 32.Kb2

After 79...Rf7

651) Taimanov,M-Fischer,R [5/20/71] Candidates Match, Vancouver [3] E97/05 King's Indian [E:Queen + Rook + minor pieces] **1.d4 Nf6 2.c4 g6 3.Nc3 Bg7 4.e4 d6 5.Nf3 0-0 6.Be2 e5 7.0-0 Nc6 8.d5 Ne7 9.Bd2 Ne8 10.Rc1 f5 11.Qb3 b6** [To prevent 12.c5] **12.ef5 gf5 13.Ng5 Nf6 14.f4! h6 15.fe5 de5 16.c5!?** [Planning 17.d6] **Nfd5 17.Nd5 Nd5 18.cb6 ab6** [18...hg5 19.Bg5 Qd6 20.b7 +-] **19.Rc6 Kh8 20.Nf3?!** [20.Qh3! Nf6 21.Bc3 Ng4 22.Rg6! Qe8 23.Qh5 +-] **Bb7 21.Rg6 Nf4 22.Bf4 ef4 23.Rd1 Qe7 24.Re6 Qc5 25.Kf1 Rfd8 26.Rd8 Rd8 27.Qa4 Qc1 28.Kf2 Bf8 29.b4 Be4 30.Re8?** [30.Qb5 =] **[D] Bc6 31.Qc6 Qc6 32.Rd8 Qf6! 33.Rc8 Qe7 34.Kf1 Kh7 35.Nd4 Bg7 36.Nb5 Be5 37.a3 Qd7 38.Ra8 f3! 39.gf3 Bh2 40.Kg2 Qg7 41.Kh2 Qe5 42.Kg1 0-1**

After 30.Re8?

652) Fischer,R-Taimanov,M [5/25/71] Candidates Match, Vancouver [4] B47/05 Sicilian [E:Minor piece] **1.e4 c5 2.Nf3 Nc6 3.d4 cd4 4.Nd4 Qc7 5.Nc3 e6 6.g3 a6 7.Bg2 Nf6 8.0-0 Nd4 9.Qd4 Bc5 10.Bf4! d6 11.Qd2 h6 12.Rad1 e5 13.Be3 Bg4** [13...Be3 14.fe3! Ke7 15.Rf6 ++-] **14.Bc5 dc5 15.f3 Be6 16.f4 Rd8 17.Nd5 Bd5 18.ed5 e4 19.Rfe1** [19.c4!?] **Rd5 20.Re4 Kd8 21.Qe2 Rd1 22.Qd1 Qd7 23.Qd7 Kd7 24.Re5 +=** [Bishop vs. Knight with pawns on both wings] **b6 25.Bf1 a5 26.Bc4 Rf8 27.Kg2 Kd6 28.Kf3 Nd7 29.Re3 Nb8 30.Rd3 Kc7 31.c3 Nc6 32.Re3 Kd6 33.a4!** [Fixing the weakened b5, b6] **Ne7 34.h3 Nc6 35.h4 h5 36.Rd3 Kc7 37.Rd5 f5 38.Rd2 Rf6 39.Re2 Kd7 40.Re3 g6 41.Bb5 Rd6 42.Ke2 Kd8?** [42...Kc7] **43.Rd3 Kc7 44.Rd6 Kd6 45.Kd3 Ne7 46.Be8 Kd5 47.Bf7 Kd6 48.Kc4 Kc6 49.Be8 Kb7 50.Kb5 Nc8 51.Bc6 Kc7 52.Bd5 Ne7 53.Bf7 Kb7 54.Bb3 Ka7 55.Bd1 Kb7 56.Bf3 Kc7 57.Ka6 Nc8 58.Bd5 Ne7 59.Bc4 Nc6 60.Bf7 Ne7 61.Be8 Kd8 [D] 62.Bg6! ++- Ng6 63.Kb6 Kd7 64.Kc5 Ne7 65.b4 ab4 66.cb4 Nc8 67.a5 Nd6 68.b5 Ne4 69.Kb6 Kc8 70.Kc6 Kb8 71.b6 1-0**

After 61...Kd8

653) Taimanov,M-Fischer,R [5/27/71] Candidates Match, Vancouver [5] D80/06 Grunfeld **1.d4 Nf6 2.c4 g6 3.Nc3 d5 4.Bg5 Ne4 5.Bh4 Nc3 6.bc3 dc4?!** [6...Bg7; 6...c5] **7.e3 Be6 8.Rb1 b6 9.Be2!** [Planning 9...Bg7 10.Bf3 c6 11.Ne2, 12.Nf4] **Bh6!** [Preventing the Ne2-f4 maneuver] **10.Nf3 c6 11.Ne5 Bg7 12.f4 Bd5 13.0-0 Nd7 14.Nc4 0-0 15.a4 +=/+ c6 16.Ne5 Ne5 17.de5! f6 18.Rb2 Be6 19.Rd2 Qc7 20.Bg4 Qc8 21.Bf3 Rb8 22.Qe2 Rd8 23.Rfd1 Rd2 24.Qd2** [24.Rd2] **Qe8 25.ef6 ef6 26.Qd6 Rc8 27.a5 Bf8 28.Qd2 Be7 29.Bd5 Qf7 30.Be6 Qe6 31.Qd7 Kf7 32.Qa7 ba5! 33.e4 Qc6 34.Rd7 Qe4 35.h3 a4 36.Bf2 Kf8 37.c4 a3 38.Qa3 Ra8 39.Qb2 Ke8 40.Qb5 Kf8 41.Rd1 Qf4 42.Bc5 Bc5 43.Qc5 Kg7 44.Rf1 Qe4 45.Qc7 Kh6 46.Rf6?? [D] Qd4 0-1** [47.Rf2 Ra1]

After 46.Rf6??

654) Fischer,R-Taimanov,M [6/1/71] Candidates Match, Vancouver [6] B44/03 Sicilian [E:Rook + minor piece] **1.e4 c5 2.Nf3 Nc6 3.d4 cd4 4.Nd4 e6 5.Nb5 d6 6.Bf4 e5 7.Be3 Nf6 8.Bg5 Be6 9.N1c3 a6 10.Bf6 gf6 11.Na3 Nd4** [11...d5! ∞] **12.Nc4 f5 13.ef5 Nf5 14.Bd3 Rc8 15.Bf5!** [Now 15...Bf5 16.Ne3 dominates d5 and f5] **Rc4 16.Be6 fe6 17.Qe2** [17.Qh5 Kd7 leads to nothing] **Rd4?** [17...Qc7] **18.0-0 Qg5 19.Rad1 Qf5 20.Rd4 ed4 21.Ne4 Be7? 22.Rd1 Qe5 [D]** [22...e5 23.Rd4! ed4 24.Nd6] **23.Qd3 Rf8 24.Qd4 Qd4 25.Rd4 d5 26.Nc3 Bc5 27.Rd2 Rf4 28.g3 Rc4 29.Ne2 Ra4 30.a3 Kd7 31.Kg2 b5 32.c3 a5 33.Nd4 b4 34.Nb3 Bb6 35.ab4 ab4 36.c4 Kc6 37.c5 Bc7 38.Nd4 Kd7 39.f4 e5 40.c6 Kc8 41.Nb5 Ra2 42.f5 Bd8 43.Rd5 Rb2 1-0**

After 22...Qe5

655) Fischer,R-Larsen,B [7/6/71] Candidates Match, Denver [1] C19/03 French **1.e4 e6 2.d4 d5 3.Nc3 Bb4 4.e5 Ne7 5.a3 Bc3 6.bc3 c5 7.a4 Nbc6 8.Nf3 Bd7 9.Bd3 Qc7 10.0-0 c4 11.Be2 f6 12.Re1 Ng6 13.Ba3!** [A prepared pawn sacrifice] **fe5 14.de5 Nce5 15.Ne5 Ne5 16.Qd4 Ng6 17.Bh5 Kf7 18.f4 Rhe8 19.f5 ef5 20.Qd5 Kf6** [20...Be6 21.Re6 Re6 22.Qf5 Rf6 23.Qd5 Re6 24.Rf1 ++-] **21.Bf3 Ne5 22.Qd4 Kg6 23.Re5 Qe5 24.Qd7 Rad8 25.Qb7 Qe3 26.Kf1 Rd2 27.Qc6 Re6 [D] 28.Bc5 Rf2 29.Kg1 Rg2 30.Kg2 Qd2 31.Kh1 Rc6 32.Bc6 Qc3 33.Rg1 Kf6 34.Ba7 ++-** [Outside pawn] **g5 35.Bb6 Qc2 36.a5 Qb2 37.Bd8 Ke6 38.a6 Qa3 39.Bb7 Qc5 40.Rb1 c3 41.Bb6 1-0**

After 27...Re6

After 37.Bc4?

656) Larsen,B-Fischer,R [7/8/71] Candidates Match, Denver [2] B36/08 Sicilian [E:Rook + Bishop] **1.c4 c5 2.Nf3 g6 3.d4 cd4 4.Nd4 Nc6 5.e4 Nf6 6.Nc3 d6 7.Be2 Nd4 8.Qd4 Bg7 9.Bg5 h6 10.Be3 0-0 11.Qd2 Kh7 12.0-0 Be6 = 13.f4 Rc8 14.b3 Qa5 15.a3 a6 16.f5 Bd7** [16...gf5? 17.ef5 Bf5 18.Rf5 ++-] **17.b4 Qe5!** [The Queen is safe and centralized here] **18.Rae1** [18.Bd4 Ne4] **Bc6** [18...Ne4 19.Ne4 Qe4 20.Bd3 Qc6 21.fg6 fg6 22.Bh6! Bh6 23.Re7 ++-] **19.Bf4 Ne4 20.Ne4 Qe4 21.Bd3 Qd4 22.Kh1 Rce8 23.Be3 Qc3 24.Bh6 Qd2 25.Bd2 Be5 26.Bf4 Bf4 27.Rf4 gf5 28.Rf5** [28.Re3 Rg8] **Kg7 29.Rg5 Kh6 30.h4 e6 31.Rf1 f5 32.Rb1 Rf7 33.b5 ab5 34.cb5 Bd7 35.g4 Ra8 36.gf5 ef5 37.Bc4?** [37.Rbg1 =] **[D] Ra4! 38.Rc1 Bb5 39.Bf7 Rh4 40.Kg2 Kg5 -++ 41.Bd5 Ba6 42.Rd1 Ra4 43.Bf3 Ra3 44.Rd6 Ra2 45.Kg1 Kf4 46.Bg2 Rb2 47.Rd7 b6 48.Rd8 Be2 49.Bh3 Bg4 50.Bf1 Bf3 51.Rb8 Be4 52.Ba6 Ke3 53.Rc8 Rb1 54.Kh2 Kf4 0-1**

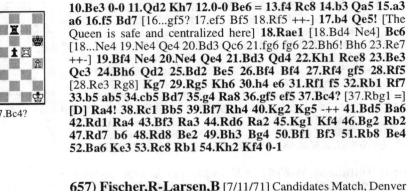

After 13...fe6

657) Fischer,R-Larsen,B [7/11/71] Candidates Match, Denver [3] B88/14 Sicilian [E:Rook + minor pieces] **1.e4 c5 2.Nf3 d6 3.d4 cd4 4.Nd4 Nf6 5.Nc3 Nc6 6.Bc4 e6 7.Bb3 Be7 8.Be3 0-0 9.f4 Bd7 10.0-0 a6 11.f5 Qc8?!** [11...Nd4 12.Bd4 b5 13.a3 Qc7 =] **12.fe6 Be6 13.Ne6 fe6 [D] 14.Na4! Rb8 15.Nb6 Qe8 16.Be6 Kh8 17.Bf5 ++- Ne5 18.Qd4 Qh5 19.Nd5 Nd5 20.Qd5 Qe2 21.Ba7 Rbe8 22.Rf2 Qb5 23.c3 Bh4 24.g3 Qd5 25.ed5 Bf6 26.Raf1 Nc4 27.Be6 Ra8 28.Bd4 Bd4 29.cd4 Rf2 30.Rf2 b5 31.Kf1 g6 32.b3 Na3 33.Ke2 Ra7 34.Rf8 Kg7 35.Rd8 b4 36.Rd6 Nb5 37.Rb6 Nd4 38.Kd3 Ne6 39.Re6 a5 40.Kd4 Kf7 41.Re2 1-0**

After 29.Kh1

658) Larsen,B-Fischer,R [7/13/71] Candidates Match, Denver [4] E97/16 King's Indian **1.c4 g6 2.Nf3 Bg7 3.d4 Nf6 4.Nc3 0-0 5.e4 d6 6.Be2 e5 7.0-0 Nc6 8.d5 Ne7 9.Nd2 c5** [9...a5; 9...Ne8; 9...Nd7] **10.Rb1 Ne8 11.b4 b6 12.a4** [12.bc5 +=] **f5 13.a5 Nf6 14.Qa4 Bd7 15.Qa3 Bh6!** [Activating the Bg7 and pressuring e4] **16.Bd3 Qc7 17.bc5 bc5 18.ef5 gf5 19.Bc2 a6! 20.Nde4? Bc1** [20.Ba4] **21.Nf6 Rf6 22.Rfc1 Raf8 23.Rb6 Bc8 24.Ne2 f4! -+** [Kingside attack] **25.Be4 Nf5 26.Rc6 Qg7 27.Rb1 Nh4 28.Qd3 Bf5 29.Kh1 [D] f3! 30.Ng3 fg2 31.Kg1 Be4 32.Qe4 Nf3 33.Kg2 Nd2 0-1**

After 18...d5

659) Fischer,R-Larsen,B [7/18/71] Candidates Match, Denver [5] B88/06 Sicilian [E:Rook + minor piece] **1.e4 c5 2.Nf3 d6 3.d4 cd4 4.Nd4 Nf6 5.Nc3 Nc6 6.Bc4 e6 7.Bb3 Be7 8.Be3 0-0 9.0-0 Bd7 10.f4 Qc8 11.f5 Nd4 12.Bd4 ef5** [12...Bc6] **13.Qf3!? fe4 14.Ne4 Ne4 15.Qe4 Be6 16.Rf3** [16.Rae1 +=] **Qc6 17.Re1 Qe4 18.Re4 d5 [D] 19.Rg3 g6 20.Bd5 Bd6?** [20...Bd5 =] **21.Re6! Bg3 22.Re7 Bd6 23.Rb7 Rac8 24.c4 a5 25.Ra7 Bc7 26.g3 Rfe8 27.Kf1 Re7 28.Bf6 Re3 29.Bc3 h5 30.Ra6! ++- Be5 31.Bd2 Rd3 32.Ke2 Rd4 33.Bc3 Rcc4 34.Bc4 Rc4 35.Kd3 Rc5 36.Ra5 Ra5 37.Ba5 Bb2 38.a4 Kf8 39.Bc3 Bc3 40.Kc3 Ke7 41.Kd4 Kd6 42.a5 f6 43.a6 Kc6 44.a7 Kb7 45.Kd5 h4 46.Ke6 1-0**

660) Larsen,B-Fischer,R [7/20/71] Candidates Match, Denver [6] B21/06 Sicilian [by transposition] **1.f4 c5 2.Nf3 g6 3.e4 Bg7 4.Be2 Nc6 5.0-0 d6 6.d3 e6 7.Na3 Nge7 8.c3 0-0 9.Be3 a6 10.d4 cd4 11.Nd4** [11.cd4 f5] **b5 12.Nc6 Nc6 13.Qd2 Qc7 14.Rad1 Rd8 15.Nc2 Rb8 16.a3 Na5 17.e5 Bf8 18.b4!?** = / ∞ **Nc6** [18...Nc4 19.Bc4 Qc4 20.Bd4, followed by Ne3-g4 +-] **19.Nd4 de5 20.fe5 Ne5 21.Bg5 Rd5! 22.Qf4 Bg7 23.h4 Rb7 24.Bf6 Bf6 25.Qf6 Qc3 26.h5 gh5 27.Kh1** [27.Ne6 +=] **Ng4 28.Bg4 hg4 29.Qh6 Bd7 30.Rf4 f5 31.Qf6** [31.Qg5 +=] **Bc8 32.Rff1 Rf7 33.Qh6 Bb7 34.Ne6 Qf6 35.Qe3 Re7 36.Rde1** [D] **Rd6 37.Qg5 Qg5 38.Ng5 Re1 39.Re1 Bd5 40.Re8 Kg7 0-1**

After 36.Rde1

661) Fischer,R-Petrosian,T [9/30/71] Candidates Match, Buenos Aires [1] B44/03 Sicilian [E:Rook + Knight] **1.e4 c5 2.Nf3 e6 3.d4 cd4 4.Nd4 Nc6 5.Nb5 d6 6.Bf4 e5 7.Be3 Nf6 8.Bg5 Be6 9.N1c3 a6 10.Bf6 gf6 11.Na3 d5!** [Specially prepared] **12.ed5** [12.Nd5 ∞] **Ba3 13.ba3 Qa5 14.Qd2 0-0-0 15.Bc4 Rhg8 16.Rd1 Bf5 =+ 17.Bd3 Bd3 18.Qd3 Nd4 19.0-0 Kb8 20.Kh1 Qa3 21.f4 Rc8 22.Ne4 Qd3 23.cd3 Rc2 24.Rd2! Rd2 25.Nd2 f5 26.fe5 Re8 27.Re1 Nc2 28.Re2 Nd4 29.Re3 Nc2 30.Rh3 Re5 31.Nf3 Rd5 32.Rh7 Rd3 33.h4 Ne3?** [33...Nd4 =] **34.Rf7 Rd1 35.Kh2 Ra1 36.h5 f4 37.Rf4 Ra2 38.Re4 Ng2 39.Kg3 Ra5 40.Ne5** [D] **1-0**

Final position

662) Petrosian,T-Fischer,R [10/5/71] Candidates Match, Buenos Aires [2] D82/05 Grunfeld **1.d4 Nf6 2.c4 g6 3.Nc3 d5 4.Bf4 Bg7 5.e3 c5 6.dc5 Qa5 7.Rc1 Ne4 8.cd5 Nc3 9.Qd2 Qa2 10.bc3 Qa5 11.Bc4 Nd7 12.Ne2 Ne5** [12...Nc5 =] **13.Ba2 Bf5 14.Be5!** [Unexpectedly giving up the Bishop, but Petrosian sees a strong initiative] **Be5 15.Nd4 Qc5 16.Nf5 gf5 17.0-0** +=/+- [f5 is weak, and White has attacking chances] **Qa5 18.Qc2 f4 19.c4 fe3 20.c5! Qd2 21.Qa4 Kf8 22.Rcd1 Qe2 23.d6! Qh5 24.f4** [D] **e2 25.fe5 ed1=Q 26.Rd1 Qe5 27.Rf1 f6 28.Qb3 Kg7 29.Qf7 Kh6 30.de7 f5 31.Rf5 Qd4 32.Kh1 1-0**

After 24.f4

663) Fischer,R-Petrosian,T [10/7/71] Candidates Match, Buenos Aires [3] C11/16 French **1.e4 e6 2.d4 d5 3.Nc3 Nf6 4.Bg5 de4 5.Ne4 Be7 6.Bf6 gf6 7.g3 f5! 8.Nc3 Bf6 9.Nge2 Nc6! 10.d5 ed5 11.Nd5 Bb2 12.Bg2 0-0 13.0-0** = / ∞ [Black has an extra pawn, but many weaknesses] **Bh8 14.Nef4 Ne5 15.Qh5 Ng6 16.Rad1 c6 17.Ne3 Qf6 18.Kh1 Bg7 19.Bh3 Ne7 20.Rd3 Be6 21.Rfd1 Bh6 22.Rd4** [Better was 22.Ne6 fe6 23.Rd7 +-] **Bf4 23.Rf4 Rad8 24.Rd8 Rd8 25.Bf5 Nf5 26.Nf5 Rd5 27.g4 Bf5 28.gf5 h6 29.h3 Kh7 30.Qe2 Qe5 31.Qh5 Qf6 32.Qe2 Re5 33.Qd3 Rd5** [33...b5! -+] [D] **1/2-1/2**

Final position

664) Petrosian,T-Fischer,R [10/12/71] Candidates Match, Buenos Aires [4] B36/05 English/Sicilian **1.c4 c5 2.Nf3 g6 3.d4 cd4 4.Nd4 Nc6 5.e4 Nf6 6.Nc3 d6 7.f3 Nd4 8.Qd4 Bg7 9.Be3 0-0 10.Qd2 Qa5 11.Rc1 Be6 12.b3** [12.Nd5, when either 12...Qa2 13.Ne7 Kh8 14.Bd4 +=, or 12...Qd2 13.Kd2 Bd5 14.cd5 += was better] **Rfc8 13.Be2 a6 14.Nd5 Qd2 15.Kd2 Nd5 16.cd5 Bd7 17.Rc8 Rc8 18.Rc1 Rc1 19.Kc1 Kf8 20.Kc2 e6** [D] **1/2-1/2**

Final position

After 17...g6

After 42.Ne2

Final position

After 33...Nf4

After 22.d5?

665) Fischer,R-Petrosian,T [10/14/71] Candidates Match, Buenos Aires [5] C42/12 Petroff [E:Minor piece] **1.e4 e5 2.Nf3 Nf6 3.Ne5 d6 4.Nf3 Ne4 5.d4 Nf6 6.Bd3** [6.c4 +=] **Be7 7.h3!** [Restricting the Bc8] **0-0 8.0-0 c6 9.Re1 Nbd7 10.Bf4 Re8 11.c4 Nf8 12.Nc3 a6 13.Qb3** [13.d5 += with more space] **Ne6 14.Bh2 Bf8 15.Re2 b5 16.Qc2 Bb7 17.Rae1 g6** [D] **18.b4 bc4 19.Bc4 Nc7! 20.Bb3 Re2 21.Re2 Ncd5 22.a3?! a5 23.Nd5 cd5!** [The doubled pawns control important squares] **24.b5 a4 25.Ba2 Qb6 26.Qb1 Ra5 27.Rb2 Ne4?** [27...Ne8 -+] **28.Bf4 Nc3 29.Qc2 Rb5 30.Rb5 Nb5 31.Qa4 Qa6 32.Qa6 Ba6 33.Be3 Na3 34.Bd5 Bc4 35.Bc6 Nc2 36.Bd2 Be2 37.Be4 Bf3 38.Bc2 1/2-1/2**

666) Petrosian,T-Fischer,R [10/17/71] Candidates Match, Buenos Aires [6] A06/04 Nimzowitsch/Larsen [E:Rook + minor piece] **1.Nf3 c5 2.b3 d5 3.Bb2?** [Allowing a strong central pawn wedge] **f6! 4.c4 d4 5.d3 e5 6.e3 Ne7 7.Be2 Nec6 8.Nbd2 Be7 9.0-0 0-0 10.e4 a6 11.Ne1 b5 12.Bg4 Bg4 13.Qg4 Qc8! 14.Qe2 Nd7 15.Nc2 Rb8 16.Rfc1 Qe8 17.Ba3 Bd6 18.Ne1 g6 -+** [Space advantage] **19.cb5 ab5 20.Bb2 Nb6 21.Nef3 Ra8 22.a3 Na5 23.Qd1 Qf7 24.a4 ba4 25.ba4 c4?!** [Too direct. 25...Rfc8 was better] **26.dc4 Nbc4 27.Nc4 Nc4 28.Qe2 Nb2 29.Qb2 Rfb8 30.Qa2 Bb4 31.Qf7 Kf7 32.Rc7 Ke6 33.g4! Bc3 34.Ra2 Rc8** [34...Rb1! -++] **35.Rc8 Rc8 36.a5 Ra8 37.a6 Ra7 38.Kf1 g5 39.Ke2 Kd6 40.Kd3 Kc5 41.Ng1 Kb5 42.Ne2** [D] **Ba5 43.Rb2 Ka6 44.Rb1 Rc7 45.Rb2 Re7 46.f3?! Ka5 47.Rc2 Rb7 48.Ra2 Kb5 49.Rb2 Bb4 50.Ra2 Rc7 51.Ra1 Rc8 52.Ra7 Ba5 53.Rd7 Bb6 54.Rd5 Bc5 55.Nc1 Ka4 56.Rd7 Bb4 57.Ne2 Kb3 58.Rb7 Ra8 59.Rh7 Ra1 60.Nd4 ed4 61.Kd4 Rd1 62.Ke3 Bc5 63.Ke2 Rh1 64.h4 Kc4 65.h5 Rh2 66.Ke1 Kd3** [D] **0-1**

667) Fischer,R-Petrosian,T [10/19/71] Candidates Match, Buenos Aires [7] B42/10 Sicilian [E:Rook + minor piece] **1.e4 c5 2.Nf3 e6 3.d4 cd4 4.Nd4 a6 5.Bd3 Nc6 6.Nc6 bc6 7.0-0 d5 8.c4 Nf6 9.cd5 cd5 10.ed5 ed5 11.Nc3 Be7 12.Qa4 Qd7! 13.Re1!** [Avoiding 13.Bb5 ab5 14.Qa8 0-0 with counterplay] **Qa4 14.Na4 Be6 15.Be3 0-0 16.Bc5 Rfe8 17.Be7 Re7 18.b4! Kf8 19.Nc5 Bc8 20.f3 Rea7 21.Re5 Bd7 22.Nd7!!** [The remaining Bishop will dominate the Knight] **Rd7 23.Rc1 Rd6 24.Rc7 Nd7 25.Re2 g6 26.Kf2 h5 27.f4 h4 28.Kf3 f5 29.Ke3 d4 30.Kd2 Nb6 31.Ree7 Nd5 32.Rf7 Ke8 33.Rb7 Nf4** [D] **34.Bc4 1-0**

668) Petrosian,T-Fischer,R [10/23/71] Candidates Match, Buenos Aires [8] D40/10 Queen's Gambit Declined **1.d4 Nf6 2.c4 e6 3.Nf3 d5 4.Nc3 c5 5.e3 Nc6 6.a3 Ne4!? 7.Qc2** [7.Bd3] **Nc3 8.bc3 Be7 9.Bb2 0-0 10.Bd3 h6 11.0-0 Na5 12.Nd2 dc4 13.Nc4 Nc4 14.Bc4 b6 15.e4** [15.d5!?] **Bb7 16.Qe2 Rc8 17.Bb3 b5 18.f4 Qb6 19.Kh1 cd4 20.cd4 b4! 21.ab4 Bb4 22.d5?** [22.Rf3 =+] [D] **Bc3 23.Bc3 Rc3! 24.Bc2 ed5 25.e5 Re3 26.Qd2 d4 27.Rab1 Qa6 28.Rf2 Rd8 29.Kg1 Be4 30.Be4 Re4 31.h3 d3 32.Rb3 Qc4 33.Rb2 Rdd4 34.g3 Rd5 35.Kh2 Rb5 36.Ra2 Rb1 37.g4 Re2 38.Re2 de2 39.Qe2 Qf4 40.Kg2 Rg3 0-1**

669) Fischer,R-Petrosian,T [10/26/71] Candidates Match, Buenos Aires [9] C10/04 French [E:Knight vs. pawns] **1.e4 e6 2.d4 d5 3.Nc3 Nc6 4.Nf3 Nf6 5.ed5 ed5 6.Bb5! Bg4 7.h3 Bf3 8.Qf3 Be7 9.Bg5 a6 10.Bc6 bc6 11.0-0 0-0 12.Rfe1** += [Better pawn structure] **h6 13.Bh4 Qd7** [13...Re8!?] **14.Re2 a5 15.Rae1 Bd8 16.b3 Rb8 17.Na4 Ne4 18.Bd8 Rbd8 19.Qf4 Qd6 20.Qd6 cd6?** [20...Nd6] **21.c4! Nf6 22.Rc1 Rb8 23.cd5 cd5 24.f3 Nh5 25.Rc6 Nf4 26.Rd2 Rfe8 27.Rd6 Re1 28.Kf2 Rh1 29.Kg3 Nh5 30.Kh4 g6 31.Rd5 Re8 32.Ra5 Ree1 33.Nc3 Nf4 34.Kg4 Ne6 35.Re5 f5 36.Kg3 f4 37.Kh4 Kh7 38.Ne4 g5 39.Kg4 Ng7 [D] 40.Ng5 hg5 41.Re1 Re1 42.Kg5 Ne6 43.Kf5 Re2 44.Re2 Nd4 45.Ke5 Ne2 46.a4 1-0**

After 39...Ng7

1972

After 29.b5

670) Spassky,B-Fischer,R [7/11/72] World Championship Match, Reykjavik [1] E56/05 Nimzo-Indian [E:Bishop vs. pawn] **1.d4 Nf6 2.c4 e6 3.Nf3 d5 4.Nc3 Bb4 5.e3 0-0 6.Bd3 c5 7.0-0 Nc6 8.a3 Ba5 9.Ne2 dc4 10.Bc4 Bb6** [10...cd4 11.ed4 h6 =] **11.dc5 Qd1 12.Rd1 Bc5 13.b4 Be7 14.Bb2 Bd7 15.Rac1** [Better is 15.e4! += with a space advantage] **Rfd8 16.Ned4 Nd4 17.Nd4 Ba4 18.Bb3 Bb3 19.Nb3 Rd1 20.Rd1 Rc8 21.Kf1 Kf8 = 22.Ke2 Ne4 23.Rc1 Rc1 24.Bc1 f6 25.Na5 Nd6 26.Kd3 Bd8 27.Nc4 Bc7 28.Nd6 Bd6 29.b5 [D] Bh2??** [29...Ke7 =] **30.g3 h5 31.Ke2 h4 32.Kf3 Ke7** [32...h3 33.Kg4 Bg1 34.Kh3 Bf2 35.Bd2! Δ 36.Kg2 ++-] **33.Kg2 hg3 34.fg3 Bg3 35.Kg3 Kd6 36.a4 Kd5 37.Ba3 Ke4 38.Bc5 a6 39.b6 f5 40.Kh4 f4 41.ef4 Kf4 42.Kh5! Kf5 43.Be3 Ke4 44.Bf2 Kf5 45.Bh4 e5 46.Bg5 e4 47.Be3 Kf6 48.Kg4 Ke5 49.Kg5! Kd5 50.Kf5 a5 51.Bf2! g5 52.Kg5 Kc4 53.Kf5 Kb4 54.Ke4 Ka4 55.Kd5 Kb5 56.Kd6 1-0**

671) Fischer,R-Spassky,B [7/13/72] World Championship Match, Reykjavik [2] Awarded to Spassky by forfeit **0-1**

After 11.Qc2

672) Spassky,B-Fischer,R [7/16/72] World Championship Match, Reykjavik [3] A77/03 Benoni **1.d4 Nf6 2.c4 e6 3.Nf3 c5 4.d5 ed5 5.cd5 d6 6.Nc3 g6 7.Nd2 Nbd7 8.e4 Bg7 9.Be2 0-0 10.0-0 Re8 11.Qc2 [D]** [11.a4 +=] **Nh5?!** [Sacrificing pawn structure for the Bishop pair] **12.Bh5 gh5 13.Nc4 Ne5 14.Ne3 Qh4! 15.Bd2** [Better was 15.f3] **Ng4 16.Ng4 hg4 17.Bf4 Qf6 18.g3?!** [Weakening. Better was 18.Bg3] **Bd7 19.a4 b6** [19...a6 20.a5] **20.Rfe1 a6 21.Re2 b5 =+/-+** [The Queenside pawn roller and White's Kingside weaknesses] **22.Rae1 Qg6 23.b3 Re7 24.Qd3 Rb8 25.ab5 ab5 26.b4 c4 27.Qd2 Rbe8 28.Re3 h5 29.R3e2 Kh7 30.Re3 Kg8 31.R3e2 Bc3 32.Qc3 Re4 33.Re4 Re4 34.Re4 Qe4 35.Bh6 Qg6 36.Bc1 Qb1 37.Kf1 Bf5 38.Ke2 Qe4 39.Qe3 Qc2 40.Qd2 Qb3 41.Qd4 Bd3 0-1**

After 24...Be3

673) Fischer,R-Spassky,B [7/18/72] World Championship Match, Reykjavik [4] B88/15 Sicilian [E:Bishop + pawn] **1.e4 c5 2.Nf3 d6 3.d4 cd4 4.Nd4 Nf6 5.Nc3 Nc6 6.Bc4 e6 7.Bb3 Be7 8.Be3 0-0 9.0-0 a6 10.f4 Nd4 11.Bd4 b5 12.a3** [12.e5 de5 13.fe5 Nd7 14.Ne4 =] **Bb7 13.Qd3 a5 14.e5 de5 15.fe5 Nd7 16.Nb5 Nc5! 17.Bc5 Bc5 =+** [Black has the Bishop pair and attacking chances for the pawn] **18.Kh1 Qg5 19.Qe2 Rad8 20.Rad1 Rd1 21.Rd1 h5 22.Nd6 Ba8 23.Bc4 h4 24.h3 Be3 [D] 25.Qg4 Qe5 26.Qh4 g5 27.Qg4 Bc5 28.Nb5 Kg7 29.Nd4 Rh8** [29...Bd6!?; 29...Rd8 -+] **30.Nf3 Bf3 31.Qf3 Bd6 32.Qc3 Qc3 33.bc3 Be5 34.Rd7 Kf6 35.Kg1 Bc3 36.Be2 Be5 37.Kf1 Rc8 38.Bh5 Rc7 39.Rc7 Bc7 40.a4 Ke7 41.Ke2 f5 42.Kd3 Be5 43.c4 Kd6 44.Bf7 Bg3 45.c5 1/2-1/2**

674) Spassky,B-Fischer,R [7/20/72] World Championship Match, Reykjavik [5] E41/10 Nimzo-Indian **1.d4 Nf6 2.c4 e6 3.Nc3 Bb4 4.Nf3 c5 5.e3 Nc6 6.Bd3 Bc3** [Nimzowitschian strategy: doubled pawns vs. two Bishops] **7.bc3 d6 8.e4 e5 9.d5 Ne7 10.Nh4 h6 11.f4 Ng6 12.Ng6 fg6 13.fe5 ?!** [13.Qe1 =] **de5 14.Be3 b6 15.0-0 0-0 16.a4 a5 17.Rb1 Bd7 18.Rb2 Rb8 19.Rbf2 Qe7 20.Bc2 g5!** =-/-+ **21.Bd2 Qe8 22.Be1 Qg6 23.Qd3 Nh5 24.Rf8 Rf8 25.Rf8 Kf8 26.Bd1 Nf4 27.Qc2??** [D] **Ba4 0-1**

After 27.Qc2??

675) Fischer,R-Spassky,B [7/23/72] World Championship Match, Reykjavik [6] D59/07 Queen's Gambit Declined **1.c4 e6 2.Nf3 d5 3.d4 Nf6 4.Nc3 Be7 5.Bg5 0-0 6.e3 h6 7.Bh4 b6 8.cd5 Nd5 9.Be7 Qe7 10.Nd5 ed5 11.Rc1 Be6 12.Qa4 c5 13.Qa3 Rc8 14.Bb5 a6?!** [14...Qb7! =] **15.dc5 bc5 16.0-0 Ra7 17.Be2 Nd7 18.Nd4 Qf8 19.Ne6 fe6 20.e4! d4** [20...Nf6 or 20...c4 was better] **21.f4 Qe7 22.e5 Rb8 23.Bc4 Kh8** [23...Nb6 24.Qb3] **24.Qh3 Nf8 25.b3 a5 26.f5!** [The decisive breakthrough] **ef5 27.Rf5 Nh7 28.Rcf1 Qd8 29.Qg3 Re7 30.h4 Rbb7 31.e6 Rbc7 32.Qe5 Qe8 33.a4 Qd8 34.R1f2 Qe8 35.R2f3 Qd8 36.Bd3 Qe8 37.Qe4 Nf6** [D] **38.Rf6! gf6 39.Rf6 Kg8 40.Bc4 Kh8 41.Qf4 1-0**

After 37...Nf6

676) Spassky,B-Fischer,R [7/25/72] World Championship Match, Reykjavik [7] B97/25 Sicilian [E:Rook + Knight] **1.e4 c5 2.Nf3 d6 3.d4 cd4 4.Nd4 Nf6 5.Nc3 a6 6.Bg5 e6 7.f4 Qb6 8.Qd2 Qb2 9.Nb3 Qa3 10.Bd3 Be7 11.0-0 h6 12.Bh4?!** [12.Bf6 Bf6 13.e5 =] **Ne4 13.Ne4 Bh4 14.f5 ef5** [D] **15.Bb5 ab5 16.Nd6 Kf8!** [16...Ke7 17.Nb5 is too dangerous] **17.Nc8 Nc6 18.Nd6 Rd8 19.Nb5 Qe7 20.Qf4 g6 21.a4 Bg5** [Better was 21...Kg7 -+] **22.Qc4 Be3 23.Kh1 f4 24.g3! g5 25.Rae1 Qb4 26.Qb4 Nb4 27.Re2 Kg7 28.Na5 b6 29.Nc4 Nd5 30.Ncd6 Bc5?** [30...Kg6] **31.Nb7 Rc8? [31...Ne3!] 32.c4! Ne3 33.Rf3 Nc4 34.gf4 g4 35.Rd3 h5 36.h3 Na5 37.N7d6! Bd6 38.Nd6 Rc1 39.Kg2 Nc4 40.Ne8! Kg6 41.h4 f6 42.Re6 Rc2 43.Kg1 Kf5 44.Ng7 Kf4 45.Rd4 Kg3 46.Nf5 Kf3 47.Ree4 Rc1 48.Kh2 Rc2 49.Kg1 1/2-1/2**

After 14...ef5

677) Fischer,R-Spassky,B [7/27/72] World Championship Match, Reykjavik [8] A39/07 English [E:Rook + minor piece] **1.c4 c5 2.Nc3 Nc6 3.Nf3 Nf6 4.g3 g6 5.Bg2 Bg7 6.0-0 0-0 7.d4 cd4 8.Nd4 Nd4 9.Qd4 d6 10.Bg5** [10.Qd3; 10.Qd2] **Be6 11.Qf4 Qa5 12.Rac1 Rab8 13.b3 Rfc8 14.Qd2 a6 15.Be3 b5?** [D] [Losing the Exchange] **16.Ba7 bc4 17.Bb8 Rb8 18.bc4 Bc4 19.Rfd1 Nd7?? 20.Nd5! ++- Qd2 21.Ne7 Kf8 22.Rd2 Ke7 23.Rc4 Rb1 24.Bf1 Nc5 25.Kg2 a5 26.e4 Ba1 27.f4 f6 28.Re2 Ke6 29.Rec2 Bb2 30.Be2 h5 31.Rd2 Ba3 32.f5 gf5 33.ef5 Ke5 34.Rcd4 Kf5 35.Rd5 Ke6 36.Rd6 Ke7 37.Rc6 1-0**

After 15...b5

After 9.Bc4

678) Spassky,B-Fischer,R [8/1/72] World Championship Match, Reykjavik [9] D41/20 Queen's Gambit Declined **1.d4 Nf6 2.c4 e6 3.Nf3 d5 4.Nc3 c5 5.cd5 Nd5 6.e4 Nc3 7.bc3 cd4 8.cd4 Nc6 9.Bc4 [D] b5 10.Bd3** [10.Be2 +=] **Bb4 11.Bd2 Bd2** [11...a6! =] **12.Qd2 a6 13.a4 0-0 14.Qc3 Bb7 15.ab5 ab5 16.0-0** [16.Ra8 Qa8 17.Bb5 Na7] **Qb6 17.Rab1 b4 18.Qd2 Nd4 19.Nd4 Qd4 20.Rb4 Qd7 21.Qe3 Rfd8 22.Rfb1 Qd3 23.Qd3 Rd3 24.Rb7 g5 25.Rb8 Rb8 26.Rb8 Kg7 27.f3 Rd2 28.h4 h6 29.hg5 1/2-1/2**

After 29...Re7

679) Fischer,R-Spassky,B [8/3/72] World Championship Match, Reykjavik [10] C95/15 Ruy Lopez [E:Rook + minor piece] **1.e4 e5 2.Nf3 Nc6 3.Bb5 a6 4.Ba4 Nf6 5.0-0 Be7 6.Re1 b5 7.Bb3 d6 8.c3 0-0 9.h3 Nb8 10.d4 Nbd7 11.Nbd2 Bb7 12.Bc2 Re8 13.b4 Bf8 14.a4 Nb6 15.a5 Nbd7 16.Bb2 Qb8 17.Rb1!** [Veiled threats against the Qb8] **c5 18.bc5 dc5 19.de5 Ne5 20.Ne5 Qe5 21.c4 Qf4 22.Bf6! Qf6 23.cb5 Red8** [23...Rad8] **24.Qc1 Qc3 25.Nf3 Qa5? 26.Bb3!** [Suddenly White has attacking chances,and will target f7] **ab5 27.Qf4 Rd7 28.Ne5 Qc7 29.Rbd1 Re7** [29...Rd1 30.Bf7 Kh8 31.Ng6] **[D] 30.Bf7 Rf7 31.Qf7 Qf7 32.Nf7 Be4** [32...c4 was better] **33.Re4 Kf7 34.Rd7 Kf6 35.Rb7 Ra1 36.Kh2 Bd6 37.g3 b4 38.Kg2 h5 39.Rb6 Rd1 40.Kf3 Kf7 41.Ke2 Rd5 42.f4! g6 43.g4 hg4 44.hg4 g5 45.f5 Be5 46.Rb5 Kf6 47.Reb4 Bd4 48.Rb6 Ke5 49.Kf3! Rd8 50.Rb8 Rd7 51.R4b7 Rd6 52.Rb6 Rd7 53.Rg6 Kd5 54.Rg5 Be5 55.f6 Kd4 56.Rb1 1-0**

After 23...fg4

680) Spassky,B-Fischer,R [8/6/72] World Championship Match, Reykjavik [11] B97/24 Sicilian **1.e4 c5 2.Nf3 d6 3.d4 cd4 4.Nd4 Nf6 5.Nc3 a6 6.Bg5 e6 7.f4 Qb6 8.Qd2 Qb2 9.Nb3 Qa3 10.Bf6 gf6 11.Be2 h5 12.0-0 Nc6 13.Kh1 Bd7 14.Nb1 Qb4 15.Qe3 d5** [Better was 15...Ne7 16.c4 f5! 17.a3 Qa4 18.Nc3 Qc6 -+] **16.ed5 Ne7 17.c4 Nf5 18.Qd3 h4 19.Bg4! ++-** [Now White has a powerful attack] **Nd6 20.N1d2 f5 21.a3! Qb6 22.c5 Qb5 23.Qc3! fg4 [D] 24.a4 h3 25.ab5 hg2 26.Kg2 Rh3 27.Qf6! Nf5 28.c6 Bc8 29.de6 fe6 30.Rfe1 Be7 31.Re6 1-0**

After 52.Re1

681) Fischer,R-Spassky,B [8/8/72] World Championship Match, Reykjavik [12] D66/04 Queen's Gambit **1.c4 e6 2.Nf3 d5 3.d4 Nf6 4.Nc3 Be7 5.Bg5 h6 6.Bh4 0-0 7.e3 Nbd7 8.Rc1 c6 9.Bd3 dc4 10.Bc4 b5 11.Bd3 a6 12.a4 ba4!** [12...b4 13.Bf6 Nf6 14.Ne4 +- with pressure on Black's weak pawns] **13.Na4 Qa5 14.Nd2 Bb4 15.Nc3 c5 16.Nb3 Qd8 17.0-0 cd4 18.Nd4 Bb7 19.Be4! Qb8 20.Bg3** [20.Nc6+= netting the Bishop pair was best] **Qa7 21.Nc6 Bc6 22.Bc6 Rac8 23.Na4 Rfd8 24.Bf3** [24.Qf3] **a5! 25.Rc6 Rc6 26.Bc6 Rc8 27.Bf3 Qa6 28.h3 Qb5 29.Be2 Qc6 30.Bf3 Qb5 31.b3?! Be7 32.Be2 Qb4 33.Ba6 Rc6 34.Bd3 Nc5 35.Qf3 Rc8 36.Nc5 Bc5 37.Rc1 Rd8 38.Bc4 Qd2 39.Rf1 Bb4 40.Bc7 Rd7 41.Qc6 Qc2 42.Be5 Rd2 43.Qa8 Kh7 44.Bf6 gf6 45.Qf3 f5 46.g4 Qe4 47.Kg2 Kg6 48.Rc1 Ba3 49.Ra1 Bb4 50.Rc1 Be7 51.gf5 ef5 52.Re1 [D] Rf2 53.Kf2 Bh4 54.Ke2 Qf3 55.Kf3 Be1 1/2-1/2**

682) Spassky,B-Fischer,R [8/10/72] World Championship Match, Reykjavik [13] B04/14 Alekhine's [E:Rook + minor piece] **1.e4 Nf6 2.e5 Nd5 3.d4 d6 4.Nf3 g6 5.Bc4 Nb6 6.Bb3 Bg7 7.Nbd2?!** [7.Ng5+=] **0-0 8.h3 a5 9.a4** [9.a3] **de5 10.de5 Na6!** [Going after a weak pawn] **11.0-0 Nc5 12.Qe2** [D] **Qe8 13.Ne4 Nba4 14.Ba4 Na4 15.Re1 Nb6 16.Bd2 a4 17.Bg5 h6 18.Bh4 Bf5 19.g4 Be6** [19...Be4] **20.Nd4 Bc4 21.Qd2 Qd7 22.Rad1 Rfd8 23.f4 Bd5 24.Nc5 Qc8 25.Qc3** [Better was 25.e6! Nc4 26.Qe2 Nb2 27.Nf5! with good attacking chances] **e6 26.Kh2 Nd7 27.Nd3 c5 28.Nb5 Qc6 29.Nd6 Qd6 30.ed6 Bc3 31.bc3 f6** [31...a3] **32.g5 hg5** [32...c4! -++] **33.fg5 f5 34.Bg3 Kf7 35.Ne5 Ne5 36.Be5 b5 37.Rf1 Rh8 38.Bf6 a3 39.Rf4 a2 40.c4 Bc4 41.d7 Bd5 42.Kg3 Ra3 43.c3 Rha8! 44.Rh4 e5! 45.Rh7 Ke6 46.Re7 Kd6 47.Re5 Rc3 48.Kf2 Rc2 49.Ke1 Kd7 50.Red5 Kc6 51.Rd6 Kb7 52.Rd7 Ka6 53.R7d2 Rd2 54.Kd2 b4 55.h4! Kb5 56.h5 c4! 57.Ra1 gh5 58.g6 h4 59.g7 h3 60.Be7 Rg8 61.Bf8 h2 62.Kc2 Kc6 63.Rd1 b3 64.Kc3 h1=Q 65.Rh1 Kd5 66.Kb2 f4 67.Rd1 Ke4 68.Rc1 Kd3 69.Rd1?** [69.Rc3 =] **Ke2 70.Rc1 f3 71.Bc5 Rg7 72.Rc4 Rd7 73.Re4 Kf1 74.Bd4 f2** [D] **0-1**

After 12.Qe2

Final position

683) Fischer,R-Spassky,B [8/15/72] World Championship Match, Reykjavik [14] D37/14 Queen's Gambit [E:Rook + pawn] **1.c4 e6 2.Nf3 d5 3.d4 Nf6 4.Nc3 Be7 5.Bf4 0-0 6.e3 c5 7.dc5 Nc6 8.cd5 ed5 9.Be2 Bc5 10.0-0 Be6** = [The isolated pawn is compensated by excellent development] **11.Rc1 Rc8 12.a3 h6 13.Bg3 Bb6 14.Ne5 Ne7! 15.Na4 Ne4 16.Rc8 Bc8 17.Nf3 Bd7 18.Be5 Ba4 19.Qa4 Nc6 20.Bf4?** [20.Bd4 Nd4 21.Nd4 =] **Qf6! 21.Bb5 Qb2 22.Bc6 Nc3 23.Qb4 Qb4 24.ab4 bc6 25.Be5 Nb5 26.Rc1 Rc8 27.Nd4** [D] **f6?? 28.Bf6! Bd4 29.Bd4 Nd4 30.ed4 Rb8 31.Rc6 Rb4 32.Kf1 Rd4 33.Ra6 Kf7 34.Ra7 Kf6 35.Rd7 h5 36.Ke2 g5 37.Ke3 Re4 38.Kd3 Ke6 39.Rg7 Kf6 40.Rd7 Ke6 1/2-1/2**

After 27.Nd4

684) Spassky,B-Fischer,R [8/17/72] World Championship Match, Reykjavik [15] B99/17 Sicilian **1.e4 c5 2.Nf3 d6 3.d4 cd4 4.Nd4 Nf6 5.Nc3 a6 6.Bg5 e6 7.f4 Be7 8.Qf3 Qc7 9.0-0-0 Nbd7 10.Bd3 b5 11.Rhe1 Bb7 12.Qg3 0-0-0** [12...b4 ∞] **13.Bf6** [13.Bb5! ab5 14.Ndb5 Qb6 15.e5 d5 16.f5 +-] **Nf6** [13...Bf6 14.Bb5!] **14.Qg7 Rdf8 15.Qg3 b4 16.Na4 Rhg8 17.Qf2 Nd7! 18.Kb1 Kb8 19.c3 Nc5 20.Bc2 bc3 21.Nc3 Bf6 22.g3 h5 23.e5 de5 24.fe5 Bh8 25.Nf3 Rd8 26.Rd8 Rd8 27.Ng5** [27.Re3 +-] **Be5 28.Qf7 Rd7 29.Qh5 Bc3 30.bc3 Qb6 31.Kc1** [31.Ka1] **Qa5 32.Qh8 Ka7 33.a4 Nd3 34.Bd3 Rd3 35.Kc2 Rd5?** [Overlooking 35...Rd8 36.Qe5 Qa4 37.Kb1 Rd5 -++] **36.Re4 Rd8 37.Qg7 Qf5 38.Kb3 Qd5 39.Ka3 Qd2 40.Rb4 Qc1 41.Rb2 Qa1 42.Ra2 Qc1 43.Rb2 Qa1** [D] **1/2-1/2**

Final position

685) Fischer,R-Spassky,B [8/20/72] World Championship Match, Reykjavik [16] C69/16 Ruy Lopez [E:Rook + pawn] **1.e4 e5 2.Nf3 Nc6 3.Bb5 a6 4.Bc6 dc6 5.0-0 f6 6.d4 Bg4 7.de5 Qd1 8.Rd1 fe5 9.Rd3 Bd6 10.Nbd2 Nf6 11.Nc4 Ne4 12.Nce5** [12.Nfe5 Be6 13.f3 +=] **Bf3 13.Nf3 0-0 14.Be3 b5 15.c4** [Better was 15.Nd2! Nc5 16.Bc5 Bc5 17.Ne4 Bb6 18.Kf1 +=] **Rab8 16.Rc1 bc4 17.Rd4 Rfe8 18.Nd2 Nd2 19.Rd2 Re4 20.g3 Be5 21.Rcc2 Kf7 22.Kg2 [D] Rb2 23.Kf3! c3 24.Ke4 cd2 25.Rd2 Rb5 26.Rc2 Bd6 27.Rc6 Ra5 28.Bf4! Ra4 29.Kf3 Ra3 30.Ke4 Ra2 31.Bd6 cd6 32.Rd6 Rf2 33.Ra6 Rh2 34.Kf3 Rd2 35.Ra7 Kf6 36.Ra6 Ke7 37.Ra7 Rd7 38.Ra2 Ke6 39.Kg2 Re7 40.Kh3 Kf6 41.Ra6 Re6 42.Ra5 h6 43.Ra2 Kf5 44.Rf2 Kg5 45.Rf7 g6 46.Rf4 h5 47.Rf3 Rf6 48.Ra3 Re6 49.Rf3 Re4 50.Ra3 Kh6 51.Ra6 Re5 52.Kh4 Re4 53.Kh3 Re7 54.Kh4 Re5 55.Rb6 Kg7 56.Rb4 Kh6 57.Rb6 Re1 58.Kh3 Rh1 59.Kg2 Ra1 60.Kh3 Ra4 1/2-1/2**

After 22.Kg2

686) Spassky,B-Fischer,R [8/22/72] World Championship Match, Reykjavik [17] B09/06 Pirc [E:Rook + minor piece] **1.e4 d6 2.d4 g6 3.Nc3 Nf6 4.f4 Bg7 5.Nf3 c5 6.dc5 Qa5 7.Bd3 Qc5 8.Qe2 0-0 9.Be3 Qa5 10.0-0 Bg4 11.Rad1** [11.h3!?] **Nc6 12.Bc4 Nh5 13.Bb3** [13.Rd5!?] **Bc3** [Grabbing a dangerous pawn, a Fischer characteristic] **14.bc3 Qc3 15.f5 Nf6 16.h3 Bf3 17.Qf3 Na5 18.Rd3 Qc7 19.Bh6 Nb3 20.cb3 Qc5 21.Kh1 [D] Qe5?** [21...Rfc8 22.Bg5 Qe5 +=] **22.Bf8 Rf8 23.Re3 Rc8 24.fg6 hg6 25.Qf4 Qf4 26.Rf4 Nd7 27.Rf2 Ne5 28.Kh2 Rc1 29.Ree2 Nc6 30.Rc2 Re1 31.Rfe2 Ra1 32.Kg3? Kg7 33.Rcd2 Rf1 34.Rf2 Re1 35.Rfe2 Rf1 36.Re3 a6 37.Rc3 Re1 38.Rc4 Rf1 39.Rdc2 Ra1 40.Rf2 Re1 41.Rfc2 g5 42.Rc1 Re2 43.R1c2 Re1 44.Rc1 Re2 45.R1c2 1/2-1/2**

After 21.Kh1

687) Fischer,R-Spassky,B [8/24/72] World Championship Match, Reykjavik [18] B69/02 Sicilian **1.e4 c5 2.Nf3 d6 3.Nc3 Nc6 4.d4 cd4 5.Nd4 Nf6 6.Bg5 e6 7.Qd2 a6 8.0-0-0 Bd7 9.f4 Be7 10.Nf3 b5 11.Bf6 gf6 12.Bd3** [12.f5 Qb6 =] **Qa5 13.Kb1 b4 14.Ne2 Qc5 15.f5 a5 16.Nf4 a4 17.Rc1** [Maneuvering to blockade Black's attack] **Rb8 18.c3 b3 19.a3 Ne5 20.Rhf1** [20.fe6 fe6 21.Nd4 +=/+/-] **Nc4 21.Bc4 Qc4 =** [Two Bishops plus strong center pawns vs. pressure on e6 and the King position] **22.Rce1 Kd8!** [Running away from the danger zone] **23.Ka1 Rb5 24.Nd4 Ra5 25.Nd3 Kc7 26.Nb4 h5 27.g3 Re5 28.Nd3 Rb8 29.Qe2 Ra5 30.fe6 fe6 31.Rf2 e5! 32.Nf5 Bf5 33.Rf5 d5 34.ed5 Qd5 [34...Rd8] 35.Nb4 Qd7 36.Rh5 Bb4 37.cb4 Rd5 38.Rc1?!** [38.Rh4] **Kb7 39.Qe4 Rc8 40.Rb1 Kb6 41.Rh7 Rd4! 42.Qg6 Qc6 43.Rf7 Rd6 44.Qh6 Qf3 45.Qh7 Qc6 46.Qh6 Qf3 47.Qh7 Qc6 [D] 1/2-1/2**

Final position

688) Spassky,B-Fischer,R [8/27/72] World Championship Match, Reykjavik [19] B05/13 Alekhine's [E:Rook + pawn] **1.e4 Nf6 2.e5 Nd5 3.d4 d6 4.Nf3 Bg4 5.Be2 e6 6.0-0 Be7 7.h3 Bh5 8.c4 Nb6 9.Nc3 0-0 10.Be3 d5** [Fixing the d-pawn before pressuring it] **11.c5 Bf3** [11...N6d7 12.Rc1 b6 13.c6!] **12.Bf3 Nc4 13.b3 Ne3 14.fe3 b6** [14...Nc6 15.Rb1 a5 16.a3 b6 17.b4 ab4 18.ab4 bc5 19.bc5 Ra3 =] **15.e4 c6 16.b4 bc5 17.bc5 Qa5 18.Nd5! Bg5! 19.Bh5** [Better was 19.h4 Bh4 20.Ne3 +-] **cd5 20.Bf7 Rf7 21.Rf7 Qd2!** [21...Be3 22.Kh1 Kf7 23.Qh5 Ke7 24.Rf1 Nd7 25.Qf7 Kd8 26.c6] **22.Qd2 Bd2 23.Raf1 Nc6 24.ed5 ed5 25.Rd7 Be3 26.Kh1 Bd4 27.e6 Be5 28.Rd5 Re8 29.Re1 Re6** [D] **30.Rd6 Kf7 31.Rc6 Rc6 32.Re5 Kf6 33.Rd5 Ke6 34.Rh5 h6 35.Kh2 Ra6 36.c6 Rc6 37.Ra5 a6 38.Kg3 Kf6 39.Kf3 Rc3 40.Kf2 Rc2 1/2-1/2**

After 29...Re6

689) Fischer,R-Spassky,B [8/29/72] World Championship Match, Reykjavik [20] B68/03 Sicilian [E:Minor piece] **1.e4 c5 2.Nf3 Nc6 3.d4 cd4 4.Nd4 Nf6 5.Nc3 d6 6.Bg5 e6 7.Qd2 a6 8.0-0-0 Bd7 9.f4 Be7 10.Be2 0-0 11.Bf3** [11.Nf3!?] **h6** [11...Qc7!?] **12.Bh4 Ne4 13.Be7 Nd2 14.Bd8 Nf3 15.Nf3 Rfd8 16.Rd6 Kf8 17.Rhd1 Ke7 18.Na4 Be8 19.Rd8 Rd8 =** [D] **20.Nc5 Rb8 21.Rd3 a5 22.Rb3 b5 23.a3 a4 24.Rc3** [24.Re3 Rd8 25.f5 Rd5] **Rd8 25.Nd3 f6 26.Rc5 Rb8 27.Rc3 g5! 28.g3 Kd6 29.Nc5 g4 30.Ne4 Ke7 31.Ne1 =+** [Spassky has outplayed Fischer, but White's position is solid enough to draw] **Rd8 32.Nd3 Rd4 33.Nef2 h5 34.Rc5 Rd5 35.Rc3** [35.Rd5] **Nd4 36.Rc7 Rd7 37.Rd7 Bd7 38.Ne1 e5 39.fe5 fe5 40.Kd2 Bf5 41.Nd1 Kd6 42.Ne3 Be6 43.Kd3 Bf7 44.Kc3 Kc6 45.Kd3 Kc5 46.Ke4 Kd6 47.Kd3 Bg6 48.Kc3 Kc5 49.Nd3 Kd6 50.Ne1 Kc6 51.Kd2 Kc5 52.Nd3 Kd6 53.Ne1 Ne6 54.Kc3 Nd4 1/2-1/2**

After 19...Rd8

690) Spassky,B-Fischer,R [8/31/72] World Championship Match, Reykjavik [21] B46/06 Sicilian [E:Rook vs. Bishop + pawns] **1.e4 c5 2.Nf3 e6 3.d4 cd4 4.Nd4 a6 5.Nc3 Nc6 6.Be3 Nf6 7.Bd3 d5!** [Fischer's innovation, supposedly based on an old Adolf Anderssen game!] **8.ed5 ed 9.0-0 Bd6 10.Nc6 bc6 11.Bd4 0-0 12.Qf3 Be6 13.Rfe1 c5! 14.Bf6 Qf6 15.Qf6 gf6 =+** [The Bishop pair and strong c-and d-pawns outweigh the doubled f-pawns] **16.Rad1 Rfd8 17.Be2 Rab8 18.b3 c4 [D] 19.Nd5 Bd5 20.Rd5 Bh2 21.Kh2 Rd5 22.Bc4 Rd2! 23.Ba6 Rc2 24.Re2 Re2 25.Be2 Rd8 26.a4 Rd2 27.Bc4 Ra2 28.Kg3 Kf8 29.Kf3 Ke7 30.g4?** [30.Ke3 =] **f5 31.gf5 f6 32.Bg8 h6 33.Kg3 Kd6 34.Kf3?** [34.f4] **Ra1 35.Kg2 Ke5 36.Be6 Kf4 37.Bd7 Rb1 38.Be6 Rb2 39.Bc4 Ra2 40.Be6 h5?!** [40...Kg4 is more accurate] **41.Bd7 0-1**

After 18...c4

MISSING TOURNAMENT GAMES

1 = Won by Fischer
1/2-1/2 = draw
0 = Lost by Fischer

US Junior Championship, 1955

691) Rd 5 Stone,K **1/2-1/2 score not available**
692) Rd 6 Briska,J **1/2-1/2** score not available
693) Rd 8 Blair,R **1/2-1/2** score not available
694) Rd 9 Winkleman,J **1/2-1/2** score not available
695) Rd 10 Saksena,F **1** score not available

Greater New York City Open, 1956

696) Rd 1 Opponent's name and score not available
697) Rd 2 Opponent's name and score not available
698) Rd 3 Opponent's name and score not available
699) Rd 4 Opponent's name and score not available
700) Rd 5 Opponent's name and score not available
701) Rd 6 Opponent's name and score not available
702) Rd 7 Hays,R score not available

Metropolitan League, 1956. Fischer played for Manhattan "A"

703) Rd 1 Opponent's name and score not available
704) Rd 2 Opponent's name and score not available
705) Rd 3 Opponent's name and score not available
706) Rd 4 Opponent's name and score not available
707) Rd 5 Opponent's name and score not available

Manhattan Chess Club "A" Reserves, 1956

708 - 718) Rd 1 - Rd 11 names, scores and results not available

US Amateur Championship, 1956

719) Rd 1 Tilles,M **1/2-1/2** score not available
720) Rd 2 Bacardi,J.F. **1** score not available
721) Rd 3 Hurttlen,N **1/2-1/2** score not available
722) Rd 4 Klaroff,S **1** score not available
723) Rd 6 Rigler,R.R. **1** score not available

US Junior Championship, 1956

724) Rd 1 Feuerstein,A **1/2-1/2** score not available
725) Rd 3 Whisler,W **1** score not available
726) Rd 4 Geller,S **1** score not available
727) Rd 5 Baylor,G **1** score not available
728) Rd 6 Henin,C **0** score not available
729) Rd 7 Weldon,C **1** score not available

730) Rd 8 Friedman **1** score not available
731) Rd 10 Kerman,D **1** score not available

Canadian Open, 1956

732) Rd 1 Lepine,G **1** score not available
733) Rd 3 Boyer,J **1** score not available
734) Rd 5 Judzentavicius **1** score not available

Log Cabin Independent Open, 1957

735) Rd 2 Faust,E **1** score not available
736) Rd 3 Hoeflin,E **1** score not available
737) Rd 4 Sobel,C **1** score not available

Log Cabin 50-50, 1957

738) Rd 1 name, result and score not available

New Western Open, Milwaukee, 1957

739) Rd 7 Tautvaisas,P **1/2-1/2** score not available

US Open, Cleveland, 1957

740) Rd 1 Gregg,D **1** score not available

Metropolitan League, New York, 1957

741) Match 1 name and score not available
742) Match 2 name and score not available
743) Match 3 name and score not available
744) Match 4 name and score not available

Match vs. Benninson,D, 1957 (Fischer 3 1/2 - 1 1/2)

745) G1   score not available
746) G2   score not available
747) G3   score not available
748) G4   score not available
749) G5   score not available

North Central Open, Milwaukee, 1957

750) Rd 7 Szedlacsek,L **1/2-1/2** (12-1-57) score not available

Match vs. Matulovic, 1958

751) G2   score not available
752) G3   score not available
753) G4   score not available

New York State Open, 1963

754) Rd 7 Name and score not available

Exhibition and Blitz Games

Bobby Fischer's results in exhibition and blitz games are as impressive as those in serious tournament play. This section includes the very few recorded blitz games of Fischer's career. Bobby seems as invincible at five-minute chess as in other forms of chess. His blitz games at Herceg Novi, Yugoslavia, (The "unofficial" World Speed Chess Championship) in 1970 (games 782-803) and at the Manahattan Chess Club blitz tournament of August, 1971, (games 804-825) were played at the height of his powers and reveal a quality of play to be envied by any chessplayer at any speed.

After 16...Kd8

755) Fischer,R-Fine,R [1963] Skittles, New York, Evans Gambit **1.e4 e5 2.Nf3 Nc6 3.Bc4 Bc5 4.b4 Bxb4 5.c3 Ba5 6.d4 ed4 7.0-0 dc3 8.Qb3 Qe7 9.Nc3 Nf6 10.Nd5 Nd5 11.ed5 Ne5 12.Ne5 Qe5 13.Bb2 Qg5 14.h4! Qh4 15.Bg7 Rg8 16.Rfe1 Kd8** [D] **17.Qg3!! 1-0**

After 29...Kb7

756) Fischer,R-Darga,K [10/60] Berlin Team Tournament C19/00 French **1.e4 e6 2.d4 d5 3.Nc3 Bb4 4.e5 c5 5.a3 Bc3 6.bc3 Ne7 7.a4 Qc7 8.Nf3 b6 9.Bb5 Bd7 10.Bd3 Nbc6 11.0-0 c4 12.Be2 f6 13.Ba3 fe5 14.de5 Ne5 15.Re1 N7c6 16.Ne5 Ne5 17.f4 Nc6 18.Bg4 0-0-0 19.Be6 Be6 20.Re6 Rd7 21.f5 Nd8 22.Re3 Qf4 23.Rf3 Qe4 24.a5 Nc6 25.ab6 ab6 26.Qb1 Kc7 27.Bc1 Qe1 28.Rf1 Qc3 29.Bf4 Kb7** [D] **30.Qb5! 1-0**

After 8.Ne5

757) Larsen,B-Fischer,R [1962] Exhibition game, Danish Television Bird's Opening **1.f4 Nf6 2.Nf3 g6 3.d3 d5 4.Nbd2 d4 5.c3 dc3 6.bc3 Nd5 7.Qa4 Nc6 8.Ne5** [D] **Bg7** [8...Nc3 9.Qc4 Ne5 10.Qc3; or if 9...Nd5 10.Nc6] **9.Ne4 Nb6 10.Qb3 Ne5 11.fe5 Be5 12.Qb5 Nd7 13.Bh6 c6 14.Qb3 Nf6 15.Bg7 Rg8 16.Bf6 ef6 17.d4 f5 18.Nf2 Bf4 19.e4 fe4 20.Bc4 Rg7 21.0-0 b5** [Better was 21...Be3!] **22.Ne4 bc4 23.Qc4 Be3 24.Kh1 Bf5 25.Qc6 Kf8 26.Nd6 Rb8 27.Qc5 Qb6 28.Qe5 Bg5 29.Rae1 Qd8** [29...Bd7 30.Rf7!] **30.g4 Bf6 31.Qd5 Be7 32.gf5 Qd6 33.Qd6 Bd6 34.f6 Rg8 35.c4 g5 36.c5 Bf4 37.h4 Rg6** [Not 37...h6? 38.h5! and the Black Rook is locked in] **38.d5 Rf6 39.hg5 Bg5 40.d6 Rc8 41.Rf6 Bf6 42.d7 Rc5 43.Re8 Kg7 44.d8=Q Bd8 45.Rd8 Rc1 46.Kg2 Rc2 47.Kg3 Ra2 0-1**

After 21...Nf8

758) Fischer,R-Andersson,U [9/70] Exhibition Game, Siegen, Nimzowitsch/Larsen **1.b3 e5 2.Bb2 Nc6 3.c4 Nf6 4.e3 Be7 5.a3 0-0 6.Qc2 Re8 7.d3 Bf8 8.Nf3 a5 9.Be2 d5 10.cd5 Nd5 11.Nbd2 f6 12.0-0 Be6 13.Kh1 Qd7 14.Rg1 Rad8 15.Ne4 Qf7 16.g4 g6 17.Rg3 Bg7 18.Rag1 Nb6 19.Nc5 Bc8 20.Nh4 Nd7 21.Ne4 Nf8** [D] **22.Nf5 Be6 23.Nc5 Ne7 24.Ng7 Kg7 25.g5 Nf5 26.Rf3 b6 27.gf6 Kh8 28.Ne6 Re6 29.d4 ed4 30.Bc4 d3 31.Bd3 Rd3 32.Qd3 Rd6 33.Qc4 Ne6 34.Be5** [Brilliant would have been 34.Rf5!! gf5 35.Rg7 Qf8 36.Qe6!! Re6 37.f7! winning immediately] **Rd8 35.h4 Nd6 36.Qg4 Nf8 37.h5 Ne8 38.e4 Rd2 39.Rh3 Kg8 40.hg6 Ng6 41.f4 Kf8 42.Qg5 Nd6 43.Bd6 1-0**

The "BEAT BOBBY FISCHER" Contest

After the Monaco, 1967 tournamant, Fischer traveled on to the Philippines to play in a scheduled international tournament. The fact that several players did not arrive in time for the main tournament gave the sponsor, MERALCO, an idea. They decided to hold a "Beat Bobby Fischer" contest. Bobby played eight individual games against the strongest Filipino players, scoring seven and a half points. Time control was forty moves in two and a half hours. Fischer also played an exhibition game with Pascual, in which each player had one hour to complete the entire game.

759) Fischer,R-Naranja,R [4/67] Philippines "Beat Bobby Fischer" contest, Sicilian [E: Rook + pawn] **1.e4 c5 2.Nc3!?** [Fischer had never been known to play this move before, but played it against Matulovic at Skopje, 1967 (1-0), and against Bertok at Zagreb, 1970 (1-0)] **Nc6 3.Nge2 e5?! 4.Nd5! Nf6 5.Nec3 Be7 6.Bc4 0-0 7.d3 h6 8.f4 d6 9.f5 b6 10.h4! Bb7 11.a3!** [Retaining the attacking light-squared Bishop in case of ...Na4] **Rc8 12.Nf6 Bf6 13.Qh5 Ne7** [D] **14.Bg5! d5 15.Bf6 dc4! 16.Qg4 g6 17.dc4 Qd6 18.Be7 Qe7 19.fg6 fg6 20.Qg6 Qg7 21.Qg7 Kg7 22.Rd1 Rcd8 23.Rd8 Rd8 24.Nd5 b5 25.cb5 Bd5 26.ed5 c4 27.a4 Rd5 28.Ke2 Rd4 29.Rd1 Re4 30.Kf3 Rf4 31.Ke3 c3 32.b3 1-0**

After 13...Ne7

760) Fischer,R-Rodriguez,R [4/67] Philippines, "Beat Bobby Fischer" contest, Sicilian **1.e4 c5 2.Nf3 e6 3.d3 Nc6 4.g3 Nge7 5.Bg2 g6 6.0-0 Bg7 7.c3 d5 8.Qe2 0-0 9.e5! f5 10.ef6!** [Opening the position] **Bf6 11.Bh6 Re8 12.g4 e5 13.h3 Qc7 14.c4 e4 15.de4 de4** [D] **16.Ng5! Nd4 17.Qe4 Bd7 18.Nc3 Bc6 19.Qd3 Bg2 20.Kg2 Rad8 21.Nge4 Qc6 22.Rfe1 Kh8 23.Rad1 Ndf5! 24.Nd5 Nh4 25.Kf1 Ng8 26.Nef6 Re1 27.Re1 Nf6 28.Qc3! 1-0**

After 15...de4

761) Reyes,R-Fischer,R [4/67] Philippines, "Beat Bobby Fischer" contest, Sicilian **1.e4 c5 2.Nf3 d6 3.d4 cd4 4.Nd4 Nf6 5.Nc3 a6 6.Bg5 e6 7.g3 Be7 8.Be3 b5 9.a3 Bb7 10.Bg2 Nbd7 11.Qe2 Rc8 12.Rd1** [D] **Rc3 13.bc3 Ne4 14.Be4 Be4 15.0-0 Qa8!** [Positioning for the attack; White is very weak on the light squares] **16.f3 Bd5 17.Rf2 0-0 18.Re1 Rc8 19.Bd2 Bd8 20.Qd1 Bb6 21.Be3** [Stopping ...e5] **Rc3 22.Nf5 ef5 23.Bb6 Nb6 24.Qd4 Rc6 25.Re7 Be6 26.Re2 Qf8 27.Rb7 Nc4 28.h4 h5 29.g4 Ne5 30.Re3 hg4 31.fg4 f4! 32.Rc3 Rc4! 33.Qd2 Qc8 0-1** [Time]

After 12.Rd1

762) Bandal,R-Fischer,R [4/67] Philippines, "Beat Bobby Fischer" contest, Benoni [E: Bishop + pawn] **1.d4 Nf6 2.c4 c5 3.d5 e6 4.Nc3 ed5 5.Nd5 Nd5 6.Qd5 Nc6 7.Nf3 d6 8.Ng5 Qe7!** [8...Qc7? 9.Nh7! Rh7 (9...Be6 10.Qe4)10.Qe4 +-] **9.Qe4 h6 10.Qe7 Be7 11.Ne4 Be6 12.Bf4 Nb4! 13.Kd2 0-0-0 14.a3 Nc6 15.e3 d5 16.Nc3 dc4 17.Ke1 a6 18.Be2 Bf6 19.Bf3 Ne5 20.Be5 Be5 21.Ke2 b5 22.Rac1 Kc7 23.Rhd1 Kb6 24.Rc2 Rd1 25.Kd1 Rd8 26.Kc1 27.Nd1 ba3 28.ba3 Rd3 29.Nb2 Rb3 30.Rb2 Ka5 31.Ra2** [D] **c3 32.Be2 Ba2! 33.Bd3 Bb3 34.f4 c4 35.Be4 Ka4 36.Bd5 Ka3 37.Bf7 Kb4 38.e4 a5 39.e5 a4 40.Bg6 a3 41.Bb1 c2 42.Bc2 a2 43.Kb2 c3 0-1**

After 31.Ra2

After 27...Ke7

After 28...Kd7

After 24...Rd7

After 33...Qb2

After 12...e5

763) Balinas,R-Fischer,R [4/67] Philippines "Beat Bobby Fischer" contest Sicilian [E:Rook + minor piece] 1.e4 c5 2.Nf3 d6 3.d4 cd4 4.Nd4 Nf6 5.Nc3 a6 6.g3 g6 7.Bg2 Bg7 8.0-0 0-0 9.h3 Bd7 10.Nde2 Nc6 11.b3 b5 12.Be3 Qc8 13.Kh2 Qc7 14.Nd5 Nd5 15.ed5 Nd8 16.Bd4 Rc8 17.Bg7 Kg7 18.Qd4 Kg8 19.c3 e5 20.de6 fe6 21.Rad1 Nf7 22.f4 Qc5 23.Qc5 Rc5 24.Rd3 Rfc8 25.Rfd1 a5 26.g4 Kf8 27.Re3 Ke7 [D] 28.Bd5 Kf6 29.g5 Ke7 [29...Kf5?? 30.Be4#] 30.c4 Nd8 31.Nd4 bc4 32.bc4 Kf7 33.Rde1 ed5 34.Re7 Kf8 35.Rd7 Rc4 36.Ree7 Rd4 37.Rh7 Kg8 38.Rhg7 Kf8 39.Rh7 1/2-1/2

764) Fischer,R-Lontoc,R [4/67] Philippines, "Beat Bobby Fischer" contest Sicilian 1.e4 c5 2.Nf3 d6 3.d4 cd4 4.Nd4 Nf6 5.Nc3 a6 6.Bc4 e6 7.Bb3 Be7 8.f4 Nbd7 9.Qf3 h5 10.Be3 Qc7 11.0-0-0 Nc5 12.f5 e5 13.Nde2 Nb3 14.ab3 b5 15.Bg5! Bb7 16.Bf6 Bf6 17.Nd5 Bd5 18.Rd5 Rc8 19.Qd3 Ke7 20.Kb1 h4 21.Rd1 Rhd8 22.c3 Qb6 23.b4 Rc6 24.Ng1! Bg5 25.Nf3 f6 26.g3! hg3 27.Ng5 fg5 28.Qg3 Kd7 [D] 29.Qe5 Kc7 30.Qg7 Rd7 31.Qg5 1-0

765) Fischer,R-Vister,M [4/67] Philippines, "Beat Bobby Fischer" contest, Pirc/Modern 1.e4 c6 2.d3 d6 3.f4 Nf6 4.Nf3 g6 5.g3 Bg7 6.Bg2 Nbd7 7.0-0 Qb6 8.Kh1 Ng4 9.d4 Ndf6 10.Nc3 h5 11.h3 Nh6 12.Nh4 Bd7 [Planning 13...0-0-0] 13.e5 de5 14.fe5 Nfg8 15.Na4 Qc7 16.Nc5 0-0-0 17.Bf4 Bf5 18.e6 Qb6 19.ef7 Nf6 [19...Nf7 20.Nf5 gf5 21.Ne6] 20.Bh6 Bh6 21.Nf5 gf5 22.Qe2 Qb2 23.Qe6 Nd7 24.Nd7 Rd7 [D] 25.Qh6 Rdd8 26.Qe6 Rd7 27.Rab1 Qc3 28.Rf5 Qd4 29.Bc6 1-0

766) Fischer,R-Badilles,G [4/67] Philippines, "Beat Bobby Fischer" contest, Sicilian 1.e4 c5 2.Nf3 e6 3.d4 cd4 4.Nd4 Nc6 5.Nb5 d6 6.Bf4 e5 7.Be3 a6 8.N5c3 Nf6 9.Bc4 Be7 10.Nd5 Nd5 11.Bd5 0-0 12.Nc3 Kh8 13.0-0 Be6 14.Bb3! [Making room for the Knight on d5] Na5 15.Nd5 Nb3 16.ab3 Bd5 17.Qd5 Qc7 18.c3 g5 19.Ra4 Rad8 20.Rb4 Rd7 21.Rb6 Kg7 22.Ra1 f5 23.ef5 Rf5 24.Ra4 Rf8 25.Rc4! Qb8 26.Rcb4 Qa8 27.c4! a5 28.R4b5 a4 29.Rb7 ab3 30.h4 Rb7 31.Rb7 Rf7 32.Bg5 Qa1 33.Kh2 Qb2 [D] 34.Qe6! Qf2 35.Re7! 1-0 [35...Re7 36.Bh6 Kh8 37.Qc8; 35...b2 36.Bh6 Kh8 37.Re8 Rf8 38.Rf8 Qf8 39.Bf8 b1=Q 40.Qf6]

767) Fischer,R-Pascual [4/67] Philippines, Exhibition game Sicilian [Played at game - 60 minutes for each player] 1.e4 c5 2.Nf3 d6 3.d4 cd4 4.Nd4 Nf6 5.Nc3 Nc6 6.Bc4 e6 7.Be3 Be7 8.Qe2 a6 9.0-0-0 Qc7 10.Bb3 Bd7 11.g4 Nd4 12.Bd4 e5 [D] 13.g5 ed4 14.gf6 dc3 15.fe7 cb2 16.Kb1 Ke7 17.Qh5! g6 18.Qh4 f6 19.e5! de5 20.f4 e4 21.Qh6 Rae8 22.Rd4 Kd8 23.Rhd1 Kc8 [23...Re7 24.Be6!! Re6 25.Qg7] 24.Rd7 Qd7 25.Rd7 Kd7 26.Qg7 Kd6 27.Qb7 e3 28.Qb6 1-0

The following fragments are from a two-game exhibition match played between Fischer and Jude Acers as Bobby's 1964 tour took him through Louisiana. The games were played at the home of Don L. Wagner in Baton Rouge.

768) Acers,J-Fischer,R [3/64] Baton Rouge **1.e4 e5 2.Nf3 Nc6 3.Bc4 g6 4.d4 ed4 5.Nd4 Bg7 6.Be3 Nge7 7.Nc3 0-0 8.f3 Re8 9.Qd2** [D] **d5!** and later **0-1**

769) Fischer,R-Acers,J [3/64] Baton Rouge, Sicilian **1.e4 c5 2.Nf3 Nc6 3.d4 cd4 4.Nd4 e5 5.Nb5 a6 6.N5a3** and later **1-0** on time.

After 9.Qd2

Fischer beats the Greenblatt Computer

770) Greenblatt Computer Program-Fischer,R [1977] Sicilian **1.e4 c5 2.Nf3 d6 3.d4 cd4 4.Nd4 Nf6 5.Nc3 a6 6.Be2 e5 7.Nb3 Be7 8.Be3 0-0 9.Qd3 Be6 10.0-0 Nbd7 11.Nd5 Rc8 12.Ne7 Qe7 13.f3 d5 14.Nd2 Qb4 15.Nb3 de4 16.Qd1 Nd5 17.Ba7 b6 18.c3 Qe7 19.fe4 Ne3 20.Qd3 Nf1 21.Qa6 Ne3 22.Bb6 Qg5 23.g3 Ra8 24.Ba7 h5 25.Qb7 h4 26.Kf2 hg3 27.hg3 f5 28.ef5 Rf5 29.Ke1 Raf8 30.Kd2 Nc4 31.Kc2 Qg6 32.Qe4 Nd6 33.Qc6 Rf2 34.Kd1 Bg4 35.Bf2** [D] **Qd3 36.Kc1 Be2 37.Nd2 Rf2 38.Qd7 Rf1 39.Nf1 Qd1# 0-1**

After 35.Bf2

771) Fischer,R-Greenblatt Computer Program [1977] King's Gambit **1.e4 e5 2.f4 ef4 3.Bc4 d5 4.Bd5 Nf6 5.Nc3 Bb4 6.Nf3 0-0 7.0-0 Nd5 8.Nd5 Bd6 9.d4 g5** [D] **10.Ng5! Qg5 11.e5 Bh3 12.Rf2 Be5 13.de5 c6 14.Bf4 Qg7 15.Nf6 Kh8 16.Qh5 Rd8 17.Qh3 Na6 18.Rf3 Qg6 19.Rc1 Kg7 20.Rg3 Rh8 21.Qh6# 1-0**

After 9...g5

772) Greenblatt Computer Program-Fischer,R [1977] Sicilian [E:Rook vs. Bishops] **1.e4 c5 2.Nf3 g6 3.d4 Bg7 4.Nc3 cd4 5.Nd4 Nc6 6.Be3 Nf6 7.Nc6 bc6 8.e5 Ng8 9.f4 f6 10.ef6 Nf6 11.Bc4 d5 12.Be2 Rb8 13.b3 Ng4 14.Bd4 e5 15.fe5 0-0 16.Bg4 Qh4 17.g3 Qg4 18.Qg4 Bg4 19.Rf1 Rf1 20.Kf1 c5 21.Bf2 Be5 22.Be1 Rf8 23.Kg2 Rf3 24.h3** [D] **Rc3 25.Bc3 Bc3 26.Rf1 Bf5 27.Rf2 h5 28.Re2 Kf7 29.Re3 Bd4 30.Rf3 Ke6 31.c3 Be5 32.Re3 d4 33.cd4 cd4 34.Re1 d3 35.h4 d2 36.Rd1 Bc3 37.Kf2 Bg4 38.Rh1 Bd4 39.Kg2 Kd5 40.a3 Ke4 41.Rf1 Kd3 42.Kh2 Ke2 43.Kg2 Bh3 44.Kh3 Kf1 45.g4 d1=Q 46.Kh2 Qe2 47.Kh3 Qg2# 0-1**

After 24.h3

Consultation Games

773) Fischer,R & Evans,L.M.-Gersch [1960] New York Queen's Gambit Declined **1.d4 d5 2.c4 e6 3.Nc3 Nf6 4.Bg5 Nbd7 5.Nf3 c6 6.e3 Qa5 7.Nd2 Bb4 8.Qc2 Ne4 9.Nde4 de4 10.Bf4 0-0 11.Be2** [D] **e5 12.de5 Ne5 13.0-0 Bc3 14.bc3 Bf5 15.Qb3 b6 16.Rfd1 Rfd8 17.Rd4 Nd3 18.Bg3 c5 19.Rd5 Be6 20.f3 Bd5 21.cd5 c4 22.Qc4 Qd5 23.Qd5 Rd5 24.fe4 Rdd8 25.e5 Rac8 26.Rd1 Rc3 27.Bh4 Rd7 28.Be1 Rc1 29.Rc1 Nc1 30.Bc4 Rc7 31.Bd5 Nd3 32.Bd2 Rc2 33.e6 Rd2 34.e7 Rd1# 0-1**

After 11.Be2

After 14...Rfd8

774) Fischer/Barden,L-Penrose/Clarke [1961] London Radio B81/00 Sicilian [E:Rook + Bishop] **1.e4 c5 2.Nf3 e6 3.d4 cd4 4.Nd4 Nf6 5.Nc3 d6 6.g4 h6 7.h3 Nc6 8.Be3 Bd7 9.Qd2 Nd4 10.Qd4 Qa5 11.0-0-0 Bc6 12.Kb1 Be7 13.Bg2 0-0 14.Qd2 Rfd8 [D] 15.Nd5 Qd2 16.Ne7 Kf8 17.Bd2 Ke7 18.Rhe1 Rac8 19.c4 Nd7 20.b3 e5 21.Be3 Nc5 22.f3 b6 23.h4 Ne6 24.Bf1 f6 25.h5 Be8 26.Kb2 Bf7 27.a4 Rb8 28.a5 Nc5 29.Ra1 Rd7 30.Kc3 ba5 31.Bc5 dc5 32.Ra5 Rc7 33.Rea1 Rbb7 34.Rb1 Be8 35.b4 cb4 36.Rb4 Rb4 37.Kb4 Rb7 38.Kc3 Bf7 39.Bd3 Kd7 40.c5 Rb3 41.Kc2 Rb7 42.Bb5 Kd8 43.Bc6 Rc7 44.Bd5 Be8 45.Kb3 Bd7 46.Kc4 Ke7 1/2-1/2** (Adjudicated by Max Ewue)

Blitz Games (Five-minute chess)

New York Blitz, 1963

After 35...g4

775) Fischer,R-Benko,P [1963] New York Blitz Caro Kann [E: Queen vs. Rook] **1.e4 c6 2.d4 d5 3.Nc3 de4 4.Ne4 Nd7 5.Nf3 Ngf6 6.Nf6 Nf6 7.Bc4 Bf5 8.Qe2 e6 9.Bg5 Be7 10.0-0-0 0-0 11.Ne5 h6 12.Bf6 Bf6 13.f4 Qc7 14.g4 Bh7 15.h4 b5 16.Bd3 Be5 17.Bh7 Kh7 18.fe5 c5 19.Qb5 cd4 20.Rd4 Rab8 21.Qe2 Kg8 22.Rhd1 Qa5 23.a3 Rb5 24.Qd2 Qd2 25.R1d2 Re5 26.b4 g5 27.hg5 hg5 28.Rd7 a5 29.Rc7 ab4 30.ab4 Re4 31.b5 Rg4 32.c4 Rb8 33.Kc2 Rg1 34.Rdd7 Rf1 35.Kb3 g4 [D] 36.Rd4 f5 37.Rdd7 Rh1 38.Kb4 Kh8 39.Rg7 Rh3 40.c5 g3 41.b6 f4 42.Rg4 e5 43.b7 Rh1 44.Rc8 Kh7 45.Rb8 Rb1 46.Kc4 f3 47.Rg3 f2 48.Rf3 f1=Q 49.Rf1 Rf1 50.Rh8 Kh8 51.b8=Q 1-0**

After 13.e5

776) Fine,R-Fischer,R [1963] New York Blitz Nimzo-Indian **1.d4 Nf6 2.c4 e6 3.Nc3 Bb4 4.e3 d5 5.Nge2 dc4 6.a3 Bd6 7.e4 e5 8.f4 ed4 9.Qd4 Nc6 10.Qc4 0-0 11.Be3 Be6 12.Qd3 Na5 13.e5 [D] Be5 14.Qb5 Bc3 15.Nc3 c6 16.Qg5 Bc4 17.Rd1 Qe8 18.Kf2 Bf1 19.Rhf1 Nc4 20.Bc5 Ne4 21.Ne4 Qe4 22.Kg1 f6 23.Qg4 Rf7 24.Rd4 Qe3 25.Kh1 Qb3 26.Qe6 Nd2 27.Qd6 Nf1 28.Qd8 Rf8 0-1**

After 9...0-0

777) Fischer,R-Fine,R [1963] New York Blitz Philidor's Defense **1.e4 e5 2.Nf3 d6 3.d4 Nd7 4.Bc4 c6 5.0-0 Be7 6.de5 de5 7.Qe2 Ngf6 8.Rd1 Qc7 9.Ng5 0-0 [D] 10.Bf7! 1-0** [10...Rf7 11.Qc4]

After 16...Bh6

778) Fine,R-Fischer,R [1963] New York Blitz Grunfeld **1.d4 Nf6 2.c4 g6 3.Nc3 d5 4.Bf4 Bg7 5.e3 0-0 6.Qb3 c6 7.Rc1 dc4 8.Bc4 b5 9.Be2 Be6 10.Qc2 b4 11.Na4 Qd5 12.b3 Nh5 13.Bf3 Qa5 14.Ne2 Bd5 15.e4 Nf4 16.Nf4 Bh6 [D] 17.ed5 Bf4 18.dc6 Bc1 19.Qc1 Na6 20.0-0 Nc7 21.Re1 e6 22.Re5 Nd5 23.Bd5 ed5 24.h4 Rac8 25.h5 Qb5 26.c7 Qd7 27.Qe3 Rc7 28.Nc5 Qg4 29.h6 Rc6 30.Rd5 Rf6 31.Nd7 Re6 32.Re5 Qd1 33.Kh2 Re5 34.Qe5 1-0**

779) Fischer,R-Reuben,S [1963] New York Blitz Sicilian **1.e4 c5 2.Nf3 Nc6 3.d4 cd4 4.Nd4 g6 5.Be3 Bg7 6.Nc3 Nf6 7.Bc4 0-0 8.Bb3 a6 9.h4 b5 10.h5 b4 11.Nd5 Ne4 12.hg6 hg6 13.Qg4 e6 14.Qh3 f5 15.0-0-0 Na5 16.Qh7 Kf7 17.Rh6 Nb3 18.ab3 Rh8 19.Qg6 Kg8 20.Rh8 Kh8 21.Rh1 Kg8 [D] 22.Rh7 Qf8 23.Bh6 1-0**

After 21...Kg8

780) Reuben,S-Fischer,R [1963] New York Blitz English [E:King + pawn] **1.c4 Nf6 2.Nc3 d5 3.cd5 Nd5 4.g3 g6 5.Bg2 Nb6 6.Nf3 Bg7 7.d3 0-0 8.Be3 Nc6 9.0-0 e5 10.Qd2 f5 11.Bh6 f4 12.Bg7 Kg7 13.Ne4 h6 14.Rad1 g5 15.d4 ed4 16.Nd4 Ne5 17.Nf3 Qd2 18.Rd2 Nec4 19.Rc2 Bf5 20.Nfd2 Rae8 21.Nc4 Be4 22.Be4 Re4 23.Nb6 cb6 24.gf4 gf4 25.Rfc1 Rf7 26.f3 Re3 27.Kf2 Rfe7 28.Rd1 Kg6 29.Rd3 Rd3 30.ed3 Re3 31.Rd2 Kf5 32.d4 Ke6 33.Re2 Re2 34.Ke2 Kd5 35.Kd3 a5 36.a4 Kc6 37.Ke4 b5 38.ab5 Kb5 39.d5 [D] Kb6 40.Ke5 Kc7 41.Kf4 b5 42.Ke5 b4 43.f4 a4 44.Kd4 a3 45.ba3 ba3 46.Kc3 Kd6 47.Kb3 Kd5 48.Ka3 Ke4 49.Kb3 Kf4 50.Kc3 Kg4 51.Kd3 Kh3 52.Ke3 Kh2 53.Kf2 ½-½**

After 39.d5

Santa Monica Blitz, 1966

781) Fischer,R-Larsen,B [1966] Santa Monica Blitz Alekhine's Defense **1.e4 Nf6 2.e5 Nd5 3.d4 d6 4.Nf3 de5 5.Ne5 Nd7 6.Nf7 Kf7 7.Qh5 Ke6 8.Qg4 Kf7 9.Qh5 Ke6 10.Qg4 Kd6 11.c4 N7f6 12.Qg3 Ke6 13.cd5 Qd5 14.Nc3 Qd4 15.Be3 Qb4 16.a3 Qb2 17.Bc4 Kd7 18.Rd1 Ke8 [D] 19.Nb5 1-0**

After 18...Ke8

Herceg Novi Yugoslavia Blitz, April 8, 1970

Bobby's most famous blitz exhibition was the great Herceg Novi, Yugoslavia, double round-robin contest in 1970, against many of the world's strongest players (blitz and otherwise). Bobby wasn't known as a "blitz demon" at the time and was not expected to win with the likes of Tal, Korchnoi, and Petrosian present. When the show was over, however, he had scored 19 points out of a possible 22, with only one loss, (to Korchnoi) while Tal took second with 14 1/2, and Korchnoi third with 14. Below are the games in the order they were played.

782) Tal,M-Fischer,R [4/8/70] Herceg Novi Blitz [1] Sicilian [E: Rook + pawn] **1.e4 c5 2.Nf3 d6 3.Nc3 e5 4.Bc4 Be7 5.d3 Nf6 6.0-0 Nc6 7.Ne1 0-0 8.f4 a6 9.a4 ef4 10.Bf4 Be6 11.Be6 fe6 12.Bg3 Qb6 13.Qd2 Ng4 14.Nf3 Nd4 15.Rab1 Nf3 16.gf3 Ne5 17.Kg2 Ng6 18.Ne2 Nh4 19.Bh4 Bh4 20.b4 Qc7 21.bc5 dc5 22.a5 Rf6 23.f4 Raf8 24.Rb6 [D] Bg5 25.e5 Rf5 26.Re6 Qf7 27.Rd6 Bf4 28.Rf4 Rf4 29.Nf4 Qf4 30.Qf4 Rf4 31.Rd7 Ra4 32.e6 Kf8 33.Rf7 Ke8 34.Rg7 Ra5 35.Rb7 Ra2 36.Kf3 Rc2 37.Rh7 c4 38.d4 c3 39.d5 Rd2 40.Ke4 c2 41.Rc7 Kd8 42.Rc4 a5 43.h4 a4 44.Ke5 a3 45.d6 Re2 46.Kf5 Rf2 47.Kg4 a2 48.d7 Ke7 49.Rc8 Rd2 50.Re8 Kf6 51.e7 Rd7 0-1**

After 24.Rb6

After 17...Nc7

After 30...e4

After 32.ef5

After 25...Rdc8

After 10.Ne1

783) Fischer,R-Tal,M [4/8/70] Herceg Novi Blitz [2] Irregular [E: Rook + Bishop] 1.g3 g6 2.Bg2 Bg7 3.Nf3 c5 4.c3 Nf6 5.0-0 0-0 6.d4 d6 7.dc5 dc5 8.Qd8 Rd8 9.Be3 Na6 10.Na3 Nd5 11.Rfd1 Bg4 12.Bd2 h6 13.h3 Be6 14.Nb5 Ndc7 15.a4 Bb3 16.Rdc1 Nb5 17.ab5 Nc7 [D] 18.Be3 Nb5 19.Bc5 b6 20.Be7 Re8 21.Ba3 Rad8 22.e3 a5 23.Nd4 Na3 24.Ra3 Bc4 25.Bf1 Bd5 26.Bg2 Bc4 27.Ra4 Bd3 28.b4 ab4 29.Rb4 Rd6 30.Rd1 Bc2 31.Rd2 Bf5 32.Rdb2 Rd8 33.Rb6 Rb6 34.Rb6 Rc3 35.Nf5 gf5 36.Bd5 Rc7 37.Rb5 Re7 38.Bc4 Re5 39.Rb7 Kh7 40.Rf7 Kg6 41.Rc7 Bf8 42.Rc6 Kg7 43.Bd3 Be7 44.Bc2 Ra5 45.Kg2 1-0

784) Fischer,R-Ivkov,B [4/8/70] Herceg Novi Blitz [3] Pirc 1.e4 d6 2.d4 g6 3.Nf3 Bg7 4.c3 Nf6 5.Bd3 0-0 6.0-0 Nc6 7.Qe2 e5 8.h3 Nh5 9.Bg5 Bf6 10.Be3 Bg7 11.Nbd2 Re8 12.d5 Ne7 13.c4 Nf4 14.Bf4 ef4 15.Rab1 Nf5 16.b4 a5 17.ba5 Ra5 18.Nb3 Ra8 19.c5 h6 20.Bb5 Bd7 21.a4 Bb5 22.ab5 Nh4 23.cd6 cd6 24.Nh4 Qh4 25.Nd2 Bd4 26.Qf3 Ra2 27.Nc4 Qf6 28.Rbd1 Bc5 29.e5 de5 30.d6 e4 [D] 31.d7 Rd8 32.Qe4 f3 33.Qf3 Qf3 34.gf3 Rc2 35.Na5 Be7 36.Nb7 Rc7 37.Nd8 Bd8 38.Rfe1 1-0

785) Ivkov,B-Fischer,R [4/8/70] Herceg Novi Blitz [4] King's Indian 1.Nf3 Nf6 2.g3 g6 3.Bg2 Bg7 4.0-0 0-0 5.c4 d6 6.d4 Nbd7 7.Nc3 e5 8.e4 ed4 9.Nd4 Nc5 10.h3 a5 11.Re1 Re8 12.Bg5 h6 13.Bf4 Nfd7 14.Qd2 Ne5 15.Bf1 Ne6 16.Ne6 Nf3 17.Kg2 Ne1 18.Re1 Be6 19.Bh6 Bh6 20.Qh6 Qf6 21.Qd2 a4 22.f4 Qe7 23.g4 c6 24.Qd4 f6 25.Rd1 Rad8 26.Na4 c5 27.Qd3 Kg7 28.Nc3 Rh8 29.Qd2 Rh4 30.a3 Rdh8 31.Kg3 f5 32.ef5 [D] Rh3 33.Bh3 Qh4 34.Kf3 Qh3 35.Ke2 Bc4 36.Kf2 Qh2 0-1

786) Smyslov,V-Fischer,R [4/8/70] Herceg Novi Blitz [5] English [E: Rook + pawn] 1.c4 g6 2.g3 Bg7 3.Bg2 Nf6 4.Nf3 0-0 5.0-0 c6 6.d4 d5 7.cd5 cd5 8.Nc3 Ne4 9.Qb3 Nc6 10.Be3 Na5 11.Qd1 Nc3 12.bc3 b6 13.Ne5 Ba6 14.Re1 Rc8 15.Bd2 e6 16.e4 Bb7 17.ed5 Bd5 18.Bd5 Qd5 19.Qe2 Rfd8 20.Ng4 Nc4 21.Bh6 f5 22.Bg7 Kg7 23.Ne3 Ne3 24.Qe3 Rc6 25.Rac1 Rdc8 [D] 26.c4 Rc4 27.Rc4 Rc4 28.Qe6 Qe6 29.Re6 Kf7 30.Re3 Rd4 31.Ra3 a5 32.Rc3 Ke6 33.Kg2 Kd6 34.h4 Ra4 35.Rc2 b5 36.Kf3 b4 37.Ke3 Kd5 38.f3 Ra3 39.Kf4 a4 40.g4 fg4 41.fg4 b3 42.ab3 ab3 43.Rc7 Ra4 44.Kg5 Rb4 45.Rc1 Kd4 46.Kh6 Rb7 0-1

787) Fischer,R-Smyslov,V [4/8/70] Herceg Novi Blitz [6] Bird's Opening [E: Rook + pawn] 1.f4 d5 2.Nf3 Nf6 3.b3 g6 4.Bb2 Bg7 5.g3 0-0 6.Bg2 c5 7.e3 Nc6 8.0-0 d4 9.Qe2 Bf5 10.Ne1 [D] Bc2 11.Nc2 d3 12.Qd1 dc2 13.Qc2 Nb4 14.Qc4 Rb8 15.a4 b6 16.Rd1 Rc8 17.Na3 e6 18.e4 Qe7 19.e5 Nfd5 20.Nb5 Rfd8 21.a5 ba5 22.Ra5 Nb6 23.Qe2 Rd7 24.Rda1 a6 25.Nd6 Rcd8 26.Bc3 N6d5 27.Bd5 Nd5 28.Ra6 g5 29.f5 Nc3 30.dc3 ef5 31.Re1 Qe5 32.Qe5 Be5 33.Re5 Rd6 34.Rd6 Rd6 35.Rf5 Rb6 36.Rg5 Kf8 37.Rc5 Rb3 38.Kg2 Rb2 39.Kh3 Kg7 40.g4 Kf6 41.Kg3 Ke6 42.h4 h6 43.h5 Rc2 44.Rc6 Ke7 45.Kf4 f6 46.Kf5 Rf2 47.Ke4 Kf7 48.c4 Rg2 49.Kf3 Rg1 50.Rc7 Ke6 51.Rh7 Rf1 52.Kg2 Rc1 53.Rc7 Ke5 54.Kg3 Rc3 55.Kh4 Rc1 56.c5 Ke6 57.Kg3 Rg1 58.Kf3 Rf1 59.Kg2 Rc1 60.Rc8 Rc3 61.c6 Rc4 62.Kf3 Rc3 63.Kg2 Rc2 64.Kg3 1-0

788) Reshevsky,S-Fischer,R [4/8/70] Herceg Novi Blitz [7]
King's Indian [E: Rook vs. Knight] **1.d4 Nf6 2.c4 g6 3.Nc3 Bg7 4.e4 0-0 5.Be2 d6 6.Nf3 e5 7.Be3 c6 8.0-0 Ng4 9.Bg5 f6 10.Bc1 f5 11.h3 ed4 12.Nd4 Ne5 13.ef5 gf5 14.f4 Qb6 15.Be3 Ng6 [D] 16.Nf5 Qb2 17.Ng7 Qc3 18.Bd4 Qa5 19.Bg4 Na6 20.Bc8 Rac8 21.Qg4 Rc7 22.Ne6 Qf5 23.Nf8 Qg4 24.hg4 Nf8 25.f5 c5 26.Bc3 Rd7 27.Rad1 Nc7 28.Rfe1 Kf7 29.Re3 b5 30.Red3 bc4 31.Rd6 Rd6 32.Rd6 Nb5 33.Rf6 Ke7 34.Rc6 Nc3 35.Rc5 Na2 36.Rc4 Nd7 37.Ra4 Nc3 38.Ra7 Ne4 39.Kh2 Kd6 40.Kh3 Ndf6 41.Kh4 h6 42.Rg7 Ke5 43.Rg6 Kf4 44.g3 Kf3 45.Rh6 Ng4 46.Rg6 Ng3 47.Rg4 1/2-1/2**

After 15...Ng6

789) Fischer,R-Reshevsky,S [4/8/70] Herceg Novi Blitz [8]
Sicilian [E: Knight vs. pawn] **1.e4 c5 2.Nf3 e6 3.c4 Nc6 4.Nc3 Nf6 5.g3 g6 6.Bg2 Bg7 7.0-0 0-0 8.d3 d6 9.h3 e5 10.a3 a5 11.Rb1 Bd7 12.Bd2 Ne8 13.Nd5 Ne7 14.b4 Nd5 15.cd5 cb4 16.ab4 a4 17.b5 Nc7 18.b6 Nb5 19.Rb4 Qb6 20.Qa1 a3 21.Rfb1 Rfc8 22.Bf1 Rc2 23.d4 a2 24.R1b3 ed4 25.Bb5 Bb5 26.Rb5 Qd8 27.Rd3 Qe7 28.Ne1 Qe4 29.Rbb3 Rd2 30.Rd2 d3 [D] 31.Ra2 Ba1 32.Ra8 Kg7 33.Ra1 d2 34.Ng2 Qd5 35.Rbb1 b5 36.Rd1 b4 37.Ne3 Qd3 38.Nf1 b3 39.Rab1 b2 40.Rb2 d5 41.Rdd2 Qc3 42.Ne3 d4 43.Nd1 Qc4 44.Rb1 h5 45.h4 f5 46.Rdb2 f4 47.Rb3 fg3 48.Rg3 Qc2 49.Rb7 Kh6 50.Nb2 Qe4 51.Rb6 Qe1 52.Kg2 Qe4 53.Kf1 Qb1 54.Ke2 Qc2 55.Ke1 Qe4 56.Kd1 Qf5 57.Rbg6 Qg6 58.Rg6 Kg6 59.Ke2 Kf5 60.Kf3 1-0**

After 30...d3

790) Fischer,R-Hort,V [4/8/70] Herceg Novi Blitz [9] A50/00
Slav [E: King + pawn] **1.d4 Nf6 2.c4 c6 3.Nc3 d5 4.cd5 cd5 5.Bf4 e6 6.e3 Nc6 7.Bb5 Bd6 8.Bd6 Qd6 9.f4 Bd7 10.Nf3 Ne4 11.Ne4 de4 12.Nd2 Qb4 13.Qb3 Qa5 14.Qa4 Qa4 15.Ba4 [D] Nb4 16.Bd7 Kd7 17.Ke2 f5 18.Nc4 Rhc8 19.Rhc1 Nd3 20.Ne5 Ne5 21.de5 Rc1 22.Rc1 Rc8 23.Rc8 Kc8 24.Kd2 Kd7 25.Kc3 Kc6 26.Kc4 b6 27.a4 a6 28.b4 b5 29.ab5 ab5 30.Kd4 Kb6 31.h3 g6 32.g4 h5 33.gh5 gh5 34.h4 Kc6 35.Kc3 1/2-1/2**

After 15.Ba4

791) Hort,V-Fischer,R [4/8/70] Herceg Novi Blitz [10] Torre
Attack **1.d4 Nf6 2.Nf3 g6 3.Bg5 h6 4.Bh4 Bg7 5.Nbd2 g5 6.Bg3 Nh5 7.e4 d6 8.Bd3 g4 9.Nh4 Bd4 10.c3 Bf6 11.Nf5 Ng3 12.fg3 e6 13.Ne3 h5 14.0-0 Nd7 15.Qe2 Qe7 16.Rae1 Ne5 17.Ndc4 Bd7 18.Na5 b6 19.Nac4 0-0-0 20.Ne5 Be5 21.Ba6 Kb8 22.Nc4 Bg7 23.a4 h4 24.a5 hg3 25.hg3 b5 26.Ne3 c6 27.c4 b4 28.c5 Bd4 29.cd6 Qd6 30.Rf4 Rh5 31.Rd1 [D] Be3 32.Qe3 Qd1 33.Rf1 Qd6 34.Rc1 c5 0-1**

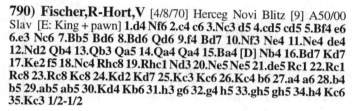

After 31.Rd1

792) Petrosian,T-Fischer,R [4/8/70] Herceg Novi Blitz [11]
Benoni **1.c4 Nf6 2.Nc3 g6 3.d4 d6 4.e4 Bg7 5.Bd3 c5 6.d5 0-0 7.Nge2 e6 8.Bg5 h6 9.Bd2 Nbd7 10.b3 ed5 11.cd5 a6 12.0-0 b5 13.f4 c4 14.bc4 Nc5 15.Bc2 b4 16.e5 de5 17.fe5 Ng4 18.Na4 Na4 19.Ba4 Be5 20.Bf4 Qb6 21.Kh1 Ba1 22.Qa1 Nf2 23.Rf2 Qf2 24.Bh6 f6 25.Bf8 Kf8 26.Ng1 Bg4 27.Qb1 Kg7 28.h3 Bf5 29.Qb4 Ra7 30.Bd1 Qa2 31.Bf3 a5 32.Qc5 Rb7 33.d6 Rb1 34.d7 Bd7 35.Qe7 Kh6 36.Qd7 Qf2 37.Kh2 Qg1 38.Kg3 Qe1 39.Kh2 Qe5 40.g3 Rb2 41.Bg2 [D] Qe4 42.Qd5 Rg2 0-1**

After 41.Bg2

After 14...bc5

After 29.Bf5

After 41.Bc2

Final position

After 16...Ba6

793) Fischer,R-Petrosian,T [4/8/70] Herceg Novi Blitz [12]
French **1.e4 e6 2.d4 d5 3.Nc3 Bb4 4.e5 c5 5.a3 Bc3 6.bc3 Qc7
7.Nf3 Ne7 8.a4 Bd7 9.Bd3 Bc6 10.0-0 Nd7 11.Ba3 h6 12.Re1 b6
13.Nd2 Ba4 14.dc5 bc5 [D] 15.Qg4 Bc6 16.Qg7 Rg8 17.Qh6 Ne5
18.Bc5 d4 19.Be4 dc3 20.Bc6 N7c6 21.Ne4 0-0-0 22.Red1 Ng4
23.Qh4 Rd1 24.Rd1 f5 25.Nd6 Kb8 26.Nb5 Qg7 27.Bd6 Kb7
28.Rb1 Kc8 29.Qg3 Qb7 30.Nc3 Qa6 31.h3 Nf6 32.Qh4 Nd7
33.Qh7 Rd8 34.Qf7 Qc4 35.Rb3 Qd4 36.Qe6 Qf6 37.Qd5 Nde5
38.Nb5 Qf7 39.Qc5 Nf3 40.Rf3 Kd7 41.Rd3 1-0**

794) Fischer,R-Bronstein,D [4/8/70] Herceg Novi Blitz [13]
French [E: Queen vs. Rook + Bishop] **1.e4 e6 2.d4 d5 3.Nc3 Bb4
4.e5 b6 5.a3 Bf8 6.f4 Nc6 7.Nf3 Nh6 8.Bd3 Nf5 9.Ne2 h5 10.g3
Bb7 11.c3 Qd7 12.Qc2 0-0-0 13.b4 f6 14.Bd2 Kb8 15.0-0 Nfe7
16.Rfb1 h4 17.Nh4 g5 18.fg5 fe5 19.Rf1 ed4 20.cd4 Bg7 21.Bc3
e5 22.Rf7 ed4 23.Rg7 Rh4 24.gh4 Qg4 25.Ng3 dc3 26.Qc3 d4
27.Qd2 Ne5 28.Rf1 Nd5 29.Bf5 [D] Nf3 30.Rf3 Qf3 31.Be4 Qa3
32.Qd4 Qc1 33.Kf2 Rf8 34.Nf5 Nc3 35.Bb7 Rf5 36.Bf3 Nd5
37.Rg8 Kb7 38.Qe4 Qd2 39.Kg3 c6 40.Qf5 Qe1 41.Kg4 Ne3
42.Kf4 Nf5 43.Kf5 Qb4 44.Rg7 Kc8 45.Be4 Qf8 46.Kg6 Qe8
47.Kf5 Qf8 1/2-1/2**

795) Bronstein,D-Fischer,R [4/8/70] Herceg Novi Blitz [14]
Sicilian [E: Rook + minor piece] **1.e4 c5 2.c3 Nf6 3.e5 Nd5 4.d4
cd4 5.Qd4 e6 6.Nf3 Nc6 7.Qe4 d6 8.Nbd2 Nb7 9.Bd3 de5 10.Ne5
Ne5 11.Qe5 0-0 12.Bc2 Bd6 13.Qh5 f5 14.Nf3 Nf4 15.Bf4 Bf4
16.0-0 g6 17.Qh3 Qf6 18.Rad1 b6 19.Rfe1 Kh8 20.g3 Bc7 21.Qh6
Qg7 22.Qg7 Kg7 23.Bb3 Re8 24.Nd4 Kf6 25.f4 a6 26.Nf3 Re7
27.h4 h6 28.Kf2 Bb7 29.Ne5 Rae8 30.a4 g5 31.hg5 hg5 32.fg5
Kg5 33.Rd4 Rh7 34.Nf3 Kf6 35.Rh4 Rh4 36.gh4 e5 37.h5 e4
38.Nd4 f4 39.Rg1 e3 40.Ke2 Be4 41.Bc2 [D] f3 42.Ke3 Bc2 43.Kf3
Be4 44.Kf2 Bh7 45.h6 Re7 46.Rg4 Bg6 47.Rh4 Rh7 48.Kf3 Kg5
49.Rg4 Kh6 and later 0-1**

796) Ostojic,P-Fischer,R [4/8/70] Herceg Novi Blitz [15]
B90/00 Sicilian **1.e4 c5 2.Ne2 d6 3.d4 cd4 4.Nd4 Nf6 5.Nc3 a6
6.a4 Qc7 7.Bd3 g6 8.f4 Bg7 9.Nf3 0-0 10.0-0 Nbd7 11.Kh1 b6
12.Qe1 Bb7 13.Qh4 Rac8 14.Bd2 e5 15.Rae1 ef4 16.Bf4 Ne5
17.Bh6 Bh618.Qh6 Nfg4 19.Qh4 Nf3 20.Rf3 f5 21.Rf4 d5 22.Rg4
fg4 23.Qg4 Rf4 24.Qg3 de4 25.Be4 Be4 26.Ne4 Re4 [D] 0-1**

797) Fischer,R-Ostojic,P [4/8/70] Herceg Novi Blitz [16]
Sicilian [E: Rook + pawn] **1.e4 c5 2.Nf3 Nc6 3.d4 cd4 4.Nd4 Nf6
5.Nc3 g6 6.Nc6 bc6 7.e5 Ng8 8.Bc4 Bg7 9.Bf4 Qa5 10.0-0 Be5
11.Be5 Qe5 12.Re1 Qc7 13.Qd4 f6 14.Bg8 Rg8 15.Qf6 d5 16.Re2
Ba6 [D] 17.Nd5 cd5 18.Qa6 Rf8 19.Rae1 Rf7 20.Qe6 Rd8 21.c3
Kf8 22.g3 d4 23.cd4 Rd4 24.Qe5 Qe5 25.Re5 Rd2 26.R1e2 Re2
27.Re2 Rf6 28.Kf1 Rc6 29.Ke1 e6 30.Kd2 Ke7 31.Re4 Rb6 32.b3
Ra6 33.a4 Kd6 34.Rh4 h5 35.Rd4 Ke7 36.Kc3 Rc6 37.Rc4 Ra6
38.Rc7 Kf6 39.Kb4 Rb6 40.Kc4 a6 41.a5 Rd6 42.b4 Rd2 43.Kc5
Rf2 44.Kb6 e5 45.Ka6 e4 46.b5 e3 47.Rc1 Ke5 48.b6 Rg2 49.b7
Rb2 50.Ka7 g5 51.b8=Q Rb8 52.Kb8 1-0**

798) Fischer,R-Uhlmann,W [4/8/70] Herceg Novi Blitz [17] French **1.e4 e6 2.d4 d5 3.Nc3 Bb4 4.a3 Bc3 5.bc3 de4 6.Qg4 Nf6 7.Qg7 Rg8 8.Qh6 Rg6 9.Qe3 Nc6 10.Bb2 b6 11.0-0-0 Bb7 12.h3 h5 13.c4 Qd6 14.Ne2 0-0-0 15.Nf4 Rgg8 16.Be2 Qe7 17.d5 ed5 18.cd5 Ne5 19.c4 Ba6 20.Qc3 Nfd7 [D] 21.d6 cd6 22.c5 Be2 23.cd6 Nc5 24.de7 Rd1 25.Rd1 Bd1 26.Qe5 Ba4 27.Kb1 Bc6 28.Nd5 Bd5 29.Qd5 1-0**

After 20...Nfd7

799) Uhlmann,W-Fischer,R [4/8/70] Herceg Novi Blitz [18] King's Indian **1.d4 Nf6 2.c4 g6 3.Nc3 Bg7 4.e4 0-0 5.Be2 d6 6.Bg5 h6 7.Be3 c5 8.d5 e6 9.Qd2 ed5 10.ed5 Kh7 11.h3 Re8 12.Bd3 Nbd7 13.Nf3 Ne5 14.Ne5 Re5 15.0-0 Bf5 16.Bf4 Bd3 17.Qd3 Re7 18.Rfe1 a6 19.g4 Qd7 20.Qg3 Rae8 21.Re7 Re7 22.Bd6 Ne4 23.Ne4 Re4 24.Bc5 Rc4 25.Qd6 Qd6 26.Bd6 Rd4 [D] 1/2-1/2**

Final position

800) Korchnoi,V-Fischer,R [4/8/70] Herceg Novi Blitz [19] King's Indian **1.d4 Nf6 2.c4 g6 3.Nc3 Bg7 4.e4 d6 5.Be2 0-0 6.Nf3 e5 7.0-0 Nc6 8.d5 Ne7 9.Nd2 c5 10.a3 Ne8 11.b4 b6 12.Rb1 f5 13.f3 f4 14.a4 g5 15.a5 Rf6 16.bc5 bc5 17.Nb3 Rg6 18.Bd2 Nf6 19.Kh1 g4 20.fg4 Ng4 21.Rf3 Rh6 22.h3 Ng6 23.Kg1 Nf6 24.Be1 Nh8 25.Rd3 Nf7 26.Bf3 Ng5 27.Qe2 Rg6 28.Kf1 [D] Nh3 29.gh3 Bh3 30.Kf2 Ng4 31.Bg4 Bg4 0-1**

After 28.Kf1

801) Fischer,R-Korchnoi,V [4/8/70] Herceg Novi Blitz [20] French [E: Rook vs. pawn] **1.e4 e6 2.d4 d5 3.Nc3 Bb4 4.e5 Ne7 5.a3 Bc3 6.bc3 c5 7.a4 Qa5 8.Bd2 Nbc6 9.Qg4 0-0 10.Nf3 f6 11.Bd3 f5 12.Qg3 c4 13.Be2 b5 14.0-0 ba4 15.Ng5 [D] Nd4 16.cd4 Qd2 17.Qh4 h6 18.Nf3 Ng6 19.Nd2 Nh4 20.Ra4 Ng6 21.Rfa1 a6 22.Nb1 Ne7 23.Ra5 Nc6 24.R5a4 Nd4 25.Bd1 f4 26.Nc3 Nc6 27.Ne2 Ne5 28.Nd4 Rb8 29.h4 Rb6 30.h5 Nc6 31.Ne2 e5 32.Nc3 Rd8 33.Bf3 e4 34.Be2 Nd4 35.Bf1 Bb7 36.Rd1 Nb5 37.Ne4 Rc8 38.Nd2 Nc3 39.Rda1 Nxa4 40.Ra4 Bc6 41.Ra5 Bb5 42.Nf3 c3 43.Nd4 Bf1 44.Kf1 Rb4 45.Rd5 a5 46.Ke2 a4 47.Kd3 Ra8 48.Kc3 Rb1 49.Rb5 Rb5 50.Nb5 a3 51.Na3 Ra3 52.Kd4 Ra2 53.Kd3 Kf7 54.g3 fg3 55.fg3 0-1**

After 15.Ng5

802) Fischer,R-Matulovic,M [4/8/70] Herceg Novi Blitz [21] Ruy Lopez **1.e4 e5 2.Nf3 Nc6 3.Bb5 f5 4.Nc3 fe4 5.Ne4 d5 6.Ne5 de4 7.Nc6 Qg5 8.Qe2 Nf6 9.f4 Qf4 10.d4 Qh4 11.g3 Qh3 12.Bg5 a6 13.Ba4 Bd7 14.Bf6 gf6 15.Qe4 Kf7 16.Ne5 fe5 17.Rf1 Ke7 18.Bd7 Kd7 19.Rf7 Ke8 20.Rc7 Bd6 21.Rb7 Rc8 22.0-0-0 Qh2 23.de5 Be7 [D] 24.Re7 Ke7 25.Qb7 Ke6 26.Qd7 Ke5 27.Qd5 Kf6 28.Rf1 Kg6 29.Qf5 Kh6 30.Qe6 Kh5 31.Rf5 Kg4 32.Rf4 Kg3 33.Qg4# 1-0**

After 23...Be7

After 33.Nd6

803) Matulovic,M-Fischer,R [4/8/70] Herceg Novi Blitz [22] Sicilian [E: Rook + minor piece] **1.e4 c5 2.Nf3 d6 3.d4 cd4 4.Nd4 Nf6 5.Nc3 a6 6.Bg5 e6 7.f4 Qb6 8.Qd2 Qb2 9.Nb3 Qa3 10.Bf6 gf6 11.Bd3 Nc6 12.0-0 Bg7 13.Rf3 f5 14.Rg3 Bf6 15.ef5 Qb416.Bf1 d5 17.Re1 Ne7 18.fe6 Be6 19.f5 Nf5 20.Nd5 Qd2 21.Nf6 Ke7 22.Nd2 Ng3 23.Nd5 Kf8 24.Nc7 Nf1 25.Rf1 Ke7 26.Na8 Ra8 27.c4 Rd8 28.Rf2 Rd4 29.Re2 Kd6 30.Ne4 Kc6 31.c5 Bc4 32.Re3 Ba2 33.Nd6 [D] b5 34.Ra3 Ra4 35.Rh3 Kc5 36.Nb7 Kc6 37.Nd8 Kc7 38.Rd3 Bc4 39.Rd4 Ra2 40.h4 a5 41.h5 a4 42.h6 a3 43.g4 Rb2 44.g5 a2 0-1**

Manhattan Blitz, 1971

Between the Larsen and Petrosian Candidates matches in 1971, Bobby was in absolute top form. He competed in the Manhattan Chess Club Blitz Tournament (8/8/71), steamrolling everyone with an unbeliveable 21-1/2 points in 22 rounds.

After 24...Be8

804) Fischer,R-Soltis,A [8/8/71] Manhattan Blitz [1] Sicilian **1.e4 c5 2.Nf3 Nc6 3.Nc3 Nf6 4.d4 cd4 5.Nd4 e5 6.Ndb5 d6 7.Bg5 a6 8.Bf6 gf6 9.Na3 f5 10.Bc4 Bg7 11.Qh5 0-0 12.ef5 Nd4 13.Bd3 f6 14.Be4 Rb8 15.Nd5 Qa5 16.c3 Rf7 17.g4 Bd7 18.0-0 Ne2 19.Kh1 Bc6 20.Rad1 Nf4 21.Nf4 Be4 22.f3 Bc6 23.Ne6 d5 24.g5 Be8 [D] 25.g6 1-0**

805) Soltis,A-Fischer R [8/8/71] Manhattan Blitz [2] Score not available. **0-1**

After 25...ef5

806) Fischer,R-Byrne,R [8/8/71] Manhattan Blitz [3] Sicilian **1.e4 c5 2.Nf3 Nc6 3.Nc3 d6 4.d4 cd4 5.Nd4 Nf6 6.Bc4 Qb6 7.Nc6 bc6 8.0-0 e6 9.Bf4 Qb2 10.Qd3 Qb4 11.Rab1 Qc5 12.Rfd1 e5 13.Bg5 Be7 14.Bf6 gf6 15.Ne2 Be6 16.Be6 fe6 17.Rb7 Kf7 18.Rdb1 d5 19.Ng3 h5 20.h4 a5 21.Qf3 Kg6 22.R1b3 a4 23.Rc3 Qd6 24.Nh5 f5 25.ef5 ef5 [D] 26.Re7 1-0**

807) Byrne,R-Fischer,R [8/8/71] Manhattan Blitz [4] B90/04 Sicilian [E: [Rook + minor piece] **1.e4 c5 2.Nf3 d6 3.d4 cd4 4.Nd4 Nf6 5.Nc3 a6 6.Be3 e5 7.Nb3 Be7 8.f3 0-0 9.Qd2 Be6 10.0-0-0 Nbd7 11.g4 b5 12.g5 Nh5 13.Nd5 Bd5 14.ed5 Rc8 15.Bh3 Rc7 16.Na5 Nb8 17.Bg4 Nf4 18.h4 f5 19.gf6 Bf6 20.Bb6 [D] Rc2 21.Qc2 Qb6 22.Nc6 Rf7 23.Nb8 Qb8 24.Kb1 Rc7 25.Qb3 Ne2 26.Qe3 Nf4 27.Rc1 h5 28.Be6 Kh7 29.Qe4 g6 30.Rhg1 Kh6 31.Rc6 Rc6 32.dc6 Qb6 33.Rc1 Ne6 34.Qd5 Nc7 35.Qd6 Bg7 36.Qe7 Kh7 37.a3 a5 38.Rd1 Qc6 39.Rd7 Ne6 40.Rd6 Qf3 41.Qe6 Qf5 42.Ka2 e4 43.Qe7 Kh6 44.Rd7 Qf6 45.Qf6 Bf6 46.Rd5 e3 47.Rd3 e2 48.Re3 Bh4 49.Re2 Bg3 50.Kb3 h4 51.a4 ba4 52.Ka4 h3 0-1**

After 20.Bb6

808) Fischer,R-Feuerstein,A [8/8/71] Manhattan Blitz [5] King's Indian Attack [E: Rook + minor piece] **1.e4 c6 2.d3 d5 3.Nd2 g6 4.g3 Bg7 5.Bg2 Nf6 6.Ngf3 0-0 7.0-0 de4 8.de4 Nbd7 9.Re1 e5 10.Nc4 Qe7 11.b3 b5 12.Ba3 b4 13.Bb2 Ba6 14.Nce5 Ne5 15.Be5 Rfd8 16.Qc1 c5 17.a3 Bb7 18.ab4 cb4 19.Qb2 Nh5 20.Bg7 Ng7 21.Qe5 Qe5 22.Ne5 Rd2 23.Ra2 Ne6 24.Nc4 Rd7 25.Na5 Rc8 26.Bh3 f5 27.Nb7 Rb7 28.ef5 Nd4 29.fg6 Rc2 30.Rc2 Nc2 31.gh7 Kg7 32.Re8 Kh7 [D] 33.Bf5 Kg7 34.Bc2 1-0**

After 32...Kh7

809) Feuerstein,A-Fischer,R [8/8/71] Manhattan Blitz [6] Score not available. **0-1**

810) Fischer,R-Mednis,E [8/8/71] Manhattan Blitz [7] French **1.e4 e6 2.d4 d5 3.Nc3 Bb4 4.e5 c5 5.a3 Bc3 6.bc3 Qc7 7.Nf3 b6 8.a4 Ba6 9.Ba6 Na6 10.Qd3 Nb8 11.0-0 Ne7 12.a5 ba5 13.Ba3 Nd7 14.dc5 Nc6 15.c4 dc4 16.Qd6 Qd6 17.ed6 0-0 18.Nd2 Nd4 19.Nc4 Rfc8 20.Ra2 Nc5 21.Na5 Nd7 22.c4 Nc6 23.Nc6 Rc6 24.c5 f6 25.Rb1 Rac8 26.h3 Nc5 27.Rc2 Nd7 28.Rc6 Rc6 [D] 29.Rb7 Nb6 30.d7 Nd7 31.Rd7 1-0**

After 28...Rc6

811) Mednis,E-Fischer,R [8/8/71] Manhattan Blitz [8] B92/10 Sicilian [E: Rook + minor piece] **1.e4 c5 2.Nf3 d6 3.d4 cd4 4.Nd4 Nf6 5.Nc3 a6 6.Be2 e5 7.Nb3 Be7 8.0-0 0-0 9.a4 Qc7 10.a5 Be6 11.f4 ef4 12.Bf4 Nbd7 13.Kh1 Ne5 14.Nd4 Rac8 15.Qe1 Kh8 16.Qg3 g6 17.Bh6 Rfe8 18.Bg5 Ng8 19.Ne6 fe6 20.Be3 Bf6 21.Bb6 Qe7 22.Bd4 Bg7 23.Rad1 Nf7 24.Bg7 Kg7 25.Qd3 Nf6 26.Qd4 Red8 27.Bc4 Ne5 28.Bb3 Rf8 [D] 29.Qd6 Qd6 30.Rd6 Ne4 31.Rf8 Rf8 32.Rd1 Nf2 33.Kg1 Nd1 34.Nd1 Kf6 35.Nf2 Ke7 36.Ne4 Nd7 37.g3 Rf5 38.Ba4 Ra5 0-1**

After 28...Rf8

812) Fischer,R-Shipman,W [8/8/71] Manhattan Blitz [9] Ruy Lopez **1.e4 e5 2.Nf3 Nc6 3.Bb5 Nge7 4.c3 d5 5.Ne5 de4 6.Qe2 Qd5 7.Nc6 Nc6 8.d4 Bf5 9.Nd2 0-0 10.0-0 Bg6 11.Nb3 f5 12.Be3 Qf7 13.Bc6 bc6 14.Qa6 Kd7 15.Na5 Qe6 16.c4 Be7 17.Rfd1 Rb8 18.d5 cd5 19.Rd5 Bd6 20.Rad1 Ke7 21.Nc6 Kf7 22.Nb8 Rb8 [D] 23.Rd6 cd6 24.Qa7 1-0**

After 22...Rb8

813) Shipman,W-Fischer,R [8/8/71] Manhattan Blitz [10] Sicilian [E: Rook + pawn] **1.Nc3 g6 2.e4 c5 3.Nf3 Bg7 4.d4 cd4 5.Nd4 Nc6 6.Be3 d6 7.Bc4 Nf6 8.f3 0-0 9.0-0 Bd7 10.Qd2 a6 11.Rad1 Rc8 12.Bb3 b5 13.Nd5 Nd5 14.ed5 Nd4 15.Bd4 Bd4 16.Qd4 a5 17.c3 a4 18.Bc2 Rc4 19.Qd2 b4 20.cb4 Qb6 21.Kh1 Qb4 22.Qb4 Rb4 23.b3 Rc8 24.Rd2 Rc3 25.Kg1 ab3 26.Bb3 Ba4 27.Ba4 Ra4 28.Re1 Kf8 29.Rb2 Rc7 30.Ra1 Ra5 31.Kf2 Rcc5 32.Rbd2 Kg7 33.h3 Kf6 34.Ke3 Ke5 35.f4 Kf5 36.g4 Kf6 37.Ke4 Ra4 38.Ke3 [D] Rd3 40.Rd3 Ra2 41.Kf3 Ra4 42.Re3 h6 43.h4 Ra7 44.Rb3 Ra5 45.Rd3 Rc5 46.Ke4 Rc4 47.Kf3 Rc1 48.Re3 Rc7 49.Rb3 Rc5 50.Ke4 Rc1 51.Kf3 Rf1 52.Kg3 Re1 53.Kf3 Rg1 54.Re3 e6 55.de6 fe6 56.Rd3 d5 57.Ra3 h5 58.gh5 gh5 59.Ra8 Rg4 60.Rf8 Ke7 61.Rh8 Rh4 62.Kg3 Rh1 63.Kg2 Rh4 64.Kg3 Rh1 65.Kg2 Ra1 66.Rh5 Ra3 67.Kf2 Kd6 68.Rh8 d4 69.Rd8 Kc5 70.Re8 Kd5 71.Re7 Ra6 72.Kf3 Ra3 73.Ke2 Re3 74.Kf2 Re4 75.Kf3 Re1 76.Rd7 Kc4 77.Kf2 Re4 78.Kf3 Re3 79.Kf2 Kd3 80.Ra7 Re2 81.Kf3 Re3 82.Kf2 Rh3 [D] 83.Ra3 Ke4 84.Rh3 Kf4 85.Rh4 Ke5 86.Kf3 Kd5 and later 1/2-1/2**

After 38.Ke3

After 30...Bg3

814) Fischer,R-Kramer,G [8/8/71] Manhattan Blitz [11] C68/19 Ruy Lopez [E:Rook + minor piece] **1.e4 e5 2.Nf3 Nc6 3.Bb5 a6 4.Bc6 dc6 5.0-0 Bg4 6.h3 Bf3 7.Qf3 Qd7 8.d3 0-0-0 9.Be3 f6 10.Nd2 Ne7 11.b4 Ng6 12.Rfb1 Be7 13.a4 b6 14.Qe2 Kb7 15.Nc4 Nf4 16.Qf3 Ne6 17.Rb3 Nd4 18.Bd4 Qd4 19.Rab1 h5 20.b5 cb5 21.ab5 a5 22.Ne3 Qd7 23.Nd5 Bc5 24.Rc3 Qd6 25.Rc4 Rd7 26.c3 f5 27.Qf5 Rf8 28.Qh5 Bf2 29.Kh1 Rdf7 30.Rc6 Bg3** [D] **31.Qf7 Rf7 32.Rd6 cd6 33.Ne3 Rf2 34.Nf5 Bf4 35.Nd6 Ka7 36.Nc4 Rc2 37.g3 Bg3 38.Ne3 Rh2 39.Kg1 Rh3 40.Kg2 1-0**

815) Kramer,G-Fischer,R [8/8/71] Manhattan Blitz [12] Score not available. **0-1**

After 25.Rf5

816) Levy,L-Fischer,R [8/8/71] Manhattan Blitz [13] B22 Sicilian **1.e4 c5 2.c3 Nf6 3.e5 Nd5 4.d4 cd4 5.cd4 d6 6.Nf3 Nc6 7.Qb3 e6 8.Bb5 Be7 9.Nc3 Nc3 10.bc3 O-O 11.O-O Bd7 12.Bf4 Na5 13.Qb2 Bb5 14.Qb5 d5 15.Nd2 a6 16.Qb2 Rc8 17.Qc2 Qd7 18.Be3 Rc6 19.f4 Rfc8 20.Rac1 Qc7 21.Nb1 Nc4 22.Qe2 Ne3 23.Qe3 b5 24.f5 ef5 25.Rf5** [D] **b4 26.Rf3 h6 27.Rc2 Qb6 28.Qf4 Rf8 29.Rg3 Bg5 30.Qf3 bc3 31.Nc3 Qd4 32.Qf2 Qf2 33.Kf2 d4 0-1.**

817) Fischer,R-Levy,L [8/8/71] Manhattan Blitz [14] Score not available.

818) Fischer,R-McKelvie [8/8/71] Manhattan Blitz [15] Score not available. **1-0**

819) McKelvie-Fischer,R [8/8/71] Manhattan Blitz [16] Score not available. **0-1**

820) Fischer,R-Kevitz [8/8/71] Manhattan Blitz [17] Score not available. **1-0**

After 23...Rac8

821) Kevitz-Fischer,R [8/8/71] Manhattan Blitz [18] Grunfeld **1.Nf3 g6 2.d4 Bg7 3.c4 Nf6 4.Nc3 d5 5.Bf4 0-0 6.e3 c6 7.Be2 Bg4 8.Qb3 b6 9.Rc1 dc4 10.Qc4 b5 11.Qc5 Nfd7 12.Qa3 a5 13.Ne4 Bf3 14.gf3 e5 15.de5 Ne5 16.0-0 Nbd7 17.Rfd1 Qh4 18.Bg3 Qh5 19.Kg2 Nb6 20.Rc2 Nec4 21.Qc5 Qc5 22.Nc5 Nb2 23.Rd6 Rac8** [D] **24.Bb5 cb5 25.Rb6 Nc4 26.Rb5 Na3 27.Ra5 Nc2** and eventually **0-1.**

Final position

822) Fischer,R-Gore,J [8/8/71] Manhattan Blitz [19] Ruy Lopez **1.e4 e5 2.Nf3 Nc6 3.Bb5 a6 4.Ba4 Nf6 5.0-0 Be7 6.Re1 b5 7.Bb3 d6 8.c3 0-0 9.h3 Na5 10.Bc2 c5 11.d4 Qc7 12.Nbd2 Nc6 13.d5 Nd8 14.a4 Rb8 15.b4 Ne8 16.Nf1 g6 17.bc5 dc5 18.Bh6 Ng7 19.Ne3 Bd6 20.Qd2 f6 21.Ng4 Bg4 22.hg4 Nf7 23.ab5 ab5 24.Ra6 Ra8 25.Rea1 Qb7 26.Ra8 Ra8 27.Ra8 Qa8 28.Be3 Qc8 29.g5 f5 30.Qe2 f4 31.Bc1 c4 32.Bd1 Qa6 33.Qb2 Ne8 34.g3 fg3 35.fg3 Nc7 36.Kg2 Kg7 37.Ne1 Qa5 38.Be2 Na6 39.Be3 Nc5 40.Bc5 Bc5 41.Nf3 Ba7 42.Bf1 Qb6 43.Kh3 Qc5 44.Qa2 Qc8 45.Kg2 Qc5 46.Qe2 Qc8 47.Qd2 Qc5** [D] **1-0**

823) Gore,J-Fischer,R [8/8/71] Manhattan Blitz [20] B92/07
Sicilian **1.e4 c5 2.Nf3 d6 3.d4 cd4 4.Nd4 Nf6 5.Nc3 a6 6.Be2 e5
7.Nb3 Be7 8.Be3 0-0 9.Qd2 Be6 10.0-0-0 Nbd7 11.Kb1 b5 12.f3
Nb6 13.Bb6 Qb6 14.Rhf1 Rfd8 15.Nd5 Bd5 16.ed5 a5 17.Qd3 a4
18.Nd2 a3 19.b3 Rab8 20.c4 bc4 21.Nc4 Qc5 22.Rd2 g6 23.Rc1
Rdc8 24.Rdd1 Qf2 25.g4 Rc5 26.Na3 Rd5 27.Qa6 Rd1 28.Bd1
d5 29.Nb5 d4 30.Nd6 Nd5 [D] 0-1**

Final position

824) Fischer,R-Brandts,P [8/8/71] Manhattan Blitz [21] Ruy
Lopez **1.e4 e5 2.Nf3 Nc6 3.Bb5 a6 4.Ba4 Nf6 5.0-0 Be7 6.Re1 b5
7.Bb3 d6 8.c3 0-0 9.h3 Na5 10.Bc2 c5 11.d4 Qc7 12.Nbd2 Nc6
13.d5 Nd8 14.a4 Qb8 15.b4 cb4 16.cb4 ba4 17.Ba4 Qb4 18.Ba3
Qb7 19.Nc4 Ne8 20.Be8 Re8 21.Bd6 f6 22.Rb1 Qa7 23.Qa4 Bd7
24.Qa3 Bb5 25.Be7 Qe7 26.Nd6 Rb8 27.Re3 Nf7 28.Ne8 Qe8
29.Nd2 Rd8 30.Rc1 Nd6 31.Rc7 Qg6 [D] 32.Rg3 Qh6 33.Rgg7
Qg7 34.Rg7 Kg7 35.f3 Kf7 36.Nb3 Ke7 37.Nc5 Rc8 38.Nb7 1-0**

After 31...Qg6

825) Brandts,P-Fischer,R [8/8/71] Manhattan Blitz [22]
King's Indian **1.d4 g6 2.c4 Bg7 3.Nc3 Nf6 4.e4 d6 5.Be2 0-0 6.Nf3
e5 7.0-0 Nc6 8.d5 Ne7 9.Ne1 Nd7 10.Nd3 f5 11.ef5 gf5 12.f4 Ng6
13.Be3 Nf6 14.Qc2 Re8 15.fe5 de5 16.Bg5 h6 17.Bf6 Qf6 18.Qb3
e4 19.Nf4 Nf4 20.Rf4 Qg5 21.Rff1 Qe3 22.Kh1 Qg5 23.c5 Kh8
24.Rad1 Be5 25.g3 Rg8 26.Nb1 f4 27.Rg1 f3 28.Bc4 Qh5 29.Qe3
[D] Rg3 30.Qe4 Qh2 0-1**

After 29.Qe3

Simultaneous Exhibition Games

Bobby Fischer played hundreds of simultaneous exhibition games, most in 1964 on a coast-to-coast tour. A large number of new games have surfaced since the last edition of this book. Readers are invited to submit unpublished Fischer simultaneous games to Hays Publishing at the address on the copyright page of this book for inclusion in future editions. Games should be accompanied by a photocopy of the original scoresheet signed by Fischer. Many of the games in this section show justifiably proud wins and draws against Bobby, but these are the exceptions. His overall winning percentage on the 1964 tour was an overwhelming 94%.

Havana, 1956

After 27.fe5

826) Fischer,R-Casado,J [2/26/56] Simultaneous, Havana Sicilian 1.e4 c5 2.Nf3 Nc6 3.d4 cd4 4.Nd4 Nd4 5.Qd4 d6 6.c4 e5 7.Qd3 Nf6 8.Nc3 Be6 9.Bg5 Be7 10.Be2 a6 11.b3 0-0 12.0-0 Re8 13.Rad1 Qa5 14.Rd2 Rac8 15.Bf6 Bf6 16.Rfd1 Red8 17.Nd5 Bd5 18.Qd5 Qd5 19.Rd5 Be7 20.f3 g6 21.c5 Kg7 22.Kf2 Rc6 23.g3 f6 24.f4 Kf7 25.Ke1 b5 26.b4 Ke8 27.fe5 [D] dc5 28.ef6 Bf6 29.bc5 Be7 30.Rd8 Bd8 31.Rd6 Rd6 32.cd6 Ba5 33.Kd1 Bb4 34.e5 Bc3 35.e6 Be5 36.d7 Ke7 37.Bg4 Bc7 38.Kc2 b4 39.Kd3 Kf6 40.Kc4 a5 41.Kc5 h5 42.Bh3 g5 43.Kc6 Bd8 44.Bg2 a4 45.Bd5 Ba5 46.Kb7 a3 47.Kc8 Ke7 48.Bc4 Bd8 1/2-1/2

Detroit 2/9/64

After 59...f5

827) Fischer,R-Witeczek,J [2/9/64] Simultaneous, Detroit King's Gambit 1.e4 e5 2.f4 ef4 3.Nf3 d5 4.ed5 Nf6 5.Bb5 c6 6.dc6 Nc6 7.d4 Bd6 8.O-O O-O 9.Bc6 bc6 10.Ne5 Be5 11.de5 Qb6 12.Kh1 Nd5 13.Qe2 Ba6 14.c4 Qd4 15.Na3 Rfe8 16.Qf2 Qf2 17.Rf2 Re5 18.Bd2 Nb6 19.Bf4 Re4 20.b3 Bb7 21.Rd1 a5 22.h3 Re7 23.Rfd2 f6 24.Bd6 Rd7 25.Bc5 Rad8 26.Rd7 Rd7 27.Rd7 Nd7 28.Bd6 Ne5 29.Bc7 Nd3 30.Ba5 Nc1 31.Bd2 Na2 32.Kg1 Kf7 33.Kf2 Ke6 34.b4 Kd6 35.g3 Bc8 36.h4 Bf5 37.Ke3 Ke5 38.b5 cb5 39.Nb5 Be6 40.c5 Bd7 41.Nd4 Kd5 42.c6 Bc8 43.c7 Kc5 44.Ne2 Kc6 45.Nf4 Kc7 46.Nh5 Bg4 47.Ng7 Kd8 48.Kf4 Bd7 49.Nf5 Ke8 50.Nd4 Kf7 51.Ke4 Kg6 52.Kd5 Be8 53.Ke6 Bf7 54.Ke7 Bd5 55.Ne6 Bc4 56.Nf8 Kg7 57.h5 Bb3 58.h6 Kg8 59.Nd7 f5 [D] 60.Nf6 Kh8 61.Kf8 Be6 62.Nd5 1-0 [Mate comes on the long diagonal]

After 21...b5

828) Fischer,R-Richburg,J [2/9/64] Simultaneous, Detroit King's Indian Attack 1.e4 c6 2.d3 d5 3.Nd2 e5 4.Ngf3 Nd7 5.g3 Ngf6 6.Bg2 g6 7.O-O de4 8.de4 Bg7 9.Qe2 O-O 10.b3 Qc7 11.Ba3 Re8 12.Nc4 c5 13.Rfd1 Bf8 14.Nfd2 Rb8 15.Ne3 Nb6 16.c4 Bd7 17.Nb1 Rbd8 18.Nc3 a6 19.Rac1 Bc8 20.Ncd5 Nbd5 21.cd5 b5 [D] 22.Bc5 Qb8 [22...Bc5 23.b4] 23.Bf8 Rf8 24.Rc6 Ne8 25.Rdc1 Nd6 26.Qd2 Kg7 27.f4 f6 28.Qb2 ef4 29.gf4 Kg8 30.e5 fe5 31.fe5 Nf5 32.Ng4 Kh8 33.e6 Ng7 34.Rc7 1-0

829) Fischer,R-Jones,J [2/9/64] Simultaneous, Detroit King's Gambit **1.e4 e5 2.f4 f6? 3.fe5 Nc6 4.d4 Be7 5.ef6 gf6 [D] 6.Qh5 Kf8 7.Bc4 Qe8 8.Bh6 1-0**

After 5...gf6??

Rochester, N.Y. 2/15/64

830) Fischer,R-Reithel, D [2/15/64] Simultaneous, Rochester, NY Sicilian **1.e4 c5 2.Nf3 d6 3.d4 cd4 4.Nd4 Nf6 5.Nc3 a6 6.Bc4 e6 7.Bb3 Be7 8.f4 b5 9.e5 de5 10.fe5 Nd5 11.Nd5 ed5 12.Qf3 O-O 13.Bd5 Ra7 14.O-O Bc5 15.c3 Be6 16.Be4 Rd7 17.Be3 Qc7 18.Ne6 fe6 19.Qh3 Be3 20.Qe3 Rf1 21.Rf1 Qa7 22.Qa7 Ra7 [D] 23.Rd1 Nd7 24.Rd6 Kf7 25.Bc2 Ne5 26.Bb3 Nc4 27.Rc6 Nb2 28.Re6 Nc4 29.Rc6 Ke7 30.Bc4 bc4 31.Rc4 Rb7 32.Ra4 Rb6 33.Kf2 Rb2 34.Kf3 Rc2 35.c4 g5 36.Ra6 Rc4 37.a4 Kf7 38.a5 Rf4 39.Ke3 Ra4 40.Ra8 Kg7 41.a6 h5 42.a7 g4 43.Kd3 Kh7 44.Kc3 Kg7 45.Kb3 Ra6 46.Kb4 Ra1 47.Kc5 Ra2 48.Kd6 Ra3 49.Ke5 Ra4 50.Kf5 Ra5 51.Kf4 Ra4 52.Kg5 Ra5 53.Kh4 Kh7 54.g3 Kg7 55.Rb8 Ra7 56.Kh5 Ra2 57.Rb7 Kf6 58.Rb6 Kf5 59.Rb5 Kf6 60.Kg4 Rh2 61.Rb6 Kf7 62.Kg5 Ra2   1/2-1/2**

After 22...Ra7

831) Fischer,R-Grant, G. [2/15/64] Simultaneous, Rochester, NY French **1.e4 e6 2.d4 d5 3.Nc3 Nf6 4.Bg5 de4 5.Ne4 Be7 6.Bf6 Bf6 7.Nf3 Bd7 8.c3 Bc6 9.Qc2 g6 10.O-O-O Nd7 11.h4 Be4 12.Qe4 c6 13.h5 Qc7 14.g4 O-O-O 15.g5 Be7 16.Bc4 Nb6 17.Bb3 Nd5 18.Rdg1 Qf4 19.Qf4 Nf4 20.Rg4?? Nd3 21.Kc2 Nf2 22.Rgg1 Nh1 23.Rh1 Bd6 24.Kd3 c5 25.d5 b5 26.Ke4 c4 27.Bc2 Rhe8 28.hg6 hg6 29.Rh7 Re7 [D] 30.Nd4?? f5 0-1**

After 29...Re7

Montreal 2/23/64

832) Fischer,R-de Gruchy, P. [2/23/64] Simultaneous, Montreal Caro Kann **1.e4 c6 2.d4 d5 3.Nc3 de4 4.Ne4 Bf5 5.Nc5 b6 6.Na6 Na6 7.Ba6 Qc7 8.Qf3 b5 9.Bd2 Qb6 10.Qf5 e6 11.Qd3 Qa6 12.a4 Nf6 13.Nf3 Be7 14.O-O Qb7 15.ab5 cb5 16.Ra5 a6 17.Rfa1 O-O 18.Bg5 Bb4 19.Bf6 gf6 20.R5a2 Kh8 21.c3 Be7 22.Nd2 Rg8 23.Qf3 Qb6 24.g3 f5 25.b4 Bg5 26.Nb3 Be7 27.Nc5 Ra7 28.Kg2 Rga8 29.Nd7 Qc7 30.Ne5 Bd6 31.Nc6 Rb7 32.Ra6 Ra6 33.Ra6 Rb6 34.Rb6 Qb6 35.d5 Kg7 36.de6 fe6 37.Nd4 Be5 38.Qe3 Bd4 39.Qd4 Qd4 40.cd4 Kf6 41.Kf3 e5 [D] 42.de5 Ke5 43.Ke3 Kd5 44.Kd3 h5 45.f4 Kc6 46.Kd4 Kd6 47.h3 1-0**

After 41...e5

833) Fischer,R-N.N. [2/23/64] Simultaneous, Montreal Two Knights **1.e4 e5 2.Nf3 Nc6 3.Bc4 Nf6 4.Ng5 d5 5.ed5 Nd4 6.c3 b5 7.Bf1 Nd5 8.cd4 Qg5 9.Bb5 Kd8 10.Qf3 [D] e4! 11.Qe4 Bd6 12.O-O Bb7 13.d3 Nf4 (13...Bh2!!) 14.Bf4 Qb5 15.d5 Qb2 16.Bd6 cd6 17.Re1 Qf6 18.Nc3 Rc8 19.Qb4 Re8 20.Qa5 Kd7 21.Qa4 1-0**

After 10.Qf3

Toronto [2/27/64]

After 26.Qf1

834) Fischer,R-Lister, M. [2/27/64] Simultaneous, Toronto
Sicilian **1.e4 c5 2.Nf3 d6 3.d4 cd4 4.Nd4 Nf6 5.Nc3 e6 6.g4 e5
7.Nf5 g6 8.Ne3 Nc6 9.h3 Be6 10.Ned5 Bg7 11.Be3 O-O 12.Qd2
Rc8 13.O-O-O Ne8 14.f3 f5 15.gf5 gf5 16.Bg5 Qd7 17.Bh6 f4
18.Bg7 Qg7 19.h4 Kh8 20.Bh3 Bh3 21.Rh3 Nd4 22.Qf2 Nf6
23.Rg1 Qd7 24.Rh2 Nd5 25.ed5 b5 26.Qf1 [D] b4 27.Ne4 Qa4
28.Qd3 Qa2 29.Ng5 Rc2 0-1**

Westerly, RI [3/1/64]

After 12...Bb7

835) Fischer,R-King, S [3/1/64] Simultaneous, Westerly, RI
Sicilian **1.e4 c5 2.Nf3 d6 3.d4 cd4 4.Nd4 Nf6 5.Nc3 Nc6 6.Bc4 e6
7.Be3 a6 8.Bb3 Be7 9.f4 O-O 10.O-O Na5 11.Qf3 b5 12.e5 Bb7
[D] 13.ef6 Bf3 14.fe7 Qe7 15.Rf3 Nc4 16.f5 Ne3 17.Re3 Qa7
18.fe6 Qd4 19.ef7 Rf7 20.Re1 Re8 21.Nd5 Kh8 22.c3 Qa7 23.g3
Re3 24.Re3 Rf3 0-1**

836) Fischer,R-Barry, R. [3/1/64] Simultaneous, Westerly, RI
Alekhine **1.e4 Nf6 2.e5 Nd5 3.d4 d6 4.c4 Nb6 5.ed6 ed6 6.Nc3 Be7
7.Bd3 d5 8.c5 N6d7 9.Nd5 Nc5 10.dc5 Bc5 11.Nf3 Nc6 12.Nc3
Qe7 13.Be2 Bg4 14.O-O Rd8 15.Qa4 Bd7 16.Re1 Nd4 17.Qd1
Be6 18.Nd4 Bd4 19.Qa4 c6 20.Be3 Be3 21.fe3 Rd2 22.Ne4 b5
23.Qa6 Rd8 24.Qc6 Bd7 25.Qc5 Qe4 26.Bb5 Qe7 27.Qe7 Ke7
28.Bf1 Rc8 29.Rac1 Rc1 30.Rc1 Kd6 31.b4 a5 32.b5 a4 33.Rd1
Ke7 34.Rd4 Ra8 35.a3 Kd8 36.Kf2 Kc7 [D] 37.b6 Kc6 38.Be2
Rd8 39.Rb4 Kb7 40.Bf3 Bc6 41.Bc6 Kc6 42.b7 Rb8 43.Ke2 Rb7
44.Rb7 Kb7 45.Kd3 Kb6 46.Kc4 1-0**

After 36...Kc7

Fitchburg, ME 3/2/64

837) Fischer,R-Dondis,H [3/2/64] Simultaneous, Fitchburg,
ME   Vienna **1.e4 e5 2.Nc3 Nf6 3.Bc4 Ne4 4.Qh5 Nd6 5.Bb3 Nc6
6.d4 Nd4 7.Nd5 Ne6! 8.Qe5 [D] c6 9.Nc3 Qf6 10.Qf6 gf6 11.Nge2
Nf5 12.g4 Nfd4 13.Nd4 Nd4 14.Be3 Nb3 15.ab3 d5 16.Ra7 Ra7
17.Ba7 Bg4 18.Bd4 Be7 19.Kd2?? c5 0-1**

After 8.Qe5

838) Fischer,R-Martin,E. [3/2/64] Simultaneous, Fitchburg, ME
French **1.e4 e6 2.d4 d5 3.Nc3 Bb4 4.e5 c5 5.a3 Bc3 6.bc3 Nc6 7.a4
Qa5 8.Bd2 Qc7 9.Qg4 Nge7 10.Nf3 Ng6 11.h4 h5 12.Qg3 c4
13.Ng5 Nce7 14.Qf3 Nf5 15.g3 Bd7 16.Bh3 Nge7 17.a5 a6 18.O-O
Bb5 19.Bc1 g6 20.Ba3 b6 21.ab6 Qb6 22.Qf4 Qb7 23.f3 Ng7
24.Kf2 Qd7 25.Rh1 Ra7 26.Bg2 Rb7 27.g4 Ng7 28.Bd6 Qd8
29.Rhb1 Rd7 [D] 30.Ra6? Ba6 31.Rb8 Bc8 32.Qc1 Ne7 33.Qa3
O-O 34.Qc5 Re8 35.Bh3 Rb7 36.Ra8 Qd7 0-1**

After 29...Rd7

839) Fischer,R-Barber, C. [3/2/64] Simultaneous, Fitchburg, ME French **1.e4 e6 2.d4 d5 3.Nc3 Bb4 4.e5 c5 5.a3 cd4 6.ab4 dc3 7.Qg4 cb2 8.Bb2 g6 9.Nf3 Nh6 10.Qf4 Nf5 11.g4 Nh4 12.b5 Nf3 13.Qf3 b6 14.h4 Nd7 15.h5 g5 16.h6 Bb7 17.Bd4 Qc7 18.Bd3 [D] Ne5 19.Qe3 f6 20.O-O-O Nd3 21.Rd3 e5 22.Bb2?? 22.d4 23.Qh3 Bh1 24.Qh1 Rc8 25.Rd2 O-O 26.Kb1 Qc4 0-1**

After 18.Bd3

Hartford [3/3/64]

840) Fischer,R-Owen,J.C. [3/3/64] Simultaneous, Hartford **1.e4 c6 2.d3 d5 3.Nd2 de4 4.de4 e5 5.Ngf3 Bg4 6.h3 Bf3 7.Qf3 Nf6 8.Bd3 Nbd7 9.O-O Bc5 10.c3 a5 11.a4 Qc7 12.Qe2 O-O 13.g4 h6 14.Nc4 Rfe8 15.Ne3 g6 16.Qf3 Bf8 17.Kh2 Bg7 18.Rg1 Nf8 19.Nf5 gf5 20.gf5 Kh7 21.Qg3 Ne6 22.fe6 fe6 23.Qg6 Kh8 24.Bh6 Bh6 25.Qf6 Bg7 26.Qh4 Kg8 27.Rg7 Kg7 28.Rg1 Kf8 29.Qh6 Ke7 30.Rg7 Kd6 31.Rc7 Kc7 32.Qg7 Kd6 33.Bc4 Rf8 34.Qh6 Rf2 35.Kg3 Raf8 [D] 36.Qe6 Kc5 37.Qe5 Kb6 38.Qd4 1-0**

After 35...Raf8

841)Fischer,R-Noderer,L [3/3/64] Simultaneous, Hartford French **1.e4 e6 2.d4 d5 3.Nc3 Bb4 4.e5 c5 5.a3 Bc3 6.bc3 Ne7 7.a4 Qa5 8.Bd2 Qc7 9.Qg4 Nf5 10.Nf3 Nc6 11.Bd3 Nce7 12.O-O Bd7 13.a5 h5 14.Qg5 Rh6 15.dc5 Qc5 16.Bc1 Qc3 17.Ba3 f6 18.ef6 gf6 19.Qc1 Rg6 20.Be7 Ke7 21.Ra3 Qb4 22.Bf5 ef5 23.Rb3 Qg4 24.g3 Bc6 25.Re1 Kf7 26.Rbe3 d4 27.Re7 Kg8 28.Nd2 Qh3 29.f3 h4 30.R1e2 [D] hg3 31.Qa3 gh2 0-1**

After 30.R1e2

842) Fischer,R-Pierce,I [1964] Simultaneous, Hartford Sicilian **1.e4 c5 2.Nf3 Nc6 3.d4 cd4 4.Nd4 Nf6 5.Nc3 d6 6.Bc4 e6 7.Bb3 Be7 8.Be3 Nd4 9.Bd4 Bd7 10.f4 Bc6 11.Qe2 Qa5 12.O-O-O O-O-O 13.Rhf1 Kb8 14.f5 e5 15.Bf2 Rhf8 16.Bh4 Rd7 17.g4 Ne8 18.Bf2 Nc7 19.Kb1 f6 20.Nd5 Bd5 21.Bd5 Nd5 22.Rd5 Qc7 23.Rfd1 Rc8 [D] 24.R1d3 Qc4 25.b3 Qc6 26.c4 b6 27.a4 Rb7 28.Kb2 a6 29.Rc3 b5 30.ab5 ab5 31.c5 dc5 32.Bc5 Bc5 33.Rcc5 Qc5 34.Rc5 Rc5 1/2-1/2**

After 23...Rc8

843) Fischer,R-Platz,J [1964] Simultaneous, Hartford French **1.e4 e6 2.d4 d5 3.Nc3 Bb4 4.e5 c5 5.a3 Ba5 6.b4 cd4 [D] 7.Qg4 Kf8 8.ba5 dc3 9.a4 f5 10.Qg3 Nc6 11.Nf3 Nge7 12.h4 Bd7 13.h5 Rc8 14.h6 g6 15.a6 Nb4 16.Qh4 Nec6 17.Ba3 d4 18.ab7 Rb8 19.Bb5 Qh4 20.Rh4 Ke8 21.Bc6 Nc2 22.Kd1 Na1 23.Bd6 Bc6 24.Bb8 Ba4 25.Ke1 Bc6 26.Nd4 Bb7 27.Bd6 Kd7 28.f3 Rc8 29.Ne2 Nb3 30.Ba3 Bd5 31.Ra4 a5 32.Nc1 Nc133.Bc1 Rc5 34.Ra3 Kc6 35.Be3 c2 36.Ra1 Rb5 37.Rc1 Bb3 0-1**

After 6...cd4

Washington, D.C. [3/8/64]

After 27.Ne2

844) Fischer,R-Evans,J [3/8/64] Simultaneous,Washington, DC *Sicilian* 1.e4 c5 2.Nf3 d6 3.d4 cd4 4.Nd4 Nf6 5.Nc3 a6 6.Bc4 e6 7.Bb3 Nc6 8.Be3 Bd7 9.f4 Qa5 10.O-O h5 11.h3 h4 12.Qf3 Qh5 13.Qf2 Rc8 14.f5 Nd4 15.Bd4 e5 16.Be3 Bc6 17.Bd5 Be7 18.Rad1 Rd8 19.Bb6 Rd7 20.Rfe1 g5 21.fg6 Qg6 22.Rf1 Bd5 23.ed5 Nh5 24.Qf5 Qf5 25.Rf5 Ng3 26.Rf2 f5 27.Ne2 [D] f4 28.Ng3 hg3 29.Re2 Bd8 30.Bd8 Kd8 31.Re4 Rdh7 32.Rd3 Rc7 1/2-1/2

After 16.fe5

845) Fischer,R-Hucks,L [3/8/64] Simultaneous Washington, DC Sicilian 1.e4 c5 2.Nf3 e6 3.d4 cd4 4.Nd4 a6 5.Bd3 Qc7 6.O-O Nc6 7.Nc6 bc6 8.Nd2 Nf6 9.b3 Bc5 10.Bb2 e5 11.Kh1 d6 12.f4 Ng4 13.Qe2 Ne3 14.Rf2 Bg4 15.Qe1 Qa7 16.fe5 [D] Nc2 17.Bc2 Bf2 18.Qf1 Bd4 19.Bd4 Qd4 20.Nc4 de5 21.h3 Be2 0-1

Pittsburgh [3/15/64]

After 28.Rf1

846) Fischer,R-Sivitz,A [3/15/64] Simultaneous, Pittsburgh Sicilian 1.e4 c5 2.Nf3 d6 3.d4 cd4 4.Nd4 Nf6 5.Nc3 a6 6.Bc4 e6 7.Bb3 Be7 8.f4 b5 9.e5 de5 10.fe5 Nd5 11.Nd5 ed5 12.Qf3 Be6 13.O-O Bc5 14.Be3 O-O 15.Rad1 Ra7 16.Kh1 Bd4 17.Bd4 Rd7 18.c3 Nc6 19.Bc2 g6 20.Qg3 Nd4 21.cd4 f5 22.ef6 Rf6 23.Bb3 Rdf7 24.Rf6 Rf6 25.Qe5 Qf8 26.Kg1 Qf7 27.Re1 Kg7 28.Rf1 [D] h5 29.h4 a5 30.a3 Qf8 31.Rf3 Qf7 32.Bc2 Qf8 33.b4 ab4 34.ab4 Qd8 35.Bb1 Bf7 36.Bd3 Be8 37.Rf4 Qd6 38.Rf6 Qf6 39.Qd5 Qh4 40.Qe5 Qf6 41.Qc5 Qc6 42.d5 Qc5 43.bc5 Kf6 44.c6 b4 45.c7 Bd7 46.Kf2 Ke5 47.Bg6 Kd5 48.Bh5 Kd6 1/2-1/2

Cleveland [3/18/64]

After 27...Kh6

847) Fischer,R-Ina,D [3/18/64] Simultaneous, Cleveland Polish 1.b4 e6 2.Bb2 d5 3.Nf3 Nf6 4.b5 b6 5.g3 a6 6.a4 ab5 7.ab5 Ra1 8.Ba1 Qd6 9.Bg2 Be7 10.O-O O-O 11.Qc1 Qb4 12.Nc3 d4 13.Na2 Qb5 14.Nd4 Qa6 15.Nc3 Bb7 16.e4 e5 17.Nf5 Bb4 18.Nd5 Nd5 19.ed5 f6 20.Qd1 Bc5 21.d4 Bd6 22.Qg4 g6 23.Nd6 cd6 24.Qe6 Kg7 25.Qd6 ed4 26.Bd4 b5 27.Qc7 Kh6 [D] 28.Ra1 Rc8 29.Be3 g5 30.Bg5 1-0

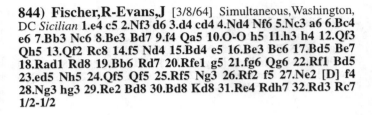

After 29...Ng4

848) Fischer,R-Zaas,D [3/18/64] Simultaneous, Cleveland Caro Kann [E: Rook vs. Bishop] 1.e4 c6 2.d3 d5 3.Nd2 de4 4.de4 Nf6 5.Ngf3 e6 6.Bd3 Bc5 7.O-O O-O 8.Qe2 Nbd7 9.b3 Re8 10.Bb2 e5 11.Rad1 Qe7 12.Nc4 Bd6 13.Nd6 Qd6 14.Nh4 Qc5 15.Nf5 Nf8 16.Qf3 Ng6 17.g3 Be6 18.h4 h5 19.Bc1 Ng4 20.Kg2 Ne7 21.Ne7 Qe7 22.Qe2 Rad8 23.f3 Nf6 24.Bg5 g6 25.Rde1 Kg7 26.f4 Bg4 27.Qf2 Qe6 28.Bc4 Bh3 29.Kh1 Ng4 [D] 30.Be6 Nf2 31.Rf2 Be6 32.Bd8 Rd8 33.f5 gf5 34.ef5 Bd5 35.Kh2 f6 36.Rd2 Rd7 37.c4 Be6 38.Rd7 Bd7 39.Rd1 Bf5 40.Rd8 c5 41.Rb8 Be4 42.Rc8 Bc6 43.a3 Kg6 44.b4 cb4 45.ab4 a6 46.Kg1 Kf5 47.Kf2 e4 48.Ke3 Kg4 49.Rg8 Kf5 50.g4 hg4 51.h5 1-0

849) Fischer,R-Gloger,J [3/18/64] Simultaneous, Cleveland
Polish **1.b4 e5 2.Bb2 f6 3.e4 Bb4 4.Bc4 Ne7 5.Qh5 Ng6 6.f4 ef4
7.Nf3 Nc6 8.Nc3 Bc3 9.Bc3 d6 10.Nh4 Ne7 11.Nf5 Kf8 12.0-0 Qe8
[D] 13.Bf6 Bf5 14.ef5 d5 15.fg6 gf6 16.Qh6 Kg8 17.g7 1-0**

After 12...Qe8

850) Fischer,R-Ellison,D [3/18/64] Simultaneous, Cleveland
French **1.e4 e6 2.d4 d5 3.Nc3 Nf6 4.Bg5 de4 5.Ne4 Be7 6.Bf6 Bf6
7.Nf3 0-0 8.Qd2 Nd7 9.0-0-0 b6 10.Qf4 Bb7 11.Bd3 Be4 12.Qe4
Bg5 13.Kb1 Nf6 14.Qe2 Nd5 15.g3 Bf6 16.h4 c5 17.c4 Nb4 18.Be4
cd4 [D] 19.a3 d3 20.Qe3 Rc8 21.ab4 Rc4 22.Bd3 Rb4 23.Bh7 Kh7
24.Rd8 Rb2 25.Kc1 Rd8 26.Ne5 Rdd2 27.Qe4 Kg8 28.Nc6 1-0**

After 18...cd4

851) Fischer,R-Kuberczyk,Z [3/18/64] Simultaneous,
Cleveland Sicilian [E:Rook vs. Bishop] **1.e4 c5 2.Nf3 Nc6 3.d4
cd4 4.Nd4 Nf6 5.Nc3 a6 6.Nc6 dc6 7.Qd8 Kd8 8.Bf4 e6
9.0-0-0 Bd7 10.Na4 b5 11.Nb6 Ra7 12.f3 Bc5 13.Nd7 Rd7
14.Bd3 Nh5 15.Bd2 Nf6 16.g4 h6 17.h4 Kc7 18.Rh2 e5 19.Rg2
Ne8 20.f4 Bd6 21.f5 f6 22.Be3 Be7 23.Rdg1 Kb7 24.Be2 c5 25.c3
Kc6 26.a4 Nd6 27.ab5 ab5 28.Kc2 Ra8 29.g5 hg5 30.hg5 Kb6
31.gf6 gf6 32.Rg7 Ra4 33.R1g4 Re4 34.Re4 Ne4 [D] 35.b4 Kc7
36.Bb5 cb4 37.cb4 Nd6 38.Bd7 Kd7 39.Rh7 Nf5 40.Bg1 Kc6
41.Kb3 Kb5 42.Rh8 Kc6 43.Ka4 Kd6 44.b5 Nd4 45.Bd4 1-0**

After 34...Ne4

852) Fischer,R-Costaras,B [3/18/64] Simultaneous,
Cleveland Sicilian **1.e4 c5 2.Nf3 Nc6 3.d4 cd4 4.Nd4 d5 5.Nc6 bc6
6.ed5 Qd5 7.Nd2 e6 8.Be2 Nf6 9.0-0 Bc5 10.Bf3 Qd6 11.Nc4 Qc7
12.g3 Nd5 13.b3 0-0 14.Bb2 Ba6 15.Be2 Rad8 16.Qe1 Nb4 17.Rc1
Bc4 18.Bc4 Na2 19.Ra1 Nb4 20.Qe4 Nd5 21.Kh1 Qe7 22.Ra6
Rc8 23.Bd5 cd5 24.Qe5 [D] Qf6 [d4!] 25.Qf6 gf6 26.Bf6 Bb6 27.c3
Rfe8 28.f4 Rc7 29.g4 h6 30.h4 Rd7 31.h5 Bd8 32.Bd4 Rb7 33.Ra7
Rb3 34.g5 Bb6 35.Rb7 1-0**

After 24.Qe5

853) Fischer,R-Mobley,H [3/18/64] Simultaneous, Cleveland
Caro Kann **1.e4 c6 2.d4 d5 3.Nc3 de4 4.Ne4 Bf5 5.Nc5 b6 6.Na6
e6 7.Bf4 Bd6 8.Qf3 Ne7 9.0-0-0 0-0 10.Nb8 Rb8 11.Ne2 Nd5
12.Bd6 Qd6 13.Ng3 Bg6 14.h4 h6 15.h5 Bh7 16.Bd3 f5 17.Rhe1
b5 18.Ne2 Nb4 19.Kb1 Nd3 20.Rd3 f4 21.Rdd1 b4 22.Nc1 a5
23.Qe2 Rf6 24.Qe5 Qd8 25.b3 Rb5 26.Qe2 Qa8 27.Qc4 Bf5 [D]
28.Nd3 Rd5 29.Nf4 Bc2 30.Qc2 Rf4 31.Re6 Rfd4 32.Rd4 Rd4
33.Rc6 Qd8 34.Rc8 Rd1 35.Kb2 a4 36.Rd8 Rd8 37.ba4 1-0**

After 27...Bf5

Toledo [3/19/64]

After 26.Nd2

854) Fischer,R-Dillard,W. [3/19/64] Simultaneous, Toledo Evans Gambit **1.e4 e5 2.Nf3 Nc6 3.Bc4 Bc5 4.b4 Bb4 5.c3 Be7 6.d4 d6 7.de5 de5 8.Qb3 Nf6 9.Bf7 Kf8 10.Ng5 Bd6 11.O-O b6 12.Nd2 Na5 13.Qb5 a6 14.Qd3 Qe7 15.Bd5 Nd5 16.Qd5 Bb7 17.Ne6 Ke8 18.Ng7 Qg7 19.Qe6 Qe7 20.Qh3 Bc8 21.Qh6 Kd7 22.Nf3 Kc6 23.Bg5 Qe6 24.Qh4 Qg6 25.Be7 Bg4 26.Nd2 [D] Be7 27.Qe7 Bh3 28.g3 Bf1 29.Rf1 Qd6 0-1**

After 17.Kb1

855) Fischer,R-Underhill,R. [3/19/64] Simultaneous, Toledo King's Gambit **1.e4 e5 2.f4 Bc5 3.Nf3 Nc6 4.fe5 d6 5.d4 Bb6 6.ed6 Qd6 7.c3 Bg4 8.Bd3 O-O-O 9.Be3 Ne5 10.Be2 Bf3 11.gf3 f6 12.Nd2 Qe7 13.Qb3 g5 14.O-O-O Nh6 15.Nc4 Nc4 16.Bc4 Kb8 17.Kb1 [D] Nf5 18.Bc1 Nh4 19.Rhf1 f5 20.ef5 Nf5 21.Rfe1 Qg7 22.Rg1 h6 23.Bd3 Rhf8 24.Qc2 Nh4 25.f4 g4 26.Qf2 Nf5 27.Rde1 h5 28.Re5 Nd4 29.Rh5 Nf3 30.Qf3 gf3 31.Rg7 Rd3 0-1**

After 14...O-O

856) Fischer,R-Blaine,R [3/19/64] Simultaneous, Toledo French **1.e4 e6 2.d4 d5 3.Nc3 Be7 4.Nf3 Nf6 5.e5 Nfd7 6.Bd3 c5 7.dc5 Nc5 8.O-O Nbd7 9.Re1 b6 10.Be3 Qc7 11.Bd4 Ba6 12.a4 Nd3 13.cd3 Rc8 14.Rc1 O-O [D] 15.Nd5 Qd8 16.Rc8 Bc8 17.Nc3 Qc7 18.Ne4 Bb7 19.Qd2 Nc5 20.Bc5 bc5 21.Qf4 h6 22.Rc1 Be4 23.Qe4 f6 24.d4 Qb6 25.d5 fe5 26.Qe5 Rf6 27.de6 Re6 28.Qd5 Qc6 29.Qc4 Kh7 30.Nd4 Qe4 31.Ne6 Qe6 32.Qe6 1-0**

After 31.Qe7

857) Fischer,R-Fink,B [3/19/64] Simultaneous, Toledo Ruy Lopez **1.e4 e5 2.Nf3 Nc6 3.Bb5 a6 4.Ba4 Nf6 5.O-O Be7 6.Re1 b5 7.Bb3 O-O 8.c3 d6 9.h3 Bb7 10.d4 Qd7 11.Nbd2 Na5 12.de5 Nb3 13.ef6 Nd2 14.fe7 Nf3 15.Qf3 Qe7 16.Qg3 Qf6 17.f3 Rfe8 18.Be3 Re6 19.a4 Qg6 20.Qf2 Bc6 21.ab5 Bb5 22.b3 Bc6 23.c4 f5 24.ef5 Qf5 25.Bd4 Re1 26.Re1 Re8 27.Ra1 Bb7 28.Bb2 Qd3 29.Re1 Re1 30.Qe1 Qg6 31.Qe7 [D] Bf3 32.Qd8 Kf7 33.Qc7 Kg8 34.Qc8 Kf7 1/2-1/2**

Chicago [3/22 and 3/23/64]

After 17...Qf6

858) Fischer,R-Sandrin,A [3/22/64] Simultaneous, Chicago King's Gambit **1.e4 e5 2.f4 ef4 3.Bc4 Nf6 4.Nc3 Bb4 5.Nf3 Qe7 6.Qe2 0-0 7.e5 Bc3 8.dc3 Nh5 9.0-0 Re8 10.Qe4 c6 11.Qd4 b5 12.Bd3 g6 13.Bf4 c5 14.Qe3 Nc6 15.Bb5 Bb7 16.Rae1 d5 17.ed6 Qf6 [D] 18.Qe8 Re8 19.Re8 Kg7 20.Bc6 Nf4 21.d7 Ne2 22.Re2 Bc6 23.Ne5 1-0**

After 28.Kg2

859) Fischer,R-Fulk,W [3/22/64] Simultaneous, Chicago French **1.e4 e6 2.d4 d5 3.Nc3 Bb4 4.e5 c5 5.a3 cd4 6.ab4 dc3 7.Nf3 Qc7 8.Bd3 Ne7 9.0-0 Nbc6 10.Re1 Nb4 11.bc3 Nd3 12.cd3 0-0 13.Ba3 Re8 14.Qd2 Bd7 15.Nd4 Nf5 16.Bb4 Nd4 17.cd4 Rec8 18.Qf4 Qc2 19.Qg3 Qb2 20.Be7 Qd4 21.Bf6 g6 22.Qg5 Rc2 23.Rf1 Qc5 24.Rae1 Rc8 25.g4 Bb5 26.Re3 Rc1 27.Rc1 Qc1 28.Kg2 [D] d4 29.Qh6 Bc6 30.Kh3 Qf1 31.Kh4 Qf2 32.Rg3 Qh2 33.Rh3 1/2-1/2**

860) Fischer,R-Mott-Smith,K [3/22/64] Simultaneous, Chicago King's Gambit [E: Knight vs. pawns] **1.e4 e5 2.f4 ef4 3.Nf3 d6 4.d4 g5 5.Bc4 h6 6.0-0 Bg7 7.c3 Ne7 8.g3 Ng6 9.Qb3 0-0 10.gf4 gf4 11.Kh1 Nc6 12.Qc2 Nce7 13.Nbd2 Be6 14.Rg1 Bc4 15.Nc4 d5 16.Nce5 de4 17.Qe4 Qd5 18.Qd5 Nd5 19.Ng6 fg6 20.Rg6 Kh7 21.Rg2 Rae8 22.Bd2 Ne3 23.Re2 Nc4 24.Rae1 Re2 25.Re2 Nd2 26.Nd2 Rf6 27.Nf3 Bf8 28.Re8 a5 29.b3 Bd6 30.c4 b6 31.Kg2 Kg6 32.Kf2 Kf5 33.h3 Rf8 34.Nh4 Kg5 35.Rf8 Bf8 36.Ng2 Bg7 37.d5 Be5 38.Kf3 Kf5 39.Ne1 Bc3 40.Nd3 Be5 41.a3 Bd6 42.b4 ab4 43.ab4 Be7 44.c5 bc5 45.bc5 Bg5 46.Nb4 Be7 47.Na6 Ke5 [D] 48.d6! cd6 49.c6 Bd8 50.c7 Bc7 51.Nc7 d5 52.Na6 Kf5 53.Nb4 d4 54.Nd3 Kg5 55.Nf4 Kh4 56.Kg2 h5 57.Kh2 1-0**

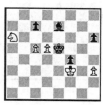

After 47...Ke5

861) Fischer,R-Sillars,K [3/22/64] Simultaneous, Chicago Sicilian **1.e4 c5 2.Nf3 d6 3.d4 cd4 4.Nd4 Nf6 5.Nc3 a6 6.Bc4 e6 7.Be3 Be7 8.Bb3 0-0 9.f4 Nbd7 10.Qf3 Nc5 [D] 11.g4 b5 12.g5 Nfe4 13.Ne4 Bb7 14.Nc5 Bf3 15.Nce6 Bh1 16.Nd8 Bd8 17.Nf5 d5 18.Bd4 f6 19.Ng3 Bf3 20.Kf2 fg5 21.Kf3 Rf4 22.Ke3 Kf8 23.Bd5 Rb8 24.Nh5 Rh4 25.Rf1 Ke8 26.Ng7 Kd7 27.Rf7 Kd6 28.Be6 Bb6 29.c3 Rf4 30.Rd7 Kc6 31.Nf5 Re8 32.Rd6 Kb7 33.Rb6 Kc7 34.Ng7 Re7 35.Ra6 1-0**

After 10...Nc5

862) Fischer,R-Dibert,G [3/22/64] Simultaneous, Chicago French **1.e4 e6 2.d4 d5 3.Nc3 Bb4 4.e5 c5 5.a3 Bc3 6.bc3 Ne7 7.a4 Nbc6 8.Nf3 Bd7 9.Bd3 Qa5 10.Qd2 c4 11.Be2 b5 12.Ba3 ba4 13.0-0 0-0 14.Nh4 f6 15.ef6 Rf6 16.f4 Nf5 17.Nf3 Rh6 18.Rab1 Qd8 19.g3 Qe8 20.Rf2 Rb8 21.Re1 Qg6 22.Ref1 Rb7 23.Ne5 Qe8 24.g4 Nfe7 25.g5 Rh4 26.Nf3 Rh3 27.Kg2 Qh5 28.Kh1 Nf5 29.Kg1 Ng3 30.Ne5 Nf1 31.Bf1 Rh4 32.Nf3 Rg4 33.Kh1 Rb1 34.Ne5 Rh4 35.Nf3 Rh3 36.Qe3 [D] e5 37.fe5 Bf5 38.e6 Be4 39.e7 Rf3 0-1**

After 36.Qe3

863) Fischer,R-Sax,B [3/22/64] Simultaneous, Chicago Evans Gambit **1.e4 e5 2.Nf3 Nc6 3.Bc4 Bc5 4.b4 Bb6 5.a4 a6 6.Bb2 d6 7.b5 Na5 8.Ba2 Be6 9.Be6 fe6 10.0-0 Nf6 11.d4 Nc4 12.Bc3 Ne4 13.de5 d5 14.Bd4 Bd4 15.Nd4 Qe7 16.f3 Nc5 17.Qe2 ab5 18.Nb5 Ra4 19.Ra4 Na4 20.N1c3 Nc3 21.Nc3 [D] Qc5 22.Kh1 Qe3 23.Qe3 Ne3 24.Ra1 Kd7 25.Ra2 Rf8 26.Ne2 g5 27.Kg1 Nc4 28.Ra7 Rb8 29.f4 gf4 30.Nf4 Ne5 31.Ra3 Rf8 32.Ne2 Nc4 33.Rh3 Rf7 34.g4 e5 35.Rh5 Ne3 36.Ng3 Kd6 37.g5 Nc2 38.h4 Ne3 39.Rh6 Kd7 40.h5 Ng4 0-1**

After 21.Nc3

864) Fischer,R-Lococo,A [3/22/64] Simultaneous, Chicago Evans Gambit **1.e4 e5 2.Nf3 Nc6 3.Bc4 Bc5 4.b4 Bb4 5.c3 Ba5 6.d4 ed4 7.0-0 Nge7 8.Ng5 d5 9.ed5 Ne5 10.Bb3 0-0 11.Nf7 Kf7 12.Qh5 Kg8 13.Qe5 dc3 14.Nc3 Bc3 15.Qc3 Nd5 16.Qd3 c6 17.Bb2 h6 18.Bc2 Be6 19.Qg6 Nf4 20.Qe4 Qd6 21.Bc1 Nd5 22.Qh7 Kf7 23.Bg6 Ke7 24.Qg7 Kd8 25.Qb7 Rb8 26.Qa7 Rh8 27.g3 Rf8 [D] 28.Ba3 1-0**

After 27...Rf8

After 21...Rf8

After 18.Qe3

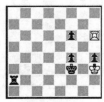

After 22...Nd3

After 60...f4

865) Fischer,R-Silverman,S [3/22/64] Simultaneous, Chicago French **1.e4 e6 2.d4 d5 3.Nc3 Nf6 4.Bg5 Bb4 5.e5 h6 6.Bd2 Bc3 7.bc3 Ne4 8.Qg4 g6 9.Bd3 Nd2 10.Kd2 c5 11.h4 Nc6 12.Rh3 cd4 13.cd4 Qb6 14.Ne2 Bd7 15.Qf4 0-0-0 16.a3 f6 17.Qf6 Rdf8 18.Qg6 Rf2 19.Ke3 Rff8 20.Rf3 Rfg8 21.Qf6 Rf8 [D] 22.Qf8 Rf8 23.Rf8 Kc7 24.g4 Ne5 25.g5 hg5 26.hg5 Nd3 27.cd3 Qd6 28.Rf6 Qe7 29.Raf1 e5 30.Nc3 ed4 31.Kd4 Qa3 32.Nd5 Kd8 33.g6 Qb2 34.Ke4 Qg2 35.Kd4 Qb2 36.Ke4 Qg2 37.Ke5 Qb2 1/2-1/2**

866) Fischer,R-Manter,L [3/22/64] Simultaneous, Chicago King's Gambit **1.e4 e5 2.Nc3 Nf6 3.Bc4 Bc5 4.f4 d6 5.Nf3 Nc6 6.d3 0-0 7.f5 Na5 8.Bg5 c6 9.Bb3 Re8 10.Qe2 Nb3 11.ab3 b5 12.Nd1 d5 13.Ne3 de4 14.de4 Qb6 15.Bf6 Be3 16.Be5 f6 17.Bc7 Qc7 18.Qe3 [D] Bf5 19.Nd2 Be4 20.Ne4 Qe5 21.0-0 Qe4 22.Qe4 Re4 23.Rf5 Rd8 24.h3 Rd2 25.Rf2 Ree2 26.Re2 Re2 27.Ra7 Rc2 28.Ra2 b4 29.Kh2 f5 30.Kg3 g5 31.Kf3 h5 32.g4 fg4 33.hg4 h4 34.Ra5 c5 35.Ke4 h3 36.Ra8 Kf7 37.Rh8 h2 38.Kd5 Kg7 39.Rh5 Kg6 40.Rh8 Rb2 41.Kc5 Rb3 42.Rh2 Kf6 43.Rf2 Kg6 44.Rd2 Rb1 45.Rd6 Kf7 46.Kc4 b3 47.Kc3 b2 48.Rd4 Rf1 49.Kb2 Rf4 50.Kc3 Ke6 51.Kd3 Ke5 52.Rd8 Rg4 53.Ke3 Rh4 54.Kf3 Rf4 55.Kg3 Rf6 1/2-1/2**

867) Fischer,R-Crown,S [3/22/64] Simultaneous, Chicago, Irregular **1.e4 e5 2.Nf3 Nc6 3.d4 Bb4 4.c3 Bd6 5.Bc4 h6 6.0-0 Nf6 7.de5 Be5 8.Ne5 Ne5 9.Bb3 d6 10.f4 Nc6 11.e5 de5 12.Qd8 Nd8 13.fe5 Ne4 14.Be3 b6 15.Na3 a6 16.Nc2 Be6 17.Nd4 Bb3 18.ab3 0-0 19.b4 Re8 20.Rfe1 c5 21.bc5 Nc5 22.Nf3 Nd3 [D] 23.Reb1 b5 24.Bd4 Nc6 25.b4 Nce5 26.Ne5 Ne5 27.Ra2 Nc4 28.h3 f6 29.Rf1 Re6 30.Rf5 Rc8 31.Rd5 Rcc6 32.Rd8 Kf7 33.Ra8 g5 34.Rf2 Nd6 35.Kh2 Ne4 36.Rf3 h5 37.g4 h4 38.Kg2 Ng3 39.Ra7 Kg6 40.Ra8 Re2 41.Kg1 Rce6 42.Rg8 Kh7 43.Rf8 Re1 44.Kg2 R6e2 45.Rf2 Ne4 46.Re2 Re2 47.Kf3 Re1 48.Ra8 Nd2 49.Kf2 Re6 1/2-1/2**

868) Fischer,R-Warren,J [3/22/64] Simultaneous, Chicago Sicilian **1.e4 c5 2.Nf3 Nc6 3.d4 cd4 4.Nd4 Nf6 5.Nc3 d6 6.Bc4 e6 7.Be3 Be7 8.0-0 0-0 9.Bb3 Bd7 10.f4 Nd4 11.Bd4 Bc6 12.Qe2 b5 13.Nb5 Bb5 14.Qb5 Ne4 15.f5 Bf6 16.Qd3 Bd4 17.Qd4 d5 18.c4 dc4 19.Qd8 Rfd8 20.Bc4 Nd2 21.Rfc1 Nc4 22.Rc4 ef5 23.b4 Rd2 24.a4 g6 25.b5 Re8 26.Kh1 Ree2 27.Rg1 Ra2 28.h3 Re4 29.Rgc1 Ra4 30.Ra4 Ra4 31.Rc7 h5 32.Kg1 h4 33.Kf2 Kg7 34.Rb7 Kf6 35.Rc7 Rb4 36.Ra7 Rb5 37.Rc7 Re5 38.Ra7 g5 39.Rb7 g4 40.Rb6 Re6 41.Rb4 Kg5 42.Rb5 Kf4 43.Rb4 Re4 44.Rb7 f6 45.Rb6 Kg5 46.Rb5 Re5 47.Rb8 Ra5 48.Rb2 Ra3 49.Rc2 gh3 50.gh3 Rh3 51.Rc8 Ra3 52.Rg8 Kf4 53.Rh8 Ra2 54.Kg1 Kg3 55.Rg8 Kf3 56.Rh8 Rg2 57.Kh1 Rg4 58.Kh2 Ra4 59.Rh6 Ra2 60.Kh3 f4 [D] 61.Rf6 Ke3 62.Kh4 f3 63.Kg3 Rg2 64.Kh3 Rg8? 65.Ra6 f2 66.Ra3 Ke2 67.Ra2 1/2-1/2**

869) Fischer,R-Sullivan,J [3/22/64] Simultaneous, Chicago
Sicilian **1.e4 c5 2.Nf3 e6 3.d4 cd4 4.Nd4 Nc6 5.Nb5 d6 6.Bf4 e5
7.Be3 a6 8.N5c3 b5 9.Nd5 Rb8 10.Be2 h6 11.Bg4 Bg4 12.Qg4 Nge7
13.Nbc3 b4 14.Ne7 Ne7 15.Ne2 Ng6 16.0-0 Qc8 17.Qc8 Rc8 18.c3
bc3 19.Nc3 Be7 20.Rfc1 0-0 21.Nd5 Bg5 22.b4 Ne7 23.Ne7 Be7 24.a4
[D] d5 25.ed5 Bb4 26.Rc6 a5 27.Kf1 Rc6 28.dc6 Rc8 29.Rc1 Bd6
30.Ke2 f5 31.f3 Kf7 32.Bb6 Bc7 33.Bc7 Rc7 34.Rc5 Ke6 35.Kd3 Kd6
36.Ra5 Rc6 37.Ra7 g6 38.a5 h5 39.a6 Kc5 40.Ra8 Re6 41.h4 Kb6
42.Ke3 e4 43.a7 Kb7 44.Rg8 Ka7 45.fe4 Re4 46.Kf3 Rg4 47.g3 Kb7
48.Re8 1/2- 1/2**

After 24.a4

870) Fischer,R-Garwin,C [3/23/64] Simultaneous, Chicago
Evans Gambit 1964, Chicago, IL **1.e4 e5 2.Nf3 Nc6 3.Bc4 Bc5
4.b4 Bb4 5.c3 Ba5 6.d4 ed4 7.O-O Bb6 8.cd4 d6 9.Nc3 Na5
10.Bg5 Qd7 11.Bd3 h6 12.Be3 Ne7 13.Na4 Nac6 14.Nb6 ab6
15.d5 Ne5 16.Ne5 de5 17.f4 Ng6 18.f5 Nf8 19.a4 Qd6 20.Qg4 g5
21.h4 Rg8 22.hg5 hg5 23.Rf3 Bd7 24.Bc2 Qb4 25.Rh3 Qb2
26.Rc1 O-O-O 27.Rh6 Ng6 28.Bd3 Rh8 29.Qg5 Rh6 30.Qh6 Nf4
31.Bf4 ef4 32.Qf4 Qd4 33.Qf2 Qd3 34.Qb6 [D] Qd1 35.Rd1 cb6
36.Kf2 Ba4 37.Rd4 b5 38.g4 Re8 39.g5 Rg8 40.Kf3 Rg5 41.Kf4
Rg1 42.Ke5 Rd1 43.Rb4 Kd7 44.Kf6 Ke8 45.Rb2 Rd4 46.e5 Rd5
47.Rh2 b4 48.Rh4 Rb5 49.e6 fe6 50.fe6 Kd8 51.e7 Kc7 52.e8=Q
Rb6 53.Qe6 Re6 54.Ke6 Bd7 55.Ke5 1/2-1/2**

After 34.Qb6

871) Fischer,R-Gruenberg,F [3/23/64] Simultaneous,
Chicago Two Knights **1.e4 e5 2.Nf3 Nc6 3.Bc4 Nf6 4.Ng5 d5 5.ed5
Nd5 6.d4 Be7 [D] 7.Nf7 Kf7 8.Qf3 Ke6 9.Nc3 Bb4 10.Bd5 Kd6
11.Bc6 Bc3 12.bc3 bc6 13.Ba3 Ke6 14.0-0 Qd5 15.Qh5 e4 16.Qh4
g5 17.Qh5 Qf5 18.f3 Qg6 19.Qg4 Qf5 20.Qf5 Kf5 21.fe4 Ke4
22.Rae1 Kd5 23.Re5 1-0**

After 6...Be7

872) Fischer,R-Kuhn,J [3/23/64] Simultaneous, Chicago Two
Knights **1.e4 e5 2.Nf3 Nc6 3.Bc4 Nf6 4.Ng5 d5 5.ed5 Nd5 6.d4 f6
[D] 7.de5 Ne5 8.Bd5 fg5 9.0-0 Bd7 10.Re1 Qf6 11.Qh5 Qg6
12.Re5** and **1-0** in 22 moves

After 6...f6

873) Fischer,R-Panzer,F [3/23/64] Simultaneous, Chicago
Evans Gambit **1.e4 e5 2.Nf3 Nc6 3.Bc4 Bc5 4.b4 Bb4 5.c3 Bc5 6.d4
ed4 7.0-0 d6 8.cd4 Bb6 9.Nc3 Bg4 10.Qa4 Bf3 11.d5 Nge7 12.dc6
Bg4 13.cb7 Bd7 14.ba8=Q Qa8 15.Bf7 Kf7 16.Qd7 Rd8 17.Qh3
Kg8 18.Qe6 Kf8 19.Bg5 Re8 20.Nd5 Nd5 21.Qd5 Qc8 22.Rac1
Bc5 [D] 23.Rc3 Re5 24.Rf3 1-0**

After 22...Bc5

After 8...c6

874) Fischer,R-Redman,L [3/23/64] Simultaneous, Chicago Two Knights **1.e4 e5 2.Nf3 Nc6 3.Bc4 Nf6 4.Ng5 d5 5.ed5 Nd5 6.d4 f6 7.de5 Ne5 8.Bd5 c6 [D] 9.Ne6 Qa5 10.Bd2 Qb6** and **1-0** after 34 moves

After 17...Kf8

875) Fischer,R-Rouse [3/23/64] Simultaneous,Chicago Two Knights **1.e4 e5 2.Nf3 Nc6 3.Bc4 Nf6 4.Ng5 d5 5.ed5 Nd5 6.d4 ed4 7.0-0 Be7 8.Nf7 Kf7 9.Qf3 Ke6 10.Re1 Ne5 11.Bf4 Bf6 12.Nc3 c6 13.Re5 Kf7 14.Nd5 Be6 15.Re6 Ke6 16.Nf6 Ke7 17.Re1 Kf8 [D] 18.Qa3 1-0**

After 9...Kf8

876) Fischer,R-Sugerman,P [3/23/64] Simultaneous, Chicago Evans Gambit **1.e4 e5 2.Nf3 Nc6 3.Bc4 Bc5 4.b4 Bb4 5.c3 Ba5 6.d4 ed4 7.0-0 d6 8.Qb3 Bb6 9.Bf7 Kf8 [D] 10.Bg8 Rg8 11.Ng5 Ne5 12.Nh7 1-0**

After 28.Bb5

877) Fischer,R-Thornell,G [3/23/64] Simultaneous, Chicago Alekhine's Defense **1.e4 Nf6 2.Nf3 Ne4 3.d4 d5 4.Bd3 c5 5.0-0 e6 6.c4 Nf6 7.Nc3 dc4 8.Bc4 cd4 9.Nd4 Be7 10.Be3 0-0 11.Qe2 Nd5 12.Nd5 ed5 13.Bd3 Nc6 14.Rac1 Nd4 15.Bd4 Bf6 16.Qe3 Bd4 17.Qd4 Be6 18.f4 Qb6 19.Qb6 ab6 20.f5 Bd7 21.Rc7 Bc6 22.a3 Rfe8 23.Rd1 b5 24.Kf2 Re5 25.Rc1 d4 26.R1c6 bc6 27.Rc6 Re3 28.Bb5 [D] Rb3 29.Bc4 Rb2 30.Kf3 Rd8 31.Ke4 Rg2 32.Rc7 Rh2 33.Rf7 Kh8 34.Kd3 Rh3 35.Kd2 d3 36.Be6 Rh2 37.Kd1 d2 38.Bd7 Kg8 0-1**

After 14...h6

878) Fischer,R-Wagenhals,W [3/23/64] Simultaneous, Chicago Pirc **1.e4 d6 2.d4 Nf6 3.Nc3 g6 4.f4 Bg7 5.Nf3 0-0 6.Bd3 a6 7.0-0 Bg4 8.h3 Bf3 9.Qf3 c6 10.Be3 Nbd7 11.e5 Ne8 12.g4 e6 13.Ne4 Qe7 14.g5 h6 [D] 15.Nf6 Ndf6 16.ef6 Nf6 17.gf6 Qf6 18.c3 Qd8 19.Rf2 f5 20.Rg2 Kh7 21.Kh2 Bf6 22.Rag1 Rg8 23.c4 d5 24.b4 Rg7 25.a4 Qb6 26.b5 ab5 27.ab5 Bd4 28.Bd4 Qd4 29.cd5 cd5 30.Bb1 Ra4 31.Re1 Qb4 32.Rge2 Ra3 33.Qf2 Rb3 34.Bc2 Rc3 35.Re6 d4 36.Rg6 Rg6 37.Bf5 Kg7 38.Bg6 Kg6 39.Qg2 Kf6 40.Rg1 Qf8 41.Qg6 Ke7 42.Qh7 Kd6 43.Qg6 Kc5 1/2-1/2**

879) Fischer,R-Wolf,P [3/23/64] *[This was not Grandmaster Patrick Wolff-Ed.]* Simultaneous, Chicago French 1.e4 e6 2.d4 c5 3.d5 ed5 4.ed5 d6 5.Nc3 Nf6 6.h3 g6 7.g4 Bg7 8.Bg2 0-0 9.Nge2 b6 10.O-O Ba6 11.a4 Nbd7 12.Bf4 Ne8 13.Re1 f5 14.g5 Ne5 15.Nb5 Nc7 16.Nec3 Re8 17.h4 Nb5 18.ab5 Bb7 19.Bf1 Re7 20.Re3 Ng4 21.Rf3 h6 22.gh6 Bh6 23.Bh6 Nh6 24.Qd2 Rh7 25.Qg5 Qg5 26.hg5 Ng4 27.Rh3 Rh3 28.Bh3 Ne5 29.Kg2 a6 30.ba6 Ra6 31.Re1 b5 32.f4 b4 33.Nb5 Bd5 34.Kf2 Bc4 35.Nc7 Ra7 36.Ne8 Nf7 37.Nf6 Kg7 38.Re8 [D] Nh6 39.Rd8 Ng4 40.Bg4 fg4 41.Rd6 Ra2 42.Ng4 Rb2 43.Ne5 Rc2 44.Kf3 b3 45.Rg6 Kf8 46.Rb6 Bd5 47.Kg4 b2 48.Nd3 c4 49.Nb2 c3 50.Nd3 Be4 51.Ne1 Rc1 1/2-1/2

After 38.Re8

880) Fischer,R-Kral [3/23/64] Simultaneous, Chicago French 1.e4 e6 2.d4 d5 3.Nc3 de4 4.Ne4 Nd7 5.Nf3 Ngf6 6.Nf6 Nf6 7.Bd3 Be7 8.Qe2 0-0 9.Bg5 c5 10.dc5 Qa5 11.c3 Qc5 12.0-0-0 b5 13.Bf6 Bf6 [D] 14.Qe4 g6 15.Qa8 b4 16.c4 1-0

After 13...Bf6

New Orleans [3/26/64]

881) Fischer,R-Chavez,F [3/26/64] Simultaneous, New Orleans B32/33 Sicilian 1.e4 c5 2.Nf3 Nc6 3.d4 cd4 4.Nd4 e5 5.Nb5 d6 6.N1c3 Nf6 7.Bg5 Be7 8.Bf6 gf6 9.Nd5 Kf8 10.c3 Rg8 11.Ne7 Ke7 12.Qd2 a6 13.Na3 Be6 14.g3 [D] d5 15.Bg2 d4 16.0-0 Rc8 17.Rad1 Ba2 18.f4 Bb3 19.fe5 fe5 20.Qh6 Rg6 21.Qh7 Qg8 22.Qh4 f6 23.Rd2 Qg7 24.Qh5 Rh8 25.Qf3? Qh6 0-1

After 14.g3

882) Fischer,R-Parham,F [3/26/64] Simultaneous, New Orleans Evans Gambit 1.e4 e5 2.Nf3 Nc6 3.Bc4 Bc5 4.b4 Bb4 5.c3 Ba5 6.d4 d6 7.Qb3 Qd7 8.de5 Bb6 9.ed6 Na5 10.Qb4 Nc4 11.Qc4 cd6 12.O-O Nf6 13.Ba3 O-O [D] 14.e5 Qg4 15.Nbd2 Nh5 16.Qg4 Bg4 17.Bd6 Rfc8 18.c4 Nf4 19.Rab1 Bf5 20.Rb3 Be6 21.g3 Ne2 22.Kg2 Bc4 23.Nc4 Rc4 24.Re1 Rc2 25.Rf1 Ra2 26.Ng5 Rc8 27.Rf3 Nd4 28.Rd3 Rcc2 29.Ne4 Nf5 30.g4 Ne3 31.Re3 Be3 32.Kg3 Rc1 33.Rc1 Bc1 34.f4 Re2 35.Nc5 b5 36.f5 Ba3 0-1

After 13...0-0

Houston [3/28/64]

883) Fischer,R-Hale,K [3/28/64] Simultaneous, Houston Caro Kann 1.e4 c6 2.d4 d5 3.Nc3 de4 4.Ne4 Nd7 5.Nf3 Ngf6 6.Nf6 Nf6 7.Ne5 e6 8.Bd3 Be7 [8...Qd4? 9.Nf7 Kf7 10.Bg6] 9.c3 c5 10.dc5 Bc5 11.Bb5 Bd7 12.Nd7 Nd7 13.0-0 a6 14.Be2 0-0 15.Bf3 Qc7 16.Qe2 Be7 17.g3 h6 18.Rd1 Rfd8 19.Bf4 Qb6 20.Rd2 Nf6 21.Rad1 Rd2 22.Rd2 Rd8 23.Rd8 Bd8 24.b4 Be7 25.a4 a5 26.Be3 Qc7 27.ba5 Qa5 [D] 28.Qb5 Qc3 29.Qb7 Bb4 30.Bb6 Qa1 31.Kg2 Qa4 32.Qc8 Qe8 33.Qc4 Qe7 34.Bd4 Bd6 35.Qc8 Qe8 36.Qb7 Qe7 37.Qc8 Qe8 1/2-1/2 [Note by Hale]

After 27...Qa5

After 14...h6

After 21...e6??

After 20...Kh7

After 48...a1=Q

Final position

After 20...Qe6

884) Fischer,R-Moffitt,S [3/28/64] Simultaneous, Houston Caro Kann **1.e4 c6 2.d4 d5 3.Nc3 de4 4.Ne4 Bf5 5.Nc5** [Fischer played this move often on the 1964 tour, and indicates (in his notes to game 49 of "My 60 memorable games") that White has more space. He also notes that the Knight on d3 (after 7.Nd3) makes the freeing maneuvers ...c5 and ...e5 difficult for Black. Moffitt still feels that his reply 5...Qc7 was probably not best and deserves a ?!] **Qc7?! 6.Bd3 Bd3 7.Nd3 e6 8.Bf4 Bd6 9.Qg4 g6 10.Nf3 Bf4 11.Nf4 Nf6 12.Qh4 Qe7 13.0-0 Nbd7 14.c4 h6** [D] **15.d5! cd5 16.cd5 0-0-0 17.de6 Nb6 18.ef7 Qf7 19.Ne5 1-0**

885) Fischer,R-Bone,C.H. [3/28/64] Simultaneous, Houston Sicilian **1.e4 c5 2.Nf3 d6 3.d4 cd4 4.Nd4 Bd7 5.Nc3 Nc6 6.Bc4 Nf6 7.0-0 g6 8.f4 Bg7 9.Nc6 Bc6 10.Qe2 0-0 11.Bd3 a6 12.a4 Rc8 13.f5 Nd7 14.Kh1 Ne5 15.Bg5 Nd3 16.cd3 Bd7 17.Nd5 f6 18.Be3 Rc6 19.b4 b5 20.ab5 ab5 21.Ra7 e6??** [D] **22.fe6 1-0** [22...Be6 23.Ne7]

886) Fischer,R-Bell,C. [3/28/64] Simultaneous, Houston, Ruy Lopez **1.e4 e5 2.Nf3 Nc6 3.Bb5 Bb4 4.c3 Bc5 5.d4 ed4 6.cd4 Bb4 7.Nc3 Bc3 8.bc3 Nf6 9.0-0 0-0 10.Bg5 h6 11.Bh4 Ne7 12.Bf6 gf6 13.Nh4 d6 14.f4 f5 15.Qh5 Kh7 16.ef5 Nf5 17.Bd3 Kg7 18.Bf5 Qf6 19.Rf3 Bf5 20.Nf5 Kh7** [D] **21.Nh6 Qh6 22.Qf5 1-0**

887) Fischer,R-Bills,W [3/28/64] Simultaneous, Houston French **1.e4 e6 2.d4 d5 3.Nc3 Nf6 4.Bg5 de4 5.Ne4 Be7 6.Bf6 gf6 7.g3 f5 8.Nc3 c6 9.Bg2 b6 10.d5 Bb7 11.de6 Qd1 12.Rd1 fe6 13.Nge2 Kf7 14.0-0 Na6 15.Nd4 Nb4 16.a3 Nd5 17.Nd5 cd5 18.Rfe1 Bf6 19.Ne6 Bb2 20.Bd5 Bd5 21.Rd5 Rhe8 22.Rf5 Kg6 23.g4 Ba3 24.h4 h6 25.h5 Kh7 26.Rf7 Kh8 27.Re3 Bc1 28.Re1 Bd2 29.Rd1 Re6 30.Rd2 a5 31.Rdd7 a4 32.Kg2 b5 33.f4 Re2 34.Kf3 Rc2 35.g5 Rac8 36.Rh7 Kg8 37.Rh6 R2c7 38.Rc7 Rc7 39.Ra6 Rc3 40.Kg4 a3 41.Ra8 Kf7 42.g6 Kf6 43.Ra6 Kg7 44.Ra7 Kf6 45.Rf7 Ke6 46.f5 Kd6 47.g7 a2 48.g8=Q a1=Q** [D] **49.Qd8 Kc5 50.Rc7 Kb4 51.Qd4 1-0**

888) Fischer,R-Boatner,J [3/28/64] Simultaneous, Houston Evans Gambit **1.e4 e5 2.Nf3 Nc6 3.Bc4 Bc5 4.b4 Bb4 5.c3 Be7 6.d4 d6 7.Qb3 Nh6 8.Bh6 gh6 9.Bf7 Kf8 10.Bh5!** [D] **1-0**

889) Fischer,R-Bone,E [3/28/64] Simultaneous, Houston French **1.e4 e6 2.d4 d5 3.Nc3 Nf6 4.Bg5 Be7 5.e5 Nfd7 6.h4 a6 7.Qg4 f5 8.Qh5 g6 9.Qh6 Bg5 10.hg5 Qe7 11.Nh3 Qf8 12.Qh4 c5 13.Nf4 Qf7 14.0-0-0 cd4 15.Ncd5 ed5 16.e6 Qg8 17.Nd5 Kd8 18.ed7 Qd5 19.Rd4 Qa2 20.Ra4 Qe6** [D] **21.Qd4??** [Uncharacteristically, Bobby blunders very badly] **Qe1 0-1**

890) Fischer,R-Brieger,R [3/28/64] Simultaneous, Houston Nimzowitsch Defense [World Class Grandmaster vs. World Class Chess composer!] **1.e4 Nc6 2.Nf3 e6 3.d4 d5 4.Nc3 Nf6 5.ed5 ed5 6.Bb5 Be7 7.Ne5 Bd7 8.Nd7 Qd7 9.0-0 0-0 10.h3 h6 11.Be3 a6 12.Bd3 Bb4 13.Ne2 Bd6 14.c3 Rfe8 15.Nf4 Bf4 16.Bf4 Ne4 17.f3 Nf6 18.Qd2 Ne7 19.Rfe1 c6 20.Be5 Nh7 21.Re2 f6 22.Bg3 Nf5 23.Bf2 Re2 24.Qe2 Nd6 25.Qc2 Nf8 26.Bg3 Re8 27.b3 g5 28.Rd1 Kg7 29.c4 Qe6 30.Re1 Qf7 31.Re8 Ne8 32.Qe2 Qe6 33.Qd2 Qd7 34.cd5 cd5 35.Qb4 Kf7 36.a4 Qe7 37.Qd2 Qa3 38.Bc2 Ne6 39.Kh2 Nf8 40.Qc3 Qe7 41.b4 Qd7 42.Bb3 Ne6 43.Qd3 Nf8 44.b5 ab5 45.ab5 Ng6 46.Qe4 Ne7 47.Qh7 Ke6 48.Qh6 Qb5 49.Ba2 Qa4 50.Bb1 Qd4 51.f4 Qe3 52.h4 [D] gh4?? 53.f5 [Oops!] Nf5 54.Bf5 Kf5 55.Qe3 hg3 56.Kg3 Nd6 57.Kf3 Ne4 58.Qb6 Ng5 59.Ke3 Ne6 60.Qb7 d4 61.Kd2 1-0**

After 52.h4

891) Fischer,R-Chalker,R [3/28/64] Simultaneous, Houston Petroff **1.e4 e5 2.Nf3 Nf6 3.d4 ed4 4.e5 Ne4 5.Qe2 Bb4 6.Kd1 Nc5?? [6...d5] [D] 7.Bg5! d3 8.cd3 f6 9.ef6 Kf7 10.Ne5 Ke6 11.Nc6 1-0** [Years later, Chalker became a master]

After 6...Nc5??

892) Fischer,R-Chaney,K [3/28/64] Simultaneous, Houston Philidor **1.e4 e5 2.Nf3 d6 3.d4 f5 4.de5 fe4 5.Ng5 d5 6.Nc3 Ne7 7.e6 [D] Ng6 8.Nf7 Qf6 9.Nh8 1-0**

After 7.e6

893) Fischer,R-Cunningham,T [3/28/64] Simultaneous, Houston King's Gambit **1.e4 e5 2.f4 ef4 3.Bc4 d5 4.Bd5 Nf6 5.Nc3 Nc6 6.Nf3 Nd5 7.Nd5 g5 8.d4 Bg7 9.h4 g4 10.Ne5 Ne5 11.de5 Be5 12.Bf4 Qd6 13.0-0 Bf4 14.Rf4 h5 15.Qd4 Rf8 16.Rf6 Be6 17.c4 c6 [D] 18.Rd1 cd5 19.cd5 Ke7 20.e5 Qb6 21.Qb6 ab6 22.de6 fe6 23.Rf8 Rf8 24.Rd6 Rf5 25.Rb6 Re5 26.Rb7 Kd6 27.Kf2 Rd5 28.a4 Rd2 29.Kg3 Rd3 30.Kf4 Rd4 31.Kg5 Ra4 32.Kh5 e5 33.b4 Kc6 34.Rb8 Kc7 35.Re8 Kd6 36.Kg4 Rb4 37.Kg5 e4 38.h5 Rb5 39.Kg6 Kd5 40.h6 Rb6 41.Kg5 Rb2 42.g4 Rb7 43.Kg6 Rb6 44.Kh5 Rb3 45.h7 1-0**

After 17...c6

894) Fischer,R-Dudley,B.G. [3/28/64] Simultaneous, Houston Sicilian **1.e4 c5 2.Nf3 d6 3.d4 cd4 4.Nd4 Nf6 5.Nc3 e6 6.g4 Nc6 7.g5 Nd7 8.Be3 Be7 9.h4 a6 10.Qd2 Nde5 11.0-0-0 Qc7 12.f4 Ng4 13.Bg1 Nd4 14.Qd4 e5 15.Qd2 ef4 16.Nd5 Qc6 17.Qf4 Bf8 18.Bh3 Ne5 19.Bd4 Ng6 20.Qf2 Be6 [D] 21.Rhf1 Bh3 22.Qf7 Kd8 23.Rf3 Bg4 24.Bb6 Kc8 25.Rc3 Bd7 26.Rc6 bc6 27.Nc3 Ne5 28.Qf2 Be7 29.Bd4 Rf8 30.Qg2 Kc7 31.Be5 de5 32.Na4 Rf4 33.Qd2 Rd8 34.Qa5 1-0**

After 20...Be6

After 30.Qd6

895) Fischer,R-Ermidis,N [3/28/64] Simultaneous, Houston
Vienna Gambit **1.e4 e5 2.Nc3 Nc6 3.Bc4 Nf6 4.f4 d6 5.Nf3 Bg4
6.Bb5 a6 7.Bc6 bc6 8.h3 Bf3 9.Qf3 Be7 10.fe5 de5 11.d3 0-0
12.Nd1 Ne8 13.Ne3 Bg5 14.0-0 Nd6 15.Kh1 Be3 16.Be3 Qd7
17.Qg3 Rae8 18.Bc5 Re6 19.Rf3 Rfe8 20.Raf1 Rg6 21.Qf2 f6
22.Rg3 Rg3 23.Qg3 Qe6 24.b3 Nb5 25.a4 Nd4 26.Bd4 ed4 27.Qc7
Qc8 28.Qg3 Kh8 29.Rf5 c5 30.Qd6 [D] Re5 31.Re5 fe5 32.Qe5
Qf8 33.Qf5 Qf5 34.ef5 Kg8 35.g4 Kf7 36.Kg2 Kf6 37.Kf3 Ke5
38.Kg3 a5 39.h4 h5 40.gh5 1-0**

After 20...Qf6

896) Fischer,R-Gould,D [3/28/64] Simultaneous, Houston Two
Knights **1.e4 e5 2.Nf3 Nc6 3.Bc4 Nf6 4.Ng5 d5 5.ed5 Na5 6.Bb5
c6 7.dc6 bc6 8.Be2 Bc5 9.d3 0-0 10.Nc3 h6 11.Nge4 Ne4 12.Ne4
Be7 13.0-0 Nb7 14.Kh1 Nd6 15.Bf3 Bf5 16.Be3 Ne4 17.Be4 Be4
18.de4 a6 19.Qg4 Bg5 20.Rad1 Qf6 [D] 21.Bg5 Qg5 22.Qg5 hg5
23.Rd6 Rac8 24.Rfd1 Rfe8 25.Kg1 f6 26.h3 Kh7 27.Rd7 Kg6
28.Ra7 Ra8 29.Ra8 Ra8 30.Rd7 Rb8 31.b3 Kh6 32.Rc7 Rb6
33.a4 a5 34.Kf1 Ra6 35.Ke2 Kg6 36.Kd3 f5 37.f3 f4 38.Kc4 1-0**

After 43...c4

897) Fischer,R-Heising,C [3/28/64] Simultaneous, Houston Ruy
Lopez **1.e4 e5 2.Nf3 Nc6 3.Bb5 a6 4.Ba4 b5 5.Bb3 Nge7 6.Ng5 d5
7.ed5 Nd4 8.Nf7 Kf7 9.d6 Nb3 10.de7 Be7 11.ab3 Bb7 12.0-0 Rf8
13.Nc3 b4 14.Ne2 Qd5 15.f3 Kg8 16.Ng3 Qd4 17.Kh1 Bd6 18.d3
Qh4 19.Ne4 Rf5 20.Be3 Raf8 21.Bf2 Qh6 22.c4 g5 23.Qe2 Qg6 24.c5
Be7 25.d4 Qe6 26.de5 Qe5 27.Bg3 Qe6 28.c6 Qc6 29.Rac1 Qe6 30.h3
c5 31.Rfe1 R8f7 32.Qd2 Qd5 33.Qc2 Qc6 34.Qc4 a5 35.Rcd1 Ba6
36.Qc2 Rd5 37.Rd5 Qd5 38.Nf2 Bf8 39.Ng4 Qf5 40.Qc1 h6 41.Re8
Kh7 42.Qe3 Qb1 43.Kh2 c4 [D] 44.Rf8 Rf8 45.Qe7 Kg6 46.Qf8 Qb2
47.Ne5 1-0**

After 24...Bd4

898) Fischer,R-Jacobs,S [3/28/64] Simultaneous, Houston
Sicilian **1.e4 c5 2.Nf3 d6 3.d4 cd4 4.Nd4 Nf6 5.Nc3 g6 6.Be3 Bg7
7.f3 Nc6 8.Qd2 Nd4 9.Bd4 0-0 10.0-0-0 Qa5 11.Bc4 Bd7 12.Kb1
Rfc8 13.Bb3 Rc7 14.h4 h5 15.g4 hg4 16.h5 gh5 17.Bf6 Bf6 18.fg4
Bg4 19.Rdg1 Qg5 20.Qf2 Rc5 21.Nd5 Be5 22.Ne7 Kh8 23.Nf5 Rc7
24.Ne3 Bd4 [D] 25.Rg4 Qg4 26.Ng4 Bf2 27.Nf2 Rc5 28.Bd5 Kg7
29.Rh5 Rc7 30.a3 Rh8 31.Rh8 Kh8 32.Ng4 Re7 33.Nh6 Kg7?
34.Nf5 1-0**

After 16.Bf4

899) Fischer,R-Jones,B [3/28/64] Simultaneous, Houston
Sicilian **1.e4 c5 2.Nf3 Nf6 3.Nc3 d5 4.ed5 Nd5 5.Bb5 Bd7 6.Ne5
Bb5 7.Nb5 e6 8.Qf3 Qf6 9.Qf6 gf6 10.c4 a6 11.cd5 ab5 12.Ng4 f5
13.Ne3 f4 14.Ng4 Bg7 15.d4 Bd4 16.Bf4 [D] Bb2 17.Rb1 Bc3
18.Kf1 b4 19.de6 fe6 20.g3 Nc6 21.Kg2 h5 22.Ne3 Ra2 23.Nc4
0-0 24.Nd6 Bd4 25.Nb7 e5 26.Bh6 Rff2 27.Kh3 c4 28.Nd6 Rf6
0-1** [A well-played game by Jones]

900) Fischer,R-Kelley,J [3/28/64] Simultaneous, Houston
Sicilian **1.e4 c5 2.Nf3 d6 3.d4 cd4 4.Nd4 Nf6 5.Nc3 a6 6.f4 Qc7
7.Be2 e6 8.0-0 Be7 9.Bf3 0-0 10.g4 h6 11.Qe2 Nbd7 12.Qg2 Rb8
13.h4 d5 14.e5 Ne4 15.Ne4 de4 16.Be4 Nc5 17.Bf3 Bh4 18.Be3 g5
19.Bf2 Bf2 20.Qf2 Bd7 21.Rae1 b5 22.Qh2 Kg7 23.f5 ef5 24.gf5
Qa7 25.f6 Kh7 26.Rf2 Rg8 [D] 27.Qh6 1-0** [27...Kh6 28.Rh2 Kg6
29.Bh5 Kh7 30.Bf7 with mate next]

After 26...Rg8

901) Fischer,R-Longcobe,E [3/28/64] Simultaneous, Houston
Philidor **1.e4 e5 2.Nf3 d6 3.d4 Nc6 4.Bb5 Bd7 5.Nc3 Be7 6.Bc6
Bc6 7.de5 de5 8.Qd8 Rd8 9.Ne5 Bf6 10.Nc6 bc6 11.f3 Bc3 12.bc3
Rb8 13.0-0 Ne7 14.Ba3 Rb5 15.Rab1 Nc8 16.c4 Rb1 17.Rb1 Kd7
18.Rb7 Re8 19.c5 f6 20.Bc1 g5 21.Kf2 Re5 22.Be3 Re6 [D]** and
1-0 in 38 moves.

After 22...Re6

902) Fischer,R-Lynch [3/28/64] Simultaneous, Houston Pirc
**1.e4 d6 2.d4 Nf6 3.Nc3 g6 4.f4 Bg7 5.Nf3 0-0 6.Bd3 Nc6 7.e5 de5
8.fe5 Nh5 9.Be3 Bg4 10.Be4 e6 11.0-0 f6 12.ef6 Nf6 13.Bc6 bc6
14.h3 Bf3 15.Rf3 Nd5 16.Rf8 Qf8 17.Nd5 cd5 18.Qd2 Qe7 19.Re1
Qd7 20.Bf4 c6 21.Be5 Be5 22.Re5 Rf8 23.Qe2 Rf6 24.c3 Kg7
25.g4 Qc8 26.h4 h6 27.Qe3 Qd7 28.Qd3 Qc8 29.c4 Qb7 30.Qc3
Qd7 31.cd5 cd5 32.Qb3 Qc7 33.Qe3 Qc6 34.Kh2 Qd6 [D] 35.g5
hg5 36.hg5 Rf8 37.Kg1 Re8 38.a4 a6 39.a5** and **1-0** in 43 moves.

After 34...Qd6

903) Fischer,R-McGregor,R.F [3/28/64] Simultaneous,
Houston Irregular **1.e4 e5 2.Nf3 f6?! [D]** [Bluffing. McGregor,
actually a strong player, wanted Fischer to think he was a beginner]
**3.Ne5 Qe7 4.Nf3 d5 5.d3 de4 6.de4 Qe4 7.Be2 Bf5 8.Nd4 Nc6
9.Nf5 Qf5 10.0-0 Bd6 11.Bg4 Qb5 12.Nc3 Qc4 13.Be2 Qf7 14.Bb5
0-0-0 15.Qg4 f5 16.Qh3 Nge7 17.Ne4 h6 18.Nd6 Rd6 19.Bf4 Rd4
20.Be3 Rb4 21.Bc6 Nc6 22.b3 Re4 23.Rfd1 Rd8 24.Rd8 Nd8
25.Rd1 Qe6 26.g3 Re3 1/2-1/2**

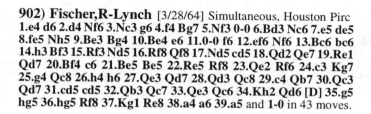

After 2...f6?!

904) Fischer,R-Michalopoulos [3/28/64] Simultaneous,
Houston King's Gambit **1.e4 e5 2.f4 f5? 3.ef5 d6 4.Qh5 Kd7 5.fe5
de5 6.Nf3 Qf6 7.Nc3 Ne7 8.Ne4 Qf5 9.Ne5 Ke6 10.Bc4 Ke5 [D]
11.d4 Kd4 12.Be3 Ke5 13.Bf4 Kd4 14.0-0-0 Ke4 15.Qf3# 1-0**

After 10...Ke5

905) Fischer,R-Nuchod,J [3/28/64] Simultaneous, Houston
Bishop's Opening **1.e4 e5 2.Bc4 Nf6 3.Nc3 Bb4 4.f4 d6 5.Nf3 ef4
6.d3 Bc3 7.bc3 Be6 8.Be6 fe6 9.Bf4 e5 10.Bd2 Nc6 11.0-0 0-0
12.Qe2 Qe7 13.Nh4 g6 14.Bg5 Qe6 15.Nf3 Ng4 16.h3 Nf6 [D]
17.Bh6 Rf7? 18.Ng5 Qe7 19.Nf7 Qf7 20.Bg5 Qe6 21.Rf6 Qe7
22.Rg6 1-0**

After 16...Nf6

After 17.Re1

906) Fischer,R-Patteson,B [3/28/64] Simultaneous, Houston Nimzowitsch Defense **1.e4 Nc6 2.d4 e5 3.de5 Ne5 4.f4 Ng6 5.Nf3 Bc5 6.Bc4 Nf6 7.f5 Ne7 8.Nc3 0-0 9.Bg5 d5 10.Bf6 gf6 11.Nd5 Nd5 12.Qd5 Qd5 13.Bd5 Re8 14.0-0-0 c6 15.Bb3 Re4 16.Rd8 Kg7 17.Re1 [D] Bb6 18.Re8 Re1 19.Ne1 Bc7 20.Nf3 Rb8 21.Re7 Bf4 22.Kb1 Bf5 23.Rf7 Kg6 24.Nh4 Kg5 25.Nf5 Kf5 26.Rh7 Rd8 27.a4 Rd2 28.Rb7 Be3 29.Rg7 Rd1 30.Ka2 Rh1 31.h3 Bb6 32.Bc4 Bd4 33.Bd3 Ke6 34.Be4 Kd6 35.Rh7 Re1 36.Bd3 Re3 37.Rg7 f5 38.Rg6 Ke5 39.Rc6 Rg3 40.Ra6 Rg2 41.Ra5 1-0**

After 8...Qf6

907) Fischer,R-Peil [3/28/64] Simultaneous, Houston *Evans Gambit* **1.e4 e5 2.Nf3 Nc6 3.Bc4 Bc5 4.b4 Bb4 5.c3 Ba5 6.d4 ed4 7.0-0 dc3 8.Qb3 Qf6 [D] 9.e5 Ne5 10.Re1 Ne7 11.Re5 0-0 12.Bg5 Qg6 13.Be7 c2 14.Nbd2 Bd2 15.Nd2 Re8 16.Bd6 Re5 17.Be5 Qg5 18.Qe3 Qe3 19.fe3 d6 20.Bb2 Bg4 21.Rc1 Bd1 22.Bd3 Re8 23.e4 c6 24.Bc2 Bc2 25.Rc2 f6 26.Kf2 Kf7 27.Kf3 d5 28.ed5 cd5 29.Rc7 Re7 30.Re7 Ke7 and 1-0 in 48 moves.**

After 16...f6

908) Fischer,R-Limoh [Pimoh?], L.C. [3/28/64] Simultaneous, Houston Sicilian **1.e4 c5 2.Nf3 Nc6 3.d4 cd4 4.Nd4 Nf6 5.Nc3 a6 6.Bc4 e6 7.0-0 d6 8.Be3 Be7 9.Bb3 0-0 10.f4 Bd7 11.Qf3 Rc8 12.f5 Nd4 13.Bd4 Kh8 14.g4 Ng8 15.Rad1 Bc6 16.Rf2 f6 [D] 17.h4 Be8 18.Rg2** [The score becomes unreadable at this point. Fischer apparently played h5 followed by hg6 and Black resigned on move 24] **1-0**

After 25...g5

909) Fischer,R-Plaster,J [3/28/64] Simultaneous, Houston French **1.e4 e6 2.d4 d5 3.Nc3 Nf6 4.Bg5 Be7 5.e5 Nfd7 6.Be7 Qe7 7.f4 a6 8.Nf3 c5 9.dc5 Nc5 10.Qd2 Bd7 11.0-0-0 Bc6 12.Bd3 Nd3 13.cd3 b5 14.Nd4 Bb7 15.Kb1 Nc6 16.Nce2 Nd4 17.Nd4 0-0 18.Rde1 Bc8 19.g4 Bd7 20.f5 ef5 21.gf5 f6 22.e6 Be8 23.Rhg1 Kh8 24.Rg3 g6 25.Reg1 g5 [D] 26.h4 h6 27.hg5 hg5 28.Rh1 Kg8 29.Rgh3 1-0**

After 23...h6?

910) Fischer,R-Schmid,A.D. [3/28/64] Simultaneous, Houston Petroff **1.e4 e5 2.Nf3 Nf6 3.d4 ed4 4.e5 Ne4 5.Qe2 Nc5 6.Nd4 Be7 7.Nc3 c6 8.Be3 d6 9.0-0-0 Be6 10.Ne6 Ne6 11.ed6 Bf6 12.d7 Nd7 13.Ne4 Be7 14.f4 f5 15.Qc4 fe4 16.Qe6 Qc7 17.Bc4 Rf8 18.Qe4 Nf6 19.Qe6 b6 20.Rhe1 Rd8 21.Rd8 Kd8 22.Rd1 Ke8 23.g3 h6? [D] 24.Bd3 Nd5 25.c4 Qd7 26.cd5 Qe6 27.de6 Rf6 28.f5 Bd6 29.Be4 Ke7 30.Bd4 Rf8 31.Bg7 Rg8 32.Bh6 c5 33.Bf4 Bf4 34.gf4 Kf6 35.Rd7 Rg7 36.Rg7 Kg7 37.e7 1-0**

911) Fischer,R-Smith,G [3/28/64] Simultaneous, Houston Falkbeer Counter Gambit **1.e4 e5 2.f4 d5 3.ed5 e4 4.Nc3 Nf6 5.Qe2 Nd5 6.Qe4 Be6 7.f5 Nc3 8.bc3 Qd5 9.Bd3 Qe4 10.Be4 Bc8 11.Nf3 Bd6 12.d4 Nd7 13.c4 Nf6 14.Bd3 c6 15.0-0 0-0 16.Re1 b6 17.a4 Bb4 18.Bd2 a5 19.Rab1 Bd2 20.Nd2 Rb8 21.c5 Nd5 22.Nc4 Ba6 [D] 23.Nb6 Bd3 24.Nd5 Rb1 25.Rb1 Bc2 26.Ne7 Kh8 27.Ra1 Be4 28.Re1 1-0**

After 22...Ba6

912) Fischer,R-Staight,G [3/28/64] Simultaneous, Houston King's Gambit **1.e4 e5 2.f4 Bc5 3.Nf3 [D] Nf6? 4.fe5 Ne4 5.d4 Bb6 6.Bd3 Nc5?** [6...d5] **7.dc5 Bc5 8.Nc3 d6 9.Qe2 0-0 10.Be3 and 1-0** in 50 moves.

After 3.Nf3

Little Rock [3/29/64]

913) Fischer,R-Hurt,J Simultaneous,Little Rock French **1.e4 e6 2.d4 d5 3.Nc3 Bb4 4.a3 Bc3 5.bc3 Ne7 6.Bd3 O-O 7.Nf3 Nd7 8.e5 f5 9.ef6 gf6 10.O-O Rf7 11.Re1 Nf8 12.Nh4 Nfg6 13.Qh5 Nh4 14.Qh4 Kh8 15.Re3 Nf5 16.Bf5 ef5 17.Rg3 Qe7 18.Bf4 Bd7 19.Bc7 Ba4 20.Bf4 Bc2 21.Re3 Qd7 22.Rae1 Rg8 23.h3 Ba4 24.Re6 Qd8 25.g3 Re8 26.Qh6 Re6 27.Re6 Qf8 28.Qh5 Bd7 29.Rd6 Qe8 30.Kh2 Be6 31.a4 Qe7 32.a5 Rg7 33.a6 b6 34.Qe2 Bd7 35.Qa2 Qe8 [D] 36.Rf6 Re7 37.Be5 Re5 38.de5 Qe5 39.Rf8 Kg7 40.Ra8 f4 41.Ra7 fg3 42.fg3 Qe6 43.Rd7 1-0**

After 35...Qe8

914) Fischer,R-Long,R Simultaneous, Little Rock Sicilian **1.e4 c5 2.Nf3 Nc6 3.d4 cd4 4.Nd4 a6 5.Nc3 e6 6.Bc4 Qc7 7.Bb3 b5 8.O-O Bb7 9.Re1 Rc8 [D] 10.Nd5 Qe5 11.Nf3 Qh5 12.Be3 Nf6 13.Nf4 Qh6 14.Ne6 g5 15.Bg5 Qg6 16.Nh4 Qh5 17.Bf6 Qd1 18.Rad1 de6 19.Bh8 1-0**

After 9...Rc8

915) Fischer,R-Weaks,H Simultaneous, Little Rock Caro Kann **1.e4 c6 2.Nc3 d5 3.Nf3 Bg4 4.h3 Bf3 5.Qf3 e6 6.d4 Nf6 7.Bd3 de4 8.Ne4 Ne4 9.Be4 Nd7 10.O-O Be7 11.Rd1 O-O 12.c4 Nf6 13.Bc2 Qc7 14.Bf4 Bd6 15.Bg5 Be7 16.Rac1 Rfd8 17.Bb3 Rd7 18.d5 ed5 19.cd5 Rad8 20.dc6 Rd1 21.Bd1 bc6 22.Bb3 c5 23.Be3 h6 24.Qf5 Kf8 25.Bc5 Bc5 26.Rc5 Qd7 27.Qf4 Qd6 28.Qc4 Rd7 29.Rc8 Ne8 30.g3 [D] Rc7 31.Ba4 Rc8 32.Qc8 Qe5 33.Qe8 Qe8 34.Be8 Ke8 35.Kg2 Kd7 36.Kf3 Kd6 37.Ke4 1-0**

After 30.g3

Wichita [4/4/64]

After 12...f6

916) Fischer,R-Ballard, D La Pierre [4/4/64] Simultaneous, Wichita, Kansas Sicilian [Notes by Ballard] **1.e4 c5 2.Nf3 Nc6 3.d4 cd4 4.Nd4 g6 5.Nc3 Bg7 6.Be3 Nf6 7.Bc4 0-0 8.Bb3 Ng4 9.Qg4 Nd4 10.Qd1 Nb3 11.ab3 b6 12.Bd4 f6** [D] [Black weakens his light squares] **13.h4** [13.Bf6 followed by 14.Qd5 leads only to a draw] **Bb7 14.h5 Kf7 15.Qg4 d5 16.ed5 Bd5 17.0-0-0 Be6 18.Qg3 Qb8 19.Qf3 Qc8 20.Ne4 Bg4 21.hg6 hg6 22.Qd3 Bd1 23.Rd1 Qc6 24.Rh1 Rac8 25.c3 Rh8 26.Re1 Rhd8 27.f4 Qd5 28.Kb1 Qb3 29.f5!!** [dominating the light squares] **gf5 30.Ng5!! fg5 31.Qf5 Bf6 32.Bf6** [According to Fischer, White should now have played 32.Qh7] **Rd1 33.Rd1 Qd1 34.Ka2 Rc5 0-1** [White soon runs out of checks]

Ogden, UT 4/4/64]

After 21...Bg6

917) Fischer,R-Hartwell, T Simultaneous, Ogden, Sicilian **1.e4 c5 2.Nf3 Nc6 3.d4 cd4 4.Nd4 Nf6 5.Nc3 g6 6.Be3 Bg7 7.Bc4 d6 8.f3 O-O 9.Qd2 a6 10.O-O-O Ne5 11.Bb3 b5 12.h4 h5 13.g4 hg4 14.f4 Nf3 15.Nf3 gf3 16.f5 b4 17.Nd5 Ne4 18.Qh2 Bf5 19.h5 g5 20.h6 Be5 21.Qh5 Bg6** [D] **22.Ne7 Qe7 23.Qg6 Kh8 24.Qf5 Ng3 25.Qf3 Nh1 26.Rh1 f5 27.Bd2 Qf6 28.Bb4 Bb2 29.Kb1 Be5 30.Rg1 Rac8 31.Bd2 g4 32.Qd5 Ba1 33.Bc1 Qd4 34.Qh1 a5 35.Rd1 Qf6 36.Rd6 Qd6 37.Ka1 Kh7 38.Qg2 a4 39.Bd5 a3 40.Bb3 Rb8 41.Qf2 Rb4 42.Qa7 1-0**

After 22...Be4

918) Fischer,R-Hunt,S Simultaneous, Ogden Sicilian **1.e4 c5 2.Nf3 d6 3.d4 cd4 4.Nd4 Nf6 5.Nc3 Nc6 6.Bg5 e6 7.Qd2 Be7 8.O-O-O Qa5 9.Nb3 Qd8 10.f3 a6 11.g4 b5 12.a3 Bb7 13.Be3 Ne5 14.Be2 h6 15.h4 Rc8 16.g5 hg5 17.hg5 Rh1 18.Rh1 Nfd7 19.Rh8 Nf8 20.f4 Nc4 21.Bc4 Rc4 22.Kb1 Be4** [D] **23.Bd4 e5 24.Ne4 ed4 25.Nd4 Qb6 26.c3 d5 27.Ng3 g6 28.f5 b4 29.ab4 gf5 30.Ngf5 Qg6 31.Rh6 Rd4 32.Qd4 Qf5 33.Ka2 Ng6 34.Rh1 Qe4 35.Rd1 Nf4 36.Qe4 de4 37.Re1 Bg5 38.Re4 Ne6 39.Re5 Be7 40.b5 ab5 41.Rb5 Nc7 42.Rh5 Kd7 43.b4 Bd6 44.Kb3 Ke6 45.c4 f5 46.c5 Bg3 47.Kc4 f4 48.b5 f3 49.b6 Na6 50.Kb5 Nb8 51.c6 Nc6 52.Kc6 f2 53.Rh1 Ke5 54.b7 Ke4 55.Rf1 Ke3 1/2-1/2**

Hollywood, CA [4/12/64]

After 35.g4

919) Fischer,R-Sacks,A Simultaneous, Hollywood, CA Sicilian **1.e4 c5 2.Nf3 d6 3.d4 cd4 4.Nd4 Nf6 5.Nc3 a6 6.Bc4 e6 7.O-O Be7 8.Be3 Qc7 9.Bb3 O-O 10.f4 b5 11.f5 e5 12.Nde2 Bb7 13.Ng3 Nbd7 14.Nh5 Nh5 15.Qh5 Nf6 16.Qf3 Rfd8 17.Bg5 b4 18.Bf6 Bf6 19.Nd5 Bd5 20.Bd5 Rac8 21.Rf2 Qa7 22.Kh1 Qd4 23.Rb1 Rc7 24.Re2 Rdc8 25.Qb3 a5 26.g3 Ra7 27.a3 Rb8 28.a4 Rc8 29.Qf3 Rac7 30.Bb3 Rc6 31.Kg2 R8c7 32.h4 Rc8 33.Kh3 R8c7 34.Rg2 h6 35.g4** [D] **Rc3 36.bc3 Rc3 37.Qc3 Qc3 38.Rg3 Qd2 39.Rbg1 Qe2 40.Bd5 Kf8 41.R3g2 Qf3 42.Rg3 Qe2 1/2-1/2**

920) Fischer,R-Rogosin,D [4/12/64] Simultaneous, Hollywood
Sicilian **1.e4 c5 2.Nf3 d6 3.d4 cd4 4.Nd4 Nf6 5.Nc3 a6 6.Bc4 e6
7.0-0 Be7 8.Bb3 0-0 9.f4 Qc7 10.Qf3 Nc6 11.Be3 Nd4 12.Bd4 b5
13.e5 de5 14.fe5 Bb7 [D] 15.ef6 Bf3 16.fe7 Qe7 17.Rf3 Rad8
18.Be3 Qb7 19.Raf1 Rfe8 20.Ne2 a5 21.c3 Qe4 22.Ng3 Qg6
23.Rf7 a4 24.Bc2 Qc2 25.Nh5 Rf8 26.Rg7 Kh8 0-1**

After 14...Bb7

San Francisco [4/13/64]

921) Fischer,R-Walters, K Simultaneous, San Francisco
Polish **1.b4 Nf6 2.Bb2 e6 3.b5 d5 4.Nf3 c6 5.e3 cb5 6.Bb5 Bd7
7.Bd7 Nbd7 8.O-O Be7 9.d3 O-O 10.Nbd2 Qc7 11.c4 dc4 12.Nc4
Rac8 13.a4 Rfd8 14.Qe2 b6 15.Rfc1 Qb7 16.h3 Nc5 17.Nd4 Rd4
18.Bd4 Nb3 19.Rcb1 Na1 20.Ra1 Nd7 21.Qb2 f6 22.Rb1 e5
23.Bc3 Nc5 24.Qa2 Qd5 25.Rd1 Nd3 26.Rd3 Qc4 27.Qd2 Qa4
28.Rd7 Qa3 29.Qd5 Kf8 30.Bd2 h6 31.Qe6 Re8 32.e4 b5 33.Be3
a5 34.Kh2 Qb4 35.Bb6 [D] Qe4 36.Bc5 Qf4 37.g3 1-0**

After 35.Bb6

922) Fischer,R-Burger,R [4/13/64] San Francisco Two Knights
**1.e4 e5 2.Nf3 Nc6 3.Bc4 Nf6 4.Ng5 d5 5.ed5 Nd4 6.c3 b5 7.Bf1 Nd5
8.cd4 Qg5 9.Bb5 Kd8 10.Qf3 Bb7 11.0-0 ed4 12.Qf7 Nf6! [D]**
[Stopping mate, threatening 13...Qg2# and hitting the Bb5] **0-1**

After 12...Nf6!

923) Fischer,R-Gross, H [4/13/64] Simultaneous, San
Francisco Vienna **1.e4 e5 2.Nc3 Nf6 3.f4 d5 4.d3 de4 5.fe5 Nd5
6.Ne4 Nc6 7.Nf3 Bg4 8.Be2 Bf3 9.Bf3 Ne5 10.O-O Be7 11.d4 Nf3
12.Qf3 O-O 13.c3 c6 14.Ng3 [D] Bg5 15.Nf5 Bc1 16.Rac1 Ne7
17.Rce1 Nf5 18.Qf5 Qc7 19.Re3 Rae8 20.Rh3 g6 21.Qf6 Re6
22.Qh4 f5 23.Rhf3 Rfe8 24.Qf4 Qe7 25.R3f2 Re4 26.Qd2 Qe6
27.a3 Qc4 28.h3 Qb5 29.Qg5 Re1 30.Re1 Re1 31.Kh2 Qd5
32.Qf6 Re6 33.Qh4 1/2-1/2**

After 14.Ng3

924) Fischer,R-Wilkerson,M [4/13/64] Simultaneous, San
Francisco Caro Kann/Panov Attack **1.e4 d5 2.ed5 Nf6 3.c4 c6 4.d4
cd5 5.Nc3 Nc6 6.c5 e6 7.Bb5 Be7 8.Nf3 O-O 9.Bc6 bc6 10.O-O
a5 11.Bf4 Ra6 12.Re1 Nd7 13.Na4 Re8 14.Ne5 Ne5 15.Be5 Bf8
16.Nb6 f6 17.Bg3 e5 18.de5 Bc5 19.Nc8 fe5 20.Rc1 Bb4 21.Re5
Qc8 [D] 22.Rd5 Re1 23.Qe1 Be1 24.Bh4 Qe6 25.Rd8 Kf7
26.Rcd1 Ra7 27.a3 c5 28.R1d3 Bd2 29.g3 g5 30.Rd2 gh4 0-1**

After 21...Qc8

After 41...Kb7

925) Fischer,R-Kane,G [4/13/64] Simultaneous, San Francisco, Center Counter **1.e4 d5 2.ed5 Qd5 3.Nc3 Qa5 4.d4 c6 5.Nf3 Nf6 6.Bd3 Bg4 7.h3 Bf3 8.Qf3 e6 9.O-O Bd6 10.Bd2 Qc7 11.Ne4 Ne4 12.Qe4 Nd7 13.c4 Nf6 14.Qf3 O-O-O 15.Be3 c5 16.dc5 Bc5 17.Rfd1 Be3 18.Qe3 Kb8 19.Be2 Ka8 20.b4 Rd1 21.Rd1 Rd8 22.Rd8 Qd8 23.a4 Qd6 24.c5 Qd8 25.b5 Nd5 26.Qe5 Qf6 27.Qd6 Qe7 28.Qe5 Qf6 29.Qd6 Qe7 30.Qg3 g6 31.Qe5 Qf6 32.Qg3 Qf4 33.Qf4 Nf4 34.Bf3 Kb8 35.a5 Kc7 36.Kf1 Nd3 37.b6 ab6 38.ab6 Kb8 39.c6 bc6 40.Bc6 Ne5 41.Ba4 Kb7 [D] 42.Be8 Kb6 43.f4 Nd3 44.Bf7 Nf4 1/2-1/2**

After 25...Rf8

926) Fischer,R-Blackstone, J [4/13/64] Simultaneous, San Francisco Sicilian **1.e4 c5 2.Nf3 Nc6 3.d4 cd4 4.Nd4 e6 5.Nb5 d6 6.Bf4 e5 7.Be3 a6 8.N5c3 Be6 9.a4 Nge7 10.Nd5 Bd5 11.ed5 Qa5 12.Nc3 Nb8 13.Bd3 Nd7 14.O-O Nb6 15.b4 Qb4 16.Rb1 Qc3 17.Rb6 Nd5 18.Bb5 ab5 19.Qd5 Qc4 20.Qb7 Qc8 21.Qd5 ba4 22.Rb7 Be7 23.f4 f6 24.fe5 de5 25.Rfb1 Rf8 [D] 26.Re7 1-0**

After 22.h3

927) Fischer,R–Henry,R. & Thacker,R [4/13/64] Simultaneous, San Francisco Two Knights **1.e4 e5 2.Nf3 Nc6 3.Bc4 Nf6 4.Ng5 Bc5 5.Bf7 Ke7 6.Bd5 Rf8 7.O-O h6 8.Nf3 d6 9.Bc6 bc6 10.d4 ed4 11.Nd4 Kf7 12.Nc3 Kg8 13.Nc6 Qe8 14.Nd5 Nd5 15.ed5 Ba6 16.c4 Bc4 17.Bh6 Bf1 18.Qg4 Bf2 19.Kh1 Bg2 20.Qg2 Qf7 21.Rf1 Rae8 22.h3 [D] Bg3 23.Rf7 Re1 24.Qg1 Rg1 25.Kg1 Rf7 26.Be3 a6 27.Kg2 Be1 28.b4 Kh7 29.a3 Rf5 30.Nb8 a5 31.ba5 Ba5 0-1**

After 6...de4

928) Fischer,R-Benson,A [4/13/64] Simultaneous, San Francisco, Caro Kann **1.e4 c6 2.Nc3 d5 3.Nf3 Bg4 4.h3 Bf3 5.Qf3 Nf6 6.d4 de4 [D] 7.Ne4?! Ne4 8.Qe4 Nd7 9.Bd3 Nf6 10.Qh4 e6 11.O-O Nd5 12.Qg3 Qc7 13.Qf3 Bd6 14.c3 O-O-O 15.a4 Bf4 16.c4 Bc1 17.cd5 Bg5 18.dc6 Rd4 19.cb7 Kd8 20.Rfd1 Ke7 21.Ba6 Rb4 22.Qa3 Qc5 1-0**

Sacramento [4/15/64]

After 20...Qd7

929)Fischer,R-Sanders,M [4/15/64] Simultaneous, Sacramento Caro Kann **1.e4 c6 2.Nc3 d5 3.d4 de4 4.Ne4 Bf5 5.Nc5 e6 6.Nb7 Qc7 7.Nc5 Nf6 8.Nb3 Be7 9.Nf3 h6 10.Bd3 O-O 11.Bf5 ef5 12.O-O Nbd7 13.Qd3 Ne4 14.g4 fg4 15.Qe4 Nf6 16.Qf5 gf3 17.Qf3 Bd6 18.Bh6 Bh2 19.Kh1 Qd7 [D] 20.Bg7 Kg7 21.Nc5 Qd4 22.Rg1 Bg1 23.Rg1 Kh8 0-1**

930) Fischer,R-Holgerson,M [4/15/64] Simultaneous, Sacramento Vienna 1.e4 e5 2.Nc3 Nf6 3.f4 d5 4.Qf3 Bc5 5.ed5 Bg4 6.Qg3 O-O 7.h3 Bd7 8.Nge2 e4 9.Qh4 Na6 10.a3 c6 11.b4 Bd6 12.dc6 bc6 13.Bb2 Qb6 14.O-O-O Rfe8 15.g4 c5 [D] 16.g5 Nh5! 17.Bg2 cb4 18.Nd5 Qb7 19.Nf6 Nf6 20.gf6 ba3 21.Bc3 a2 22.d3 e3! 0-1

After 15...c5

931) Fischer,R-Singleton,C [4/15/64] Simultaneous, Sacramento Sicilian 1.e4 c5 2.Nf3 b6 3.d4 cd4 4.Nd4 Bb7 5.Nc3 e6 6.Bd3 Bb4 7.Qg4 Qf6 8.Be3 h5 9.Qg3 Bc3 10.bc3 Qg6 11.Qc7 Be4 12.Nb5 Bd3 13.cd3 Qg2 14.O-O-O Na6 15.Qe5 f6 16.Qd4 Qc6 17.c4 Ne7 18.Nd6 Kf8 19.Rhg1 e5 [D] 20.Qe4 Qe4 21.de4 Nb4 22.a3 Nbc6 23.c5 Nc8 24.Nc8 Rc8 25.Rd7 Rg8 26.Kb2 b5 27.Rgg7 Rg7 28.Bg7 Kg7 30.Re7 Kg6 31.Ra7 Rc5 32.h4 Rc4 33.f3 Rd4 34.Rc7 Rd3 35.Rc3 Rd2 36.Rc2 Rd3 37.Rc3 Rd2 38.Kb3 Rh2 39.Kb4 Rh4 40.Kb5 f5 41.ef5 Kf5 42.a4 Rh1 43.a5 h4 44.Rc4 h3 45.Rh4 h2 46.Ka6 Kg5 47.Rh3 Kf4 48.Ka7 e4 49.fe4 Ke4 50.a6 Kd5 51.Ka8 Kc6 52.a7 Kc7 53.Rh8 Kd7 1/2-1/2

After 19...e5

932) Fischer,R-Rubin,S [4/15/64] Simultaneous, Sacramento Vienna 1.e4 d5 2.ed5 Nf6 3.c4 c6 4.dc6 Nc6 5.Nc3 e5 6.d3 Bc5 7.Be2 Bf5 8.Nf3 Ng4 9.O-O Qb6 10.Qe1 Nb4 11.h3 Nf2 12.d4 ed4 13.Na4 Nh3 14.gh3 d3 15.Kh1 Qe6 16.Nc5 Qe2 17.Nd4 Qe1 18.Re1 Kf8 19.Nf5 Rd8 [D] 20.Bf4 Nc2 21.Bd6 Kg8 22.Ne7 Kf8 23.Ng6 Kg8 24.Nh8 Ne1 25.Re1 d2 26.Rd1 Rd6 27.Ne4 Rd8 28.Nf7 Kf7 29.Rd2 Rd2 30.Nd2 Ke6 31.Kg2 Ke5 32.Kf3 Kd4 33.Ke2 h6 34.b4 g5 35.c5 a6 36.a4 a5 37.Nb3 Kc4 38.Na5 Kb4 39.Nb7 1-0

After 19...Rd8

Davis, California (Clock Simultaneous) [4/16/64]

933) Fischer,R-Blackstone,J [4/16/64] Davis Clock Simultaneous Sicilian 1.e4 c5 2.Nf3 d6 3.d4 cd4 4.Nd4 Nf6 5.Nc3 a6 6.Bc4 e6 7.0-0 Be7 8.Bb3 Qc7 9.f4 b5 10.f5 b4 [D] 11.fe6 bc3 12.ef7 Kf8 13.Bg5 Ng4 14.Bf4 cb2 15.Rb1 Nc6 16.Bd5 Nd4 17.Ba8 Qa7 18.Kh1 Nb5 19.Qd2 Qa8 20.c4 Na7 21.Bd6 Nc6 22.Be7 Ne7 23.Qg5 Kf8 24.Qc5 Ne7 25.Qc7 Nf6 26.e5 Qc6 27.Qd8 Kf7 28.Qh8 Bb7 29.Rb2 Qc4 30.Rbf2 Ng6 31.Rf6 gf6 32.Rf6 Ke7 33.Qh7 Kd8 34.Rd6 Kc8 35.Qd7 Kb8 36.Qd8 Ka7 37.Qb6 Ka8 38.Rg6 1-0

After 10...b4

934) Fischer,R-Celle,O [1964] Davis Clock Simultaneous Evans Gambit 1.e4 e5 2.Nf3 Nc6 3.Bc4 Bc5 4.b4 Bb4 5.c3 Be7 6.d4 d6 7.de5 Ne5 8.Ne5 de5 9.Qh5 g6 10.Qe5 Nf6 11.Ba3 Rf8 12.0-0 Ng4 13.Qg3 Ba3 14.Na3 Qe7 15.Bb5 c6 [D] 16.Nc4 Qe6 17.Rad1 cb5 18.Qc7 Bd7 19.Nd6 Ke7 20.Nf5 gf5 21.ef5 Rac8 22.Rd7 Qd7 23.f6 Nf6 24.Re1 Ne4 25.Re4 Kf6 26.Qd7 Rfd8 27.Qg4 1-0

After 15...c6

After 23...dc4

935) Fischer,R-Hoppe,R [4/16/64]Davis Clock Simultaneous French **1.e4 e6 2.d4 d5 3.Nc3 Bb4 4.e5 Ne7 5.a3 Bc3 6.bc3 b6 7.Qg4 Ng6 8.h4 h5 9.Qg3 Ba6 10.Ba6 Na6 11.Ne2 c5 12.Nf4 Nf4 13.Bf4 Kf8 14.Bg5 Qd7 15.0-0 Rc8 16.f4 Nb8 17.Rad1 cd4 18.cd4 Nc6 19.c4 Ne7 20.Be7 Ke7 21.Qg7 Rcg8 22.Qf6 Ke8 23.f5 dc4 [D] 24.d5 ed5 25.e6 Qe7 26.ef7 Qf7 27.Rde1 Kf8 28.Qd6 Kg7 29.Re7 Qe7 30.Qe7 Kh6 31.Re1 Rg7 32.Qf6 Kh7 33.Re7 1-0**

After 24...Nb5

936) Fischer,R-Janushkowsky,A [4/16/64]Davis Clock Simultaneous Evans Gambit **1.e4 e5 2.Nf3 Nc6 3.Bc4 Bc5 4.b4 Bb4 5.c3 Ba5 6.d4 ed4 7.0-0 d6 8.Qb3 Qe7 9.e5 de5 10.Ba3 Qf6 11.cd4 e4 12.Ne5 Nh6 13.Nc6 bc6 14.Qa4 Bb6 15.Nc3 Bd7 16.Ne4 Qf4 17.Nc5 Bc5 18.Bc5 Nf5 19.Rfe1 Kd8 20.Bf7 Nd6 21.Be6 Re8 22.g3 Qf6 23.Bd7 Kd7 24.d5 Nb5 [D] 25.Red1 Kc8 26.Qa6 Kd8 27.dc6 Nd6 28.Bd6 cd6 29.Qb7 1-0**

After 38...Ra2

937) Fischer,R-McCaskey,E [4/16/64] Davis Clock Simultaneous Alekhine's Defence [E: Rook + minor piece] **1.e4 Nf6 2.e5 Nd5 3.d4 d6 4.c4 Nb6 5.ed6 ed6 6.Nc3 Be7 7.Bd3 N8d7 8.Nge2 Nf6 9.b3 d5 10.c5 Nbd7 11.b4 c6 12.0-0 0-0 13.Qc2 Re8 14.f4 Nf8 15.f5 b6 16.Bf4 Bd7 17.h3 Kh8 18.g4 Ng8 19.Qd2 h6 20.Kg2 Bg5 21.Ng1 Bf4 22.Qf4 Qg5 23.Qg5 hg5 24.Nf3 f6 25.h4 gh4 26.Rh1 Nh6 27.Rh4 Kg8 28.Kf2 Kf7 29.Ne2 Ke7 30.Ng3 Kd8 31.g5 fg5 32.Ng5 Kc7 33.Nf3 bc5 34.bc5 Rab8 35.Rb1 Rb1 36.Bb1 Bb8 37.Bd3 Rb2 38.Ke3 Ra2 [D] 39.f6 Nf5 40.Nf5 gf6 41.Rh8 Ne6 42.Nd6 a5 43.Bf5 Ng5 44.Ng5 Bf5 45.Nf5 fg5 46.Rh7 Kd8 47.Ne7 a4 48.Nc6 Kc8 49.Ne7 Kd7 50.Nd5 Ke6 51.Ke4 a3 52.Re7# 1-0**

After 44...hg4

938) Fischer,R-Osbun,E [4/16/64] Davis Clock Simultaneous Evans Gambit **1.e4 e5 2.Nf3 Nc6 3.Bc4 Bc5 4.b4 Bb4 5.c3 Ba5 6.d4 ed4 7.0-0 d6 8.Qb3 Qd7 9.cd4 Bb6 10.Bb5 Kf8 11.d5 Na5 12.Qa4 c6 13.dc6 bc6 14.Bd3 Nb7 15.Nc3 Nc5 16.Qc2 Ne7 17.Ba3 Ng6 18.Rfd1 Nf4 19.Bf1 Kg8 20.Ne5 Qc7 21.Nc4 Be6 22.Nd6 Rd8 23.e5 f6 24.Bc5 Bc5 25.Nce4 Bd6 26.ed6 Qc8 27.Nc5 Bd5 28.d7 Qc7 29.g3 Ne6 30.Ne6 Be6 31.Bc4 Kf7 32.Be6 Ke6 33.Re1 Kf7 34.Qc4 Kg6 35.Re7 Rhg8 36.Rae1 h5 37.Qf7 Kh6 38.R1e6 Rdf8 39.Rf6 gf6 40.Qh7 Kg5 41.h4 Kg4 42.Re4 Kh3 43.Qf5 Rg4 44.Rg4 hg4 [D] 45.Qd3 1-0**

After 25.Qa4

939) Fischer,R-Rubin,S [4/16/64] Davis Clock Simultaneous Center Counter [E:Rook + minor piece] **1.e4 d5 2.ed5 Nf6 3.c4 c6 4.d4 cd5 5.Nc3 e6 6.Nf3 Be7 7.c5 0-0 8.Bd3 Nc6 9.a3 a5 10.Na4 Nd7 11.Qc2 h6 12.0-0 Qc7 13.Re1 Bf6 14.Be3 b6 15.cb6 Nb6 16.Rac1 Na4 17.Qa4 Bb7 18.Bb5 Rfc8 19.Ne5 Be5 20.de5 Qd7 21.Bd4 Rab8 22.Rc3 Ba8 23.Rec1 Rb5 24.Qb5 Rb8 25.Qa4 [D] Ne5 26.Qd7 Nd7 27.Rc8 Kh7 28.Rb8 Nb8 29.Rc8 Nc6 30.Bc5 Bb7 31.Rc7 Ba8 32.b4 ab4 33.ab4 d4 34.b5 1-0**

940) Fischer,R-Shifrine,M [4/16/64] Davis Clock Simultaneous
**1.e4 e5 2.Nc3 Nc6 3.Bc4 Nf6 4.f4 Bc5 5.Nf3 d6 6.d3 Bg4 7.h3 Bf3
8.Qf3 Qe7 9.Bb5 a6 10.Bc6 bc6 11.Ne2 Nd7 12.f5 h6 13.Bd2 a5
14.a4 Nf6 15.g4 d5 16.Ng3 de4 17.de4 Nd7 18.h4 f6 19.g5 0-0-0
20.gh6 gh6 21.0-0-0 Bb4 22.Be3 Nb6 23.Bb6 cb6 24.Nh5 Rhg8
25.Rhg1 Rd1 26.Rd1 Bc5 27.Qd3 Bd4 28.c3 Bc5 29.Qa6 Kb8 [D]
30.Nf6 Be3 31.Kb1 Rd8 32.Rd8 Qd8 33.Qe2 Bc5 34.Nh5 Qh4
35.f6 Qh3 36.f7 Qc8 37.Nf6 1-0**

After 29...Kb8

941) Fischer,R-Von Oettingen,S [4/16/64] Davis Clock
Simultaneous Center Counter **1.e4 d5 2.ed5 Nf6 3.c4 c6 4.d4 cd5
5.Nc3 Nc6 6.Nf3 e6 7.c5 Be7 8.Bb5 0-0 9.0-0 Bd7 10.Bf4 Ne4
11.Rc1 f5 12.Bc6 Bc6 13.Ne5 Qe8 14.f3 Nc3 15.Rc3 Bf6 16.Re1
g5 17.Nc6 Qc6 18.Be5 Qd7 19.b4 a5 20.b5 Qb5 21.Rb3 Qd7
22.Qb1 Be5 23.Re5 Rf7 24.Rb6 Re7 25.Qb3 a4 26.Qe3 Kf7
27.Qg5 Ra6 28.Ra6 ba6 29.g4 Re8 30.gf5 Qd8 [D] 31.fe6 1-0**

After 30...Qd8

942) Fischer,R-Wilkerson [4/16/64] Davis Clock Simultaneous
Sicilian **1.e4 c5 2.Nf3 Nc6 3.d4 cd4 4.Nd4 Nf6 5.Nc3 d6 6.Bc4 g6
7.Nc6 bc6 8.e5 Nd7 9.ed6 ed6 10.0-0 d5 11.Nd5 Nc5 12.Qd4 cd5
13.Bb5 Bd7 14.Bd7 Qd7 15.Qh8 f5 16.Re1 Ne6 [D] 17.Qf6 1-0**

After 16...Ne6

Santa Barbara [4/18/64]

943) Fischer,R-Allen,B [4/18/64] Simultaneous, Santa Barbara
Sicilian **1.e4 c5 2.Nf3 Nc6 3.d4 cd4 4.Nd4 Nf6 5.Nc3 d6 6.Bc4
Na5 7.Bd3 e5 8.Bb5 Bd7 9.Bd7 Qd7 10.Nb3 Nc4 11.Bg5 Nb2
12.Qf3 [D] Qg4 13.Bf6 Qf3 14.gf3 gf6 15.Nd5 Rc8 16.Rb1 Rc2
17.0-0 Nd3 18.Nf6 Kd8 19.Rbd1 Nf4 20.Rd2 Rd2 21.Nd2 Be7
22.Ng4 h5 23.Ne3 Rg8 24.Kh1 Nh3 25.Nd5 Bh4 0-1**

After 12.Qf3

Santa Monica [4/19/64]

944) Fischer,R-Clement,C [4/19/64] Simultaneous, Santa
Monica French **1.e4 e6 2.d4 d5 3.Nc3 Bb4 4.e5 Ne7 5.a3 Bc3
6.bc3 c5 7.a4 Qc7 8.Nf3 cd4 9.cd4 Nbc6 10.Qd2 Bd7 11.Ba3 Nf5
12.g4 [D] Nfd4 13.Nd4 Qe5 14.Qe3 Qd4 15.Qd4 Nd4 16.0-0-0 e5
17.Bb2 Bg4 18.Rd2 Nc6 19.Rg1 Be6 20.Rg7 0-0-0 21.Bb5 Rdg8
22.Rg8 Rg8 23.Bc6 bc6 24.Be5 Rg1 25.Kb2 Rg4 26.Rd4 Rd4
27.Bd4 1/2-1/2**

After 12.g4

After 18...Rhe8

945) Fischer,R-House,J[4/19/64] Simultaneous, Santa Monica Vienna Game **1.e4 e5 2.Nc3 Nf6 3.g3 d5 4.ed5 Nd5 5.Bg2 Be6 6.Nge2 c5 7.0-0 Nc6 8.f4 Nc3 9.bc3 Bd5 10.fe5 Bg2 11.Kg2 Ne5 12.Nf4 g6 13.Re1 Qc7 14.d4 cd4 15.cd4 0-0-0 16.Qe2 Nc4 17.c3 Bd6 18.Rb1 Rhe8 [D] 19.Qe8 Re8 20.Re8 Kd7 21.Re2 Qc6 22.Kg1 b5 23.Ng2 a6 24.Bf4 Qf3 25.Rbe1 Qc3 26.Bd6 Qd4 27.Kh1 Qd6 28.Ne3 Ne3 29.Re3 Qd5 30.Kg1 Qa2 31.Rd1 Kc6 32.Rc1 Kb6 33.Re7 b4 34.Rcc7 Qd5 35.Rcd7 Qc5 36.Kg2 b3 37.Rb7 Ka5 38.Rf7 h5 39.h4 Qc2 40.Kg1 b2 41.Rf1 Ka4 0-1**

After 37.b4

946) Fischer,R-Neustaedter,R [4/19/64] Simultaneous,Santa Monica Sicilian **1.e4 c5 2.Nf3 d6 3.d4 cd4 4.Nd4 Nf6 5.Nc3 a6 6.Bc4 e6 7.Be3 Nbd7 8.f4 b5 9.Bb3 Bb7 10.f5 e5 11.Nf3 Nc5 12.Bg5 Nb3 13.Bf6 Qf6 14.ab3 Qd8 15.O-O Be7 16.Nd5 O-O 17.c4 bc4 18.bc4 Bd5 19.Qd5 Qb6 20.Rf2 Rac8 21.g3 Rc5 22.Qd3 Rfc8 23.b3 Rb8 24.Nd2 Bg5 25.Nf3 Be7 26.Nd2 Bg5 27.Nf3 Be7 28.Rb1 Ra5 29.Kg2 Ra3 30.Rfb2 a5 31.Qe2 Qb4 32.Qc2 Qc5 33.Ra2 Ra2 34.Qa2 Qe3 35.Qc2 h6 36.h4 a4 37.b4 [D] d5 38.cd5 Rb4 39.Rb4 Bb4 40.Qa4 Qe2 41.Kh3 Qf3 42.Qb4 Qh1 1/2-1/2**

After 31...Qc5

947) Fischer,R-Hunt,J [4/19/64] Simultaneous,Santa Monica Sicilian **1.e4 c5 2.Nf3 d6 3.d4 cd4 4.Nd4 Nf6 5.Nc3 a6 6.Bc4 e6 7.O-O Qc7 8.Bb3 Nc6 9.Be3 Bd7 10.f4 Be7 11.f5 Nd4 12.Bd4 ef5 13.ef5 Bc6 14.Qd3 d5 15.Rae1 O-O-O 16.a4 Bd6 17.g3 h5 18.Bf6 gf6 19.Nd5 Bc5 20.Kg2 Bd5 21.Bd5 h4 22.c4 hg3 23.hg3 Bd6 24.Rh1 Rhg8 25.Rh3 Be5 26.b4 Qd6 27.b5 a5 28.Re3 Qb4 29.Re2 Rg7 30.Qe4 Qe7 31.c5 Qc5 [D] 32.Bb7 Kb8 33.Ba6 Rd5 34.Rh8 1-0**

Ventura, California [4/22/64]

After 24...fe6

948) Fischer,R-Bedford,M [4/22/64] Ventura Pirc **1.e4 g6 2.d4 Bg7 3.Nf3 d6 4.Bc4 c6 5.Bb3 Nf6 6.Nc3 O-O 7.O-O Na6 8.h3 Nc7 9.Be3 Be6 10.d5 cd5 11.ed5 Bd7 12.Nd4 Qc8 13.Kh2 b5 14.a3 a5 15.Qf3 Rb8 16.a4 b4 17.Ncb5 Nb5 18.ab5 Bb5 19.Nb5 Rb5 20.Qe2 Rb8 21.Ra5 Nh5 22.g4 Nf6 23.Ra7 e6 24.de6 fe6 [D] 25.Bh6 1-0**

Denver [4/26/64]

949) Fischer,R-Kraft, B [4/26/64] Simultaneous, Denver
Alekhine **1.e4 Nf6 2.e5 Nd5 3.d4 d6 4.c4 Nb6 5.ed6 cd6 6.Nc3 g6
7.Bd3 Nc6 8.Nge2 Bg7 9.Be3 Bd7 10.O-O Nb4 11.b3 Nd3 12.Qd3
Bf5 13.Qd2 Nd7 14.h3 h5 15.Rad1 Nf6 16.d5 Qd7 17.Bd4 [D] g5
18.Qg5 O-O-O 19.Ba7 Bh6 20.Qh4 Rdg8 21.Ng3 Bg5 22.Qd4
Bh3 23.Na4 Qg4 24.Qg4 Bg4 25.f3 Bh4 26.Ne2 Bd7 27.Nb6 Kc7
28.Nd7 Kd7 29.Bd4 Rh6 30.b4 e5 31.de6 fe6 32.a4 Ne8 33.c5 e5
34.Be5 Re6 35.f4 Reg6 36.g3 Bg3 37.f5 Bh2 38.Kh1 Rg2 39.Bh2
Re2 40.f6 Rgg2 41.Bg1 Rg4 42.Rd4 Rd4? 43.Bd4 1-0**

After 17.Bd4

950) Fischer,R-Koehler,W [4/26/64] Simultaneous, Denver
Sicilian **1.e4 c5 2.Nf3 d6 3.d4 cd4 4.Nd4 Nf6 5.Nc3 a6 6.Be2 e6
7.f4 b5 8.Bf3 Ra7 9.Be3 Rc7 10.O-O b4 11.Na4 Bb7 12.c3 Ne4
13.cb4 Nd7 14.b5 Qa8 15.ba6 Ba6 16.Re1 d5 17.Rc1 Rc1 18.Qc1
Bb4 19.Rd1 O-O 20.Qc6 Ndf6 21.a3 Bd6 22.Qa8 Ra8 23.Rc1 Rc8
24.Rc8 Bc8 25.b4 Bd7 26.Nb6 Be8 27.Nb3 Kf8 [D] 28.a4? Bb4
29.Be2 Nc3 30.Bd3 Na4 31.Na4 Ba4 0-1**

After 27...Kf8

951) Fischer,R-Haskins,M [4/26/64] Simultaneous, Denver
French **1.e4 e6 2.d4 d5 3.Nc3 Bb4 4.e5 a5 5.a3 Bc3 6.bc3 c5 7.Qg4
Ne7 8.Qg7 Rg8 9.Qh7 Qc7 10.Qd3 b6 11.Nf3 Ba6 12.Qd2 cd4
13.cd4 Bf1 14.Kf1 Nf5 15.g3 Qc4 16.Kg2 Nc6 17.c3 a4 18.Rb1
b5 19.Re1 Na5 20.Qe2 Rb8 21.Qc4 dc4 22.Ng5 Rg7 23.g4 Nb3
24.f4 Ne7 25.h4 Nd5 26.Kg3 Nc3 27.Rb2 Nd4 28.h5 b4 29.h6 Rg8
30.Rb4 Rb4 31.ab4 Nce2 32.Kf2 Nc1 33.Rc1 a3 34.Rc4 a2 35.h7
Rh8 36.Rc8 Ke7 37.Rh8 [D] a1=Q 38.Re8 Ke8 39.h8=Q Kd7
40.Ne4 Qb2 41.Kg3 Qb3 42.Kh4 1/2-1/2**

After 37.Rh8

Cheltenham, Pa. [5/3/64]

952) Fischer,R-Koppany,A [5/3/64] Simultaneous,
Cheltenham, PA Pirc **1.e4 g6 2.d4 Bg7 3.Nc3 d6 4.f4 Nf6 5.Nf3
O-O 6.Bd3 c5 7.dc5 Bd7 8.cd6 ed6 9.O-O Bc6 10.f5 gf5 11.ef5
Nbd7 12.Kh1 d5 13.Ne2 Kh8 14.Ng3 Qb6 15.Ng5 Rae8 16.Nh5
Bb5 17.Ng7 Kg7 18.Nh3 Rg8 19.Nf4 Kh8 20.b3 Bc6 21.Bb2 d4
22.Bc4 Re4 23.Bf7 Rg4 24.Qd2 Ref4 25.Rf4 [D] Rg2 26.Qg2 Bg2
27.Kg2 Qc6 28.Kg1 Kg7 29.Bc4 b5 30.Bd3 Ne5 31.Raf1 Kf7
32.Bd4 Nd3 33.cd3 Qc2 34.R4f3 Ng4 35.Rh3 h6 36.Rh4 Qe2
37.Ba7 Ne5 38.Rh3 Ng4 39.a4 ba4 40.ba4 Qa2 41.Rh4 Qa4
42.Be3 Qe8 43.Rg4 Qe3 44.Kh1 Qd3 1/2-1/2**

After 25.Rf4

953) Fischer,R-Nickel,R [5/3/64] Simultaneous, Cheltenham,
PA Latvian Gambit **1.e4 e5 2.Nf3 f5 3.Ne5 Qf6 4.d4 d6 5.Nc4 fe4
6.Nc3 Qf7 7.Be2 Nf6 8.O-O Be6 9.Ne3 d5 10.f3 ef3 11.Bf3 c6
12.Ng4 Bd6 13.Nf6 Kd8 [D] [13...Qf6 and 13...gf6 are met by
14.Bh5] 14.Na4 Qc7 15.Bg5 1-0**

After 13...Kd8

Boston [5/10/64]

After 12.g4

954) Fischer,R-Codman,R [5/10/64] Simultaneous, Boston, MA French **1.e4 e6 2.d4 Ne7 3.Nc3 g6 4.h4 Bg7 5.h5 d5 6.h6 Bf8 7.Bg5 a6 8.Bf6 Rg8 9.Nf3 Nd7 10.e5 Nf6 11.ef6 Nf5 12.g4 [D] Qf6 13.gf5 Qf5 14.Bd3 Qf4 15.Rh4 Qf6 16.Qe2 Bd7 17.Ne5 Qh4 18.Qf3 f5 19.O-O-O Bh6 20.Kb1 Qd4 21.Qe2 Bg7 22.Nd7 Kd7 23.Bf5 Qe5 0-1**

Milwaukee [5/10/64]

After 21.Bg5

955) Fischer,R-Meifert,H [5/14/64] Simultaneous, Milwaukee, Sicilian **1.e4 c5 2.Nf3 a6 3.c4 Nc6 4.d4 cd4 5.Nd4 Nf6 6.Nc3 e5 7.Nf5 d5 8.cd5 Bf5 9.ef5 Nd4 10.Bd3 Nd5 11.Be4 Bb4 12.Bd2 Bc3 13.bc3 Nc6 14.Qb3 Nce7 15.Qb7 O-O 16.Rd1 Rb8 17.Qa6 Qc7 18.O-O Rfd8 19.Qe2 Rb2 20.Qf3 Ra2 21.Bg5 [D] Nf6 22.Bf6 gf6 23.Qg3 Kh8 24.Qh4 Ng8 25.Bd5 Ra3 26.c4 Ra6 27.Rd3 Qe7 28.Rh3 h6 29.Rg3 Kh7 30.h3 Qf8 31.Re1 Rdd6 32.Re4 Ne7 33.Rb3 Nd5 34.cd5 Ra5 35.Qh5 Ra1 36.Kh2 Rd5 37.Rh4 Rd4 38.Rd4 ed4 39.Qh4 Ra6 40.Qd4 Ra2 41.Rd3 Qb8 42.g3 Qb2 1/2-1/2**

After 23...Re5

956) Fischer,R-Zvers,J [5/14/64] Simultaneous, Milwaukee Philidor [E: Rook vs. minor pieces] **1.e4 e5 2.Nf3 d6 3.d4 ed4 4.Nd4 Be7 5.Nc3 c6 6.Bc4 Nf6 7.a4 Bg4 8.f3 Bh5 9.Be3 Ne4 10.Ne4 d5 11.Ng3 dc4 12.Ndf5 Bg6 13.Ng7 Kf8 14.Bh6 Qa5 15.c3 Qe5 16.Qe2 Qe2 17.Ke2 Kg8 18.N7f5 Bf8 19.Bf8 Kf8 20.Rhd1 Na6 21.Rd4 Nc5 22.Rc4 Re8 23.Kf1 Re5 [D] 24.f4 Rf5 25.Nf5 Nb3 26.Rd1 Bf5 27.Rd8 Kg7 28.Rh8 Nd2 29.Ke2 Nc4 30.Rb8 Nb2 31.Rb7 Na4 32.Kd2 Nc5 33.Ra7 1/2-1/2**

Flint,MI [5/16/64]

After 20.Kf1

957) Fischer,R-Dubois,D [5/16/64] Simultaneous, Flint, MI. Center Counter **1.e4 d5 2.ed5 Nf6 3.c4 c6 4.d4 cd5 5.Nc3 g6 6.Nf3 Bg7 7.c5 0-0 8.b4 Nc6 9.b5 Ne4 10.bc6 Nc3 11.Qb3 Ne4 12.cb7 Bb7 13.Qb7 Qa5 14.Bd2 Nd2 15.Nd2 Bh6 16.Qb2 Rab8 17.Qc2 e5 18.Rd1 ed4 19.Be2 Rfe8 20.Kf1 [D] Re2 21.Ke2 Qa6 22.Kf3 Qf6 23.Ke2 Qa6 24.Kf3 1/2-1/2**

After 13...Be6

958) Fischer,R-Snuske,R [5/16/64] Simultaneous, Flint, MI Two Knights **1.e4 e5 2.Bc4 Nc6 3.Nf3 Nf6 4.Ng5 d5 5.ed5 Nd5 6.d4 Be7 7.Nf7 Kf7 8.Qf3 Ke6 9.Nc3 Bb4 10.Bd5 Kd6 11.Bc6 Bc3 12.bc3 bc6 13.O-O Be6 [D] 14.de5 Kd7 15.Rd1 Bd5 16.c4 Rf8 17.Qh3 1-0**

959) Fischer,R-Murdock,W [5/16/64] Simultaneous, Flint, MI Sicilian **1.e4 c5 2.Nf3 Nc6 3.d4 cd4 4.Nd4 d6 5.Nc3 a6 6.Bc4 g6 7.Be3 Bg7 8.Qd2 e6 9.O-O-O Nf6 10.Nc6 bc6 11.Qd6 Qd6 12.Rd6 Bb7 13.f3 O-O 14.Na4 [D] Ne8 15.Rd2 Nf6 16.Nc5 Rfd8 17.Nb7 Rab8 18.Nc5 Rb2 19.Kb2 Ne4 20.Kc1 Nd6 21.Bd4 Rb8 22.Bg7 1-0**

After 14.Na4

Columbus, OH [5/18/64]

960) Fischer,R-Lense,E [5/18/64] Simultaneous, Columbus, OH Alekhine's **1.e4 Nf6 2.e5 Nd5 3.d4 d6 4.c4 Nb6 5.ed6 ed6 6.Nc3 Nc6 7.Nf3 Be7 8.Bd3 Bg4 9.Be3 Qd7 10.O-O O-O 11.h3 Bf5 12.a3 Bf6 13.b4 a5 14.b5 Ne7 15.Rc1 c5 16.bc6 bc6 17.d5 Rab8 18.Bf5 Nf5 19.dc6 Qc6 20.Bb6 Bc3 21.Rc3 Rb6 22.Nd4 Nd4 23.Qd4 Qc5 24.Qc5 dc5 25.Rd1 a4 26.Rd7 Rfb8 27.Rf3 [D] R6b7 28.Rff7 Rd7 29.Rd7 Rb3 30.Rc7 Ra3 31.Rc5 Rc3 32.Kh2 1/2-1/2**

After 27.Rf3

961) Fischer,R-Mantia,T [5/18/64] Simultaneous,Columbus, OH Caro Kann **1.e4 c6 2.Nc3 d5 3.d4 de4 4.Ne4 Bf5 5.Nc5 e5 6.Nb7 Qd4 7.Qd4 ed4 8.Bd3 Bd3 9.cd3 Nd7 10.Nf3 Rb8 11.Na5 Bb4 12.Bd2 Bd2 13.Nd2 Nc5 14.Ke2 Kd7 15.Rhc1 Ne6 16.Nc6 Rb2 17.Ne5 Ke7 18.Rcb1 Rb1 19.Rb1 Nh6 20.Ne4 Rc8 21.Rb7 Kf8 22.Nd6 Rc7 23.Rc7 Nc7 24.Nc6 Ne6 25.g3 a6 26.a4 f6 27.a5 Nf7 28.Nf5 [D] g6 29.Nfd4 Nd4 30.Nd4 Nd6 31.Ne6 Ke7 32.Nc5 h6 33.Ke3 Kd8 34.Kd4 Nb5 35.Kc4 Nc7 36.d4 f5 37.Nd3 Ke7 38.Kc5 Kd7 39.d5 g5 40.Ne5 1/2-1/2**

After 28.Nf5

962) Fischer,R-Lutes,W [5/18/64] Simultaneous,Columbus, OH Center Counter **1.e4 d5 2.ed5 Qd5 3.Nc3 Qa5 4.d4 c6 5.Nf3 Nf6 6.Bc4 Bg4 7.h3 Bf3 8.Qf3 e6 9.Bd2 Qc7 10.O-O-O Nbd7 11.Kb1 O-O-O 12.g4 Nb6 13.Bf4 Bd6 14.Bd6 Rd6 15.Bb3 Rhd8 16.Ne2 c5 17.c3 c4 18.Bc2 Nbd5 19.Ng3 Ra6 20.Ne2 Rd7 21.Nc1 Qa5 22.Ka1 b5 23.a3 Ne8 24.Na2 Nec7 25.h4 b4 26.cb4 Nb4 27.Nb4 Qb4 28.Rc1 Nb5 29.Qc6 Rc6 30.ab4 Rd4 31.Kb1 c3 32.bc3 Nc3 33.Kb2 Rb4 34.Bb3 Na4 35.Ka3 Rb3 36.Kb3 Nc5 37.Ka2 Kd7 38.Rh3 e5 39.Rhc3 Kd6 40.Rd1 Ke6 41.Rdc1 Kd5 [D] 42.Rd1 Ke6 1/2-1/2**

After 41...Kd5

Cicero, IL [5/20/64]

963) Fischer,R-Puto,E [5/20/64] Simultaneous, Chicago Giuoco Piano **1.e4 e5 2.Nc3 Nc6 3.Bc4 Bc5 4.f4 Nf6 5.Nf3 d6 6.d3 0-0 7.f5 Nd4 8.Bg5 c6 9.a3 h6 10.Bh4 b5 11.Ba2 a5 12.g4 g5 13.fg6 Bg4 14.Bf7 Kg7 [D] 15.Nd4 Bd4 16.Ne2 Bb2 17.Rb1 Bc3 18.Kf2 Ne4 19.de4 Qh4 20.Kg2 Qh3 21.Kg1 Qe3 0-1**

After 14...Kg7

After 31...Nf5

964) Fischer,R-Bikulcius,,J [5/20/64] Simultaneous, Cicero,Ill
French **1.e4 e6 2.d4 d5 3.Nc3 Bb4 4.e5 Ne7 5.a3 Bc3 6.bc3 0-0 7.Nf3 Nd7 8.Bd3 h6 9.a4 a5 10.0-0 c5 11.Re1 Qc7 12.Bf4 Ng6 13.Be3 c4 14.Bf1 f6 15.ef6 Nf6 16.g3 Qf7 17.Bh3 Bd7 18.Nd2 Rab8 19.f4 Rfe8 20.Bg2 Bc6 21.Rf1 Qd7 22.h4 Ba4 23.h5 Ne7 24.g4 b6 25.Bh3 Rf8 26.Nf3 Bc6 27.Ne5 Qc8 28.g5 hg5 29.fg5 Ne4 30.Rf8 Kf8 31.Qf1 Nf5 [D] 32.Bf5 ef5 33.Nc6 Qc6 34.Qf5 Ke7 35.Qe5 Qe6 36.Qg7 Kd8 37.Qf8 Kd7 38.Qb8 Qg4 39.Kh2 Qe2 40.Kg1 Qg4 1/2-1/2**

After 13...c5

965) Fischer,R-Fajkus,,J [5/20/64] Simultaneous, Cicero,Ill
Vienna Game **1.e4 e5 2.Nc3 c6 3.d4 Qc7 4.de5 Qe5 5.Nf3 Qc7 6.Bd3 d6 7.0-0 Be6 8.Nd4 Qc8 9.f4 d5 10.f5 Bd7 11.e5 Bc5 12.Be3 Bd4 13.Bd4 c5 [D] 14.Qg4 g6 15.e6 cd4 16.ef7 Kf8 17.Qd4 Bf5 18.Qh8 Qc5 19.Kh1 Kf7 20.Bf5 1-0**

After 18...Rhg8

966) Fischer,R-Goranson,W [5/20/64] Simultaneous, Cicero,Ill Vienna Game **1.e4 e5 2.Nc3 Nf6 3.Bc4 Bc5 4.f4 d6 5.Nf3 Bg4 6.h3 Bh5 7.g4 Ng4 8.hg4 Bg4 9.Na4 Nc6 10.c3 Qf6 11.f5 g6 12.Nc5 dc5 13.Rf1 gf5 14.Qe2 Bf3 15.Qf3 Qh4 16.Kd1 f4 17.d3 0-0-0 18.Kc2 Rhg8 [D] 19.Rh1 Qg3 20.Qg3 Rg3 21.Rh7 f6 22.Bd2 Na5 23.Be6 Kb8 24.Rd7 Rd7 25.Bd7 c4 26.d4 c6 27.Rh1 Rg7 28.Bf5 Kc7 29.Rh6 Rf7 30.Be1 Rg7 31.Rf6 Rg2 32.Bd2 ed4 33.cd4 Nb3 34.ab3 cb3 35.Kd3 Rb3 36.Kc4 b5 37.Kc5 1-0**

After 13...Bf6

967) Fischer,R-Kral,G [5/20/64] Simultaneous, Cicero,Ill
French **1.e4 e6 2.d4 d5 3.Nc3 de4 4.Ne4 Nd7 5.Nf3 Ngf6 6.Nf6 Nf6 7.Bd3 Be7 8.Qe2 O-O 9.Bg5 c5 10.dc5 Qa5 11.c3 Qc5 12.O-O-O b5 13.Bf6 Bf6 [D] 14.Qe4 g6 15.Qa8 b4 16.c4 a5 17.Rd2 Bd7 18.Qe4 a4 19.Qe3 Qe7 20.h4 a3 21.b3 Bc3 22.Rc2 f5 23.c5 Qf6 24.Bc4 Bb2 25.Kb1 f4 26.Qe4 Kg7 27.c6 Bc8 28.Rd1 e5 29.Rd7 Bd7 30.cd7 Rd8 31.Rd2 Qe7 32.Bb5 Qc5 33.Qc6 Qf8 34.Ng5 Qf5 35.Qe4 1-0**

After 6...Be7

968) Fischer,R-Kumro,T [5/20/64] Simultaneous, Cicero,Ill
Vienna Game **1.e4 e5 2.Nc3 Nf6 3.f4 d6 4.Nf3 Nc6 5.Bb5 Bd7 6.d3 Be7 [D] 7.Bc6 Bc6 8.fe5 de5 9.Ne5 0-0 10.Nc6 bc6 11.0-0 Qd7 12.Qf3 Ng4 13.h3 Ne5 14.Qg3 Bd6 15.Bf4 f6 16.d4 Ng6 17.Bd6 cd6 18.Rad1 Qe6 19.d5 cd5 20.Rd5 Rfd8 21.Rfd1 Ne5 22.Nb5 Rab8 23.Nd6 Rf8 24.Nf5 Ng6 25.Rd7 Qb6 26.Kh1 Rbd8 27.Rg7 Kh8 28.Rf1 Qb2 29.Qg4 Rg8 30.Rh7 1-0**

969) Fischer,R-Nyman,W [5/20/64] Simultaneous, Cicero,Ill
King's Gambit **1.e4 e5 2.f4 ef4 3.Bc4 d5 4.Bd5 Nf6 5.Nc3 Bb4
6.Nf3 0-0 7.0-0 Bc3 8.dc3 c6 9.Bc4 Qb6 10.Kh1 Ne4 11.Qe1 Re8
12.Bf4 Nd6 [D] 13.Bd6 Re1 14.Rae1 Bd7 15.Ng5 Na6 16.Rf7 1-0**

After 12...Nd6

970) Fischer,R-de Parry,T [5/20/64] Simultaneous, Cicero,Ill
French **1.e4 e6 2.d4 d5 3.Nc3 Bb4 4.e5 f6 5.a3 Ba5 6.Qg4 Qe7
7.Nf3 Nc6 8.Bb5 Bd7 9.0-0 Qf7 10.Qh4 g5 11.Na4 h5 12.Qh4 g5
13.Qg3 g4 14.Nb6 ab6 15.Bc6 Bc6 16.Ne1 f5 17.Nd3 Bb5 18.Rd1
h4 19.Qe3 Ne7 20.Nf4 Ng6 21.Ng6 Qg6 22.Qg5 Kf7 23.Qg6 Kg6
24.Bf4 Ra4 25.c3 h3 26.g3 Rha8 27.Bc1 [D] c5 28.bc5 bc5 29.dc5
Rc4 30.Bd2 Rc5 31.Rdb1 Ba6 32.Rb6 Kf7 33.Rd6 Rac8 34.Rd7
Ke8 35.Rh7 R8c7 36.Rh6 Kd7 37.Rh7 Kc6 38.Rh6 Re7 39.Rb1
Bd3 40.Rb4 Rb5 41.Be3 Rb4 42.ab4 Kd7 43.Rh8 b5 1/2-1/2**

After 27.Bc1

971) Fischer,R-Sandrin,A [5/20/64] Simultaneous, Cicero,Ill
Philidor **1.e4 e5 2.Nf3 d6 3.d4 Nd7 4.Bc4 c6 5.0-0 Be7 6.de5 de5
7.Qe2 Ngf6 8.Rd1 Qc7 9.Ng5 Rf8 10.a4 h6 11.Nf3 Nc5 12.Nc3
Bg4 13.h3 Bh5 14.g4 Bg6 15.Nh4 Bh7 16.Nf5 Rg8 17.Qf3 Ne6
18.Be3 a6 19.a5 c5 20.Nd5 Nd5 21.Bd5 0-0-0 [D] 22.Be6 fe6
23.Ne7 Qe7 24.Qg3 Qc7 25.f3 Rgf8 26.Kg2 Rd1 27.Rd1 Rf7
28.Bg1 Rd7 29.Rd7 Kd7 30.Qe1 b5 31.ab6 Qb6 32.Qc3 Qb4
33.Qe5 Qd2 34.Bf2 Qc2 35.Qg7 Kc6 36.Qh7 Qb2 37.Qh6 Qb3
38.g5 1-0**

After 21...0-0-0

972) Fischer,R-Sillars,K and Manter,L [5/20/64]
Simultaneous, Cicero,Ill Sicilian **1.e4 c5 2.Nf3 d6 3.d4 cd4 4.Nd4
Nf6 5.Nc3 a6 6.h3 e5 7.Nde2 Be6 8.g4 d5 9.ed5 Nd5 10.Bg2 Nc3
11.Qd8 Kd8 12.Nc3 Nc6 13.Be3 Bb4 14.0-0-0 Ke7 15.Ne4 Rhd8
16.a3 Ba5 17.Bc5 Ke8 18.Nd6 Rd6 19.Rd6 Bc7 [D] 20.Rc6 1-0**

After 19...Bc7

973) Fischer,R-Warren,J [5/20/64] Simultaneous, Cicero,Ill
Sicilian **1.e4 c5 2.Nf3 Nc6 3.d4 cd4 4.Nd4 Nf6 5.Nc3 d6 6.Bc4 e6
7.Bb3 Be7 8.Be3 0-0 9.0-0 Bd7 10.f4 Nd4 11.Bd4 Bc6 12.Qe2 b5
[D] 13.Nb5** [After this 13th move, Fischer looked up from the board
at me and said "Didn't I make this mistake against you before?"
Bear in mind that this was two months after the first game (Chicago
Simul), many simuls and hundreds of games later, as he was on tour
with many simuls throughout the country. What a memory! - *Note
by Jim Warren*] **Bb5 14.Qb5 Ne4 15.f5 Bf6 16.Qd3 Bd4 17.Qd4
d5 18.c4 dc4 19.Qe4 cb3 20.fe6 Qb6 21.Kh1 fe6 22.ab3 Qb3 23.h3
Qb2 24.Qe6 Kh8 25.Qe7 Rf1 26.Rf1 h6 27.Rf8 Rf8 28.Qf8 Kh7
29.Qf5 Kg8 30.Qc8 Kh7 31.Qf5 g6 32.Qa5 Qb6 33.Qa2 Qb7
34.Qa1 Qc7 1/2-1/2**

After 12...b5

New York City [5/24/64]

After 16...Bg5

974) Fischer,R-McDermott,M [5/24/64] Simultaneous, New York Bishop's Opening **1.e4 e5 2.Bc4 Nf6 3.Nc3 Bc5 4.f4 d6 5.Nf3 Bg4 6.h3 Bf3 7.Qf3 Nc6 8.d3 Nd4 9.Qg3 Nc2 10.Kd1 Na1 11.Qg7 Rf8 12.fe5 de5 13.Rf1 Be7 14.Bg5 Ne4 15.Ne4 f5 16.Qh7 Bg5 [D] 17.Qg6 1-0**

After 15...Be7

975) Fischer,R-Terrone,J [5/24/64] Simultaneous, New York Ruy Lopez **1.e4 e5 2.Nf3 Nc6 3.Bb5 a6 4.Ba4 Nf6 5.0-0 Be7 6.Re1 d6 7.Bc6 bc6 8.d4 Nd7 9.Nbd2 Bf6 10.Nc4 Nb6 11.Na5 Bd7 12.b3 0-0 13.de5 de5 14.Ba3 Re8 15.c4 Be7 [D] 16.c5 Nc8 17.Nb7 1-0**

After 21.g3

976) Fischer,R-Morrison,S [5/24/64] Simultaneous, New York Vienna **1.e4 e5 2.Bc4 Nf6 3.Nc3 Nc6 4.f4 Ne4 5.Nf3 Nc3 6.dc3 Be7 7.fe5 d6 8.Bf4 de5 9.Qd8 Bd8 10.Ne5 Ne5 11.Be5 O-O 12.O-O-O c6 13.Rhf1 Be7 14.Bd6 Bd6 15.Rd6 Bg4 16.h3 Bh5 17.Rd7 b5 18.Bb3 a5 19.a4 Bg6 20.Rfd1 Be4 21.g3 [D] Bf5 22.Rc7 Bh3 23.Rc6 ba4 24.Ba4 g6 25.Bb3 a4 26.Ba2 Bg4 27.Rd4 h5 28.Rg6 Kh7 29.Rf6 Kg7 30.Rdf4 Ra7 31.Bd5 Re7 32.c4 Kg8 33.Kd2 Re2 34.Kc3 Re3 35.Kd4 Re7 36.c5 Rc7 37.c6 Rd8 38.Kc5 Rdd7 39.Ra4 Kg7 40.Rd6 Re7 41.b4 1-0**

977) Fischer,R-Westing,E [5/24/64] Simultaneous, New York Caro Kann **1.e4 c6 2.Nc3 d5 3.d4 de4 4.Ne4 Bf5 5.Nc5 Qc7 6.Nf3 Nd7 7.Bd3 Bd3 8.Nd3 e6 9.O-O Bd6 10.c4 Ngf6 11.Qe2 O-O 12.b3 c5 13.Bb2 cd4 14.Bd4 Rfe8 15.Nde5 Ne5 16.Ne5 Bc5 17.Bb2 Rad8 18.g3 Bd4 19.Bd4 Rd4 20.Nf3 Rd6 21.Rfd1 Red8 22.Rd6 Qd6 23.Re1 Qd3 24.Kg2 Qe2 25.Re2 Kf8 26.h3 Ke7 27.g4 h6 28.Rc2 b6 29.b4 a5 30.a3 ab4 31.ab4 Rc8 32.Nd4 Nd7 33.f4 g5 34.f5 Ne5 35.c5 bc5 36.Rc5 Rc5 37.bc5 Kd7 38.Kg3 Nc6 39.fe6 fe6 40.Nf3 [D] Ke7? 41.Kf2 e5 42.Ke3 Ke6 43.Ke4 Ne7 44.Ne5 Nc8 45.Nc6 Kd7 46.Kd5 Kc7 47.Ne5 Ne7 48.Ke6 1-0**

After 40.Nf3

New York, 1965

After 35...Re7

978) Fischer,R-Martinez,G [1965] Simultaneous, New York French **1.e4 e6 2.d4 Bb4 3.c3 Ba5 4.a4 c6 5.e5 Ne7 6.Nd2 d5 7.ed6 Qd6 8.Nc4 Qd5 9.Na5 Qa5 10.Nf3 b5 11.Bd3 Nd7 12.0-0 Nd5 13.Ng5 N7f6 14.f4 b4 15.c4 Ne7 16.f5 Nf5 17.Bf5 ef5 18.Qe1 Kf8 19.Bd2 Rb8 20.Bf4 Rb7 21.Bd6 Kg8 22.Be5 Qd8 23.Bf6 gf6 24.Nf3 h6 25.Kh1 Kh7 26.Rd1 Be6 27.d5 cd5 28.Nd4 Qc8 29.Qh4 dc4 30.Qf6 Rg8 31.Nf5 Rg6 32.Qe5 Qc6 33.Nh4 Bh3 34.Rf2 Rg5 35.Qf4 Re7 [D] 36.Nf3 Be6 37.Ng5 hg5 38.Qg5 1-0**

979) Fischer,R-Leayza,L [1965] Simultaneous, New York
Caro Kann **1.e4 c6 2.d4 d5 3.Nc3 de4 4.Ne4 Bf5 5.Ng3 Bg6 6.Nf3
Nf6 7.h4 h6 8.Bd3 Bd3 9.Qd3 e6 10.Bf4 Nbd7 11.0-0-0 Be7
12.Kb1 0- 0 13.Bc1 Qa5 14.Ne4 Ne4 15.Qe4 Nf6 16.Qe2 Rfd8
17.Ne5 c5 18.g4 cd4 19.g5 Nd5 20.gh6** [D] **Nc3 21.bc3 Rd5 22.Qe4
Rb5 23.Ka1 0-1**

After 20.gh6

Athens, Greece, 8/68

980) Fischer,R-Anastasopoulos [8/68] Simultaneous, Athens
Ruy Lopez [E: Rook + minor piece] **1.e4 e5 2.Nf3 Nc6 3.Bb5 a6
4.Bc6 dc6 5.0-0 f6 6.d4 ed4 7.Nd4 c5 8.Nb3 Qd1 9.Rd1 Bd7 10.a4
0-0-0 11.Be3 b6 12.Nc3 Bd6 13.a5 c4** [D] **14.ab6 cb3 15.Ra6 Ne7
16.Ra8 Kb7 17.Ra7 Kb8 18.Nd5 Nd5 19.ed5 Bc8 20.bc7 Bc7
21.c4 Bb7 22.Rd3 Rd7 23.Rb3 Bd6 24.Ra5 Kc8 25.Rab5 Bb8
26.g3 Re8 27.c5 Ba7 28.c6 Bc6 29.dc6 Rc7 30.Rb7 1-0**

After 13...c4

981) Kokkoris,L-Fischer,R [8/68] Simultaneous, Athens
Sicilian [E: Rook + minor piece]**1.e4 c5 2.d4 cd4 3.Nf3 d6 4.Nd4
Nf6 5.Nc3 a6 6.Bg5 e6 7.Bc4 h6 8.Bh4 b5 9.Bb3 g5 10.Bg3 b4
11.Na4 Ne4 12.Qf3 Bb7 13.0-0-0 Nd7 14.Rhe1 g4 15.Qg4 Qg5
16.Qg5 hg5 17.f3 Ng3 18.hg3 0-0-0 19.Bc4 d5 20.Bd3 Bd6 21.g4
Rh2 22.Re2 Kb8 23.c3 Rc8 24.Kb1 bc3 25.Nc3 Be5 26.Bc2 Bg7
27.a3 Rc4 28.Red2** [D] **Rd4 29.Rd4 Bd4 30.Rd4 Rg2 31.Bd1 Ne5
32.f4 Ng4 33.fg5 Ne5 34.Na4 Rg5 35.Nc5 Bc8 36.Be2 a5 37.Ra4 Rg1
38.Kc2 Rg2 39.Kd1 Nc6 40.Nb3 e5 41.Na5 Nd4 42.Bh5 Be6 43.Rb4
Kc8 44.Nb7 Kc7 45.a4 Rg5 0-1**

After 28.Red2

982) Fischer,R-Ornithopoulos,N [8/68] Simultaneous, Athens
Sicilian [E: Rook + Bishop] **1.e4 c5 2.Nc3 Nc6 3.Nge2 e6 4.d4 cd4
5.Nd4 Nf6 6.Ndb5 Bb4 7.a3 Bc3 8.Nc3 d5 9.ed5 Nd5 10.Bd2 Nc3
11.Bc3 Qd1 12.Rd1 f6 13.f4 Bd7 14.Bc4 0-0-0 15.0-0 Rhe8
16.Rde1 Re7 17.b4 Kc7 18.b5 Nb8 19.Bb4 Ree8 20.Rf3 Kb6
21.a4 a5 22.Ba3 Bc8 23.Bb3 h6 24.Rc3 Ka7 25.Rc7 Rd7 26.Bc5
Ka8** [D] **27.Bb6 e5 28.fe5 fe5 29.Ba5 e4 30.Rc4 e3 31.Rc7 g6
32.Bb6 Rc7 33.Bc7 Nd7 34.a5 Nc5 35.Bd5 Ne6 36.Be6 Re6
37.Bb6 Bd7 38.c4 Re4 39.Re3 Rc4 40.Rd3 Rc1 41.Kf2 Rc2
42.Kg3 Bf5 43.Rf3 Bd7 44.Rf7 Be8 45.Rh7 h5 46.Rh8 Rc8 47.Be3
h4 48.Kf2 and 1-0 in 64 moves.**

After 26...Ka8

983) Fischer,R-Trikaliotis,G [8/68] Simultaneous, Athens
Sicilian [E: Rook + minor piece] **1.e4 c5 2.Nf3 Nc6 3.Bb5 a6 4.Bc6
bc6 5.Nc3 d5 6.b3 Bg4 7.h3 Bf3 8.Qf3 e6 9.0-0 Nf6 10.d3 Be7
11.Na4 0-0 12.Re1 Nd7 13.Ba3 Qa5 14.Qg3 Rfc8 15.f4 Nb6
16.Bb2 d4 17.Nb6 Qb6 18.Bc1 Qd8 19.Qf3 Qd7 20.Bd2 Re8
21.Rec1 Rac8 22.Kh1 Bf8 23.Rd1 f6 24.c3 e5 25.f5 Kh8 26.cd4
cd4 27.g4 c5 28.Rg1 Rc6 29.g5 fg5 30.Rg5 Qf7 31.Rag1 a5 32.Be1
Ra6 33.Qg4 Rc6 34.Ba5 Ra6 35.b4 cb4 36.Bb4 h6** [D] **37.Bf8 hg5
38.Bb4 Rh6 39.Rg3 Qh5 40.Qh5 Rh5 41.Kg2 Kg8 42.Bd2 Ra8
43.Bg5 Ra2 44.Kf3 Kf7 45.h4 Ra3 46.Kg4 Rh8 47.Rg2 Rc8
48.Rb2 Rac3 49.Rb5 R3c5 50.Rb7 R5c7 1/2-1/2**

After 36...h6

After 29.N7f6

984) Vyzantiadis,L-Fischer,R [8/68] Simultaneous, Athens
1.d4 Nf6 2.c4 e6 3.Nf3 d5 4.Nc3 c5 5.Bg5 cd4 6.Nd4 e5 7.Nf3 d4
8.Nd5 Be7 9.Bf6 Bf6 10.g3 Nc6 11.Nd2 Bg5 12.Bg2 0-0 13.0-0
Kh8 14.Qc2 f5 15.f4 Bh6 16.Rad1 ef4 17.gf4 g6 18.Nb3 Bg7 19.e3
de3 20.Ne3 Qf6 21.Rf2 Rb8 22.Nd5 Qh4 23.Qd3 Be6 24.Qg3 Qd8
25.Rfd2 Bg8 26.Qf2 Re8 27.Nc5 Qa5 28.Nd7 Rbd8 29.N7f6 [D]
Qa2 30.Ne8 Re8 31.Qc5 h6 32.b4 Qb3 33.b5 Na5 34.Ne7 Bf7
35.Rd8 Kh7 36.Re8 Qd1 0-1

Solingen, 9/29/70

985) Fischer,R-Christoph,M [9/29/70] Simultaneous,
Solingen Reti 1.Nf3 g6 2.g3 Bg7 3.Bg2 d6 4.0-0 Nf6 5.c4 0-0 6.b3

After 36.Bf5

d5 7.Bb2 c6 8.d3 a5 9.Nbd2 Na6 10.a3 b5 11.Rc1 bc4 12.bc4 Bd7
13.Be5 Ne8 14.Bg7 Ng7 15.Nb3 Rb8 16.Ne5 Be8 17.cd5 cd5
18.Nd4 Rb2 19.Nec6 Qd6 20.a4 Nb4 21.Nb5 Qe6 22.Nb4 Rb4
23.Nc7 Qe5 24.Nd5 Ra4 25.Qd2 Nf5 26.e3 Qd6 27.d4 Bb5
28.Rfe1 Bc4 29.Nc3 Rb4 30.Ne4 Qb6 31.Nc5 Rd8 32.Nb7 Rc8
33.Ra1 a4 34.Nc5 Qb5 35.Bh3 Rd8 36.Bf5 [D] Qc5 37.Bc2 Qb5
38.Ra3 Rb8 39.Qc3 Bb3 40.Bb3 ab3 41.Qb2 Rc8 42.Raa1 Rc2
43.Qa3 b2 44.Rab1 Kg7 45.d5 Qc5 46.Qd3 Rbc4 47.Qb3 Qa5
48.Rf1 Qc3 49.Qb7 Qf6 50.Kg2 Rd2 51.Qb8 g5 52.Rbd1 Rd1
53.Rd1 Rc2 54.Rf1 Qc3 55.d6 ed6 56.Qd6 Qe3 57.Qb4 Qd3
58.Re1 Re2 59.Rf1 Qd5 60.Kg1 Qe5 61.h3 Rc2 62.Qb3 Rc1
63.Qd3 Qe1 64.Qd4 f6 0-1

Madrid, 1970

After 24...Rc6

986) Fischer,R-Bachiller,G [1970] Simultaneous, Madrid
B43/00 Sicilian 1.e4 c5 2.Nf3 e6 3.d4 cd4 4.Nd4 a6 5.Nc3 Qc7
6.Bd3 Nf6 7.0-0 b5 8.Re1 Bb7 9.e5 Nd5 10.Nd5 Bd5 11.a4 b4
12.Be4 Be4 13.Re4 Nc6 14.Bf4 Rc8 15.Rc1 Qa7 16.c3 bc3 17.Rc3
Bc5 18.Be3 0-0 19.Rc5! Qc5 20.Ne6 Qa5 21.b4 Nb4 22.Nf8 Nd5
23.Nd7 Nc3 24.Qg4 Rc6 [D] 25.Nf6! Kh8 [25...Kf8 26.Qg7!]
26.Qg7! 1-0 [26...Kg7 27.Rg3 and mate follows]

Buenos Aires, 11/11/71 and 11/14/71

After 30.Rh6

987) Fischer,R-Rubinstein,J [11/11/71] Simultaneous,
Buenos Aires Sicilian 1.e4 c5 2.Nf3 d6 3.d4 cd4 4.Nd4 Nf6 5.Nc3
Nc6 6.Bc4 e6 7.Bb3 Be7 8.Be3 0-0 9.Qe2 a6 10.0-0-0 Qc7 11.g4
Nd7 12.Rhg1 Nc5 13.g5 b5 14.Qh5 b4 15.Nce2 Nb3 16.ab3 Nd4
17.Nd4 g6 18.Qh6 e5 19.Nf5 Bf5 20.ef5 Rfc8 21.Rd2 Bf8 22.Qh4
gf5 23.f4 a5 24.Rg3 a4 25.Rh3 Bg7 26.Kd1 ab3 27.cb3 Ra1
28.Ke2 Qc1 29.Qf2 e4 30.Rh6 [D] Rc2! 0-1 [The pinned Rd2 no
longer defends d1!]

988) Fischer,R-Szmetan,J [11/14/71] Simultaneous, Buenos Aires C31/01 King's Gambit [E: Rook + pawn] **1.e4 e5 2.f4 d5 3.Nf3 de4 4.Ne5 Nd7 5.Nc3 Ngf6 6.Bc4 Ne5 7.fe5 [D] Qd4 8.Bf7 Kf7 9.ef6 Bc5 10.Qe2 gf6 11.Rf1 h5 12.b3 e3 13.Qc4 Qc4 14.bc4 ed2 15.Bd2 Re8 16.Kd1 Bg4 17.Kc1 Ba3 18.Kb1 Rad8 19.Nd5 Re6 20.Bc1 Be2 21.Re1 Bc5 22.a4 Bc4 23.Re6 Ke6 24.Nc7 Kf5 25.a5 Rd7 26.Ra4 Bf7 27.Nb5 Rd1 28.Kb2 Be8 29.Rc4 Bg1 30.Nc3 Rd4 31.Rc7 Bc6 32.Ne2 Rb4 33.Kc3 Rb1 34.Ng1 Rc1 35.Ne2 Rb1 36.Nd4 Ke5 37.Nc6 Kd6 38.Rf7 Kc6 39.Rf6 Kc7 40.Rf5 h4 41.h3 Ra1 42.Rg5 Kc6 43.Kc4 Ra2 44.Kb3 Ra1 45.Rg6 Kb5 46.Rg5 Ka6 47.Rg4 Rb1 48.Kc4 Ka5 49.Kc3 Rg1 50.Rg7 Kb6 51.Kc4 Rc1 52.Rg6 Ka5 53.Kd3 Kb5 54.Rg4 a5 55.Rh4 a4 56.Kc3 a3 57.Rb4 Kc5 58.Ra4 Rg1 [D] 59.Ra3 Rg2 60.Kb2 Rh2 61.Rc3 Kb5 62.Kb3 Rh1 63.Rg3 b6 64.Rg5 Ka6 65.Rh5 Rb1 66.Kc3 Rh1 67.Rh8 Kb5 68.h4 Rh3 69.Kd4 Kb4 70.h5 Rh4 71.Ke5 Kc3 72.h6 Kc2 73.Kf6 b5 74.Kg5 Rh1 75.Rb8 Rg1 76.Kf5 Rh1 77.Kg6 Rg1 78.Kf7 Rh1 79.Kg7 Rg1 80.Kh8 Rg5 81.h7 Kc3 82.Rc8 Kd4 83.Rg8 Rh5 84.Rg4 Kc3 1-0**

After 7.fe5

After 58...Rg1

989) Fischer,R-Seidler,A [11/14/71] Simultaneous, Buenos Aires Sicilian **1.e4 c5 2.Nf3 Nc6 3.d4 cd4 4.Nd4 Nf6 5.Nc3 e5 6.Ndb5 d6 7.Bg5 a6 8.Bf6 gf6 9.Na3 f5 10.Qh5 d5 11.0-0-0 Ba3 12.ba3 fe4 13.Rd5 Qe7 14.Ne4 Qa3 15.Kd1 Be6 [D] 16.Nd6 Ke7 17.Qg5 Kf8 18.Qh6 Ke7 19.Qg5 Kf8 20.Qh6 Ke7 21.Qg5 ½-½**

After 15...Be6

Miscellaneous games

After 19...h5

990) Fischer-N.N. [Conditions and location unknown] Ruy Lopez **1.e4 e5 2.Nf3 Nc6 3.Bb5 a6 4.Bc6 dc6 5.0-0 Bg4 6.h3 Bf3 7.Qf3 Qd7 8.d3 0-0-0 9.Be3 f6 10.Nd2 Ne7 11.b4 Ng6 12.Rfb1 Be7 13.a4 b6 14.Qe2 Kb7 15.Nc4 Nf4 16.Qf3 Ne6 17.Rb3 Nd4 18.Bd4 Qd4 19.Rab1 h5 [D] 20.b5 cb5 21.ab5 a5 22.Ne3 Qd7 23.Nd5 Bc5 24.Rc3 Qd6 25.Rc4 Rd7 26.c3 f5 27.Qf5 Rf8 28.Qh5 Bf2 29.Kh1 Rdf7 30.Rc6 Bg3 31.Qf7 Rf7 32.Rd6 cd6 33.Ne3 Rf2 34.Nf5 Bf4 35.Nd6 Ka7 36.Nc4 Rc2 37.g3 Bg3 38.Ne3 Rh2 39.Kg1 Rh3? 40.Kg2 1-0**

After 28.Ke4

991) Reshevsky,S-Fischer,R [6/13/57] New York *Played at 10 seconds per move with Reshevsky blindfolded* **1.c4 Nf6 2.Nc3 g6 3.Nf3 Bg7 4.d4 O-O 5.e4 d6 6.Be2 c6 7.O-O a6 8.Re1 b5 9.b3 b4 10.e5 de5 11.de5 bc3 12.ef6 Bf6 13.Bh6 Qd1 14.Rad1 Re8 15.Bd3 Nd7 16.Be4 Nc5 17.Bc6 Bf5 18.g4 Bg4 19.Kg2 Bf5 20.Ba8 Ra8 21.Nd4 Nd3 22.Nf5 Ne1 23.Re1 gf5 24.Rd1 e5 25.c5 Rc8 26.b4 f4 27.Kf3 Be7 28.Ke4 [D] Rc6 29.Rg1 Rg6 30.Rg6 fg6 31.Kd3 Kf7 32.Kc3 g5 33.c6 Ke6 34.Kc4 Kd6 35.b5 ab5 36.Kb5 e4 37.Kc4 Bf6 38.h4 f3 39.hg5 e3 40.Bf8 Be7 41.Be7 Ke7 42.c7 Kd7 0-1**

After 36...Ra7

992) Fischer,R-Harris,W [5/11/58] Live TV Simultaneous, New York Center game **1.e4 e5 2.d4 ed4 3.c3 d5 4.Qd4 c6 5.ed5 Qd5 6.Qd5 cd5 7.Nf3 Nf6 8.Bf4 Nc6 9.Nbd2 Bf5 10.Nb3 Be7 11.Bb5 O-O 12.Bc6 bc6 13.O-O Rfc8 14.Rfe1 Ne4 15.Nfd4 Be6 16.f3 Nc5 17.Ne6 Ne6 18.Nd4 Bc5 19.Be3 Bd4 20.Bd4 Nd4 21.cd4 Re8 22.Kf2 Re1 23.Re1 Kf8 24.Rc1 Rc8 25.Ke3 g5 26.Rc5 f5 27.b4 f4 28.Kd2 Ke7 29.Ra5 Rc7 30.a4 Kd6 31.Ra6 Ke7 32.Ra5 Kd7 33.g3 Kd6 34.gf4 gf4 35.Rc5 a6 36.Ra5 Ra7 [D] 37.b5 cb5 38.ab5 Kc7 39.Ra6 Ra6 40.ba6 Kb6 41.Kc3 Ka6 42.Kb4 Kb6 43.Ka4 Ka6 44.h3 h6 45.Kb4 Kb6 46.Ka4 Ka6 47.h4 h5 1/2-1/2**

After 26.ed5

993) Forbes,Cathy-Fischer,R [1992] Skittles game (played on Fischer's pocket set!) at the Fischer-Spassky match King's Indian **1.d4 Nf6 2.Nf3 g6 3.Bf4 Bg7 4.Nc3 d6 5.e4 O-O 6.h3 c5 7.dc5 Qa5 8.Bd2 Qc5 9.Bd3 a6 10.a4 b6 11.O-O Bb7 12.Re1 Nbd7 13.Be3 Qc7 14.Qe2 e6 15.Bf4 e5 16.Bg3 Nc5 17.Nd2 Nh5 18.Bh2 Nf4 19.Bf4 ef4 20.Nb3 Nd7 21.Qd2 f3 22.g3 Ne5 23.Bf1 h5 24.Rad1 Rad8 25.Nd5 Bd5 26.ed5 [D] Nc4 27.Qd3?? Nb2 0-1** (Cathy Forbes is a British reporter who was covering the match).

1992 World Championship
Rematch vs Boris Spassky

994) Fischer,R-Spassky,B [1992] Sveti Stefan, World Championship Rematch [1] Ruy Lopez C95 **1.e4 e5 2.Nf3 Nc6 3.Bb5 a6 4.Ba4 Nf6 5.O-O Be7 6.Re1 b5 7.Bb3 d6 8.c3 O-O 9.h3 Nb8 10.d4 Nbd7 11.Nbd2 Bb7 12.Bc2 Re8 13.Nf1 Bf8 14.Ng3 g6 15.Bg5 h6 16.Bd2 Bg7 17.a4 c5 18.d5 c4 19.b4 Nh7** [19...cb3!?] **20.Be3 h5 21.Qd2 Rf8 22.Ra3 Ndf6 23.Rea1 Qe7 24.R1a2 Rfc8 25.Qc1 Bf8 26.Qa1 Qe8 27.Nf1** [Beginning an interesting maneuver to b1!] **Be7 28.N1d2 Kg7 29.Nb1!** [D] [Threatening to trade everything on the a-file followed by Na3, winning a pawn. Spassky sacs a piece for play] **Ne4 30.Be4 f5 31.Bc2 Bd5 32.ab5 ab5 33.Ra7 Kf6 34.Nbd2 Ra7 35.Ra7 Ra8 36.g4 hg4 37.hg4 Ra7 38.Qa7 f4 39.Bf4 ef4 40.Nh4 Bf7 41.Qd4 Ke6 42.Nf5! Bf8** [42..gf5 Bf5#] **43.Qf4 Kd7 44.Nd4 Qe1 45.Kg2 Bd5 46.Be4 Be4 47.Ne4 Be7 48.Nb5 Nf8 49.Nbd6 Ne6 1-0**

After 29.Nb1

995) Spassky,B-Fischer,R [1992] Sveti Stefan, World Championship Rematch [2] King's Indian E80 [E: R + minor piece] **1.d4 Nf6 2.c4 g6 3.Nc3 Bg7 4.e4 d6 5.f3 c5 6.dc5 dc5 7.Qd8 Kd8 8.Be3 Nfd7 9.Nge2 b6 10.O-O-O Na6 11.g3 Nc7 12.f4 e6 13.Bh3 Ke7 14.Rhf1 h6 15.e5 Bb7 16.g4 Rad8 17.Ng3 f6 18.Nce4 fe5 19.f5 Be4 20.Ne4 gf5 21.gf5 Nf6 22.Rg1 Rd1 23.Kd1 Bf8 24.Nf6 Kf6 25.Rf1 ef5 26.Rf5 Kg7 27.Re5 Bd6 28.Re4 Bh2 29.Ke2 h5 30.Re7 Kf6 31.Rd7 Be5 32.b3 h4 33.Kf3 Rg8 34.Bg4 h3 35.Rh7 h2 36.Bf4 Rf8 37.Be5 Kg6 38.Ke4 Kh7 39.Bh2 Re8 40.Kf5 Ne6 41.Kf6 Nd4 42.Bd6 Re4 43.Bd7 Re2 44.a4 Rb2 45.Bb8 a5 46.Ba7 Rb3 47.Ke5 Nf3 48.Kd6 Nd2 49.Be6 Rb4 50.Kc6** [D] **Nb3 51.Bd5 Ra4 52.Bb6 Ra1 53.Bc5 a4 54.Bb4 a3 55.c5 Nd4 56.Kd7 Rd1 57.Ba3 Nc2 58.c6 Rd5 59.Bd6 1/2-1/2**

After 50.Kc6

996) Fischer,R-Spassky,B [1992] Sveti-Stefan, World Championship Rematch [3] Ruy Lopez C95 [E: R + minor piece] **1.e4 e5 2.Nf3 Nc6 3.Bb5 a6 4.Ba4 Nf6 5.O-O Be7 6.Re1 b5 7.Bb3 d6 8.c3 O-O 9.h3 Nb8 10.d4 Nbd7 11.Nbd2 Bb7 12.Bc2 Re8 13.Nf1 Bf8 14.Ng3 g6 15.Bg5 h6 16.Bd2 ed4 17.cd4 c5 18.Bf4 cd4! 19.Nd4 Ne5 20.b3** [D] **d5 21.Qd2 de4 22.Ne4 Nd5 23.Bg3 Rc8 24.Re2 f5 25.Be5 Re5 26.Ng3 Re2 27.Nge2 Nb4 28.Rd1 Nc2 29.Nc2 Qd2 30.Rd2 Rc7 31.Ne3 Kf7 32.h4 Bc8 33.Nf4 g5 34.hg5 hg5 35.Nd3 Bg7 36.Nd5 Rc6 37.N5b4 Rc7 38.Nd5 Rc6 39.N5b4 Rc7 1/2-1/2**

After 20.b3

997) Spassky,B-Fischer,R [1992] Sveti-Stefan, World Championship Rematch [4] Queen's Gambit D27 [E: R + minor piece] **1.d4 d5 2.c4 dc4 3.Nf3 Nf6 4.e3 e6 5.Bc4 c5 6.O-O a6 7.dc5 Qd1 8.Rd1 Bc5 9.b3 Nbd7 10.Bb2 b6 11.Nc3 Bb7 12.Rac1 Be7 13.Nd4 Rc8 14.f3 b5 15.Be2 Bc5 16.Kf1!? Ke7 17.e4? g5! 18.Nb1 g4 19.Ba3 b4? 20.Rc5! Nc5 21.Bb4 Rhd8 22.Na3 gf3 23.gf3 Nd7 24.Nc4 Ba8 25.Kf2 Rg8 26.h4 Rc7 27.Nc2 Rb8 28.Ba3 h5? 29.Rg1 Kf6 30.Ke3 a5 31.Rg5 a4? 32.b4 Nb7 33.b5 Nbc5 34.Nd4 e5?** [D] **35.Ne5 Ne5 36.Rf5 Kg7 37.Re5 Ne4! 38.Bd3! Rc3 39.Bb4! Rd3 40.Kd3 Nf6 41.Bd6 Rc8 42.Rg5 Kh7 43.Be5 Ne8 44.Rh5 Kg6 45.Rg5 Kh7 46.Bf4 f6 47.Rf5 Kg6 48.b6 Rd8 49.Ra5 Bf3 50.h5! 1-0**

After 34...e5?

After 23...Qe7

After 45...Re3!

Final Position

After 37.Bf1

998) Fischer,R-Spassky,B [1992] Sveti Stefan, World Championship Rematch [5] Ruy Lopez C95 **1.e4 e5 2.Nf3 Nc6 3.Bb5 a6 4.Ba4 Nf6 5.O-O Be7 6.Re1 b5 7.Bb3 d6 8.c3 O-O 9.h3 Nb8 10.d4 Nbd7 11.Nbd2 Bb7 12.Bc2 Re8 13.Nf1 Bf8 14.Ng3 g6 15.Bg5 h6 16.Bd2 ed4 17.cd4 c5 18.d5 Nb6 19.Ba5?! Nfd7 20.b3 Bg7 21.Rc1 Qf6 22.Rb1 b4 23.Ne2 Qe7** [D] **24.a3?! ba3 25.Bc3 f5! 26.Bg7 Qg7 27.Nf4 fe4 28.Nh4 g5! 29.Ne6 Qf6 30.Qg4 Nd5 31.Ng5 hg5 32.Qd7 Nb4! 33.Qb7 Nc2 34.Re4 a2 35.Rf1 Nb4! 36.Rg4 a1=Q 37.Ra1 Qa1 38.Kh2 Qg7 39.Qf3 Qe5 40.g3? Rf8 41.Qg2 Qf6 42.f4 Ra7! 43.Rg5 Rg7 44.Rh5 Qe6 45.g4 Rf4** **0-1**

999) Spassky,B-Fischer,R [1992] Sveti Stefan, World Championship Rematch [6] Queen's Gambit D27 [E: R + minor piece] **1.d4 d5 2.c4 dc4 3.Nf3 Nf6 4.e3 e6 5.Bc4 c5 6.O-O a6 7.dc5 Qd1 8.Rd1 Bc5 9.b3 Nbd7 10.Bb2 b5 11.Be2 Bb7 12.Nbd2 Ke7 13.a4 ba4 14.Ra4 Rhb8?! 15.Rc1! Bd5 16.Ne5! Bd6 17.Nd7 Nd7 18.Ra6 Ra6 19.Ba6 f6? 20.Bc4 Bc4 21.Rc4 Nc5 22.Rc3 f5 23.Ba3 Ne4!? 24.Rc7 Kd8 25.Bd6 Nd2 26.Rg7 Rb3 27.h4 h5 28.Bf4 Ke8 29.Kh2 Rb2 30.Kh3 Ne4 31.f3 Nf2 32.Kg3 Nd3 33.Bg5 e5 34.Kh3 Nf2 35.Kh2 Nd3 36.Bh6 Ne1 37.Kg1 Nd3 38.Bg5 Rb1 39.Kh2 Rb2 40.Re7 Kf8 41.Re6 Kg7 42.Kh3 Re2 43.Rd6 Ne1 44.Bf6 Kg8 45.Be5 Re3!** [D] **46.Bf4? Re2 47.Rg6 Kf7 48.Rg5 Ke6 49.Bc7 Ra2 50.Bb6 Nd3 51.Kh2 Ne1 52.Kh3 Nd3 53.Bc7 Rc2 54.Bb6 Ra2 55.Kg3 Ne1 56.Rh5 Rg2 57.Kf4 Nd3 58.Ke3 Ne5 59.Rh6 Kd5 60.Bc7 Rg7 61.Be5 Ke5** **1/2-1/2**

1000) Fischer,R-Spassky,B [1992] Sveti Stefan, World Championship Rematch [7] Ruy Lopez [E: minor piece] C90 **1.e4 e5 2.Nf3 Nc6 3.Bb5 a6 4.Ba4 Nf6 5.O-O Be7 6.Re1 b5 7.Bb3 d6 8.c3 O-O 9.d3 Na5 10.Bc2 c5 11.Nbd2 Re8 12.h3 Bf8 13.Nf1 Bb7 14.Ng3 g6 15.Bg5 h6 16.Bd2 d5? 17.ed5 c4 18.b4! cd3 19.Bd3 Qd5 20.Be4! Ne4 21.Ne4 Bg7 22.ba5 f5 23.Ng3 e4 24.Nh4 Bf6? 25.Ng6 e3 26.Nf4! Qd2 27.Re3 Qd1 28.Rd1 Re3 29.fe3 Rd8 30.Rd8 Bd8 31.Nf5 Ba5 32.Nd5! Kf8 33.e4 Bd5 34.ed5 h5 35.Kf2 Bc3 36.Ke3 Kf7 37.Kd3 Bb2 38.g4 hg4 39.hg4 Kf6 40.d6 Ke6 41.g5! a5 42.g6 Bf6 43.g7 Kf7 44.d7** [D] **1-0**

1001) Spassky,B-Fischer,R [1992] Sveti Stefan, World Championship Rematch [8] King's Indian E84 **1.d4 Nf6 2.c4 g6 3.Nc3 Bg7 4.e4 d6 5.f3 O-O 6.Be3 Nc6 7.Nge2 a6 8.Qd2 Rb8 9.h4 h5 10.Bh6 e5!? 11.Bg7 Kg7 12.d5 Ne7 13.Ng3 c6 14.dc6 Nc6!? 15.O-O-O Be6! 16.Kb1 Ne8 17.Nd5 b5! 18.Ne3! Rh8 19.Rc1 Qb6 20.Bd3 Nd4 21.Nd5 Qa7! 22.Nf1 Nf6!? 23.Nfe3 Bd5 24.cd5 Rbc8 25.Rcf1 Qe7 26.g4 Nd7 27.g5 Kf8?! 28.Rf2 Ke8 29.Bf1! Nc5 30.Bh3! Rc7 31.Rc1!? Ncb3 32.ab3 Nb3 33.Rc6! Nd2 34.Rd2 Kf8 35.Ra6 Ra7! 36.Rc6 Kg7 37.Bf1** [D] **Ra1! 38.Ka1 Qa7 39.Kb1 Qe3 40.Kc2 b4** **0-1**

1002) Fischer,R-Spassky,B [1992] Sveti Stefan, World Championship Rematch [9] Ruy Lopez C69 [E: R + minor piece] **1.e4 e5 2.Nf3 Nc6 3.Bb5 a6 4.Bc6 dc6 5.O-O f6 6.d4 ed4 7.Nd4 c5 8.Nb3 Qd1 9.Rd1 Bg4 10.f3 Be6 11.Nc3 Bd6 12.Be3 b6 13.a4 O-O-O 14.a5 Kb7 15.e5! Be7 16.Rd8 Bd8 17.Ne4! Kc6?? 18.ab6 cb6 [D] 19.Nbc5!! Bc8 20.Na6 fe5 21.Nb4 1-0**

After 18...cb6

1003) Spassky,B-Fischer,R [1992] Sveti Stefan, World Championship Rematch [10] Nimzo-Indian E35 [E: R + minor piece] **1.d4 Nf6 2.c4 e6 3.Nc3 Bb4 4.Qc2 d5 5.cd5 ed5 6.Bg5 h6 7.Bh4 c5 8.dc5 Nc6 9.e3 g5 10.Bg3 Qa5 11.Nf3 Ne4 12.Nd2 Nc3 13.bc3 Bc3 14.Rb1 Qc5 15.Rb5 Qa3 16.Rb3 Bd2 17.Qd2 Qa5 18.Bb5 Qd2 19.Kd2 Bd7 20.Bc6 Bc6 21.h4 Ke7 22.Be5 f6 23.Bd4 g4 24.Rc1 Ke6 25.Rb4 h5 26.Rc3 Rhc8 27.a4? b6 28.Kc2 Be8 29.Kb2 Rc3 30.Bc3 Rc8 31.e4? Bc6 32.ed5 Bd5 33.g3 Bc4 34.Bd4 Kd5 35.Be3 Rc7 36.Kc3 f5 37.Kb2 Ke6 38.Kc3 Bd5 39.Kb2 Be4 40.a5 ba5 41.Rb5 a4 42.Rc5 Rb7 43.Ka3 a6 44.Ka4 Bd5 45.Ka5 Ke5 46.Ka6 [D] Rb3 47.Rc7 Ke4 48.Rh7 Re3 49.fe3 Ke3 50.Rh5 Be4 51.Rh8 Kf3 52.Re8 Kg3 53.h5 Bd3 54.Kb6 f4 55.Kc5! f3 56.Kd4 Bf5 57.Rf8 Kf4 58.h6 g3 59.h7 g2 60.h8=Q g1=Q 61.Kc4 Qc1 62.Kb3 Qc2 63.Kb4 Qe4 64.Kc3 Qc6 65.Kb3 Qd5 66.Kc3 Qc5 67.Kb2 Qb4 68.Ka2 1/2-1/2**

After 46.Ka6

1004) Fischer,R-Spassky,B [1992] Sveti Stefan, World Championship Rematch [11] Sicilian B31 [E: R + minor piece] **1.e4 c5 2.Nf3 Nc6 3.Bb5 g6 4.Bc6!? bc6 5.O-O Bg7 6.Re1 e5 7.b4! cb4 8.a3 c5? 9.ab4 cb4 10.d4 ed4 11.Bb2 d6 12.Nd4! Qd7 13.Nd2 Bb7 14.Nc4 Nh6 15.Nf5!! Bb2 16.Ncd6 Kf8 17.Nh6 f6? 18.Ndf7 Qd1 19.Rad1 Ke7 20.Nh8 Rh8 21.Nf5! gf5 22.ef5 Be5 23.f4 Rc8 24.fe5 Rc2 25.e6! Bc6 26.Rc1! Rc1 27.Rc1 Kd6 28.Rd1 Ke5 29.e7 a5 30.Rc1 Bd7 31.Rc5 Kd4 32.Ra5 [D] b3 33.Ra7 Be8 34.Rb7 Kc3 35.Kf2 b2 36.Ke3 Bf7 37.g4 Kc2 38.Kd4 b1=Q 39.Rb1 Kb1 40.Kc5 Kc2 41.Kd6 1-0**

After 32.Ra5

1005) Spassky,B-Fischer,R [1992] Sveti Stefan, World Championship Rematch [12] King's Indian E83 [E: minor piece] **1.d4 Nf6 2.c4 g6 3.Nc3 Bg7 4.e4 d6 5.f3 O-O 6.Be3 Nc6 7.Nge2 a6 8.h4 h5 9.Nc1 e5?! 10.d5 Ne7 11.Be2 Nh7 12.Nd3 f5 13.a4! Nf6 14.Nf2 a5? 15.Qc2 c5? 16.O-O-O b6 17.Rdg1 Nh7 18.Nb5 Kh8? 19.g4 hg4 20.fg4 f4 21.Bd2 g5 22.hg5 Ng6 23.Rh5 Rf7 24.Rgh1 Bf8 25.Qb3 Rb8 26.Qh3 Rbb7 27.Nd3 Kg8 28.Ne1 Rg7 29.Nf3 Rbf7 30.Rh6 Qd7 31.Qh5! Qg4 32.Rg6 Qh5 33.Rg7 Rg7 34.Rh5 Bg4 35.Rh4 Bf3 36.Bf3 Ng5 37.Bg4! Rh7 38.Rh7 Kh7 39.Kc2 Be7 40.Kd3 Kg6 41.Nc7 Kf7 42.Ne6 Nh7 43.Bh5 Kg8 44.Be1 Nf6 45.Bh4 Kh7 46.Bf7 [D] Nd5 47.cd5 Bh4 48.Bh5 Kh6 49.Be2 Bf2 50.Kc4 Bd4 51.b3 Kg6 52.Kb5 Kf6 53.Kc6 Ke7 54.Ng7 1-0**

After 46.Bf7

1006) Fischer,R-Spassky,B [1992] Belgrade, World Championship Rematch [13] Sicilian B31 [E: R + minor piece] **1.e4 c5 2.Nf3 Nc6 3.Bb5 g6 4.Bc6 bc6 5.O-O Bg7 6.Re1 f6 7.c3 Nh6 8.d4 cd4 9.cd4 O-O 10.Nc3 d6 11.Qa4?! Qb6! 12.Nd2 Nf7 13.Nc4 Qa6! 14.Be3 Qa4 15.Na4 f5! 16.ef5 Bf5 17.Rac1 Rfc8 18.Na5 Bd7 19.b3 Rab8 20.Nc3 Kf8 21.a3 Nh6 22.b4 Nf5 23.Red1 Ke8 24.Ne4 Rb5 [D] 25.h3 h5 26.Rd2 a6 27.Kf1 Rd5 28.Rcd1 Rb5 29.Ke2 Be6 30.Rc1 Kd7 31.Nc3 Rbb8 32.Kf1 h4 33.Ke2 Bf6 34.Ne4 Bd5 35.Kd3 Bg7 36.Rdc2 Rc7 37.Re1 Rf8 38.f3 Rb8 39.Nc3 Bg8 40.Ne2**

After 24...Rb5

Bf7 41.Bd2 Bf6 42.Rec1 Rbc8 43.Nc4 Rb7 44.Na5 Rbc7 45.Nc4 Rb7 1/2-1/2

After 24...Bc7

1007) Spassky,B-Fischer,R [1992] Belgrade, World Championship Rematch [14] Queen's Gambit D27 [E: minor piece] **1.d4 d5 2.c4 dc4 3.Nf3 Nf6 4.e3 e6 5.Bc4 c5 6.O-O a6 7.dc5 Qd1 8.Rd1 Bc5 9.b3 b5 10.Be2 Bb7 11.Bb2 Nbd7 12.Nbd2 O-O 13.Rac1 Rfc8 14.h3 Kf8 15.Kf1 Ke7 16.Ne1 Bd6 17.a4 Bc6 18.ab5 ab5 19.Rc2 Rc7 20.Rdc1 Rac8 21.Bf3 Bf3 22.Ndf3 e5 23.Rc7 Rc7 24.Rc7 Bc7** [D] **25.Nc2 Ne4 26.Na3 b4 27.Nc4 f6 28.Ne1 Ndc5 29.Nc2 Nb3 30.Nb4 Nbd2 31.Nd2 Nd2 32.Ke2 Nc4** 1/2-1/2

After 27.Ke1

1008) Fischer,R-Spassky,B [1992] Belgrade, World Championship Rematch [15] English Opening E07 **1.c4 e6 2.Nf3 Nf6 3.g3 d5 4.Bg2 Be7 5.O-O O-O 6.d4 Nbd7 7.Nbd2 b6 8.cd5 ed5 9.Ne5 Bb7 10.Ndf3 Ne4 11.Bf4 Ndf6 12.Rc1 c5 13.dc5 bc5 14.Ng5 Ng5 15.Bg5 Ne4 16.Be7 Qe7 17.Be4 de4 18.Nc4 e3 19.f3 Rad8 20.Qb3 Rfe8 21.Rc3 Bd5! 22.Rfc1 g6 23.Qa3 Bf3 24.ef3 e2 25.Re1 Rd1 26.Kf2 Re1 27.Ke1** [D] **Qd7! 28.Qb3! Qh3 29.Ne3 Qh2 30.g4 Rb8! 31.Qd5 Rb2 32.Qd8 Kg7 33.Nf5 gf5** 1/2-1/2

After 32...e5!

1009) Spassky,B-Fischer,R [1992] Belgrade, World Championship Rematch [16] Benoni E70 **1.d4 Nf6 2.c4 c5 3.d5 d6 4.Nc3 g6 5.e4 Bg7 6.Bg5 h6 7.Bh4 g5 8.Bg3 Qa5 9.Bd3? Ne4 10.Be4 Bc3 11.bc3 Qc3 12.Kf1 f5 13.Rc1 Qf6 14.h4 g4 15.Bd3? f4 16.Ne2 fg3 17.Ng3 Rf8 18.Rc2 Nd7? 19.Qg4 Ne5 20.Qe4 Bd7 21.Kg1 O-O-O 22.Bf1 Rg8 23.f4 Nc4! 24.Nh5 Qf7 25.Qc4 Qh5 26.Rb2 Rg3! 27.Be2 Qf7 28.Bf3 Rdg8 29.Qb3 b6 30.Qe3 Qf6 31.Re2 Bb5 32.Rd2 e5!** [D] **33.de6 Bc6 34.Kf1 Bf3** 0-1

After 49...Rd3

1010) Fischer,R-Spassky,B [1992] Belgrade, World Championship Rematch [17] Sicilian B23 [E: R + minor piece] **1.e4 c5 2.Nc3 Nc6 3.Nge2 e6 4.g3 d5 5.ed5 ed5 6.Bg2 d4 7.Nd5 Nf6 8.Nef4 Nd5 9.Nd5 Bd6 10.O-O O-O 11.d3 Be6 12.Nf4 Bf5? 13.h3 Rb8 14.Bd2 Re8 15.Re1 Re1 16.Qe1 Qd7 17.g4 Re8 18.Qd1 Bf4 19.Bf4 Be6 20.Qf3! Nb4!? 21.Qb7 Nc2 22.Rc1 Qb7 23.Bb7 Nb4 24.Be4 Ba2 25.Bd2! Bd5 26.Bd5 Nd5 27.Rc5 Nb6 28.Kf1 f6 29.Ra5 Re7 30.Bb4 Rd7 31.Bc5 Kf7 32.Ke2 g5 33.Kf3 Kg6 34.Ke4! h5 35.Bd4 Re7 36.Kf3 h4 37.Bc5 Re1! 38.Ra7 Nd5! 39.Bf8! Re8 40.Bd6 Re6 41.Rd7 Nb6 42.Rd8 Nd5 43.b4 Re1! 44.b5! Rb1 45.Rb8 Rb3? 46.Ke4! Nc3 47.Kd4 Nb5 48.Kc4 Rc3 49.Kb5 Rd3** [D] **50.Kc6 Rh3 51.Kd5! Rf3 52.Ke6 Rf2 53.Rg8 Kh7 54.Kf7! Ra2 55.Rg7 Kh6 56.Bf8 Ra7 57.Kf6! Ra6 58.Kf7** 1-0

After 21.Ndb3

1011) Spassky,B-Fischer,R [1992] Belgrade, World Championship Rematch [18] Queen's Gambit D27 [E: minor piece] **1.d4 d5 2.c4 dc4 3.Nf3 a6 4.e3 Nf6 5.Bc4 e6 6.O-O c5 7.dc5 Qd1 8.Rd1 Bc5 9.Nbd2 O-O 10.a3 b5 11.Be2 Bb7 12.b4 Be7 13.Bb2 Nbd7 14.Rac1 Rfc8 15.Nb3 Rc1 16.Rc1 Rc8 17.Rc8 Bc8 18.Nfd4 Nb8 19.Bf3 Kf8 20.Na5 Bd6 21.Ndb3** [D] **e5! 22.Nc5 Ke7 23.h3 Nfd7 24.Nd3 f6 25.Be4 g6 26.f4 ef4 27.ef4 Nb6 28.Nb7 Bc7 29.Nbc5 Nc4 30.Bc1 Nd7 31.Kf1 Nc5 32.Nc5 Bb6 33.Bd3 Bc5 34.bc5 Be6 35.Kf2 Kd7 36.Bc4 Bc4** 1/2-1/2

1012) Fischer,R-Spassky,B [1992] Belgrade, World Championship Rematch [19] Sicilian B23 [R + minor piece; Q + pawn] **1.e4 c5 2.Nc3 Nc6 3.Nge2 e5 4.Nd5 Nge7 5.Nec3 Nd5 6.Nd5 Be7 7.g3 d6 8.Bg2 h5! 9.h4 Be6 10.d3 Bd5 11.ed5 Nb8 12.f4 Nd7 13.O-O g6 14.Rb1 f5! 15.b4 b6 16.bc5 bc5 17.c4 O-O 18.Qa4 Bf6 19.Rb7 Nb6 20.Qb5 Rf7 21.Rf7 Kf7 22.Bd2 Rb8 23.Qc6 Nc8? 24.Re1 Ne7 25.Qa4 Qc7 26.Kh2 ef4? 27.Bf4 Be5 28.Re2 Rb6 29.Kh3 Ng8?? 30.Re5! de5 31.Be5 Qe7 32.d6 Rd6 33.Bd6 Qd6 34.Bd5 Kf8 35.Qa7 Ne7 36.Qa8 Kg7 37.Qb7 Kf8 38.a4 f4! 39.a5 fg3 40.a6 Qf4 41.Bf3 Nf5 42.Qe4 g2 43.Qf4 g1=Q 44.Be4 Qa1 45.a7 Qa7 46.Bf5 gf5 47.Qf5 Kg7 48.Qg5 Kf8 49.Qh6 Kg8 50.Qh5 Qc7 51.Qg6 Kh8 52.Qf6 Kg8 53.Qe6 Kh8 54.Qd5 Qf7 [D] 55.Kg2 Qg6 56.Kh3 Qf7 57.Qe5 Kh7 58.Kg4 Qg6 59.Kf4 Qh6 60.Kf3 Qg6 61.Qe4 Kh8! 62.Ke2 Qd6 63.Qe3 Qh2 64.Kd1 Qh1 65.Kd2 Qh2 66.Kc3 Qh4 67.d4 Kh7 68.d5? Qf6 69.Kc2 Qd6 70.Qg5 Kh8 71.Kd2 Qb6 72.Qe5 Kg8 73.Qe8 Kg7 74.Qb5 Qc7 75.Kc2 Kf8 76.Qa6 Qh2 77.Kb3 Qb8 78.Qb5 Qc7 79.Ka3 Qa7 80.Kb3 Ke7 81.Kc2 Kd8 82.Kd2 Qc7 83.Qa6 Qf4 84.Kc2 Qe4 1/2-1/2**

After 54...Qf7

1013) Spassky,B-Fischer,R [1992] Belgrade, World Championship Rematch [20] Sicilian B24 [E: R + minor piece] **1.e4 c5 2.Ne2 Nf6 3.Nbc3 e6 4.g3 Nc6 5.Bg2 Be7 6.O-O d6 7.d3 a6 8.a3 Qc7 9.f4 b5 10.Kh1 O-O 11.Be3 Bb7 12.Bg1 Rab8 13.h3 Ba8 14.g4 b4?! 15.ab4 cb4 16.Na4 Nd7 17.Qd2 Rfc8 18.b3 a5 19.g5 Bf8 20.Ra2 Ne7 21.Nd4! g6 22.Nb2 Bg7 23.Nc4 d5?! 24.Na5 de4 25.de4 e5 26.Ne2 ef4 27.Nf4 Ne5 28.Nd3 Rb5 29.Ne5 Qe5 30.Nc4 Qg5 31.Be3 Qh4 32.Nd6 [D] Bc3 33.Qf2 Qf2 34.Rf2 Rbb8 35.Nc8 Rc8 36.Ra7 Kf8 37.Bh6 Ke8 38.Bg5 f6 39.Bf6 Bf6 40.Rf6 Bc6 41.Kg1 Bd7 42.Rd6 Bc6 43.Bf1 1-0**

After 32.Nd6

1014) Fischer,R-Spassky,B [1992] Belgrade, World Championship Rematch [21] Sicilian B44 [E: R + pawn] **1.e4 c5 2.Nf3 Nc6 3.d4 cd4 4.Nd4 e6 5.Nb5 d6 6.c4 Nf6 7.N5c3 Be7 8.g3 O-O 9.Bg2 a6 10.O-O Rb8 11.Na3 Qc7 12.Be3 Bd7 13.Rc1 Ne5 14.h3 Rfc8 15.f4 Ng6 16.Qd2 Be8 17.Rfd1 b6 18.Qf2 h6 19.Kh2 Qa7 20.Qe2 Qc7?! 21.Bf3 Bc6 22.Nab1 Qb7 23.Nd2 b5 24.cb5 ab5 25.b4 Qa8 26.Rc2 d5!? 27.e5 Ne4 28.Be4! de4 29.Bc5! Bc5 30.bc5 Rd8 31.Re1 Ne7 32.Nce4 Nf5 33.Nb3 Nd4 34.Nd4 Rd4 35.Nd6 Qa4 36.f5! Ra8 37.Rb2 Qa3! 38.fe6 fe6 39.Nb5 Bb5 40.Qb5 Rd3 41.Rg2! Qc3 42.Ree2! Ra3 43.Rc2 Qe5 44.Rce2 Re3 45.Re3 Re3 46.a4 Rc3 47.c6! Qd6 48.c7! Rc7 49.Qb8 Kh7 50.a5 h5 51.h4 Qc5? 52.a6 Rf7 53.Qb1 Kh6 54.Qa2 Re7 55.Qd2 Kg6 56.Re2 Kh7 57.Qc2 Qc2 58.Rc2 [D] Kg6 59.Ra2 Ra7 60.Ra5 e5 61.Kg2 Kf6 62.Kf2 Ke6 63.Ke3 Kf5 64.Kf3 g6 65.Ra3 g5 66.hg5 Kg5 67.Ke4 1-0**

After 58.Rc2

1015) Spassky,B-Fischer,R [1992] Belgrade, World Championship Rematch [22] Sicilian B20 **1.e4 c5 2.Ne2 Nf6 3.Nbc3 d6 4.g3 Nc6 5.Bg2 g6 6.O-O Bg7 7.d3 O-O 8.h3 Rb8 9.f4 Bd7 10.Be3 b5 11.a3 Ne8 12.d4 cd4 13.Nd4 b4 14.Nc6 Bc6 15.ab4 Rb4 16.Ra7 Rb2 17.e5 Bg2 18.Kg2 Nc7 19.ed6 ed6 20.Na4 Ra2 21.Bb6 Qe8! 22.Rc7 Qa4 23.Qd6 Rc2 24.Rc2 Qc2 25.Bf2 Qe4 26.Kg1 [D] 1/2-1/2**

Final Position

After 58.a8=Q

1016) Fischer,R-Spassky,B [1992] Belgrade, World Championship Rematch [23] Sicilian B23 [E: minor piece] **1.e4 c5 2.Nc3 e6 3.Nge2 Nc6 4.g3 d5 5.ed5 ed5 6.d3 Nf6 7.Bg2 Be7 8.Bg5! d4 9.Bf6 Bf6 10.Ne4 Be7 11.Nf4 O-O 12.O-O Re8 13.Qh5 g6! 14.Qd5 Bf5! 15.Rfe1 Kg7 16.a3 Rc8 17.h3 Qd5 18.Nd5 Bf8 19.g4 Be6 20.Nef6 Red8 21.g5 Bd6 22.Re4 Ne7! 23.Rh4 Rh8 24.Re1 Nf5 25.Rhe4 h6!26.h4 hg5 27.hg5 Rh4 28.Rh4 Nh4 29.Re4! Nf5! 30.Nf4 Ba2!? 31.N4d5 Bd5 32.Nd5 Kf8 33.Kf1 Re8 34.Re8 Ke8 35.Nf6 Kd8 36.Bb7 Bf4 37.Ne4 Bc1 38.a4 Bb2 39.Nc5 Bc1 40.Be4 Bg5 41.Bf5 gf5 42.Nb3 Bf6 43.Kg2 Kd7 44.Kg3 Ke6 45.Na5 Be5 46.Kh4 Bf6! 47.Kh5 Kd5 48.Kh6 Kc5! 49.Kh7 Kb4 50.Nc6 Kc3 51.Kg8 Kc2 52.Kf7 Bh8 53.a5? Kd3 54.a6 Ke2 55.Na7 d3 56.Nc6 d2 57.a7 d1=Q 58.a8=Q [D] Qd5 59.Kg6? Qe6 60.Kh7 Bc3 61.Nd8 Qe7? 62.Kg6 Qf6 63.Kh5 Qh8? 64.Kg6 Qg7 65.Kf5 Qf6 66.Kg4 Qg6 67.Kf4 Bd2 68.Ke5 Bc3 69.Kf4 Qd6 70.Kf5 Qd7 71.Kg5 Qe7 72.Kf5 Qf6 73.Kg4 Qg7 74.Kf5 Qf6 75.Kg4 Qg6 76.Kf4 Bd2 77.Ke5 Qg5 78.Ke6 Qg4 79.Kf7 Qd7 80.Kg6 1/2-1/2**

After 39.Rc1

1017) Spassky,B-Fischer,R [1992] Belgrade, World Championship Rematch [24] Sicilian B20 [E: R + minor piece] **1.e4 c5 2.Ne2 Nf6 3.Nbc3 d6 4.g3 g6 5.Bg2 Nc6 6.O-O Bg7 7.d4 cd4 8.Nd4 Bg4 9.Nde2 Qc8 10.f3 Bh3! 11.Bh3 Qh3 12.Bg5 O-O 13.Qd2 h6 14.Be3 Kh7 15.Rac1 Qd7 16.Nd5 Nd5 17.ed5 Ne5 18.b3 b5! 19.Bd4 Rac8 20.f4 Ng4 21.Bg7 Kg7 22.Nd4 Nf6 23.c4 bc4 24.bc4 e6! 25.de6 fe6 26.Rfe1 Rfe8 27.Nb3 a6 28.Qd4! Rc6 29.Red1 e5 30.fe5 Re5 31.Qe5 de5 32.Rd7 Nd7 33.Rd1 Nf6 34.c5 Kf7 35.Rc1 Nd7 36.Kf2 Ke6 37.Ke3 Kd5 38.Rd1 Ke6 39.Rc1 [D] Kd5 1/2-1/2**

After 32...Rf8

1018) Fischer,R-Spassky,B [1992] Belgrade, World Championship Rematch [25] Sicilian B80 **1.e4 c5 2.Nc3 Nc6 3.Nge2 d6 4.d4 cd4 5.Nd4 e6 6.Be3 Nf6 7.Qd2 Be7 8.f3 a6 9.O-O-O O-O 10.g4 Nd4 11.Bd4 b5 12.g5 Nd7 13.h4 b4? 14.Na4 Bb7? 15.Nb6! Rb8 16.Nd7 Qd7 17.Kb1 Qc7 18.Bd3 Bc8 19.h5 e5 20.Be3 Be6 21.Rdg1 a5 22.g6! Bf6 23.gh7 Kh8 24.Bg5 Qe7 25.Rg3 Bg5 26.Rg5 Qf6 27.Rhg1 Qf3! 28.Rg7! Qf6 29.h6 a4 30.b3 ab3 31.ab3 Rfd8 32.Qg2 Rf8 [D] 33.Rg8 Kh7 34.Rg7 Kh8 35.h7! 1-0**

After 56...Nc7

1019) Spassky,B-Fischer,R [1992] Belgrade, World Championship Rematch [26] Benoni E90 [E: minor piece] **1.d4 Nf6 2.c4 c5 3.d5 d6 4.Nc3 g6 5.e4 Bg7 6.Bd3 O-O 7.Nf3 Bg4 8.h3 Bf3 9.Qf3 Nbd7 10.Qd1 e6 11.O-O ed5 12.ed5 Ne8 13.Bd2 Ne5 14.Be2 f5!? 15.f4 Nf7? 16.g4! Nh6?! 17.Kg2 Nc7 18.g5 Nf7 19.Rb1 Re8 20.Bd3 Rb8 21.h4 a6 22.Qc2 b5 23.b3! Rb7 24.Rbe1 Re1 25.Re1 Qb8 26.Bc1! Qd8 27.Ne2! bc4 28.bc4 Ne8 29.h5 Re7 30.h6! Bh8 31.Bd2 Rb7 32.Rb1 Qb8 33.Ng3 Rb1 34.Qb1 Qb1 35.Bb1 Bb2 36.Kf3 Kf8 37.Ke2 Nh8 38.Kd1 Ke7 39.Kc2 Bd4 40.Kb3 Bf2 41.Nh1!? Bh4 42.Ka4 Nc7 43.Ka5 Kd7 44.Kb6 Kc8 45.Bc2 Nf7 46.Ba4 Kb8 47.Bd7 Nd8 48.Bc3 Na8 49.Ka6 Nc7 50.Kb6 Na8 51.Ka5 Kb7 52.Kb5 Nc7 53.Ka4 Na8 54.Kb3 Kc7 55.Be8 Kc8 56.Bf6 Nc7 [D] 57.Bg6 hg6 58.Bd8 1-0**

1020) Fischer,R-Spassky,B [1992] Belgrade, World Championship Rematch [27] Ruy Lopez C69 [E: minor piece] **1.e4 e5 2.Nf3 Nc6 3.Bb5 a6 4.Bc6 dc6 5.O-O f6 6.d4 ed4 7.Nd4 c5 8.Ne2 Qd1 9.Rd1 Bd7 10.Nbc3 Ne7 11.Bf4 O-O-O 12.Rd2 Ng6 13.Bg3 Ne5 14.Be5 fe5 15.Rad1 c4 16.Kf1 Bc5 17.Ng1 Bg4 18.Rd8 Rd8 19.Rd8 Kd8 20.Nce2 Ke7 21.Ke1 b5 22.c3 Kf6 23.h3 Bh5 24.Ng3 Bf7 25.Nf3 g6 26.Nf1 g5 27.Ke2 Bg6 28.N3d2 h5 29.Ne3 c6 30.Kf3 Bf7 31.Ndf1 a5 32.Ke2 Be6 33.Ng3 Kg6 34.a3 Bf7 35.Ngf5 Be6 36.Kf3 Bd7 37.Kg3 Be6 38.Kf3 Bd7 39.Kg3 Be6 40.h4 Bd7 41.hg5 Kg5 42.Nh4 Bg4 43.Ng4 hg4 44.Nf5 a4 45.f3 gf3 46.Kf3 [D] Bf8 47.Ne3 Kh5 48.Nf5 Bc5 1/2-1/2**

After 46.Kf3

1021) Spassky,B-Fischer,R [1992] Belgrade, World Championship Rematch [28] King's Indian E83 **1.d4 Nf6 2.c4 g6 3.Nc3 Bg7 4.e4 d6 5.f3 O-O 6.Be3 Nc6 7.Nge2 a6 8.h4 h5 9.Nc1 e5 10.d5 Nd4 11.Nb3 Nb3 12.Qb3 Kh7! 13.Be2 Bh6 14.Bh6 Kh6 15.O-O-O Kg7 16.Kb1 Qe7 17.Rdg1 Rh8 18.g4! hg4 19.fg4 Nd7 20.g5 Nc5 21.Qd1 a5 22.Rf1 Bd7 23.Qe1 Rh7 24.Qg3 Rf8 25.Rf6 Rfh8 26.b3 Be8 27.Bg4 Bd7 28.Bd1 Be8 29.Bg4 Bd7 30.Bd1 Be8 31.Rf2!? [D] c6! 32.a4 Qd8 33.Ka2 Qe7 34.Bg4 Bd7 35.Bd1 Be8 1/2-1/2**

After 31.Rf2!?

1022) Fischer,R-Spassky,B [1992] Belgrade, World Championship Rematch [29] Ruy Lopez C95 [E:R + minor piece] **1.e4 e5 2.Nf3 Nc6 3.Bb5 a6 4.Ba4 Nf6 5.O-O Be7 6.Re1 b5 7.Bb3 d6 8.c3 O-O 9.h3 Nb8 10.d4 Nbd7 11.c4 c6 12.cb5 ab5 13.Nc3 Bb7 14.Bg5 b4 15.Nb1 h6 16.Bh4 c5 17.de5 Ne4! 18.Be7 Qe7 19.ed6 Qf6! 20.Nbd2 Nd6 21.Nc4 Nc4 22.Bc4 Nb6 23.Ne5 Rae8 24.Bf7 Rf7 25.Nf7 Re1 26.Qe1 Kf7 27.Qe3 Qg5 28.Qg5 hg5 29.b3 Ke6 30.a3 Kd6? 31.ab4 cb4 32.Ra5! Nd5 33.f3 Bc8 34.Kf2 Bf5 35.Ra7 [D] g6 36.Ra6 Kc5 37.Ke1 Nf4 38.g3 Nh3 39.Kd2 Kb5 40.Rd6 Kc5 41.Ra6 Nf2 42.g4 Bd3 43.Re6 Kd5 44.Rb6 Kc5 45.Re6 1/2-1/2**

After 35.Ra7

1023) Spassky,B-Fischer,R [1992] Belgrade, World Championship Rematch [30] King's Indian E83 **1.d4 Nf6 2.c4 g6 3.Nc3 Bg7 4.e4 d6 5.f3 O-O 6.Be3 Nc6 7.Nge2 a6 8.h4 h5 9.Nc1 Nd7 10.Nb3 a5! 11.a4?! Nb4 12.Be2 b6! 13.g4!? hg4 14.fg4 c5 15.h5 cd4 16.Nd4? Nc5 17.Nd5? Bb7! 18.Nf5?! gf5 19.gf5 Bd5 20.ed5 [D] Bb2 21.Kf1 Qd7 22.Qb1 Ba1 23.Rg1 Kh8 24.Qa1 f6 25.Qb1 Rg8 26.Rg6 Rg6 27.hg6 Kg7 0-1**

After 20.ed5

LAST MINUTE ADDITIONS

After 6.Bb3

1024) Altusky,J-Fischer,R [1954] Brooklyn NY, C71 Ruy Lopez **1.e4 e5 2.Nf3 Nc6 3.Bb5 a6 4.Ba4 d6 5.d4 b5 6.Bb3 [D] Bg4 7.Bf7?? Kf7 8.Ng5 Qg5 0-1**

After 9...Nge5??

1025) Fischer,R-Altusky,J [1954] Brooklyn NY, E90 King's Indian **1.d4 g6 2.c4 Nf6 3.Nc3 Bg7 4.e4 O-O 5.Bg5 d6 6.Nf3 Nbd7 7.e5 de5 8.de5 Ng4 9.Nd5 Nge5?? [D] 10.Ne7 Kh8 11.Ng6 hg6 12.Bd8 1-0**

After 40.Kg4

1026) Fischer,R-Hense,K [1961] Los Angeles, Ruy Lopez **1.e4 e5 2.Nf3 Nc6 3.Bb5 a6 4.Ba4 d6 5.c3 Bd7 6.O-O g6 7.d4 Bg7 8.d5 Nb8 9.c4 Ne7 10.Nc3 O-O 11.Bd7 Nd7 12.Ne1 f5 13.Nd3 f4 14.f3 g5 15.Bd2 Qe8 16.b4 Qg6 17.c5 h5 18.Rc1 g4 19.c6 bc6 20.dc6 Nf6 21.Kh1 h4 22.Rg1 Nh5 23.h3 gh3 24.gh3 Qe6 25.Rg4 Nf6 26.Rg2 Nc6 27.Nd5 Ne4 28.fe4 Qh3 29.Kg1 Qd3 30.Rc6 Rf7 31.Rc7 Rc7 32.Nc7 Ra7 33.Ne8 h3 34.Rg5 Kf8 35.Qh5 Qd4 36.Kh1 Qd2 37.Ng7 Qe1 38.Kh2 Qf2 39.Kh3 Qf1 40.Kg4 [D] Qe2 41.Kh4 Qh2 42.Kg4 Qe2 0-1**

After 17...Nc5

1027) Fine,R-Fischer,R [1963] New York B87 Sicilian /Najdorf **1.e4 c5 2.Nf3 d6 3.d4 cd4 4.Nd4 Nf6 5.Nc3 a6 6.Bc4 e6 7.Bb3 b5 8.Qe2 Be7 9.g4 b4 10.Nb1 d5 11.e5 Nfd7 12.Bf4 Qb6 13.Nf3 a5 14.Ba4 O-O 15.Be3 Qc7 16.Bd4 Ba6 17.Qe3 Nc5 [D] 18.Bc5 Bc5 19.Nd4 Qb6 0-1**

After 33...Kf6

1028) Fischer,R-Green,M [1963] Poughkeepsie, NY Sicilian **1.e4 c5 2.Nf3 e6 3.d4 cd4 4.Nd4 d6 5.Bd3 Nc6 6.Nc6 bc6 7.O-O d5 8.ed5 cd5 9.c4 Nf6 10.cd5 Nd5 11.Be4 Bd6?! 12.Nc3 Nc3 13.Bc6! Ke7 14.bc3 Rb8 15.Qg4 Rg8 16.Qh4 f6 17.Qh7 Bb7 18.Bb7 Rb7 19.Re1 Qc8 20.h3 Kf7 21.Qh5 g6 22.Qf3 Rb5 23.a4 Rf5 24.Qe2 Bc5 25.Be3 Re5 26.Qf3 Rd8 27.Rab1 Be3 28.Re3 Re3 29.Qe3 Rd7 30.Qh6 f5 31.c4! Qd8 32.Kh2 a5 33.f4 Kf6 [D] 34.Rb7! Re7** [34...Rb7?? Qg5 wins the Black Queen] **35.c5 1-0**

1029) Fischer,R-Burns,N [1964] Flint, Michigan, Simultaneous French **1.e4 e6 2.d4 d5 3.Nc3 Nf6 4.Bg5 Bb4 5.e5 h6 6.Be3 Ne4 7.Ne2 c5 8.a3 Nc3 9.Nc3 cd4 10.Bd4 Be7 11.f4 Nc6 12.Bb5 Bd7 13.Bc6 bc6 14.Na4 Qa5 15.c3 c5 16.Nc5 Bc5 17.b4 Bb4 18.ab4 Qc7 19.O-O Bb5 20.Rf3 g6 21.Bc5 a5 22.Qd4 a4 23.Ra3 h5 24.Rh3 Kd7 25.Re3 Qc6 26.Re1 Rhc8 27.Rd1 Kc7 28.Qf2 Kb7 29.Qh4 Rh8 30.Qf6 Rh7 31.h4 Rg8 32.Kh2 Ra8 [D] 33.Qe7 Qc7 34.Qg5 Re8 35.Qg3 Ra8 36.Qe3 Rhh8 37.Rda1 Qc6 1/2-1/2**

After 32...Ra8

1030) Fischer,R-Dedinsky,J [1964] Milwaukee, Simultaneous French **1.e4 e6 2.d4 d5 3.Nc3 Bb4 4.e5 c5 5.a3 Bc3 6.bc3 Ne7 7.a4 Qa5 8.Bd2 c4 9.Nf3 Nd7 10.Ng5 h6 11.Qh5 g6 12.Qh3 Nb6 13.Nf3 Bd7 14.Qh4 Ba4 15.Qf6 Rh7 16.h4 Nf5 [D] 17.h5 Nd7 0-1**

After 16...Nf5

1031) Fischer,R-Flynn,G [1964] Sacramento, CA, Simultaneous **1.e4 g6 2.d4 Bg7 3.Nc3 c5 4.dc5 Qa5 5.Nf3 Nc6 6.Bd3 Bc3 7.bc3 Qc3 8.Bd2 Qc5 9.O-O Nf6 10.Re1 d6 11.Rb1 a6 12.Be3 Qh5 13.h3 Nd7 14.Qd2 Nde5 15.Ne5 Qe5 16.f4 Qa5 17.c3 b5 18.e5 d5 19.a4 d4 20.Be4 de3 21.Bc6 Kf8 22.Qe3 Rb8 23.ab5 ab5 24.c4 b4 25.c5 Bf5 26.Ra1 Qc7 27.Be4 Be4 28.Qe4 Qc5 29.Kh2 e6 30.Rec1 Qb5 31.Rc7 Kg7 32.Raa7 Rhf8 33.Rcb7 Rb7 34.Rb7 Qd5 35.Qd5 ed5 36.Rb4 Rd8 [D] 37.Rd4 f6 38.g3 f5 1-0**

After 36...Rd8

1032) Fischer,R-Gale,W [1964] Boston, Simultaneous French **1.e4 e6 2.d4 d5 3.Nc3 Nf6 4.Bg5 Be7 5.e5 Nfd7 6.h4 f6 7.Qh5 g6 8.ef6 Nf6 9.Qe2 Nc6 10.O-O-O O-O 11.Nf3 a6 12.Kb1 b5 13.Bh6 Re8 14.Ng5 Bf8 15.Bf8 Kf8 16.h5 h6 17.Nf3 Nh5 18.Qe3 Ng7 19.Qh6 Qf6 20.Bd3 Ke7 21.Bg6 Rf8 22.Rhe1 Kd8 23.Ne5 Ne7 24.Re3 Ngf5 25.Qh7 Ne3 26.fe3 Ng6 27.Ng6 Qf7 28.Nf8 Qf8 29.g4 c5 30.dc5 Qc5 [D] 31.g5 Ra7 32.Qh8 1-0**

After 30...Qc5

1033) Fischer,R-Kaufer,W [1964] Columbus, OH Simultaneous French **1.e4 e6 2.d4 d5 3.Nc3 Nf6 4.Bg5 Be7 5.e5 Nfd7 6.h4 c5 7.Be7 Qe7 8.Nb5 Na6 9.Nd6 Kd8 10.Ba6 ba6 11.f4 Rb8 12.b3 a5 13.Qd2 cd4 14.Nf3 Nb6 15.Nd4 Qd7 16.Qa5 a6 17.Qc5 Rb7 18.Nc6 Kc7 19.Na5 Kd8 20.Nab7 Bb7 21.Qb6 [D] Ke7 22.Nb7 Re8 23.O-O-O 1-0**

After 21.Qb6

After 43...Rh3

1034) Fischer,R-Kord,H [1964] Detroit, Simultaneous French
1.e4 e6 2.d4 d5 3.Nc3 Bb4 4.e5 Ne7 5.a3 Bc3 6.bc3 c5 7.a4 Qa5
8.Bd2 Nbc6 9.Nf3 c4 10.Ng5 h6 11.Nh3 Bd7 12.Nf4 O-O-O
13.Be2 f6 14.ef6 gf6 15.O-O e5 16.Nh5 Rdf8 17.Kh1 Kb8 18.Rb1
Ka8 19.Qc1 Qc7 20.Bh6 Rf7 21.de5 Rfh7 22.Bg7 Rh5 23.Bh5
Rh5 24.Bf6 Ne5 25.Qf4 N7g6 26.Be5 Qe5 27.Qe5 Ne5 28.a5 Kb8
29.h3 Kc7 30.Kg1 b5 31.ab6 ab6 32.f4 Nf7 33.Rf3 b5 34.g4 Rh8
35.Kg2 Bc6 36.Re1 Nd6 37.Re7 Kd8 38.Ra7 d4 39.f5 d3 40.cd3
cd3 41.Ra6 d2 42.Ra1 Bf3 43.Kf3 Rh3 [D] 44.Kf4 Rc3 45.Rd1
Nc4 0-1

After 49.Nf2

1035) Lunefeld,R-Fischer,R [1964] Waltham, Mass.
Simultaneous Sicilian 1.e4 c5 2.Nf3 d6 3.d4 cd4 4.Nd4 Nf6 5.Bc4
Ne4 6.Qh5 e6 7.Be6 Be6 8.Ne6 Qe7 9.O-O Qe6 10.Re1 Be7
11.Qb5 Qd7 12.Qd7 Nd7 13.Re4 Nf6 14.Re2 Kd7 15.Nc3 Rhc8
16.Bg5 Ng8 17.Bf4 Rc4 18.Bg3 Rac8 19.Rd1 R8c6 20.Red2 Nf6
21.Rd4 Nh5 22.Rc4 Rc4 23.Rd2 Ng3 24.hg3 Bg5 25.f4 Bf6
26.Nd1 b5 27.Kf2 b4 28.Ke3 a5 29.Kd3 Rc5 30.Ke4 h5 31.c3 bc3
32.bc3 Bc3 33.Rc2 Bb4 34.Rc5 dc5 35.Kd5 Be1 36.Kc5 Ke6
37.Kb5 Bg3 38.Ka5 Bf4 39.Kb6 g5 40.a4 h4 41.a5 Bh2 42.a6 Bg1
43.Kb7 g4 44.a7 Ba7 45.Ka7 f5 46.Kb6 Ke5 47.Kb5 Kd4 48.Kc6
f4 49.Nf2 [D] h3 50.gh3 g3 0-1

After 33...Kc8

1036) Fischer,R-O'Keefe,J [1964] Flint, Mich. Simultaneous
Sicilian 1.e4 c5 2.Nf3 Nc6 3.d4 cd4 4.Nd4 g6 5.Nc3 Bg7 6.Be3 Nf6
7.Bc4 Qa5 8.O-O a6 9.Nb3 Qc7 10.Be2 b5 11.f4 d6 12.Nd5 Nd5
13.ed5 Na5 14.Bd4 Nb3 15.ab3 Bd4 16.Qd4 O-O 17.Bd3 Bb7
18.b4 a5 19.ba5 Ra5 20.Ra5 Qa5 21.b4 Qa2 22.Re1 Qd5 23.Qd5
Bd5 24.Re7 Rc8 25.Kf2 Rc3 26.Bb5 Rc2 27.Re2 Rc3 28.Rb2 Bb7
29.Be2 Kf8 30.b5 Ke7 31.Bf3 Bf3 32.gf3 Kd7 33.b6 Kc8 [D] 34.b7
Kb8 35.Rb6 Rc7 36.Rd6 Kb7 1/2-1/2

After 20...Nf6

1037) Fischer,R-Reubens,J [1964] Simultaneous French 1.e4
e6 2.d4 d5 3.Nc3 Bb4 4.a3 Bc3 5.bc3 c5 6.Qg4 Ne7 7.Qg7 Rg8
8.Qh7 Qc7 9.Nf3 cd4 10.Bb5 Bd7 11.Bd7 Nd7 12.O-O Nf6
13.Qh4 Ne4 14.Bf4 Qc3 15.Ne5 Nf5 16.Qh7 O-O-O 17.Qf7 Rg2
18.Kg2 Nh4 19.Kg1 Qh3 20.Qg7 Nf6 [D] 21.Nc6 Nf3 22.Kh1 e5
23.Ne7 1-0

After 34.Kd5

1038) Fischer,R-Thackrey,D [1964] Flint, Mich. Simultaneous Sicilian 1.e4 c5 2.Nf3 Nc6 3.d4 cd4 4.Nd4 g6 5.Nc3 Bg7
6.Be3 Nf6 7.Bc4 O-O 8.Bb3 Qa5 9.f3 d5 10.ed5 Nb4 11.Qd2 Nbd5
12.Nd5 Qd2 13.Kd2 Nd5 14.Bd5 Rd8 15.Bb3 Bd4 16.Bd4 Rd4
17.Ke3 Rd8 18.Rhd1 Bd7 19.Rd4 Bc6 20.Rad1 Rd4 21.Rd4 Kf8
22.Bd5 Bd5 23.Rd5 Ke8 24.c4 Rc8 25.Kd4 e6 26.Rd6 Ke7 27.c5
b6 28.b4 Rb8 29.Rc6 Kd7 30.b5 bc5 31.Kc5 e5 32.a4 f5 33.Ra6
Rb7 34.Kd5 [D] e4 35.fe4 f4 36.e5 1-0

1039) Fischer,R-Acers,J [1964] New Orleans, Simultaneous C43 Petroff **1.e4 e5 2.Nf3 Nf6 3.d4 d5 4.Ne5 Ne4 5.Bd3 c5 6.Bb5 [D]** and 1/2-1/2 in 78 moves.

After 6.Bb5

1040) Fischer,R-Snitzer,F [1965] New York, Ruy Lopez **1.e4 e5 2.Nf3 Nc6 3.Bb5 a6 4.Ba4 Nf6 5.O-O b5 6.Bb3 Bc5 7.Ne5 Ne5 8.d4 d6 9.dc5 dc5 10.f4 Qd1 11.Rd1 c4 12.fe5 cb3 13.Nc3 bc2 14.Rd2 Ng4 15.Nd5 O-O 16.Rc2 Ne5 17.Bf4 Ng6 18.Bc7 Bb7 19.Nb6 Ra7 20.e5 Re8 21.Re1 Nf4 22.Bd6 Bg2 23.Rg2 Rb7 24.Rg4 Rb6 25.Rd1 Ng6 26.Rc1 h6 27.Re4 f6 28.Rc7 Ne5 29.Be5 Re5 30.Re5 fe5 31.Kf2 Re6 32.Ke3 e4 33.Ra7 Kh7 34.b3 h5 35.a4 ba4 36.ba4 Kg6 37.a5 Kf6 38.Rb7 g5 39.h3 g4 40.hg4 hg4 41.Rb6 Ke5 42.Rb8 Rc6 [D] 43.Rg8 Rc3 44.Ke2** Result given as 1/2-1/2

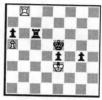

After 42...Rc6

1041) Fischer,R-Zhukov,E [1965] New York, French **1.e4 e6 2.d4 d5 3.Nc3 de4 4.Ne4 Nd7 5.Nf3 Ngf6 6.Bd3 Be7 7.Qe2 c5 8.Nf6 Nf6 9.dc5 Qa5 10.Bd2 Qc5 11.O-O-O Bd7 12.Ne5 Ba4 13.g4 Rc8 14.b3 Bc6 15.Nc6 bc6 16.g5 Nd5 17.Qe5 O-O 18.Kb1 a5 19.h4 Nb4 20.Qc5 Bc5 21.Bb4 ab4 22.f4 Be3 23.f5 e5 [D] 24.Rde1 Bd4 25.h5 h6 26.gh6 gh6 27.f6 Kh8 28.Bc4 Rc7** 1/2-1/2

After 23...e5

1042) Fischer,R-Middendorf,F [1970] Germany, Sicilian/ Najdorf **1.e4 c5 2.Nf3 d6 3.d4 cd4 4.Nd4 Nf6 5.Nc3 a6 6.Bc4 e6 7.Bb3 b5 8.O-O Bb7 9.Re1 Nbd7 10.Bg5 Qa5 11.Bf6 Nf6 12.e5! de5 13.Ne6! b4 14.Ng7 Bg7 15.Qd6 Nd7 16.Bf7 Kf7 17.Qd7 Kf6 18.Rad1 Rhg8 19.Rd6 Kg5 20.h4 Kh4 21.Qf5 [D] Bg2 22.Kg2 Bh6 23.Kf3** 1-0

After 21.Qf5

1043) Fischer,R-Weberg [1971] Buenos Aires, Simultaneous Ruy Lopez **1.e4 e5 2.Nf3 Nc6 3.Bb5 a6 4.Ba4 Be7 5.O-O Be7 6.Re1 b5 7.Bb3 O-O 8.c3 d5 9.ed5 Nd5 10.Ne5 Ne5 11.Re5 c6 12.d4 Bd6 13.Re1 Qc7 14.g3 Bh3 15.Nd2 Rae8 16.Nf1 Re7 17.Be3 Rfe8 18.Qd3 Re4 19.Nd2 R4e7 20.Nf1 f5 21.Bd5 cd5 22.a4 g5 23.ab5 ab5 24.Qb5 f4 25.Bd2 Bf1 26.Rf1 Qb7 27.Qb7 Rb7 28.gf4 Bf4 29.Bf4 gf4 30.Kg2 Rb2 31.Kf3 Re4 32.Rg1 Kf7 33.Rg4 Rc2 34.Ra3 Ree2 35.Rg2 Ke6 36.Kf4 [D] Rf2 37.Rf2 Rf2 38.Kg3 Rc2** 1/2-1/2

After 36.Kf4

TOURNAMENT RESULTS AND CROSSTABLES

1955

July 15 - 24, 1955

US Junior Championship - Lincoln, Nebraska
10 round swiss

(1) Kalme 9 (2) Remlinger 7 1/2 (3-4) Gross, Staklis 6 (5-9) Rinaldo Lorber, Greene, Pupols, Lewis 5 1/2(10-20) Fromes, Warner, Shaeffer, Whisler, Ruth, Stone, Burkett, Ames, Briska, FISCHER, Thomason (21) Winkelman 4 (22-23) Dick, Blair 3 1/2 (24) Saksena 1

1956

May 25 - 27, 1956

US Amateur Championship - New Jersey
6 round swiss - 88 players

(1-3) Hudson, Cotter, Lyman 5 1/2 (4-6) Parmelee, C. McCormick, Mechner 5 (7-10) Nash, Weininger, Garfinkell, Hutaff 4 1/2 (11-23) Pennington, Hobson, Gersch, Wysowski, Hurttlen, N., Bartholy, Hurttlen,R., Jones, R., Scott, Goldsmith, FISCHER, Jones, W., Krauhs 4

July 1 - 7, 1956

US Junior Championship
10 round swiss - 28 players

(1) FISCHER 8 1/2 (2-3) Henin, Feuerstein 8 (4) Geller,S. 7 (5-6) Baylor, Levine 6

July 17 - 28, 1956

US Open Championship
Oklahoma City, Oklahoma
12 round swiss - 102 players

(1-2) Bisguier, Sherwin 9 1/2 (3) Steinmeyer 9 (4-8) Saidy, DiCamillo, Mednis, Popel, FISCHER 8 1/2

August 25 - September 2, 1956

Canadian Open - Montreal
10 round swiss - 88 players

(1-2) Evans, Lombardy 8 (3-7) Sherwin, Mednis, Vaitonis, Joyner, DiCamillo 7 1/2 (8-12) Yanofsky, Anderson, Williams, Bakos, FISCHER 7

October 7 - 24, 1956

Rosenwald Memorial
New York City
(crosstable page 255)

November 23 - 25, 1956

Eastern States Open - Washington, D.C.
7 round swiss - 56 players

(1) Berliner 6 (2-5) Feuerstein, FISCHER, Lombardy, Rossolimo 5 1/2

December, 1956 - January, 1957

Manhattan Chess Club Championship Semi-final 1956
(crosstable page 255)

1957

February 22 - 24, 1957

Log Cabin Open - West Orange, New Jersey
6 round swiss - 61 players

(1-5) Feuerstein, Santasiere, Green, Fuster, Wanetick 5 (6-11) FISCHER, O'Rourke, Bass, Hearst, Lombardy, Whitaker 4

March, 1957

Match vs. Euwe, New York
(result page 255)

March 31, 1957

Log Cabin 50-50 - West Orange, New Jersey

July 4 - 7, 1957

New Western Open - Milwaukee, Wisconsin
8 round swiss - 122 players

(1-2) Byrne, D., Evans 7 (3-5) Berliner, Popel, Tautvaisis (6-12) diCamillo, FISCHER, Weinberger, Addison, Theodorovych, Ragan, Surgies 6

July 8-14, 1957

US Junior Championship - San Francisco, California
9 round swiss - 33 players

(1) FISCHER 8 1/2 (2) Ramirez 7 1/2 (3) Sholomson 6 1/2 (4) Thacker 6

August 5 - 17, 1957

US Open - Cleveland, Ohio
12 round swiss - 175 players

(1-2) FISCHER, Bisguier 10 (3) Byrne,D 9 1/2 (4-7) Byrne,R, Santasiere, Mednis, Shipman 9

August 30 - September 2, 1957
New Jersey State Open - East Orange, New Jersey
7 round swiss - 81 players

(1) FISCHER 6 1/2 (2) Saidy 6 (3-4) Feuerstein, Sobel 5 1/2

September, 1957
Match vs. R. Cardoso
New York City
(result page 256)

November 29 - December 1, 1957
North Central Open - Milwaukee, Wisconsin
7 round swiss - 93 players

(1) Popel 6 (2-4) Byrne,D., Szeldascek, Brasket 5 1/2 (5-11) FISCHER and four others 5

December 17, 1957 - January 7, 1958
US Championship - New York City
1957-58
(crosstable page 256)

1958

July, 1958
Training Match vs. Janosevic
Yugoslavia
(result page 256)

July 20 - 26, 1958
Match vs. Matulovic
Belgrade
(result page 256)

August 5 - September 10, 1958
Portoroz Interzonal
(crosstable page 257)

December 12, 1958 - January 1, 1959
US Championship 1958-59
(crosstable page 258)

1959

March 23 - April 9, 1959

Mar del Plata International Tournament
Santiago Chile, 1959
(crosstable page 258)

April ? - May 6, 1959

Santiago, Chile International Tournament
(crosstable page 259)

May - June, 1959

Zurich International Tournament
(crosstable page 260)

September 7 - October 29, 1959

Candidates Tournament (Quadruple round robin)
Belgrade-Bled-Zagreb
(crosstable page 259)

December 18, 1959 - January 1, 1960

US Championship
New York City
(crosstable page 263)

1960

March 29 - April 15, 1960

Mar Del Plata, International Tournament
(crosstable page 261)

June 23 - July 21, 1960

Buenos Aires International Tournament
(crosstable page 262)

October 5 - 10, 1960

Reykjavic
(crosstable page 260)

October 17 - November 9, 1960

Liepzig Olympiad
Board 1 FISCHER 13 / 18

December 18, 1960 - January 3, 1961
US Championship
New York City
(crosstable page 263)

1961

July 16 - August 10, 1961
Match vs. Reshevsky
New York-Los Angeles
(result page 264)

September 3 - October 3, 1961
Bled, Yugoslavia
Alekhine Memorial International Tournament
(crosstable page 264)

1962

January 27 - March 6, 1962
Interzonal
Stockholm, Sweden
(crosstable page 265)

May 2 - June 26, 1962
Candidates Tournament
Curacao, 1962
(crosstable page 266)

September 16 - October 9, 1962
Varna Olympiad Board 1 FISCHER 12 / 17

December 16, 1962 - January 3, 1963
US Championship 1962/63
(crosstable page 266)

1963

July 4 - 7, 1963
Western Open
Bay City, Michigan
8 round swiss
(1) FISCHER 7 1/2

August 30 - September 2, 1963
New York State Open
Poughkeepsie
7 round swiss 57 players
(1) FISCHER 7

December 15, 1963 - January 2, 1964
US Championship
New York City
(crosstable page 267)

1965

August 25 - September 26, 1965
Capablanca Memorial
Havana
(crosstable page 268)

December, 1965
US Championship - New York
(crosstable page 269)

1966

July 20 - August 15, 1966
Piatigorsky Cup
Santa Monica, California
(crosstable page 267)

October 26 - November 11, 1966
Havana Olympiad
Board 1 FISCHER 15 /17

December 11, 1966 - January 1, 1967
US Championship
New York City
(crosstable page 269)

1967

March 24 - April 4, 1967
Monaco Grand Prix International Tournament
(crosstable page 270)

August 6 - September 30, 1967
Skopje International Tournament
(crosstable page 270)

October 16 - November 16, 1967
Sousse Interzonal

Fischer withdrew from the tournament after 14 rounds (10 games actually played) while leading the tournament.His individual results: vs. Barczay 1-0; vs. Portisch 1/2; vs. Miagmasuren 1; vs. Cuellar 1; vs. Sarapu 1; vs. Kavalek 1/2; vs. Stein 1; vs. Korchnoi 1/2; vs. Reshevsky 1; vs. R. Byrne 1.

1968

June 17 - July 1, 1968
Netanya International Tournament, 1968
(crosstable page 271)

September 7 - 23, 1968
Vinkovci International Tournament, 1968
(crosstable page 271)

1969

No serious games played in 1969

1970

March 29 - April 4, 1970
USSR vs. the Rest of the World - Board 2
(crosstable page 272)

April 8, 1970
Herceg Novi Blitz Tournament
(5-minutes per player)
(crosstable page 272)

April 12 - May 8, 1970
Rovinj / Zagreb
Tournament of Peace
(crosstable page 273)

July 18 - August 15, 1970
Buenos Aires International Tournament
(crosstable page 274)

September 6 - September 24, 1970
Siegen Olympiad
Board 1 FISCHER10 / 13

November 9 - December 12, 1970
Interzonal - Palma de Mallorca
(crosstable page 275)

1971

May 16 - June 1, 1971
Candidates Match vs. M. Taimanov - Vancouver
(result page 275)

July 6 - 20, 1971
Candidates Match vs. B. Larsen - Denver
(result page 276)

August 8, 1971
Manhattan Chess Club Blitz Tournament
New York City
22 Rounds(1) FISCHER 21 1/2

September 30 - October 26, 1971
Candidates Match vs. T. Petrosian - Buenos Aires
(result page 276)

1972

July 11 - August 31, 1972
World Championship Match vs. B. Spassky - Reykjavic
(result page 276)

1992

September2 - November 5, 1992

World Championship Rematch vs. B. Spassky - Sveti Stefan / Belgrade
(result page 276)

ROSENWALD MEMORIAL, 1956

	1	2	3	4	5	6	7	8	9	10	11	12	Total
1. Reshevsky	x	1	½	1	1	0	1	1	½	1	1	1	9
2. Bisguier	0	x	½	½	0	½	1	1	1	½	1	1	7
3. Feuerstein	½	½	x	0	1	0	0	½	1	1	1	1	6½
4. Mednis	0	½	1	x	1	1	1	½	½	0	½	½	6½
5. Bernstein	0	1	0	0	x	1	0	½	1	½	1	½	5½
6. Byrne, D	1	½	1	0	0	x	1	0	0	1	0	1	5½
7. Turner	0	0	1	0	1	0	x	1	0	1	1	½	5½
8. FISCHER	0	0	½	½	½	1	0	x	1	0	½	½	4½
9. Seidman	½	0	0	½	0	1	1	0	x	0	½	1	4½
10. Hearst	0	½	0	0	½	0	0	1	1	x	0	1	4
11. Pavey	0	0	0	½	0	1	0	½	½	1	x	½	4
12. Shainswit	0	0	0	½	½	0	½	½	0	0	½	x	2½
	1	2	3	4	5	6	7	8	9	10	11	12	Total

MANHATTAN CHESS CLUB CHAMPIONSHIP (SEMI-FINAL) 1956

	1	2	3	4	5	6	Total
1. Pavey	x	½	½	1	1	1	4
2. Turner	½	x	½	1	1	½	3½
3. Vine	½	½	x	½	1	1	3½
4. FISCHER	0	0	½	x	1	1	2½
5. Tamargo	0	0	0	0	x	1	1
6. Baron	0	½	0	0	0	x	½
	1	2	3	4	5	6	Total

MATCH VS. EUWE, NEW YORK, 1957

	1	2	Total
1. FISCHER	0	½	½
2. Euwe	1	½	1½

MATCH VS R. CARDOSO, NEW YORK, 1957

	1	2	3	4	5	6	7	8	Total
1. FISCHER	1	1	0	1	1	½	½	1	6
2. Cardoso	0	0	1	0	0	½	½	0	2

US CHAMPIONSHIP, NEW YORK, 1957-58

	1	2	3	4	5	6	7	8	9	10	11	12	13	14	Total
1. FISCHER	x	½	1	1	½	½	1	1	½	1	1	1	½	1	10½
2. Reshevsky	½	x	0	0	1	1	1	½	1	½	1	1	1	1	9½
3. Sherwin	0	1	x	½	½	1	0	½	½	1	1	1	1	1	9
4. Lombardy	0	1	½	x	½	½	½	½	0	1	0	1	1	1	7½
5. Berliner	½	0	½	½	x	0	0	½	½	1	1	1	½	1	7
6. Denker	½	0	0	½	1	x	0	1	½	0	1	0	1	1	6½
7. Feuerstein	0	0	1	½	1	1	x	½	1	0	0	½	½	½	6½
8. Mednis	0	½	½	½	½	0	½	x	0	1	½	½	1	1	6½
9. Seidman	½	0	½	1	½	½	0	1	x	0	1	0	1	0	6
10. Bernstein	0	½	0	0	0	1	1	0	1	x	0	1	½	0	5
11. Bisguier	0	0	0	1	0	0	1	½	0	1	x	½	0	1	5
12. Di Camillo	0	0	0	0	0	1	½	½	1	0	½	x	0	1	4½
13. Turner	½	0	0	0	½	0	½	0	0	½	1	1	x	½	4½
14. Kramer	0	0	0	0	0	0	½	0	1	1	0	0	½	x	3
	1	2	3	4	5	6	7	8	9	10	11	12	13	14	Total

MATCH VS JANOSEVIC, YUGOSLAVIA, 1958

	1	2	Total
1. FISCHER	½	½	1
2. Janosevic	½	½	1

MATCH VS MATULOVIC, BELGRADE, 1958

	1	2	3	4	Total
1. FISCHER	½	?	?	?	2½
2. Matulovic	½	?	?	?	1½

INTERZONAL, PORTOROZ, 1958

	1	2	3	4	5	6	7	8	9	10	11	12	13	14	15	16	17	18	19	20	21	Total
1. Tal	x	½	1	½	½	½	½	½	0	½	1	1	1	½	½	1	½	1	½	1	1	13½
2. Gligoric	½	x	½	½	½	0	½	½	½	1	½	½	1	½	1	1	0	1	1	1	1	13
3. Benko	0	½	x	½	1	½	1	½	1	½	½	½	0	1	½	½	½	½	1	1	1	12½
4. Petrosian	½	½	½	x	½	½	½	½	1	1	½	½	½	½	½	0	1	1	1	½	1	12½
5. FISCHER	½	½	0	½	x	0	½	½	½	½	½	½	½	1	½	1	1	½	1	1	1	12
6. Olafsson	½	1	½	½	1	x	1	0	½	½	1	½	½	½	0	1	0	0	1	1	1	12
7. Averbach	½	½	0	½	½	0	x	½	1	½	0	½	½	1	1	1	½	1	½	½	1	11½
8. Bronstein	½	½	½	½	½	1	½	x	½	1	½	½	½	½	½	½	1	½	0	½	1	11½
9. Matanovic	1	½	0	0	½	½	0	½	x	½	1	½	½	½	½	1	1	½	1	½	1	11½
10. Pachman	½	0	½	0	½	½	½	0	½	x	½	½	½	½	1	1	1	½	1	1	1	11½
11. Szabo	0	½	½	½	½	0	1	½	0	½	x	1	½	½	0	½	1	1	1	1	1	11½
12. Filip	0	½	½	½	½	½	½	½	½	½	0	x	½	½	1	½	½	½	1	1	1	11
13. Panno	0	0	1	½	½	½	½	½	½	½	½	½	x	1	½	½	1	½	1	½	½	11
14. Sanguinetti	½	½	0	½	0	½	0	½	½	½	½	½	0	x	1	½	1	1	½	1	½	10
15. Neikirch	½	0	½	½	½	1	0	½	½	0	1	0	½	0	x	0	½	1	½	1	1	9½
16. Larsen	0	0	½	1	0	0	0	½	0	0	½	½	½	½	1	x	1	1	½	0	1	8½
17. Sherwin	½	1	½	0	0	1	½	0	0	0	0	½	0	0	½	0	x	1	0	1	1	7½
18. Rossetto	0	0	½	0	½	1	0	½	½	½	0	½	½	0	0	0	0	x	1	½	1	7
19. Cardoso	½	0	0	0	0	0	½	1	0	0	0	0	0	½	0	½	1	0	x	1	1	6
20. de Greiff	0	0	0	½	0	0	½	½	½	0	0	0	½	0	½	1	0	½	0	x	0	4½
21. Fuster	0	0	0	0	0	0	0	0	0	0	0	0	0	½	½	0	0	0	0	1	x	2

US CHAMPIONSHIP, NEW YORK, 1958-59

	1	2	3	4	5	6	7	8	9	10	11	12	Total
1. FISCHER	x	1	1	1	½	½	½	½	½	1	1	1	8½
2. Reshevsky	0	x	1	½	½	1	1	½	½	1	½	1	7½
3. Sherwin	0	0	x	½	1	1	½	1	1	½	½	½	6½
4. Bisguier	0	½	½	x	1	0	½	½	½	1	1	½	6
5. Byrne,D	½	½	0	0	x	1	1	½	1	½	½	½	6
6. Evans	½	0	0	1	0	x	0	1	1	½	1	1	6
7. Lombardy	½	0	½	½	0	1	x	1	½	½	½	1	6
8. Benko	½	½	0	½	½	0	0	x	1	½	1	1	5½
9. Byrne,R	½	½	0	½	0	0	½	0	x	½	1	½	4
10. Kalme	0	0	½	0	½	½	½	½	½	x	½	½	4
11. Mednis	0	½	½	0	½	0	½	0	0	½	x	½	3
12. Weinstein	0	0	½	½	½	0	0	0	½	½	½	x	3
	1	2	3	4	5	6	7	8	9	10	11	12	

MAR DEL PLATA, 1959

	1	2	3	4	5	6	7	8	9	10	11	12	13	14	15	Total
1. Najdorf	x	½	½	1	½	1	½	1	1	½	1	1	½	1	½	10½
2. Pachman	½	x	1	½	1	½	½	½	1	0	1	1	1	1	1	10½
3. FISCHER	½	0	x	½	0	1	1	½	1	½	1	1	1	1	1	10
4. Ivkov	0	½	½	x	1	½	1	1	½	1	½	1	1	½	1	10
5. Letelier	½	0	1	0	x	1	½	½	0	1	1	1	½	1	1	9
6. Rossetto	0	½	0	½	0	x	½	½	½	1	½	1	1	1	1	8
7. Wexler	½	½	0	0	½	½	x	½	½	½	½	1	½	1	1	7½
8. Sanchez	0	½	½	0	½	½	½	x	1	½	½	½	1	1	0	7
9. Sanguinetti	0	0	0	½	1	½	½	0	x	1	½	½	1	½	1	7
10. Emma	½	1	½	0	0	0	½	½	0	x	1	0	1	0	½	5½
11. Bolbochan	0	0	0	½	0	½	½	½	½	0	x	½	½	1	0	4½
12. Pilnik	0	0	0	0	0	0	0	0	½	½	1	½	x	0	1	1	4½
13. Shocron	½	0	0	0	½	0	½	0	0	0	½	1	x	0	1	4
14. Souza Mendes	0	0	0	½	0	0	0	0	½	1	0	0	1	x	1	4
15. Redolfi	½	0	0	0	0	0	0	1	0	½	1	0	0	0	x	3

SANTIAGO, CHILE, 1959

	1	2	3	4	5	6	7	8	9	10	11	12	13	Total
1. Ivkov	x	½	1	1	1	1	1	½	½	0	1	½	1	9
2. Pachman	½	x	½	1	1	0	1	1	1	½	1	½	1	9
3. Pilnik	0	½	x	0	½	½	1	1	1	1	1	1	½	8
4. FISCHER	0	0	1	x	0	1	½	0	1	1	1	1	1	7½
5. Sanguinetti	0	0	½	1	x	½	½	½	½	1	1	1	1	7½
6. Sanchez	0	1	½	0	½	x	½	1	½	1	½	1	1	7½
7. Flores	½	0	0	½	½	½	x	1	1	0	½	1	½	6
8. Jauregui	½	0	0	1	½	0	0	x	1	1	1	0	1	6
9. Letelier	1	0	0	0	½	½	0	0	x	½	½	½	½	4
10. Romo	0	½	0	0	0	0	1	0	½	x	1	0	1	4
11. Ader	½	0	0	0	0	½	½	0	½	0	x	½	1	3½
12. Stekel	0	½	0	0	0	0	0	1	½	1	½	x	0	3½
13. Souza Mendez	0	0	½	0	0	0	½	0	½	0	0	1	x	2½
	1	2	3	4	5	6	7	8	9	10	11	12	13	

CANDIDATES TOURNAMENT, 1959
BELGRADE-BLED-ZAGREB

	1	2	3	4	5	6	7	8	Total
. Tal	x	0010	½½½½	01½1	1111	1½11	111½	111½	20
. Keres	1101	x	0½½½	1½½0	0101	½½11	1110	1111	18½
. Petrosian	½½½½	1½½½	x	½½0½	11½½	0½½1	100½	½11½	15½
. Smyslov	10½0	0½½1	½½1½	x	½½10	0½10	½1½1	½011	15
. FISCHER	0000	1010	00½½	½½01	x	10½½	01½1	½1½1	12½
. Gligoric	0½00	½½00	1½½0	1½01	01½½	x	½½10	½1½½	12½
. Olafsson	000½	0001	011½	½0½0	10½0	½½01	x	00½1	10
. Benko	000½	0000	½00½	½100	½0½0	½0½½	11½0	x	8
	1	2	3	4	5	6	7	8	

ZURICH INTERNATIONAL TOURNAMENT 1959

	1	2	3	4	5	6	7	8	9	10	11	12	13	14	15	16	Total
1. Tal	x	0	½	½	1	1	½	1	1	0	1	1	1	1	1	1	11½
2. Gligoric	1	x	1	0	1	½	0	1	½	1	½	1	1	½	1	1	11
3. FISCHER	½	0	x	1	½	1	½	1	1	1	1	0	1	½	½	1	10½
4. Keres	½	1	0	x	½	1	½	½	1	½	1	1	½	1	1	½	10½
5. Larsen	0	0	½	½	x	½	0	1	½	½	1	1	1	1	1	1	9½
6. Unzicker	0	½	0	0	½	x	½	½	1	1	1	½	1	1	1	1	9½
7. Barcza	½	1	½	½	1	½	x	0	0	0	½	1	0	1	1	1	8½
8. Olafsson	0	0	0	½	0	½	1	x	0	1	½	1	1	½	1	1	8
9. Kupper	0	½	0	0	½	0	1	1	x	½	0	½	½	1	½	1	7
10. Bhend	1	0	0	½	½	0	1	0	½	x	1	1	0	0	½	½	6½
11. Donner	0	½	0	0	0	0	½	½	1	0	x	0	1	1	1	1	6½
12. Keller	0	0	1	0	0	½	0	0	½	0	1	x	1	1	1	0	6
13. Duckstein	0	0	0	½	0	0	1	0	½	1	0	0	x	0	1	1	5
14. Walther	0	½	½	0	0	0	0	½	0	1	0	0	1	x	½	1	5
15. Blau	0	0	½	0	0	0	0	0	½	½	0	0	0	½	x	½	2½
16. Nievergelt	0	0	0	½	0	0	0	0	0	½	0	1	0	0	½	x	2½
	1	2	3	4	5	6	7	8	9	10	11	12	13	14	15	16	

REYKJAVIC, 1960

	1	2	3	4	5	Total
1. FISCHER	x	1	1	1	½	3½
2. Johannsson	0	x	½	1	1	2½
3. Olafsson	0	½	x	1	½	2
4. Gudmundsson	0	0	0	x	1	1
5. Thorbergsson	½	0	½	0	x	1
	1	2	3	4	5	

MAR DEL PLATA, 1960

	1	2	3	4	5	6	7	8	9	10	11	12	13	14	15	16	Total
1. FISCHER	x	0	½	1	1	1	1	1	1	1	1	1	1	1	1	1	13½
2. Spassky	1	x	½	1	1	½	1	1	1	1	1	1	1	1	½	1	13½
3. Bronstein	½	½	x	½	1	1	½	1	½	½	½	1	1	1	1	1	11½
4. Olafsson	0	0	½	x	1	1	0	1	1	½	½	1	1	1	1	1	10½
5. Bazan	0	0	0	0	x	1	½	½	½	1	1	½	1	1	1	1	9
6. Wexler	0	½	0	0	0	x	1	½	½	½	1	1	½	1	1	1	8½
7. Letelier	0	0	½	1	½	0	x	0	½	1	1	1	0	½	1	1	8
8. Foguelman	0	0	0	0	½	½	1	x	0	1	0	0	1	1	1	½	6½
9. Incutto	0	0	½	0	½	½	½	1	x	0	½	½	1	½	½	½	6½
10. Redolfi	0	0	½	½	0	½	0	0	1	x	1	½	1	0	½	1	6½
11. Bielicki	0	0	½	½	0	0	0	1	½	0	x	½	½	1	½	1	6
12. Eliskases	0	0	0	0	½	0	0	1	½	½	½	x	½	1	½	1	6
13. Alvarez	0	0	0	0	0	½	1	0	0	0	½	½	x	0	½	1	4
14. Gadia	0	0	0	0	0	0	½	0	½	1	0	0	1	x	1	0	4
15. Marini	0	½	0	0	0	0	0	0	½	½	½	½	½	0	x	1	4
16. Saadi	0	0	0	0	0	0	0	½	½	0	0	0	0	1	0	x	2
	1	2	3	4	5	6	7	8	9	10	11	12	13	14	15	16	

BUENOS AIRES INTERNATIONAL, 1960

	1	2	3	4	5	6	7	8	9	10	11	12	13	14	15	16	17	18	19	20	Total
1. Korchnoi	x	½	½	½	1	0	½	½	1	1	½	1	1	½	1	1	½	1	0	1	13
2. Reshevsky	½	x	½	0	1	1	½	½	½	½	½	1	½	½	1	1	½	1	1	1	13
3. Szabo	½	½	x	1	0	1	1	½	½	½	0	½	½	½	1	½	½	1	1	1	12
4. Evans	½	1	0	x	0	1	½	½	½	1	1	½	½	½	0	½	½	1	½	1	11
5. Guimard	0	0	1	1	x	0	1	0	½	1	1	1	1	0	1	½	½	0	½	1	11
6. Rossetto	1	0	0	0	1	x	½	½	0	½	1	1	1	0	½	1	½	1	½	1	11
7. Taimanov	½	½	0	½	0	½	x	½	1	½	1	0	½	½	½	½	1	1	1	1	11
8. Unzicker	½	½	½	½	1	½	½	x	½	½	½	½	½	1	0	0	½	1	1	½	10½
9. Olafsson	0	½	½	½	½	1	0	½	x	½	1	1	½	½	½	½	½	1	1	0	10½
10. Gligoric	0	½	½	0	0	½	½	½	½	x	0	½	½	½	1	1	1	½	1	1	10
11. Uhlmann	½	½	1	0	0	0	0	½	0	1	x	0	½	1	½	1	½	0	1	1	9
12. Benko	0	0	½	½	0	0	1	½	0	½	1	x	½	1	½	0	1	1	0	1	9
13. Ivkov	0	½	½	½	0	0	½	½	½	½	½	½	x	½	1	½	½	½	½	½	8½
14. FISCHER	½	½	½	½	1	1	½	0	½	½	0	0	½	x	0	½	0	½	1	½	8½
15. Wexler	0	0	0	1	0	½	½	1	½	0	½	½	0	1	x	0	1	½	1	½	8½
16. Pachman	0	0	½	½	½	0	½	1	½	0	0	1	½	½	1	x	½	0	1	½	8½
17. Eliskases	½	½	½	½	½	½	0	½	½	0	½	0	½	1	0	½	x	1	½	0	8
18. Bazan	0	0	0	0	1	0	0	0	0	½	1	0	½	½	½	1	0	x	1	0	6
19. Wade	1	0	0	½	½	½	0	0	0	0	0	1	½	0	0	0	½	0	x	1	5½
20. Foguelman	0	0	0	0	0	0	0	½	1	0	0	0	½	½	½	½	1	1	0	x	5½
	1	2	3	4	5	6	7	8	9	10	11	12	13	14	15	16	17	18	19	20	

US CHAMPIONSHIP, NEW YORK 1959-60

	1	2	3	4	5	6	7	8	9	10	11	12	Total
1. FISCHER	x	½	½	1	1	½	1	½	1	1	1	1	9
2. Byrne, R.	½	x	½	1	½	1	½	½	1	½	1	1	8
3. Reshevsky	½	½	x	½	1	1	0	1	1	1	0	1	7½
4. Benko	0	0	½	x	½	1	1	½	½	1	1	1	7
5. Bisguier	0	½	0	½	x	½	½	1	½	1	1	1	6½
6. Weinstein	½	0	0	0	½	x	1	0	1	1	1	1	6
7. Seidman	0	½	1	0	½	0	x	½	1	0	1	1	5½
8. Sherwin	½	½	0	½	0	1	½	x	½	0	½	1	5
9. Mednis	0	0	0	½	½	0	0	½	x	1	1	1	4½
10. Bernstein	0	½	0	0	0	0	1	1	0	x	½	1	4
11. Denker	0	0	1	0	0	0	0	½	0	½	x	1	3
12. Ault	0	0	0	0	0	0	0	0	0	0	0	x	0
	1	2	3	4	5	6	7	8	9	10	11	12	

US CHAMPIONSHIP, NEW YORK, 1960-61

	1	2	3	4	5	6	7	8	9	10	11	12	Total
1. FISCHER	x	1	1	1	½	1	½	½	1	½	1	1	9
2. Lombardy	0	x	0	½	½	½	1	½	1	1	1	1	7
3. Weinstein	0	1	x	1	1	½	0	½	½	1	½	½	6½
4. Bisguier	0	½	0	x	½	½	1	1	0	1	1	½	6
5. Reshevsky	½	½	0	½	x	½	½	½	1	½	1	½	6
6. Sherwin	0	½	½	½	½	x	½	1	1	0	½	1	6
7. Kalme	½	0	1	0	½	½	x	1	½	0	½	½	5
8. Benko	½	½	½	0	½	0	0	x	½	1	0	1	4½
9. Berliner	0	0	½	1	0	0	½	½	x	0	1	1	4½
10. Byrne,R	½	0	0	0	½	1	1	0	1	x	0	½	4½
11. Saidy	0	0	½	0	0	½	½	1	0	1	x	1	4½
12. Seidman	0	0	½	½	½	0	½	0	0	½	0	x	2½
	1	2	3	4	5	6	7	8	9	10	11	12	

MATCH VS RESHEVSKY
NEW YORK - LOS ANGELES, 1961

	1	2	3	4	5	6	7	8	9	10	11	Total
1. FISCHER	0	1	½	½	1	½	0	½	½	½	½	5½
2. Reshevsky	1	0	½	½	0	½	1	½	½	½	½	5½

BLED, 1961

	1	2	3	4	5	6	7	8	9	10	11	12	13	14	15	16	17	18	19	20	Total
1. Tal	x	0	½	½	½	½	½	1	1	1	½	1	1	1	½	1	1	1	1	1	14½
2. FISCHER	1	x	1	½	½	1	1	½	1	½	½	½	½	1	1	½	½	1	½	½	13½
3. Petrosian	½	0	x	½	1	½	½	1	½	½	½	½	1	1	0	½	1	1	1	1	12½
4. Keres	½	½	½	x	½	½	½	½	0	½	½	1	½	1	1	1	1	½	1	1	12½
5. Gligoric	½	½	0	½	x	½	½	½	1	1	½	½	½	½	½	1	1	1	1	1	12½
6. Geller	½	0	½	½	½	x	½	1	0	½	½	½	½	0	1	1	½	1	1	½	10½
7. Trifunovic	½	0	½	½	½	½	x	½	½	½	½	½	½	½	½	½	1	½	1	1	10½
8. Parma	0	½	0	½	½	0	½	x	½	½	½	½	½	1	½	1	½	½	1	1	10
9. Bisguier	0	0	½	1	0	1	½	½	x	0	½	0	1	0	½	1	½	½	1	1	9½
10. Matanovic	0	½	½	½	0	½	½	½	1	x	½	½	0	1	½	½	0	1	1	½	9½
11. Darga	½	½	½	½	½	½	½	½	½	½	x	½	½	0	½	0	½	1	0	1	9
12. Donner	0	½	½	0	½	½	½	½	1	½	½	x	1	0	½	1	½	0	0	1	9
13. Najdorf	0	½	0	½	½	½	½	½	0	1	½	0	x	1	½	0	½	1	1	½	9
14. Olafsson	0	0	0	0	½	1	½	0	1	0	1	1	0	x	1	½	½	½	½	½	8½
15. Portisch	½	0	1	0	½	0	½	½	½	½	½	½	½	0	x	0	½	½	½	1	8
16. Ivkov	0	½	½	0	0	0	½	0	0	½	1	0	1	½	1	x	1	½	½	½	8
17. Pachman	0	½	0	0	0	½	0	½	½	1	½	½	½	½	½	0	x	½	½	½	7
18. Bertok	0	0	0	½	0	0	½	½	½	0	0	1	0	½	½	½	½	x	½	1	6½
19. Germek	0	½	0	0	0	0	0	0	0	0	1	1	0	½	½	½	½	½	x	½	5½
20. Udovic	0	½	0	0	0	½	0	0	0	½	0	0	½	½	0	½	½	0	½	x	4
	1	2	3	4	5	6	7	8	9	10	11	12	13	14	15	16	17	18	19	20	

INTERZONAL, STOCKHOLM, 1962

	1	2	3	4	5	6	7	8	9	10	11	12	13	14	15	16	17	18	19	20	21	22	23	Total
1. FISCHER	x	½	½	1	½	½	½	½	1	½	1	½	1	1	1	1	1	1	1	1	½	1	1	17½
2. Geller	½	x	½	½	½	1	½	1	1	1	½	0	1	½	1	1	½	1	½	½	1	0	1	15
3. Petrosian	½	½	x	½	½	½	½	½	½	½	1	1	½	½	1	½	1	½	1	1	1	½	1	15
4. Korchnoi	0	½	½	x	1	½	½	½	0	½	1	1	½	1	1	½	1	½	½	1	1	0	1	14
5. Filip	½	½	½	0	x	½	½	1	½	0	½	½	1	1	½	½	½	1	1	½	1	1	1	14
6. Benko	½	0	½	½	½	x	½	½	½	1	0	½	½	½	1	1	1	0	1	1	½	1	1	13½
7. Gligoric	½	½	½	½	½	½	x	0	½	½	1	½	½	1	0	1	½	1	½	1	½	1	1	13½
8. Stein	½	0	½	½	0	½	1	x	1	0	0	½	1	½	½	1	½	1	½	1	1	1	1	13½
9. Portisch	0	0	½	1	½	½	½	0	x	1	½	½	½	½	½	1	1	1	0	1	1	1	0	12½
10. Uhlmann	½	0	½	½	1	0	½	1	0	x	1	1	½	0	1	1	1	0	1	1	0	1	0	12½
11. Olafsson	0	½	0	0	½	1	0	1	½	0	x	½	½	0	½	½	1	½	1	1	1	1	1	12
12. Pomar	½	1	0	0	½	½	½	½	½	0	½	x	0	0	1	½	½	1	1	½	1	1	1	12
13. Bolbochan	0	0	½	½	0	½	½	0	½	½	½	1	x	½	½	½	½	1	1	½	½	1	1	11½
14. Barcza	0	½	½	0	0	½	0	½	½	1	1	1	½	x	½	½	½	½	½	½	1	0	1	11
15. Bilek	0	0	0	0	½	0	1	½	½	0	½	0	½	½	x	½	½	1	1	1	1	1	1	11
16. Bisguier	0	0	½	½	½	0	0	0	0	0	½	½	½	½	½	x	½	½	1	½	1	1	1	9½
17. Bertok	0	½	0	0	½	0	½	½	0	0	0	½	½	½	½	½	x	½	½	0	½	1	½	7½
18. Yanofsky	0	0	½	½	0	1	0	0	0	1	½	0	0	½	0	½	½	x	1	½	½	0	½	7½
19. German	0	½	0	½	0	0	½	½	1	0	0	0	0	½	0	0	½	0	x	½	½	1	1	7
20. Schweber	0	½	0	0	½	0	0	0	0	0	0	½	½	½	0	½	1	½	½	x	1	½	½	7
21. Teschner	½	0	0	0	0	½	½	0	0	1	0	0	½	0	0	0	½	½	½	0	x	1	1	6½
22. Cuellar	0	1	½	1	0	0	0	0	0	0	0	0	0	1	0	0	0	1	0	½	0	x	½	5½
23. Aaron	0	0	0	0	0	0	0	0	1	1	0	0	0	0	0	0	½	½	0	½	0	½	x	4
	1	2	3	4	5	6	7	8	9	10	11	12	13	14	15	16	17	18	19	20	21	22	23	

CANDIDATES TOURNAMENT
CURACAO, 1962

	1	2	3	4	5	6	7	8	Tota
1. Petrosian	x	½½½½	½½½½	½1½½	½½11	½½1½	11½-	½11½	17½
2. Keres	½½½½	x	½½½½	0½1½	½½1½	1110	1½1-	½11½	17
3. Geller	½½½½	½½½½	x	11½0	½½1½	½½½1	½11-	½11½	17
4. FISCHER	½0½½	1½0½	00½1	x	010½	01½1	½1½-	1½1½	14
5. Korchnoi	½½00	½½0½	½½0½	101½	x	½½½0	10½-	1111	13½
6. Benko	½½0½	0001	½½½0	10½0	½½½1	x	10½-	011½	12
7. Tal	00½-	0½0-	½00-	½0½-	01½-	01½-	x	10½-	7
8. Filip	½00½	½00½	½00½	0½0½	0000	100½	01½-	x	7

US CHAMPIONSHIP, NEW YORK, 1962-63

	1	2	3	4	5	6	7	8	9	10	11	12	Total
1. FISCHER	x	1	1	½	1	½	1	0	½	½	1	1	8
2. Bisguier	0	x	1	½	½	½	½	1	½	1	½	1	7
3. Addison	0	0	x	½	1	½	1	1	½	½	1	½	6½
4. Evans	½	½	½	x	½	½	1	½	1	½	0	½	6½
5. Reshevsky	0	½	0	½	x	½	1	1	1	½	1	½	6½
6. Byrne,R	½	½	½	½	½	x	½	½	½	1	½	½	6
7. Berliner	0	½	0	0	0	½	x	1	½	½	1	1	5
8. Mednis	1	0	0	½	0	½	0	x	½	1	½	1	5
9. Benko	½	½	½	0	0	½	½	½	x	0	1	½	4½
10. Rossolimo	½	0	½	½	½	0	½	0	1	x	½	½	4½
11. Steinmeyer	0	½	0	1	0	½	0	½	0	½	x	1	4
12. Sherwin	0	0	½	0	½	½	0	0	½	½	0	x	2½

US CHAMPIONSHIP, NEW YORK, 1963-64

	1	2	3	4	5	6	7	8	9	10	11	12	Total
1. FISCHER	x	1	1	1	1	1	1	1	1	1	1	1	11
2. Evans	0	x	1	½	½	½	0	1	1	1	1	1	7½
3. Benko	0	0	x	1	½	1	1	1	½	1	½	½	7
4. Saidy	0	½	0	x	0	½	1	1	1	1	½	1	6½
5. Reshevsky	0	½	½	1	x	½	0	½	1	1	1	½	6½
6. Byrne,R	0	½	0	½	½	x	0	½	1	1	1	½	5½
7. Weinstein	0	1	0	0	1	1	x	0	0	0	1	1	5
8. Bisguier	0	0	0	0	½	½	1	x	1	0	½	1	4½
9. Addison	0	0	½	0	0	0	1	0	x	½	½	1	3½
10. Mednis	0	0	0	0	0	0	1	1	½	x	½	½	3½
11. Steinmeyer	0	0	½	½	0	0	0	½	½	½	x	½	3
12. Byrne,D	0	0	½	0	½	½	0	0	0	½	½	x	2½

PIATIGORSKY CUP, SANTA MONICA, 1966

	1	2	3	4	5	6	7	8	9	10	Total
1. Spassky	x	1½	½1	½½	1½	½½	½½	½½	1½	½1	11½
2. FISCHER	0½	x	01	½1	½½	½½	½1	01	11	½1	11
3. Larsen	½0	10	x	1½	½0	11	½1	1½	01	½0	10
4. Portisch	½½	½0	0½	x	½½	1½	½½	½½	½1	½1	9½
5. Unzicker	0½	½½	½1	½½	x	½½	½½	½½	1½	½½	9½
6. Petrosian	½½	½½	00	0½	½½	x	½½	11	½½	½1	9
7. Reshevsky	½½	½0	½0	½½	½½	½½	x	½1	½½	1½	9
8. Najdorf	½½	10	0½	½½	½½	00	½0	x	1½	½1	8
9. Ivkov	0½	00	10	½0	0½	½½	½½	0½	x	½1	6½
10. Donner	½0	½0	½1	½0	½½	½0	0½	½0	½0	x	6

CAPABLANCA MEMORIAL, HAVANA 1965

	1	2	3	4	5	6	7	8	9	10	11	12	13	14	15	16	17	18	19	20	21	22	Total
1. Smyslov	x	0	½	0	½	½	1	½	1	½	1	1	1	1	0	1	1	1	1	1	1	1	15½
2. FISCHER	1	x	0	0	0	½	1	1	1	1	½	1	1	½	1	½	½	1	1	½	1	1	15
3. Geller	½	1	x	½	½	½	½	½	1	1	½	½	½	½	1	½	1	1	½	1	1	1	15
4. Ivkov	1	1	½	x	0	½	1	0	1	½	½	½	1	1	1	½	1	1	1	1	0	1	15
5. Kholmov	½	1	½	1	x	½	½	½	½	½	½	½	½	1	1	1	½	½	½	1	1	1	14½
6. Pachman	½	½	½	½	½	x	1	0	½	½	½	½	½	½	½	½	1	½	1	1	1	1	13
7. Donner	0	0	½	0	½	0	x	1	1	½	1	1	1	½	1	½	½	½	½	½	1	1	12½
8. Robatsch	½	0	½	1	½	1	0	x	½	½	0	1	½	½	½	½	½	½	½	1	1	1	12
9. Bilek	0	0	0	0	½	½	0	½	x	½	½	½	½	½	½	1	1	1	1	1	1	1	11½
10. Parma	½	½	0	½	½	½	½	½	½	x	1	0	½	½	1	½	½	½	1	½	½	½	11
11. Pietzsch	0	0	½	½	½	½	0	1	½	0	x	0	½	1	½	½	½	½	½	1	1	1	10½
12. Szabo	0	0	½	½	½	½	0	0	½	1	1	x	½	½	½	1	0	½	1	1	1	0	10½
13. O'Kelly	0	½	½	0	½	½	0	½	½	½	½	½	x	½	½	0	1	½	½	½	1	1	10
14. Tringov	0	0	½	0	0	½	½	½	½	½	0	½	½	x	0	½	1	1	1	1	1	½	10
15. Jimenez	1	½	0	0	0	½	0	½	½	0	½	½	½	1	x	½	½	½	½	½	1	½	9½
16. Ciocaltea	0	½	½	½	0	½	½	½	0	½	½	0	1	½	½	x	½	0	1	0	1	½	9
17. Doda	0	0	0	0	½	0	½	½	0	½	½	1	0	0	½	½	x	1	0	1	1	½	8
18. Lehmann	0	0	0	0	½	½	½	½	0	½	½	½	½	0	½	1	0	x	1	½	0	½	7½
19. Wade	0	½	½	0	½	0	½	½	0	0	½	0	½	0	½	0	1	0	x	½	1	1	7½
20. Cobo	0	0	0	0	0	0	½	0	0	½	0	0	½	0	½	1	0	½	½	x	½	1	5½
21. Garcia,G	0	0	0	1	0	0	0	0	0	½	0	0	0	0	0	0	0	1	0	½	x	1	4
22. Perez	0	0	0	0	0	0	0	0	0	½	0	1	0	½	½	½	½	½	0	0	0	x	4
	1	2	3	4	5	6	7	8	9	10	11	12	13	14	15	16	17	18	19	20	21	22	

US CHAMPIONSHIP, NEW YORK, 1965

	1	2	3	4	5	6	7	8	9	10	11	12	Total
1. FISCHER	x	0	0	½	1	1	1	1	1	1	1	1	8½
2. Byrne,R	1	x	½	½	½	1	0	1	1	½	½	1	7½
3. Reshevsky	1	½	x	1	½	½	½	1	0	1	½	1	7½
4. Addison	½	½	0	x	½	½	½	1	1	1	1	0	6½
5. Zuckerman	0	½	½	½	x	½	1	½	1	½	½	1	6½
6. Rossolimo	0	0	½	½	½	x	1	1	0	1	1	½	6
7. Benko	0	1	½	½	0	0	x	½	0	½	1	1	5
8. Evans	0	0	0	0	½	0	½	x	1	1	1	1	5
9. Saidy	0	0	1	0	0	1	1	0	x	½	1	½	5
10. Bisguier	0	½	0	0	½	0	½	0	½	x	½	½	3
11. Burger	0	½	½	0	½	0	0	0	0	½	x	1	3
12. Suttles	0	0	0	1	0	½	0	0	½	½	0	x	2½
	1	2	3	4	5	6	7	8	9	10	11	12	

US CHAMPIONSHIP, NEW YORK 1966-67

	1	2	3	4	5	6	7	8	9	10	11	12	Total
1. FISCHER	x	½	1	1	1	½	1	½	1	1	1	1	9½
2. Evans	½	x	½	½	1	1	½	½	1	1	0	1	7½
3. Benko	0	½	x	0	1	0	½	1	½	1	1	½	6
4. Sherwin	0	½	1	x	½	1	1	½	½	0	1	0	6
5. Bisguier	0	0	0	½	x	½	1	0	½	1	1	1	5½
6. Addison	½	0	1	0	½	x	1	0	1	½	½	0	5
7. Saidy	0	½	½	0	0	0	x	1	1	½	1	½	5
8. Byrne,R	½	½	0	½	1	1	0	x	½	½	0	0	4½
9. Reshevsky	0	0	½	½	½	0	0	½	x	½	1	1	4½
10. Rossolimo	0	0	0	1	0	½	½	½	½	x	½	1	4½
11. Byrne,D	0	1	0	0	0	½	0	1	0	½	x	1	4
12. Zuckerman	0	0	½	1	0	1	½	1	0	0	0	x	4
	1	2	3	4	5	6	7	8	9	10	11	12	

	1	2	3	4	5	6	7	8	9	10	Total
1. FISCHER	x	½	0	1	½	1	1	1	1	1	7
2. Smyslov	½	x	½	½	1	½	½	1	1	1	6½
3. Geller	1	½	x	0	½	½	1	½	1	1	6
4. Larsen	0	½	1	x	0	1	1	½	1	1	6
5. Matanovic	½	0	½	1	x	½	½	½	½	1	5
6. Gligoric	0	½	½	0	½	x	½	½	1	1	4½
7. Lombardy	0	½	0	0	½	½	x	1	1	1	4½
8. Forintos	0	0	½	½	½	½	0	x	1	1	4
9. Mazzoni	0	0	0	0	½	0	0	0	x	½	1
10. Bergraser	0	0	0	0	0	0	0	0	½	x	½
	1	2	3	4	5	6	7	8	9	10	

MONACO, 1967

	1	2	3	4	5	6	7	8	9	10	11	12	13	14	15	16	17	18	Total
1. FISCHER	x	0	1	1	1	1	1	1	½	½	1	1	1	0	1	½	1	1	13½
2. Geller	1	x	1	½	1	1	½	1	½	½	½	1	½	½	½	1	1	1	13
3. Matulovic	0	0	x	½	1	1	1	1	1	½	½	1	1	1	½	1	1	1	13
4. Kholmov	0	½	½	x	½	½	½	½	1	1	1	½	½	½	1	1	1	1	11½
5. Bukic	0	0	0	½	x	½	½	1	½	½	½	1	½	1	1	½	½	1	9½
6. Maric	0	0	0	½	½	x	½	½	½	½	½	½	½	1	1	½	1	1	9
7. Minic	0	½	0	½	½	½	x	½	½	½	½	½	1	0	½	½	1	1	8½
8. Damjanovic	0	0	0	½	0	½	½	x	½	1	½	½	0	1	½	1	1	1	8½
9. Popov	½	½	0	0	½	½	½	½	x	½	½	0	½	1	1	½	1	½	8½
10. Knezevic	½	½	½	0	½	½	½	0	½	x	½	0	½	1	½	1	½	1	8½
11. Sofrevski	0	½	½	0	½	½	½	½	½	½	x	1	½	½	½	½	1	0	8
12. Dely	0	0	0	½	0	½	½	½	1	1	0	x	1	0	1	1	0	1	8
13. Soos	0	½	0	½	½	½	0	1	½	½	½	0	x	1	0	0	1	1	7½
14. Janosevic	1	½	0	½	0	0	1	0	0	0	½	1	0	x	1	1	0	1	7½
15. Nicevski	0	½	½	0	0	0	½	½	0	½	½	0	1	0	x	½	½	1	6
16. Ilievski	½	0	0	0	½	½	½	0	½	0	½	0	1	0	½	x	½	1	6
17. Panov	0	0	0	0	½	0	0	0	0	½	0	1	0	1	½	½	x	0	4
18. Danov	0	0	0	0	0	0	0	½	0	0	1	0	0	0	0	0	1	x	2½
	1	2	3	4	5	6	7	8	9	10	11	12	13	14	15	16	17	18	

SKOPJE 1967

	1	2	3	4	5	6	7	8	9	10	11	12	13	14	Total
1. FISCHER	x	½	1	1	1	1	½	1	1	½	1	1	1	1	11½
2. Yanofsky	½	x	½	0	1	½	1	½	½	1	1	½	½	½	8
3. Czerniak	0	½	x	1	1	½	½	0	½	½	½	1	1	1	8
4. Hamann	0	1	0	x	0	1	0	½	1	1	½	0	1	1	7
5. Kagan	0	0	0	1	x	½	½	½	½	1	1	1	0	1	7
6. Ciocaltea	0	½	½	0	½	x	1	½	½	½	½	0	1	1	6½
7. Kraidman	½	0	½	1	½	0	x	½	1	½	0	0	½	1	6
8. Aloni	0	½	1	½	½	½	½	x	0	½	0	1	1	0	6
9. Domnitz	0	½	½	0	½	½	0	1	x	½	½	1	0	1	6
10. Porath	½	0	½	0	0	½	½	½	½	x	½	1	1	½	6
11. Troianescu	0	0	½	½	0	½	1	1	½	½	x	0	0	1	5½
12. Geller,U	0	½	0	1	0	1	1	0	0	0	1	x	½	0	5
13. Ree	0	½	0	0	1	0	½	0	1	0	1	½	x	½	5
14. Bernstein	0	½	0	0	0	0	0	1	0	½	0	1	½	x	3½

NETANYA, 1968

	1	2	3	4	5	6	7	8	9	10	11	12	13	14	Total
1. FISCHER	x	½	1	½	1	½	1	1	½	1	1	1	1	1	11
2. Hort	½	x	½	½	½	1	½	1	½	½	½	1	1	1	9
3. Matulovic	0	½	x	½	½	1	1	½	1	1	½	1	½	1	9
4. Gheorghiu	½	½	½	x	½	½	½	½	½	½	1	1	1	1	8½
5. Ivkov	0	½	½	½	x	½	½	½	1	½	1	1	1	1	8½
6. Byrne,D	½	0	0	½	½	x	0	1	½	1	1	1	1	1	8
7. Matanovic	0	½	0	½	½	1	x	½	½	½	1	1	1	½	7½
8. Bertok	0	0	½	½	½	0	½	x	½	½	½	1	1	1	6½
9. Robatsch	½	½	0	½	0	½	½	½	x	½	½	½	1	1	6½
10. Minic	0	½	0	½	½	0	½	½	½	x	½	½	1	1	6
11. Wade	0	½	½	0	0	0	0	½	½	½	x	½	1	1	5
12. Nikolic	0	0	0	0	0	0	0	0	½	½	½	x	1	1	3½
13. Jovanovac	0	0	½	0	0	0	0	0	0	0	0	0	x	1	1½
14. Matov	0	0	0	0	0	0	½	0	0	0	0	0	0	x	½
	1	2	3	4	5	6	7	8	9	10	11	12	13	14	

VINKCOVCI, 1968

USSR VS THE REST OF THE WORLD - BOARD 2
BELGRADE, 1970

	1	2	3	4	Total
1. FISCHER	1	1	½	½	3
2. Petrosian	0	0	½	½	1

HERCEG NOVI BLITZ TOURNAMENT
(5-MINUTE CHESS)

	1	2	3	4	5	6	7	8	9	10	11	12	Total
1. FISCHER	x	2	1	2	1½	1½	2	2	1½	1½	2	2	19
2. Tal	0	x	2	1	0	2	1½	½	2	1½	2	2	14½
3. Korchnoi	1	0	x	½	0	2	2	2	1	1½	2	2	14
4. Petrosian	0	1	1½	x	1	1	1½	1	1	1½	2	2	13
5. Bronstein	½	2	2	1	x	½	½	1	½	1½	1½	2	13
6. Hort	½	0	0	1	1½	x	1	2	2	1	1	2	12
7. Matulovic	0	½	0	½	1½	1	x	½	2	2	1½	1	10
8. Smyslov	0	1½	0	1	1	0	1½	x	½	1	1	2	9
9. Reshevsky	½	0	1	1	1½	0	0	1½	x	½	1½	1	8
10. Uhlmann	½	½	½	½	½	1	0	1	1½	x	0	2	8
11. Ivkov	0	0	0	0	½	1	½	1	½	2	x	2	7½
12. Ostojic	0	0	0	0	0	0	1	0	1	0	0	x	2
	1	2	3	4	5	6	7	8	9	10	11	12	Total

ROVINJ / ZAGREB
TOURNAMENT OF PEACE, 1970

	1	2	3	4	5	6	7	8	9	10	11	12	13	14	15	16	17	18	Total
1. FISCHER	x	½	1	½	½	½	1	½	1	0	1	½	1	1	1	1	1	1	13
2. Hort	½	x	½	½	½	½	½	1	½	1	½	1	½	½	½	½	1	1	11
3. Gligoric	0	½	x	1	½	1	½	½	½	½	½	½	1	½	½	1	1	1	11
4. Smyslov	½	½	0	x	½	½	½	1	½	½	1	1	½	1	½	1	½	1	11
5. Korchnoi	½	½	½	½	x	½	0	1	0	1	½	1	½	1	1	½	1	1	11
6. Petrosian	½	½	0	½	½	x	½	½	½	1	½	1	½	½	1	½	1	1	10½
7. Minic	0	½	½	½	1	½	x	½	½	½	1	½	½	½	½	0	½	1	9
8. Ivkov	½	0	½	0	0	½	½	x	½	½	½	1	½	½	1	½	1	1	9
9. Bertok	0	½	½	½	1	½	½	½	x	0	½	½	½	½	½	½	½	1	8½
10. Kovacevic	1	0	½	½	0	0	½	½	1	x	1	0	½	½	½	½	1	½	8½
11. Uhlmann	0	½	½	0	½	½	0	½	½	0	x	1	1	1	½	1	1	0	8½
12. Browne	½	0	½	0	0	0	½	0	½	1	0	x	½	½	½	1	1	1	7½
13. Ghitescu	0	½	0	½	½	½	½	½	½	½	0	½	x	½	½	½	0	½	6½
14. Kurajica	0	½	½	0	0	½	½	½	½	½	0	½	½	x	½	½	½	½	6½
15. Parma	0	½	½	½	0	0	½	0	½	½	½	½	½	½	x	½	½	½	6½
16. Marovic	0	½	0	0	½	½	1	½	½	½	0	0	½	½	½	x	0	½	6
17. Udovic	0	0	0	½	0	0	½	0	½	0	0	0	1	½	½	1	x	1	5½
18. Nicevski	0	0	0	0	0	0	0	0	0	½	1	0	½	½	½	½	0	x	3½
	1	2	3	4	5	6	7	8	9	10	11	12	13	14	15	16	17	18	

BUENOS AIRES INTERNATIONAL, 1970

	1	2	3	4	5	6	7	8	9	10	11	12	13	14	15	16	17	18	Total
1. FISCHER	x	1	1	1	½	½	½	½	1	1	1	1	1	1	1	1	1	1	15
2. Tukmakov	0	x	1	½	½	½	½	½	1	1	½	½	1	½	½	1	1	1	11½
3. Panno	0	0	x	½	½	½	½	1	½	1	1	½	1	1	½	1	1	½	11
4. Gheorghiu	0	½	½	x	½	½	½	½	½	1	½	1	½	1	1	½	½	1	10½
5. Najdorf	½	½	½	½	x	½	½	½	0	1	½	1	1	1	1	½	0	1	10½
6. Reshevsky	½	½	½	½	½	x	½	½	½	½	½	1	1	1	½	½	½	1	10½
7. Smyslov	½	½	½	½	½	½	x	½	½	½	½	½	1	½	½	½	½	½	9
8. Mecking	½	½	0	½	½	½	½	x	½	½	½	½	0	½	½	½	1	1	8½
9. Quinteros	0	0	½	½	1	½	½	½	x	0	½	1	0	½	½	½	1	1	8½
10. Damjanovic	0	0	0	0	0	½	½	½	1	x	½	½	½	½	1	1	½	1	8
11. O'Kelly	0	½	0	½	½	½	½	½	½	½	x	0	½	½	½	½	1	1	8
12. Bisguier	0	½	½	0	0	0	½	½	0	½	1	x	1	½	0	½	1	1	7½
13. Szabo	0	0	0	½	0	0	0	1	1	½	½	0	x	½	1	½	1	1	7½
14. Garcia,R	0	½	0	0	0	0	½	½	½	½	½	½	½	x	1	1	0	1	7
15. Rubinetti	0	½	½	0	0	½	½	½	½	0	½	1	0	0	x	½	½	1	6½
16. Rossetto	0	0	0	½	½	½	½	½	½	0	½	½	½	0	½	x	0	½	5½
17. Schweber	0	0	0	½	1	½	½	0	0	½	0	0	0	1	½	1	x	0	5½
18. Agdamus	0	0	½	0	0	0	½	0	0	0	0	0	0	0	0	½	1	x	2½
	1	2	3	4	5	6	7	8	9	10	11	12	13	14	15	16	17	18	

PALMA DE MALLORCA INTERZONAL, 1970

	1	2	3	4	5	6	7	8	9	10	11	12	13	14	15	16	17	18	19	20	21	22	23	24	Total
1. FISCHER	x	0	1	½	1	1	½	1	½	1	1	1	1	1	1	1	1	½	1	1	½	½	1	½	18½
2. Larsen	1	x	½	½	0	1	½	½	½	½	1	1	0	½	½	1	½	1	½	1	1	½	1	½	15
3. Geller	0	½	x	1	½	1	½	1	½	½	½	1	½	½	1	½	1	½	½	½	1	1	½	½	15
4. Hubner	½	½	0	x	½	1	½	0	½	½	0	½	½	1	½	1	1	1	1	½	1	1	1	1	15
5. Taimanov	0	1	½	½	x	½	½	½	½	½	½	0	½	0	1	1	½	1	½	1	½	1	1	1	14
6. Uhlmann	0	0	0	0	½	x	1	½	½	1	½	½	1	½	0	1	½	1	1	½	1	1	1	1	14
7. Portisch	½	½	½	½	½	0	x	½	0	1	½	1	1	½	½	½	1	½	½	1	½	1	1	0	13½
8. Smyslov	0	½	0	1	½	½	½	x	1	½	½	0	½	½	½	½	½	½	1	1	½	1	1	1	13½
9. Polugaevsky	½	½	½	½	½	½	1	0	x	½	1	½	½	½	½	1	0	½	1	1	½	½	½	½	13
10. Gligoric	0	½	½	½	½	0	0	½	½	x	1	½	1	½	1	½	½	1	0	½	1	½	1	1	13
11. Panno	0	0	½	1	½	½	½	½	0	0	x	½	½	½	1	1	½	½	½	½	1	1	½	1	12½
12. Mecking	0	0	0	½	1	½	0	1	½	½	½	x	1	½	½	½	½	0	½	½	1	1	1	1	12½
13. Hort	0	1	½	½	½	0	0	½	½	0	½	0	x	1	½	1	½	½	½	½	1	½	1	½	11½
14. Ivkov	0	½	½	0	1	½	½	½	½	½	½	½	0	x	½	½	0	½	½	½	½	1	½	½	10½
15. Suttles	0	½	0	½	0	1	½	½	½	0	0	½	½	½	x	0	½	½	1	½	0	1	½	1	10
16. Minic	0	0	½	0	0	0	½	½	0	½	0	½	0	½	1	x	1	½	½	½	1	½	1	1	10
17. Reshevsky	0	½	0	0	½	½	0	½	1	½	½	½	½	1	½	0	x	½	½	½	0	0	½	1	9½
18. Matulovic	½	0	½	0	0	0	½	½	½	0	½	1	½	½	½	½	½	x	½	½	0	0	½	1	9
19. Addison	0	½	½	0	½	0	½	0	0	1	½	½	½	½	0	½	½	½	x	½	0	0	1	1	9
20. Filip	0	0	½	½	0	½	0	0	0	½	½	½	½	½	½	½	½	½	½	x	½	1	½	0	8½
21. Naranja	½	0	0	0	½	0	½	½	½	0	0	0	0	½	1	0	1	1	1	½	x	0	0	1	8½
22. Uitumen	½	½	0	0	0	0	0	0	½	½	0	0	½	0	0	½	1	1	1	0	1	x	1	½	8½
23. Rubinetti	0	0	½	0	0	0	0	0	½	0	½	0	0	½	½	0	½	½	0	½	1	0	x	1	6
24. Jimenez	½	½	½	0	0	0	1	0	½	0	0	0	½	½	0	0	0	0	0	1	0	½	0	x	5½
	1	2	3	4	5	6	7	8	9	10	11	12	13	14	15	16	17	18	19	20	21	22	23	24	

CANDIDATES MATCH VS TAIMANOV, VANCOUVER 1971

	1	2	3	4	5	6	Total
1. FISCHER	1	1	1	1	1	1	6
2. Taimanov	0	0	0	0	0	0	0

CANDIDATES MATCH VS LARSEN, DENVER, 1971

	1	2	3	4	5	6	Total
1. FISCHER	1	1	1	1	1	1	6
2. Larsen	0	0	0	0	0	0	0

CANDIDATES MATCH VS PETROSIAN, BUENOS AIRES, 1971

	1	2	3	4	5	6	7	8	9	Total
1. FISCHER	1	0	½	½	½	1	1	1	1	6½
2. Petrosian	0	1	½	½	½	0	0	0	0	2½

WORLD CHAMPIONSHIP MATCH VS SPASSKY, REYKJAVIC, 1972

	1	2	3	4	5	6	7	8	9	10	11	12	13	14	15	16	17	18	19	20	21	Total
1. FISCHER	0	0F	1	½	1	1	½	1	½	1	0	½	1	½	½	½	½	½	½	½	1	12½
2. Spassky	1	1F	0	½	0	0	½	0	½	0	1	½	0	½	½	½	½	½	½	½	0	8½

WORLD CHAMPIONSHIP REMATCH VS SPASSKY, SVETI STEFAN / BELGRADE, 1992

(First player to win ten games - draws not counting)

	1	2	3	4	5	6	7	8	9	10	11
1. FISCHER	1	½	½	0	0	½	1	1	1	½	1
2. Spassky	0	½	½	1	1	½	0	0	0	½	0

SVETI   STEFAN

	12	13	14	15	16	17	18	19	20	21	22	23	24	25	26	27	28	29	30	Total
1. FISCHER	0	½	½	½	1	1	½	½	0	1	½	½	½	1	0	½	½	½	1	10
2. Spassky	1	½	½	½	0	0	½	½	1	0	½	½	½	0	1	½	½	½	0	5

BELGRADE

PLAYER INDEX

* **Blitz Games**
** **Simultaneous Games**

OPENING INDEX

(Tournament and Match games)

ECO INDEX

(Tournament and Match games only)

ENDGAME INDEX

(Tournament and Match games only)

This is a general endgame index. Examples: **King and pawn** can mean King and pawn(s) vs. King and pawn(s) or King vs. King and pawns. **Bishop and pawn** means Bishop and pawn(s) vs. Bishop and pawn(s), or Bishop vs. pawn(s). The same holds true for **Knight and pawn, Minor piece** (Bishop vs. Knight), **Rook and pawn,** and **Queen and pawn.** **Rook and minor piece** is defined as any combination of Rook(s) and minor piece(s) vs. any other combination of Rook(s) and minor piece(s), including cases where one side is the exchange up. **Other Queen Endings** include Queen vs. any combination of other pieces, or Queen + another piece(s) vs. Queen + another piece(s).